Ilse Graham

Goethe
Portrait of the Artist

Walter de Gruyter · Berlin · New York
1977

Library of Congress Cataloging in Publication Data

Graham, Ilse, 1914—
    Goethe , portrait of the artist.
    Bibliography: p.
    Includes index.
    1. Goethe, Johann Wolfgang von, 1749—1832-- Criticism and
interpretation.
    PT2177.G67 1977 831'.6 76-54974
    ISBN 3-11-006928-8

CIP-Kurztitelaufnahme der Deutschen Bibliothek

Graham , Ilse
Goethe , portrait of the artist. — 1. Aufl. — Berlin, New York :
de Gruyter, 1977.
    ISBN 3-11-006928-8

©

Satz und Druck: Walter de Gruyter & Co., Berlin
Umschlaggestaltung: Rudolf Hübler, Berlin
Bindearbeiten: Lüderitz & Bauer, Berlin
Printed in Germany

To

ERICH TRUNZ

who lit a beacon for Goethe scholars and lovers everywhere
this book is gratefully inscribed.

Author's Note

Except where otherwise indicated, quotations from Goethe are cited according to the text of the *Hamburger Ausgabe in 14 Bänden*, herausgegeben von Erich Trunz, zehnte, überarbeitete Auflage, München 1974, a copy of which was most kindly put at my disposal by Verlag C. H. Beck for the purposes of this book. I should like to thank the editors of *German Life and Letters* for permitting me to reprint, with slight modifications, Chapter 7 which appeared in *New Series, Vol. XXIV*, October 1970, No. 1, dedicated to Mary E. Gilbert; also to the editors of the *Jahrbuch der deutschen Schillergesellschaft*, where a German version of Chapter 1 appeared in Jahrgang 18, 1974. A radically shortened German version of Chapter 11 was given as an address to the I.V.G. Congress held in Cambridge, August 1975, and will in due course be published in the proceedings of the Congress.

My most heartfelt thanks go to my friend Mary Gilbert who followed the writing of these pages with her usual keen interest and gave me her unstinting help in the preparation of the manuscript for press.

Easter 1975

Table of Contents

Nichts ist vergänglich, als der eine, der genießt und zuschaut.

Foreword

The reader of these pages will find them to contain neither one more 'study of Goethe' nor a collection of essays loosely bound together by his illustrious name. In this book I have attempted to define the nature of that poet's artistic sensibility and to isolate that quality of his structuring imagination by which we instantly recognise almost any page from his hand as being unmistakably and uniquely Goethean. This quality pervades his scientific writings no less than his lyrical poetry, his dramas or his fiction. And of necessity so, since all the multifarious interests and activities of that figure sprang from one and the same creative centre, from what he himself on occasion termed his 'exakte sinnliche Phantasie'.

To show this structuring principle at work, I have indeed singled out a number of his major writings for close critical scrutiny. Here as always, the work of art has had my first allegiance, and I have permitted no thesis or theory of mine to obscure its contour or violate its integrity of meaning. Yet a focus every critic must have. He may only speak *about* works of art; he cannot perform them as a conductor will perform a musical score. To speak *about* a work of art means adopting a specific angle from which to approach it. And this inevitably spells selectivity and even a degree of one-sidedness.

I have availed myself of the freedom entailed by this critical necessity and have endeavoured to choose such viewpoints as shall lead into the heart of whatever work I might be discussing, and at the same time elucidate the structuring imagination of which it is the product. Thus, for instance, I have treated of the *Italian Journey* from the vantage point of what happened to Goethe's drama *Torquato Tasso* on that trip: a facet which in my view vitally contributes to the understanding of that strange venture and also furthered me in my specific enquiry. Analogously, I had to be selective in my handling of the vast narrative panorama of *Die Wahlverwandtschaften*. The angle from which I approached it — the structure of experiencing evinced by the main character, Ottilie — enabled me to make a reasonably balanced and inclusive statement of what this novel is 'about', and to pursue my investigation regarding the structure of experiencing that has left its mark on this figure and, indeed, this work. Similarly, an analysis of the diverse perceptual modes which are explored in *Wilhelm Meister* and determine the inner form of that novel yielded much valuable material regarding the model of perception which is characteristic of Goethe himself and has left its unmistakable imprint on all his writing and thinking.

All in all, the preoccupations that governed my choice and treatment of individual works — preoccupations at all times geared to the work in hand — are gathered up and made fully apparent in the concluding chapter which does indeed make explicit the intellectual backbone of a coherent argument carried on throughout these pages.

The division of this study into separate sections aims at pinpointing the particular aspect of my composite portrait exhibited most clearly by the works treated under that heading. But in the case of an artistic phenomenon as homogeneous and organically indivisible as is Goethe any compartmentalisation is bound, in the last resort, to remain unsatisfactory. Facets I had to isolate run fluid into one another in the living organisms of the works. *Die Wahlverwandtschaften* could equally well be treated under the heading of *Gegenständlichkeit* as under that of *The Symbolic Mode*. The discussion of *Faust* might have been slotted into that pigeon-hole as readily as into the section on *Dauer im Wechsel*. The subject-object relation, the symbolic mode of experiencing, permanence in transience — these are all bound up with one another and re-appear variously interlaced in every work from Goethe's hand. Nevertheless, I have endeavoured to build up my running argument in a meaningful and ascending order.

Chronological considerations played some part in devising that order, but had at times to give way to more decisive ones. The opening chapter of the section entitled *Chameleon* for instance deals with an early phase in Goethe's life, the phase we associate with *Werthers Leiden*. It would have been true to biographical fact to follow up this discussion with the chapters of the second section, which concern themselves with the maturing of a very young and labile poet to manhood. But thematic continuity was felt to be more important than biographical correctness; and accordingly the second chapter of the opening section pursues the recurrence of the same aspect of Goethe's artistic personality — his creative ambivalence — into a much later phase of his life.

Similarly, much might have argued in favour of grouping together the chapter on *Die Natürliche Tochter* with that on *Pandora*. These two works are fairly close in point of time as well as in their thematic materials and the poet's way of handling them. Nevertheless, I grouped the chapter on *Pandora* together with that on the much earlier *Italian journey* for the reason that both reflect, and enable us to understand, what were eminently times of critical transition in the poet's development. And it is the rhythms of that development and this poet's characteristic way of living through creative crises that form an important feature of the portrait I endeavour to put before my readers.

Needless to say, that portrait is far from complete. I may well be charged with showing excessive concern for some features at the cost of others. Again, selectivity is a must which may even be salutary. I can only hope that those traits on which I felt it proper to concentrate are indeed basic to Goethe's artistic physiognomy and that my subject will be readily recognised in the likeness I have endeavoured to create of him.

I   Chameleon

'Die wenigen, die was davon erkannt' — (Goethe) —
Wovon eigentlich?
Ich nehme an: vom Satzbau.

G. Benn

Goethe's own Werther:
An artist's truth about his fiction

'Yet coolness is derived from all that heat . . .'
Elizabeth Jennings

I.

In the beginning was ambivalence. Although these words cannot claim the status of Gospel truth, a certain amount of validity attaches to them in the human sphere, certainly in that of the creative artist. Goethe's first novel which brought him world fame is full of ambivalences, and so too his lifelong reaction towards his progeny was to be — a fact which is reflected in the title of this chapter. Was I to place the 'own' in 'Goethe's own Werther' into inverts? To do so would have indicated something of the vast difference between author and character which is plain from the novel itself, and would have done justice to the almost anguished way in which Goethe dissociated himself from his extravagant creation. But it would have belied the streak of possessive tenderness Goethe paradoxically evinced towards his illustrious misfit; a protective love otherwise exclusively reserved for 'das himmlische Kind', Ottilie. On balance, I decided to let the complexity of the case speak for itself and not to prejudge a lifelong love-hate relationship by a crude parodistic device.

Again, ambivalence — Goethe's own though of a different power — dogged me in the choice of my subtitle. Would not 'An Artist's Fiction about his Truth' have been more appropriate? *Dichtung und Wahrheit* Goethe called his autobiography, not *vice versa*. Yet for the longest time he had in fact called it *Wahrheit und Dichtung* and had decided on the order he finally adopted on grounds — so he tells Riemer[1] — of euphony. As for the title itself, in whatever order, it had caused Goethe some considerable headache. To Ludwig I of Bavaria he writes on January 1, 1830 that he had plumped for it in a kind of Mephistophelian *Widerspruchsgeist*. Sad experience had made him very much alive to the fact that the public would in any case query the 'truth' of such biographical undertakings as his own: they would want it truer still; and so he decided to call their bluff. 'Diesem zu begegnen, bekannte ich mich zu einer Art von Fiktion, . . . denn' — and here we must attend closely — 'es war mein ernstestes Bestreben das eigentliche Grundwahre, das, insofern ich es einsah, in meinem Leben obgewaltet hatte, möglichst

---

[1] *Mitteilungen über Goethe*, ed. A. Pollmer, Leipzig 1921, p. 188 f.

darzustellen und auszudrücken.'[2] This 'denn' is baffling. The 'Grundwahre', Goethe then proceeds to explain, which is distilled from a long and multi-coloured life in the retrospect of old age, is anything but a photographic truth. It is truth selected, telescoped and condensed; a dialectical reversal Goethe sums up as follows: 'Dieses alles, was dem Erzählenden und der Erzählung angehört, habe ich hier unter dem Worte: Dichtung, begriffen, um mich des Wahren, dessen ich mir bewußt war, zu meinem Zweck bedienen zu können.'[3] Clearly, the word 'Dichtung' in *Dichtung und Wahrheit* is designed to confound any expectations of verisimilitude the naive reader might harbour. It signifies that 'Grundwahre' which, in the case of an artist's biography, cannot help but be formed truth; and such formed truth we shall encounter in whatever appertains to 'dem Erzählenden und der Erzählung'.

The year following, on March 30th, 1831, he tells Eckermann: 'Ich nannte das Buch "Dichtung und Wahrheit", weil es sich durch höhere Tendenzen aus der Region einer niederen Realität erhebt . . . ', to which he adds: 'Aber die Deutschen wissen nicht leicht, wie sie etwas Ungewohntes zu nehmen haben, und das Höhere geht oft an ihnen vorüber, ohne daß sie es gewahr werden.'

When Goethe has his knife in the Germans — and how often he and Schiller did so with relish — he usually has in mind their particular kind of earnestness which is essentially 'stofflich' and fails to detect, and respect, the high seriousness of the playful, the aesthetic, the formed, which Goethe and Schiller rated incomparably higher than any profundity of matter. We note that he now quotes the title in its reversed, and final, order, as *Dichtung und Wahrheit*; and by the prominence he thus gives to *Dichtung* emphasises that 'höhere Wahrheit' which is truth formed; (and here we might do well to remember the dictum of the very young poet who, in his early twenties already, knew: 'Jede Form, auch die gefühlteste, hat etwas Unwahres').[4] A *höhere Wahrheit*, then, we must conclude, precisely by virtue of being *höher*, that is to say, formed, inevitably contains 'etwas Unwahres'. These definitions are like contradictory signals flashing past our eye at one and the same moment and confusing it. And to make confusion complete, here is Kanzler von Müller's report of how Goethe reacted to his suggestion that the poet write about the life and atmosphere at Tierfurt as it was at the time of the Dowager Duchess Amalia. Goethe replied that this should not prove too difficult an undertaking: 'man dürfte nur die Zustände *ganz treu** so schildern, wie sie sich dem *poetischen Auge** in der Erinnerung darstellten; Dichtung und Wahrheit, ohne daß Erdichtung dabei wäre.'[5] Evidently it is the relation between pairs

[2] Letter to Zelter, 15. II. 1830.
[3] *Ibid.*
[4] *Aus Goethes Brieftasche*, XII, p. 22.
[5] 13. VI. 1825.
* my italics.

of seemingly contradictory terms which Goethe continually couples that needs
to be explained: *Fiktion* and *Grundwahrheit; Dichtung* and *höhere Wahrheit*
(which occurs in Eckermann's record of the conversation from which I
quoted); and, finally, *ganz treu* and *poetisches Auge:* time and again these
appear bracketed together in a number of paradoxical statements which are
clearly of the most fundamental. During sixty long years, from that early
aperçu Aus Goethes Brieftasche which I have quoted, to those late utterances
vis à vis Eckermann and Riemer, he maintains one and the same position. At
first sight, such continuity of vision may appear baffling; on second thoughts,
it becomes readily understandable. For the problem behind these formulations
is absolutely central to the creative mode of experiencing as such, and is bound
to crop up, in one form or another, in every phase of an artist's development.
It is the problem of how the artist experiences. Does he experience what
others experience and the way they do, and then set about shaping artistically
what he has first shared with his fellow-men? Or does he experience differently
from the very start, at least on occasion? This is the question I shall pursue in
this chapter, in relation to the youthful creator of *Werther* and to the author
of *Dichtung und Wahrheit*, as he looks back upon the early phase of his poetic
career in the retrospect of old age.

Two distinguished American critics have summed up their own findings
on this thorny problem as follows: ' ... we must not forget that the artist
may "experience" life differently in terms of his art: actual experiences are
seen with a view to their use in literature and come to him partially shaped by
artistic traditions and preconceptions.'[6] I wholeheartedly subscribe to the view
expressed here. The artist's experiencing — this is my thesis — evinces a
structure that is subtly, decisively and from the very moment of inception
at variance from that of others. However much he may appear to be like the
next man, he is busy assimilating the world 'immer in sich lebend, strebend
und arbeitend'[7]; he seizes the outer world 'durch die innre Welt die alles
packt, verbindet, neuschafft, knetet und in eigner Form, Manier, wieder
hinstellt.'[8] His loving and his suffering may look like everyone else's; but
always his experience is tied up, by a clandestine thread as it were, with his
medium, his artmaking. And sometimes the threads cross and get tangled.
He is always the one of whom Leonore Sanvitale says:

> Er scheint sich uns zu nahn, und bleibt uns fern;
> Er scheint uns anzusehn, und Geister mögen
> An unsrer Stelle seltsam ihm erscheinen.
>
> (*Tasso*, I, 2).

[6] René Wellek and Austin Warren, *Theory of Literature*, New York 1949, p. 72. A similar
point is made by V. Lange, 'Goethe's Craft of Fiction', *PEGS* (New Series) XXII,
1952—1953, pp. 34ff. and p. 40.
[7] Letter to Auguste Gräfin zu Stolberg, 13. II. 1775.
[8] Letter to F. H. Jacobi, 21. VIII. 1774.

Such secret estrangement results in a curiously doubled, iridescent sense of self; a condition the young Goethe may be presumed to have experienced for the first time as being a potential threat at the time of writing his *Werther*. On the whole, he was, and remained, reticent about this experience — a central one in the life of any artist[9]. 'Den besondern Charakter seines poetischen Bildungstriebes mögen andere bezeichnen', he cursorily notes in the *Selbstschilderung* of 1797[10]. Only very occasionally did he lift the veil and grant us a glimpse into 'diese Geheimnisse des Lebens'[11], as he has it in the last letter he ever wrote: in *Torquato Tasso*, in the eery cycle of sonnets which will occupy us in a later chapter[12] and in some poems of the *Westöstliche Divan*, say, *Die schön geschriebenen*. These insights are most closely guarded in largely autobiographical works such as *Werther* or *Dichtung und Wahrheit*; and it is precisely this that makes them so alluring. I have elsewhere endeavoured to isolate the distinctive structure of experiencing peculiar to the young author of *Werther* — so different from that of Werther himself — in a structural analysis of that novel[13]. Here I would only touch on that precocious self-awareness of the young poet. My main concern, in this chapter, is to illuminate the young Goethe's awareness of the questionable nature of an artist's life as it is mirrored in the retrospect of *Dichtung und Wahrheit*.

It is sometimes maintained that the author of *Dichtung und Wahrheit*, adopting a well worn literary topos, stylised his portrait of the *Werther*-poet in such a way as to obliterate all distinguishing lines between himself and his fictional character. By this, as well as his notorious dictum that all his published works were in any case only 'Bruchstücke einer großen Konfession', he is said to have precluded any interpretation of his novel other than on biographical lines. If this were so, the autobiography would have to tell us precious little about the young man 'im grauen Biber-Frack mit dem braunseidnen Halstuch und Stiefeln' who, a secret double of the Carnival-Goethe, experienced the world 'immer in sich lebend, strebend und arbeitend'[14]. I hardly think the matter is as simple as that. As we have seen, the author of *Dichtung und Wahrheit* was well aware of the complexity of the concept of

[9] Of the genesis of a verbal work of art Gottfried Benn writes as follows: 'Der Autor besitzt: Erstens einen dumpfen schöpferischen Keim, eine psychische Materie. Zweitens Worte, die in seiner Hand liegen, zu seiner Verfügung stehen, mit denen er umgehen kann, die er bewegen kann, er kennt sozusagen seine Worte. Es gibt nämlich etwas, was man die Zuordnung der Worte zu einem Autor nennen kann. Vielleicht ist er auch an diesem Tag auf ein bestimmtes Wort gestoßen, das ihn beschäftigt, erregt, das er leitmotivisch glaubt verwenden zu können . . .' (In: *Gespräch über Gedichte*, ed. W. Urbanek, Bamberg 1961, p. 69).
[10] X, p. 530.
[11] Letter to W. v. Humboldt, 17. III. 1832.
[12] Cf. Chapter II.
[13] In *Goethe and Lessing. The Wellsprings of Creation*, London and New York 1973, Chapter VI.
[14] Letter to Auguste Gräfin zu Stolberg, 13. II. 1775.

'truth' with which he operates. He is not likely to have sacrificed the poetic truth about the young author of *Werther* to the regard for historical verisimilitude of 'what happened'. For, in the last resort, *Dichtung und Wahrheit* is an artist's reading of a life that was creative through and through. Goethe's creativity was 'das Gesetz, wonach er angetreten'. But where may we expect to find those 'Spezialissima' appertaining to his artistic existence, to use a term Goethe himself coined for suchlike insights late in life[15]? Surely where the artist's shaping hand is at work, that is to say, in 'was dem Erzählenden und der Erzählung angehört', in the ordering of his narrative, the idiom he employs, the images he uses.

> Dichter ist umsonst verschwiegen,
> Dichten selbst ist schon Verrat

says the author of the *Westöstliche Divan*. I suggest we take our cue from that and try to ferret out the artist's truth about the young poet of *Werther* in those places where the forming artist articulates *das Grundwahre* of his life's story in poetic images.

2.

Werther destroys himself. Goethe went on living in order to write. He himself tells us so, saying that there were two of them, Werther and himself, of whom one perished and the other went on living *in order* to write the story of his double, 'so wie es in Hiob (1, 16) heißt: Herr, alle deine Schafe und Knechte sind erschlagen worden und ich bin allein entronnen, Dir Kunde zu bringen'[16]. We note the repeated final construction and suspect that the decision to stay alive was not entirely motivated by the need to supply the grisly details of Werther's death, but by the deeper compulsion 'Kunde zu bringen'. Like Ishmael in *Moby Dick*, he survived to tell the story. He lived in order to give utterance[17]. This was his destiny and its creative compulsion was stronger than the lure of the abyss in which his Werther perished.

Of course, one can also see it the other way around. There are plenty of statements which would seem to reverse the emphasis. One of them in

---

[15] Letter to Zelter, 27. III. 1830.

[16] Caroline Sartorius to her brother, 27. X. 1808 (In: *Goethe über seine Dichtungen*. Versuch einer Sammlung aller Äußerungen des Dichters über seine poetischen Werke, ed. Hans G. Gräf, Teil 1—3, Frankfurt a. Main 1901—1914, Vol. I, 2, p. 584).

[17] A friend of Kestner's, A. A. F. von Hennings, reports going to see Moses Mendelssohn and finding him steeped in Goethe's *Werther*. Hennings told Mendelssohn that neither Goethe's infatuation with Lotte nor Jerusalem's suicide were the models for Werther's own end, whereupon Mendelssohn exclaimed: 'Ach, ich verstehe; Goethe fand es poetisch schön, sich zu erschießen, und zog es vor, in richtiger Person am Leben zu bleiben!' (From an unpublished biography of August Adolph Friedrich von Hennings, legation councillor at the Danish Embassy in Berlin from Nov. 1772 to Oct. 1774. I am indebted to Professor Ritschl, a descendant of Hennings, for permitting me to publish the extract).

Dichtung und Wahrheit. There Goethe reports on his suicidal tendencies, on his resolve to get them out of his system and to live, and adds: 'Um dies aber mit Heiterkeit tun zu können mußte ich eine dichterische Aufgabe zur Ausführung bringen wo alles was ich über diesen wichtigen Punkt empfunden, gedacht und gewähnt, zur Sprache kommen sollte' (III, 13, p. 585). So he wrote in order to live? Is this the burden of the introductory poem to the *Trilogie der Leidenschaft* where the poet states

Zum Bleiben ich, zum Scheiden du erkoren,

not without adding, however, that Werther's premature departure had not deprived him of much that he, Goethe, would have regretted missing? So perhaps writing to live meant living in order to write yet more, not because it was such a fine thing to live, but because the creative addiction overrode all other considerations. And how strong these creative drives must have been we may glean from one of the strangest of the many utterances Goethe made about *Werther*, in a conversation with Eckermann, a couple of months before he wrote the *Trilogie der Leidenschaft*. Speaking of the hapless hero of his youth, he says "das ist auch so ein Geschöpf, das ich gleich dem Pelikan mit dem Blut meines eigenen Herzens gefüttert habe"[18]. The pelican is an ancient symbol for Christ who gave his life for those who fed of his flesh and drank of his blood. The pattern is reversed. It is not Werther who dies that his creator might live. It is the poet who dies — and dies a sacrificial death at that — so that his creation might live. We shall have something more to say about the vicissitudes — one feels inclined to say the passion — undergone by the young author of *Werther* as he suffered, for his work's sake, a creative death that is matched only by the strangeness surrounding his resurrection.

These comments by themselves show the distance between the author of the *Herausgeberbericht*, whose life is unconditionally pledged to his work, and the hero of the novel who consumes his vitality in boundless subjectivism. He lives for his creation; he feeds it with his heart's blood. But what does this figure of speech really signify? A few illustrations showing how the young Goethe fed motifs from his own life into the life-stream of his hero, to articulate *his* destructive passion, will readily illuminate this point.

Some two and a half years before he composed his novel, Goethe writes to his friend Salzmann, apologising for his dilatoriness as a correspondent. 'Sie rathen nicht warum ich nicht schreibe', we read: 'Es ist eine Leidenschafft, eine ganz unerwartete Leidenschafft, Sie wissen wie mich dergleichen in ein Cirkelgen werfen kann, daß ich Sonne, Mond und die lieben Sterne darüber vergesse.'[19] In his letter of I, June 19, he lets his Werther pick up these very

---

[18] To Eckermann, 2. I. 1824.

[19] Letter to J. D. Salzmann, 28. XI. 1771. Lange stresses that there is little in *Werther* that is not experienced and could not be biographically documented. ('Goethe's Craft of Fiction', in *PEGS (New Series) XXII*, 1953, pp. 35ff..)

words to describe his total infatuation with Lotte. The absurd incongruency of this echo is hardly likely to have escaped the poet. For he himself, a full-blooded young man no less than his Werther, had used the same image in a very different context indeed: to tell his friend of the creative *furore* in which he found himself over his new drama, *Götz von Berlichingen*. What a high-handed and matter-of-fact transposition into a new key!

Again, in the famous letter of May 10 Werther laments his inability to put the oppressive intensity of his feelings on paper.

'Mein Freund! Wenn's dann um meine Augen *dämmert**, und die Welt um mich her und der Himmel ganz in meiner Seele ruhn wie die Gestalt einer Geliebten — dann sehne ich mich oft und denke: Ach könntest du das wieder ausdrücken, könntest du dem Papier das einhauchen, was so voll, so *warm** in dir lebt . . .'

This motif, too, in which the tragic potentialities of his character are sounded for the first time, has its origin in Goethe's own experience. More than two years earlier he, too, had watched a similar sunset in a rather doleful frame of mind — the separation from Lotte was still fresh in his mind. But what did he do? He ran to friends, borrowed pencil and paper and — so he reports to Kestner — 'zeichnete zu meiner großen Freude, das ganze Bild *so dämmernd warm** als es in meiner Seele stand.'[20] Goethe does where Werther dreams. He articulates the phenomenon of dusk, objectifies and enjoys it; and, remembering no doubt the occasion, lets poor Werther sigh ineffectually for the paper he has not got, and his eyes grow dim — *dämmern* is the word he actually uses — with the frustration of it all. The degree of awareness and objectivity implied by such conscious manipulation is truly astonishing.

And did he not know about the absurdity of Werther's posture in that early letter? Years earlier, at the beginning of 1772, on sending the manuscript of his *Urgötz* to Herder, Goethe writes that he has now stepped back from his easel to gain distance from his work, so far no more than a sketch, and to see the distance he has to cover in order to reach his final goal[21]. Of course he knew! The youngster who had written to Herder, in that famous letter of July 1772, 'Dreingreiffen, packen ist das Wesen ieder meisterschafft', adding 'dass ieder Künstler' — poets included — 'so lang seine Hände nicht plastisch arbeiten nichts ist'[22], was not likely to fool himself about Werther: a painter lying lazily on the bosom of nature without lifting as much as a

---

[20] Letter to J. Ch. Kestner, 25. XII. 1772.
[21] Letter to Herder, beginning of 1772.
[22] Letter to Herder, about 10. VII. 1772. Cf. E. M. Wilkinson, 'Goethe to Herder, July 1772', in: *GLL (New Series) XV*, Oct. 1961, and my *Goethe and Lessing*, Chapter V, pp. 79ff. W. Kayser quotes this passage to allude, in passing, to the difference it reveals between Goethe and Herder ('Die Entstehung von Goethe's "Werther"', in: *D. Vjschrift 19*, 1941, p. 451f.). Klaus Scherpe uncritically takes it for granted that Werther is a creative artist. (*Werther und Wertherwirkung. Zum Syndrom bürgerlicher Gesellschaftsordnung im 18. Jahrhundert*, Homburg, Zurich, Berlin 1970, p. 58 and 60.)
* my italics.

finger, was not, and could never be, an artist, his own protestations notwithstanding; no more than a Raphael born without hands.

Such autobiographical source-material dating back to a period well before
he took his novel in hand illuminates the extraordinary insight the young
poet had into himself, into his own characteristically creative reaction-
patterns, and the full consciousness with which he made use of these, his
artistic addictions to give voice to the uncreative passion of his hero.

But then, if the differences are patent, so are the likenesses between Werther and his young creator. In recent times it is perhaps Barker Fairley who
has been most insistent on pointing out the resemblances, saying, not only
with regard to that novel but to all of Goethe's creations of the *Sturm und
Drang*, that the thinnest of dividing lines runs between author and his characters which as often as not is in danger of altogether vanishing[23]. He certainly makes his point vividly and, at times, persuasively. And he has the
older Goethe on his side, at least as far as *Werther* goes. Or does he? In
Part III, Book 12 of *Dichtung und Wahrheit* we read: 'Ruht nun, wie man
sagt, in der Sehnsucht das größte Glück, und darf die wahre Sehnsucht nur
auf ein Unerreichbares gerichtet sein; so traf wohl alles zusammen, um den
Jüngling, den wir gegenwärtig auf seinen Irrgängen begleiten' — Goethe
means himself —

> 'zum glücklichsten Sterblichen zu machen. Die Neigung zu einer versagten Braut, das
> Bestreben, Meisterstücke fremder Literatur der unsrigen zu erwerben und anzueignen,
> die Bemühung, Naturgegenstände nicht nur mit Worten, sondern auch mit Griffel und
> Pinsel, ohne eigentliche Technik, nachzuahmen: jedes einzeln wäre schon hinreichend
> gewesen, das Herz zu schwellen und die Brust zu beklemmen.' (III, 12, IX, p. 546).

'Whose heart and whose chest?', we may ask; the young poet's or that of
his hero? Every word in Goethe's self-portrait has its exact correspondence
in the hero of his novel: the positing of an ideal that must needs remain
unattainable, the attachment to a girl already engaged (one of the many
expressions of this ethos), the derivative relation to the literary genius of
foreign nations — Homer, Ossian or Goldsmith as the case may be —[24]

---

[23] In: *A Study of Goethe*, London 1947.

[24] Georg Jäger has discussed the role of the 'passionate reader' in the Age of Sensibility
who — in close correspondence to the attitude developed *vis-à-vis* the didactic literature
of the time — aims at a maximal identification with his subject. 'Die Bücher wurden
nicht gelesen, sie wurden durchlebt', he writes. According to Jäger, Goethe supports this
model of reception, both by the dedication of the editor and by Werther's own reaction
to literary experiences; more than that, the conception of the contemporary reader becomes
an overt subject of discourse. (In: 'Die Wertherwirkung. Ein rezeptionsästhetischer
Modellfall.' In: *Historizität in Sprach- und Literaturwissenschaft*. Vorträge und Berichte der
Stuttgarter Germanistentagung, ed. W. Müller-Seidel, Munich 1974.)

Jäger's observations are historically interesting and relevant to the interpretation of
Goethe's novel. But he ignores the ironic use the author makes of this 'model' to characterise the tragic subjectivism of his hero. This irony is most patent in the double allusion
to Lessing's *Emilia Galotti*. Undoubtedly the poet, in this case, operates with a different

the illstarred and dilettantish attempts at artistic utterance in a recalcitrant medium —: all these forms of uncreativeness which Goethe here ascribes to himself — he actually speaks of 'Mangel oder Stockung von Produktions-kraft' (III, 12, p. 539) — his Werther encounters, too. And given the neoplatonic premise — subtly ironised by the modifying 'wie man sagt' — the premise that only the unattainable, the ideal hatched and harboured in the pure inwardness of the mind, is supremely worth having, we inevitably arrive at the state of inner congestion and outer constriction which, in the end, drives Werther to put a bullet through his brain. Again, there are repeated allusions, in *Dichtung und Wahrheit*, to those 'übertriebene Forderungen an sich selbst' which destroyed the best of Germany's youth in the midst of peace and plenty[25]; and these bear all too clearly on Werther's predicament.

Must we then subscribe to the thesis that the author of *Dichtung und Wahrheit* stylised the poet of *Werther* and his whole generation in such a way that life and poetry run fluid into one another and that any attempt to distinguish between them must remain an idle undertaking?

model and presupposes a different reaction-pattern on the part of his readers. The novel all but begins with an oblique reference to the prince's conversation with the painter Conti, and closes with the bare statement of fact that *Emilia Galotti* lay open on Werther's desk. It is however noteworthy that Werther's first allusion is dated May 10, 1771, that is to say, predates the publication of Lessing's drama which took place in the spring of 1772. This means that the reader of 1774 was aware of an echo, at least in retrospect, at the end of the novel, of which Werther himself cannot have had any knowledge. What is the message of that echo? Conti's assertion that he is a great painter at all times, but that his hand fails him, and the more overtly paradoxical assertion that Raphael would have been the greatest painterly genius even if he had perchance been born without hands surely signify, in the light of the tragic action, that the worth of the mind's ideal is independent of its realisation or non-realisation. This is the common theme of the initial conversation and the tragedy as a whole. (Cf. my *Goethe and Lessing*, Chapter I.) It is precisely this theme of neoplatonic inwardness which dominates Goethe's *Werther* and is enunciated for the first time in his letter of May 10.

Neither the opening allusion nor the closing reference to Lessing's drama which are the frame within which Goethe sets his narrative is mediated by the hero; both address themselves to the reader above Werther's head as it were. This means that the narrator, in this one case at least, does not aim at an identification of the readers' reaction with that of Werther. Quite on the contrary, the narrator requires the reader to make a highly differentiated, independent judgment on these allusions, a judgment which of necessity critically distances him from Werther. He is to identify in Werther's first allusion to the Conti-conversation the theme which governs drama and novel alike, and to anticipate the tragic development of this resonant motif. Werther's allusion is like a police warrant he flourishes without knowing its content.

Analogously, W. Kayser ignores the subtleness Goethe displays in the use of the then fashionable pronoun 'mein' at which Lichtenberg scoffs, calling it an *albernes Modeprono-men*. Goethe does not let Werther speak of 'his Homer' for nothing. With the utmost economy of means, such touches drive home Werther's fatal egocentricity. To see in them proof of Werther's 'Reichtum an eigenem seelischen Besitz' as Kayser does, is to miss the point. (*Loc. cit.*, p. 455 f.)

[25] III, 12. HA IX, p. 539; III, 13, p. 583; III, 14, HA X, p. 7.

We here have a perfect example of that 'Wiederholte Spiegelung' in which a work of art, itself significantly reflecting life, radiates back into life and enhances its image. Such a repeated mirroring was precisely what Goethe intended in *Dichtung und Wahrheit*, his avowed aim being 'den Menschen in seinen Zeitverhältnissen darzustellen' and to show 'wie er sich eine Welt- und Menschenansicht daraus gebildet, und wie er sie, wenn er Künstler, Dichter, Schriftsteller ist, wieder nach außen abgespiegelt' (I, p. 9). In his auto-biography he appears doubly reflected, a mirrored image of the mirror-image he had once held up to himself and to his time, representative, modelling himself together with his whole generation on his Werther, blue frockcoat, yellow waistcoat and all.

But where, in this stylised presentation, do we find the artist who created Werther and survived him? We must ferret him out in his language, in the images behind which he sought refuge. Images are the surest store-houses of a poet's memory; the constant companions of a poet's life, they are most likely to preserve, consciously or subconsciously, the *Grundwahre* of a creative existence.

3.

One of the image patterns which would, at first sight at least, seem to con-firm the close resemblance between the young author of *Werthers Leiden* and the hero of that novel is the complex clustered around the notion of warmth and heat. In attempting to explain that curious phenomenon of *taedium vitae* which, at the time immediately preceding the composition of *Werther*, attacked the best of the young, and not least himself, like a killer virus, Goethe, in his autobiography, adduces 'ein siedend jugendliches Blut' as an important symp-tom in the pathology of the time. Especially undermining, in his view, is the experience of repetition to fullblooded youngsters convinced of the uniqueness of their feelings at their first arousal[26]. A little later on, he con-fesses, in a more personal vein, to the sense of passionate personal involvement with which he had received the news of Jerusalem's suicide, committed to end

---

[26] W. Kayser underpins his thesis that Goethe falsified the genesis of *Werther* in the retro-spect of *Dichtung und Wahrheit* by a two-pronged argument. The first is that none of the three causes Goethe adduces in the autobiography for the *taedium vitae* experienced by the young in fact play any part in *Werther*. The second is that the experience of repetition will only become fatal to persons of maturer age. Both parts of this argument, as I see things, are equally untenable. 'Die arme Leonore' in fact preceded Lotte, and it is not by chance that the novel opens on this motif (I, May 4, 1871); as for the alternation between favour and disfavour, this is an experience Werther makes in relation to the aristocracy (II, March 15—24), not to speak of the personal sphere (II, October 26); and it is the awareness of his own weak will which gradually undermines his morale (I, July 26 and 30). As regards Kayser's second argument, it would seem to me that the experience of repetition is at its most devastating in the case of the young who look upon their experience as absolute.

a triangular situation which was so much like his own. He writes: 'So konnte es nicht fehlen, daß ich jener Produktion, die ich eben unternahm' — i. e. *Die Leiden des jungen Werther* — 'alle die Glut einhauchte, welche keine Unterscheidung zwischen dem Dichterischen und dem Wirklichen zuläßt' (III, 13, p. 587). These words would seem to support those critics who insist that no distinction between poetry and personal experience is feasible. And not only by their matter, but quite as much by their manner. For with this 'Glut', this 'siedend jugendliches Blut' the poet had indeed endowed his hero in plentiful measure. The early and seemingly innocuous allusions to the warmth of Werther's empathy with nature and the lives of those around him soon give way to more worrying statements. We are alarmed at his identification with the 'feurige Natur' of the girl who kills herself because her lover has jilted her, and his defence of suicide as no less inevitable than a 'bösartiges Fieber'; we are troubled by his excessive response to the trifling social slight he suffers — mortification and rage, we are told, 'lief mir wie siedend Wasser durch die Adern' — and by the culminating simile of the whole series, that of the noble breed of horses, 'die, wenn sie schrecklich erhitzt und aufgejagt sind, sich selbst aus Instinkt eine Ader aufbeißen, um sich zum Atem zu helfen' — a scarcely veiled adumbration of Werther's own way of finding release from intolerable constriction. Thus, when the Editor, near the close of the novel, records that Werther's frantic attempt to save the peasant lad — now become murderer — 'war das letzte Auflodern der Flamme eines erlöschenden Lichtes' (II, 98), an image pattern is rounded off which has by and by helped to articulate the hero's feverish intensity of feeling, an overworking of one function at the expense of the rest which inevitably leads to the collapse of the whole man. Again we are left with a disturbing — because seemingly incontestable — parallel between hero and author. Both are at the mercy of elemental drives. If we consider in addition that the violent reaction Goethe's novel triggered off in his contemporaries was commonly referred to as 'Werther-Fieber'[27] — a coinage which sharply pinpoints the blurring of reality and fiction, on the part of the poet as well as of his public — any attempt to distinguish between the one and the other must seem hopelessly academic[28].

However, it would seem advisable at this point to turn our attention to another image-pattern. This is the imagery of water which has a central

---

[27] Cf. Lange's salutary reminder of the redeeming quality of the narrator's irony. (*Loc. cit.*, p. 39 f.)

[28] Hennings reports Moses Mendelssohn as saying about *Werther:* 'Nun, so waffnen Sie sich, wenn Sie ihn lesen. Mich hat er sehr angegriffen. Was sollen die Leute, die nichts als Glut erregen und der erhitzten Phantasie keinen Führer lassen, um sicher hindurch zu kommen.' (*Op. cit.*) Valuable documentation as to the reaction triggered off by *Werther* and the whole phenomenon of 'Werther-Fieber' is provided by K. Scherpe (*op. cit.*) and G. Jäger (*loc. cit.*).

place in Goethe's *opus* and, together with that of the *Schleier*, is presumably
to be regarded as being his archetypal symbol of creativeness, as I have shown
elsewhere.[29]

A letter to Zelter, written when the youngest son of the latter had committed
suicide, may serve as an opening illustration. It so happened that Goethe was
working on a scheme for the section on the *Werther-Zeit* in *Dichtung und Wahrheit* when the news reached him. Consoling his friend in the midst of reliving
intimately similar problems, he writes that it is once again the old story of
taedium vitae, an illness as natural as it is unnatural, which had raged through
him in his own youth in all its symptoms, as no one who had read his
Werther would doubt. 'Ich weiß recht gut, was es mich für Entschlüsse und
Anstrengungen kostete, damals den Wellen des Todes zu entkommen, so wie
ich mich aus manchem späteren Schiffbruch auch mühselig rettete und mühselig erholte.'[30] This is a weighty statement indeed, and one which deserves
to be regarded as serious evidence of how Wertherish Goethe was and, perhaps,
remained.

In *Die Leiden des jungen Werther*, too, the imagery of water plays a decisive
part in the structuring of form and theme. Indeed, so pervasive is it in the fabric
of the novel that there can be no doubt of the symbolic import it carries by
the end. From the moment, early on in the novel, when Werther asks 'warum
der Strom des Genies so selten ausbricht, so selten in hohen Fluten herein-
braust und eure staunende Seele erschüttert' and answers his own question, saying 'Liebe Freunde, da wohnen die gelassenen Herren auf beiden Seiten des
Ufers, denen ihre Gartenhäuschen, Tulpenbeete und Krautfelder zu Grunde
gehen würden . . .' (I, 26. Mai) —: from that moment onward, water, by the
inexorable logic of poetic diction, comes to be associated with Werther's
measurelessness and instability until, in the end, the floods which seethe and
swirl through 'his' valley, inundating every place which had betokened security,
stand revealed as the palpable symbol of those elemental drives Werther has
ruthlessly unleashed in himself, forces which are about to destroy him as they
sweep away his last moorings this side of death.

It is very much with this significance that Goethe employs the imagery of
water in his account of the *Werther*-time, in *Dichtung und Wahrheit*. Strangely
enough, references to the element, clearly of a metaphorical nature, flank his
narrative with striking symmetry. They neatly 'frame' the subject, as it were.
Approaching his main topic somewhat tardily after more than two-thirds of
Book 12, Goethe writes — and this sentence literally contains the first mention
of the novel —: 'Jener Vorsatz, meine innere Natur nach ihren Eigenheiten
gewähren, und die äußere nach ihren Eigenschaften auf mich einfließen zu
lassen, trieb mich an das wunderliche Element, in welchem Werther ersonnen

---

[29] In *Goethe and Lessing*, Chapter XII.
[30] 3. XII. 1812.

und geschrieben ist.' (III, 12, p. 540f.) The final summarising words about himself in relation to his work run as follows: '... ich hatte mich durch diese Komposition, mehr als durch jede andere, aus einem stürmischen Elemente gerettet, auf dem ich durch eigne und fremde Schuld, durch zufällige und gewählte Lebensweise, durch Vorsatz und Übereilung, durch Hartnäckigkeit und Nachgeben auf die gewaltsamste Weise hin und wider getrieben worden' (III, 13 p. 588).

The fact that the same image, in much the same signification, occurs over a span of nearly 40 years, in a compelling fashion within Goethe's novel, in the author's retrospective account of the period of its creation as well as in a personal document recalling the initial situation with brute force, would seem pretty conclusive evidence of the resemblance between Werther and his author, at least in the days of his youth[31]. And indeed, a little poem written as early as 1775 in reply to Nicolai's foolish skit on *Werther* would seem to drive the same point home yet more forcefully. Goethe included it in his autobiography, and this is how it runs:

> Mag jener dünkelhafte Mann
> Mich als gefährlich preisen;
> Der Plumpe, der nicht schwimmen kann,
> Er will's dem Wasser verweisen[32]!

A strong statement, this, and a strange one, too. The poet is not merely *exposed* to the element: he *is* the element. But, at the same time, he is its master, genius, god; a Neptune-like figure. For in this case, the element itself can — swim.

A youngster likening himself to water that can swim may be said to know how to keep his own head above water, for all his inner fluidity. And the poet who knows himself to be element and master in one is, after all, very different from 'his' Werther.

Yet exposure and instability seem to predominate in the retrospective account of the *Werther-Zeit*. In the paragraph immediately preceding the mention of Jerusalem's suicide and the catalytic effect this event had on him, Goethe recalls his resolution to stop playing about with the idea of killing himself — (a very un-Wertherish resolve, and a very un-Wertherish method of putting it into effect, incidentally) — and instead to compose his obsession into poetry. 'Ich versammelte hierzu die Elemente, die sich schon ein paar Jahre in mir herumtrieben . . .' he writes, 'aber es wollte sich nichts gestalten' (III, 13, p. 585). The *Elemente* — in this beautifully precise image — are the bits and pieces of matter as yet untransmuted by form and therefore envisaged

---

[31] W. Kayser regards this letter and the experience connected with it as the true nucleus of Goethe's retrospective — and falsifying — account of the genesis of *Werther*.

[32] This poem, composed in the early months of 1775, was slightly modified for inclusion in *Dichtung und Wahrheit*. Cf. Max Morris, *Der junge Goethe*, Leipzig 1912, Vol. VI, p. 447. Morris' assessment is accepted by E. Trunz, ed. *HA* X, p. 586f.

materially, like driftwood aimlessly floating in the total fluidity of his mind: for we must not overlook the fact that the image, by implication, tells us once again, as the little poem to Nicolai had done, that his very mind is liquid element.

But once we come to the account of Jerusalem's death and the shaping processes it sparked off in the young Goethe, the picture changes out of all recognition. 'Auf einmal erfahre ich die Nachricht von Jerusalems Tode, . . . und in diesem Augenblick war der Plan zu 'Werthern' gefunden, das Ganze schoß von allen Seiten zusammen und ward eine solide Masse, wie das Wasser im Gefäß, das eben auf dem Punkte des Gefrierens steht, durch die geringste Erschütterung sogleich in ein festes Eis verwandelt wird' (III, 13, p. 585)[33]. This passage is so hackneyed that one hardly dares quote it. But has the fact been sufficiently noted how carefully the poet has prepared for its coming, by embedding the whole crucial account in the imagery of water, symbol — up to now — of amorphous elemental drives? And who has explored the relevance of the image complex as a whole, and of this particular simile, for the whole tortured question of the relation between Werther and Goethe, between fiction and the artist's truth as he reveals it to us in *Fiction and Truth*, as it were between the lines? I scarcely think that anyone has. So let us look at this simile.

4.

Water is a curious phenomenon. Whether its temperature is 99 degrees or 1, it remains the same: fluid, the unstablest of elements, taking what shape it has from its firmer surroundings, be it the cup or the vessel or the riverbed that bounds it. But let the temperature drop by just one point on the thermometer, just below zero, and a mere difference of degree will become a difference of quality: what was liquid and utterly amorphous will turn into a solid crystalline mass, evenly structured throughout and so cohesive that you can tip it out of its container and it will firmly stand on its own; fluidity formed. And yet ice represents nothing more than an allotropy of water. However radical the permutation it undergoes, its physical substance remains unchanged.

In this specific passage, however, Goethe is referring to a rather less common constellation which may also turn water into ice. Ordinarily water will become ice when the temperature drops below freezing-point. In

---

[33] It is well known that in fact fifteen months elapsed between Jerusalem's death on October 30, 1772 and the actual writing down of *Werther*, begun on Feb. 1, 1774. Between these milestones the revision of the *Urgötz* (February and March 1773) and the wedding of Maximiliane La Roche to P. A. Brentano (Jan. 15, 1774) and their subsequent move to Frankfurt took place. Goethe himself hints at the length of the gestation period of *Werther* in *Dichtung und Wahrheit*, III, 13, where he describes the complex circumstances in which the novel was written, 'nach so langen und vielen geheimen Vorbereitungen' (*HA* IX, p. 587).

rare cases, however, water which is supercooled — that is to say, well below freezing-point — will remain liquid. This may occur when, by design or by a freak of nature, it is kept absolutely still, sheltered from even such slight interferences as particles of dust settling on its surface. A sudden jolt will then have the instant effect of turning such supercooled water to ice.

In both cases, the common and the more rare one to which Goethe here refers, a drop of temperature is involved. In the ordinary course of events this immediately precedes the process of freezing. In the far rarer case with which Goethe operates here, empirically, no doubt, since the phenomenon was to be theoretically formulated much later, the drop of temperature takes place well before the solidification of water into ice.

In this extended simile, then, Goethe gives expression to a double paradox. Firstly the paradox that the difference between water and ice is both qualitative and non-qualitative. This is highly relevant; for under the image of water at freezing-point, the poet is speaking of the difference between himself as he was before he composed *Werther*, and as he was after the permutation which had made his composition fall into shape. He was the same, yet irreversibly different. Besides, by implication, he is telling us something about himself, the artist, in contradistinction to his Werther for whom water remains, at all times, the fluid and amorphous element. The difference between 'before and after' is qualitative in that, what in the pre-*Werther* Goethe as well as in his tragic hero, remained pure fluid element, in the author of *Werther* assumes a form which stands on its own, like ice tipped out of a bowl, entirely independent of its creator. It is non-qualitative, on the other hand, not only because Goethe remained Goethe, but because that form itself he had created is no extraneous mould superimposed upon the element — like a pie-dish placed on top of a pie — but the product of an enabling predisposition on the part of what is elemental to become structured, without in any wise changing its basic substance.

The second paradox lies in the fact that a severe emotional jolt — the news of Jerusalem's death — which made the author 'breathe all his own *Glut*' into the ensuing art-product, should at the same time be associated with the lowering of his and its inner temperature to beyond freezing-point, and that the shaking-up he received should result in a sudden stabilising of the very lability he had, up to that moment, shared with Werther and his unfortunate model, the suicide Jerusalem.

What is it that this metaphor tells us about the enabling creative act? As I see it, two things. Firstly that, in the case of an artist, form is concealed in what seems sheer amorphous flux, to become manifest instantly and spontaneously. Secondly, that a process of stabilisation corresponding to that of the flux which spontaneously assumes form takes place in the artist himself, a stabilisation which precedes the material work of art and is indeed its presupposition. Even before water crystallises, we recall, it is supercooled and sheltered from all disturbing agencies. Here, between the lines, as it were, we come upon an artist's truth; and this, to my mind, points to a different order of events in the creative act than that generally assumed to be implied by Goethe's notorious statement that all his works are but the 'Bruchstücke einer großen Konfession'. This is commonly interpreted as meaning that by composing a work of art, the poet 'got it', and the pathological elements contained in it, 'out of his system', and *as a result* of such a cathartic art regained serenity and composure.

But is this what our simile tells us? Where does the cooling off and the composure set in? After the water has become a crystalline mass, or, to say the same thing in different terms, after the act of composing? Does an artistic composition come into being in the midst of soul-shaking upheaval and hotheaded passion? If so, Werther might have fared better and a bullet might have been saved. In fact, his *Glut* and his excess of emotional instability — paradoxically Werther is rigid in his very insistence on absolute fluidity of response — are such that he is never in the right frame to produce art and to be restored in the process. Either he is cool and distanced, and then he has nothing of import to compose. Or he is in a white heat of excitement and feels shaken; and then he is so riveted upon the object of his emotion that he cannot transfer his excitement to another arena altogether, to the encounter of vision and medium in the creative act.

Werther's psychic household is split down the middle as it were. His energies are divided as between personal and formal impulses. They run parallel, like rail-lines. What stirs him most deeply goes unsung. It is not seized, willy-nilly, by a powerful shaping impulse clamouring to pass it 'durch die innere Welt die alles packt, verbindet, neu schafft, knetet und in eigner Form, Manier, wieder hinstellt'[34]. Such a 'tampering' he at bottom repudiates as a sacrilegious *Herumbosseln an der Natur*. That fluid and labile interaction between both spheres of experiencing — the personal and the formal one — which characterises the true artist, to him is profoundly alien[35]. Werther's experiencing, fixedly geared to personal objectives, is never seized by artistic energies lying in wait to claim kindred emotional materials and to lift them into their own domain, there to be assimilated into the structuring

---

[34] Letter to F. H. Jacobi, 21. VIII. 1775.

[35] Cf. P. Valéry: 'Zwischen den Absichten und den Mitteln, zwischen den Vorstellungen, was werden soll, und den Verrichtungen, aus denen die *Form* hervorgeht, klafft kein Gegensatz mehr. Zwischen den Gedanken des Künstlers und dem Stoffe seiner Kunst schwingt nunmehr das Band einer innigen Entsprechung, deren *bemerkenswerte Eigenschaft eine Wechselwirkung ist,* die sich *jene die sie nicht erlebten, nicht vorzustellen vermögen.* Das Wesen von all dem hat Michelangelo in zwei Versen umrissen . . . :

Non ha l'ottima alcun concetto
Ch'un marmo solo in se circonscriva.'

(In: *Über Kunst,* trs. Carlo Schmidt, Frankfurt a. Main 1965 p. 87).

imagination[36]. But precisely this is what happens in the act of artistic conception: an experiential nucleus is gradually weaned from a purely personal nexus and transplanted into the artistic domain, there to be fertilised by formative energies drawing on a store of remembered forms. The obstinacy with which Werther cleaves to the personal sphere *from the very outset* precludes the inception of such an aesthetic structure.

The personal documents of the young Goethe we have discussed, whose ironic deployment within his novel we have noted, demonstrate to what extent 'human experiencing', for this young author, from the beginning took place under the aegis of its poetic usefulness, and that it was in all cases grist to his poetic mill. It is this predisposition to entertain all manner of things, from their very inception onwards, within an artistic imagination governed by the artist's relation to his medium, which marks the characteristically creative structure of experiencing and determines what is to be the artist's 'truth'; a mode of response and a 'truth' radically opposed to Werther's, who impassively receives what is offered to him without transforming it.

These observations are confirmed by the simile of water at freezing-point suddenly becoming structured. For this simile tells us that for Goethe, on this occasion at least, the enabling process of organising experiential materials set in spontaneously, at a stage long *before* composition proper, let alone the writing down, may be said to have begun. 'Das Ganze', that is to say the experience structured in and by the artistic imagination, is there, latent; and all its elements are organised before they 'von allen Seiten zusammenschossen und eine solide Masse wurden'[37]. On the contrary, this predisposition to let the inner temperature drop, to disengage, or shelter, oneself, somehow, from the habitual encroachments of experience, is the *conditio sine qua non* of the process of composition. Schiller knew this, too, when he warned the poet that there is no such thing as passionate poetry, but a poetry of passion conceived in the state of *fernende Erinnerung*[38]. The psychical distance — at which the supercooled water hints — is a pre-requisite of composition as much as its result. It is a "frame of mind", a latent disposition to stand back and perceive pattern in the welter of experiential elements, a response itself capable of creating the illusion of time lapsed or spaces intervening[39] (this is the force of Schiller's *fernend*) —; and this disposition it is which enables the artist to transfer his inital *Glut* from the material to the formal aspects of any situation which has arrested his attention, and to 'compose' it in terms of his chosen medium.

If then Goethe describes the feverish excitement into which he was plunged at the news of Jerusalem's death, adding 'so konnte es nicht fehlen, daß ich

---

[36] Cf. my *Goethe and Lessing*, Chapter VI.
[37] Cf. *Dichtung und Wahrheit*, III, 13, p. 585, ll. 27—30.
[38] In: 'Bürgers Gedichte a) Rezension'. *Sämtliche Werke, Säkular-Ausgabe*, Vol. 16, p. 239.
[39] Cf. Chapter VII, p. 178.

jener Produktion, die ich eben unternahm, alle die Glut einhauchte, welche keine Unterscheidung zwischen dem Dichterischen und dem Wirklichen zuläßt', we may now look upon this passage as evidence of a mode of connection between life-experience and artistic experience which is diametrically opposed to the one that is usually said to hold. The two spheres *are* indistinguishable; this is absolutely true. But not because the 'Glut' Goethe here avows is directed to the personal sphere, in a manner which would permit us to reduce the composition to its all too human elements and to *zerrupfen* (the term Goethe uses) the weave of the finished work in order to track down 'the truth' of it in its material ingredients[40]. No, the spheres are indistinguishable because the 'Glut' of which Goethe speaks is the 'coolness' which 'is derived from all that heat', the cold fire of the artist whose experiencing, from the very beginning, took place under the aegis of the secret formative impulse and, *for this reason*, is no longer capable of being separated out from the creative domain.

5.

I have, on several occasions, used the word 'frame' and have done so advisedly. Goethe himself, we saw, 'frames' his narrative of the *Werther-Zeit*, by embedding it in references to water, for all its fluidity. But then, at the heart of the whole account, at its climactic point, water emerges in its extreme permutation as ice, solidly structured; eloquent token, within this related if incongruous frame, of the mysterious self-organisation of a work of art, seemingly in the midst of overwhelming pressures and distress.

In a manner exactly parallel to this device, Goethe, in Book XIII, insulates his analysis of that disturbing phenomenon of *taedium vitae* which he had shared with so many of his contemporaries, and the ensuing account of the actual composition of *Die Leiden des jungen Werther* — the novel in which the young saw their own sickness reflected — by setting it into a framework of objectivity. He does so, in the beginning, by gently drawing our attention to the surprising kinship of his epistolary novel with that most objective of literary genres — the drama (III, 13, pp. 576ff.). It was his dramatic subjects, he tells us, which at that time had the strongest pull over him; not least because he was by nature and temperament an outgoing and social being rather than an introvert. Even his solitary hours, he tells us, he would cheer by turning them into so many imaginary parties, summoning up in his mind all manner of people he knew, with whom he would then discuss his current preoccupation. These presences, he tells us, were never chosen from amongst the circle of his intimate friends; they were, rather, acquaintances, often geographically distant or otherwise remote (III, 13, p. 577).

---

[40] *Dichtung und Wahrheit*, III, 13, p. 592.

With such imaginary visitors — they sound much like Lotte and Kestner in general type — he would then converse, listening to their opinions, expatiating on what appeared to please *them* and often politely deferring to their judgment. It is with the aid of such invisible counsellors, Goethe then reveals — and this revelation hits one like a bolt — that his *Werther* came to be written. 'Jene in diesem Geiste geschriebenen Wertherischen Briefe haben nun wohl deshalb einen so mannigfaltigen Reiz', Goethe concludes, 'weil ihr verschiedener Inhalt erst in solchen ideellen Dialogen mit mehreren Individuen durchgesprochen worden, die sodann aber, in der Komposition selbst, nur an *einen* Freund und Teilnehmer gerichtet erscheinen' (III, 13, p. 577f.).

What a fascinating transition from that most objective of literary genres — the drama[41] — to the epistolary soliloquy, and from Goethe's own geniality to those *Zöglinge der Einsamkeit* stricken by *taedium vitae*, and to Werther in particular! Even the young Goethe who stood behind the extreme subjectivism of his Werther created him in that object-impregnated mode, with that *Gegenständlichkeit* of perception and poetry-making which he himself was so joyfully to acclaim as the mainspring of his genius in all its manifestations. It was thus, by proliferating, as it were, his own objectivity in a number of imaginary assessors positioned all round his subject, that the young author ensured for his novel as a whole that stereoscopic depth of vision[42] which

---

[41] In fact, the epistolary novel restricting itself to the letters of only one character represents a more exacting form even than the drama, in point of the author's objectivity. Both genres are at one in that the figure's, or figures', statements are in character, if we except the *Herausgeberbericht* in which the narrator's voice is heard. The total statement made by the drama, however, is the result of the dialectical interaction of diverse characters' pronouncements complementing or modifying one another, as the case might be. Such a counterpoint, in Goethe's novel, is absent. It is for this reason that critics often maintain that, with the exception of motifs such as that of the peasant-lad which were added later, the main portion of the novel is devoid of landmarks enabling the reader to distance himself from Werther from the very start (cf. M. Mendelssohn (note 29); K. Scherpe (*op. cit.*, p. 27); Gerhard Kaiser (in: 'Zum Syndrom modischer Germanistik. Bemerkungen über Klaus Scherpe, Werther und Wertherwirkung . . . ', in: *Euphorion 65*, 1971, p. 197); G. Jäger (*loc. cit.*, p. 407)). Such readings fail to do justice to Goethe's telling employment of poetic motifs and, most of all, to the unrivalled expressive power and *finesse* of his language. In my own structural analysis of the novel I have traced some of these motifs and discussed some linguistic devices with a view to showing how the poet succeeds in ironising and quietly disproving Werther's own pronouncements. In my view, the reader who has taken in Werther's letter of May 10 and has paid sufficient attention to literary allusions, choice and order of words and syntactical features, is already alerted to Werther's disturbed relation to reality and established in his aesthetic distance from the soliloquising hero.

[42] G. Lucács convincingly writes: 'Nur in der Stimmung Werthers verdrängt am Schluß die Nebelhaftigkeit Ossians die klare Plastik des volkstümlich verstandenen Homer. Der junge Goethe bleibt als Gestalter im ganzen Werk ein Schüler dieses Homer.' (In: *Goethe und seine Zeit*, Bern 1947, p. 26.) This divergence between the speaker and the narrator in a novel in which the narrator nowhere intrudes, can only be explained in terms of the

Werther's single pair of blinkered eyes could never have achieved. And it is thus, by prefacing the retrospective account of an emotion-charged time and of the emotion-charged work sprung from it, with an analysis of his own, utterly contrary, mode of approach to that very work — sociable, objective, *gegenständlich* — that he at one stroke insulates the ensuing tale of woe. He sets it as it were within the frame of his own sanity; for this same attitude is highlighted once again at the end of his account, when he contrasts the distance he himself has gained from his novel with its frenzied reception by the general public. Thus, from the very outset he distances himself and the alert reader from the morbidity of the subject-matter with which he must at long last come to grips.

We have no grounds for doubting the correctness of Goethe's recollection, neither with regard to the genesis of *Werther* nor with regard to the sense of shock and distress its reception caused him; all of which is attested by a host of contemporaneous evidence. How much of that objectivity and circumspection which makes the novel itself so un-Wertherish is revealed here, between the lines, through the mere arrangement of the events that are reported, and through the frame within which they are placed!

But Goethe himself actually uses the image of the frame in his account of the *Werther-Zeit;* and this image is well worth looking at, both for the prominent position it holds in the second, climactic, section of the narrative, and for its intrinsic significance.

As we have remarked, Book 12 of *Dichtung und Wahrheit* somewhat tardily approaches its central topic, the biographical antecedents of the *Werther* story. It is in the following book, the thirteenth, that the poet reveals the genesis proper of the work which has some of its roots in Wetzlar, a genesis, however, which becomes interwoven with the account of his stay at Schloß Ehrenbreitstein and his relations, there, and later on in Frankfurt, with the La Roche family, especially with the eldest daughter, Maxe. As for this relation, it was a curious repetition, and reflection, of that with Lotte from whom he had fled. There, in Wetzlar, he had been the outsider, however cherished. He had become both more involved and more alienated than he had ever anticipated. Now, here, in Ehrenbreitstein, the tragi-comedy repeated itself, but this time with different players. Maxe was soon to be married to an older man in Frankfurt, and although she was not happy, and continued her former unselfconscious intimacy with Goethe, he once again found himself in the role of the odd man out. In his description of the La Roche set-up, he gives expression to his sense of alienation with the greatest frankness:

astonishing stratification of the linguistic idiom employed by the speaker; and this multi-layered character of the language in turn is illuminated by Goethe's own account of the novel's genesis. Cf. Victor Lange 'Goethe's Craft of Fiction', *(loc. cit.).*

'In so viel neue Familienverhältnisse war ich ohne wirklichen Anteil, ohne Mitwirkung eingeklemmt. War man mit einander zufrieden, so schien sich das von selbst zu verstehn; aber die meisten Teilnehmer wendeten sich in verdrießlichen Fällen an mich ... Es dauerte nicht lange, so wurde mir dieser Zustand ganz unerträglich, aller Lebensverdruß, der aus solchen Halbverhältnissen hervorzugehn pflegt, schien doppelt und dreifach auf mir zu lasten, und es bedurfte eines neuen gewaltsamen Entschlusses, mich auch hiervon zu befreien.' (III, 13, p. 587).

It all sounds very much like Goethe's own Werther: painfully aware of being the odd man out after some weeks of idyllic coexistence with Kestner, leaving, and returning, to find the same situation again, only more intolerable. But the difference is as subtle as it is striking. Werther goes back to the original scene and any distance he may have achieved in those wintry days away from Lotte melts away in the white-heat of a now hopeless passion. An experience which, in the first part of the novel, was still structured, becomes chaotic in its frenzied repetition: the appearance of the mad secretary and the *Bauern-bursche* become murderer merely serve to confirm and to enhance Werther's pathological mixture of involvement and alienation: what pattern there is in these recurrences, is not Werther's, but the poet's.

And now for Goethe himself. He too undergoes a similar experience twice over, but what was pristine and probably largely unconscious the first time, in its second phase is transferred to a new locality and a new inner arena and experienced, from the very start, in a subtly different way, predisposing him to perceive pattern and to compose it, given the necessary catalyst. And here the image of the frame on which I touched earlier on, becomes important. At the very outset of Chapter 13, the central *Werther* chapter, Goethe tells of his arrival at Ehrenbreitstein. After the shortest of introductory sentences about the La Roche family, he straight away plunges into a description of the locality. This is what he selects for his — and for our — first impression:

Das Haus, ganz am Ende des Tals, wenig erhöht über dem Fluß gelegen, hatte die freie Aussicht den Strom hinabwärts. Die Zimmer waren hoch und geräumig, und die Wände galerieartig mit aneinanderstoßenden Gemälden behangen. Jedes Fenster, nach allen Seiten hin, machte den Rahmen zu einem natürlichen Bilde, das durch den Glanz einer milden Sonne sehr lebhaft hervortrat; ich glaubte nie so heitere Morgen und so herrliche Abende gesehen zu haben.' (III, 13, p. 557).

Werther too experiences lovely mornings and splendid sunsets. But he would have baulked at such an artificial setting. 'Muß es denn immer gebosselt sein, wenn wir teil an einer Naturerscheinung nehmen sollen?' he would have contemptuously asked, had he looked upon a natural scene as insulated by art as this one here.

This opening of Chapter 13 is, I think, a subtle hint on the part of the poet that he came to his second love experience in a changed 'frame' of mind. From the beginning he perceived what he encountered as through a frame, 'ein natürliches Bild' surrounded by compositions designed and framed by

artists' hands and itself composed within its window-frame. Some may say
that the ageing author of *Dichtung und Wahrheit* looked back upon, and thus
very neatly 'composed', the tumultuous phase of his youth of which he was
shy even in retrospect. I am not so sure. For at the end of his account of
the genesis of the work, in the paragraph immediately following the description of the effect Jerusalem's suicide had on him and the creative act it
precipitated, Goethe resorts to the image again: and this time he clearly
remembers what the young author did in fact do: 'Das nunmehr fertige
Manuskript lag im Konzept ... vor mir. Es ward sogleich geheftet: denn
der Band dient der Schrift ungefähr wie der Rahmen einem Bilde: man sieht
viel eher, ob sie denn auch wirklich in sich selbst bestehe' (III, 13, p. 587).

6.

As the report of the genesis of the novel is flanked by references to frames,
so Goethe's experience itself of the second phase of the double-encounter
which issued in the actual composition of *Werther* takes place, I would
suggest, in a 'frame of mind' that is delicately different from his own former
states, from that of other mortals, and certainly from Werther's. He came
to Ehrenbreitstein, ready not only to endure a repetition but to perceive a
pattern, in the enhanced reflection of the Wetzlar episode. And perceiving
pattern always means distance, just as does experience 'reflected', taking the
word in both its meanings. This time, one feels, his *Lebensweise* was more
gewählt than *zufällig*. He felt alienated as he had done before, in Wetzlar,
perhaps more so. But it is a different alienation in kind from that to which
Werther falls victim. He was capable of turning it into the alienation of the
artist who articulates the pattern he perceives and, in order to do so, steps
back from it in a kind of disinterested enchantment. It is surely no accident
that his complaint about being a bystander caught up in a host of 'Halbverhältnisse' should, without break, lead on to one of the most crucial
paragraphs, i. e. the description of the act of composition itself, accomplished
at break-neck speed, and in a state of total creative alienation. We read:

> 'Ich hatte mich äußerlich völlig isoliert, ja die Besuche meiner Freunde verbeten, und so
> legte ich auch innerlich alles beiseite, was nicht unmittelbar hierher gehörte. Dagegen
> faßte ich alles zusammen, was einigen Bezug auf meinen Vorsatz hatte, und wiederholte
> mir mein nächstes Leben, von dessen Inhalt ich noch keinen dichterischen Gebrauch
> gemacht hatte. Unter solchen Umständen, nach so langen und vielen geheimen Vorbe-
> reitungen, schrieb ich den "Werther" in vier Wochen ...' (III, 13, p. 587).

We know of course that Goethe's memory played him a trick here; the
composition of *Werther* was taken in hand fifteen months after the time named
here, and the catalyst was not Jerusalem's suicide, but the marriage of Maxe
La Roche and the tensions resulting from it. But one might argue that the

telescoping vision of the poet here was truer than reality. For what is the scene between Brentano and Goethe in which the poet was forbidden the house, if not a mirroring of the unpleasantnesses surrounding Jerusalem's end, and what were these but an enhanced *Wiederspiegelung* of the events in Wetzlar? Of more consequence still than this condensation would seem to be the concealed connection between the two successive paragraphs. The one describing the *human* alienation of one caught up in 'Halbverhältnissen' is seamlessly joined to the ensuing account of that *creative* alienation which preceded the actual composition. Goethe treats as one continuous whole what was so different and yet evinced the same pattern. His artistic eye discerned reflection within reflection, reiterated a repeated event 'von dessen Inhalt ich noch keinen dichterischen Gebrauch gemacht hatte'[43]. And what better supplementation, on the reality-level, of the simile of supercooled water which, artificially sheltered from all disturbances, remains at freezing-point, than the description the poet gives of himself? Like the water he remains quite still, almost artificially insulated against all external influences which at this point would be extraneous and distracting, in the strangest equipoise between passivity and deliberation — 'Vorsatz' — contemplativeness and emotion —: a state of unadulterated latency. And for all Goethe's insistence, in that very passage, that he breathed into this product 'alle die Glut . . ., welche keine Unterscheidung zwischen dem Dichterischen und dem Wirklichen zuläßt' (III, 13, p. 587), we are perhaps less taken aback by the image he nonetheless chose for the process — that of water *freezing* into a solid structure — more able to understand the seeming paradox between being, at one and the same time, full of *Glut* and ice, and more inclined, finally, to perceive a substantial difference between Werther's truth and that of his creator, *qua* creator, than the poet himself chose to reveal at this point.

The lack of involvement, of active participation; 'Die Halbheit solcher Zustände', 'solche Halbverhältnisse': for a Werther this would — and did — amount to a verdict of death. For Goethe they were not just tormenting — that they were beyond all doubt — but he also availed himself of his freedom to stand back from the scene, to perceive its essential pattern and to use it *für seine Zwecke* when the time was ripe.

---

[43] There is a good deal of evidence showing that the young Goethe did in fact systematically collect impressions and experiences with the explicit purpose of utilising such materials artistically as occasion arose. Cf. his letters to Charlotte von Stein dated 1. I. 1780, 11. III. 1781 and 12. XII. 1781. Such documentation may be chastening to adherents of the *Erlebnis*-school of aesthetics; in fact, the storing up of materials for future use is a thoroughly familiar trait of the artistic sensibility. One thinks of Kleist's *Ideenmagazin* and of Keats' letter to B. R. Haydon, expecting full understanding for his 'looking upon the Sun, the Moon, the Stars, the Earth and its contents, as materials to form greater things' (10. III. 1817). Cf. also Chapter II of this book for Goethe's utilisation of motifs he found in the letters of Bettina von Arnim.

7.

'To use it' seems a rather harsh thing to say, suggesting a certain uncommitted-
ness of the artist in the midst of seeming commitment. But this is precisely how
it was, and is, and my words were circumspectly chosen. Maxe followed upon
Lotte. And although Goethe, in his general diagnosis of that strange phenomenon of *taedium vitae*, emphasises the disillusionment caused by the 'Wiederkehr der Liebe' (III, 13, p. 578), he himself reacted quite differently, and with
much more creative resilience. *Wiederkehr*, for him, meant reflection; and
reflection, so we learn from the essay *Wiederholte Spiegelungen* written in 1823,
means enhancement. Early on in Book 13 he writes, with an unselfconscious
frankness which is both charming and a trifle callous: 'Es ist eine sehr
angenehme Empfindung, wenn sich eine neue Leidenschaft in uns zu regen
anfängt, ehe die alte noch ganz verklungen ist. So sieht man bei untergehender
Sonne gern auf der entgegengesetzten Seite den Mond aufgehn und erfreut
sich an dem Doppelglanz der beiden Himmelslichter' (III, 13, p. 561f.). *Halbverhältnisse*, just because they are *Halbverhältnisse* and leave the artist free to
perceive, abstract and combine superimposed patterns reflecting one another,
for him may assume an enhanced significance, that *Doppelglanz*, in fact, which
illuminates the figure of the incomparable Lotte. Goethe himself tells us so
later on in the book, again with the same engaging frankness: 'Bei meiner
Arbeit war mir nicht unbekannt,' he writes, 'wie sehr begünstigt jener Künstler gewesen, dem man Gelegenheit gab, eine Venus aus mehreren Schönheiten
herauszustudieren, und so nahm ich mir auch die Erlaubnis, an der Gestalt
und den Eigenschaften mehrerer hübscher Kinder meine Lotte zu bilden,
obgleich die Hauptzüge von der geliebtesten genommen waren' (III, 13,
p. 593). Yes, Goethe 'used' this alienation, this half-commitment, to perceive
and articulate essential and authentic pattern. He used it creatively, as one
who is wholly committed only to one quest: to Venus Urania[44], to form *per
se*, to the making of art. It is the author of *Künstlers Erdewallen* — composed
roughly at the time of *Werther* — and the creator of Tasso as Leonore
Sanvitale sees him, who speaks here; not just the ageing author of *Truth and
Fiction* who could afford to be serene or maybe wished to appear so.

Yet Goethe also confessed to torment and anxiety at this time. To perceive
the *Doppelglanz* of two luminaries, one setting and the other rising, may have
its charms in retrospect. Experienced from nearby, however, such ambivalence may be far from pleasant and breed its own anguish, in a young man

[44] Regarding the invocation of the Muse — the speaker of 'Künstlers Erdewallen' apostrophizes Venus Urania — Gottfried Benn writes perspicaciously and wittily: 'An wen ist
ein Gedicht gerichtet?' Benn asks and quotes the 'bemerkenswerte Antwort, die ein
gewisser Richard Wiburn darauf gibt: Ein Gedicht, sagt er, ist an die Muse gerichtet,
und diese ist unter anderem dazu da, die Tatsache zu verschleiern, daß Gedichte an
niemanden gerichtet sind.' (In: *Gespräch über Lyrik, op. cit.* p. 66.)

capable of love and care. Again, the complexity of his reaction, as Jerusalem's fate — reflected in and merged with his own most recent trauma, the banishment from Maxe Brentano — together with his own composition burst on him, as it were, in one breath, must have been nothing short of frightening. It was an uncanny state likely to alienate him not only from others (he himself emphasises his monastic seclusion whilst putting *Werther* on paper) — but, far worse, from himself. For, at one and the same moment, he breathed his own *Glut* into the nascent work, and was distanced from its experiential materials to the point of iciness[45]. Worst of all, perhaps, was the alienation from those he loved, about whom he had written, and who thought that they still knew him, when in fact he had been so radically transformed in the strange processes of transposing truth — and an artist's truth at that which is different from the start — into fiction, that he hardly knew himself any longer. Such a situation carries the seeds of a deep inner disorientation. How could the others understand that *Werther* stood by itself, like the manuscript in its binding, like ice tipped out of its container? How could they suspect that the poet himself, in weaving his feelings and Lotte and Kestner and Maxe into a symbolic structure and transforming them — and his own relation to them — in the process, was a different person from the one they thought they knew? And indeed, how could they understand the connection between these 'untruths' and the higher truth of his novel? About these torments Goethe is quite frank in that almost tragic letter to Kestner written on November 21, 1774, after the latter had protested against the alleged indiscretions and distortions of 'reality' the poet had perpetrated in his novel. Years later, he returns to these unhappinesses in the retrospect of his autobiography. But in this reticent account we are forced to read between the lines. Once again, he feels alienated from his friends: but — "Freilich war es hier abermals der Stoff, der eigentlich die Wirkung hervorbrachte" (III, 13, p. 588), Goethe now reports, and this laconic comment is far more devastating than his subsequent account of the tumultuous response he sparked off in his contemporaries, at the very moment when he had regained his composure. For 'Le style, c'est l'homme': and if ever this was true of any book, it is of *Werther*. Only in its form had the metamorphosis its author had undergone in the process of composing found its proper precipitate. Only there — not

---

[45] This shift of interest Goethe articulated for the first time in 'Künstlers Morgenlied' (Stanzas 13 and 14), that is to say, roughly a year before he composed *Werther*. In later works, he treated of this re-orientation from the point of view of others, e. g. the princess in *Torquato Tasso* (V, 4), and the figure of the beloved in the cycle of sonnets (esp. No. XV). In this connection, cf. Chapter II of this book. John Keats says of the poet that 'he looks upon fine phrases as a lover' (Letter to B. Bailey, 14. VIII. 1809). Exactly this infatuation with his art shows through Goethe's promise to the Kestners that, in his revision of *Werther*, he would, within the year, expurgate everything that had caused them offence and hurt 'auf die *lieblichste einzigste innigste Weise* ... ' (21. XI. 1774).

in its *Stoff* — was *he* to be found. Not to understand the form of his book was not to understand the book; worse still, it was not to understand the man the author had become in the writing of it. The inane and universal quest for 'the truth' 'behind' the fiction was terrifying to one for whom the truth had in increasing measure changed and become that highly complex and iridescent phenomenon — an artist's truth[46]. And it is no doubt the sense of alienation, from others and from his erstwhile self, which prompted him to travel incognito for years after *Werther* was written (III, 13, p. 593). To nail him down to it, and to insist that he was the pre-Werther Goethe, was not only irksome in the extreme. It meant inflaming a mortal crisis of identity which had burst upon him as he wrote *Werther* and which was to remain associated with that work as long as he lived.

8.

How the experiential elements 'die sich ... in mir herumtrieben' (III, 13, p. 585) became transformed in the act of composing — and he along with them — one last example may show. Just before beginning his narrative of the *Werther-Zeit*, in Book 12, Goethe confesses to a deep sense of emptiness. He had left Friederike in Sesenheim and his friends in Frankfurt and Darmstadt. Thus, transplanted to a strange scene, 'war mir eine Leere im Busen geblieben, die ich auszufüllen nicht vermochte; ich befand mich daher in einer Lage, wo uns die Neigung ... unversehens überschleichen ... kann' (III, 12, p. 541). This 'Leere im Busen' Goethe was to feel twice again, in a short space of time: first, when he left Lotte in Wetzlar and, later, when he wrenched himself away from Maximiliane.

Meanwhile, he also 'used' it for his Werther as he was wont to 'use' so many elements of his personal experience. 'Ach diese Lücke!' Werther cries out, 'diese entsetzliche Lücke, die ich hier in meinem Busen fühle! — Ich denke oft, wenn du sie nur *einmal*, nur *einmal* an dieses Herz drücken könntest, diese ganze Lücke würde ausgefüllt sein' (II, Oct. 19). More surprisingly, the same image is taken up by the Editor with reference to the level-headed Lotte, in one of the most frankly revelatory passages of this section of the novel: 'Alles, was sie Interessantes fühlte und dachte, war sie gewohnt mit ihm zu teilen, und seine Entfernung drohete in ihr ganzes Wesen eine Lücke zu reißen, die nicht wieder ausgefüllt werden konnte' (II, p. 106).

Here, in the autobiography, the evocation of his post-Sesenheim depression ushers in the most amazing of modulations. In the paragraph immediately following that admission of emptiness he felt on coming to Wetzlar, the poet switches over to a different level of discourse altogether. The *Verfasser* — as

---

[46] Cf. *Dichtung und Wahrheit*, III, 13, p. 592, ll. 11—23 in which Goethe formulates this dilemma and the 'unleidliche Qual' it caused him.

he now calls himself — confesses to his sense of relief at having arrived, at long last, at the point where he may speak of his *Werther*, the topic which forms the gravitational centre of the book. 'Es hat sich nicht als selbständig angekündigt; es ist vielmehr bestimmt, die Lücken eines Autorlebens auszufüllen, manches Bruchstück zu ergänzen und das Andenken verlorner und verschollner Wagnisse zu erhalten' (III, 12, p. 541). What an audacious transposition into a new key! The pain and the anguish which originally attached to a personal context and which the poet, within the fictional framework of his novel, continued to use in such a context, for himself have become transmuted into the — quite unshareable — pain and anguish endured by the artist *qua* artist as he thinks of the gaps in the articulation of his life's picture and of the refractoriness of the 'elements' he seeks to integrate into a coherent whole. What a different connotation the word 'Bruchstück' assumes here from the one we traditionally associate with it, thinking as we do of the notorious 'Bruchstücke einer großen Konfession'! It signifies nothing whatever *confessional* here. The poet's concern is, in its entirety, with the *compositional* aspect of his life's picture.

Such failures of communication as this potential one here, the young author, in his time, must have encountered over and over again as he wrote his *Werther*. For, notwithstanding the fact that complicating sensations connected with his creativity had entered into his experience and shot it through with a strange new thread, he was blithely 'recognised' and hailed as the immutable model of his incurable character. No wonder that, by the time he came to write up the *Werther*-period in *Fiction and Truth*, he resignedly observed 'daß Autoren und Publikum durch eine ungeheuere Kluft getrennt sind, wovon sie, zu ihrem Glück, beiderseits keinen Begriff haben' (III, 13, p. 593). The public, because they do not know anything about the transformation in 'their' author, once the alchemy of the shaping-impulse is beginning to work in him; and the author because, by some saving grace, the trauma of alienation he endures — from his own habitual self as well as from others — in the act of patterning reality into a symbolic structure is turned into the serene containment which attends the process of 'composing' and is mercifully forgotten afterwards, like the pains of childbirth.

Goethe perhaps never said anything truer or more enigmatic than he did in the only letter he addressed to Maxe's mother[47] in more than five years. In this letter he summed up his being, saying

'Ich bin, wie immer, die warme Kälte.'

This is an artist's truth, the truth of any artist, in all places and at all times.

---

[47] To Sophie La Roche, 1. IX. 1780.

Strange encounter:
The Cycle of Sonnets 1807/8

Du Doppeltgänger! Du bleicher Geselle!
Was äffst du nach mein Liebesleid...
                                              Heine

I.

There is hardly a major work of Goethe's which has aroused such controversy as the cycle of sonnets written in 1807 to 1808. In fact, its very status
as a major work has been called in question. Gundolf roundly declares the
cycle and the almost contemporaneous *Pandora* to be works 'die man aus
Goethes Dasein weglassen könnte, ohne dies dadurch wesentlich anders zu
sehen'[1]. Summing up an otherwise interesting argument to which we shall
return, Gundolf concludes: 'Bestimmt sich der Wert nach der Fülle und
Ursprünglichkeit des ausgedrückten Lebens, so nehmen Episteln und Sonette
Goethes, da bloß aus Spiel und Spiegelung entstanden, unter Goethes Werken
keinen hohen Rang ein.'[2] At the other end of the critical spectrum stand
P. Hankamer, and E. Reitmeyer, in her *Studien zum Problem der Gedichtsamm-
lung mit eingehender Untersuchung der Gedichtsammlungen Goethes und Tiecks*. Reitmeyer suggests a symmetrical principle at work in the cycle and claims that,
in its final form, it ' ... zeigt die schöne, klare Symmetrie des Baues, die so
schön ist, daß das Ganze wirklich selig in sich selbst ruht'[3]. In a far less
formalistic approach Hankamer sees the artistic precipitate of Goethe's critical
transition to old age between 1805 and 1810 in the *Wahlverwandtschaften*,
Pandora and the cycle of sonnets, all of which he regards as works 'deren Rang
unzweifelhaft ist ... '. The form of the sonnet, with its 'gemeisterte Wider-
streit polarer Lebenskräfte'[4] was to become the perfect lyrical vessel in which
Goethe for the first time articulated that archetypal experience of *Entsagung*
which was to dominate his old age.

Between such extremes of rejection and acceptance we find the more
'middle of the way' assessments of M. Kommerell, E. Staiger and, more
recently, H. J. Schlütter. Kommerell, assessing the sonnets as 'einen merk-

---

[1] In: *Goethe*, Berlin 1916, p. 577.

[2] p. 579.

[3] Bern 1935, p. 89.

[4] In: *Spiel der Mächte. Ein Kapitel aus Goethes Leben und Goethes Welt*, Stuttgart 1943, p. 10
and 81.

würdigen, weit unterschätzten Gedichtkreis'[5], nevertheless sees it as a tentative forerunner to the *Westöstliche Divan*. Staiger too sees the Sonette as an 'Ankündigung von neuen Möglichkeiten'[6] but regards the cycle as a whole as falling short of the high pitch set by *Mächtiges Überraschen* and concludes that the only two works in which the new maturity of the poet has come to full fruition, are the *Wahlverwandtschaften* and *Pandora*. Schlütter considers that this cycle is 'nur ein opusculum auf dem Wege von Goethes klassischer zur Altersdichtung'[7], and distinguishes sharply between the poetic merit of the sonnets written after Goethe's return to Weimar at the end of 1807 and the earlier ones composed, in his view, during the preceding stay in Jena. In his opinion, the heart-pieces of the cycle are the letter-sonnets VIII to X 'die' — in the words of the blurb — 'zu den schönsten Sonetten des 19. Jahrhunderts gehören'. This biographically orientated approach is taken to an extreme by H. M. Wolff[8] who does not concern himself with the problem of evaluation but merely reconstructs an order of 'action' which would establish the cycle as the direct precipitate of Goethe's relationship with Sylvie von Ziegesar.

However varied the individual estimates of the cycle as a whole and of the relative merits of single poems or groups of poems in it, one feature is characteristic of all critics alike: they operate with the assumption of a basic polarity in the poet between 'spirit' and 'passion' which on the one hand called for the sonnet as its appropriate form whilst leading, on the level of subject matter, to a well-marked differentiation between the love-sonnet proper and those 'artists' poems' carrying a heavier intellectual freight and composed from a greater distance. This basic scheme is articulated time and again, most fully and incisively by Hankamer and by E. Trunz in the notes to Vol. I of the Hamburg edition of Goethe's works. Trunz is well worth quoting because of the succinctness of his formulations: the sonnets, we read, are 'gespannt in die Polarität von Leidenschaft und Geist'[9], in clear continuation of the classical Petrarchan tradition with its 'Antithese von Leidenschaft und Entsagung'[10]. Poems such as XIV articulate 'die innerste Möglichkeit dieser Form, die Antithese von Chaos und Kosmos'[11]. Thus this genre is eminently suited for a cycle nourished by a 'Hintergrundsspannung von Dämonie und sittlichem Willen . . .'[12].

---

[5] In: *Gedanken über Gedichte*, Frankfurt/Main 1943, p. 308.

[6] In: *Goethe*, Vol. II, Zurich 1956, p. 444 ff.

[7] Hans-Jürgen Schlütter, *Goethes Sonette. Anregung Entstehung Intention* in: *Goethezeit* Bd. I, Bad Homburg v. d. H. Berlin Zurich 1969, p. 122.

[8] In: *Goethe in der Periode der Wahlverwandtschaften (1802—1809)*, Munich 1952.

[9] In *HA* I, ed. E. Trunz, p. 632.

[10] *Ed. cit.*, p. 633.

[11] *Ibid.*

[12] *Ed. cit.*, p. 634.

The basic presupposition of all critics alike is that there is a well-defined experiential core in the shape of a human love relationship at the heart of the cycle, and that to a greater or lesser degree the poems, through their form as well as through their overt content, register the assimilation of this *donnée* in terms of resistance, proviso or affirmation. The polarity which governs these poems is seen as being one between human emotions engendered in the first place in a human encounter and the complex of reactions this precipitates in a poet no longer young and concerned to protect his inner universe. Putting it quite simply, it stems from the dialectic of love as encountered by an ageing, representative and vulnerable man. It is this unchallenged basic assumption as to the identity of the partners in this poetic conversation that the following pages seek to investigate.

2.

In the late essay *Bedeutende Fördernis durch ein einziges geistreiches Wort* Goethe, with evident delight, approves the contention put forward by Heinroth

> 'daß nämlich mein Denkvermögen gegenständlich tätig sei, womit er aussprechen will:
> daß mein Denken sich von den Gegenständen nicht sondere, daß die Elemente der
> Gegenstände, die Anschauungen in dasselbe eingehen und von ihm auf das innigste durch-
> drungen werden, daß mein Anschauen selbst ein Denken, mein Denken ein Anschauen
> sei . . .'[13]

And indeed, Heinroth had scored a bull's eye with his observation. From Goethe's earliest beginnings, he shows a genius in letting the object speak undistorted by the subjectiveness of the percipient. This is true even of the products of his *Sturm und Drang;* and it is in a large measure due to his strange 'object-permeatedness' that this labile and threatened young man steered through a turbulent period in which not a few of his lesser companions suffered shipwreck. The evocation of Lotte and her world in all their wholesome soundness — and an evocation through Werther's eyes at that! — is, I suppose, the most astonishing achievement of a very young poet in the midst of emotional turmoil. But even at a time prior to the composition of *Werther* Goethe had given proof of his *Gegenständlichkeit* in his treatment of the most refractory of subject-matters: his love-lyrics. For in them he succeeded in evoking a total situation, in which he was an emotionally engaged partner, with a perception at once tender and so translucent as though he himself stood clear of it. This is the secret of, say, *Mailied* or *Willkommen und Abschied*. In the former of the two poems, the event of first human love is not 'set' against the background of cosmic burgeoning: it is so consistently envisaged as an integral part of the encompassing event — the urgent bursting of a thousand buds into blossom and a thousand throats into song, the

---

[13] *HA* XIII, p. 37.

reflection of radiance all around, in the shimmering field and the glistening
eye — and so consistently enacted in the short expletives interlacing the
human and the natural spheres, that the pervasiveness and reciprocity of young
love and the very act of singing emerge with spontaneous conviction. Loving
is an 'organ' disclosing a world that is itself in love with life. And the world
thus disclosed gives the cosmic resonance to the personal event, permeating
it with its enhancing reality. There is no description of 'him' or 'her', no
depiction of any characteristic scene. And yet a young couple in the glory of
perfect reciprocity, giving as receiving, crystallises in the halo of radiance
that surrounds it.

Similarly, in *Willkommen und Abschied*, the storm-swept elemental coming
and going of the young lover is delicately reflected in her:

> Ein rosenfarbnes Frühlingswetter
> Lag auf dem lieblichen Gesicht . . .

and for all the difference of the mood that goes into the parting, the heart-
scene, realised with one stroke, once again captures a reciprocity of love
transcending the different modalities of male and female, of acting and suffering, a reciprocity beautifully enacted in the chiastic balance of the concluding
lines:

> Und doch, welch Glück, geliebt zu werden!
> Und lieben, Götter, welch ein Glück!

It is surprising enough how the young poet evokes a relationship in the
vibrant give and take of the sexes without in the least obtruding himself on
the picture. More surprising yet is his capacity to let a stressful relationship
emerge before our eyes, in such a manner that we can see it in the round, in
its distilled essence, uncluttered and undistorted by the perceiving I of the
speaker, however tellingly his tensions are conveyed. A quick glimpse at the
slightly later *An Belinden* will give some measure of this rare gift. So far
from being overweening, the clearly disturbed I of the speaker is malleable
and receptive in the extreme: 'ich guter Junge', he calls himself. There is a
slight distancing in that appellation. He sees himself in his little world as
though he were another. And thus, looking into his *Zimmerchen* from the outside, he conjures up his picture and hers, a picture that has deeply imprinted
itself on one unreservedly susceptible to the girl he loves and to all the stress
such loving brings:

> Ahndungsvoll hatt' ich dein Bild empfunden
> Tief in meiner Brust.

Stress is what is conveyed in the first stanza, with the unscannable syncopa-
tions in its long lines and the helpless trailing off of the short ones. The more
peaceful, flowing metres of the second and third stanzas, together with the
images he uses, speak of his own law: a budding creativeness cradled close
to nature. It is in such solitude that she, and her world, imprint themselves
on him with merciless clarity. At the same time, he himself experiences him-

self as he is in this *milieu*, as a double of himself whom he now sees in the third person. Who could exhaustively analyse the way in which the stabbing brightness of the vowels and the accumulation of monosyllabic words of the first two lines of stanza 4 evoke the bewildering glitter of this Rococo scene, the glaring chandeliers and the alien distractions? Or the way in which the choice of generalised words, in the second part of the stanza, the stressful syncopation of the *unerträglichen* and the reflected cacophony of the consonant scheme — e. g. *Ge-sichtern ge-genüberstellt* — combine to create the harshness of surface confrontations in a meaningless social bustle? And yet, so great is the speaker's willingness to let himself be permeated by what is so alien, and to permeate it in turn, that in the end he has made himself one with the object he so intimately feels:

Wo du bist, Natur.

He has literally achieved that phenomenon which the late words from *Bedeutende Fördernis durch ein einziges geistreiches Wort* were to articulate discursively and interpret for us: 'daß die Elemente der Gegenstände, die Anschauungen in dasselbe — [i. e. das Denken] — eingehen und von ihm auf das innigste durchdrungen werden'.

In the two great poetic cycles, the *Roman Elegies* and the *Westöstliche Divan*, that innate *Gegenständlichkeit* of Goethe's perceiving has found exemplary expression. 'Jeder neue Gegenstand, wohl beschaut, schließt ein neues Organ in uns auf', we read in *Bedeutende Fördernis*[14]. The creative encounter with classical Rome in which 'der nackete Armor' was revered discloses possibilities of simple sensual loving undreamt of by the disciple of Charlotte von Stein; and that loving, in turn, to him unlocks the very spirit of Rome and the ancient world and makes it his own. How vividly the figure of his beloved springs to life, strictly guarded as an unmarried Roman girl would be, swift to surrender, expertly dedicated to the care and bodily comforts of the 'freien, rüstigen Fremden' whom she loves, who has brought pleasure and plenty to her life, versed in love-making and all the domestic skills that make a home into an asylum of love, exquisitely cunning in the silent language of lovers in public places, and in deceiving her guardian, yet movingly chaste in her fearless dedication. How the nights spent with her make him a Roman under Amor's protection, and give him a lineage back to those days

Da er den nämlichen Dienst seinen Triumvirn getan.

It is his love, she who gave herself to him at the right moment, that reveals to him the deity of *Gelegenheit*, protectress of those that know how to seize and prize the swift present, be they Romans by birth or by affinity:

Einst erschien sie auch mir, ein bräunliches Mädchen, die Haare
Fielen ihr dunkel und reich über die Stirne herab,

[14] *HA* XIII, p. 38.

Kurze Locken ringelten sich ums zierliche Hälschen,
    Ungeflochtenes Haar krauste vom Scheitel sich auf.
Und ich verkannte sie nicht, ergriff die Eilende: lieblich
    Gab sie Umarmung und Kuß bald mir gelehrig zurück.

Her swift Southern loving[15] to him unlocks the whole company of the
immortals and the band of those mythological figures who enshrine the spirit
of antiquity, whose seed created Rome:

In der heroischen Zeit, da Götter und Göttinnen liebten,
    Folgte Begierde dem Blick, folgte Genuß der Begier.

Through the vivifying love-experience of a supremely receptive self a whole
world, a whole culture springs to life; and, saturated by such enriching contacts, the self receives itself back, transformed and surprised by its own new
simplicity.

A similar recognition of himself through the medium of a new world — and
of that new world through the medium of a transformed self — takes place
on that second journey, the spiritual *Hegire* to the East of which the *Westöstliche Divan* speaks. 'Der Mensch kennt nur sich selbst, insofern er die Welt
kennt, die er nur in sich und sich nur in ihr gewahr wird', we read in
Bedeutende Fördernis[16]. Swiftly and surely, the ageing lover of a sensitive younger
woman recognises the affinity to his own condition of Hafis' world — its
wrought translucency, its extravagant playfulness, its blend of intellectuality
and lightness — and appropriates it. This world, once seized, in turn discloses an inner 'organ' through which to experience and interpret Marianne's
loving and his. With what *Gegenständlichkeit* this relationship springs to life
— a loving developed to a high art by two virtuosi, a play with passion so
formed that in the very act of surrender they delight in the abstract pattern
of their game, and smile to one another across the distances between them.

Freude des Daseins ist groß,
Größer die Freud' am Dasein,
Wenn du, Suleika,
Mich überschwenglich beglückst,
Deine Leidenschaft mir zuwirfst,
Als wär's ein Ball,
Daß ich ihn fange,
Dir zurückwerfe
Mein gewidmetes Ich;
Das ist ein Augenblick![17]

---

[15] An aspect of Goethe's Italian stay which still reverberates in Hermann's rapid development to sexual maturity. Cf. the pastor's *apologia* for Hermann's instantaneous decision
to marry Dorothea, in Canto 5, *HA* II, p. 471 f.

[16] *Ed. cit.*, Vol. XIII, p. 38.

[17] In this connection, cf. Max Rychner, *J. W. Goethe. Westöstlicher Divan*, Zurich 1952,
p. 513 and Ehrhard Bahr, *Die Ironie im Spätwerk Goethes. ' . . . diese sehr ernsten Scherze'*,
Berlin 1972, p. 75.

Equally realised is the relation to Saki, adoring adolescent who feels protective of his exuberant and carelessly carousing master and finally drops healthily asleep, watched over by his charge who in the midst of intoxication has the wakefulness of age.

This self is dedicated, shadowlessly absorbed into these relationships, and yet strangely aware of its own contour as he receives it back from Suleika's and Saki's hands; a self both light and wise, reverent and urbane, at home with the universe as with the midget and marvelling at its own width and extravagant range which reflects the extravagant richness of the world to which it has become attuned.

It is in this late cycle as it has been from this poet's beginnings: the supreme receptivity to which a whole world and the relations that have mediated this world to him, have become *gegenständlich*, envisages itself as receiving no less than giving. In *Mailied* and in *Willkommen und Abschied* he is loved as much as loving; in *Ganymed* 'umfangend umfangen'; in 'Warum gabst du uns die tiefen Blicke' he experiences himself as the learner who

fühlte sich in deinem Auge gut;[18]

in the *Roman Elegies* he is happy to confess:

Und umwunden bin ich, römische Flechten, von euch;

and so, too, even the sovereign mind of the *Westöstliche Divan* feels himself to be the creation he receives from the hands of his beloved:

Wie sie sich an mich verschwendet,
Bin ich mir ein wertes Ich;
Hätte sie sich weggewendet,
Augenblicks verlör' ich mich.

As we approach the cycle of sonnets written in 1807 and 1808, we must bear in mind those basic and constant features of Goethe's poetry which the brief survey of these pages have revealed: the disclosure of a saturated relationship in which the poet's being is shadowlessly absorbed, and of a whole world that has been mediated to him through this relation; and the reciprocal disclosure of a transformed self mediated to him through a transforming personal and cultural encounter: a *gegenständliches* self gratefully experienced as a gift from the hands of his beloved.

3.

To enter the world of the cycle with which we are concerned in this chapter is to enter a very bare and austere world indeed: the abstract world of the sonnet. Here, in the sonnets, we enter the world of the troubadours and Petrarch. Yet how marginal it all remains, how little there is of the plasticity

18 Cf. Chapter VII.

with which the classical world had saturated the *Roman Elegies* or indeed of the Eastern aura that pervades Goethe's *Divan* as with a delicate perfume. One poem in which the most illustrious ancestor of the genre, Petrarch, takes a bow, a couple of allusions to the courtly world of *Minne*, a passing and not very serious reference to the Last Judgment, and that is all. What is more, such atmospheric touches are neutralised, and even ironically undermined, by the poet glancing over his shoulder at a contemporary drama interspersed with sonnets by one W. v. Schütz. It has often been remarked that this cycle lacks the coherence of a world in which it is set or an action it unfolds. Trunz sums up this paucity succinctly: 'Äußerliche Situations-malerei gibt es kaum. Ein paar bildhafte Situationen sind angedeutet, aber sie sind mehr symbolisch ... Sie zeigen fast keine Umwelt, sondern nur zwei Gestalten in bedeutenden Bewegungen und Haltungen. Auch ist keine eigentliche Handlung in den Sonetten.'[19]

Are we then to see the cycle of sonnets as centred in 'zwei Gestalten in bedeutenden Bewegungen und Haltungen'? This, at first sight, seems a likely enough supposition. We seem to be dealing with a group of poems concerned with a love-relationship: two figures, that of the poet and that of the *Mädchen;* a series of recollected encounters in the more distant past (V), two actual encounters (II and IV); one contemplated encounter (III); two actual dialogues between the lovers (XIV and XV), foreshadowed by a monologue of the lover on a related topic (XI); three love-letters by *die Liebende* (VIII, IX and X); one by her lover (XII); nostalgic reflections by him after their separation (VI and VII); musings on the nature of their love (XIII and XVI); and the definitive if enigmatic revelation of the girl's identity (XVII): this, with the exception of the opening poem which seems to move on a more abstract level altogether (although it, too, has an encounter for its topic), comprises the situations and themes sounded in the cycle as a whole. How can we doubt that it is 'about' a love-relation?

But as soon as we narrow our focus and scrutinise the partners in that love-relation, new doubts begin to arise. It has often been noted that the girl portrayed in sonnet IV — *Das Mädchen spricht* — bears little or no resemblance to the writer of the letters in sonnets VIII, IX and X. The one is forceful, the other feminine and yielding. Moreover, neither of them seems to fit together with the frivolous shrew the poet warns about the consequences of her dilly-dallying in sonnet XIII, nor indeed with the mediaeval *Frauen* or *Fürstin* or *Herrin* invoked in II, V and XVI respectively[20]. To which it

[19] *HA* I, p. 632.

[20] Cf. Hankamer who operates with the hypothesis that the cycle is inspired by Goethe's passionate attachment to Minna Herzlieb and who has to concede that 'für Minna-Ottilie ist der Ton der Mädchensonette meist zu spielerisch frei. Er ist nicht artig, sondern selbstgewiß bis zum Scherz.' (*Op. cit.*, p. 71.) Staiger argues that the contour of the *Mädchen* remains blurred: 'Das Mädchen der Sonette ... wandelt sich und entschwindet

must be added — and this has oddly enough not been remarked upon — that the voice we hear in the two dialogue-poems (XIV and XV) does not tune in with any other we have heard, except perhaps remotely with that of the speaker of sonnet IV: it is a delicate voice betraying a high degree of intellectual and, indeed, aesthetic sophistication.

Biographical data, some factual and others of a speculative nature, have been advanced to explain this incongruence. The degree of Goethe's emotional engagement with Minna Herzlieb has been variously assessed by different critics[21]. Whatever the truth of this matter, it has been convincingly shown by R. Steig that Goethe made extensive use of letters written to him by Bettina Brentano shortly before and during the composition of his cycle[22]. To complicate matters further, the thesis has been advanced that the real figure 'behind' these poems is not Minna Herzlieb but Sylvie von Ziegesar[23]. To the Goethe biographer these questions may be of burning interest. In the present context the only relevance attaching to such inquiries is, firstly, that the protracted controversy about the identity of the female partner does suggest some lack of unification in Goethe's portrayal, and, secondly, that

uns, sobald wir es anzuschauen versuchen . . .' *(op. cit.,* Vol. II, p. 445 f.). Schlütter criticises the 'sentenzenhafte [Redeweise] des Mädchens' which, here as much as in XIV and XV, gives rise to an 'unbeabsichtigte Komik'. *(Op. cit.,* pp. 87 ff.) Schlütter reads the three poems in which the *Mädchen* makes a substantial contribution to the theme of life-experience and art-experience — in my view the overriding theme of the cycle as a whole — as being expressive of that 'Humor, in jenem offenen, der Geselligkeit gemäßen Sinn' (p. 96) which betrays Goethe's uneasiness with the form of the sonnet; and this supposed uneasiness of the poet with a genre as yet unfamiliar to him makes Schlütter relegate these poems to the initial phase of the composition in Jena, preceding Christmas 1807. I would take exception to Schlütter's estimate of these sonnets as being sociably 'scherzhaft' (p. 87), to his equation of humorousness with uneasiness which he culls from a tortuous interpretation of one of Goethe's maxims (p. 98), and thus, ultimately, with the whole chronology he bases on such shaky foundations. Cf. note 33 for an assessment of his critical method. I hope to show that the sonnets he thus stigmatises as lacking in displacement and, therefore, infers to have been composed early on, in fact are amongst the most substantial — and exciting — of the entire cycle. Joachim Müller, on the other hand, considers the very sonnets Schlütter so highhandedly dismisses as constituting 'die tiefere Einheit' of the cycle. Unfortunately his detailed observations are often too difficult to follow to form a concrete contribution to the scholarly discussion. (*Goethes Sonette — Lyrische Epoche und motivische Kontinuität,* Berlin 1966.)

[21] For a summary of critical discussion on this point, cf. Schlütter, *op. cit.,* p. 131 ff.

[22] In: *Bettinas Briefwechsel mit Goethe, auf Grund ihres handschriftlichen Nachlasses,* ed. Reinhold Steig, Leipzig 1922.

[23] By Wolff, whose study is wholly concerned with the role played by Sylvie von Ziegesar in the poetic works of that period and, in the treatment of the *Sonette,* exhausts itself in the effort to trace a coherent love-plot. Wolff would scarcely approve of Thomas Mann's description of Goethe's love relationships: A 'dichterisch zweckhafte, jedenfalls dichterisch fruchtbare Liebesleidenschaft' he calls Goethe's relation to Marianne von Willemer, whilst the engagement to Lili Schönemann is brushed aside as a 'werkwidrige Dummheit'. (In: *Neue Studien,* Stockholm 1948, pp. 13 and 26.)

the love-relationship articulated in the cycle is such that the poet felt free to draw on motifs and formulations deriving from a woman with whom he was assuredly in no melodious rapport — Bettina. If the later inclusion, in the *Westöstliche Divan*, of poems actually written by Marianne von Willemer suggests a high degree of consolidation between personal and artistic engagement (even though her contributions retain a subtly different tone from Goethe's own Suleika poems), the procedure adopted here would seem to point in the opposite direction[24].

To form some picture of the *Liebende* in this work, it would seem advisable to turn to that group of sonnets in which she is allowed to speak for herself, that is to say, the three letter-poems which take up the central portion of the cycle. Acclaimed as the heart-piece of the whole collection by a modern critic[25], these sonnets were already singled out from the rest by Goethe's contemporary Caroline Sartorius soon after their appearance. 'Schön waren sie alle', we read in a letter to her brother;

> 'am schönsten aber die in welchen er *Sie* sprechen ließ und mit deren Zartheit ich nichts zu vergleichen wüßte, wie es denn wohl noch nie einen Dichter gegeben hat, der in das Weibliche Gemüth so tiefe Blicke gethan, und es ist als habe das ganze Geschlecht von der Edelsten bis zur Niedrigsten bei ihm beichte gesessen.'[26]

There is a good deal of truth in this assessment. These sonnets portray a feminine sensibility *par excellence*. The voice we hear is receptive in the highest degree. She is pure response as it were. He, and the hours spent with him, are the sole content of her consciousness. His glance, his kiss, the caressing words he once spoke to her: no more. She turns these memories over in her mind, weeps, feels him to be near even while he is far, and reaches out for confirmation:

> Vernimm das Lispeln dieses Liebewehens!
> Mein einzig Glück auf Erden ist dein Wille,
> Dein freundlicher zu mir; gib mir ein Zeichen! (VIII)

She writes that she has nothing to write about; and refrains from saying what is unspeakable, as she was silenced already once before by his fulfilling presence:

> So stand ich einst vor dir, dich anzuschauen,
> Und sagte nichts. Was hätt' ich sagen sollen?
> Mein ganzes Wesen war in sich vollendet. (IX)

---

[24] Staiger tentatively suggests that the poetic exploitation of motifs supplied by Bettina may point to some doubt, on the part of the poet, as to his creative capacity (*op. cit.*, II, p. 445), a possibility Schlütter vehemently rejects (*op. cit.*, p. 107).

[25] Schlütter (*op. cit.*, esp. p. 116 and 121), whose whole argumentation and dating are determined by his high regard for these letter-poems, considers this generality of conception to be their prime virtue.

[26] In: *Goethes Briefwechsel mit Georg und Caroline Sartorius*, ed. Else v. Monroy, Weimar 1931, p. 83 f.

She imagines sending him a sheet of blank paper and responds to the imaginary reply with which he might grace it:

> Sogar dein Lispeln glaubt' ich auch zu lesen,
> Womit du liebend meine Seele fülltest
> Und mich auf ewig vor mir selbst verschöntest. (X)

Caroline Sartorius is not far off the mark: these poems do not outline an individual, characteristic profile. They portray, rather, the distilled and somewhat generalised essence of feminity[27]: the woman who lives for her love, and has no being apart from that loving. She is pure receptacle, void of any content bar what he pours into it. This lack of individual identity becomes progressively more marked. In the concluding tercet of the last sonnet she dreams up the very whispers she still remembers in the corresponding portion of the first. As no message from him reaches, and fills, her, she has progressively less to say. The dominant image of the last poem — the blank sheet — is an eloquent symbol of this vacuity. And, turning back to our brief digression in the previous section, we note a striking reversal of the pattern we had seen to be characteristically Goethean: from the early *Sturm und Drang* poems to the *Divan*, it is he, the poet, who feels himself to be the recipient in the love-relationship; a pattern which finds its culmination in the *Marienbader Elegie: she* raises him up into her arms; he feels received

> Als wärst du wert des ewig schönen Lebens;

his heart beats, 'für alles ihr zu danken'; a gratitude which finds its ultimate formulation in the words 'fromm sein!'

This pattern here is dramatically reversed. It is he, the speaker of these poems, the *Dichter*, who is the giving one; he that completes her being and raises it to a higher pitch of significance. She is the blank sheet he fills, a mirror which reflects back, not her image at all, but his, enhanced by the magnitude of her devotion.

Not that this pattern is isolated in Goethe. It is well marked in his dramas. Gretchen and Klärchen boundlessly adore their lovers, and Egmont (when he surprises Klärchen in his full ceremonial regalia) no less than Faust mirror themselves in the naively worshipful admiration they inspire[28]. But then these figures are conceived in the dramatic mode and their function, at least in part, is precisely to reflect back a magnified image of the hero. Here, in the lyric mode, the reversal of the customary pattern is all but unique, and powerfully contributes to the overall effect of these 'heart-pieces' on the reader: they fail to give any individual profile to the partner in the love-relationship, portraying a generic femininity which is implemented in terms of pure responsiveness.

---

[27] Cf. Schlütter (*op. cit.*), p. 121.

[28] Thomas Mann has noted this 'narzißhaften Einschlag' of Goethe's eroticism. In: *Adel des Geistes*, Stockholm 1955, p. 609f.

This generic character of the female partner was praised by Caroline Sartorius and has been declared as fulfilling the 'poetic programme' outlined by Goethe in a letter to Minna Herzlieb's foster father, the printer Frommann, in a letter dated December 26, 1807, in which he announces his intention to portray in his sonnets 'ein zwar irdisches und gegenwärtiges, aber doch auch warmes und treues Wohlmeynen und Lieben . . . '. Before venturing on any value judgment of our own, it is important to emphasise two facts: the figure of the *Mädchen*, in the poems where she speaks for herself and could be justly expected to come to life most vividly, fails to do so. She lacks all the *Gegenständlichkeit* that is characteristic of the female partners in Goethe's lyrical poetry of, say, Lili in *An Belinden*, of Frau von Stein in 'warum gabst du uns die tiefen Blicke . . . ', of Faustina, or indeed of Ulrike von Levetzow in the *Marienbader Elegie*. She is a void filled by him, a mirror reflecting his magnified image. This may be connected with the genesis of these sonnets, which demonstrably utilise motifs ocurring in Bettina Brentano's contemporaneous letters to Goethe without being addressed to her. Now Bettina's masculine and active wooing of Goethe stands in the sharpest possible contrast to the passive responsiveness evinced by the writer of these letter-poems. Goethe lifted the material Bettina offered him from her letters, transposed it into a new key and adapted it to his purpose of portraying his partner in her own right.

As I see it, he failed in this intention, if indeed he ever had it. And this is in turn connected with the poetic quality of the three sonnets given over to 'the beloved'. They are charming poems; as sonnets they are decidedly weak. They lack the dynamic which is the hallmark of the genre. The sonnet is a strictly dialectical form. It demands tension between its two asymmetrical and all but self-contained halves, the octet and the tercets, differentiated as the latter are by new rhymes and new rhyme schemes, apart from being intrinsically shorter. This structure asks for increasing concentration and an energetic acceleration towards a climax. Over and above the central divide, polar tensions may play between the two quartets or the first and second tercet respectively — qualities which are displayed in an exemplary fashion by the opening sonnet of the cycle, *Mächtiges Überraschen*. The girl's letter-poems, with their uninterrupted lyrical flow, lack such dynamic; and this is true in increasing measure, in the degree in which her feeling loses definition and direction. In the first of these letter-poems, the incision between octet and tercets still marks a reversal. A low is reached with the words 'da fang' ich an zu weinen'; and this surprisingly ushers in a hopeful turn which is intensified in the second tercet. In the middle poem, *Die Liebende abermals*, the break between octet and tercet is slurred over by the repetition of the same motif: the 'Wonnen, Hoffnungen, Entzücken, Plagen' at the end of the second quartet are too suavely echoed in the 'Sinnen, Wünschen, Wähnen, Wollen' of the first tercet. It is true that the speaker decides not to communicate these preoccupations which she had initially wanted to describe to her lover: but the fluid verbal transition blurs the sharpness of contour and overlays the architecture of the form. In *Sie kann nicht enden* the flow of associations is entirely unidirectional; and in the leisurely and lyrical gait of the poem the antithetical power and precision of the form and the tensions it generates are all but completely dissipated.

In his masterly exposition of the inner structure of the sonnet, W. Mönch insists on its 'Zweigliedrigkeit' and its 'dialektische Struktur'[29]. The prescribed change of rhyming words and rhyme scheme as from octet to tercets 'verlangt Umschwung des Inhalts. Wenn der Gedanke von dem einen Gedichtteil in den andern hinübergeschleift wird, läuft die Komposition dem inneren Gesetze des Sonetts zuwider'[30]. In increasing measure this is the formal flaw of the three letter-sonnets. If, a little later on, Mönch describes the sonnet as being 'die gegebene Form für den Geist-Menschen, den Denker, der, wie Schaeffer sagt, "im Zustand einer Leidenschaft eine Befeuerung seines Wesens und somit auch der Verstandeskräfte erfährt"'[31], he identifies the slightness of feeling the poet musters for his female partner as the cause of the essential weakness of these poems *qua* sonnets. W. Kayser's observations on the genre are a similarly apt comment on the poems we are considering: 'Es läßt an sich keinen strömenden Rhythmus und als Haltung kein schlichtes Hinsingen und kein leidenschaftliches Hinausströmen zu. Es verlangt Bau, und zwar ganzheitlichen Bau des rhythmischen Gefüges ... es verlangt damit bewußtes, diszipliniertes Sprechen.'[32]

Thus the 'heart-piece' of this cycle diverges in a number of important points from the features which we have reason to believe are characteristic of Goethe's love-lyrics seen as a whole. Unlike the two great cycles, unlike single poems even, such as *An Belinden*, this group of poems does not mediate any *gegenständliche Anschauung* of the world in which the loving encounter takes place. Nor does the figure of the female partner, here conceived as a passive vessel in the very poems one could reasonably expect to bespeak her individuality, attain the felt-through contour this poet is so adept at evoking. He has not permeated himself with the life he has created; and this underexposure, ill concealed by the foreign material he introduced, is reflected in the low pitch of the sonnets given over to her. As we have seen in the previous chapter, Goethe readily and successfully amalgamated materials from diverse strata of his experience in a given composition. Bettina's own mother, Maxe Brentano, had lent her features to the portrait of Lotte. Indeed, many motifs taken from different contexts of his own experiencing found their way

---

[29] In: *Das Sonett. Gestalt und Geschichte*, Heidelberg 1955, p. 33.
[30] *Ibid.*
[31] *Op. cit.*, p. 36.
[32] W. Kayser, *Das sprachliche Kunstwerk. Eine Einführung in die Literaturwissenschaft*, Bern 1948, p. 262.

into *Werther* and were assimilated into a homogeneous whole which bears all the marks of authenticity. Why did he not succeed here, by the same procedure, in evoking a compelling image of the partner in the central relationship in her own right? Could it be that to do so was a peripheral concern which failed to command the best energies of the structuring imagination? We must bear this possibility in mind.

4.

The picture changes out of all recognition as we broach the group of sonnets in which the relationship between the lovers is brought before our eyes in actual, concrete encounters. The sonnets concerned — II, IV, XIV and XV — show us 'zwei Gestalten in bedeutenden Bewegungen und Haltungen' (Trunz). They portray a vital, dynamic relationship eminently fitted to the character of the genre and indeed giving rise to powerful sonnets that fully realise the rich dialectical texture and structured energy inherent in the form. What makes the sparks fly?

Quite generally we may describe the life of these sonnets as springing from a polarity of stimulus and resistance. These poems move, not singly, but in waves, and the direction of the movement is reversed, usually more than once. Their dynamic may be compared to the restless to-ing and fro-ing in the first tercet of *Mächtiges Überraschen*. The pattern is exhibited at its simplest in the first sonnet of the cycle to be composed, *Das Mädchen spricht* (IV). Resistance, mounting, issues in stimulus. This basic polarity is thematically explored on a number of levels, with *Freundliches Begegnen* unequivocally on the plane of personal feeling and the following sonnets of the group steadily moving into less charted borderlands where love and art meet and inextricably mingle: 'Sonnettenwut und Raserei der Liebe'.

The first poem of this series, *Freundliches Begegnen*, makes full use of the dialectical possibilities of the sonnet. It is in continual movement, the second quartet reversing the direction of the first one, a dialectic which is re-enacted, in greatly intensified form, in the two tercets. This wave-like rhythmicity of the movement means that the coming to rest at the end of the last tercet — 'sie lag in meinen Armen' — is felt to be provisional if forceful. The movement which has swept through the poem twice might well start up again after a temporary lull. The sonnet certainly comes to a close, a dramatic close even; yet its unexhausted impetus points beyond its confines: a perfect combination for a sonnet virtually inaugurating a cyclic action, and an apt annunciation of the cycle's inner beat[33].

---

[33] Cf. Schlütter who judges, incomprehensibly in my view: 'Dieses Spiel von Überraschung und Wiederholung gibt der Fabel den humoristischen Einschlag.' This assessment is important in that it forms the basis of Schlütter's evaluation of the cycle as a whole and of his chronological inferences. Citing Goethe's maxim: 'Der Humor entsteht, wenn die

The speaker, in the first quartet, is resistance personified to any impingement from the outside. 'Zur nahen Flucht gewillet', wrapped up in his cloak and intent on making do with the internal warmth generated by such protective covering, he walks alone on a rocky path declining into a wintry scene. In an abrupt reversal the second quartet introduces the — highly stylised — figure of the girl. Everything is turned about: the wintry greyness gives way to a sense of the heavens opening, the *unruhige Sinn* of the fourth line is pacified in the 'Mein Sehnen war gestillet' of the eighth; and the girl, 'musterhaft' — a favourite typifying epithet of the old Goethe — like 'jene lieben Frauen der *Dichter*welt'* is greeted as 'der neue Tag', the image Tasso had used to express the revolution engendered by the princess' entry into his life. The lineaments of an artistic encounter are faintly discernible. The first tercet repeats the initial movement by taking up the identical image. The poet — we may by now address the speaker by this name — wraps himself more firmly into his own warmth, that 'innre Wärme, Seelenwärme, Mittelpunkt' the young Goethe had so passionately invoked, more than thirty years earlier, in *Wandrers Sturmlied*, to which the symbolism of the protective covering of genius is essential. Another abrupt turn in the second tercet: he throws off his cloak in an impetuous movement and entrusts himself to the warmth of the loving encounter.

The same imagery is continued into the next meeting, *Das Mädchen spricht*, and here again images of warmth — or its opposite — are dialectically intertwined with inaccessibility. The figure of the poet has doubled. He stands side by side with his own marble bust. The girl senses that his stony likeness is the projection of his unapproachable self. He is as contained in himself as is the work of art that is his externalised image. And as protected.

'Der Feind verbirgt sich hinter seinem Schilde', the girl complains. Both, artist and image, appear equally cold to the onlooker, if anything the man who is called alive more so than the stone.

>   Mit dir verglichen zeigt der Stein sich milde ...

the girl comments and, later on, complains:

>   Sollt' ich von beiden Kälte leiden müssen,
>   Da dieses tot und du lebendig heißest?

Vernunft nicht im Einklang mit den Dingen ist, sondern sie entweder zu beherrschen strebt und nicht damit zu Stande kommen kann ... oder sich ihnen gewissermaßen unterwirft und mit sich spielen läßt', he substitutes 'die Sonettform' for 'Dinge' and Goethe's 'noch immer nicht ganz geschwundene Skepsis' [towards the sonnet] for 'Vernunft' and arrives at the conclusion, central to his argument, that the greater the humour (in his reading) which prevails in a given sonnet, the greater the uneasy distance of the poet from his chosen form and the earlier the date of its composition. Conversely he argues 'daß die Komik sich desto mehr aus den Sonetten zurückzieht, je mehr das Sonett als Kunstform geschätzt wird.' (*Op. cit.*, p. 98.) It will be seen that Schlütter's manipulation of Goethe's maxim is arbitrary in the extreme.

* my italics.

Eventually she decides to coax the hidden fire out of the live man and to rouse his jealousy by bestowing passionate kisses on the stone.

It may be relevant to note the similarity, and contrast, of the situation articulated here with that of the Pygmalion myth. Pygmalion falls in love with one of his own statues and is wretched at its unresponsiveness. To comfort him, Aphrodite animates the marble and the union between artist and image is consummated. The situation depicted here is the exact obverse. Artist and image — the image of himself *qua* artist, inviolate from external impingements, resting in his inner harmonies — are in unbroken silent rapport. The artist, doubled, is shown in the undisturbed, consummated relation to himself. This artistic Eros, in the classical myth pacified by the goddess, here is abruptly invaded by the girl seeking to divert it into an outside relationship of an overtly erotic character. From the two contemporary accounts we have of the incident with Bettina, it becomes clear that the poet himself had done not a little to provoke this attack[34]. Interestingly enough, the sonnet has dropped this motif altogether. It squarely focuses on a situation of an inward turned narcissistic eroticism, which is immune to relationship and thus felt to be a resistant stance, as it is interfered with by a powerful erotic stimulus from an outside source seeking to redirect its force. The dynamic of resistance and stimulus which informs the poems of this group is becoming defined as having its centre of gravity in the artistic consciousness. The girl is the occasion revealing the lability of the artistic Eros, no more. Whether or not she succeeds in transmuting and rechannelling it, the poem does not say.

This shift to the internal scene of experience impinging on the artistic domain is completed in the remaining two sonnets depicting actual encounters, Nos. XIV and XV. The first of these poems would seem to invalidate this statement from the start: for do not *Die Liebenden* form a firm phalanx against *Die Zweifelnden* and counter them with the voice of solidarity? However, this question merely raises further ones that have to do with the identity of the speakers. Who are *Die Zweifelnden* that ask

Was quält ihr euch und uns ...

with the Sisyphus-labour of their sonneteering? What outsider, rather than the poet himself, would be tormented by the fruitlessness of such exacting labour? Again, who is the speaker of the second quartet who seems to articulate — and critics have noticed this — the very defence of the sonnet as being the appropriate form for wary hearts which the poet of these sonnets might himself have advanced? Who, finally, are the 'ihr' addressed by *Die Zweifelnden*, the 'wir' of *Die Liebenden*? Do they now both compose sonnets —

Ihr liebt, und schreibt Sonette!

---

[34] Cf. R. Steig (*ed. cit.*), pp. 304 and 413.

and

> Im Gegenteil, wir sind auf rechtem Wege!

— as Marianne von Willemer and Goethe were to collaborate in the composition of the *Westöstliche Divan*?

I would suggest that it is the poet's voice we hear throughout this sonnet, refracted first in the dialectic between doubt, defence and renewed doubt, and then again in the culminating dialectic between artistic and personal Eros. Resistance and stimulus once again is the underlying dynamic generating the polar movement that patterns this densely structured poem. Resistance in the first quartet, analogous to that expressed in the opening line of 'Natur und Kunst, sie scheinen sich zu fliehen': what is the use of tinkering with the sophisticated form of the sonnet when the loving heart seeks to reveal itself in immediate utterance? The second quartet reverses the position. The heart is no longer young. It is precisely a resistant form that may act as a stimulus for a heart that has outgrown *ganz ungebundne* utterance. The first tercet again reverses its direction.

> Was quält ihr euch und uns, auf jähem Stege
> Nur Schritt vor Schritt den läst'gen Stein zu wälzen,
> Der rückwärts lastet, immer neu zu mühen?

After this renewed reversal, stimulated by the sense of insuperable resistance, the lovers jointly speak. And in the culminating tercet resistance and stimulus are once more dialectically intertwined.

> Im Gegenteil, wir sind auf rechtem Wege!
> Das Allerstarrste freudig aufzuschmelzen,
> Muß Liebesfeuer allgewaltig glühen.

This is said by both lovers. But again we must pause. The imagery of warmth, hugely intensified here, has permeated the poems depicting the lovers' actual encounters. And so far it has been the 'innre Glut' of the artist, contained in himself, passionately absorbed in his creative Eros. We shall presently add some further links to this associative chain. What is decisive here is the logical direction of the statement made by this unusual pair of lovers. They do not say that the melting down of resistances in the creative act serves to bring about a conflagration of love. Quite the contrary: a mighty conflagration of love is invoked because such energy will melt down such resistance as inhibits the consummation of the creative act itself. The love relation is the means; the end — contained in the final clause — unequivocally refers us to the artistic domain. This fact has, to my knowledge, not been noted: it indubitably reverses the customary emphasis[35] and identifies the poet as the true speaker. Of course, 'love', Eros, is involved here, and, with it, the figure of *Die Liebende* who knew how to strike sparks from marble. But

---

[35] Cf. for instance J. Müller's summarising observation in an otherwise sensitive appraisal. (*Op. cit.*, 20f.)

this love is a means, an occasion: it will turn into the artistic Eros which will — and at this very moment does — smelt down the rigid form of the sonnet and make it molten metal in the poet's hand.

The last poem in this series of 'encounters' is again cast into the form of a dialogue, between the girl and the poet (now the male voice is unequivocally identified as that of the *Dichter*). It is a marvellous sonnet, second to none in the whole cycle for the sheer power with which, through a series of retardations, it mounts to a climax which truly enacts what it says: the force of it fairly blows one over. In this sonnet the poet has certainly not hesitated

Sein Innerstes von Grund aus umzuwühlen;

a necessary reminder to all those who insist that virtuosodom, and poems about virtuosodom, are playful and 'second-grade art' in that they are not directly nourished by biographically accredited love-involvements. The artistic engagement, especially when its Eros is crossed by personal arousal, is a play with fire; and nowhere, except in his *Tasso* and in the *Wahlverwandtschaften*, has Goethe expressed the deadly seriousness of this game of chance more devastatingly than in this sonnet[36].

Formally, the immense power of this sonnet incongruously derives from the interlocking of the quartets with the first tercet. The girl has, in the first quartet, expressed the qualms which *Die Zweifelnden* had already advanced in the corresponding quartet of the previous poem: she has pinpointed the polarity between sincere loving and the virtuoso performance demanded from the sonneteer: the niceties of the form he is handling with its 'verschränkte Zeilen', its 'Silbespielen' and the filing processes it necessitates. The girl knows all about the narcissistically tinged erotic pleasure her 'süßer Freund' derives from such pursuits; and sadly and ironically contrasts his *Ernst* with the *Ernst* of emotional commitment in relationship.

The second quartet elaborates the point she has made. The artist may be ruthless *with* himself, but if so, he is only ruthless *for* himself, for his art's sake. Here, as in the last tercet of the preceding sonnet, the customary expectations are reversed: he does not arouse interest because his existence is fraught with emotional crises; on the contrary, he churns himself up so as to arouse the interest of his readers and entertain them stylishly. The whole cycle of emotions to which he exposes himself — his burns and his balms — is self-induced and internal. Like the artist holding secret intercourse with his own bust, he is contained, exclusively related to himself and to his art. His art is his heaven and his hell.

---

[36] Perhaps this is the kind of thing E. Staiger has in mind when he writes: 'Etwas Ungeheures geistert hin und wieder zwischen den Zeilen'; but one does not know because in the sequel (as so often) he keeps his options open: 'Öfter aber scheint alles doch nur artistische Sprachgebärde zu sein'. (*Op. cit.*, II, p. 446.)

The *Dichter*, in his reply, fully confirms all she has said. And he confirms it in the self-same terms. If she knows that the artist drives secret shafts into his depths, so does he:

> Irrgänglich-klug miniert er seine Grüfte;

if she knows that he is a professional at his game, he counters by calling himself a trained — *ausgelernt* is the word Goethe uses — 'Feuerwerker'; if she knows that his burns are controlled, inflicted on himself to lend fire to his 'Silbespiele' and his play with 'verschränkten Zeilen', he can go one better: he is an adept at arranging superbly timed artistic fire-works,

> Drauf ausgelernt, wie man *nach Maßen** wettert . . .

This apparent assent of the tercet creates an impression of stasis which runs counter to the sonnet form. All seems to have been said that can be said, about artists and art-making. But it is the lull before the storm. In the second tercet hell breaks loose:

> Allein die Macht des Elements ist stärker,
> Und eh' er sich's versieht, geht er zerschmettert
> Mit allen seinen Künsten in die Lüfte.

What a statement, like a streamer swishing past all the earlier provisos across three lines, in a huge arc, with its 'zerschmettert' — it rhymes with 'wettert' — bursting in midair and 'alle seine Künste' audibly dissolving in the 'Lüfte'! Interestingly, with the exception of *Mächtiges Überraschen*, which stands apart anyway, such resounding enjambments between the last two lines are only to be found in *Kurz und Gut* (III) and *Nemesis* (XI), and the end of all three sonnets alike speaks of — fire.

But the slurring of the second quartet and the first tercet which is here so cunningly employed to delay, and intensify, the climax, has another function yet. It also blurs the dividing line between the two speakers. It is the poet to whom the fire imagery belongs on which the girl touches. He it is that knows the secrets of the artistic household, its ruthless squanderings and its ruthless economy, his immunity from searing contact, the deep fraudulence of his existence. The girl is no more than the externalisation of his own voice; and that warning voice uttering those inner provisos it is which in the end will generate the spark and set off the charge of high explosives — the sudden illumination of the devastating risks of being a virtuoso. This is the Goethe of the *Wahlverwandtschaften* holding a monologue with his self, one of the most intimately tragic monologues we may overhear in the whole of his work: the partner in this conversation is a poetic fiction.

In fact, Goethe has already introduced us to the secret partner with whom the poet holds his dialogue. He very appropriately comes on to the scene in *Kurz und Gut*, that is to say in the sonnet preceding the one in which we

---

* my italics.

encounter his double in the unequivocal shape of his marble bust. *Kurz und Gut* again very appropriately sets in where *Freundliches Begegnen* had left off. In that poem resistance is not spent; and at the beginning of the next poem it is once again to the fore. She, who had been the subject of the previous encounter, the first one, in this poem becomes an outside object about which the poet negotiates with his partner: and this partner is his heart.

In a perceptible effort to take the whole affair casually — the accumulation of trivial words in the first two lines tells us so — the poet decides to retire gracefully from an encounter in which he may become unduly involved. No easy matter this, as is betrayed by the words 'dem vielgewohnten Schönen', resonant as they are with the suffering strains of *Pandora*, the *Trilogie der Leidenschaft* and the second *Faust*.

The second quartet essays an answer to the question raised by the first. The poet must have his heart's assent. It cannot be denied outright. What about diverting the Eros that has been roused into artistic channels, and writing a poem 'about' her? This would be an innocuous way of being *liebevoll* and, yet, out of harm's way.

The creative partnership works. The poet can pull off the conversion-trick, together with his heart. They are old hands at this game.

> Siehst du, es geht! Des Dichters Wink gewärtig,
> Melodisch klingt die durchgespielte Leier,
> Ein Liebesopfer traulich darzubringen.

Here, as in sonnet XV which we have just discussed, the division between the octet and the tercets is slurred; the mental movement inaugurated with the poet turning to his heart continues, even beyond the first tercet, into the second which begins with what is a virtual repetition of the first line of its forerunner:

> Du denkst es kaum, und sieh: das Lied ist fertig;

and here, as in that high-explosive later sonnet, this retardation is used to twist the end, with its bold enjambment, into a biting dialectic:

> Allein was nun? — Ich dächt', im ersten Feuer
> Wir eilten hin, es vor ihr selbst zu singen.

Undoubtedly, this is both a very good and a light-handed sonnet. In fact, the poet who is here coming to terms with his heart, *is* the *Feuerwerker* of the climactic sonnet, the fifteenth, who feels himself to be in full control of his craft, and his own craftiness. The 'durchgespielte Leier' here corresponds to the *ausgelernten Feuerwerker* in the later poem. But the coda of that later poem is still missing, at this point in the cycle.

And yet, what depths are sounded even in this seemingly light-weight poem. What abysmal irony in that resolution,

> Ein Liebesopfer traulich darzubringen.

Lightly, Goethe here touches on ranges of experience he had lived through at the time of *Werther* and later, of *Tasso*. Is the poet who 'files' at his words, who, in the white-heat of creation, falls in love with them, still making an offering of love to the person his poem is 'about'? And most importantly, does the poet whose structuring imagination has achieved the wrought miracle of, say, a *Werther* feel that its authenticity still speaks the plain language of emotional sincerity? An authenticity bought at the price of overlaying experience with experience, Charlotte Buff with Maxe Brentano, until he has coaxed the abiding pattern from the individual encounter? I have dealt with this range of problems at length in the preceding chapter; they were not problems specific to Goethe's youth: they reverberate even here, in this *trauliche Liebesopfer*, coined at the threshold of old age[37].

In his youth, everything had had the radiance of innocence: loving, the spring of creativity — *ein Quell gedrungner Lieder* — that welled up from such loving, even the wretchedness of inner betrayal. All had been fresh and singular and sacred. But then experience — the mere fact of repetition which the author of *Dichtung und Wahrheit* claims to be one of the prime causes of the *taedium vitae* that befell the young — had claimed its inevitable toll: repeated loving, the gradual adaptation to the shock of being able to convert emotional disasters into creative triumphs and to survive, the very awareness even that he could command ever richer and more beguiling poetic registers, all this had left its mark. It was a different thing to sing at a time

Da wir noch von Liebe litten

or
. . . ins bekannte Saitenspiel
Mit Mut und Anmut einzugreifen,

or, indeed, to elicit mellifluous strains from 'die durchgespielte Leier', as he is asking his heart to do in the sonnet we are considering.

Perhaps this 'Liebesopfer' the poet here prepares is not so much an offering of love as an immolation of his very loving. After the very first encounter, itself ambivalent in the highest degree, he withdraws into the safety of creative containment, into the luxury 'zu sagen, wie ich leide',

In liebevollen, traurig heitern Tönen.

Such sacrifice is not one to be thought of lightly[38], or as giving rise to 'poetry of the second grade'[39]. Far from it. The fifteenth sonnet, and others yet in this cycle, should teach us to think again before we judge these poems to be 'scherzhaft' or springing from 'scherzhafter Übertreibung', as critics

---

[37] For radically different readings of this sonnet in a light-hearted humorous vein, cf. Schlütter (*op. cit.*, p. 96), Wolff (*op. cit.*, p. 142) and Müller (*op. cit.*, p. 24). On the other hand, Thomas Mann roundly declares 'daß . . . seine Treuherzigkeit treuloser Art und sein Lieben ein Mittel zum Zweck, ein Mittel zum Werke war.' (In: *Neue Studien*, p. 58.)

[38] Schlütter (*op. cit.*, p. 87) in relation to XIV and XV, and p. 96 in relation to II, III and IV.

[39] Cf. Gundolf, *op. cit.*, p. 577.

have described them[40]. It is a sacrifice of immediacy at the first stirring of love and an all but instantaneous withdrawal of the erotic energies that have been released, into an inwardness that preserves and transmutes them into the incessant creative labour to which this vulnerable and ageing man is committed. We must not be fooled by the poet's

> Ich dächt', im ersten Feuer
> Wir eilten hin, es vor ihr selbst zu singen.

This is a temporary deflection of the magnet-needle, and the next sonnet will find the girl *vis à vis* that impenetrable paradox of a poet who is 'wie immer, die warme Kälte'[41]: the artist who, for all that he glows with a concealed fire, faces all outside impingements as frozen as his bust. Here, in the third sonnet, written to follow the first encounter, the decision to internalise the newly awakened Eros and to sublimate it into creative Eros is taking shape before our very eyes: it is a shunting of the nascent feeling onto a new track, a lifting of it into a new context within which it is from now on experienced and progressively structured. It is this early transference of the total emotional complex from the personal to the creative arena which accounts for the — uncharacteristic — wavering in the delineation of the girl the cycle is 'about'[42]. The direct emotional exposure of the poet to his fictitious partner has been too short for him to have permeated himself with her being and to be able poetically to implement it with that *Gegenständlichkeit* which attaches to Belinde or Lida or Faustina or Suleika. In lieu of such a patient personal exposure and the felt-through poetic image it would yield, Goethe utilised the raw materials he derived from a tributary source — the Bettina letters — and, adapting them to the requirement in hand — the portrayal of a mirroring receptivity — merged them with the features of whoever had sparked off the creative Eros in him — in all probability Minna Herzlieb — into a generalised and uneven portrait.

5.

Thus, the strange encounter which has fed this cycle of poems has yielded no cultural landscape comparable to that revealed in the *Roman Elegies* or in the *Westöstliche Divan*. Nor has it issued in a poetically saturated evocation of the woman who has, in those other cycles, mediated such a cultural encounter. The withdrawal of libidinal energy from the central female personage of this cycle occurs too early on to permit of such an envisagement in the round, in her own right as it were. She is marginally realised as a function of the figure of the poet: as resistance, stimulus and mirror.

---

[40] Cf. Schlütter, *op. cit.*, p. 87 and Grete Schaeder, *Gott und Welt. Drei Kapitel Goethescher Weltanschauung*, Hameln 1947, p. 278.

[41] Cf. Chapter I, note 51.

[42] Cf. Chapter I, p. 22 f.. Cf. also my *Goethe and Lessing*, Chapter V.

But there remains one figure this cycle does evoke with an almost uncanny *Gegenständlichkeit*, an etched sort of sharpness: and that is the figure of the poet. Over-lifesized, the austere image of one disturbed by Eros in a *Mächtiges Überraschen* and set on damming it back into the interior reservoir of his creativity meets us in these pages. There is an almost demoniacal objectivity about this self-portrait: the rhetoric of gesture about the cloaked forbidding figure striding through rocky regions, iced over and made, one feels, of sheer granite, the stone whose 'einsame stumme Nähe' the shaken heart of the young poet had already once sought, in which Jarno-Montan will seek the communion of the solitary; the incessant ironic doubling of himself, who is double, in his immobile bust, in his true, if labile, partner, his heart, and in those immense internal dialogues conducted with his shadow image, the girl; the mirroring back of his hugely magnified self in the reflecting surface of those letter-sonnets, in which she is dwarfed and he appears as the sole owner and dispenser of what life she has, a Promethean creator, unmoved mover, a God incapable of being transfigured by the glory of his creation and reborn in it.

Not that the withdrawal into creative solitude which sets in after the very first encounter is effected painlessly or once and for all. The Eros which feeds love and art alike is much too strong a power, and too Janus-faced, to permit of any surgery that would excise the disturbance and yet keep the creative core intact. The centrality of the impingement, and its violence, can be gauged from a sonnet like *Nemesis*. Chary of infections of all kinds, the poet shuns poetic and personal involvement alike, only to be ruthlessly persecuted by both in one:

Sonettenwut und Raserei der Liebe.

In a few poems the inner dialectic — not between passion and renunciation in the ordinary sense of those words, but between personal and artistic Eros — is pacified; and there the poet speaks in those 'liebevollen, traurig heitern Tönen' he had elicited from his heart, attains to that 'reine, gesättigte Spiegelung' Kommerell has seen as the culminating achievement of this stressful cycle. Significantly, these are the sonnets that usher in and consummate the separation: *Wachstum* and, more specifically, *Reisezehrung* and *Abschied*. These poems reflect the progressive stages of internalisation, the withdrawal of libidinal energies to an inviolate centre where they become creative[43], by that long and patient process of sublimation and transmutation the poet was to describe, in a less taciturn and more bountiful period of his life, in the poem *Die schön geschriebenen*. There are no such extravagant riches bequeathed to him by the beloved of this cycle, riches to be treasured even as they are being exchanged. The exposure was too short and, maybe, the answering voice too faint to warrant such reckless surrender as will regenerate him in the

---

[43] For a similar assessment cf. Staiger, *op. cit.*, II, p. 448.

midst of renunciation, in the *Westöstliche Divan.* Here he parts from a child, a younger sister, a *Fürstin,* different facets of one visualised just long enough for him to sense that he must withdraw by casting her into the mould of the unattainable. *Reisezehrung* and *Abschied* are incandescent with loving and renunciation, because it is in pain that he loses, and retrieves, the energies he has himself fed into the encounter with his Eros. What is left and what he retrieves, is creativity distilled, that sense of love understood as a symbol which we shall have occasion to discuss in later chapters and which has found consummate expression in the *Divan* line

Mir bleibt genug! Es bleibt Idee und Liebe!

These words are adumbrated in the concluding lines of those poems in which Eros, internalised, is pacified at the price of renouncing all outward possessions, of renouncing the relationship even that, fructifying the creative self, has threatened to invade it at its core. Now that Eros is safely taken back into the inviolate centre:

> So kann ich ruhig durch die Welt nun reisen;
> Was ich bedarf, ist überall zu haben,
> Und Unentbehrlich's bring' ich mit — die Liebe.

And:

> Ich suchte mein Verlornes gar verdrossen.
> Da war es gleich, als ob der Himmel glänzte;
> Mit schien, als wäre nichts mir, nichts entgangen,
> Als hätt' ich alles, was ich je genossen.

The heavens that opened at the sight of the beloved has become an interior radiance, pure landscape of the sore and shining heart.

6.

There remain the two flanking poems of the cycle, *Mächtiges Überraschen* and *Scharade:* incomparable in poetic power and human displacement, both are set a little apart from the body of it. The chiffres they employ attract our attention: they veil as much as they reveal.

The first of these, the opening poem of the cycle, has been universally acclaimed as perhaps the finest sonnet Goethe ever wrote. It is a majestically perfect sonnet; and to say this is tantamount, almost, to emphasising its austerely abstract quality[44]. For so powerful are the dynamics of this genre and so self-structuring is the dialectical play of its polarities that all the content it needs is its own internal movement manifested in sound. It is as it were geometry become music. This ultimate purity of form Goethe has realised in *Mächtiges Überraschen;* and one feels hesitant to blur it by a search for any too concrete meaning-equivalent. The image he has chosen echoes

---

[44] W. Mönch explores the possibility of essentially 'abstract' sonnets. (*Op. cit.*, p. 50.)

one that he had previously used in *Mahomets-Gesang* and *Gesang der Geister über den Wassern* as well as in the opening scene of *Faust II*. It is that of a fast flowing mountain torrent, faceless, elemental force, pure dynamics become audible in time. Unstructured and anonymous, its contour and personality are carved out by what it encounters on its course; in this case, by the prefigured course of the sonnet-form itself, and the encounters it holds in store.

In the opening quartet we meet this energy rushing under an irresistible momentum towards its destination, impatient of being held up, oblivious of its own power to transmute impetus into image, untrammelled force into bounded form. In an abrupt reversal, the second quartet introduces the counter-energy: a mountain, demoniacally animated, flinging itself and its whirling entourage into the way of the stream, arresting its downward course. Another reversal in the first tercet: 'Mächtiges Überraschen'. The waters, seeking an outlet, restlessly fluctuate to and fro. As they mount the unrelenting barrier, they are deflected, fall back and are met, and drunk, by the newly oncoming waves. A seething welter of energies fruitlessly warring and confounded by cross-currents simultaneously surging forward and retreating. The last line of that tercet takes up, in intensified form, the message of the first quartet:

> Gebannt ist nun zum Vater hin das Streben.

Then, in the second tercet, comes the gathering up of all the previous strands and the resolution of the dialectic, still reverberating in the *Schwanken* — an important word for Goethe as we shall see — the *Blinken*, the *Wellenschlag* and even the *neue Leben*. The waters come to rest in the 'weite Schale', now become a lake. Force is contained and transmuted into form, a self-contained form. And the waters now discover that power to reflect which they had sought to bypass in their impatient striving to their destination. They reflect — themselves, as they had done early on in their course, and as they are now, lapping against the rocks — and they reflect the stars that mirror their eternity in the *neue Leben*: infinite momentum pacified in the infinity of the symbolic moment.

What is there to interpret about this poem that is not contained in its own form, except for saying that it mirrors the strange encounter that is the substance of this cycle? Libidinal energy flowing out, austerely, majestically towards its destination; Eros crossing and all but catastrophically confounding it; and the final miracle: all this force being cupped and contained through the transforming power of creative Eros, and reflecting in a symbol the infinity of energies to which direct discharge is denied. The anonymity of the carrying symbol — water — corresponds to the anonymity of the libidinal force the course of which is traced in this cycle of poems, from its first arousal to its final sublimation: Protean Eros. Oreas and Eros — the words are all but the same.

And the concluding sonnet? *Scharade* has been taken as a tender and good-humoured bow to Minna Herzlieb to whom Zacharias Werner had already paid a compliment in *verschränkten Reimen*. And this no doubt it is[45]. But I think that Goethe has concealed more in the chiffre language of this poem than the two innocuous syllables 'Herz' and 'Lieb' betray at first sight. He himself indicates as much in the first quarter of the poem:

> Zwei Worte sind es, kurz, bequem zu sagen,
> Die wir so oft mit holder Freude nennen,
> Doch keineswegs die Dinge deutlich kennen,
> Wovon sie eigentlich den Stempel tragen.

It is a good thing, the poet tells us,

> Eins an dem andern kecklich zu verbrennen;

but again, what does this mean? Is the heart being seared by love, or love seared by contact with the heart? If the former, is the pain 'was Herzen redlich fühlen' or that self-inflicted burn that the poet himself 'weiß ... auszukühlen'? If the latter, is the poet describing the self-immolation of love he was to articulate in *Selige Sehnsucht*, or the far more dubious *Liebesopfer* that is proposed in *Kurz und Gut*? There is no clear-cut answer to these questions. The poet himself has warned us that we are dealing with words the reference of which is far from certain.

We have, I think, gained some insight into the confusing signification both these words have taken on in these poems. 'Herz' is what *die Liebende* means when she reminds the poet of 'was Herzen redlich fühlen'. It is also the poet's ambivalent partner who colludes with him in evading the impact of the emotional encounter by giving utterance to it in 'traurig heitern Tönen'. 'Lieb' is what the poet experiences when he says

> Ich fühl' im Herzen heißes Liebetoben.

It fills the pages of her letter-sonnets. But it is also present in that highly dubious 'Liebesopfer' the poet and his heart decide 'ihr traulich darzubringen'; and that love is riveted as unrelentingly to the artistic Eros in

> Sonettenwut und Raserei der Liebe ...

as the two sides of that Janus-faced power, Eros himself, are fixed to one another. It is precisely this inner ambivalence *within* the terms to be polarised which informs the best of Goethe's sonnets with their dense dialectical texture.

Could it be that in that moving supplication of the poet

> In Einem Bild sie beide zu erblicken,
> In Einem Wesen beide zu umfangen

---

[45] Through his identification of the girl 'behind' the sonnets with Sylvie von Ziegesar H. M. Wolff is reduced to arguing that this poem, 'genau genommen', does not belong to this cycle but should have been placed into the group 'An Personen'. (*Op. cit.*, p. 149.)

a deeply resigned man gives utterance to the wish to be single once more, and to be able to say, with his own Tasso:

> Was auch in meinem Liede wiederklingt,
> Ich bin nur *einer, einer* alles schuldig?

Such a second innocence was once again to be granted to the author of the *Westöstliche Divan* and *Trilogie der Leidenschaft*. Here, in this painfully etched encounter with himself against a blurred backcloth, he seems to be asking his reader:

> Fühlst du nicht an meinen Liedern,
> Daß ich eins und doppelt bin?[46]

---

[46] *Gingo Biloba, Westöstlicher Divan, Buch Suleika.*

II A Master in the Making

Stillness and tranquillity set things in order in the universe.

La Tsu

One trifling Word:
'Zwischen uns sei Wahrheit'

'My way is to share my love, not share my hate.
Sophocles

I.

The plaster cast which has enveloped the figure of Iphigenie for so long, has audibly begun to crack. A number of critics have raised their voices against the increasing unreality to which the idealisation of the heroine of Goethe's first classical verse-drama has inevitably led. And although their protests have been heard and the school of thought is rapidly dying out which insisted on seeing in her an all too simple incarnation of Winckelmann's concept of 'edle Einfalt, stille Größe'[1], it may yet prove useful to identify the critical fallacy from which such an oversimplification has sprung in the first place.

The common root of E. M. Butler's[2], R. Peacock's[3] and B. Fairley's[4] assessment — to mention only some — can, I believe, be traced to the rubric 'Charlotte-poetry'. The period into which inception and execution of Goethe's classical drama falls, is that of his close association with Charlotte von Stein. His manifold utterances dating from that time — poetic utterances such as 'Warum gabst du uns die tiefen Blicke', letters and diary entries as the case may be — have attuned us to the idea that it was Goethe who was the disturbed and unbalanced partner in this relationship, whilst Charlotte acted as the wise and moderating influence on her younger friend. From this it was easy and tempting to extrapolate to the figures, and the emotional constellations between them, that appear in the dramatic works of the time. Tasso and Orestes, labile and driven as they are, were taken to be masks of their creator; and the fact that Goethe himself acted the part of Orestes invited such an identification. Conversely, the figures of Iphigenie and of Eleonore D'Este were with equal aplomb identified with the person of Charlotte von Stein. These latter figures thus became a convenient repository for all that

---

[1] E. M. Butler apodictically states: 'Goethe created in *Iphigenia* what Winckelmann had seen in Laocoon: noble simplicity and serene greatness in the heroine, and the conquest of pain and suffering by sublimity of soul.' (In: *The Tyranny of Greece over Germany*, Cambridge 1935, p. 101).

[2] Cf. note 1.

[3] Ronald Peacock, 1) 'Goethe's version of Poetic Drama', *PEGS* XVI, 1947 and 2) *Goethe's Major Plays*, Manchester 1959.

[4] Barker Fairley, *A Study of Goethe*, Oxford 1947.

Goethe himself was not, for all those qualities he lacked in himself. The qualities associated with him were perceived in the threatened figures of the male protagonists. An easy equation, this, but a fallacious one. Goethe is in truth to be found in Orestes *and* Iphigenie, and in Pylades and Thoas and Arkas as well. And the same holds good, *mutatis mutandis*, for the personages of *Torquato Tasso*. If Iphigenie were in fact all that her creator was not, how could the interaction between her and Orestes possibly be explained? And — more crucially yet — how could we possibly account for the balance of contour and proportions this truly classical drama so patently achieves? Both, interaction and resolution of dramatic conflict as well as the beneficial symmetry of this play can only be explained on the assumption that its heroine was, at best, an *internalised* Charlotte von Stein, that she was as much flesh of her creator's flesh and bone of his bone as was her male counterpart, in short, that she and Orestes share both the problems and the disposition to transcend these problems which Goethe himself evinced in his relationship with Charlotte von Stein, a relationship which was, after all, both viable and of his own choosing.

The legacy with which a predominantly biographical approach has saddled us, then, is an untroubled and pure Iphigenie, a dramatic figure who has no problems[5] and, therefore, undergoes no real development.

This sad emaciation has been vigorously, and justly, attacked by a number of critics, notably by Arthur Henkel[6], S. P. Jenkins[7], Oskar Seidlin[8] and

---

[5] This trend is most uncompromisingly represented by Peacock (*op. cit.*, 2) who describes Iphigenie as 'innocent, saintly and remote' (p. 65). He stresses the similarity of Iphigenie to Charlotte von Stein and of her problem to the feminism of the period (p. 78). Nonetheless, in his earlier article (*loc. cit.*, 1) he warns against easy biographical inferences as from Orestes to Goethe and Iphigenie to Frau von Stein (p. 35).

Walter Rehm is similarly preoccupied with Iphigenie's unruffled purity and calm. (In: *Götterstille und Göttertrauer*, Bern 1961.) However, for all its onesidedness this study conveys what is certainly a decisive aspect of this character, and the drama in which she figures, with such hypnotic intensity of vision that one hesitates to voice any criticism. His point had to be made once, and it has never been made more movingly. Similar considerations determine one's reactions *vis à vis* Adolf Beck's 'der "Geist der Reinheit" und die "Idee des Reinen". Deutsches und Frühgriechisches in Goethes Humanitätsideal.' I in: *Goethe* (neue Folge) 7, 1942 and II in: *Goethe* (neue Folge) 8, 1943.

[6] In 'Iphigenie auf Tauris', in: *Das Deutsche Drama*, ed. B. von Wiese, Vol. I, Düsseldorf 1960. He bluntly and correctly describes the play as 'gescholten als Dokument einer Lebensanschauung, die vor den Abgründen des Daseins die Augen verschließt. Zudem ist keins zugleich von Klischees — gerade der Bewunderer — so zugedeckt worden wie Goethe's "Iphigenie auf Tauris"' (p. 169).

[7] Sylvia P. Jenkins has made notable contributions towards a more realistic approach to the play and, especially, to the character and development of the heroine. Cf. 1) *The Versions of Goethe's Iphigenie of Tauris. A comparative and critical study.* Unpublished Thesis for the MA, London 1950. 2) 'The Image of the Goddess in *Iphigenie auf Tauris*', in: *PEGS* (New Series) XXI, 1952, and 3) in *Iphigenie auf Tauris* ed. S. P. Jenkins, London and Edinburgh 1958. In 2) she stresses the 'diabolical' aspect of Iphigenie's purism and its

Günther Müller[9]. Such recent trends are greatly to be welcomed. It is never-theless my opinion that the final move to end the vicious critical polarisation of the two characters has as yet to be taken, that is to say, the polarisation of Orestes as the receptacle of Goethe's deepest existential problem, on the one hand, and Iphigenie as a denizen of more trouble-free zones and dispenser of solutions that lie beyond Orestes' reach, on the other[10]. I propose to consider the heroine of the drama as a figure no less internalised and 'experienced' than Orestes, that is to say, as a conception springing from the same central stratum of a creator envisaging tragic possibilities of the most radical kind and transcending them as does her brother. Such an approach will not merely restore the full depth-dimension to the figure of the heroine and her interaction with her brother; it will demonstrate the balance of this play which has been overwhelmingly felt but not convincingly explained in terms of its structure and, ultimately, show up what is of the greatest interest in the context of this book: the enormous achievement this drama represents both inherently and in its author's career, human and creative: the two cannot readily be com-partmentalised.

2.

Brother and sister are the offspring of one tribe, heirs to one shared heritage — a common-place enough thing to say; and yet, how often has this shared ancestry been scrutinised with a view to Iphigenie? Indeed, how often has it been looked at closely at all? It is a grisly story the priestess tells the King, and we cannot afford glibly to brush past a catalogue of deeds the poet him-self, assuredly in no melodramatic vein, expects us to stomach. He rams home these antecedents, not merely because they explain Iphigenie's dread of barbarism and her humanitarian aspirations — not to speak of Orestes' mental unbalance — but also because they have moulded her — and her brother's — very conception of a deed.

---

all but inhuman consequences (p. 75), while in 3) she is concerned to show the initial unrelatedness of Iphigenie to her saviours and her gradual surmounting of what is an essentially negative attitude.

[8] Oskar Seidlin has perhaps gone furthest in exploding the myth of a 'remote' Iphigenie. Cf. 1) 'Goethe's Iphigenie and the human Ideal' in: *Mod. Lang. Quart.*, 10, 1949 and 2) 'Goethe's Iphigenie — "verteufelt human"?' in: *Von Goethe zu Thomas Mann. Zwölf Versuche*, Göttingen 1963.

[9] Günther Müller, 'Das Parzenlied in Goethes *Iphigenie*', in *PEGS* (New Series) XVII, 1953, emphasises Iphigenie's smouldering resentment of her priestly office and shows the *Parzenlied* as being an expression of *her* rebelliousness in that it is a 'Konzentration der tantalidischen Kräfte, die greifbar und ungreifbar das Ganze durchwaltet haben.' (p. 104.)

[10] This dichotomy is epitomised by Peacock's statements that 'opposite his sister, pictured as ineffably pure and noble, he [Orestes] on his side appears as guilt incarnate' (*op. cit.*, 2, p. 63); and 'Neither before nor after did Goethe conceive innocence and evil so absolutely separated.' (*Op. cit.*, 2, p. 91.)

Vernimm! Ich bin aus Tantalus' Geschlecht . . .

Iphigenie, after protracted hesitation, confesses; to which the king replies:

Du sprichst ein großes Wort gelassen aus.

Well might he say so; the genealogy that follows is murderous. Tantalus' son, Pelops, gains his wife by a callous ruse. Promised by her father to the contestant that beats him in a chariot race, Pelops bribes the charioteer to unhinge a wheel, and King Oeinamaus is dragged to death by his own horses. The sons of Pelops and Hippodameia, Thyestes and Atreus, jealously watch their father's love for a son born of a previous marriage: Joined in common hatred

und heimlich wagt
Das Paar im Brudermord *die erste Tat*.*

Suspected by Pelops of being the murderess, Hippodameia kills herself. For a while the brothers rule jointly. Presently Thyestes commits adultery with his brother's wife. The latter expels him from Mycena. But Thyestes, 'auf schwere Taten sinnend', has long since kidnapped one of his nephews and reared him in the belief that he is his own son. This youth he sends back to his brother and, filled with ill-founded hatred, he seeks to murder his own father in the supposed person of his uncle. His plot is discovered and he is cruelly tortured and killed by Atreus who never recognises his own son in his victim. Eventually he discovers whom he has murdered and plots an 'unerhörte Tat'. Seemingly reconciled, he invites his brother Thyestes and his boys, takes and slaughters them and offers their cut-up bodies to their father at the welcome dinner: 'die ekle, schaudervolle Speise'. At this point in her recital, Iphigenie, shaken with horror, breaks off and summarily adds that she will spare her interlocutor 'viel Taten des verworrnen Sinnes', taking up the thread of her story with an account of her own father's fate. Agamemnon is the firstborn son of Atreus, the grisly cook. His wife, Chlytemnestra, bears him three children: herself, Iphigenie, her sister Electra and Orestes, the youngest and the heir. All seems peaceful until, waiting for a favourable wind to take the Greek army to Troy, the king shows himself willing to sacrifice his eldest daughter Iphigenie, to pacify the irate goddess Diana. Iphigenie is saved and carried to Tauris in a cloud. This is all she knows of the history of her family, and we must turn to Orestes' recapitulation of the end of the exposition to his friend Pylades. Chlytemnestra, out of revulsion against Agamemnon's infanticide, has taken Aegisthus for a lover. When Agamemnon returns victorious from the Trojan wars, she and her lover entangle the unsuspecting king in a dense net —

ein faltenreich
Und künstlich sich verwirrendes Gewebe —

* my italics.

caught in which the king is slain by his rival. On this day Elektra hides her young brother, the image of his father. He is given into the keeping of Agamemnon's brother-in-law Strophius, where he is received like a son and educated together with Strophius' own Pylades. Both youths burn with longing to avenge Agamemnon. In disguise they make their return to Mycena, ostensibly to bring the queen news of Orestes' death. His vengefulness, abated by his mother's presence, is blown into full flame by his sister's account of the 'verruchte Tat' and by the sight of the crime's bloody trail; and with his sister's dagger he desperately stabs his own mother to death.

These are the antecedents of Iphigenie. Such are the deeds that have imprinted themselves on her mind, and Orestes'. Homicide, suicide, fratricide, rape, infanticide in its most hideous form — cannibalism. Neither she nor he knows of a different kind of deed.

This recital of a nauseating history is necessary for a number of related reasons. These deeds do not only fill, and mould, the consciousness of brother and sister; they also tell us a great deal about the genetic material from which they stem, and the psychological antecedents under which they labour. The poet himself has told us succinctly about both.

> Zwar die gewalt'ge Brust und der Titanen
> Kraftvolles Mark war seiner Söhn' und Enkel
> Gewisses Erbteil;

So much for the genetic material of Tantalus' tribe: excessive vitality. As for the psychological pattern evolved from such a legacy, we read:

> doch es schmiedete
> Der Gott um ihre Stirn ein ehern Band.
> Rat, Mäßigung und Weisheit und Geduld
> Verbarg er ihrem scheuen, düstern Blick:
> Zur Wut ward ihnen jegliche Begier,
> Und grenzenlos drang ihre Wut umher.

The operative lines in this analysis are the two last: excessive vitality again, unchecked, so the previous lines tell us, by any patient prompting of reflection, moderation or wisdom. Nothing but desire magnified to an orgiastic fury that knows no bounds. Desire for what? In the early instances of Pelops and Thyestes certainly incestuous desire, for the woman that belongs to the father-figure or the brother: and, after that, desire to act out the emotions unleashed by these primal promptings: hatred and vengefulness followed by more hatred and vengefulness, in an incessant and ever more accelerated chain-reaction, a raging of instincts ever untutored by higher promptings, ever more deeply ingrained by the law of blood-vengeance which, itself a rationalisation of such self-perpetuating fury, ostensibly sanctions it; and — most important of all — a paroxysm discharging itself in an ever narrowing circle: for presently all the members of the tribe are affected by, and actively drawn into, the network of murder and vengeance, in such a fashion that the ensuing deeds assume an ever more grossly incestuous character.

Such then is the simple mechanism unleashed by the excess of vitality which is the heritage of Tantalus' race: lust, rage, rape, lustful rage, murder, more lustful rage, more murder, and so on *ad infinitum* without a breathing space. We are entitled to speak of a mechanism as, earlier on, we spoke of a chain-reaction. A mechanistic terminology is the only apt one to describe the type of relational pattern that is being evolved in and by this primitive tribal society. To prove this point it will be necessary once more to look at the detailed circumstances in which the majority of these criminal deeds are perpetrated.

What strikes the reader who cares to delve into the recital of atrocities, is the fact that, in most of the instances the poet cites, victim or criminal or both are unconscious of one another's identity at the time the evil deed is done. Thyestes and Atreus commit their 'erste Tat' 'heimlich', that is to say in such a fashion that their half-brother does not know who his murderers are. Atreus' son attempts to assassinate his estranged father, thinking that he is his uncle, and Atreus avenges himself on the youth, thinking he is Thyestes' son. Thyestes eats his own children's flesh — or meat — without suspecting the ingredients of his dinner. Agamemnon is slain by he knows not whom. Orestes returns to kill his mother in disguise.

The poet presents the reader with a strange and constant concatenation here: murderer and victim are closely related — we have remarked on the ever-narrowing circle of incestuousness — yet unknown to one another. 'Nahverwandte Meuchelmörder' — that is how the last and most sensitive survivor of that savage breed, Orestes, has it, glad to be destined to end his life in a strange land, at the hands of a strange priestess:

> Soll ich wie meine Ahnen, wie mein Vater
> Als Opfertier im Jammertode bluten:
> So sei es! Besser hier vor dem Altar,
> Als im verworfnen Winkel, wo die Netze
> Der nahverwandte Meuchelmörder stellt.

'Opfertier', 'nahverwandte Meuchelmörder': It is the prehuman anonymity of incestuous relations the poet pinpoints in these words, and in the chain of action and reaction from which they derive their resonance.

This claustrophobic raging — for all the lust of Tantalus' overvital race turns to rage — is time and again articulated in metaphors expressive of those two components — closeness and anonymity which between them produce a catastrophic configuration that is rife with destruction — destruction of others and self-destruction. And the prehuman primitiveness of such inter-action finds expression in the fact that such symbolism is inevitably drawn from the subhuman realm of animals and plants. By way of illustration, I shall only quote two formulations which equally bring out the salient features of these constellations: proliferating vitality, suffocating closeness and anonymity. The objective import of these metaphors is vouchsafed by the fact that they are given over to different, if related, speakers.

Hearing of the manner of her father's death, itself claustrophobic in the highest degree, Iphigenie laments:

> Weh dir, unseliges Mycen!
> So haben Tantals Enkel Fluch auf Fluch
> Mit vollen wilden Händen ausgesät!
> Und, gleich dem Unkraut, wüste Häupter schüttelnd
> Und tausendfält'gen Samen um sich streuend,
> Den Kindeskindern nahverwandte Mörder
> Zur ew'gen Wechselwut erzeugt!

Later in the same scene, Orestes responds:

> Gut, Priesterin! Ich folge zum Altar;
> Der Brudermord ist hergebrachte Sitte
> Des alten Stammes . . .
> Wie sich vom Schwefelpfuhl erzeugte Drachen,
> Bekämpfend die verwandte Brut, verschlingen,
> Zerstört sich selbst das wütende Geschlecht.

'Nahverwandte Meuchelmörder', 'nahverwandte Mörder', 'verwandte Brut' —: the poet's meaning is too persistently voiced to be overlooked. Moreover, the stifling closeness that is conveyed by these metaphors is supported by a host of subsidiary images. There is the 'dunkle Decke' of her oppressive brooding that Orestes' mother spreads about the young child's head, the 'dunkle Blume', half-frozen and immobile, to which Orestes likens his boyhood self, or the 'breite Nacht' of his guilt which pursues and covers him wherever he turns his steps, like the furies with their suffocating vapours. In turn, such images recall the hemmed-in state of which Arkas accuses Iphigenie:

> Solang' ich dich an dieser Stätte kenne,
> Ist dies der Blick, vor dem ich immer schaudre;
> Und wie mit Eisenbanden bleibt die Seele
> Ins Innerste des Busens dir geschmiedet —

a description with which she herself concurs when she describes her existence as that of a shadow incessantly circling around its own grave, or when she confesses her deep dread of untying her tongue and opening her soul to her benefactor. Even after she has spoken, Thoas, reverting to the most fateful image of all, that of the perilous net, rounds off the claustrophobic pattern. Hearing Iphigenie's trusting words, he bitterly surmises:

> So haben die Betrüger, künstlich dichtend,
> Der lang' Verschloßnen, ihre Wünsche leicht
> Und willig Glaubenden, ein solch Gespinst
> Ums Haupt geworfen.

Agamemnon's fate, of which the king knows nothing, symbolically ensnaring Iphigenie once again! Stroke by merciless stroke, the poet has built up a picture of a race all but hopelessly enmeshed in a web of mutual oppression and destruction which has driven the last survivors into a stifled inwardness.

These then are the psychological antecedents, not only of Orestes, but of Iphigenie, too. Such are the impressions which have imprinted themselves on the child's soul, to which, in the case of Orestes, must be added the haunting and fixed memory of stabbing to death his 'doch verehrte Mutter':

Doch sein geschwungner Arm traf ihre Brust.

With such formative impressions taken into account, who could seriously maintain that Iphigenie is serenely untroubled and needful of no development? To do so is to make a mockery of the poet's carefully articulated intentions, and a hollow farce of the humanity which in the end flowers from the darkest abysses of an all but inhuman landscape.

3.

And yet this landscape is all the time gaining a more ideal aspect, in the solitude of Diana's sanctuary. Not only because Iphigenie longs to go home to be reunited with those she loves, but also because the very fabric of her loving and her recollection has undergone a profound transformation. Transported, in a cloud, to the distant isle, she has been lifted, bodily, out of the closely forged chain of furious action and reaction spelling inevitable disaster. She has been removed from the subhuman scene of blind instinctuality running its mindless course. Her transplantation to Tauris means more than physical survival: it inaugurates the birth of a spiritual self. For in the stillness of the temple, revered from afar by the king and his people, those violent impingements which were her past recede. In the quiet rhythm of her daily rites the storm of feeling abates, thought begins to crystallise and, as she tends the holy flame, 'in kindlicher Beschäftigung', she for the first time experiences a doing which does not destroy, but sustains[11]. There is space around her and time to breathe and be. Trauma becomes recollection shot through with the thread of a reflection which is cleansed and nourished by the pure and steady intercourse with the divine. It is precisely this habit of reflection which later on, when Pylades presses for the rapid execution of his deceitful plot, will make her pause and say 'O laß mich zaudern'; and this moment it is which turns the scales.

Gradually, in the stillness of such 'ewig frommer Kindheit', the tangle of lives lived out in furious instinctuality begins to unravel itself, and she perceives the pattern in the madness: vitality without restraint breeds the monstrous:

---

[11] This is the aspect of Iphigenie W. Rehm so vividly evokes (*op. cit.*, cf. note 5).

Und die Gestalt des zufällig Ermordeten
Wird auf des traurig-unwilligen Mörders
Böse Stunden lauern und schrecken.

The panorama of the human landscape as she knows it lies spread out before her, monotonous, barren and infinitely sad. Yet as she understands it, and the blind, ever-repeated suffering of the race that calls itself human, she embraces 'des Menschenlebens schwere Bürden' in a sisterly compassion at once tender and removed from the hard clasp of desire.

In such forgiveness even her father, the dearly loved 'traurig-unwillige Mörder', is included. Indeed, he more than anyone: for her first love went to him and it was he, the 'göttergleiche Agamemnon', that imprinted himself on the child's imagination as the 'Muster des vollkommnen Manns'[12], he that interpreted for her the splendour of the divine. She herself remembers the moment when he and his illustrious companions embarked for Troy:

Sie zogen aus,
Als hätte der Olymp sich aufgetan,
Und die Gestalten der erlauchten Vorwelt
Zum Schrecken Ilions herabgesendet,
Und Agamemnon war vor allen herrlich!

Vaterbild, Vatergötter, Götterbilder — those are the words in which she encompasses all that to her is dear and sacred.

Strange irony of life, and doubly strange irony of a life lived in exile, however much of a saving sanctuary it be, this nostalgic idealisation of a past she herself knows to have been far from idyllic; this fervent idolising of a father who, however 'traurig-unwillig', offered her up to the furtherance of his ruthless aspirations!

Dies sind die Ahnherrn deiner Priesterin;

Iphigenie had said at the end of her grisly recital to Thoas. She knows it all. And yet so great is the trauma of nature turned monstrous, so ardent the longing for childhood's first loving and revering, so great the transfiguring power of an imagination unchecked by reality, that what was ugly and stifling, in the distant recollection glows with the semblance of joyous life and warmth, whilst the shelter of the sanctuary to her takes on the hue of night and the chill of death.

There is in every sensitive soul a deep refusal to write off the past which is source and origin, which is an inextricable part of what one has become; and the more so, the earlier those nurturing bonds are broken, waiting as yet to be resolved. The self-same Iphigenie who likens her tribe to an untended

---

[12] Cf. Detlev W. Schumann in 'Die Bekenntnisszenen in Goethe's "Iphigenie"'. In: *JbdSG*, IV, 1960, p. 230. Cf. also M. Kommerell who writes: 'Väterlich-töchterliche Beziehungen haben die Gefühlskraft, nur nicht die Sinnlichkeit der hohen Leidenschaft . . . ' (*op. cit.*, p. 403).

jungle of weeds sowing their wild seeds all about themselves 'zur ew'gen Wechselwut', will transpose this sickening image into an idealised key as soon as it is suggested that she has grown estranged from the land of her birth in a second home that has served her better. Passionately she replies to Arkas:

> Das ist's, warum mein blutend Herz nicht heilt.
> In erster Jugend, da sich kaum die Seele
> An Vater, Mutter und Geschwister band,
> Die neuen Schößlinge, gesellt und lieblich,
> Vom Fuß der alten Stämme himmelwärts
> Zu dringen strebten, leider faßte da
> Ein fremder Fluch mich an und trennte mich
> Von den Geliebten, riß das schöne Band
> Mit ehrner Faust entzwei. Sie war dahin,
> Der Jugend beste Freude, das Gedeihn
> Der ersten Jahre. Selbst gerettet, war
> Ich nur ein Schatten mir, und frische Lust
> Des Lebens blüht in mir nicht wieder auf.

And so, too, in her opening monologue, she longingly envisages her ancestral halls

> wo die Sonne
> Zuerst den Himmel vor ihm aufschloß, wo
> Sich Mitgeborne spielend fest und fester
> Mit sanften Banden an einander knüpften.

What irony: that sun which she remembers shining on her childhood is the very sun which — so she told Thoas — turned away his face and turned his chariot off course at the sight of the monstrosities perpetrated by her race,

> und läßt
> Uns nur in grauenvolle Dämmrung sehn.

Those 'Mitgeborne' are the survivors of the fourfold slaughter perpetrated by Atreus and Thyestes who, having killed off their half-brother, serve up one another's children — the uncles of Orestes and Iphigenie — at a macabre dinner party. Those *sanfte* or *schöne Bande*, as she calls them, are the unrelenting bonds forged by lust and rage between 'nahverwandte Meuchelmörder'. And by the strangest reversal, the healing days in the quiet sanctuary, removed from murderous proximity, filled with pious and life-tending deeds, by a starved imagination are repudiated as 'ein unnütz Leben' and 'ein zweiter Tod'; an existence v*ertrauert*

> an der heil'gen Stätte,
> Gleich einem Schatten um sein eigen Grab.

The voluntary bonds here, in her second home, which tie her to the divine and to a people eager to be drawn towards the divine, unstifling, leaving her space to live and breathe and grow in understanding, to the exile become 'ernste, heil'ge Sklavenbande', as *ehern* as the relentless bonds of rage laid upon the unreflecting brows of her accursed race.

And, exile that she feels, she clings to those insubstantial phantoms of the past and closes her heart against the living people to whom she owes survival and the burgeoning of that very humanity by which she hopes to redeem her own star-crossed tribe. Her heart is locked and her tongue is tied by those very unrelenting bonds — *Eisenbanden* — which fetter the members of her tribe to one another and her to them. She cannot flow out in relatedness.

It is not only that, priestess and 'sister' as she is, she recoils from Thoas' silent courtship. That inner shyness betokens her obedience to her nature and, indeed, her destiny. But her reticence has another root yet, deep in her allegiance to an unresolved past. To her, all that is revered is encompassed in the image of her father, the 'göttergleichen Agamemnon'. Him, and the 'Götterbilder' of his illustrious crew and 'die Gestalten der erlauchten Vorwelt', and them alone, her imagination has invested with the aura of divinity. The image of the divine is encaged within her heart, unable to flow out so as to transfigure the strangers amongst whom she lives. As yet, the gods live in solitary confinement. That rediffusion of the divine, enabling her to encounter it in unreserved and reverent relatedness in the 'rohe Skythen', will have to await the recovery of her lost world in the figure of Orestes.

4.

In this disturbed presence the complex mental frame of Iphigenie is astonishingly re-enacted, albeit in intensified form[13]. He, too, is an exile, turned in upon himself and shunning relatedness because he has been seared by the relationships of his youth; and he, too, hankers after a past he knows to have been murderous. Incessantly, 'gleich einem Schatten um sein eigen Grab' as Iphigenie has it, his mind circles around the misdeeds of the past, his father's murder at the hand of his mother and her lover, and his own avenging murder of his mother. Giddyingly and unendingly, the vapours of Acheron swirl around his guilty head:

> In seinen Wolkenkreisen wälzet sich
> Die ewige Betrachtung des Geschehnen
> Verwirrend um des Schuld'gen Haupt umher.

Like his sister who experiences life in the sanctuary as a living death, the way to redemption to him seems the way downward, to death, the way *of* death even.

> Es ist der Weg des Todes, den wir treten:

---

[13] Although Seidlin is at pains to stress the parallelism of brother and sister (*loc. cit.* 2, p. 14), he emphasises that 'die Richtung ihres Sehens ist polar entgegengesetzt; Iphigenie, ungebrochen von der Todesverführung, will zurückkehren, heimkehren ins Leben ... Iphigeniens Richtung ist der Weg aus dem Tode, Orests Richtung der Weg in die Nacht.' (*Loc. cit.*, 2, p. 17.) Seidlin does not acknowledge the symbolic signification which such images as 'Tod' and 'Nacht' have, for Iphigenie as well as for her brother. This is where we part company.

these are his first words. As Iphigenie appears a phantom to herself, so Orestes feels a larva in the Taurian day.

> Laßt mich, ich komme bald zu euch hinab . . .

he explains to the furies, his constant companions:

> Das Licht des Tags soll euch nicht sehn, noch mich.
> Der Erde schöner grüner Teppich soll
> Kein Tummelplatz für Larven sein.

Yet, as with Iphigenie, his blighted youth, the stifling bonds that tied him to a vengeful, guilty mother —

> Des Lebens dunkle Decke breitete
> Die Mutter schon mir um das zarte Haupt . . .

he reminisces — the fiery hatred of Electra, plotting murder: all this is present and real to him, and all is nostalgically transfigured. His father who, for all he knows, murdered his sister and thus laid the wretched burden of bloody vengeance upon him —

> wie sehr
> Verlangt' ich, ihn zu sehn, bei ihm zu sein! —

the boyhood days with Pylades, in reality spent preparing himself for patricide, in memory seem peaceful, calm and free. Those were the days when

> Die Welt so weit, so offen vor uns lag —

days in reality spent forging yet another link in the relentless chain of rage and remorse. Those were the days when he dared think, in the starlit nights, of myriads of deeds; and 'große Taten' they were to be. Even in the paroxysm of horror, at his past and at himself, which seizes him as he confesses his guilt, he beseeches Iphigenie and Pylades to go back to the hell that is home, urging:

> Geht ihr, daheim im schönen Griechenland
> Ein neues Leben freundlich anzufangen.

Irony indeed, this double-life the past leads in an exile's heart. Unresolved bonds are tied ever faster by a fretting imagination and slowly contract a soul that is unable to flow out into the present. It is with Orestes as it is with Iphigenie: as she idolises the father who all but murdered her and is unable, in her threefold account of her sacrifice, so much as to mention his name —

> Sie lockten mit der Mutter mich ins Lager;
> Sie rissen mich vor den Altar . . .

she recounts the event to Thoas, with vague and careful circumlocution — so, too, Orestes' memory is split, his heart is torn between conventional condemnation and love of his 'doch verehrten Mutter'.

In this play, as in *Torquato Tasso*[14], the poet has fastened upon a moment of transition and reversal: the 'pregnant moment' when his figures are compelled to step forth from their cocoon — Tasso from his creative engrossment and brother and sister from their solitary brooding upon moral issues inextricably tied up with what is past — and face the changed configuration of a present demanding, above all, living relatedness.

5.

This movement towards the present, uneasily prefigured in the opening 'Heraus' of the drama[15] and accelerated by Thoas' wooing for Iphigenie's hand, finally links up with the now, in the encounter of brother and sister.

> ... willst du mir durch ihn
> Und ihm durch mich die sel'ge Hilfe geben ...:

these are the words in which Iphigenie beseeches Diana not to let her new-found brother rage in madness. From the beginning this strangest of all literary meetings in the pre-Freudian era takes place under the aegis of strict mutuality; a fact which has understandably been overlooked by critics who deem Iphigenie to be unneedful of help, but has equally eluded those with a more realistic approach to her[16]. And from the beginning this troubled pair, children of the same parents and heirs to the same legacy, bring their unresolved past into the present. Iphigenie is anxious to hear about one thing alone — the fate of her idolised father; with an indifference which borders on the callous, she brushes aside Orestes' mention of their mother, peremptorily saying

> Sie rettet weder Hoffnung, weder Furcht.[17]

[14] Cf. my *Goethe and Lessing*, Chapter VII, section 4.
[15] Here again I disagree with Seidlin. He reads the first word of the drama, 'Heraus', as having an entirely positive significance. (*Loc. cit.*, 2, p. 17.) I interpret it in conjunction with the subsequent 'in eure Schatten' and indeed the lines that follow: and shade, shadow, being deployed, by her as by Orestes, as synonymous with death, I see her opening gesture as clouded by that ambivalence and reticence which indeed the opening monologue articulates in its entirety.
[16] Both J. G. Robertson (in: *The Life and Work of Goethe*, London 1932, p. 119) and J. Boyd, ed. *Iphigenie auf Tauris: An Interpretation and Critical Analysis*, Oxford 1942, p. 77), have drawn attention to the similarity between the situation of brother and sister and modern psycho-analytical techniques. They could hardly be expected to operate with the more recent concept of counter-transference which is indeed most surprisingly prefigured in Iphigenie's psychological involvement with, and dependence on, Orestes. Kommerell writes: ' ... geschwisterliche Beziehungen verwandeln so tief, ja fast tiefer als Liebesbegegnungen.' (*Op. cit.*, p. 403.)
[17] A fact noted by Boyd but accorded an extraordinary explanation. (*Op. cit.*, p. 65, cf. also p. 141f.)

Equally, for all his protestations that he does not wish to divulge the awful secret of his guilt[18], Orestes compels his sister to ask the fatal question.

How does this confidence come about? In the presence of this stranger what empowers him to face up to the deed

> die ich so gern
> Ins klanglos-dumpfe Höhlenreich der Nacht
> Verbergen möchte . . . ?

He can do so because Iphigenie's 'holder Mund' awakens in him all the love of his 'doch verehrte Mutter' which had lain buried beneath the ashes of his guilt and the inhuman law of vengeance which drove him into it. He can face his conflict and acknowledge it. And, in doing so, himself.

> Ich bin Orest!

he says; and his words signify his emergence from the anonymity of the tribal group, the birth of a human self capable, as such, of relatedness.

But in the last resort Iphigenie empowers Orestes to lay his bruised soul open to her because she is his sister; his sister by birth, and in spiritual empathy. They are the members of one tribe, they have the same parents. They share the self-same memories, both of their antecedents and of those intimate childhood events that bind siblings together 'mit sanften Banden'. But they share more yet: those almost interchangeable mirror-experiences of Iphigenie being offered up by their 'traurig-unwillige' father, and a 'traurig-unwillige' Orestes offering up their mother. And now, above all, the 'liebe-volle Schwester' who seeks his eyes as beseechingly as his mother had done when he slew her[19] — the sister who had herself trembled at the altar — by the strangest reversal is compelled, or so it seems, to sacrifice him as he himself immolated his mother's life. Iphigenie herself reveals to Thoas the spring of her sympathy:

> Löst die Erinnerung des gleichen Schicksals
> Nicht ein verschloßnes Herz zum Mitleid auf?
> Wie mehr denn meins! In ihnen seh ich mich.
> Ich habe vorm Altare selbst gezittert . . .

But the deepest spring of her compassionate understanding flows through the sanctuary; the still place where she had been able to recollect in tranquillity what had been unendurable in brute reality, where, in meditation sustained by a steady rhythm of pious acts, she had gradually perceived the universal pattern in her tribe's story of lust and rage, and embraced the whole hard-pressed human race in pitying love. The 'fromme Klarheit' of such deep sisterliness it is which transmits itself to Orestes and unties his tongue.

---

[18] D. W. Schumann has noted Orestes' reticence but has failed to explain it or indeed to spot his driving eagerness to make Iphigenie probe further. (*Loc. cit.*, p. 237.)

[19] This subtle touch was detected by Düntzer as early as 1899. In: 'Goethes "Iphigenie auf Tauris"', in: *Erläuterungen zu den deutschen Klassikern*, I. Abt., Band 14, Leipzig 1899, p. 131.

But the help is mutual. And it is here, in the reciprocal resolution of the conflict as well as in its shared antecedents, that the inner balance of a drama handling materials so profoundly unclassical is rooted.

> Willst du mir durch ihn
> Und ihm durch mich die sel'ge Hilfe geben ...

is Iphigenie's supplication. As the sister helps the brother by the sheer quality of her loving compassion, so Orestes and, to a lesser degree, Pylades, help Iphigenie through the sheer glory of a *Wiederfinden* which ends a long spell of austerity and unalleviated emptiness. She had loved her father, she had even forgiven him: but never again had she set eyes on his face. The seed of her loving and forgiving had not been nourished by contact with the present.

> Weh dem, der fern von Eltern und Geschwistern
> Ein einsam Leben führt!

she had lamented:

> Ihm zehrt der Gram
> Das *nächste** Glück vor seinen Lippen weg.
> Ihm schwärmen abwärts immer die Gedanken
> Nach seines Vaters Hallen ...

To see[20] that father's features come to life again in those of his son — Agamemnon's *Ebenbild* — to remember in a flash, and actually to see and touch that scar across her brother's brow, that starshaped birthmark on his hand which she had known when they were children together, as she had known her own face and hands: this is fulfilment standing before her, unfathomable in its bounty, huge — *ungeheuer* — as the image of the 'schönste Tochter des größten Vaters'. And as huge — *ungeheuer* — as is 'das Recht der Gegenwart', to quote the Goethe of *Die Wahlverwandtschaften*. All that was lost and mourned, at one stroke is recovered and enriched. The unfinished relation to the father, her love and forgiveness of him, is refructified, lived through in the fiercely compassionate love of the brother and absorbed in it, even as Orestes' injured love for his mother is made whole and transcended in the healing balm of the sister's embrace. The unrelenting fetters — *eherne Bande* — which kept these two in thrall to an irretrievable past, are resolved. They are free for each other and for the present.

But by this release an even greater good is recovered. The divine is set free from the constricting bonds that have kept it fettered to the tribal image. As the fixation, Iphigenie's and Orestes', to past and parents is resolved, the divine flows out into the present, into their loving of each other and thence into the humanity they embrace in such liberated loving. The captive gods

---

[20] For an analysis of the development undergone by such early perceptual materials and the bearing of this development on the maturation of the whole person, cf. Chapters VIII and XIII of this book.

* my italics.

are freed. They are recovered throughout a world of beings like Iphigenie and Orestes, bounded by instinct yet craving for the divine whose image they bear, and through this release that whole world becomes divinised. Iphigenie will vindicate that enlarged vision presently, in the working out of her relationship with Thoas; and Orestes is granted a foretaste of it as, in his healing trance[21], he sees once 'nahverwandte Meuchelmörder' peaceably walk side by side, now 'göttergleich und ähnlich'.

It is in this drama as so often in Goethe's poetry. Imprints made early on the personality are deep and lasting, and it takes a felicitous interaction between self and world to bring about the flowering of even the best gifts and the noblest dispositions. *Iphigenie,* up to the meeting of brother and sister, is a drama without world, and in the measure in which this is so, it is a potential tragedy. Like Mignon and the Harfner, Iphigenie and Orestes are exiled[22]. Like these two tragically romantic figures they are in danger of being hollowed out by their craving for a past which has become objectless[23]. It is through their fructifying encounter with one another and the sturdy presence of Pylades, that true child of the world, that their latent disposition to love, arrested and warped through traumatic impressions early in life, finds an answering object and is able to mature. This swift and organic burgeoning it is to which Iphigenie gives such moving, and extravagant, utterance:

> Vernehm' ich dich, so wendet sich, o Teurer,
> Wie sich die Blume nach der Sonne wendet,
> Die Seele, von dem Strahle deiner Worte
> Getroffen, sich dem süßen Troste nach.
> Wie köstlich ist des gegenwärt'gen Freundes
> Gewisse Rede, deren Himmelskraft
> Ein Einsamer entbehrt und still versinkt.
> Denn langsam reift, verschlossen in dem Busen,
> Gedank' ihm und Entschluß; die Gegenwart
> Des Liebenden entwickelte sie leicht.

[21] In an otherwise highly sophisticated reading of the play, Sigurd Burckhardt argues that Orestes' swoon signifies the 'intoxicated surrender to the curse, which transforms Tartarus into an idyll' (in: *The Drama of Language,* Baltimore 1970, p. 52 and note 11 (p. 166). I am unable to follow Burckhardt here, and find myself in total agreement with Staiger who describes Orestes' swoon as 'Gnade des Vergessens'. (*Op. cit.,* Vol. I, p. 369.) On the other hand, Staiger's refusal to concede that the very act of 'confessing' to his crime induces a relaxation which is therapeutic in itself (p. 368), strikes me as obscurantist, as does also, in supreme measure, his insistence that we must read Orestes' invocation of 'vergoßnen Mutterblutes Stimme' in terms of Goethe's own sense of guilt *vis à vis* Friederike Brion and Lili Schönemann, a complex the poet finally lived down in his relation with Charlotte von Stein, 'der reinen *Schwester*'. (P. 352.) Such wilful blindness, here and elsewhere, mars an otherwise exquisitely sensitive study.

[22] Cf. Chapters VIII and XIII of this book.

[23] Staiger writes: 'Mignon und der Harfner sind aus früheren Jahren übernommen, ein später Nachklang des Orest.' In: *Die Zeit als Einbildungskraft des Dichters* (2), Zurich 1963, p. 128.

Such slow unfolding and maturing of early imprints through liberating contact with reality is the developmental process Goethe traces in *Iphigenie*[24]. It is the marvelling recognition, in an answering world, of the image she carried in her innermost heart, which will enable Iphigenie to say to Thoas:

> Wert und teuer,
> Wie mir mein Vater war, so bist du's mir,
> Und dieser *Eindruck** bleibt in meiner Seele.

It is this which will empower Orestes to perceive the archetypal image of the Goddess in the stranger who is in truth his kin.

6.

Yet how fraught with danger is this dazzling encounter with the present! Reality, 'Gegenwart', is the operative word of Iphigenie's eulogy of Pylades. Without it there is no growth, only inner stagnation. But the sudden influx of the present into minds attuned to the phantom world of the past carries its own risks. Iphigenie's joy and liberation, after the isolation of exile and inwardness, threaten to engulf her by the sheer immensity of their impact.

> In meinen Armen hielt ich das Unmögliche

she will recall later, and:

> meinen Bruder
> Ergriff das Herz mit einziger Gewalt.

This is the vehemence of a child of Tantalus' tribe; words from one whose feelings, starved too long, now break loose, threatening the very freedom her brother has only just recovered. 'Einziger Gewalt': where, but a moment earlier, love had widened to embrace all in the one, and the divine in him, it now seems to have contracted again and to have taken on a frightening intensity. Orestes, damaged by the harsh impingements of his youth, recoils like one seared. Picking up the echo of former violence in the elemental outpouring of her joy, he draws back:

> Ist hier Lyäens Tempel? und ergreift
> Unbändig-heil'ge Wut die Priesterin?

And, overwhelmed by a proximity he cannot endure, he retreats into unconsciousness, first hallucinating the retribution against himself which his violated feeling demands, finally to lapse into a healing vision.

How delicate is the balance in this play between fulfilment and restraint, between vitality and desctruction! How precariously narrow is the ridge of the present! One intemperate word betraying excess, one wrong nuance of

[24] Cf. Chapter VIII of this book.
* my italics.

look or gesture is enough to precipitate disaster. For disaster threatens for the
three protagonists, for brother and sister as well as for the Taurian king.
There is madness round the corner for Orestes as he hallucinates the
'liebevolle Schwester' enacting the retribution that is his desert, looking at
him as his mother had done. What he now imaginatively experiences is the
vindication of the accursed mechanism of crime breeding crime which he had
hoped against hope he might live down. There is ultimate despair round the
corner for Iphigenie as she sees her brother, scarcely recovered, losing himself in raving madness.

> Es greift die Furie
> Vielleicht den Bruder auf dem Boden wieder
> Des ungeweihten Ufers grimmig an . . .

she muses. Had her loving been 'unbändig-heilig', or as still and pure as the
consecrated flame of the sanctuary? Moreover, Thoas, whom she had all but
forgotten in the ecstasy of the reunion, has unaccountably registered the
vehemence of her emotions.

> Sie sinnt sich nun ein eigen Schicksal aus . . .

he grimly says, as if he had been present at that *Wiederfinden* or heard the extravagant words in which she recalled her transport.

> Mein Schicksal ist an deines festgebunden . . .

she had assured her brother, and

> Meinen Bruder
> Ergriff das Herz mit einziger Gewalt;

and to this contraction of her sympathies, however unspoken, on to one single
object, he responds by an ominous narrowing of his own: he orders that the
sacrifice of strangers be resumed. And this means not only peril for her brother,
but the collapse of a turbulent young people's striving towards the light. It
seems as though the several destinies of the two ends of the world — the
brother and the foreign island king — were resting on two swaying scales
within her heart: one feeling too many on this one, one caring thought too
little on that one, and the cosmic balance is disturbed. Either way disaster
lies. The sacrifice of the strangers has been decided, and Iphigenie who had
tended the sacred flame in the hope that one day she might expiate the crimes
of her tribe and nurse what is left of it into a purer life, will plunge a desperate
brother into insanity and death —

> Mit welchen Blicken
> Kann ich von meinem Bruder Abschied nehmen,
> Den ich ermorde?

she will ask: with Chlytemnestra's? — will herself be plunged from her stead-
fast believing in a divine cosmos into the 'grauenvolle Dämmrung' of primal
chaos.

Tragedy upon tragedy. What abysses did this poet envisage who is so readily charged with evading the tragic possibilities inherent in human life, and nowhere more so than *vis-à-vis* a play supposed to propound an all too glib humanitarian gospel! Is a corpse-strewn stage an existential poet's only credential, and are our sensibilities so blunted that thousandfold death and hell endured in the imagination will no longer do?

7.

But between such cataclysm and the untried present there lies Iphigenie's patient schooling in purity of participation; there lies, besides, the lesson brother and sister have taught one another in the dizzy moments of their first encounter.

The closest kin have found one another. Iphigenie has been granted the realisation of her dream,

> Der Seligkeit, dem Liebsten, was die Welt
> Noch für mich tragen kann, das Haupt zu küssen,
> Mit meinen Armen, die den leeren Winden
> Nur ausgebreitet waren, dich zu fassen!

Orestes has responded, saying:

> Seit meinen ersten Jahren hab' ich nichts
> Geliebt, wie ich dich lieben könnte, Schwester.

Yet how does this vehement drawing together end? Orestes raves and faints and Iphigenie is wafted away in a cloud of forgetful ecstacy, as she was once before, when she was saved from imminent death. Brother and sister, immersed in a stream of unconscious oblivion — he uses the image of Lethe, she that of the returning tide — have suffered an eclipse of their individual selves, the very selves which, announcing their identity, had entered into mutual relatedness. They have temporarily regressed into the anonymity of their tribe, have relived the perilous pattern of their race, that of incestuous closeness leading to estrangement. Quite unconsciously, Orestes reminds us of this pattern in what may be considered the heart-speech of the entire drama. Casting away the disguise in which he had, up to this point, communicated with Iphigenie — he had related his misdeed in the third person — he abruptly breaks into the first person and says:

> Ich kann nicht leiden, daß du große Seele
> Mit einem falschen Wort betrogen werdest.
> Ein lügenhaft Gewebe knüpf' ein Fremder
> Dem Fremden, sinnreich und der List gewohnt,
> Zur Falle vor die Füße; zwischen uns
> Sei Wahrheit!
> Ich bin Orest!

'Ein Fremder dem Fremden'? This is not what this drama has told us. Brothers and brothers, sons and fathers, sons and mothers, wives and husbands — it is they that have waylaid and slain one another in a web or trap,

> im verworfnen Winkel, wo die Netze
> Der nahverwandte Meuchelmörder stellt;

Thyestes and Atreus their half-brother, Atreus his own son, Thyestes his two boys, Chlytemnestra Agamemnon and Orestes Chlytemnestra: this had been the monotonous list of hunter and hunted; 'Nahverwandte' all. Had not all these kins been 'Meuchelmörder', that is to say, killers going about their business secretly, in disguise? And 'Nahverwandte Meuchelmörder', 'verwandte Brut', 'Opfertier': are not all these synonyms expressive of the profound anonymity of the mechanism of orgiastic rage that governs this race? Lust raging within the narrow confines of a tribal group knit together by incestuous ties, proliferating and exterminating each other in turn: such claustrophobic closeness, paradoxically, means radical strangeness between each and all, between victim and murderer, pursuer and pursued, huddling together like animals surprised by a storm in a den.

One dip into that ocean of regression, one taste of the orgiastic estrangement from Orestes, from Thoas, from her very being, and Iphigenie is restored to her true self. That sea to which, in a surge of elemental feeling, she has momentarily entrusted her being, now seems an alien element; and she longs once again to tread

> Den festen Boden deiner Einsamkeit.

Not for her the estrangement of oblivion. For her the tempered strangeness of her solitary calling, that 'ewig fromme Klarheit' which is ever responsive to the divine surrounding her as with an invisible aura. This is her element, a pure medium permeating, and transforming, all human concerns; clarifying them and filtering them into the purity of universal sisterly compassion. The river of exclusive love is turbid and clogged. It is the spring of true humanity alone — humanity filtered through the divine — which flows through the unimpeded heart and reaches all.

For her, then, not the primitive kinship which estranges, but that strangeness which, grounded in an inalienable proximity to the Numinous, calls true kinship into being. For her not the 'Nahverwandten Meuchelmörder' but the mediated relatedness in which humans walk side by side, 'göttergleich und ähnlich'. This is the task for which the discipline of the sanctuary has prepared her, for which the encounter with Orestes has liberated her. It has purged her love of the constricting ties to the past, and, in a short and sharp schooling, has freed it from all self-centredness. She is ready to go out to the divine wherever there are human beings.

This is the frame in which the ugly conflict precipitated by the strangers' arrival and Thoas' hardening finds her. She must choose, or so it seems, between her brother and the king. To Pylades it seems a clearcut situation, and an easy choice:

> Den Bruder, dich und deinen Freund zu retten,
> Ist nur *ein* Weg; fragt sich's, ob wir ihn gehn?

On the one side, there are the close bonds of love and kinship. To sacrifice them is unthinkable. On the other side, the remote regard for the stranger, the barbarian. To sacrifice that bond costs but a trifle, a single word. When Iphigenie demurs at this argument, Pylades spells it out in all clarity:

> Man sieht, du bist nicht an Verlust gewohnt,
> Da du, dem großen Übel zu entgehn,
> Ein falsches Wort nicht einmal opfern willst.

Who would choose the lesser good and the lesser sacrifice it involves but one enamoured with her own perfection and unversed in the school of life?

> Ganz unbefleckt genießt sich nur das Herz ...

— the heart, we remember, which is open to the voice of true humanity only as long as the spring of life, and love, flows through it in unalloyed purity — Iphigenie had argued; and Pylades had replied:

> So hast du dich im Tempel wohl bewahrt;
> Das Leben lehrt uns, weniger mit uns
> Und andern strenge sein; du lernst es auch.
> So wunderbar ist dies Geschlecht gebildet,
> So vielfach ist's verschlungen und verknüpft,
> Daß keiner in sich selbst, noch mit den andern
> Sich rein und unverworren halten kann.

These words touch on the life-nerve of the drama, and on the life-nerve of Iphigenie's being. They once more revert to the image of the net, symbol, in this drama, of the fateful interlacing of destinies too closely knit together. But to Iphigenie's perception and to hers alone in this play — except for the sharp crisis articulated in the *Parzenlied* — the web of human destinies lies spread out, and she repudiates the fatalistic associations which have accrued to it in the course of the drama. She perceives that it is spun of one stuff — human beings capable of goodness all — and that the intactness of a fabric so finely spun is inseparably bound up with the soundness of each single thread: tear it in one place and the whole will give. The 'falsche Wort' smoothly offered to Thoas[25] will not merely mean the sacrifice of Orestes, herself and their friend — this the king's hardening has already taught her: it will rend the tissue of humanity.

---

[25] Provocatively and persuasively, Burckhardt speaks of the world of Goethe's drama as 'the world of a language-school'. (*Op. cit.*, p. 36.) Only whilst he sees the surpassing word in Thoas' final 'Lebt wohl!', I would divide the honours between that and Orestes' 'zwischen' in 'Zwischen uns // Sei Wahrheit!' which, as D. Schumann points out, is placed at the exact mathematical centre of the play. (*Loc. cit.*, p. 238.) Cf. the end of this chapter.

It is Pylades' role to remind Iphigenie that an outside world with its own implacable demands exists. She and her brother are in danger of forgetting this fact. To reconcile these demands, real and urgent as they are, with the inner voice of conscience — no less real and urgent — falls outside his competence. This is left to Iphigenie. For her there can be no choice in terms of sacrificing either her brother or her benefactor. For her, there is only one choice: whether to sacrifice that indivisible fabric of humanity or to keep it inviolate. She opts for the latter. Not that she loves Orestes less than Thoas, now her 'zweiter Vater'. How could she? In entrusting his fate and hers to the king's hands, she heroically and graciously affirms that she abides by the quality of relatedness she has learnt in Diana's service, a tempered love that is mediated through the divine and includes every being made in its image. It is a gesture of including Thoas between Orestes and herself, of taking him, even, into her deepest loving.

> O trüg' ich doch ein männlich Herz in mir,

she exclaims, as, in defiance of Pylades' pragmatism, she prepares herself for her surpassing deed. For a surpassing deed it is, her faithfulness to the indivisibility of love in this cruel dilemma, as 'unerhört' and elemental as are the deeds of her ancestors[26].

> Hat denn zur unerhörten Tat der Mann
> Allein das Recht? Drückt denn Unmögliches
> Nur er an die gewalt'ge Heldenbrust?

she asks. As she gathers courage to confront Thoas with the truth, images of fire and bold avengers course through her mind. She is, and remains, a true child of Tantalus, 'verteufelt human'.

Her open speech rings true. It springs from that inner openness to the divine which empowers her to flow out in pure and unimpeded love towards the 'rohe Skythe' as much as to her kin by birth — a liberation, paradoxically, her own kin has brought about: and her voice reaches Thoas' heart. Her vision of undivided and inviolate humanity is made good in the bond of hospitality that will tie together the farthest ends of the inhabited world.

> Wert und teuer,
> Wie mir mein Vater war, so bist du's mir,
> Und dieser Eindruck bleibt in meiner Seele.
> Bringt der Geringste deines Volkes je
> Den Ton der Stimme mir ins Ohr zurück,
> Den ich an euch gewohnt zu hören bin,
> Und seh ich an dem Ärmsten eure Tracht:
> Empfangen will ich ihn wie einen Gott . . .

---

[26] Schumann points out the range of *unerhörte Taten* of which this is one, though qualitatively different from its predecessors. (*Loc. cit.*, p. 243.) It is, precisely, a verbal deed.

What a rich and ample vision, and how rich in resonances! These are, virtually, the words she had addressed to Orestes when he first came; words which at that time she could only address to a 'werter Landsmann'. Then she had said:

> Selbst der letzte Knecht,
> Der an den Herd der Vatergötter streifte,
> Ist uns in fremdem Lande hoch willkommen:
> Wie soll ich euch genug mit Freud' und Segen
> Empfangen, die ihr mir das Bild der Helden,
> Die ich von Eltern her verehren lernte,
> Entgegenbringet ...

Now Thoas, and his people, bear the imprint of those that she loved and revered most, that opened up Olympus to her spirit. He has become her second father, no less treasured than the 'göttergleiche Agamemnon': for even the humblest of the Taurians, to her, is 'göttergleich und ähnlich'. There is something of that 'inn're Jauchzen', which told her that the grown man before her was her own Orestes, about her loving description now of how she will recognise a Taurian, should he land at her distant shore; the same intimacy of recollection, of their features, the very sound of their voices, that have impressed themselves upon a mind which will cherish these trifling memories for ever after. There is something of the childlike and inconsolable grief which informs her opening monologue as she now thinks of the wind swelling the sails of the ship that will carry her away from the land which has become her second home. Only now the tears flow freely, and all bitterness is drained from her. The whole wide world is Iphigenie's now, sweet as childhood and home and sacred as first love.

How exquisite is the blend, in these last *ernst-lieblichen* speeches, as Goethe has it in another context, of graveness and spontaneity! What was an alternating rhythm at the beginning of the drama, sometimes even a violent oscillation, has now fused into a singular strain, at once wholly tender and wholly pure. And what a grandiose span has been covered from this beginning to this end: from the monstrous deeds, the very telling of which threatens to stain the dignity of language, to the reticent word, to the true and open word, to the ineffably chaste and gracious farewell words at the end, Iphigenie's 'holde Worte' and Thoas' final 'Lebt wohl'! It is the two-pillared arc which stretches from the animal-pride to society and civilisation, from the dawn of time when human beings are mindlessly offered in bloody sacrifice, to the epoch-making moment when the sacrifice of even one guarded word is repudiated as a mortal crime. And all this development within one generation, indeed within the compass of three single lives — Orestes, Thoas and Iphigenie herself.

From deeds to words, from titanically obsessed actions inaugurating an unending chain of destruction to the word that creates newness of life and

inaugurates humanity, in both senses of the word, as a living reality — this is
the span this drama sustains: and it reflects the span of one man's development
over a very few years, from his turbulent youth to maturity. That one word
which ushers in civilisation is the word Iphigenie enacts and Orestes speaks:
'Zwischen uns sei Wahrheit': the utterance which declares war on the
sacrifice of anything human, in any shape or form. More precisely, it is the
humble preposition 'zwischen'. A profoundly ambiguous word, doing double
duty here and, on closer inspection, a very profound word indeed. It tells us
that 'Wahrheit', integrity of relatedness, is a force that bridges and binds the
participants in the human conversation. At the same time, it affirms, however
delicately, the very distance it spans. It is of the essence of 'Wahrheit' that it
creates, and preserves, that vital space, that aura of solitude in the other in
which his encounter with the divine takes place. It is not too much to say
that the word 'zwischen' defines the precise quality of relatedness as it emerges
from this play. 'Zwischen' — kinship between individuals joined in reverence
of their own and the other's groundedness in the divine — this *is* 'Wahrheit',
the truth of relatedness.

In *Wilhelm Meisters Wanderjahre*, the carpenter Joseph tells Wilhelm of the
confinement of the young widow Marie, whom he loved at first sight.
'Frau Elisabeth trat zu ihr, gleichsam um mich zu melden', he recounts,
'hub etwas vom Bette auf und brachte mir's entgegen: in das weißeste Zeug
gewickelt den schönsten Knaben. Frau Elisabeth hielt ihn gerade zwischen
mich und die Mutter, und auf der Stelle fiel mir der Lilienstengel ein, der sich
auf dem Bilde zwischen Maria und Joseph als Zeuge eines reinen Verhältnisses aus der Erde hebt'.

It does not take weapons to resolve the issue 'between' the contestant parties,
as Thoas believes.

> Das Bild, o König, soll uns nicht entzweien!

Orestes tells the king. What stands 'between' them is Iphigenie herself, sister
to Orestes and the Taurian people alike, the holy one, tender and austere,
like the lily 'Zeuge eines reinen Verhältnisses'[27].

Absolute immediacy of relationship, be it the instinctual immediacy of
Tantalus' race or Faust's and Tasso's claim to radical immediacy of feeling,
in this drama is presented as nothing short of catastrophic. It is heroically
infantile and prehuman. Only the relation which is filtered through the
divine on its course to the other is accounted truly human; as creative and
free-ranging as are the symbolisms of language and art — the image of Diana,

---

[27] Cf. Chapter VIII, pp. 205 and 208. Altogether, *Iphigenie* is a forerunner of *Wilhelm Meisters
Wanderjahre*, in that already here that quality of responding which the later Goethe would
have termed *Entsagung* transforms a tangle of — largely incestuous — relationships into
a network of affinities which spans the ends of the world. Cf. Chapter VIII, pp. 222 ff..

for instance — which are man's most liberating possessions, his most nego-
tiable currency.

Iphigenie is a drama enacting the birth, in three individuals, of civilisation
and a humanity which puts an end to all human sacrifice, bar one —: the
sacrifice exacted in the name of mediacy. It is of this, the immolation of youth
in the name of committed adulthood, that the word 'zwischen' speaks with
gentle urgency.

'Rat, Mäßigung und Weisheit und Geduld':
The Diaries of a young Man (1775—1782)

There's a divinity that shapes our ends,
Rough-hew them how we will.

Shakespeare

I.

'Kind, Kind! nicht weiter! Wie von unsichtbaren Geistern gepeitscht, gehen die Sonnen-
pferde der Zeit mit unsers Schicksals leichtem Wagen durch, und uns bleibt nichts als
mutig gefaßt die Zügel festzuhalten, bald rechts, bald links, vom Steine hier, vom
Sturze da, die Räder wegzulenken. Wohin es geht, wer weiß es? Erinnert er sich doch
kaum, woher er kam.'

These are the last words of Goethe's autobiography, the words of Egmont,
passionately quoted by the author to Demoiselle Delph as the coachman,
waiting to take him to Weimar, impatiently blew his horn. It is indeed a fitting
end for an autobiography which had begun with the precise description of the
planetary constellation at the minute of his entry into this world. For Egmont,
too, feels his life's course to be governed by suprapersonal powers, by the
sunsteeds of time running their predetermined heavenly course and by
invisible spirits whipping him along in his light chariot at break-neck
speed. In *Egmont*, Goethe had undertaken to portray 'das Dämonische,
was von beiden Seiten im Spiel ist'[1]; and by interpolating the discussion of the
demonic in the narrative of his life immediately before it races towards its
climactic end — a young man taking the reins of his destiny into his own
resolute hands — he had indicated what the beginning of the narrative had
foreshadowed: that he saw his own life directed by higher and mysterious
powers. For all that he repudiates, elsewhere, that he himself was a demonic
figure, here, at the end of *Dichtung und Wahrheit*, he releases his readers with
just this impression, phrased, it is true, in his usual understating way: he speaks
of his little life, 'dem aber doch auch seltsame Ereignisse, wenigstens mit einem
dämonischen Schein bekleidet, bevorstanden'[2]; the events being, precisely,
his imminent departure for Italy and the last minute change of course to the
duchy where he was going to spend the rest of his life.

By a neat coincidence, Goethe's diary begins a few days before that impassioned moment when he took leave from Demoiselle Delph, the idea of

Quotations from the Diaries are according to the *Artemis Gedenkausgabe der Werke, Briefe
und Gespräche.*

[1] *Dichtung und Wahrheit*, IV, 20, *HA* X, p. 176.
[2] *Ibid.*, p. 177.

an Italian journey and future plans of a career in Mannheim, quoting his hero's words. The first entry is dated 'Auf der Reise von Frankfurt nach Heidelberg, Oktober 30, 1775', in other words, on the first lap of the trip which was to take him away from Lili Schönemann to Italy, or so the thought. It is an extraordinary glimpse these jottings afford us into the immediate pre-Weimar Goethe, the young author of *Götz*, *Werther* — written eighteen months before — *Clavigo*, *Stella*, of the *Urfaust* and the great *Sturm und Drang* hymns, the 'Künstlergedichte' and those disturbingly lovely Lili lyrics. Like his *Egmont*, he is surrendered to a demonic force beyond his controlling — 'das liebe unsichtbaare Ding das mich leitet und schult', and 'das Weitere steht bey dem lieben Ding das den Plan zu meiner Reise gemacht hat', we read; yet, like his dramatic heroes — Weislingen, Faust, Clavigo, Fernando — he asks, and not without a touch of narcissistic pleasure, 'Bin ich denn nur in der Welt mich in ewiger unschuldiger Schuld zu winden —'. He flirts with his *Verworrenheit* — the word occurs three times — idiom and punctuation are wilful in the extreme and, at the end, in true Wertherish fashion, he announces: 'Will ich doch allen Launen den Lauf lassen'. It is a strange document of transition, not unlike the famous letter to Herder written three years earlier, in July 1772, pregnant with intimations of meanings scarcely glimpsed, yet still dithyrambically topsy-turvy, 'entsetzlich durcheinander'[3].

In the entries of the early days in Weimar subjectivity still seems to predominate and, with it, the sense of being a prey to his own intense and confused emotions. We find him describing himself as 'dumpf', 'dumpfsinnig' (June 17, 18, 21, 1776), 'dunkel' (June 15, July 7, August 27, 1777); he notes 'Fieberhaffte Wehmuth.' (December 31st, 1776), 'fieberhaffte Schläfrigkeit' (January 1st, 1777), 'Umhergewandelt Scheis weh.' (January 11, 1777), 'viel gelitten . . . tiefes Leiden' (December 25, 1776); expressions all reminiscent of Werther's wilful introversion, of those 'übertriebene Forderungen an sich selbst' giving way to that sense of exhaustion he so insistently stresses, in *Dichtung und Wahrheit*, as being the prime cause of the *taedium vitae* which attacked him and his young contemporaries at and after the time of *Werther*[4].

On April 13, 1777, there is the laconic entry: 'Viel in der Seele umgeworfen.' On June 17, the day after he heard of his sister's death: 'Leiden und Träumen.' On July 4 of that year, his depiction of Bohemian life, with its abrupt changes of mood, recalls the flash-back scenes in the poem *Ilmenau*. We read: 'Früh nach Dornburg leidlich helle. Dort ward mir's wohl. Gezeichnet. Abends nach Kunitz. Das Schloss gefährlich erstiegen. im Regen zurück. Nachts auf der Streue mit d. Herzog, Prinzen [Konstantin], Dalberg u 2 Einsiedels vorher tolles Disputiren mit Einsied d. jüngern.' The suicide of Christel

---

[3] Cf. my *Goethe and Lessing*, Chapter V part 1; also E. M. Wilkinson, 'Goethe to Herder, July 1772', *GLL* (New Series), Vol. XV, October 1961.
[4] III, 13, *HA* IX, p. 590 and III, 14, *HA* X, p. 7. Cf. Chapter I of this book (pp. 16 ff.) and my *Goethe and Lessing*, Chapter VI.

von Lasberg leaves Goethe a prey to different, and contrary, impingements. He writes: 'In stiller Trauer einige Tage beschäfftigt um die Scene des Todts, nachher wieder gezwungen zu theatralischem Leichtsinn.' (January 19, 1778). Altogether the diary for that year — Goethe's thirtieth — is interspersed with entries which show him to be changeable, now outward turned and participating in events, now relapsing into himself, deep in ferment. The entry of March 27 reads: ♃ [the duke] war viel in Milit. gedancken, und ich ganz fatal gedruckt von allen Elementen es währte noch einige Tage.' Between April 1 and 12: 'Weiter vegetirt in tausend Gedancken an unsre Verhältnisse und unser Schicksaal. Unruhe des ♃ [duke]. erwachend Kriegsgefühl ... Wühlte ich still an Felsen und Ufer fort.' On July 14, 1778: 'Im stillen fortgekrabelt. körperlich gelitten. Fatale Lichter über allerley Verhältnisse.' And still, as late as December 8 of that year: 'Nach Tiefurt wo mich alles an den Menschen ärgerte. Drum macht ich mich weg nach Hause. Hatte Lust zu nichts. (Zeichnete wenig an den Moulures.) Aristophanes konnte mich des Schlafs nicht erwehren.' To complete the picture, Goethe's extraordinary susceptibility to the weather must be alluded to. We frequently find him expressing this dependence through an uncommented equation such as 'Bewegung des Herzens Frühlings Thauwetter.' (February 24, 1777), 'In dunckler Unruhe früh ... Grauer Morgen.' (July 7, 1777), 'Dumm Wetter und Sinn.' (July 14, 1777) or 'War diese Zeit her wie das Wetter klar, rein, fröhlich.' (March 29—31, 1779), this last type of entry becoming ever more characteristic.

Such entries show a young man tossed about this way and that, labile, a prey to moods from within and impingements from without, lacking an abiding sense of purpose, a firm centre, perhaps even a continuing sense of identity.

As perhaps the most typical example of that Wertherish mood we may cite an early entry made on August 9, 1776: 'Verduselter, verzeichneter, verwarteter verschlafener Morgen', we read under that date. Rarely can the prefix 'ver' have been used to more purpose than in this entry. It graphically depicts that total futility and lack of any purposeful activity, that absence of any inner economy which we associate with Werther's drift towards destruction. With one difference: where Werther would have been effusive, Goethe is to the point and pithy. And indeed, from the beginning of this intimate venture, this is the characteristic idiom he employs, concise and — often in curious contradiction to the prevailing mood — as impersonal as a telegraph message. The most striking thing is the all but total absence of the pronoun 'I' — he seems almost deliberately to avoid it — and the astrological symbols he uses for the principal figures in his life — Charlotte von Stein, the Duke Karl August and others. This latter habit does not appear to be a mystifying trick — a chiffre language in a secret conversation: rather does it seem to be expressive of some sense of being a party to a suprapersonal constellation which determines his destiny along with that of the others.

Soon, moreover, that self-satisfied indulgence begins to disappear with which, not many moons earlier, he had invoked 'das liebe Ding'. Increasingly his persistent musings about destiny — that *Rat* which earned Tantalus a place at the table of the Gods — are marked by humility and a sense of accountability which he accepts as the price of being chosen for an uncommon fate. On November 7, 1776, we read: '... Was ist der Mensch dass du sein gedenckst und das Menschenkind dass du dich sein annimmst.' On April 6, 1777, we read, without further comment: ' = Schwere Hand der Götter.' On September 5 of the same year: '... das Buch Hiob gelesen.' On December 10, standing on the Brocken surrounded by mist and clouds, under a clear sky: 'Was ist der Mensch dass du sein gedenckst.' True, very occasionally there is a proud awareness of privilege, a note even of hubris. But far more often his awareness of being different takes the form of an unflinching sense of duty. On July 14, 1779, after giving high praise to George Batty, the minister in charge of agricultural affairs, he continues: 'Aber ich spüre zum voraus, es ist auch nicht für mich. Ich darf nicht von dem mir vorgeschriebnen Weeg abgehn, mein Daseyn ist einmal nicht einfach ...'; and some ten days later, on July 25, after helping to put out a fire in Apolda: 'Ich dancke nur Gott dass ich im Feuer und Wasser den Kopf oben habe, doch erwart ich sittsam noch starcke Prüfungen ...'. And, later in the same entry:

> 'Das Elend wird mir nach und nach so prosaisch wie ein Kaminfeuer. Aber ich lasse doch nicht von meinen gedancken und ringe mit dem unerkannten Engel sollt ich mir die Hüfte ausrencken. Es weis kein Mensch was ich thue und mit wieviel Feinden ich kämpfe um das wenige hervorzubringen. Bey meinem Streben und Streiten und Bemühen bitt ich euch nicht zu lachen, zuschauende Götter. Allenfalls lächlen mögt ihr, und mir beystehen.'

It is not 'der gepriesene Halbgott' of Goethe's *Sturm und Drang* years that is speaking here; not even his Egmont, except for that inimitable lightness of touch with which the writer minimises his own *cri de cœur;* rather it is the surveying poet of *Grenzen der Menschheit, Gesang der Geister über den Wassern,* or the author of *Iphigenie.* Survey, envisagement of perspectives in which to view the human condition and, within it, his own life: *Rat;* such is the prevailing frame of these reflective utterances.

The question arises, how and by what means it was possible that the 'Strudelkopf' who wrote that first head over heels entry on October 30 1775, wayward, moody, indulgent and utterly in ferment, should within a matter of a few years, before our very eyes almost, have developed the manly sense of purpose, self-awareness and discipline which so rapidly take over in these entries. To trace this development and to show the several strands perceptible within it as concretely as possible is the task of this chapter.

2.

The word Goethe uses time and again, in the early entries, with an almost magic, incantatory force, is *rein*. So much has been written about this word, in connection with *Iphigenie*, with regard to Goethe's relation to Frau von Stein and as a key concept *per se*[5], that it may be useful to follow it back to its source here, in these private jottings. This much is certain, in whatever context and in whatever meaning-nuance we encounter it, it always seems to imply and, indeed, to presuppose moderation.

In the first instance, it occurs in association with words such as *abgezogen*, *entfremdet* and *still*. Like Iphigenie in the seclusion of her sanctuary, Goethe keeps himself to himself, and endeavours to do so even when he is in company. Incessantly, he relates what happens to him in the here and now to an inner core he cherishes and seeks to strengthen in solitude. A few illustrations: on February 4, 1777, he states 'Reiner Tag'. On November 13 of the same year, in a similar vein, 'Reine Ruh'. On the Wartburg he writes on October 4, 1777: 'Tiefes Gefühl des Alleinseyns . . . Mich störte Knebels Ankunft, der mir auch Grüse brachte, in meinem Gefühl gänzlicher Abge-schnittenheit, seine Erzählungen wie seine Gegenwart, zerrten mich in die alten Verhältnisse hinüber.' Four days later, still from the Wartburg:

> Stund inwärts gewendet wieder auf . . . Grimms Eintritt [schloß mich] wieder zu. Ich fühlte so inniglich dass . . . ich dem Manne nichts zu sagen hatte . . . die Klufft zwischen mir und denen Menschen allen fiel mir so grass in die Augen, da kein Vehikulum da war . . . Ins Herzogs Zimmer! konnts nicht dauern, sah den Mond über dem Schlosse und herauf. Hier nun zum letztenmal, auf der reinen ruhigen Höhe . . . Gern kehr ich doch zurück in mein enges Nest, nun bald in Sturm gewickelt, in Schnee verweht. Und wills Gott in Ruhe vor den Menschen mit denen ich doch nichts zu theilen habe. Hier hab ich weit weniger gelitten als ich gedacht habe, bin aber in viel Entfremdung bestimmt, wo ich doch noch Band glaubte.' (October 8).

On the first day of 1778, we find the entry: 'Rein ruhig hatte das alte Jahr zusammen gepackt.' 'Diese Woche viel auf dem Eis, in immer gleicher fast zu reiner Stimmung . . . Stille und Vorahndung der Weisheit' (beginning of February, 1778). 'fortdauernde reine Entfremdung von den Menschen' (February 12). '. . . blos vegetirt, still und rein' (beginning of April). 'Diese letzte Zeit meist sehr still in mir. Architecktur gezeichnet um noch abgezogner zu werden. Leidlich reine Vorstellung von vielen Verhältnissen' (end of December). ' . . . in der Stille . . . Ich bin zu abgezogen um die rechten Verhältnisse die meist Lumperey und Armuth Geists und Beutels sind zu finden und zu benuzzen doch muss es gehn. Da ich viel klärer bin . . .' (January 10, 1779). 'Das beste ist die tiefe Stille in der ich gegen die Welt lebe und wachse, und gewinne was sie mir mit Feuer und Schwert nicht nehmen können' (on May 13, 1780). And, perhaps most astonishingly, on December 9, 1778: 'sie (Char-

---

[5] Cf. Chapter III, note 5.

lotte von Stein) kommt mir immer liebenswürdig vor, obgleich fremder'; and, similarly, 'War ⊙ sehr lieb. War ich sehr in mir' (January 6—8, 1799).

Like his Iphigenie, Goethe is seeking inner seclusion in order to gain distance from the pressures of the day, the too close involvement in the practical and emotional concerns of others and, most of all, from the labile fluctuations of his own feelings. When he permits himself to be dragged back 'in die alten Verhältnisse', he will run up against a toll-bar or smash his sledge. His irritable impressionableness and susceptibility are such that any impingement makes a disproportionately violent impact upon him, to the extent that he is engulfed by them and loses sight of his self. To emerge from this feverish flux, to find living and breathing space in which, gradually, a stable self crystallises and an abiding sense of his own identity awakens, this is his first concern, as it is the basis of Iphigenie's spiritual development. And even Frau von Stein is included in this process. As he loves her more, he registers a growing sense of distance, perhaps even of estrangement, from the complex of deep emotions she represents. In all the manifold relations and involvements of his life, Goethe is striving to emerge from ephemeral flux and to develop a self which is the master rather than the prey of its impingements. A little more than a year after his arrival in Weimar, we find the gratified statement 'wie sich mein innres seit einem Jahr befestigt hat' (September 2, 1777); and such surveying judgements are to be found period-ically throughout these entries.

It is in this connection that we must see two characteristic traits of these diaries we already observed in passing: their telegraphic style and the use of astrological symbols denoting those especially close to him. As for the first, it signifies an emotional economy or even reticence. The I of the person who is affected in this or that way, is safely tucked away, in some unreachable seclusion, even from his own susceptible self. It is in this way that we must read an entry such as that strange 'War zugefroren gegen alle Menschen.' (beginning of December, 1778), or that laconic entry à propos of his re-read-ing of *Werther*: 'Las meinen Werther, seit er gedruckt ist das erstemal ganz und verwunderte mich' (April 30, 1780). What distance and what inner chastity *vis à vis* this extravagant work of his youth! And all the more so since the tell-tale word 'my' slips in unawares. And does not the employment of astrological symbols for the circle of people closest to him argue the desire for distance and lasting perspectives? Might one not even say that he conceives of those relations as being of symbolic significance and nurtures them in such a fashion? Such need for distance does not imply lack of partici-pation; rather does it argue the need for purity of participation, a quality of relatedness which guards, and helps to liberate, the core of his individuality rather than to smother it; which remains mindful of the suprapersonal ties of the participants and reveres them. The word *abgezogen* which recurs in connection with relationships, tells its own tale. It is synonymous with 'abstract', and thus presupposes a high degree of mental activity exercised on the raw material of experience: subsuming what is particular and singular — the pure flux of the moment — under more generalised modes of apprehension and thus placing it into universal and lasting perspectives. To experience things thus, *sub specie aeternitatis*, is to experience them 'rein'. When we read, as we do on November 2, 1776, as on so many other occasions, 'Nachts gebadet', and remember other similar occasions such as that described in a letter to Gustel von Stolberg — which is accompanied by the poem he sang as he emerged from his ablution: 'Alles geben die Götter ihren Lieblingen ganz' — we feel that this immersion in the element and the subsequent emerging onto the moonlit banks is a purifying act of symbolic import. In one of the most crucial entries in which he takes stock of his youthful errors with that sternness which suggests that he has only just left this state behind, Goethe writes that he stands 'wie einer der sich aus dem Wasser rettet und den die Sonne anfängt wohlthätig abzutrocknen' (August 7, 1779). Ablution from the dross of daily involvement, emergence from elemental flux of sheer susceptibility, this is purity.

This mental 'abstraction', however, is not attained in a void. From early on, Goethe is aware that the temperance which leads to such purity of perception is based on moderation and discipline on the most primitive physical plane. In *Wilhelm Meisters Lehrjahre*, Therese confesses to Wilhelm: 'Ich . . . gestehe gern, ich habe vom Sittlichen den Begriff als von einer Diät, die eben dadurch nur Diät ist, wenn ich sie zur Lebensregel mache, wenn ich sie das ganze Jahr nicht außer Augen lasse.'[6] Her words are fully borne out by the measures towards moral self-education we see Goethe adopting in his diaries. He does think of it as grounded in the strictest physical hygiene. In that first confused entry, on the way to Heidelberg, we read, not surprisingly: 'Ominose Überfüllung des Glases'; an indulgence which leads to more indulgence. For when the innkeeper apologises for the vats and wine-barrels standing about as a result of a particularly rich harvest, his young guest exclaims that he should not worry, 'denn es sey sehr selten daß einen der Segen Gottes inkommodire' — a sentiment no doubt accompanied by appropriate action — and concludes that he intends to give free rein to his every whim.

On January 13, 1779, an entry which is as un-Wertherish as any we may find, concludes with the observation: 'Dass ich nur die Hälfte Wein trincke ist mir sehr nützlich, seit ich den Caffee gelassen die heilsamste Diät.' Self-exhortations to abstain from drinking wine and English beer continue (April 1 and end of April, 1780). On the latter occasion we find the gratified entry: 'War sehr ruhig und bestimmt, die letzten Tage wenig eingezogen. Ich trincke fast keinen Wein. Und gewinne täglich mehr in Blick und Geschick zum thätigen Leben.' Within four years of his turbulent trip to Heidelberg, in

---

[6] VII, 6, *HA* VII, p. 459f.

that other crucial entry which draws up the balance of his wasted youth, Goethe ends with a kind of prayer: 'Lasse uns von Morgen zum Abend das gehörige thun und gebe uns klare Begriffe von den Folgen der Dinge. Dass man nicht sey wie Menschen die den ganzen Tag über Kopfweh klagen und alle Abend zu viel Wein zu sich nehmen. Möge die Idee des reinen die sich bis auf den Bissen erstreckt den ich in Mund nehme, immer lichter in mir werden.' (August 7, 1779)[7]. The moderation of physical appetites is firmly embedded in the lively notion of a moral diet — Therese's notion. We are less than a year from the inception of Tasso to whom the poet has lent precisely this physical immoderation and a *laissez faire* in matters dietetic which is based, precisely, upon an inability and unwillingness to survey, and obey, the law of cause and consequence — a basic lack of *Rat* in Goethe's sense of the word. Antonio makes much play of this infantile adherence to the pleasure principle and Goethe leaves us in no doubt that he is correct in regarding such lassitude as a root cause of Tasso's moral immaturity[8]. As for Goethe himself, his abstinence from food and drink on the voyage to Sicily will occupy us in a later chapter[9]; and Erich Trunz has drawn attention to the poet's extreme regularity and moderation in matters of diet throughout his life[10]. There is little doubt that he regarded the physical habits which we see him acquiring here, in his early Weimar years, as the biological base of his long life and unimpeded creativity.

Two entries dating from February 1782, that is to say, the very end of the period we are considering, once more gather together the diverse elements that are compounded in Goethe's experience of purity; physical abstinence, withdrawnness, discipline and, most of all, stillness; on February 10, he writes: 'Enthielt ich mich stille.', and one week later, on February 17, he echoes his own words: 'Enthielt mich zu Hause und war fleisig.', we read. The person writing here is the future author of the work to which he was to give the subtitle *Die Entsagenden*.

3.

But here an urgent question announces itself. Is this somewhat distant, pure and reflective young man we see in the mirror of his diary a 'feiner Paradies-vogel' as Aurelie, in *Wilhelm Meister*, accuses the idealistic hero of being, that 'poetic fiction' of which lore maintains 'sie hätten keine Füße, sie schwebten in der Luft und nährten sich vom Äther'[11]? Is the Goethe of the

[7] In this connection, cf. A. Beck, 'der "Geist der Reinheit" und die "Idee des Reinen"' I and II, *loc. cit.*

[8] *Torquato Tasso*, V, 1.

[9] Chapter V, p. 121.

[10] In: 'Ein Tag aus Goethes Leben', *Goethe-Jahrbuch 90*, 1973.

[11] *Wilhelm Meisters Lehrjahre*, V, 10.

early Weimar years a superior kind of Werther, turned in upon himself, shunning a good day's work and everything that smacks of the humdrum chores that make a man of a dreamer? Quite on the contrary. The Goethe we encounter in those pages is — need we say it even? — Lotte and Albert as well as Werther, Prometheus no less than Ganymed. He seeks activity as a fish seeks the water. From the beginning onwards he shows a tendency to seek refuge in some sort of ordered activity when he is inward-turned, reflective or confused. On November 7, 1776, for example, we read: 'Mit den Bienen beschäfftigt und sie zur Winterruh gebracht . . . Was ist der Mensch dass du sein gedenckst und das Menschenkind dass du dich sein annimmst. Abends Bau Grillen im Garten, und Feldzug gegen die Jahrs zeit.' Similarly, on December 25 of the same winter: 'Zu⊙. [Charlotte von Stein], viel gelitten allein gessen. noch zu Schardts tiefes Leiden. Zu Kalben. in Garten. Ordnung gemacht . . . '. And then the rider: 'zu Herdern vergnügter Abend . . . '. This inborn disposition will be articulated with full insight within a couple of years, as in February 1779, when we read, 'Diese Zeit her habe ich meist gesucht mich in Geschäfften aufrecht zu erhalten und bey allen Vorfällen fest zu seyn und ruhig' (between February 15 and 23).

True, at first there are occasional grumbles, as when he complains that the duke vents his own fitful temper on him, when, like his own Egmont, he frets at the hollow pomp and the stuffy air in the council room (December 9, 1778 and February 1, 1779), or groans about 'Bevorstehende neue Eckel Verhältn. durch die Kriegs Comiss.' (end of December, 1778). But in increasing measure he gives all of himself to the job in hand and finds himself steadied by thus going all out. At the beginning of February, 1778, we read: 'Bestimmteres Gefühl von Einschränckung, und dadurch der wahren Ausbreitung', a sentence which announces the future creator of Jarno. Similarly, on February 12: 'Stille und Bestimmtheit im Leben und handeln', which like a counterpoint follows the observation: 'fortdauernde reine Entfremdung von den Menschen.' He has no patience with theorists and know-alls that criticise where others do. On May 13, 1780, barely a fortnight after re-reading his Werther and 'wondering', we read:

'Für Krafft ists schade er sieht die Mängel gut, und weis selbst nicht eine Warze wegzunehmen. Wenn er ein Amt hätte würf er alles mit dem besten Vorsatz durcheinander, daher auch sein Schicksaal . . . In der Nähe ists unangenehm so einen Nage wurm zu haben, der, untätig einem immer vorjammert was nicht ist wie es seyn sollte. Bey Gott es ist kein Canzellist der nicht in einer Viertelstunde mehr gescheuts reden kan als ich in einem Vierteljahr Gott weis in zehn iahren thun kann.'

This same entry begins with the clear insight of what he had practised intuitively some three years earlier, when he had found refuge from perturbation by doing a gardening job. 'War die Zeit manigfaltig beschäfftigt. . . .' he writes, adding: 'Verzogen sich einige hypochondrische Gespenster.'

But what is the kind of activity into which this poet puts his all? The war commission, the road commission, the agricultural commission, even the fire service: these are the concerns we hear about. We have alluded to the fire in Apolda in which he was 'den ganzen Tag gebraten und gesotten' (July 25, 1779). He has long and detailed sessions about agricultural matters with George Batty, and so far from feeling that he is being side-tracked from concerns of greater moment, he looks upon the expertise of the latter in his craft with unstinted admiration and, in an entry full of interest which will engage our attention later, compares his mastery in his chosen field with that of the artist.

'Diese Nähe zu allen Saiten der Harfe,'

he notes on July 14, 1779,

'die Gewissheit und Sicherheit wo mit er sie rührt mag den Meister anzeigen in jeder Art. Er geht wenn er bemerken soll grad auf das los, wie Batty auf einem Landgut, er träumt nicht im allgemeinen wie unser einer ehmals um Bildende Kunst. Wenn er handeln soll greift er grad das an was iezt nötig ist. Gar schön ist der Feldbau weil alles so rein antwortet wenn ich was dumm oder was gut mache, und Glück und Unglück die primas vias der Menschheit trifft.'

Goethe's joy in watching a master of his craft — a craft so alien to his own vocation as he presently states — lies in observing the fine correspondence between what needs to be done and the response elicited, between pure receptivity and pure activity[12]. 'Jeder neue Gegenstand, wohl beschaut, schließt ein neues Organ in uns auf', Goethe was to write many years later. Here, in Batty's fruitful activity, he saw an example of a faculty, a physical instinct almost, responding with appropriate activity to an object to which he felt natively attuned, by which he was permeated: he saw a living embodiment of what he was to call 'gegenständliche Anschauung' and no doubt actively developed his own inborn understanding of the needs of things growing through such illuminating intercourse.

This concern with the pure interaction between self and world, with the pure answer received from an object and in turn given to its purely perceived need, goes to explain his special gratification at his activities in the war commission which, so he explicitly and somewhat startlingly states, offer no food whatever to his imagination and his creative self. 'Die Kr. Comm. werd ich gut versehn', he writes on February 1st, 1779, 'weil ich bey dem Geschäfft gar nichts hervorbringen will, nur das was da ist recht kennen, und ordentlich haben will.' Again it is the exercise of submitting himself to the needs of the object before him in pure receptivity, without intrusion of his own mind, its preconceived notions or fantasies, and the discovery in himself of what activity will answer to these needs, which delights him.

[12] Cf. Chapter VIII, sections 7, 8 and 9.

Perhaps the most astonishing of these entries is the relatively early one dated January 13, 1779, in which he announces that he has been placed in charge of the selfsame war commission. We read:

'Die Kriegs Comiss. über nommen Erste Session. Fest und ruhig in meinen Sinnen, und scharf. Allein dies Geschäffte diese Tage her. Mich drinn gebadet ... Der Druck der Geschäffte ist sehr schön der Seele, wenn sie entladen ist spielt sie freyer und geniest des Lebens. Elender ist nichts als der behagliche Mensch ohne Arbeit, das schönste der Gaben wird ihm eckel.'

This passage, written just over five years after the composition of *Werther*, by itself abundantly explains Goethe's abhorrence of being identified with his hero. In two sentences he has put his finger on the *malaise* of his artistic *Schwärmer*: the idle hunt for experience unsupported by purposeful action. The Goethe of these diaries knows what he knew when he created the world of Lotte and Albert next to Werther's, what his Werther fails to understand: that in straining all the powers of his heart and imagination to 'experience' the world, he will never come to know this world as it is, because he will always project himself and his own need onto the experience of it. To know it, he must listen to its voice and test his understanding by appropriate action eliciting an answering echo. He must listen to the world as the world responds to his answer.

Goethe has articulated gist and image of this diary observation in a verse written decades later:

Im Atemholen sind zweierlei Gnaden:
Die Luft einziehn, sich ihrer entladen.
Jenes bedrängt, dieses erfrischt;
So sonderbar ist das Leben gemischt.
Du danke Gott, wenn er dich preßt,
Und dank' ihm, wenn er dich wieder entläßt.[13]

These lines clarify — if such clarification be needed still — the most extraordinary sentence in Goethe's gleeful entry concerning his military duties. 'Mich drinn gebadet.' Werther seeks to bathe in the sea of fragrances around him (I, May 4), or, later, to submerge himself in the fathomless ocean of Lotte's eyes (II, December 6) which, significantly and paradoxically, are inside him. The Goethe of these diaries, still a young man this side of thirty, knows that he bathes himself clean of himself and gains true refreshment, not when he obtrudes himself on the other in the quest to 'experience' it, but when he submits himself to the other and loses himself in it; 'wenn er lernt, ... seiner selbst in einer pflichtmäßigen Tätigkeit zu vergessen.'[14] What eyes would Werther have made, if Albert had told him that he was bathing himself clean in his files! The young Goethe knew better.

[13] *Westöstlicher Divan, Buch des Sängers.*
[14] *Wilhelm Meisters Lehrjahre,* VII, 9.

And yet, here and there, amid all this eulogy of pure *Tätigkeit*, we hear something resembling a suppressed sob. On April 1, 1780, he reports having read the journal of his Swiss trip to friends; the trip he took to escape from Lili. And he adds: ' . . . da wir alle nicht mehr verliebt sind und die Lava Oberfläche verkühlt ist, giengs recht munter und artig, nur in die Rizzen darf man noch nicht visitieren. da brennts noch.' Towards the end of April 1780, immediately following the gratified statement that every day he is developing more aptitude for the active life, we find the entry: 'Doch ist mirs wie einem Vogel der sich in Zwirn verwickelt hat ich fühle, dass ich Flügel habe und sie sind nicht zu brauchen. Es wird auch werden' — he adds somewhat lamely — 'in dess erhohl ich mich in der Geschichte, und tändle an einem Dram oder Roman.' We recall the lines to Lili Schönemann in which a creative crisis is hinted at in the same image — the very crisis which prompted him to break off the relation:

> Wie ein Vogel, der den Faden bricht
> Und zum Walde kehrt,
> Er schleppt des Gefängnisses Schmach,
> Noch ein Stückchen des Fadens nach,
> Er ist der alte freigeborne Vogel nicht,
> Er hat schon jemand angehört.

So, too, the poem *Der Adler und die Taube* comes to mind. A similar *cri de cœur* is heard in an entry dated between May 26 and June 22, 1780, that is to say, a couple of months after the statement we have considered. He writes: 'NB. vom 26 [Mai] bis 22 folgenden Monats habe nichts geschrieben . . . Meine Tage waren von Morgends bis in die Nacht besetzt. Man könnte noch mehr, ia das unglaubliche thun wenn man mäsiger wäre. das geht nun nicht.'

Is Goethe asking too much of himself? Is the poet forcing his protesting genius into too rigid a mould? Is all this cult of practical activity dissociated from his true poetic vocation and inimical to it, perhaps even a device to save himself from his vulnerability? Is he a tight-lipped Pooh-Bah, a self-appointed Lord High Everything Else, in order to eradicate — as has so often been maintained — the waywardness of an artistic temperament which had by the skin of its teeth escaped from the perils of its *Sturm und Drang*? The entries we have just been considering certainly raise this question; and we must seek to answer it from the same source, that is to say, from the diaries themselves.

4.

From early on, these diaries are punctuated by a series of entries relating to the poet's own household. It soon becomes apparent that such allusions are metaphorical rather than literal in character, and gradually the image becomes a shorthand for some symbolic meaning.

At first these references mirror the confused mental frame of the owner. On December 31, 1776, for instance — the last day of the year and a time for taking stock — he reports that he has smashed his sledge and, without transition, comments: 'Wunderbare Wirthschafft in der Laube.' Half way through the following year, on August 27, he reports from a trip to Kochberg and Ilmenau: 'Ritt ich Nach Tische dunckel von W. weg, ich sah offt nach meinen Garten zurück, und dachte so was alles mir durch die Seele müsse biss ich das arme Dach wieder sähe.' 'Das arme Dach' is clearly to be understood metaphorically. Master and abode are in tune with one another, and, looking back upon his home, it reflects back to him such manifold batterings as he, poor devil, will have to take on his journey.

For two months or so, we hear no more in this strain. But clearly, what was a vaguely perceived correspondence has continued to gestate in his imagination, and in an entry dated November 14, 1777 emerges as a fully matured symbol. In one of those periodic surveys of his doings which punctuate his diary, he writes, in a kind of prayer:

> 'Heiliges Schicksaal du hast mir mein Haus gebaut und aus staffirt über mein Bitten, ich war vergnügt in meiner Armuth unter meinem halbfaulen Dache ich bat dich mirs zu lassen, aber du hast mir Dach und Beschräncktheit vom Haupte gezogen wie eine Nachtmüzze. Laß mich nun auch frisch und zusammengenommen der Reinheit geniessen. Amen Ja und Amen winckt der erste Sonnenblick d. 14. Nov.
> Acht in der Haushaltung keinen Ritz zu eng, eine Maus geht durch.'

In the preceding entry of this diary there had been an unmistakable touch of self-pity at being called away from his muddled inner *ménage* to answer for himself in the world, and pity mixed with relief at the thought of returning to his refuge. Here now is a man challenged by holy destiny to raise the pitch of his life from the very foundations upwards, and accepting the uncomfortable illumination that he can no longer lazily shelter in an inner set-up he knows to be corrupt. 'Halbfaul': what a magnificently ambiguous coinage, coupling idleness with corruption. In the clear light of the morning sun he perceives that all his attempts at bettering himself have been piecework, and that the time has come to put his inner house in order which is in disarray and in bad repair, a liability reflecting the owner's dreamy indolence. For the first time in these pages the notion of an inner economy makes its appearance, expressed in the words *Armuth* and *halbfaul*, and in the image of the mice which, once they find a crack, carry away the provisions and undermine fabric and foundations of the whole. It takes briskness and resolution to sustain this illumination in its purity, and to translate it into action. And it takes realism and integrity to bear with the lively perception of corruption in the greater economy of the social whole he is serving and yet to remain true to his own standards without unavailing bitterness.

Both these related preoccupations, with his own household and the leaks in the social fabric to which he is actively committed, continue to gestate and to gain increasing clarity. Three months later, early in February, 1778, we read:

> '... in immer gleicher fast zu reiner Stimmung. Schöne Aufklärungen über mich selbst und unsre Wirthschafft, Stille und Vorahndung der Weisheit. Immer fortwährende Freude an Wirtschafft, Ersparniss. Auskommen. Schöne Ruhe in meinem Hauswesen gegen vorm Jahr. Bestimmteres Gefühl von Einschränckung, und dadurch der wahren Ausbreitung.'

On April 12 of that year we read: 'Mit Ordnen des Hauswesens beschäfftigt.', and, in a similar strain, on October 3: 'Immer nähere Ordnung des Hauswesens.' Three days later, we read: 'Mancherley gedacht über vorige und iezzige Wirthschafft auch mit eignem Hauswesen beschäfftigt.' (October 6). Clearly the cracks through which the mice enter have been stopped up; the assets are outweighing the debits, what comes in is greater than what goes out, the balance sheet presents a flourishing budget. Within his own affairs, Goethe, reflecting and acting, feels that he is achieving a healthy economy of energies.

This inner affluence he strives to defend *vis à vis* the larger household of the state, in the running of which he is actively engaged. After a session with the duke in which the maintenance of law and order is discussed, he notes that he held back with his true opinion.

> 'Indem man unverbesserliche Ubel an Menschen und Umständen verbessern will verliert man die Zeit und verdirbt noch mehr statt dass man diese Mängel annehmen sollte gleichsam als Grundstoff und nachher suchen diese zu kontrebalanciren. Das schönste Gefühl des Ideals wäre wenn man immer rein fühlte warum man's nicht erreichen kann.' (December 14, 1778).

In practice, however, such a discrepancy between private and public standards is disillusioning, and a source of irritation. There is a good deal of fretting about the damage wrought by the 'Lumperei' and selfish greed of others, traits moreover which tend to escape him in his innocence. 'Ich bin nicht zu dieser Welt gemacht,' we read in an entry near the end of December, 1778, 'wie man aus seinem Haus tritt geht man auf lauter Koth.' And similar outbursts recur on January 10 of the year following as well as on February 1, 1779.

These, however, are peripheral trials in the quest for an inner economy. And an entry dated July 14, 1779 confirms how much headway this stubborn young official has been making in this, his principal concern. There we read:

> '... gute Unterredung mit Batty über seine lezte Exkursion. Wills Gott dass mir Acker und Wiese noch werden und ich für dies simpleste Erwerb der Menschen Sinn kriege.
> Gedancken über den Instinckt zu irgend einer Sache. Jedes Werck was der Mensch treibt, hat möcht ich sagen einen Geruch. Wie im groben Sinn der Reuter nach Pferden riecht, der Buchladen nach leichtem Moder und um den Jäger nach Hunden. So ists auch im Feinern. Die Materie woraus einer formt, die Werckzeuge die einer braucht, die Glieder die er dazu anstrengt das alles zusammen giebt eine gewisse Häuslichkeit und Ehstand dem Künstler mit seinem Instrument. Diese Nähe zu allen Saiten der Harfe, die Gewissheit und Sicherheit wo mit er sie rührt mag den Meister anzeigen in ieder Art.'

There follows the description I have already quoted of the mutual affinity between master and medium, be it Batty with his fields — an enviable profession 'weil alles so rein antwortet' — or anyone else in his own area of activity, together with the recognition that such simple harmonies are not for him, the writer:

'... nur wünsch ich dass nach und nach alles anmasliche versiege, mir aber schöne Krafft übrig bleibe die wahren Röhren neben einander in gleicher Höhe aufzuplumpen.'

Then he concludes:

'Man beneidet ieden Menschen den man auf seine Töpferscheibe gebannt sieht, wenn vor einem unter seinen Händen bald ein Krug bald eine Schaale, nach seinem Willen hervorkommt. Den Punkt der Vereinigung des mannigfaltigen zu finden bleibt immer ein Geheimniss, weil die Individualitet eines ieden darinn besonders zu Rathe gehn muss und niemanden anhören darf.'

This statement deserves to be quoted in full; for not only is it the culminating statement of the whole series — in it, 'Häuslichkeit', by a significant *Steigerung*, becomes intensified to 'Ehstand' — but also it gives us the most intimately convincing explanation of the fact that Goethe stuck out his many and diversified activities as a public servant and found such an existence rewarding. This sense of authenticity derives, in a large measure, from the fact that Goethe is here viewing a large spectrum of activities at their point of coincidence with his own craft, the making of art[15]. In using the analogy of the artist with his instrument — the harpist plucking the strings of his harp or the potter whose hands are riveted to the turntable — he is as it were speaking his own language, the language of mind in relation to its medium, and vindicating in his own terms — aesthetic terms — the virtue of, say, agriculture. And whatever activity his thoughts encompass, he is able to demonstrate the same excellence, the excellence he has most at heart: the feedback experienced by the artist at living in any activity to which he chooses to apply his faculties. Given that one man is better at one thing than another — 'Der Mensch versteht nichts, als was ihm gemäß ist', Montan-Jarno maintains in *Wilhelm Meisters Wanderjahre*[16] — it is immaterial whether we apply ourselves to riding, or bookselling, or harp playing, or sowing and tilling, or potting, or, for that matter, to military affairs: self and world, mind and medium, together with the limbs and tools employed to work these media, are partners in a symbiotic relationship, together forming one economy: the object that is understood, the need that is sensitively registered and supplied, will yield rich dividends in terms of material gain and enhanced skill. Horse and rider, welded together 'voll Gefühl der doppelten centaurischen Gewalt'[17],

---

[15] Cf. *Wilhelm Meisters Wanderjahre*, I, 4, *HA* VIII, p. 37, ll. 26—30, and Chapter VIII of this book.
[16] I, 3.
[17] *Die Natürliche Tochter*, I, 6.

will together perform feats neither could have accomplished without this mutual bond. The symbol, or token, of such an intimate community is the smell shared by both — the bookish smell which clings to the salesman or the horsy smell which clings to the rider or stable-boy; and this in turn is the analogue of that affinity which unites the plant and the gardener with green fingers or, for that matter, the nursing mother and her baby. Feedback there is in all these situations (and none exhibits this more patently than the nursing situation where the fulfilment of the baby's need increases the supply of milk in the mother), and continued interaction leads to an ever more intimate attunement and reciprocal enrichment of the partners[18].

In this crucial statement Goethe's intuition once again circles around that notion of *gegenständliches Anschauen* which was to become so important a clue to his own being, later in life. His 'Gedancken über den Instinckt zu irgend einer Sache' here foreshadow his maxim 'Jeder neue Gegenstand, wohl beschaut, schließt ein neues Organ in uns auf.' It is important to realise, however, that Goethe is here not primarily concerned with the feedback he, born artist that he is, receives from his art, but that he is using this special source of insight to demonstrate, with impeccable aesthetics, analogous possibilities in other fields of activity. His prime concern, at this point, is to develop as many 'organs' or faculties as possible in a variety of skills, to develop his self to the full by making an art of living, and to justify this choice[19].

But in the last resort, this reading of the life he leads as a public servant as a generalised art of living was bound to leave the specialist in him — the born poet — unconvinced. Within three weeks of the entry we have been considering, we come upon another reckoning with himself, this time in a minor key. On August 7, he takes a stern look at the inner man and his development, and comes up with an answer suggesting that his economy is after all not as thriving as he had pretended in his more euphoric moments. He reports having burnt a host of papers, takes stock of his past literary endeavours and condemns the lot for their dilettantism, their short-term perspectives and their narcissistic mock-humility. 'Wie des Thuns, auch des Zweckmäsigen Denckens und Dichtens so wenig,' — he continues his self-accusations — 'wie in zeitverderbender Empfindung und Schatten Leidenschafft gar viel Tage verthan, wie wenig mir davon zu Nuz kommen und da die Hälfte nun des Lebens vorüber ist, wie nun kein Weeg zurückgelegt ...'. There is no glimmering of a feedback here, only the stinging awareness of a consumption of time and energy with nothing to show for it on the front

---

[18] Cf. Chapter VIII, section 8.

[19] This philosophy, which dominates *Wilhelm Meisters Lehrjahre,* will be substantially modified in the *Wanderjahre* with their emphasis on specialisation in an age of specialisation. Cf. II, 11, *HA* VIII, p. 282.

that concerns him most. There are no entries against his poetic ledger, only
debts booked to a life that is half spent.

Whether this assessment is objectively correct or not is immaterial. What
concerns us here, in this context, is the fact that Goethe felt that in his inner
economy to date his inborn gift, his poetic genius, had received short thrift.
He might have said, with his own Wilhelm Meister: ' . . . was [hilft es mir],
ein Landgut in Ordnung zu bringen, wenn ich mit mir selber uneins bin?'[20]
There were, after all, many cracks in his poetic house that had been left
untended, and unobserved; the mice had nibbled away at his most precious
store of grain.

5.

How Goethe dealt with this inner crisis — for a crisis we must call it — in
the days and weeks that immediately followed, we do not know. For a while,
there is no mention of it. Then, two months later, he went on a Swiss trip
— his second — with the duke. Fresh impressions tend to be beneficial. The
entries of the winter months following that diversion are level-headed and
cheerful. On March 21 Goethe notes that he can only think and create while
walking[21]. Five days later, on March 26, he walks on foot to Tiefurt. And
on that congenial occasion a truly breathtaking illumination comes to him,
a wholly wise, and original, solution to the problem that had so exercised him.

'Die Geheimnisse der Lebenspfade darf und kann man nicht offenbaren',
we read in *Makariens Archiv;* 'Es gibt Steine des Anstoßes, über die ein jeder
Wanderer stolpern muß. Der Poet aber deutet auf die Stelle hin.'[22] In this
case, it was the poet in Goethe, his 'singende Dämon'[23], who, in the rhythm
of walking, pointed up illness and cure.

As he moved along, many thoughts crossed in his mind. He realises that
we inevitably make mistakes, and that those mistakes, grievous as they are,
turn out to have been unavoidable in that they served to bring about good.
One cannot even wish them away; they are a ruse of our genius. 'war ein-
gehüllt den ganzen Tag', he continues, 'und konnte denen vielen Sachen die
auf mich drucken weniger widerstehen.' This awareness of his own susceptibility which accompanies him through life like his own shadow, all of a
sudden gives him an idea. How about going along with his deeper self? How
about assuming that what appears to be waywardness and fitfulness, in fact
are manifestations of some inner rhythm, capable of being brought to consciousness and utilised? We read:

---

[20] *Wilhelm Meisters Lehrjahre,* V, 3.
[21] Cf. *Wandrers Sturmlied* and E. M. Wilkinson and L. A. Willoughby on this poem. [In:
   Goethe Poet and Thinker, London 1962, Chapter III.] Cf. also *Wilhelm Meisters Wanderjahre,*
   III, 1, *HA* VIII, p. 312, ll. 4—10.
[22] *HA* VIII, p. 460.
[23] Cf. note 21.

'Ich muss den Cirkel der sich in mir umdreht, von guten und bößen Tagen näher be-
mercken, Leidenschafften, Anhänglichkeit Trieb dies oder iens zu thun. Erfindung,
Ausführung Ordnung alles wechselt, und hält einen regelmäsigen Kreis. Heiterkeit,
Trübe, Stärcke, Elastizität, Schwäche, Gelassenheit, Begier eben so. Da ich sehr diät lebe
wird der Gang nicht gestört und ich muss noch heraus kriegen in welcher Zeit und
Ordnung ich mich um mich selbst bewege.'

This idea is epoch-making in more ways than one. Epoch-making in that
it marks the decisive point in Goethe's development from a youth who does
not know what to do with his own riches, to wisdom and maturity. And
epoch-making in that this project to understand his own unconscious —
indeed the notion that the unconscious is an ordered part of the psyche capable of being understood — prefigures insights first systematically explored
and made publicly available in our own century, through Freud's solitary
venture. And epoch-making in yet a third sense. For Western thought,
although conditioned to the notion that a certain rhythmicity, grounded in
the biological endowment of women, is characteristic of the feminine psyche,
is slow to accept the possibility that the male psyche, too, may be subject
to analogous cycles. And here is Goethe, in the year 1780, confidently
assuming his feminine heritage and undertaking a solitary journey into the
realm of the mothers, matrix of his deepest creativity!

It is scarcely possible to exaggerate the magnitude, the pluck and the
eventual implications of this undertaking as it presented itself to him on his
walk to Tiefurt. Four and a half years earlier, in his first diary entry, he had
declared his intention of giving free rein to his every whim and mood; a
strategem which places him into the closest proximity to his Werther announcing: 'Auch halte ich mein Herzchen wie ein krankes Kind; jeder Wille wird
ihm gestattet', and using his letters in precisely this fashion. Now Goethe
approaches these very moods and whims which, welling up from the unconscious, continually cross his conscious purpose, in a radically different spirit:
disputing that they are intractable *Poltergeister* in his inner household, and
instead viewing them as law-abiding, and vital, members of his psyche which
must be integrated in its total economy. Treat them as enemies and the
conscious mind can do little, and what it does achieve will be fortuitous,
determined by forces outside its control. Treat them, and the unconscious
of which they are the overt manifestations, as equal partners, and a man will
act in unison with himself, with the full force of his libidinal drives coming
to the support of his conscious intention. To do so, he must study these
hidden resources, and their laws, with the disinterestedness of the scientific
observer. He must submit to them, and permit himself to be permeated by
them, not so as to be ruled by them — this would be a regression, in theoret-
ical guise, to Werther and to his own beginnings — but in order to marshal
them to the purposes sanctioned by the whole man. It is again a matter of
developing 'den Instinckt zu irgend einer Sache', of gaining a *gegenständliche*

Anschauung of an object: this time the object being the most important of all in the life of a born artist, namely the creative resources stored away in the recesses of his unconscious.

It is on this epoch-making walk to Tiefurt on March 26, 1780, that a life-long development was inaugurated which the poet surveys, with deserved gratification and even admiration, in the last letters to come from his pen, to his friend Wilhelm von Humboldt. Here the foundation-stone was laid of that incomparable artifice of Goethe's life and work in which there are passage-ways from cellar to roof. Here that wise and cunning interlacing of conscious and unconscious drives begins which enabled the poet to 'command his muse', and to bring forth, with the minimum of inner resistance and a maximum of creative energy, a body of work of unparalleled magnitude, unity in diversity, and depth. On that day, on that walk, Goethe solved the problem of his inner economy, by enlarging that notion to include his unconscious drives. As long as he had neglected them, in an all too rigid effort to be a universal man and an official, they had been as mice, nibbling away at his resources and leaving him with a deficit. As soon as he had the wisdom to acknowledge their legitimate existence, the leak was stopped, and the mice turned into benign dwarfs, guarding, and increasing, his innermost treasure.

The days that followed his momentous discovery see Goethe eagerly putting his hypothesis to the test. On March 29, he writes: 'frühe hat ich den aufräumenden und ordnenden Tag. Viel Briefe weggeschrieben und alles ausgepuzt.' The next day, March 30, we read — and we scarcely trust our eyes — 'Hatt ich den erfindenden Tag. Anfangs trüblich ich lenckte mich zu Geschäfften, bald wards lebendiger. Brief an Kalb. Zu Mittag nach Tiefurt zu Fus Gute Erfindung Tasso ...'; to which he adds: 'Abends wenig Momente sinckender Krafft. darauf acht zu geben. Woher.'

Within four days of entering into partnership with his unconscious, one of the most seminal of all his works was conceived! This is in itself sufficient cause for surprise. But surprise grows into amazement when we ask what work it was in particular that came to him in a flash the moment he released his creative energies and permitted them to fructify his consciousness. It is the tragedy of the poet; tragedy, precisely, because the hero is an absolute artist, an elemental, unconscious organ of nature who refuses to integrate his inborn gift into the embracing organisation of a fully developed, conscious humanity[24]. It is ironic and paradoxical in the highest degree that Goethe should have conceived this of all subject matters at the precise juncture of his life when he himself achieved the synthesis between his conscious and his unconscious drives, a highly creative synthesis as the result was to prove. Tasso, the human silkworm, as a controlled invention: this retrospectively vindicates

[24] Cf. my *Goethe and Lessing*, Chapter VII.

the endeavours of his creator to develop his being in all directions — conscious as well as unconscious, practically and reflectively as well as emotionally and imaginatively — and to achieve a full humanity by manifold contacts with the world; moreover, it calls into question the truth of the warning the Duke of Ferrara gives to Tasso:

Der Mensch gewinnt, was der Poet verliert.

As I endeavour to show in another chapter[25], these words, which are frequently regarded as containing the essence of the play, are only conditionally true. Undoubtedly the Weimar official forewent many an opportunity — inwardly as well as outwardly — to give his genius free rein. Yet the exercise of the human qualities of 'Rat, Mäßigung und Weisheit' — the supreme wisdom of harnessing his unconscious drives to the purposes of his conscious mind — 'und Geduld' were to stand the poet in him in excellent stead: they empowered him to activate his creative potential to the full — so fully as to articulate the tragedy of the absolute artist — and to nurse along this precious yet precarious gift *in* the context of his humanity without letting himself be destroyed by it.

6.

Geduld —: what tremendous patience and staying power it took to raise his being to this pitch, in how many directions and on how many levels he had to learn to practise this virtue! 'Viel Arbeit in mir selbst zu viel Sinnens,' — we read in a diary entry towards the end of 1778 — 'dass Abends mein ganzes Wesen zwischen den Augenknochen sich zusammen zu drängen scheint.' (end of December). This remark is a fair measure of the patient concentration this thirty year old mustered in working out the manifold problems of these early years in Weimar and, moreover, in working away at himself. The formulation he chooses gives us a preliminary clue as to the manner in which he set about his work. Like Werther who sees Lotte's eyes 'hier in meiner Stirne, wo die innere Sehkraft sich vereinigt', Goethe carries the image of his whole being inside his head. But what a difference! Where Werther hallucinates, Goethe perceives, and perceives the object of his preoccupation with an almost painful clarity.

To begin with, much patience was needed to get physical excess and mental instability under some sort of control. The youth that came to Weimar drank, kept irregular hours, worked obsessively and in snatches, was moody and indulgent, prone to sudden depressions and corresponding elations in which he would do foolhardy things: and now all of a sudden he was catapulted into public eminence, had to hold down a number of responsible jobs and act as mentor to a turbulent and wilful patron eight years his junior who

---

[25] Cf. Chapter V.

was going through the very teething troubles he was himself trying to
outgrow. It was relatively easy to see what he ought to be doing, and to do
it once in a while; it was infinitely harder to adopt a physical and moral diet
as a daily and hourly rule. The matter of physical moderation will serve as
a handy illustration. As early as August 1779, he is able to see physical abstinence as a symbol of that inner stillness and purity he — like his own
Iphigenie — strives to attain. 'Möge die Idee des reinen die sich bis auf den
Bissen erstreckt den ich in Mund nehme, immer lichter in mir werden', he
prayerfully writes on the 7th of that month. Eight months later he notes with
evident satisfaction that he has not drunk any wine for three whole days,
and a week or so after that, with a touch of resignation, 'Ich trinke fast
keinen Wein.'

Habits grow slowly; and although Goethe kept on chivying himself in the
direction he wanted to go, he also had an innate disposition to go along with
himself. Had he not possessed this resilience, his task *vis à vis* his princely
ward would have been an impossible one. The foibles of the younger man
would have constituted too big a threat for one not able to bear with his
own regressions. As it was, he showed an exquisite patience blended with
firmness in his handling of the temperamental duke. Time and again, he
would try to help him in his troubles and tactfully indicate ways and means
of avoiding them in the future. An entry dated February 1, 1779 is entirely
typical:

'mit ♃ gessen nach Tisch einige Erklärung über: zu viel reden, fallen lassen, sich
vergeben, seine Ausdrücke mässigen, Sachen in der Hizze zur sprache bringen die nicht
geredt werden sollten . . . ♃ steht noch immer an der Form stille. Falsche Anwendung auf
seinen Zustand was man bey andern gut und gros findet. Verblendung am äusserlichen
Ubertünchen. Ich habe eben die Fehler beym Bauwesen gemacht.'

Only one patiently in touch with his own past can muster such patience *vis
à vis* one who holds up a mirror to his own transgressions. But when the
occasion demanded it, he could be firm and shoulder the responsibility of
being the older and wiser of the two. There is a delightful illustration of
this at the time of their Swiss journey. The two had climbed a mountain, the
Tschingel glacier, and were fooling about throwing stones into the valley.
'Der Herzog wolte es auch noch immer toller, ich sagt ihm das wäre das
und mehr fänden wir nicht' (October 10, 1779).

Basically, Goethe's patience with his own youthful turbulence and with
the excesses of the duke springs from that intimate understanding of growing
process which was to inform his morphological insights. 'Aber auch ausser
dem Herzog ist niemand im Werden,' he notes (July 13, 1779). He has outgrown earlier phases and will continue to grow in accordance with an inner
law; and so, too, will the younger man, in his own good time:

Weiß doch der Gärtner, wenn das Bäumchen blüht.

The extreme patience he was expected to practise in his relationship with Charlotte von Stein, and with his own 'heißen Blut', is readily apparent from the monosyllabic terseness of his entries regarding her. Not one effusion, not a single epithet expressive of his emotions, not so much as an exclamation mark or a dash even. But it was patience of a different complexion that was demanded of him when he wrote: 'sie kommt mir immer liebenswürdig vor, obgleich fremder. Wie die übrigen auch' (December 9, 1778). How much of a riddle he must have felt to himself, obeying a call for solitariness that was all of his own demanding, and standing aloof from the very relation in which he was so passionately engrossed, a stranger not only to the other, but to himself. This was the pain of consciousness, a self-awareness that stamped him as different, which was to find expression in the poem 'Warum gabst du uns die tiefen Blicke . . . '[26]; it is a puzzled pain which reverberates in every one of the many diary entries noting his 'fortdauernde reine Entfremdung', not just from the woman he loved but from the whole circle of people to whose being he so sensitively responded. It is almost as though he were bound by a secret vow, the purpose of which he himself does not fully understand, any more than he understands the powers that keep exacting it from him; a loneliness borne patiently and never more than touched on restrainedly in these diaries, until it was to find full-throated utterance in Mignon's song

Heiß mich nicht reden, heiß mich schweigen,
Denn mein Geheimnis ist mir Pflicht . . .

A similar dogged obedience tied him to the meticulous execution of professional duties which must, at many a moment, have seemed utterly foreign to him, for all his conscious knowledge that such manifold contacts with the external world were an invaluable discipline and, even, enrichment. ' . . . Gewissheit des Ausharrens', we read after days of devoting all his time and energies to the military commission (January 13, 1779); and again, in February of that year, 'Diese Zeit her habe ich meist gesucht mich in Geschäften aufrecht zu erhalten und bey allen Vorfällen fest zu seyn und ruhig.' (between February 15 and 23). Or, on January 17, 1780: 'Kriegs Comm. waren mir die Sachen sehr prosaisch.' And then, despite it all, on May 13, 1780: 'Ruckte wieder an der Kr. Komm Repositur. Hab ich das doch in anderthalb Jahren nicht können zu stand bringen! es wird doch! Und ich wills so sauber schaffen als wenns die Tauben gelesen hätten. Freilich es ist des Zeugs zu viel von allen Seiten, und der Gehilfen wenige.' The entry closes with the words: 'Ich fühle nach und nach ein allgemeines Zutrauen und gebe Gott dass ichs verdienen möge, nicht wies leicht ist, sondern wie ichs wünsch. Was ich trage an mir und andern sieht kein Mensch.' What inner vision is it to which he feels pledged, which makes him drive himself so relentlessly? One last illus-

---

[26] Cf. Chapter VII.

tration, taken from an entry in which he notes that he has not written anything for a month, because he was kept on his feet from morn to night: 'Man könnte noch mehr, ia das unglaubliche thun wenn man mäsiger wäre. das geht nun nicht. Wenn nur ieder den Stein hübe der vor ihm liegt. doch sind wir hier sehr gut dran. alles muss zulezt auf einen Punckt, aber Ehrne Gedult, ein steinern Aushalten' (June 22, 1780). 'Ehrne Gedult, ein steinern Aushalten': those are, or so it would seem, the words of a stoic, one possessed by the ideal of absolute discipline in the exercise of abnegation. Yet the dating of this entry, and the one previously quoted, do not admit of such an interpretation. For these unrelenting stipulations are made *after* that momentous decision to watch his own inner cycles and to go along with his inner rhythm: and this is not the resolution of a stoic. Again, as in the matter of his increasing sense of estrangement, we are here confronted with patience within patience, a patience as it were of the second power: he doggedly persists with his duties, and yet that persistence itself is embedded in an encompassing pursuit: the endeavour to tap his unconscious resources and to bring them into consonance with his conscious striving. That is to say, self-denial is carefully built into surrender, abnegation into a larger affirmation, iron discipline into a *laissez faire* which itself is a discipline of a higher order. It is in such a context that a statement such as 'Niemand als wer sich ganz verläugnet ist werth zu herrschen, und kan herrschen', needs to be placed (May 13, 1780). Only he can be master who commands his resources to the full; and only he commands his resources to the full who dares to set them free. This is the goal that is meant when Goethe writes 'regieren' or, as in the present entry, 'Ich will doch herr werden.'

What a complex goal, and what a complex mental state. Conscious striving in a specific direction as part of an experiment in unconscious liberation which is in its turn conceived, and executed, in the context of an encompassing consciousness. This is the image of his being, his 'ganze Wesen', the imprint of which lodges 'zwischen den Augenknochen', in painful clarity. This is the 'Punckt der Vereinigung des manigfaltigen' towards which he is working (July 14, 1779 and May 26 to June 22, 1780); words reflecting those written to Herder eight years earlier — 'und doch muß das Alles ein's seyn' (July, 1772).

And how multifarious are the elements that must be brought into consonance. There are the many specialised activities he is pursuing in his capacity as a man of public affairs, and, allied to them, scientific pursuits such as mineralogy, botany and comparative anatomy. All these activities called forth in him answering skills, or 'organs' of perception.

Yet there was another organ — that for poetry apart — another 'Instinckt zu irgend einer Sache', as Goethe calls it in that crucial entry in which art appears as an analogue of that intimate attunement, or symbiosis, between self and object in any given sphere, which so fascinates Goethe. That 'Sache' was himself, in the totality of his conscious-unconscious being, with all its ramified skills. The task of that organ was, precisely, to divine, by the closest contact with himself, the point of intersection of all these multifarious activities and aptitudes, and to synthesise them into an encompassing economy of maximal creativeness. To achieve that flexible synthesis was vital; not only because it was vital to be a unified organism, but also because Goethe's growing social consciousness readily divined that he lived in a time of transition from the universally educated individual to a more specialised education demanded of the members of an increasingly industrialised community. He had to be specialised and yet whole, many and yet one. 'Mache ein Organ aus dir', Montan says to Wilhelm[27]; and to do this was the young Goethe's overriding concern. This meant perceiving himself in all the complexity of his practical activities, perceiving himself in relation to his principal and inborn skill, his poetic gift, and perceiving himself *vis à vis* that incommensurable mainspring of his energies, his unconscious. Small wonder that he felt he had an unspeakable load to bear, and that, time and again, he invoked those unknown higher powers he obeyed, as he doggedly went about his enigmatic task.

In developing that supreme organ, or instinct, for his many-layered self, Goethe was certainly becoming more close-knit and intimately in touch with himself. Equally certainly he developed a doubled, or even tripled, self-awareness, a complexity which is not an easy burden to bear and which called for a patience all its own. He was immersed, in many directions and on many levels, and yet he was an onlooker to his own engrossments. He was creating many things in many areas, and over and above that he was creating himself. He perceived that manifold which was himself with a pure and penetrating perception, as though — rich and spontaneous human being that he was — he stood free of himself. He perceived himself as he perceived all other objects and beings, however close to him and however beloved, with a kind of 'gegenständlicher Anschauung'. With an objective passion, as though he were something else, he perceived his own inner law, and worked away at his matter to give it its own appropriate form. Here, in these diaries, in relation to his own self, we find that characteristic subject-objectivity, that active submission to the object — in this instance himself — which was to be the hallmark of his thinking and his poetry.

In *Bekenntnisse einer schönen Seele* we read:

Das ganze Weltwesen liegt vor uns wie ein großer Steinbruch vor dem Baumeister, der nur dann den Namen verdient, wenn er aus diesen zufälligen Naturmassen ein in seinem Geiste entsprungenes Urbild mit der größten Ökonomie, Zweckmäßigkeit und Festigkeit zusammenstellt. Alles außer uns ist nur Element, ja ich darf wohl sagen, auch alles in uns;

[27] *Wilhelm Meisters Wanderjahre*, I, 4.

aber tief in uns liegt diese schöpferische Kraft, die das zu erschaffen vermag, was sein soll, und uns nicht ruhen und rasten läßt, bis wir es außer uns oder an uns auf eine oder die andere Weise dargestellt haben.'[28]

Goethe was this mason, or perhaps this sculptor. He worked on what he took in hand, until it was 'was es sein soll', until he had realised its inner form, whether that was his work for the community, or *Iphigenie* and *Tasso*, or — his self. Where in *Tasso* the three senses of *Bildung* cleave tragically apart, in him they were fused into one indivisible whole. He was an educated and active member of an educated community, he brought forth works of art, and he fashioned himself. With a disinterested *furore* he sculpted and chiselled at his inner form, as Michelangelo 'discovered' the slaves in the marble rock in which they lay concealed, and liberated them from the captivity of the surrounding dross. This objective passion of the sculptor possessed by an inner image, not the abnegation of the stoic, is the force of that magnificent self exhortation 'Ehrne Gedult, ein steinern Aushalten'. Impassioned yet supremely conscious, Goethe bodied forth from out of himself that inner form of his being the image of which had wholly taken possession of him. For 'Was der Mensch leisten soll, muß sich als ein zweites Selbst von ihm ablösen, und wie könnte das möglich sein, wäre sein erstes Selbst nicht ganz davon durchdrungen'?[29]

[28] *Wilhelm Meisters Lehrjahre*, VI.
[29] *Wilhelm Meisters Wanderjahre*, I, 4.

III   Metamorphoses

And so I cross into another world
shyly and in homage linger for an invitation
from the unknown that I would tresspass on.

D. H. Lawrence

'Tasso's' Italian Journey

> 'God, deliver me from my sterile torments!'
>
> Aeschylus

1.

Packing his trunks for Italy, Goethe took with him, along with some minor works, the manuscripts of *Egmont*, *Iphigenie*, *Faust*, *Wilhelm Meisters Theatralische Sendung*, and *Tasso;* the first four in a reasonably advanced state. On the Brenner *Iphigenie* was taken out and some revision work was done, along the lines Herder had urged; Goethe gradually, and joyfully, began to versify the iambic prose of the first draft. To the rest of his literary freight he alludes collectively, in a strangely ambivalent mood: '[Ich] betrachte ... dagegen mit einem Schauer manche Pakete, von denen ich ein kurz und gutes Bekenntnis ablegen muß: sind es doch meine Begleiter, werden sie nicht viel Einfluß auf meine nächsten Tage haben!' (Auf dem Brenner, 8. September abends).

There is no mention of *Tasso* during the whole rich month in which Goethe saw Verona and Vicenza, made the living acquaintance of the revered Palladio and Mantegna, and saw the longed-for Venice. He saw and saw and saw; and to him, the 'nordischen Flüchtling' as he calls himself on October 7, the introverted Tasso seems to belong to another life. However, he was forcibly reminded of his problem child in Ferrara, where he was shown Tasso's supposed prison, too wretched, Goethe surmises, to have been the place where the poet was incarcerated. For the rest, he records, 'weiß im Haus kaum jemand mehr, was man will'. This was on October 16, and the entry of that night interestingly records the first pang of irritation Goethe has registered during the whole of his six weeks' sojourn. It is equally illuminating to see what eventually drove away the mental clouds: 'Sodann', we read,

'erheiterte mich der gute Einfall eines Malers, Johannes der Täufer vor Herodes und Herodias. Der Prophet in seinem gewöhnlichen Wüstenkostüme deutet heftig auf die Dame. Sie sieht ganz gelassen den neben ihr sitzenden Fürsten, und der Fürst still und klug den Enthusiasten an. Vor dem König steht ein Hund, weiß, mittelgroß; unter dem Rock der Herodias dagegen kommt ein kleiner Bologneser hervor, welche beide den Propheten anbellen.'

'Mich dünkt', Goethe adds, 'das ist recht glücklich gedacht.'

What else is this picture but the externalisation of the memory which had jarred on him that day, Tasso's 'Disproportion des Talentes mit dem Leben', as he summed up the theme of his play to Caroline v. Herder? There is the visionary, a stranger to the court, to its restraints and its refinements, in his *Wüstenkleide* which recalls the 'schwarze Kittel' the self-exiled poet sees himself donning; vehement, pointing at the princess, who, 'gelassen', looks at the duke whose gaze rests on the enthusiast, 'still und klug'. No scene, no reproach at Ferrara. The sophistication of the atmosphere forbids the very thought. Only the dogs bark out aloud the painter's thoughts, and, maybe, of those present: 'this man does not belong here. He is an outrage against civilisation.'[1]

Goethe's earlier prophecy seems to be coming true; Tasso, the Tasso in him, is a companion on his journey. But he is not going to let him spoil it for him.

Four blissful months go by in Rome, with not so much as a single mention of his travelling companion. The days are crowded with seeing, seeing the works of formative art and of nature, with copying what he sees and with reflecting on what he has thus actively taken in, and compared. These are the weeks in which he constantly speaks of a second birth, or a *Wiedergeburt von innen*, going on in him. His whole being seems to be pacified as his eye is satisfied and schooled. For a schooling it is, this seeing of things in the crystalline southern light, as they are in themselves. 'Ich lebe nun hier mit einer Klarheit und Ruhe', he writes on November 10,

> 'von der ich lange kein Gefühl hatte. Meine Übung, alle Dinge, wie sie sind, zu sehen und abzulesen, meine Treue, das Auge Licht sein zu lassen, meine völlige Entäußerung von aller Prätention kommen mir einmal wieder recht zustatten und machen mich im stillen höchst glücklich ... Wer sich mit Ernst hier umsieht und Augen hat zu sehen, muß solid werden, er muß einen Begriff von Solidität fassen, der ihm nie so lebendig ward ... Ich bin nicht hier, um nach meiner Art zu genießen; befleißigen will ich mich der großen Gegenstände, lernen und mich ausbilden ...'

'... der großen Gegenstände': Raphael and Michelangelo, Titian, Guido, the Venetian School, the Forum and the Palatin, St. Peter's, old coins and medals, villas; and always the southern vegetation. The idea of the *Urpflanze*, which had flashed through his mind in Padua, steadily gains weight, and its converse, perhaps even more adventurous and more decisive for his later development as artist-scientist: the idea that the classical artists had produced their works of art by intuiting and internalising the morphological laws according to which Nature herself produces variety from the simple; a parallelism formulated on December 13 and articulated with programmatic force in an entry dated January 28, 1787: 'Ich habe eine Vermutung', we read, 'daß sie [i. e. the Greeks] nach eben den Gesetzen verfuhren, nach welchen die Natur verfährt und denen ich auf der Spur bin'.[2]

This *Spur* led Goethe to Naples, and, thence, to Sicily, to the Gardens of Palermo. Gradually, amongst all this visual revel, a new longing makes

---

[1] For a discussion of Tasso's antisocial aspects see my *Goethe and Lessing*, Chapter VII.
[2] Cf. Chapters VI, section 3, and XIII.

itself felt which was bound to take the reveller away from the glut of forms which is Rome. He is beginning to tire of the 'ungeheuern und doch nur trümmerhaften Reichtum dieser Stadt', he writes in the same entry in which he articulates his epoch-making hunch; and, a few days earlier, we find the complaint that he must 'alles aus unendlichen, obgleich überreichen Trümmern zusammenstoppeln' (January 22). The first impulse of his second life is spent; he longs to be in touch, once again, with elemental nature: he resolves to see Vesuvius and, most of all, the open sea. He is aware that he is drawn into regions not only more fertile but also potentially more destructive than the ones in which he has spent the past four formative months. Curiously and incongruously, this secret craving creeps into the imagery he uses to describe his labours to make Rome his own: 'Nun wird es mir immer schwerer', we read, 'von meinem Aufenthalt in Rom Rechenschaft zu geben; denn wie man die See immer tiefer findet, je weiter man hineingeht, so geht es mir auch in Betrachtung dieser Stadt' (January 25). And again, in the same letter in which he likens Naples and Sicily to paradise and hell in one, he summarises his last Roman efforts, saying '. . . so spanne ich denn alle Segel meines Geistes auf, um diese Küsten zu umschiffen' (February 16).

On that day he had seen Tasso's grave in a corner of St. Onofrio. At the beginning of the entry he asks himself whether he would not be much wiser to do new things, e. g., to work out his plan for *Iphigenie auf Delphi*, 'als mich mit den Grillen des "Tasso" herumzuschlagen'. But he continues: 'und doch habe ich auch dahinein schon zuviel von meinem Eignen gelegt, als daß ich es fruchtlos aufgeben sollte.' Later in the same entry he describes, with patent sympathy, the wax bust of Tasso's face in the monastery library of St. Onofrio and writes that it suggests 'einen talentvollen, zarten, feinen, in sich geschlossenen Mann'.

On February 19, he writes gleefully: 'Der Vesuv wirft Steine und Asche aus, und bei Nacht sieht man den Gipfel glühen. Gebe uns die wirkende Natur einen Lavafluß! Nun kann ich kaum erwarten, bis auch diese großen Gegenstände mir eigen werden.' And two days later yet, in the midst of packing for his departure: 'Morgen gehn wir nach Neapel. Ich freue mich auf das Neue, das unaussprechlich schön sein soll, und hoffe in jener paradiesischen Natur wieder neue Freiheit und Lust zu gewinnen, hier im ernsten Rom wieder an das Studium der Kunst zu gehen.' From *Kunst* to *Natur* which, as he well knows, is heaven and hell in one.

And what is this Hafis taking along on this southern *Hegire* to *Chisers Quell?* A few paragraphs later we read: 'Eins habe ich über mich gewonnen, daß ich von meinen poetischen Arbeiten nichts mitnehme als "Tasso" allein, zu ihm habe ich die beste Hoffnung.'

From these crowded and exited entries one thing becomes clear: the return from formed Rome to elemental nature, and the inner return to *Tasso*, tragedy of the poet which had been banished while the *Augenmensch* had had his fill, in Goethe's mind are inseparably intertwined. The thought of the one vivifies the thought of the other. Tasso, the elemental creature through whom Nature herself is operating — who likens himself to the sea, whom Antonio likens to a volcano — *Tasso* could only come to final fruition by a renewed surrender to elemental flux, for all its threat of destruction. To shape that work, a return to the realm of the mothers, those matrixes of all shapes who themselves dwell in night and chaos, was needed.

2.

In Naples the poet walks about, conscious of the blend of fertility and destruction in this 'wundersamste Gegend von der Welt. Unter reinstem Himmel der unsicherste Boden' (March 1). He climbs to the top of Vesuvius for the second time, in the company of the painter Tischbein, and comments:

> 'Ihm, dem bildenden Künstler, der sich immer nur mit den schönsten Menschen- und Tierformen beschäftigt, ja das Ungeformte selbst, Felsen und Landschaften, durch Sinn und Geschmack vermenschlicht, ihm wird eine solche furchtbare Aufhäufung, die sich immer wieder selbst verzehrt und allem Schönheitsgefühl den Krieg ankündigt, ganz abscheulich vorkommen.' (March 6).

This is Goethe the artist speaking for himself; yet some *Widerspruchsgeist* in him insisted on timing the eruptions, penetrating to the very mouth of the crater between the end of one and the beginning of the next, until, fascinated by the 'ungeheuren Rachen', or 'Abgrund', as he variously has it, he overstayed his welcome and found himself overtaken by a hail of stones! Ambivalence persists and, ten days later, comes to the surface of his consciousness. 'In vierzehn Tagen muß sich's entscheiden', he writes on March 16, 'ob ich nach Sizilien gehe. Noch nie bin ich so sonderbar in einem Entschluß hin und her gebogen worden. Heute kommt etwas, das mir die Reise anrät, morgen ein Umstand, der sie abrät. Es streiten sich zwei Geister um mich.' And, sure enough, the following paragraph reveals the source of this inner conflict: he would like to throw his *Tasso* into the fire, he writes; which however does not prevent him from pursuing his labours, he adds: and, that being so, 'so wollen wir ein wunderlich Werk daraus machen' (March 16). Ambivalence persists. The next days sees the entry: 'Über meine sizilianische Reise halten die Götter noch die Waage in Händen. Das Zünglein schlägt herüber und hinüber. Wer mag der Freund sein, den man mir so geheimnisvoll ankündigt?' The frigate from Palermo has returned. Will he go back to be in Rome for Holy Week? He was going to be there, next year; in just a little less than a year's time he was to write the momentous sentence 'daß ich eigentlich zur Dichtkunst geboren bin' (February 22, 1788). But as yet he is torn by the conflict with his own daimon; he does not yet know whether he will go to Sicily any more than he knows the identity of the friend 'den man mir so geheimnisvoll ankündigt': 'Noch nie bin ich so unentschieden gewesen; ein Augenblick, eine Kleinigkeit mag entscheiden' (March 17).

Fifteen years earlier, after his departure from Lotte and Wetzlar, it had
been a pocket knife and a chance encounter with a black-eyed young woman
that had turned the scales[3]. What was it now that sealed a fate once again in
the balance? Two things: the acquaintance with the young artist Kniep who
was ready to become his companion and who, unlike Tischbein, the
bildende Künstler, had happily launched himself 'in das eigentlichste Element
des Landschaftlers'; and a vicarious erotic stimulus which moved him in
the strangest of fashions. Goethe was invited at Lord Hamilton's and there
met his beautiful mistress, 'ein schönes Weib, das Meisterstück des großen
Künstlers'. In the twinkling of an eye, the protracted conflict between art and
nature was resolved. The scale of nature went down, heavily: for did she not
herself body forth art? And strange, there was a mirroring of the experience;
and it brought with it a *Steigerung* of the impulse which was to guide him.
Kniep had a secret love affair in Naples; and before embarking for Sicily, he
showed his young woman to his friend who was himself to remain unseen.
A highly rousing experience, this secret sharing of his friend's erotic
pleasures, in imagination. And what was the result of this 'ersatz' erotic
adventure? 'Nach diesem angenehmen Abenteuer spazierte ich am Meere hin
und war still und vergnüglich. Da kam mir eine gute Erleuchtung über
botanische Gegenstände. Herdern bitte ich zu sagen, daß ich mit der Urpflanze bald zustande bin ...' (Zum 25. März).

What could testify in a more striking manner to the ubiquity of creative
Eros[4] than these two episodes and the release of energy in which they
resulted? Two stimulating erotic encounters, both in the imagination; and an
irresistible pull towards Sicily, the gateway, for this poet, to the mysteries of
Asia and Africa, to the secret point of confluence between the laws of art
and nature which he was to explore there, by pursuing the tracks Nature
herself followed in the formation of plants, and in a work of art. Not the one
he thought he would nurse along and bring to fruition: *Wilhelm Meister*, in
which art terminates in the art of living; but in the unknown friend *Torquato
Tasso*, tragedy of the artist in whom the art of living terminates in the making
of art[5].

3.

Four days later, on March 29, Goethe and Kniep embarked and set sail for
Palermo. This move and its consequences were to mark the most important lap
on the whole Italian sojourn and quite possibly the most decisive turning point
of the poet's life. That he himself had some intimation that this was so is surely
proven by the protracted conflict with his *Daimon* before he cast the die, and

[3] Cf. Chapter I, section 5.
[4] In this connection, cf. my *Goethe and Lessing*, Chapter V, especially section 5.
[5] Cf. my *Goethe and Lessing*, Chapter VII.

by the last words he wrote on the morning of the embarkation: 'Es ist denn doch, als wenn ich mein Fasanenschiff nirgends als bei euch ausladen könnte', he writes to his friends back home, and adds the heartfelt wish: 'Möge es nur erst recht stattlich geladen sein!' (March 29.) The allusion points five months back, to the first stage of the Italian journey, to a dream he had had about a fortnight before arriving in Rome. Goethe had seen St. Agatha attributed to Raphael and his mind had been led, past *Iphigenie* which he was then happily in the process of recasting in verse, to musings about the possible continuation of the play in a projected *Iphigenie auf Delphi*. Troubled, almost, by such a crowding in of poetic visions, he was reminded of a dream he had had about a year before. This he now recounts to his friends: he landed on the shores of a fertile island, knowing that the most beautiful pheasants were to be obtained there. He negotiated with the natives who soon brought him the desired fowls which, however, took on the shape and hue of peacocks or 'seltenen Paradiesvögeln'. These were stowed away in his boat, their heads pointing inwards, their tails forming a huge coloured umbrella around the rim of the craft, so bountiful 'daß für den Steuernden und die Rudernden kaum hinten und vorn geringe Räume verblieben'. However, having arrived in harbour, between gigantic ships, the dreamer, climbing from deck to deck, eventually succeeded in espying and securing a landing-place for his little treasure boat (Bologna, October 19). — The last entry before Goethe's arrival in Rome alludes to this dream, as though he expected to gather his poetic freight there, on the dry land of the capital of the world. Now the dream recurs as he is in truth setting out to a 'fruchtbaren, reich bewachsenen Insel' with its tropical flora and fauna. And now, tossed about between decision and counter-decision, the dearth of manoeuvering space for captain and rowers seems to gain an enhanced significance. What will his 'seltene Paradiesvögel' turn out to be in the land which, more even than Naples, is a paradise and a hell? And will he remain at the helm as he goes to gather his rare poetic harvest, oppressed by its riches? He himself had asked the question — clearly prefiguring the duke's admonition to Tasso — as he doubtfully wrote: 'Reisen lern' ich wohl auf dieser Reise, ob ich leben lerne, weiß ich nicht.' And he had been prepared to pay a high price for whatever initiation he might be granted, calling in question the gain of renewed life that Rome had brought him and apodeictically stating: 'Gewiß, es wäre besser, ich käme gar nicht wieder, wenn ich nicht wiedergeboren zurückkommen kann' (March 22, 1787).

In the most obvious sense of the word he did not stay at the helm of the little boat taking him to his dream-island; not even on deck. Overtaken by violent sea-sickness, he was compelled to retire to his cabin; and there, abstaining from food and drink, he lay on his bunk. '. . . abgeschlossen von der äußern Welt ließ ich die innere walten', he writes; and at once we think of Tasso's morbid introspections. But, lo and behold, the sentence continues:

'und da eine langsame Fahrt vorauszusehen war, gab ich mir gleich zu bedeutender Unterhaltung ein starkes Pensum auf.' The *Pensum* is the recasting into
blank verse of the poetic prose of the two opening acts of *Tasso* — which of
all his papers he had chosen to take along on the journey. In the earlier version
these acts 'hatten etwas Weichliches, Nebelhaftes, welches sich bald verlor,
als ich nach neueren Ansichten die Form vorwalten und den Rhythmus
eintreten ließ'. Anyone who knows what it feels like to be sea-sick cannot fail
to be impressed by the composure of this statement. *Pensum* indeed, and *Form*
and *vorwalten lassen!* The next day, March 31, almost everyone has succumbed to
sea-sickness. Of himself Goethe writes: 'Ich blieb in meiner gewohnten Lage,
das ganze Stück ward um und um, durch und durch gedacht.' We almost feel
his stomach turning around in his body, in this 'um und um, durch und
durch'; yet how sublimated is the use to which he puts these physical revol-
utions and convulsions!

At this point in the narrative Goethe tells us a most illuminating detail.
'Der schelmische Kniep', he reports, would every now and then come and
tease the sick poet with glowing reports of the foods that were being served,
regretting that he, Goethe, was missing his share. We can readily guess how
his Tasso would have reacted. Antonio tells us so. But this poet writes:
'Ich ... enthielt mich außer weißem Brot und rotem Wein aller Speisen und
Getränke und fühlte mich ganz behaglich[6].' The next day, April 1: 'Um drei
Uhr morgens heftiger Sturm. Im Schlaf und Halbtraum setzte ich meine
dramatischen Plane fort, indessen auf dem Verdeck große Bewegung war.
Die Segel mußten eingenommen werden, das Schiff schwebte auf den hohen
Fluten ... wir lavierten an und ab.' And in the midst of all this he records:
'Doch ließ ich meinen dichterischen Vorsatz nicht aus dem Sinne, und ich war
des ganzen Stücks so ziemlich Herr geworden'; a statement which reads oddly
in conjunction with the next entry, in the early hours of the following morning.
Nearing Palermo, Goethe writes: 'der Plan meines Dramas war diese Tage
daher im Walfischbauch ziemlich gediehen.'

Was he at the helm of this expedition? Yes and no. Shut up in his cabin,
in the *Walfischbauch*, he was utterly regressed. Yet he was also the master of his
regression, not only in the sense that he mastered his poem but also that he
mastered his rebelling body, by the wisdom and sobriety he had taught himself years back, in his early Weimar days. 'Ich will doch Herr werden', he had
written then. 'Niemand, als wer sich ganz verläugnet, ist werth zu herrschen
und kan herrschen.' There is much in this extraordinary chronicle, to be sure,
that is reminiscent of his own Tasso: the absolute surrender to the extremity of
the situation (some people cannot be sick). Like Tasso, after the cataclysm,
he *is* the wave, the storm-tossed sea. And Tasso, too, in the midst of ship-

---

[6] Cf. Chapter IV, section 6.

wreck, is capable of poetic utterance. But there is one difference: Tasso is driven. The poet of Tasso remains the master of his deepest regression.

Goethe learnt two things on this memorable sea-trip: to immerse himself once again in elemental flux and to derive new vitality from such total immersion. His creative impulse had spent itself in Rome; and to compose *Tasso*, of all things, the tragedy of the creative artist through whom the laws of formative nature course unimpeded, he himself had to expose himself to the workings of elemental nature within and without and obey his daimon. At the same time, and paradoxically, he found that, in serving her, he also mastered her within him. Like the speaker of that magnificent poem of transition, *Seefahrt,* he had proven himself a skipper who understood the elements, who could draw in his sails when necessary and yet remain

> Treu dem Zweck auch auf dem schiefen Wege;

like the Direktor in the *Vorspiel auf dem Theater* — and indeed like the aged poet at the finish — he could tell the artist in himself:

> Gebt ihr euch einmal für Poeten,
> So kommandiert die Poesie . . .

and set a sizeable *Pensum* to his sea-sick muse; and, like his own Faust, he could leave the arid forms of what he now called *das gestaltenverwirrende Rom* behind and, armed with his key, descend into elemental flux — whether we choose to call it *das Reich der Mütter* or *den Walfischbauch* is immaterial — thence to retrieve an image of *Natura Naturans*, still moist and gleaming from the matrix.

Had not Goethe, in nursing along his *Tasso* in these circumstances, trancended his hero as well as the warning words of the duke? It seemed that he did not need to forfeit the poet to prove himself a man capable of surrender, and in it, of restraint and mastery: his daimon and his genius worked hand in hand[7].

4.

During the six spring weeks Goethe spent in Sicily, *Tasso* is not so much as mentioned. Receptive as always, his attention is captivated by the manifold interests of the natural, human and artistic scene. Yet his creative *nisus* could not be stopped. We know that it was *Nausikaa* over which, 'auf dem über-

---

[7] Cf. Chapter IV, section 5. Clearly the complex task the poet had set himself in March 1780, i. e. to go along with his own unconscious cycles in order to master them, had not been an academic one. It is yielding dividends here, in the incongruous circumstances in which he is coming to grips with the very play the conception of which had been the first fruit of his resolution seven years earlier. Here is another milestone on that quest to interlace conscious and unconscious drives in a seamless creativity which was to find its final articulation in the last letter from his hand, the letter of March 17, 1832, to W. von Humboldt.

klassischen Boden in einer poetischen Stimmung' (*Aus der Erinnerung*, un-
dated) he *verträumte* his Sicilian stay, troubled intermittently and with ever
greater urgency by the spectre of the *Urpflanze, die alte Grille* as he tellingly
calls it. Is there any connection between these two preoccupations and the
subterraneous gestation of his travel companion? As I see it, plenty. The
search for the *Urpflanze* sprang from the quest for the laws of organising
nature. These, he felt, were the very laws according to which the classical
artists had proceeded in their works of art. In Rome, he had patiently tried to
assimilate this oneness, hoping that such contact would galvanise him into a
similar kind of organic creativity. Palladio and Winckelmann had in turn served
him as models in this ambitious quest; and later he had extrapolated from
their achievement to that of the ancients in general. Of Palladio we read as
early as October 2, 1786, that is to say, before ever he had set foot in Rome:
'Mich dünkt, ich habe nichts Höheres, nichts Vollkommeneres gesehen . . .
Denke man sich aber auch den trefflichen Künstler, . . . der erst mit unglaub-
licher Mühe sich an den Alten heranbildet, um sie alsdann durch sich wiederherzustellen.' Of Winckelmann: 'Außer den Gegenständen der Natur, die in
allen ihren Teilen wahr und konsequent ist, spricht doch nichts so laut als
die Spur eines guten, verständigen Mannes, als die echte Kunst, die ebenso
folgegerecht ist als jene' (December 13, 1786). Of the 'Kunst der Griechen' in
general: the problem is

'zu erforschen, wie jene unvergleichlichen Künstler verfuhren, um aus der menschlichen
Gestalt den Kreis göttlicher Bildung zu entwickeln, welcher vollkommen abgeschlossen
ist und worin kein Hauptcharakter so wenig als die Übergänge und Vermittlungen
fehlen. Ich habe eine Vermutung, daß sie nach eben den Gesetzen verfuhren, nach welchen
die Natur verfährt und denen ich auf der Spur bin.' (January 28, 1787).

Such creative participation in a nature which obeys the laws of art, and
in an art which was, in that highest sense, a second nature[8], was to become
a simple fact in Sicily, in the composition of *Nausikaa*, with the idea of the
Urpflanze and Homer for his joint guides. The view from those public gardens
of Palermo, 'die schwärzlichen Wellen am nördlichen Horizonte, ihr An-
streben an die Buchtkrümmungen, selbst der eigene Geruch des dünstenden
Meeres, das alles rief mir die Insel der seligen Phäaken in die Sinne sowie ins
Gedächtnis. Ich eilte sogleich, einen Homer zu kaufen . . .' (April 7, 1787).
Exactly one month later, we read that he yielded to an ever increasing urge

'. . . die gegenwärtige herrliche Umgebung, das Meer, die Inseln, die Häfen, durch poetische
würdige Gestalten zu beleben und mir auf und aus diesem Lokal eine Komposition zu
bilden, in einem Sinne und in einem Ton, wie ich sie noch nicht hervorgebracht. Die
Klarheit des Himmels, der Hauch des Meeres, die Düfte, wodurch die Gebirge mit
Himmel und Meer gleichsam in *ein* Element aufgelöst wurden, all dies gab Nahrung
meinen Vorsätzen; und indem ich in jenem schönen öffentlichen Garten zwischen blü-

---

[8] For the reverberations of this 'discovery' in the aesthetics and creative productivity of
the post-Italian Goethe, cf. Chapter VI, section 5, Chapters XI and XIII.

henden Hecken von Oleander, durch Lauben von fruchttragenden Orangen- und Zitronenbäumen wandelte und zwischen andern Bäumen und Sträuchen, die mir unbekannt waren, verweilte, fühlte ich den fremden Einfluß auf das allerangenehmste.'

The sea voyage is over, yet the sea is undisputed mistress, the element of elements in which all is dissolved: the sky, the contours of the hills, the very contours of the moulding eye — Kniep is praised in the preceding entry, 'da er mich einer Bürde entledigt, die mir unerträglich wäre, und mich meiner eigenen Natur wiedergibt'— even the constraints of the imagination —: all are dissolved, and from the enveloping fragrance there arises the figure of the Greek Don Juan, seductive tempter and traveller like Weislingen and Clavigo and Fernando, dreamily cast in the mould of the Homeric world that fills the poet's nostrils with its sea-vapours. How effortless is this creative assimilation of the spirit of the ancient poet, one who himself was a second nature, here, in sea-girded Sicily where the very plants bespoke the law of his poetry! Back in Naples, Goethe was himself to confirm this naturalness of Homer and the identity of his poetry with the organising principles of nature. 'Was den Homer betrifft', he writes to Herder, in his first letter from the mainland, dated May 17, 1787,

'ist mir wie eine Decke von den Augen gefallen. Die Beschreibungen, die Gleichnisse etc. kommen uns poetisch vor und sind doch unsäglich natürlich, aber freilich mit einer Reinheit und Innigkeit gezeichnet, vor der man erschrickt. Selbst die sonderbarsten erlogenen Begebenheiten haben eine Natürlichkeit, die ich nie so gefühlt habe als in der Nähe der beschriebenen Gegenstände.'

And he continues that he is on the point of discovering the secret of the creation and organisation of plants, a key which will not only enable him to *invent* plants animated by 'eine innerliche Wahrheit und Notwendigkeit', but, beyond that, unlock the mystery of all life!

Did he have to mention Tasso at a moment of time when, exempt from all the restraints of *terra firma*, he felt so extravagantly close to the organising energies of nature and art? Why write about Tasso while he was living him? We may be confident that the figure of the poet was in his mind when he reports in his first letter home, with clear allusion to his pheasant dream: 'ich habe unsäglich aufgeladen und brauche Ruhe, es wieder zu verarbeiten' (Neapel, May 17, 1787).

5.

The memory of the dream-like weeks spent on the island reverberates in the themes which preoccupy Goethe in Naples. Philippo Neri, 'der humoristische Heilige' and Goethe's patron saint, makes his first appearance here: a curiously free man, devout yet worldly — an Italian parallel to Luther — this figure was bound to seem attractive to Goethe, and especially now, after the releasing experience of the sea-girded paradise. It is in the same free and easy mood that he explodes the Nordic myth of Neapolitan sloth and convinces his readers by detailed observations that Neapolitans are as industrious as anyone, but that a happy temperament and a benign nature and climate have fitted them not to work 'um bloß zu *leben*, sondern um zu *genießen*, und daß sie sogar bei der Arbeit des Lebens froh werden wollen' (May 28, 1787)[9]. He has high praise for their 'ausgezeichnete Fröhlichkeit' which makes short thrift even of death (May 29), and delights in their 'freudigem Kunstsinn' which he obviously rates far above the 'strenge Handwerksfertigkeit' of the North (June 1st).

In the midst of such a carefree time the announcement of the third part of Herder's *Ideen zur Philosophie der Geschichte der Menschheit*, freshly published in Riga, reached the poet; and his acid comment illuminates not only his prevailing mood but also his expectations of the approaching future in Rome and the incessant if subterranean preoccupation with the play that had now been his sole companion for many a week. 'Auf Herders dritten Teil freu' ich mich sehr', he writes. 'Hebet mir ihn auf, bis ich sagen kann, wo er mir begegnen soll. Er wird gewiß den schönen Traumwunsch der Menschheit, daß es dereinst besser mir ihr werden solle, trefflich ausgeführt haben.' And then follows a sardonic rider: 'Auch, muß ich selbst sagen, halt' ich es für wahr, daß die Humanität endlich siegen wird, nur fürcht' ich, daß zu gleicher Zeit die Welt ein großes Hospital und einer des andern humaner Krankenwärter sein werde' (May 27, 1787). Strangely bitter words, these, reminiscent of the 'verteufelt human' which has bedevilled critics of *Iphigenie*, and anticipating, surely, the portrait, in *Tasso*, of the princess, who so laconically asks of her name-sake Leonore:

> Glücklich?
> Wer ist denn glücklich?

and for herself answers the question, saying:

> Ich bin gesund, das heißt, ich bin nicht krank; (III, 2).

Coming from Sicily and here, on the happy-go-lucky soil of Naples, he was filled with the belief in the creativity of Nature, and natural creativity. He felt vital and close to the mystery of life. What wonder that the hypochondriac North — and that meant Rome and Ferrara as well as Weimar — should act on him like an irritant, and their civilisation, the very word *Bildung* and all it entailed, which is the central word in *Tasso*, to him should seem a cruel sapping of the wellsprings of creation? His eyes were still turned towards the elemental. The splendidly spitting Vesuvius, emitting fiery vapours and huge glowing waves of lava, fertile and destructive —: this is what fascinated him in his last days in Naples; this was what to him seemed his 'ernstlichen Zwecke', this what made him kick against 'die widerwillige

---

[9] How could the creator of Egmont fail to be in tune with this philosophy of life?

Artigkeit des Tags', the last day in the vicinity of the gigantic phenomenon which was spent with footling farewell visits. The traveller from Sicily, on his way to Rome, did not have much enthusiasm for *Sitte* and *Sittlichkeit* and *Ziemlichkeit* and *Schicklichkeit*, to name only some of the synonyms the princess — and he himself — will use interchangeably in his tragedy of a poet. Now they spelt death. Goethe sided with the erupting volcano, and with the eruptive figure of his hero.

But we love what we must leave; and back in eternal Rome he feels newly initiated into a higher calling. Not accidentally he arrived on Corpus Christi; and his first letter takes its tone from the occasion. *Feierlich, eingeweiht, höhere Betrachtung, fleißig, reinigt* — these are the words that characterise the mood of those *Briefe eines Zurückgekehrten;* and by the end of the month, having once again found 'den höchsten anschauenden Begriff von Natur und Kunst' in the Gallery Colonna, he can once again write: 'Wenn ihr mein gedenkt, so denkt an mich als einen Glücklichen'.

For six weeks Goethe once again revels in training his eye, meanwhile writing portions of *Wilhelm Meister* and finishing his *Egmont*. It is interesting to note that in the middle of his *résumé* he inserts, without any obvious reason, a retrospective report of events already chronicled, first on April 17 in Naples and then in a letter to Herder written from Naples on May 17: his obsession with the *Urpflanze* and his subsequent conviction that he has found the key to the creation and organisation of plant-life and, indeed, of all things living. Even more intriguing is the insertion, following that report, of a section entitled *Störende Naturbetrachtungen*. Read closely, however, these paragraphs contain a key to the incongruous arrangement. Goethe describes the 'leidenschaftliche Bewegung' into which the idea of the metamorphosis of plants has thrown and continues to throw him. He explains 'daß ich von einem solchen Gewahrwerden wie von einer Leidenschaft eingenommen und getrieben worden': and all at once we understand two things, his portrayal of the demonic in *Egmont* — he writes that he has all but completed the fourth act — and the *Steigerung* of the drama into the visionary and poetic, a law he was later to explain to Eckermann, à propos of his *Novelle*, in precisely these terms of plant-morphology[10]. And can we wonder that in the letter announcing the completion of *Egmont* he should prophesy that 'Tasso kommt nach dem neuen Jahre'? *Tasso*, poem of the artist through whom Nature herself operates? It is as if to put his explicit seal upon this secret connection, that we are told in the paragraph following this announcement: '. . . die Kunst wird mir wie eine zweite Natur, die gleich der Minerva aus dem Haupte Jupiters, so aus dem Haupte der größten Menschen geboren worden.'

The mention of *Tasso* is dated at the end of August. We do not hear the name any more until November 3 when he speaks of this tragedy and *Faust*

[10] Jan. 18, 1827.

as two heavy stones he has yet to push uphill. And then again on January 10, when he writes, with apparent levity, that during the course of the year which has just begun he will have to fall in love with a princess in order to write *Tasso* and make a pact with the devil to get down to his *Faust*. The frivolous tone of this allusion is misleading. These words are written at the height of an existential crisis as soul-rending and violent as any Goethe ever lived through. What does the all but complete silence about his travel companion during the intervening four and a half months, and his sudden re-emergence here signify, at a point where to the perceptive reader apprehensions about the poet's mental stability seem amply justified?

We are entering upon the final phase of Goethe's Italian sojourn, a phase marked by a conflict so fierce and so protracted that victory wore the features of madness and rebirth the pallor of death. It is the struggle between the visual artist and the poet, with Torquato Tasso as the secret antagonist. Let us attempt to trace his hidden steps.

6.

From September onwards, that is to say, after the completion of *Egmont* and the prophecy that the new year will usher in *Tasso*, statements crowd in thick and fast which testify to Goethe's ever increasing awareness that the laws of nature and those of great art are identical. This awareness would, by rights, point in the direction of *Torquato Tasso*, the tragedy in which it has found its most direct poetic precipitate. Instead, and paradoxically, they are ever more closely geared to Goethe's obsession with being an artist. Speaking of his happiness to be able 'mit der größten Ruhe und Reinheit eine eingeborne Leidenschaft befriedigen zu können', and (in the following letter) of his persistent labouring, he tells us: 'Ich bin immer fleißig. Nun hab' ich ein Köpfchen nach Gips gezeichnet, um zu sehen, ob mein Prinzipium Stich hält. Ich finde, es paßt vollkommen . . . Ich sehe nun wohl, wie weit sich's mit Applikation bringen ließe . . . Es wird recht fleißig nach der Natur gezeichnet werden.' And, as if to explicate the foregoing allusion to his *eingebornen Leidenschaft*, he concludes: 'Ich mag nun von gar nichts mehr wissen, als etwas hervorzubringen und meinen Sinn recht zu üben. Ich liege an dieser Krankheit von Jugend auf krank, und gebe Gott, daß sie sich einmal auflöse.'[11] In the next letter, of September 22, he tells his friends that his labours are continuing and that he is now concentrating entirely on the human figure. The following letter, dated September 28, confirms what he had foreseen. 'Ich bin hier' — i. e. in Frascati —

---

[11] It is important to realise that Goethe speaks of his passion for the visual arts as an illness and prays, not for a fulfilment of this passion, but for a crisis relieving him of it.

'sehr glücklich, es wird den ganzen Tag bis in die Nacht gezeichnet, gemalt, getuscht, geklebt, Handwerk und Kunst recht ex professo getrieben . . . Nun hoffe ich, daß auch die Zeit des Vollendens kommen wird . . .'

He calls his eyes, charmingly, *frischgewaschen* and *gebildet* and does not tire of training them on objects offered by nature or by art. His 'eigentlicher Trieb', he surmises, 'war, durch Nachbildung von Natur- und Kunstgegenständen Hand und Augen möglichst zu steigern' (September, Bericht). We read through these pages and keep forgetting that it is a poet who is speaking. They sound like the records of a young painter or graphic artist vying with a bunch of like-minded companions to perfect himself in his craft.

Suddenly, in the midst of this abandon, a note of doubt creeps in, like a cloud running across a sunny field. 'Lebhaft vordringende Geister'[12], he notes, are not satisfied with being receptive. They want to know and this desire drives them to do; and in the end one feels

'daß man nichts richtig beurteilt, als was man selbst hervorbringen kann. Doch hierüber kommt der Mensch nicht leicht ins klare, und daraus entstehen gewisse falsche Bestre-bungen, welche um desto ängstlicher werden, je redlicher und reiner die Absicht ist. Indes fingen mir in dieser Zeit an Zweifel und Vermutungen aufzusteigen, die mich mitten in diesen angenehmen Zuständen beunruhigten; denn ich mußte bald empfinden, daß der eigentliche Wunsch und die Absicht meines Hierseins schwerlich erfüllt werden dürfte.' (Bericht. September).

This caution, no doubt prompted by his acquaintance with K. Ph. Moritz's aesthetic treatise which turns on exactly this question of the relation between receptivity and productivity in the making of art, is not heeded. Goethe goes on hectically drawing and painting; and he speaks about his obsessive activity as though he were scolding his Werther for losing himself in his introspective musings: 'Wenn man mich außer mir selbst herausbringen könnte, müßten es diese Tage tun', he writes — and, interestingly enough, the entry is dated in the slapdash manner of one for whom time has ceased to matter: 'Castle Gandolfo, den 8. Oktober, eigentlich den 12ten, denn diese Woche ist hingegangen, ohne daß ich zum Schreiben kommen konnte' — 'aber ich falle immer wieder in mich zurück, und meine ganze Neigung ist auf die Kunst gerichtet. Jeden Tag geht mir ein neues Licht auf, und es scheint, als wenn ich wenigstens würde sehen lernen.'

A slight note of resignation persists, together with unabated fascination. On October 27 he writes: 'Ich bin in diesem Zauberkreise wieder angelangt und befinde mich gleich wieder wie bezaubert, zufrieden, stille hinarbeitend, vergessend alles, was außer mir ist . . .' Angelika Kaufmann, he bashfully confesses, has given him high hopes as far as his landscape drawing goes; and adds 'Ich will wenigstens fortfahren, um mich dem zu nähern, was ich wohl nie erreiche'.

---

[12] Cf. Chapter XIII, p. 354f..

The retrospective *Bericht* for the month of October contains a clue as to that note of resignation which persisted alongside the most exhaustive efforts. The month had brought an encounter with an attractive young Milanese woman with whom Goethe had fallen in love on the spot, only to learn that she was already engaged to another man. He retired gracefully, afraid that he might be caught out in a Wertherish situation here, in Rome, of all places; and this secret wound no doubt lent his utterances of that time their surprisingly introverted and hopeless air. Yet, quite unlike his Werther and very much like his Tasso, the withdrawal of the loved object led to a marked increase of artistic energy. For he marvelled at 'die Fülle der Körperlichkeit' with which his eye saw, and almost felt, its objects; a displacement of erotic energy from its primary object into creative channels which is not surprising to those familiar with the early 'Künstlergedichte', *Torquato Tasso*[13] or indeed the poem *Cupido* which heads the *Bericht* for January, 1788. What however remains difficult to account for is the coincidence between a creative crisis and a personal embroilment entered, or so it seems, to no other end than to enhance this block. Goethe had not, and could not have, known that his Milanese friend was engaged. Yet it would be obtuse to look upon this closing-off of an outlet as a chance occurrence. The arrangement of his narration, the inclusion in it, beside this erotic adventure, of the history of his patron-saint, Philippo Neri, leaves no doubt but that he himself perceived pattern where others might have accused their ill luck. The pattern was, precisely, first the release and then the abrupt closing-off of one outlet for libidinal energies which could not be transferred to the creative arena, because Goethe clung to an artistic medium incapable of absorbing, and transmuting, acute emotional shocks. Hence he found himself in front of closed doors and in the teeth of a sharpened artistic conflict, fed by those very surplus energies he could neither assimilate nor shape.

It is precisely at this point that *Tasso* receives one of its rare mentions: 'Nun liegen noch so zwei Steine vor mir: "Faust" und "Tasso".' (Rom, November 3). It was inevitable that his travelling companion should pipe up in his mind at this moment. For in him the lability and disponibility of creative Eros figures to a fault. As against that, Goethe, obstinately standing in front of the wrong door and being a related human being into the bargain, found himself debarred from such an easy transposition, and his conflict sharpened.

Not that his pen rested during this period; but significantly he worked on minor projects, such as the *Singspiele Erwin und Elmire* and *Claudine von Villa Bella:* and these could not resolve what seemed to be an indecisive battle between greater, and unseen, opponents.

---

[13] Cf. my *Goethe and Lessing*, Chapters V, section 5 and VII.

Weighty entries testifying to his insight into the interconnection of the laws of Nature and art recur with renewed frequency during the month of December. The month sets in with the confident declaration: 'So viel versichre ich dir: ich bin über die wichtigsten Punkte mehr als gewiß, und obgleich die Erkenntnis sich ins Unendliche erweitern könnte, so hab' ich doch vom Endlich-Unendlichen einen sichern, ja klaren und mitteilbaren Begriff.' And, on the 21st of the month: 'Der Verstand und die Konsequenz der großen Meister ist unglaublich' etc. etc.

The last letter of that month, dated December 25, Christmas day, gives us a lively impression of the inner state such intimations engendered in Goethe. He notes the fact that it is Christ's birthday — a specially dramatic one as it happened since the day was ushered in by a violent storm — and thence goes on to describe his own mental frame in a language which suggests nothing short of a religious transport. 'Der Glanz der größten Kunstwerke blendet mich nicht mehr', he alarmingly writes; 'ich wandle nun im Anschauen . . .'; and we think of the cautionary lines from *Pandora*

> Daß nicht vor Helios' Pfeil erblinde mein Geschlecht,
> Bestimmt, Erleuchtetes zu sehen, nicht das Licht.

And, later in the same letter: 'Ich habe keine Worte, die stille, wache Seligkeit auszudrücken, mit der ich nun die Kunstwerke zu betrachten anfange . . .'. Such words receive their colouring from the intervening section, in which Heinrich Meyer is described in somewhat startlingly extravagant terms: 'Er hat eine himmlische Klarheit der Begriffe und eine englische Güte des Herzens', we read. And we wonder: is the innate balance of Goethe's mind beginning to give under the strain of an unacknowledged conflict — the coflict between the vocation he would have and that which is his, and is inseparably entwined with the fortunes of his silent travel companion?

The retrospective *Bericht* for the month of December suggests that our apprehensions may not be far off the mark: the most sweeping statements about the oneness of Nature and classical visual art are now presented in an indubitably religious tenor, and, moreover, embedded in reflections and reminiscences which incessantly circle around the mystery of Christ's martyrdom and transfiguration. The substance of the report is the detailed description of frescoes, in a number of churches, painted by and after Raphael: the Church of S Paolo alle Tre Fontane[14] showing frescoes of Christ and his apostles, 'einen verklärten Lehrer mit seinen zwölf ersten und vornehmsten Schülern, welche ganz an seinen Worten und an seinem Dasein hingen und größtenteils ihren einfachen Wandel mit einem Märtyrertode krönten . . .'. Raphael's 'herrliche Bild der Transfiguration', in the monastery next to the Church of St. Paul, gave rise to a violent dispute: the picture shows 'einen besessenen

---

[14] The frescoes are not in S Paolo alla Tre Fontane as Goethe remembers them to be, but in the neighbouring church of S Vincenzo e S Anastasio. Cf. *HA* XI, p. 663, note to p. 448.

Knaben' presented by his disconsolate parents to the disciples, in the absence of the Master. They are unable to exorcise the demon but point heavenward where 'der einzig Kräftige', the transfigured Christ, has appeared. The dispute which aroused and divided the friends was the question whether Raphael had here indulged himself in presenting a double action, or whether the two halves of the picture formed one whole: 'unten das Leidende, Bedürftige, oben das Wirksame, Hülfreiche, beides aufeinander sich beziehend, ineinander ein-wirkend.' Goethe emphatically takes the part of the latter school of thought, and it is here, in this incongruous, Christian, context, that we find one of his passionate declarations of the identity between the laws of an uncorrupted Nature and an uncorrupted art: '. . . der gottbegabte Mann . . . soll in der Blüte seines Lebens falsch gedacht, falsch gehandelt haben? Nein! er hat wie die Natur jederzeit recht, und gerade da am gründlichsten, wo wir sie am wenigsten begreifen.' We shall leave the identity of the possessed youth to the imagination, and quote one or two more of the statements which articulate Goethe's most obsessive concern, the concern which, by every logic, ought to point to the figure of his poet-hero, who is never so much as alluded to. Of Michelangelo's Sybillae in Maria della Pace we read: 'Ebenso ist auch hier in den Sibyllen die verheimlichte Symmetrie, worauf bei der Komposition alles ankommt, auf eine höchst geniale Weise obwaltend; denn wie in dem Organismus der Natur, so tut sich auch in der Kunst innerhalb der genausten Schranke die Vollkommenheit der Lebensäußerung kund.' And, within a few lines, the culminating utterance of all: 'Mir ward bei diesem Umgang das Gefühl, der Begriff, die Anschauung dessen, was man im höchsten Sinne die Gegenwart des klassischen Bodens nennen dürfte. Ich nenne dies die sinnlich geistige Überzeugung, daß hier das Große war, ist und sein wird.' The words *klassischer Boden* are beautifully ambiguous, encompassing both the soil and the monuments of art that have organically sprung from this soil: words in which the union between art and nature is so deeply experienced that one term suffices to embrace both.

The following insertion, entitled *Philipp Neri, der humoristische Heilige*, fits the increasingly religious tenor of Goethe's narrative from Christmas day onwards. A wordly man, richly gifted, handsome and clear-minded, and graced with charisma — Goethe uses, with evident pleasure, the Italian word *attrativa* — his late entry into the priesthood exercises '. . . einen merk-würdig steigernden Einfluß' on his spiritual powers. The celebration of the Eucharist transports him into 'einen Enthusiasmus, in eine Ekstase, wo man den bisher so natürlichen Mann gänzlich verliert'; and literally so, since he has the power of levitation which not only raised him up above the altar but is supposed, on one occasion, to have transported him to the ceiling of a room in which he was praying for one dangerously sick. Clearly Goethe is fascinated by this figure, in many ways like himself, and perhaps sharing also his own ecstatic intensity without an outlet in any palpable medium.

At the beginning of the new year — the year Goethe had forecast would see the completion of his *Tasso* — the decisive words are uttered which explain the allusions during the month preceding and afford us the key to all that is to follow.

On January 5, the first letter of the year, he writes that after an interval of several weeks he once again has 'die schönsten, ich darf wohl sagen Offenbarungen'. Clearly the word is circumspectly chosen. 'Es ist mir erlaubt, Blicke in das Wesen der Dinge und ihre Verhältnisse zu werfen, die mir einen Abgrund von Reichtum eröffnen.'[15] This is the language of a mystic. He continues, as we would expect, saying: 'Das Studium des menschlichen Körpers hat mich nun ganz. Alles andere verschwindet dagegen.' '. . . hat

---

[15] Cf. Goethe's letter to the Duke Carl August dated Jan. 25, 1788: 'Als ich zuerst nach Rom kam, bemerkte ich bald, daß ich von Kunst eigentlich gar nichts verstand und daß ich bis dahin nur den allgemeinen Abglanz der Natur in den Kunstwerken, bewundert und genossen hatte, hier tat sich eine andre Natur, ein weiteres Feld der Kunst vor mir auf, ja ein Abgrund der Kunst, in den ich mit desto mehr Freude hineinschaute als ich meinen Blick an die Abgründe der Natur gewöhnt hatte. . . . Gegen Ende Oktober kam ich wieder in die Stadt und da ging eine neue Epoche an. Die Menschengestalt zog nunmehr meine Blicke auf sich und wie ich vorher, gleichsam wie von dem Glanz der Sonne, meine Augen von ihr weggewendet, so konnte ich nun mit Entzücken sie betrachten und auf ihr verweilen.' (*HA* Briefe 2, p. 79, No. 459.)

The editor's note (p. 500, note to 79.13 f.) that the Renaissance regarded the art of antiquity — and only that — as being a second or *andere Natur* is of course correct, but does not touch upon Goethe's own most intimate and pressing 'revelations' at that 'epoch' of his life. Nor does it draw attention to the curious use of the word *Abgrund* — 'Abgrund der Kunst' and 'Abgründe der Natur' — which is juxtaposed to the more superficial perception, at an earlier phase, of the 'allgemeinen Abglanz der Natur in den Kunstwerken': clearly 'Abgrund', in this context, is synonymous with that direct perception of art-nature in the splendour of the human form which Goethe himself likens to an unblinking gaze into the light of the sun.

This letter is written some nine and a half years before Goethe saw the Rheinfall and visited the Vierwaldstätter Lake (in September and October 1797) where, as he concedes to Eckermann, the *terza rima* of the sunrise in *Anmutige Gegend* came to him. (May 6, 1827.) That is to say, he is writing these extravagant and dangerous words to his princely friend just about ten years before he had the strength to say // So bleibe denn die Sonne mir im Rücken! // and twenty years before Prometheus, in *Pandora*, will voice his concern // Daß nicht vor Helios' Pfeil erblinde mein Geschlecht, // Bestimmt, Erleuchtetes zu sehen, nicht das Licht! //

We may doubt many facets of the authenticity of the latter part of Goethe's *Italienische Reise* in which contemporaneous letters, themselves considerably edited, alternate with reports composed much later. The letter to the Duke Carl August, with its imagery of abysses and sun, is priceless source material for the authenticity of the report in so far as it turns on the severity of the crisis Goethe experienced in relation to the visual arts. The same imagery which is characteristic of that letter returns time and again in the journal (cf. the previous pages). It is indeed Faust's crisis, and Epimetheus', and we may seek the source of these later creative precipitates of near-catastrophe here, in these last weeks Goethe spent on Italian soil. The following chapter as well as Chapter XIII endeavour to show that the repercussions of the experience discussed here may be traced into Goethe's old age.

mich nun ganz': these are the words of one possessed, and we think of Raphael's fresco which had caused such acrimonious dispute. But the writer is not only the boy possessed by demons. He is also the Saviour going towards his martyrdom. We hardly believe our eyes when we read the words: 'Es spitzt sich bis gegen Ostern eine Epoche zu, das fühl' ich; was werden wird, weiß ich nicht.' And, in the following letter, dated January 10: 'Am menschlichen Körper wird fleißig fortgezeichnet, wie abends in der Perspektivstunde. Ich bereite mich zu meiner Auflösung, damit ich mich ihr getrosten Mutes hingebe, wenn die Himmlischen sie auf Ostern beschlossen haben. Es geschehe, was gut ist.'

This extraordinary passage hardly requires a comment. But we note that the self-offering which is foreseen to take place at Eastertide is envisaged as a dissolution: *meine Auflösung:* and dissolution of all contours in *one* elemental flux had been the keynote of the most poignant evocation of the Sicilian scene, and the 'dissolution' of his artistic sickness had been what he had prayed for.

And here, at this point of almost unendurable inner tenseness, the hidden conflict which had gathered force comes to the fore of the poet's consciousness. First a declaration of consuming passion: 'Das Interesse an der menschlichen Gestalt hebt nun alles andre auf. Ich fühlte es wohl und wendete mich immer davon weg, wie man sich von der blendenden Sonne wegwendet.' Now, clearly, he faces it, head-on. This is Icarus, and Euphorion, and Faust before he has sacrificed his quest for the absolute and is able to say:

> So bleibe denn die Sonne mir im Rücken!

This is the speaker of the poem *Cupido* (which will soon make its appearance in the narrative), *gesengt* by Eros, confused in his doing, *blind* and *irre*. This is the poet of *Selige Sehnsucht*, mothlike, drawn to fly towards the perilous flame.

Then comes a somewhat alarming allusion to Ariadne's thread, needed to find the way in the present labyrinth, but too short to serve as a secure guide. And then, abruptly, the declaration that he will have to fall in love with a princess to write his *Tasso* during the year that has just begun, and make a pact with the devil to get on with *Faust*.

Perversely, the letter all but ends with a statement regarding his aims which, by the use of the word *Epoche*, is overtly brought into the orbit of his religious intimations: 'Meine titanischen Ideen', he writes,

'waren nur Luftgestalten, die einer ernsteren Epoche vorspukten. Ich bin nun recht im Studio der Menschengestalt, welche das non plus ultra alles menschlichen Wissens und Tuns ist.'

And he concludes the outburst with words which unequivocally refer us back to the religious sphere, and the self-offering he sees ahead: 'Ich raffe alles mögliche zusammen, um Ostern eine gewisse Epoche, wohin mein Auge nun reicht, zu schließen . . .'.

7.

We have reached the peak point of this strange travelogue; the precipitation to the end is steep and fast. Goethes first letter, dated February 1, announces 'eine neue Not . . ., worin mir niemand raten noch helfen kann. "Tasso" muß umgearbeitet werden, was da steht, ist zu nichts zu brauchen, ich kann weder so endigen noch alles wegwerfen. Solche Mühe hat Gott den Menschen gegeben!' This is followed, on February 6, by a movingly resigned entry: 'Ich bin recht still und rein und . . . jedem Ruf bereit und ergeben. Zur bildenden Kunst bin ich zu alt, ob ich also ein bißchen mehr oder weniger pfusche, ist eins. Mein Durst ist gestillt . . . mein Genuß ist friedlich und genügsam. Zu dem allen gebt mir euern Segen.'

Two weeks later a promising young French artist died, suddenly, at the age of 25. He left behind a life-size figure of Philoctetes fanning his painful wound with the wing of a bird of prey. Goethe saw it in the abandoned studio. This event left a deep mark on Goethe who must have recognised in it an enactment of his own destiny. For the report is immediately followed by the truly breathtaking words: 'Täglich wird mir's deutlicher, daß ich eigentlich zur Dichtkunst geboren bin . . . Von meinem längern Aufenthalt in Rom werde ich den Vorteil haben, daß ich auf das Ausüben der bildenden Kunst Verzicht tue.' He adds that, as Angelika Kaufmann assures him, he *sees* more precisely than anyone else. 'Genug, ich habe schon jetzt meinen Wunsch erreicht: in einer Sache, zu der ich mich leidenschaftlich getragen fühle, nicht mehr blind zu tappen' (February 22)[16].

It is fitting that, at this moment of his artistic development, he should have recast the poem *Künstlers Erdewallen*, composed *Künstlers Apotheose* and added both to the body of the *Künstlergedichte*, that protracted hymn to the oneness of the creative Eros expressing itself now in natural, and now in art forms, and permeating the latter with the bodiliness which betokens their origin.

The time had come to leave Rome. Easter was at hand, his accounts were made. Yet the inner struggle was not yet over. The last act was still to come. On March 7 he reports: 'Ich habe angefangen, ein wenig zu modellieren. Was den Erkenntnispunkt betrifft, gehe ich sehr rein und sicher fort, in An-wendung der tätigen Kraft bin ich ein wenig konfus. So geht es mir wie allen meinen Brüdern.' The following week, the week preceding Easter, we read: 'Ferner habe ich diese Woche einen Fuß modelliert.' He works from a skeleton, he writes, from the cast of a live foot, from half a dozen of the best specimens of classical statues and several bad ones. Three or four artists come to see and advise him daily, the angelical Heinrich Meyer being the most helpful. 'Wenn mit diesem Winde auf diesem Elemente ein Schiff nicht von der Stelle

---

[16] Cf. Goethe's letter to Herder, July 10, 1772, in which he writes: 'Jetzt . . . tue ich die Augen zu und tappe.' His development has certainly come full circle.

käme, so müßte es keine Segel oder einen wahnsinnigen Steuermann haben.' In a desperate key, this image takes us back to one he had used during his earlier Roman stay, in the first flush of his visual endeavours and his musings on the common morphological laws underlying the creations of art and nature. Determined to fashion with his own hands what his mind had understood, he had written: 'und so spanne ich denn alle Segel meines Geistes auf, um diese Küsten zu umschiffen.' (February 16, 1787). It also takes us back to the pheasant dream and forward to Tasso's last and shattered metaphor. Is he still thinking of bringing home the freight of a visual artist, or is he sensing catastrophe around the corner?

Good Friday has come and gone. 'Ich habe diese Zeit wieder viel studiert', we read, 'und die Epoche, auf die ich hoffte, hat sich geschlossen und geründet. Es ist zwar immer eine sonderbare Empfindung', he adds laconically, 'eine Bahn, auf der man mit starken Schritten fortgeht, auf einmal zu verlassen, doch muß man sich darein finden und nicht zu viel Wesens machen.' And then, less laconically: 'In jeder großen Trennung liegt ein Keim von Wahnsinn.' This is written on Easter Sunday. Goethe adds: 'Soeben steht der Herr Christus mit entsetzlichem Lärm auf.'

What had Goethe 'studiert'? We do not hear about this until three weeks later. Between question and answer a vital excerpt from Karl Philipp Moritz's *Über die bildende Nachahmung des Schönen* is interpolated, an essay which, so Goethe tells us, grew from prolonged and intensive conversations with his gifted yet highly neurotic friend. The gist of this essay is a finely drawn distinction between the formative impulse in art and mere receptivity; a distinction which, in the nature of things, frequently becomes blurred, much to the detriment of the person harbouring such a confusion. 'Dem höchsten Genuß des aus sich selbst hervorgebrachten Schönen sich so nah zu dünken und doch darauf Verzicht zu tun, scheint freilich ein harter Kampf —': but let that battle be fought through to the end, and 'der Frieden in uns ist hergestellt, und das nun wieder in seine Rechte getretene Empfindungsvermögen eröffnet sich zum Lohne für sein bescheidnes Zurücktreten in seine Grenzen dem reinsten Genuß des Schönen, der mit der Natur seines Wesens bestehen kann.' (Bericht. März).

These annihilating words were written by Moritz. They pronounce Goethe's own judgment on his endeavours to be a plastic artist. And yet, what had he referred to when he wrote on that Easter Sunday, March 22, that he had been intensively studying? On April 14 he tells us. 'Die Verwirrung kann wohl nicht größer werden!' we read. 'Indem ich nicht abließ, an jenem Fuß fortzumodellieren, ging mir auf, daß ich nunmehr "Tasso" unmittelbar angreifen müßte, zu dem sich denn auch meine Gedanken hinwendeten, ein willkommener Gefährte zur bevorstehenden Reise.'

8.

What was it, we may ask in conclusion, that motivated Goethe in his bid
to be a visual artist? Why was the decision to abandon this quest such an
agonising one, comparable, in his own mind, to the passion and martyrdom
of Christ? In what sense can he have experienced this quest as a saving mission?
And lastly, why was it so supremely painful to accept his *Tasso* and, in that
work, himself and his own true vocation?

The answer, I think, lies in Goethe's deep-rooted humanism. It was the
splendour of the *Menschengestalt* 'welche' — so he writes at the beginning of the
epoch of his *Auflösung* — 'das non plus ultra alles menschlichen Wissens und
Tuns ist', which commanded his deepest loyalty. To the consummation, and
perpetuation, of that *Menschengestalt* he was most passionately pledged. This
statement is true on a number of levels which I shall try to explicate one by
one, and, as it were, from the bottom upwards. Firstly, and quite humbly, he
knew what he owed, from his boyhood days onwards, to the mere presence
of classical forms. In the epilogue to the *Italienische Reise* he tells us how profound an influence a piece of statuary he saw in Leipzig and, later, the huge
collection in the *Antikensaal* at Mannheim, had had on him. These and copies
he soon bought made up for a dearth he had felt from the start in his home.
'Diese edlen Gestalten waren eine Art von heimlichem Gegengift, wenn das
Schwache, Falsche, Manierierte über mich zu gewinnen drohte.' Once in Italy,
he had become greedy for those presences and had surrounded himself with
plaster casts of the ones he loved best. 'Wenn man des Morgens die Augen
aufschlägt, fühlt man sich von dem Vortrefflichsten gerührt; alles unser
Denken und Sinnen ist von solchen Gestalten begleitet, und es wird dadurch
unmöglich, in Barbarei zurückzufallen.'

Needless to say, this therapeutic influence rested in the profound naturalness of classical art. It was, in his view, an art itself deeply imbued with the
laws and rhythms of organic nature, and to be in its presence meant to be
deeply in touch with Nature, indoors or out of doors. 'Umgeben von antiken
Statuen, empfindet man sich in einem bewegten Naturleben, man wird die
Mannigfaltigkeit der Gestaltung gewahr und durchaus auf den Menschen
in seinem reinstem Zustande zurückgeführt, wodurch denn der Beschauer
selbst lebendig und rein menschlich wird.' What a model for a man in his
daily life, and for an artist in pursuit of his noblest mission 'wetteifernd
mit der Natur etwas Geistig-Organisches hervorzubringen'! And indeed, what
a necessary corrective for a man and an artist living amongst human, social
and natural forms which are corrupt and corrupting![17] To have reconstituted
in themselves, with the help of those classical forms, a purified concept of

---

[17] For the post-Italian repercussions of that vital experience — repercussions perceptible in
Goethe's art as well as in his theory of art — cf. Chapters VI, sections 4 and 5, and XIII.

man and Nature and to have re-educated themselves according to that abstract model and brought forth products in its likeness, to Goethe's mind was the real triumph of a Winckelmann or a Palladio, as it was Goethe's own supreme achievement in the eyes of Schiller.

But would a pocket edition of Homer — such as Goethe carried around with him in Sicily — not have done the same service to a lover of antiquity as classical statuary? And indeed, was writing the *Achilleis* or *Hermann und Dorothea* not fulfilling the same function as copying the Juno Ludovisi or modelling a human foot? For Goethe, decidedly, no. The form of the *Odyssey* or of *Iphigenie* is not palpably 'there' in the sense in which the form of the Belvedere Apollo is. In the case of a statue or even a building, the 'inner' and the outer form coalesce. Whether or not we are conscious of doing so, we take it in as we perceive it. But who knew anything of the inner form of *Werther* in Goethe's time, except for a few connoisseurs such as, say, Lichtenberg or, perhaps, Napoleon Bonaparte? The inner form of a verbal work of art is a hidden thing, latent in its pages, and to distil it from those pages costs a formidable effort on the part of disciplined sensibilities; besides, it is an immaterial form which has to be recreated at every renewed encounter with the work of art and does not 'stay put', reliably and palpably, imprinting itself on the inner eye as does a statue on the perception. Reading, of its essence, is a private, erratic and evanescent act.

And as for writing, instead of moulding or drawing or building? How much more public is the draughtsman's or sculptor's or architect's craft from its inception than the poet's! How much more geared to people and places and to the function it is to fulfil within such a context! How infinitely more difficult it is for the poet to 'see' what he is doing than for the sculptor and painter who can step back and survey the direction in which he is being led, at a glance! How infinitely more difficult to keep a sustained check on his efforts as between one occasion and the next, than with the visual artist whose palpable shapes remain unaffected by the play of his imagination or the tricks of his mood! And as for the role of others in the creative process: when Goethe modelled his foot, some three to four visitors came day by day and commented and advised. When he wrote *Werther* and *Egmont* he was *incommunicado*. *Tasso* was written 'im Walfischbauch', in the extremest seclusion. This is only in part explained by the fact that he was a good poet and a mediocre sculptor. The difference is more deeply rooted in the non-spatial nature of the verbal medium which inevitably makes for a greater degree of introversion.

And what of the completed art-product? The sculpture stands on the market place or in the public gardens; or it adorns a church. The building is inhabited; the painting hangs in an art gallery. It is not only reliably 'there'; it also forms a reliable bridge to fellow men and the public world. The poem, or even the novel, does none of these things. It becomes the private possession of this or that reader, hidden in the recesses of his study and corrupted by the figments of his imagination. It 'is' absolutely nothing apart from what it is to this or that man, at this or that moment; nothing but a *substratum* signalling to him who is willing to receive such signals but unable to defend itself against being man-handled; no more. And the author is in scarcely a better position than any other reader. He too has to reconstruct its form in his imagination, and his imagination, too, is fitful[18]. The poem, once written, can be a liability rather than a support. It cannot sustain its marvelling begetter when he is in a creative trough, let alone re-constitute him. Its articulated form can be a formidable deterrent to one in helpless and inarticulate flux. This is because, in a strange fashion, being an immaterial thing, it remains private, a part of him, and yet is no longer a part of him. Besides, the moment it is authentically articulated it ceases to be subjectively true. This is the terrifying experience Goethe underwent in the making of *Werther*, objectified, later, in *Torquato Tasso* as well as in the cycle of sonnets. 'Jede Form, selbst die gefühltetste, hat etwas Unwahres', he wrote; and the *Werther* trauma was to confirm the truth of this early *apercu*[19]. There is something repellent about any highly wrought artistic statement to him who knows the inside story of its fashioning-process; provided, of course, that the product has reached aesthetic adulthood[20]. All art lies; but none more than poetry which without warning as it were uses language that is representational — that is to say, signifies dictionary meanings and assigns them to external referents — to body forth presentational symbolic structures operating within a strictly internal frame of reference: casting poetic statements in the mould of logical propositions. It lies in the very double-faced nature of language that a mature and patently 'engaged' love-lyric dissembles incomparably more than a painted or sculpted portrait taking every artistic licence is capable of doing.

The Goethe of 'die Künstlergedichte', of *Werther* and *Tasso*, of *Pandora*, *Die Wahlverwandtschaften* and the cycle of sonnets in their proximity knew about these abysses and shunned them. 'Von seinen "Wahlverwandtschaften" sagt er', Eckermann reports, 'daß darin kein Strich enthalten, der nicht erlebt, aber kein Strich so, *wie* er erlebt worden.' And as for the sonnets! The depth of cynicism and unalleviated loneliness in lines such as those spoken by the girl in sonnet XV — these do not bear thinking about. Would they have come to Phidias? Or Picasso? There can be little doubt of the answer the poet who wrote them — the poet of *Tasso* — would have given.

In these senses, then, the visual arts are morale-savers where poetry is deeply undermining. But such a saving function is for the benefit of the artist

---

[18] Cf. Chapter XIII.

[19] Cf. Chapter I, section 7.

[20] As Goethe knew when he included the following dictum by Rembrandt amongst his *Maximen und Reflexionen*: 'An meinen Bildern müßt ihr nicht schnuffeln, die Farben sind ungesund.' (*HA* XII, p. 418, No. 818.) For a modern statement, cf. Yeats' *The Circus Animals' Desertion*.

himself, at least primarily. In the eyes of Goethe, however, the saving mission of visual art went far beyond the personal welfare of the creator. This vocation Goethe expressed perhaps most forcefully in the section entitled *Schönheit* of his *Winckelmann* essay; and the argument is developed so cogently and resonantly that I shall quote it in full.

'... das letzte Produkt der sich immer steigernden Natur ist der schöne Mensch. Zwar kann sie ihn nur selten hervorbringen, weil ihren Ideen viele Bedingungen widerstreben, und selbst ihrer Allmacht ist es unmöglich, lange im Vollkommnen zu verweilen und dem hervorgebrachten Schönen eine Dauer zu geben. Denn genau genommen kann man sagen, es sei nur ein Augenblick, in welchem der schöne Mensch schön sei.

Dagegen tritt nun die Kunst ein: denn indem der Mensch auf den Gipfel der Natur gestellt ist, so sieht er sich wieder als eine ganze Natur an, die in sich abermals einen Gipfel hervorzubringen hat. Dazu steigert er sich, indem er sich mit allen Vollkommenheiten und Tugenden durchdringt, Wahl, Ordnung, Harmonie und Bedeutung aufruft und sich endlich bis zur Produktion des Kunstwerkes erhebt ... Ist es einmal hervorgebracht, steht es in seiner *idealen Wirklichkeit** vor der Welt, so bringt es eine dauernde Wirkung, es bringt die höchste hervor: denn indem es aus den gesamten Kräften sich geistig entwickelt, so nimmt es alles Herrliche, Verehrungs- und Liebenswürdige in sich auf und erhebt, indem es die menschliche *Gestalt beseelt**, den Menschen über sich selbst ... und vergöttert ihn für die Gegenwart, in der das Vergangene und Zukünftige begriffen ist. Von solchen Gefühlen werden die ergriffen, die den olympischen Jupiter erblickten ... Der Gott war zum Menschen geworden, um den Menschen zum Gott zu erheben.'

The Italian Goethe who sought for the point of coincidence between the creative laws of Nature and art, who incessantly endeavoured to permeate himself with the forms exhibiting such unity and who unceasingly strove to body forth such forms himself, was one who in literal truth felt himself to be 'eine ganze Natur, die in sich abermals einen Gipfel hervorzubringen hat.' This peak — and here, I think, lies the source of the confusion — was to be a twin-peak: *beseelte Gestalt* — the palpable creation, *outside himself*, of a sculpted form bodying forth, in its *idealen Wirklichkeit*, the living laws of Nature and immortalising its begetter, the *schöne Mensch*, in all the depth and width of meaning to which Goethe has *emporgesteigert* that word; but also, and more importantly still, *gestaltete Seele* — the formation, *within himself*, of a supreme entelechy, fountain-head of living Art-Nature, infinitely productive of forms and perdurable. The quest for the god-like inner man who transcends humanity by re-creating it — and now in *wirklicher Idealität* — was, I think, the ultimate propelling force which drove Goethe, with a well-nigh insane intensity, to cleave to the chimera of being a visual artist. In a titanic *Steigerung* of his creative energies to the potency of *Natura Naturans*, he lived a Promethean dream, and one not free from hubris. And flying in the face of the impossible at that. For through the realisation of his vision he hoped, somehow, to vanquish man's implacable enemy — death. Even the God-Man in whose foot-

* my italics

steps he walked 'mit starken Schritten', during that agonisingly tense 'epoch', between that Christmas day 1787 and Easter Sunday 1788, had to suffer death once he had chosen to take on the shape of man.

When Goethe gave up modelling his hapless foot, shortly after that fateful Easter Sunday, a spasm in him relaxed. Something gave. His desperado dream of divinised man collapsed at its very base. An inner form grown brittle underwent the *Auflösung* he had prophesied. Released from a lifelong sickness which had become a paroxysm and a bitter passion, he arose renewed, ready to hail two travelling companions he had hitherto spurned: Torquato Tasso, and — Death. Tasso, which means the fate of the poet who — more than any artist — must surrender to the inwardness and elemental flux his insubstantial medium imposes on him[21]; and Death: the death we all die, and that waxing and waning of the creative surge which empowered him to say

> Das Lebend'ge will ich preisen
> Das nach Flammentod sich sehnet . . .

and say it as limpidly as he did.

[21] Cf. Chapters VI, XI and XIII.

The three Faces of Prometheus:
'Pandora'. A Fragment

> For last year's words belong to last year's language
> And next year's words await another voice.
>
> T. S. Eliot

I.

When Leo von Seckendorf and Dr. Stoll invited Goethe to write a contribution for their new journal *Pandora*, he readily accepted. Had the name sparked off a latent preoccupation of his? In the *Tag- und Jahreshefte* for the year 1807/08 the poet reports the event, adding 'und da der mythologische Punkt, wo Prometheus auftritt, mir immer gegenwärtig und zur belebten Fixidee geworden, so griff ich ein, nicht ohne die ernstlichsten Intentionen, wie ein jeder sich überzeugen wird, der das Stück so weit es vorliegt aufmerksam betrachten mag.'[1]

Despite the austere symmetries of the *Festspiel* which extend from the scenic *décor* to the plunge of Phileros and Epimeleia into opposing elements[2], critics have by and large maintained that it is Epimetheus who has come to dominate the outer and inner action, whilst Prometheus recedes into comparative insignificance[3]. Moreover, it is held that the aged Titan here has little or no connection with the figure of Prometheus known to us from Goethe's *Sturm und Drang*, from the ode and the dramatic fragment which bear his name[4].

Yet Goethe's own testimony in the *Tag- und Jahreshefte* should make us wary of this critical assumption. Not only does he expressly state the seminal importance for him of the Prometheus figure; the context in which this statement occurs carries considerable weight in its own right. It is a shorthand calling to mind a number of utterances which are paradigmatic for Goethe's mode of creativity. The best known of these is to be found in the late essay *Bedeutende Fördernis durch ein einziges geistreiches Wort*. There we read:

---

[1] *AGA* 11, p. 821.

[2] Sigurd Burckhardt persuasively argues that the 'furchtbare Symmetrie' (Blake) of the opposing forces in *Pandora* is such that only a miracle can bring about their synthesis. 'So ist *Pandora* notwendigerweise ein Wunder- und Erlösungsspiel, oder war als solches gedacht, obwohl es nur bis zur Verheißung gedieh.' ('Sprache als Gestalt in Goethes "Prometheus" und "Pandora"', in: *Euphorion* 50, 1956, p. 171.)

[3] This position is most emphatically formulated by P. Hankamer. (*Op. cit.*, p. 198 f.)

[4] A point Burckhardt seeks to prove above all by an analysis of the poetic idioms employed in the early and the late fragments.

'Mir drückten sich gewisse Motive, Legenden, uraltgeschichtlich Überliefertes so tief in den Sinn, daß ich sie vierzig bis funfzig Jahre lebendig und wirksam im Innern erhielt; mir schien der schönste Besitz, solche werte Bilder oft in der Einbildungskraft erneut zu sehen, da sie sich denn zwar immer umgestalteten, doch ohne sich zu verändern einer reineren Form, einer entschiednern Gegenwart entgegenreiften.'[5]

Similarly, Goethe speaks of the long gestation of his ballads to Eckermann:

'Ich hatte sie alle schon seit vielen Jahren im Kopf, sie beschäftigten meinen Geist als anmutige Bilder, als schöne Träume, die kamen und gingen und womit die Phantasie mich spielend beglückte. Ich entschloß mich ungern dazu, diesen mir seit so lange befreundeten glänzenden Erscheinungen ein Lebewohl zu sagen, indem ich ihnen durch das ungenügende dürftige Wort einen Körper verlieh. Als sie auf dem Papiere standen, betrachtete ich sie mit einem Gemisch von Wehmut; es war mir, als sollte ich mich auf immer von einem geliebten Freunde trennen.'[6]

Other statements could be adduced to corroborate what Goethe is telling us here[7]. Perhaps one more, from *Das Sehen in subjektiver Hinsicht*, will add a useful facet to the ones already quoted. Speaking of the ordered yet entirely autonomous life of visual impressions in his imagination, Goethe adds the rider:

' ... man sieht deutlicher ein, was es heißen wolle, daß Dichter und alle eigentliche Künstler geboren sein müssen. Es muß nämlich ihre innere produktive Kraft jene Nachbilder, die im Organ, in der Erinnerung, in der Einbildungskraft zurückgebliebenen Idole freiwillig ohne Vorsatz und Wollen lebendig hervortun, sie müssen sich entfalten, wachsen, sich ausdehnen und zusammenziehn, um aus flüchtigen Schemen wahrhaft gegenständliche Wesen zu werden.'[8]

The three passages quoted here share the emphasis both on the longevity of those nuclei of the poetic imagination and on the incessant process of development they undergo. They are the same and yet not the same; growing, expanding or contracting at given stages under their own impetus. This is exactly what the term 'belebte Fixidee' as applied to the *uraltgeschichtliche* figure of Prometheus is telling us. And if we glance back to the statement the poet makes in *Bedeutende Fördernis*, the time span Goethe adduces for some of his motifs would seem to fit the Prometheus figure *par excellence*. It claimed his attention as a very young man — the *Fragment* was written in the summer of 1773 and the *Ode* in 1774 — and surfaced again in *Pandora*, written when Goethe was nearly sixty years old, some thirty five or more years later. The poet's relation to this mythological figure was to be discussed in considerable detail in *Dichtung und Wahrheit* — we shall presently come to this document — and indeed, as late as 1820 its life seems far from exhausted. Replying to Zelter who has read the then as yet unpublished fragment for the first time, the

---

[5] *HA* XIII, p. 38.
[6] March 14, 1830.
[7] Conversation with Eckermann, May 6, 1827. *Ballade, Betrachtung und Auslegung, HA* I, pp. 40ff.
[8] *AGA* 16, p. 902f.

seventy-year-old poet comments: 'Merkwürdig ist es jedoch, daß dieses widerspenstige poetische Feuer schon funfzig Jahre unter poetischer Asche fortglimmt . . .'[9].

Thus we may assume that the figure of Prometheus is one of those archetypal poetic motifs which, like Faust, accompanied Goethe throughout his long life, always developing, now *sich ausdehnend*, now *sich zusammenziehend;* we must defer judgment as to which of theses phases this 'belebte Fixidee' had entered at the time of writing *Pandora* until later in this chapter.

Such continuity as Goethe ascribes to his poetic life also forces us to challenge the all too ready assumption that the aged Titan of the *Festspiel* has little or nothing to do with the figure that dominated his youthful imagination. Is this really so? To answer this question, we must turn to the early products themselves. Perhaps the most economical way of doing so is to approach them, with all due care, through the eyes of the author of *Dichtung und Wahrheit*.

The inner authenticity of his account there becomes immediately apparent from his opening paragraph. Despite the kindly guidance he had been wont to receive from his elders, he writes, he had a nagging sense of ultimately being thrown back onto his own resources: 'Ich hatte jung genug gar oft erfahren, daß in den hülfsbedürftigsten Momenten uns zugerufen wird: "Arzt, hilf dir selber!", und wie oft hatte ich nicht schmerzlich ausseufzen müssen: "Ich trete die Kelter allein." '[10] The similarity of this mood to the one expressed in the ode —

> Da ich ein Kind war,
> Nicht wußte, wo aus noch ein —

and to the opening exchange of the fragment between Prometheus and Merkur[11] is too obvious to be laboured.

It is the sense of helplessness that every child knows from experience which, so Goethe writes, made him scrutinise his own resources. And the one resource which never failed him was his own productivity, 'mein produktives Talent'. 'Es verließ mich seit einigen Jahren keinen Augenblick', we read at the outset of his memorable description of a somnambulist poetic activity so incessant that it blurred the very boundaries of day and night. This productivity, immune to all outside influences, he elected as the surest foundation upon which to ground 'mein ganzes Dasein'. It is in this frame and at this discovery that his attention was drawn to the figure of Prometheus 'der, abgesondert von den Göttern, von seiner Werkstätte aus eine Welt bevölkerte'. What attracted him first and foremost to this figure was its autonomy enabling him, 'zum Trutz höherer Wesen, zu schaffen und zu bilden . . .'; a

---

[9] May 12, 1820.
[10] *Dichtung und Wahrheit*, III, 15, *HA* X, p. 47.
[11] ll. 1—26.

dignity which went together with the fact that he represented a sort of 'Mittelfigur' in the dynasty of beings, entrusted with the creation of man and worthy
of such office as a descendant of the gods. Above all, Goethe recounts, he was
drawn to this isolated figure because he himself depended upon a state of
total isolation for his poetic productions to take shape[12]. It was this temperamental affinity between one creator and the other, rather than 'der titanisch-
gigantische, himmelstürmende Sinn' of Prometheus, which bound him to that
figure. What they shared at bottom was 'jenes friedliche, plastische, allenfalls
duldende Widerstreben, das die Obergewalt anerkannt, aber sich ihr gleich-
setzen möchte'; a deeper bond than that of protest which — Goethe concedes —
crept into his ode representing no more, however, than the exaggerated sense
of isolation which inevitably accompanied his own creative activities, together
with a temporary over-identification with the subject in hand[13].

This retrospective summary in my opinion represents an eminently fair
account of Goethe's early treatments of the Prometheus theme, both as regards
their intrinsic significance and the mental frame from which they sprang.
The central lines of the ode

> Hast du's nicht alles selbst vollendet,
> Heilig glühend Herz?

express the self-reliance of one by no means godless — the word *heilig* is proof
of that — but thrown back onto his own resources; creative resources, as
becomes clear from the concluding stanza of the poem, and resources tapped
in that solitariness which is the mode of creativity.

The Prometheus of the fragment is more obviously placed between isolation
and reverence. He scorns Zeus' offer, in that he feels his will to be autonomous;
yet he reveres Minerva and fate. And the heart beating at the centre of his
self-sufficiency is his solitary delight in creating — a motif developed in greater
breadth here than in the ode. The two monologues of the first act are given
over to this theme. As Merkur leaves, he turns to his statues, soliloquising:

> Unersetzlicher Augenblick!
> Aus eurer Gesellschaft
> Gerissen von dem Toren,
> Meine Kinder!
> Was es auch ist, das meinen Busen regt —

Sich einem Mädchen nahend.

> Der Busen sollte mir entgegen wallen!
> Das Auge spricht schon jetzt!
> Sprich, rede, liebe Lippe, mir!
> O könnt ich euch das fühlen geben,
> Was ihr seid!

[12] Cf. Chapter X, section 7 and notes 58, 59 and 60.
[13] All previous quotations are from *Dichtung und Wahrheit*, III, 15, *HA* X, pp. 47ff.

Again, at the departure of his brother Epimetheus he turns to his creations. In his silent intercourse with them he feels fulfilment:

> Hier meine Welt, mein All!
> Hier fühl ich mich;
> Hier alle meine Wünsche
> In körperlichen Gestalten.
> Meinen Geist so tausendfach
> Geteilt und ganz in meinen teuern Kindern.

Here is a man who is at peace when he is left alone to pursue his 'plastische' activity. And who feels in no way diminished by the thousandfold shapes in which his vision finds expression. There is no gap here between vision and realisation. The inner *form* glimpsed by his mind is reflected back to him inviolate in the manifold of *forms* he creates, without a sense of loss.

> Sieh diese Stirn an!
> Hat mein Finger nicht
> Sie ausgeprägt?

he marvels as he shows his products to Minerva.

This Prometheus, for all the solitariness enjoined by his being creative, lives in the double-rhythm of contraction and expansion, of that *Verselbstigung* and *Entselbstung* of which decades later the aged poet was to speak at the end of the 'Cosmogenic Myth', in the eighth book of *Dichtung und Wahrheit*[14]. For all that 'der Kreis, den meine Wirksamkeit erfüllt' is the pivot of his creative existence, his 'Eigensinn' is not blunted to the bliss

> Wenn die Götter, du,
> Die Deinigen und Welt und Himmel all
> Sich all ein innig Ganzes fühlten ...

as his brother accuses him of being. His sense of magical oneness with Minerva, the wealth of mystical experience with which he has endowed his favourite creation, Pandora, and his interpretation of Pandora's intimations of love as a process of *Stirb und Werde*: all this is eloquent testimony of the fact that he knows surrender to what is not the self as he knows assertion of the self, and knows them to be the beats of one creative pulse. It is usually said that the Prometheus of the ode only knows the systole of life[15], the complementing diastole having found articulation in *Ganymed*. This is not entirely true. The *heilig* at the centre of the poem contains the counter movement *in nuce*, as it were: but here, in the fragment, this double rhythm has been incomparably more fully and explicitly developed.

We may then say that the Prometheus figure of Goethe's youth is shown as a 'Mittelfigur' between gods and men, the absolute and the finite. Open to the

---

[14] II, 8. For a detailed analysis of that passage cf. Chapter XII.
[15] Cf. E. Trunz (ed.) in *HA* I, p. 472.

absolute, stressfully but fruitfully related to the sphere of the gods, solitary by reason of being a creator rather than a rebel, and above all 'plastisch': rapturously turned towards the products of his creativity whom he feels to be magically at one with the power that engenders them, as he himself feels magically at one with Minerva, the animating goddess, and in no way troubled by a sense of incongruity between the creative vision and its finite products, his divine heritage and his earthly legacy. His attitude may be summed up in the words by which the aged Goethe complemented the aesthetic *credo* of Plotinus:

> 'Eine geistige Form wird aber keineswegs verkürzt, wenn sie in der Erscheinung hervortritt, vorausgesetzt daß ihr Hervortreten eine wahre Zeugung, eine wahre Fortpflanzung sei. Das Gezeugte ist nicht geringer als das Zeugende, ja es ist der Vorteil lebendiger Zeugung, daß das Gezeugte vortrefflicher sein kann als das Zeugende.'[16]

2.

In Riemer's diary for May 17, 1808 — a time when Goethe was working on his *Festspiel* — we find the following entry: 'Über Pandora: über Systole und Diastole des Weltgeistes. Jene gibt die Spezifikation, diese das Unendliche.'[17]

We have no trouble in recognising in the figure of the aged Prometheus the principle of 'Spezifikation' taken to extreme lengths. Before we elucidate this point in detail, it might be useful to refer to Goethe's main source for the handling of the Prometheus myth, Plato's early dialogue *Protagoras*. According to the sophist, Prometheus and his brother Epimetheus shared the task of equipping the newly created organic species of life, Epimetheus looking after the animals and running out of resources by the time he had reached the top of the ladder, man. Prometheus steps in and 'steals in his extremity the inventive skill of Hephaestus and Athene, together with fire; for without fire it could neither be acquired, nor used by any; and presented them to the human race.'[18] But as yet man lacked 'polity', that is, the art to assert himself against the other species and of living together peaceably. To cure this condition, Zeus, at a later date, furnished them with justice and shame which, unlike the earlier skills, were distributed impartially among them.

The Prometheus we meet in the *Festspiel* is above all the dispenser of fire and those rudimentary material skills that derive from its possession. The human race has not yet learnt to live together peaceably. This higher human art is as yet withheld from them. As the smiths and the shepherds depart from the scene, and shortly before Phileros appears in brutal pursuit of Epimeleia, he dismisses them, saying:

---

16 In: *Wilhelm Meisters Wanderjahre, Aus Makariens Archiv*, HA VIII, p. 464.
17 *AGA* 22, p. 496.
18 In: *The Phaedrus, Lysis and Protagoras of Plato*, trs. J. Wright (Golden Treasury Series), London 1929, p. 197. Cf. note 32.

> Entwandelt friedlich! Friede findend geht ihr nicht.
> Denn solches Los dem Menschen wie den Tieren ward,
> Nach deren Urbild ich mir Beßres bildete,
> Daß eins dem andern, einzeln oder auch geschart,
> Sich widersetzt, sich hassend aneinander drängt,
> Bis eins dem andern Übermacht betätigte.

As yet the *Menschenvater* has not been able to humanise his race, according to the *beßre Urbild* before his inner eye. And not only is his handiwork defective. His own primal act of creation, accomplished with Minerva's aid, seems to have receded into some all but forgotten past. References to it are sparse and vague. He has taken the fire and given it to man. This is the creative act the blacksmiths celebrate above all.

> Höchstes, er hat's getan,
> Der es geraubt.
> Wer es entzündete,
> Sich es verbündete,
> Schmiedete, ründete
> Kronen dem Haupt.

Has he taken that fire from his own once 'heilig glühend Herz'? And has that heart itself ceased to be creatively alive? Certainly

> Der Kreis, den meine Wirksamkeit erfüllt

has been drawn more narrowly. The bond with the gods has snapped. Respectful memories of Athene's skill replace that youthful and ecstatic sense of a magical oneness when her speech had seemed to be his and his hers[19], when he had accepted the life-breath of his creatures from her hand. He no longer expands to merge his self with the *Weltgeist*. And such contraction is reflected in the nature and material of what he now creates. He teaches his 'children' to produce, in vigorous activity,

> Werktätig, weisekräftig, ins Unendliche.

His heart is with them,

> Die ihr, hereinwärts auf den Amboß blickend, wirkt
> Und hartes Erz nach eurem Sinne zwingend formt ...

He calls his blacksmiths to work at crack of dawn, saying:

> So ruf' ich laut euch Erzgewält'ger nun hervor:
> Erhebt die starken Arme leicht, daß taktbewegt
> Ein kräftger Hämmerchortanz, laut erschallend, rasch
> Uns das Geschmolzne vielfach strecke zum Gebrauch.

He sees and feels and hears justice wrought in iron chains. To his son he says:

---

[19] For excellent observations on that point cf. S. Burckhardt, *loc. cit.*, p. 163.

> Wo Vaterwille sich Gewalt schuf, taugst du nicht.
> Hast jene Ketten nicht gesehn, die ehernen,
> Geschmiedet für des wilden Stieres Hörnerpaar,
> Mehr für den Ungebändigten des Männervolks?
> Die sollen dir die Glieder lasten, klirrend hin
> Und widerschlagen, deinem Gang Begleitungstakt.

Most striking of all, his vision of woman is a vision wrought in metal. To this old master craftsman it is inconceivable that Pandora's beauty should not have sprung from the hands of the fire- and metal-fashioning god:

> Gereihte Gaben Amphitritens trug der Hals.
> Dann vielgeblümten Kleides Feld, wie es wunderbar
> Mit frühlingsreichem bunten Schmuck die Brust umgab.

'Die Brust' is the cue Epimetheus eagerly takes up, recalling how she pressed him to this very breast. Prometheus, relentlessly dispassionate, continues to recollect her belt:

> Des Gürtels Kunst war über alles lobenswert ...;

at which erotically charged memory Epimetheus recalls undoing this belt in the act of love. But passion talks past passion:

> Dem Drachen, um den Arm geringelt, lernt' ich ab,
> Wie starr Metall im Schlangenkreise sich dehnt und schließt.

Epimetheus' recollection of Pandora's enveloping arms is forthwith shunted onto another track:

> Die Ringe schmückend verbreiterten die schmale Hand ...,

he recalls. His thought of the loving pressure of that hand is again sidetracked by the question:

> Und glich sie wohl Athenens Hand an Kunstgeschick?

It may have been a caressing hand as Epimetheus says it was; but above all it was skilful in the extreme:

> Athenens Webstuhl offenbart' ihr Oberkleid ...,

Prometheus muses; the wavelike and iridescent charm of her trailing hem is ignored; but he remembers observing that

> Der Saum verwirrte fesselnd auch den schärfsten Blick.

Pandora's foot, according to Epimetheus

> Beweglich wie die Hand erwidernd Liebesdruck ...,

moves his brother differently:

> Auch hier nicht müde schmückte nur der Künstler mehr;
> Biegsame Sohlen, goldne, schrittbefördernde ...,

he recalls, marvelling. Epimetheus'

> Beflügelte! sie rührte kaum den Boden an ...

is countered by Prometheus'

> Gegliedert schmückten goldne Riemen schleifenhaft.

Vis à vis this stichomythic exchange we have two options. Either we see it as confirming the general view that the figure of Epimetheus has far outgrown that of his brother who here meets the lover's passionate evocation of the 'Hochgestalt' with the obtuseness of a mechanic. Or we must take seriously the stichomythic form of their exchanges which for Goethe usually signifies a clash of equally valid if opposing modes of response to a given phenomenon[20]. In addition we must take seriously the fact that the operative word, 'die Hochgestalt', is placed on the lips of the boorish Prometheus. I think that we have no option but to take that figure seriously and to concede to him a passion of his own, which the poet would have us consider a match to Epimetheus' lyrical engrossment.

It is not enough to maintain that this Prometheus speaks the language of one who drives slaves to a pragmatic and unimagined end. He speaks the demonic language of one whose whole being has contracted into a single organ seized and saturated by the — inert — material to which he is bound in passionate affinity, which he shapes even as it has invaded his imagination, stamping it with its imprint. In his fiercely kinaesthetic grasp of things we still recognise the young poet who proclaimed, more than thirty years earlier: 'Dreingreiffen, packen ist das Wesen ieder meisterschafft ... und ich finde, daß ieder Künstler so lang seine Hände nicht plastisch arbeiten nichts ist'. This is still the Titan who had once asked Minerva:

> Sieh diese Stirn an!
> Hat mein Finger nicht
> Sie ausgeprägt?

Only now he has grown old and is concerned to hammer out what had been incandesced with vision in the first fire of youth. The hot passion of the primal vision has become the cold glow of an artisan addicted to the material in which this vision must take final shape[21].

The stichomythic exchanges between the brothers are exchanges between one moved — to use S. Alexander's terminology — by a material passion and another moved by a passion that is abstract and formal[22]. Prometheus'

---

[20] Cf. *Egmont* II, Egmonts Wohnung, *HA* IV, p. 406; *Iphigenie* I, 2, *HA* V, p. 9 and IV, 4, *ibid.* p. 52; and *Die Natürliche Tochter*, II, 5, *ibid.*, p. 246.

[21] R. Petsch convincingly writes that Prometheus 'ist ein Formästhetiker von größtem Zuschnitt.' In: 'Die Kunstform von Pandora', in: *Die Antike* (6), 1930, p. 31.

[22] In: *Beauty and other Forms of Value*, London 1933.

unrelenting objectivity, opposed as it is to his brother's lyrical transports, may blind us to the obsessive quality of his engrossment. This very objectivity and impersonality is the measure of the completeness of his engagement and of the length of the experience by which this engagement is nourished. He no longer wrestles with the gods, he no longer has to do with living creation. The creative fire is the fire that burns in his smithy. Within him, it has contracted to a pinpoint spark, and thus he shapes the materials in which he is now working with an ultimate concentration on the detailed hammering out of his vision, 'weisekräftig'. He thinks and feels and sees in metal[23]. Metal is what he has become. Those very slow-moving and heavy trimeters in which he speaks, speak with the voice and texture of ore.

And he is as untiring and as undaunted as his younger self. As untiring: neither in the early ode nor in the fragment is there a *soupçon* of this creator slackening in his work, giving himself a breathing space from his labours or indeed finding his productive impetus waning. Creating to him is as natural as breathing. 'Hier sitz' ich', the speaker of the ode proclaims; a formulation full of confidence and devoid of posturing; and the figure of the fragment moves amongst his statues as through a virgin forest promising infinite growth and proliferation. Is not this creative trust borne out in retrospect by the author of *Dichtung und Wahrheit* whose 'produktives Talent' — and we know the truth of this statement from many contemporaneous reports — '... verließ mich seit einigen Jahren keinen Augenblick'?

The aged Titan of the *Festspiel* no longer creates the miracle of life (even the young one needed Minerva for that): but nonetheless, in the intermediate sphere he now inhabits, divorced from the gods and working in inert matter, he and his 'children' labour on in a relentless rhythm broken not even by night but merely by the biological need to rest a while; and nowhere in the play is there any suggestion that he distrusts this rhythm of 'Kraft und Bruderkräfte', fearing that it may fail him.

And as undaunted. The miracle of life eludes the aged creator, and the 'heilig glühend Herz' has contracted to a cold spark. Where once his finger shaped Pandora's brow, 'geschwungne Hämmer' now beat out strips of molten ore into tongues and tools capable of fashioning *Gefertigtes*, *Seltnes*. But such an increasing 'Spezifikation' and differentiation to him does not spell a diminution of the forming impulse, let alone its fragmentation. True, he had intended to fashion 'Beßres' than he did. He has not realised the 'Urbild' of his primal vision. But that vision itself has contracted and been absorbed into his medium. This medium he incessantly explores, finding ever new techniques, producing ever new forms for the one form he had envisaged in the first fire of youth — Pandora. This ultimate vision the old Prometheus rejects, concentrating vehemently on what is realisable and

---

[23] As the sculptor and goldsmith Cellini is supposed to have dreamed in gold.

moving, 'weisekräftig', in a world of his own making and his own bounding. This identification with his matter, this masterful emancipation of forms at his command used, allegorically as it were, as repositories of his sovereign if scattered wisdom rather than as precious vessels wrought by immediate inspiration, this absorption in detail constitutes what we may call Prometheus' *Altersstil;* the style, say, of Goethe's own *Wanderjahre.*

Of course there is renunciation about this intermediary and derivative mode of productivity which, closed to the Numinous, has abjured the 'Urbild' of his youth and stubbornly works in the realm of inert matter. But this is Goethe's renunciation. It belongs to the ethos of this figure to give no utterance to this awareness and scarcely to allow it to cross the threshold of his consciousness. The infinite is banished like Pandora, the one form has been translated into the many forms with the loss that realisation entails, the boundless Phileros is sent to his death 'mit starrender Gesetzlichkeit'. Prometheus has opted for his domain, the temperate and sober domain of daytime, the 'Sternenglanz' and 'Schattentiefe' of night have become dreamless caesuras between one day's work and the next, and the only diastole the Titan acknowledges is the primitive 'Ruhmal' of sleep, a biological regeneration due equally to the 'mühsam finstergründig Strebenden' and to those who 'früh zur Mühe gehn'. *Mühe* is all. Prometheus rejects the transfiguring grace of the 'gottgewählte Stunde' which grants man direct and renewing contact with the absolute; and, more guarded than Faust, has long since turned his back on the 'Flammenübermaß' of the sun, mindful

> Daß nicht vor Helios' Pfeil erblinde mein Geschlecht,
> Bestimmt, Erleuchtetes zu sehen, nicht das Licht.

He has opted for mediacy and specification[24].

3.

As against this, Epimetheus errs as one blinded and seared by the sun, yet making straight for its irresistible 'Feuermeer'.

> Wer von der Schönen zu scheiden verdammt ist,
> Fliehe mit abegewendetem Blick!
> Wie er, sie schauend, im Tiefsten entflammt ist,
> Zieht sie, ach! reißt sie ihn ewig zurück.[25]

[24] U. Wilamowitz-Möllendorf writes: 'Mit Prometheus hat der stürmende Jüngling und der enttäuschte Mann ... jener in stolzem Selbstgefühl, dieser in bitteren Stunden sympathisiert, wo er es aufgeben wollte, "bewegtem Rauchgebilde nachzustürzen, zu erreichen das, was unerreichbar ist."' (In: 'Goethes Pandora' *Goethe-Jahrbuch XIX*, 1898, p. 6*.)

[25] 'Nicht in den Sonetten, hier [in: 'Wer von der Schönen zu scheiden verdammt ist'] singt Goethe seiner Liebe zu Minna Herzlieb den innigsten wahrsten Abschiedsgesang', writes P. Hankamer (*op. cit.*, p. 197). This is a most regrettable lapse from this critic's wonted level of sophistication; besides, it constitutes a fatal flaw in his argument as a whole.

Incessantly, he woos the primal vision that was once vouchsafed to him in
his youth. His whole life asks the question, Faust's question:

> Und sollt ich nicht, sehnsüchtigster Gewalt,
> Ins Leben ziehn die einzigste Gestalt?

Who is this *Gestalt* for whose return he lives and waits? One formulation
for many may give some impression of its power and of the annihilating
intensity with which he longs for what once, for a short while, he possessed,
or thought he did.

> Sie steiget hernieder in tausend Gebilden,
> Sie schwebet auf Wassern, sie schreitet auf Gefilden,
> Nach heiligen Maßen erglänzt sie und schallt,
> Und einzig veredelt die Form den Gehalt,
> Verleiht ihm, verleiht sich die höchste Gewalt.
> Mir erschien sie in Jugend-, in Frauengestalt.

It is Pandora, and it is not Pandora. It is the *Gestalt aller Gestalten* which to
him revealed itself in the shape of Pandora: 'Mir erschien sie in Jugend-, in
Frauengestalt.'[26]
The blinding intensity of a vision glimpsed and mourned takes us back to
Goethe's Italian Journey, just about twenty years earlier. More precisely, it
takes us back to the last three months of his second stay in Rome which we
have considered in the preceding chapter. During that *Epoche*, as he calls it,
between Christmas 1787 and Easter 1788, he had time and again written of
strange and ecstatic experiences, in strange and ecstatic images as yet overriding Prometheus' cautionary words with which we concluded the last
section and, by implication, those the Faust of *Anmutige Gegend* will speak as,
dazzled by the 'Flammenübermaß' of the rising sun, he resolves:

> So bleibe denn die Sonne mir im Rücken!

Having expatiated at length — and most interestingly — on the playfulness (in the most
serious sense of the word) of a drama which perceives 'das Spiel des Lebens, das Leben
als ein Schicksalsspiel, als Spiel der Mächte' (*op. cit.*, p. 174), he goes on to stress, in a
manner that is hardly short of the simplistic, its confessional, biographical elements of
which the figure of Epimetheus is the nucleus. 'Das spielnotwendige Gleichgewicht . . .
wird durch die Bekenntnisnot des Dichters gestört . . . (198f.); so blieb Pandora durch
den übermächtigen Einfluß des Erlebens ein Fragment' (p. 206). One would like to
answer critics like Hankamer and Wolff (who reduces the works he discusses to Goethe's
passion for Sylvie von Ziegesar) in the words of Wilamowitz-Möllendorf who writes, in
1898: 'er brauchte für seine typischen Gestalten nicht nach unbedeutenden Persönchen
zu greifen, die ihm gerade ein flüchtiger Moment nahebrachte.' (*Loc. cit.*, p. 6*, note.)
Which is not merely forthright, but good aesthetics.
[26] Petsch writes: 'Diese kühne Ausweitung des Begriffs und der Wirkung der Schönheit
ist keine Willkür in den Augen Goethes, der von sich selbst bekannt hat, daß er "das
Ideelle nur unter der Form des Weibes" denken könne.' (*Loc. cit.*, p. 24.) Wilamowitz-
Möllendorf, too, insists on the' symbolische Bedeutung sämtlicher Personen'. (*Loc. cit.*,
p. 6*.)

We saw in the preceding chapter what were the revelations that gave rise to these dangerously rapturous utterances and the mental frame from which they sprang. Gradually, during his stay in Italy, Goethe had come to feel that the laws governing nature were identical with those operative in the visual classical arts. We had seen that his own unremitting efforts in the field of the plastic arts had been motivated by the intense desire himself to bring forth a product which might itself embody the laws of nature, a creation such as would raise its creator to the power and pitch of *Natura Naturans* and endow him with her own permanence. This had been the lure held out to him by the plastic arts, and to part from his dream had brought him close to a kind of insanity. 'In jeder großen Trennung liegt ein Keim von Wahnsinn', he had written shortly before quitting his modelled foot, and Rome; 'man muß sich hüten, ihn nachdenklich auszubrüten und zu pflegen.'

Could the 'nachdenkliche' Epimetheus be mourning the loss, in Pandora, of a similarly searing dream? Or are we really forced to accept the lamentably naive and aesthetically crude solution that such suffering as incandesces these pages, or those of the *Wahlverwandtschaften*, the *Sonette* or, for that matter, *Die Natürliche Tochter*, is 'about' a personal encounter such as, say, with Sylvie von Ziegesar or, in the first three works, Minna Herzlieb?

Round about the turn of the century, Goethe had hatched the plan of writing a vast poem tracing the laws of organisation throughout the diverse realms of nature — Herder's *Ideen* had given him an impetus in this direction — and as late as 1810, at the time of composing *Pandora*, he had written to Sartorius in the same vein: 'Wenn ein paar große Formeln glücken, so muß das alles Eins werden' — strange *Steigerung* of the formulation he had found for his wish to synthesise the multifarious tendencies in himself, in his famous letter to Herder of July 1772! — 'alles aus Einem entspringen und zu Einem zurückkehren . . .'[27]. Certainly the idea of an encompassing nature-poem was fermenting in his head, and was associated with his *Festspiel*[28].

Let us return to Plato's *Protagoras* from which Goethe took much of the mythological material for his *Festspiel*. According to the sophist, both brothers, Prometheus and Epimetheus, were charged with fitting the newly created organic species for their earthly career. Epimetheus entreated his brother to leave the distribution of powers to him and he proceeded as follows:

'To some he assigned strength without speed; others, that were weaker, he equipped with speed. Some he furnished with weapons; while for those whom he had left weaponless, he devised some other endowment to save them. Animals, which he clad with puny

[27] July 19, 1810.

[28] This association becomes clear from the letter to Sartorius just quoted. The second paragraph following the passage I have quoted reads as follows: 'Ein kleines Heft von mir, unter dem Titel: Pandora, ein Taschenbuch, ist in Wien gedruckt worden. Eigentlich ist es der erste Teil eines wunderlichen Dramas. Mögen und können Sie sich hineinlesen, so werden Sie es nicht ganz umsonst getan haben.'

frames, were to find safety in the flight of their wings, or subterranean retreats; those which he invested with size, were by this very size to be preserved. And so throughout the whole of the distribution *he maintained the same equalising principle;** his object in all these contrivances being to prevent any species from becoming extinct. Having thus supplied them with means of escaping mutual destruction, he proceeded to arm them against the seasons, by clothing them with thick furs and strong hides, proof against winter-frost and summer-heat, and fitted also to serve each of them, when seeking rest, as his own proper and native bed: and under the feet he furnished some with hoofs, others with thick and bloodless skins. His next care was to provide them with different kinds of food: to one class he gave herbs of the field; to another, fruits of the trees; to a third, roots; while a fourth he destined to live by making other animals their prey. Such, however, he allowed to multiply but slowly, while their victims he *compensated** with fecundity, thus ensuring preservation to the species. For as much though',

Protagoras concludes his account, saying: 'as Epimetheus was not altogether wise, he unawares exhausted all the endowments at his command on the brute creation; so he still had left on his hands without provision the human family, and he knew not what to do.'[29]

This passage, which has not to my knowledge been noted in connection with the figure of Goethe's Epimetheus, at once opens up exciting perspectives into which to place him and, indeed, in which to view the play as a whole. For in it, Plato, through the mouth of Protagoras, is formulating nothing less than the basic law Goethe evolved in his thinking on nature, the law of compensation. Charged by Zeus with the distribution of powers, Epimetheus is here shown acting as the executor of organising nature who, through a constant process of metamorphosis and *Steigerung*, held in check by the law of compensation, produces the ascending forms on the ladder of creation with the self-same economy which characterises her household at large.

Example upon example could be cited to demonstrate the coincidence of Epimetheus' creative activity with that which Goethe, in his *Farbenlehre* no less than in his more narrowly morphological writings, ascribes to organising nature herself. I shall cite a few for many. In *Allgemeine Einleitung in die Vergleichende Anatomie* we read:

'Wenn wir die Teile [des Tieres] genau kennen und betrachten, so werden wir finden, daß die Mannigfaltigkeit der Gestalt daher entspringt, daß diesem oder jenem Teil ein Übergewicht über die andern zugestanden ist.

So sind, zum Beispiel, Hals und Extremitäten auf Kosten des Körpers bei der Giraffe begünstigt, dahingegen beim Maulwurf das Umgekehrte stattfindet.

Bei dieser Betrachtung tritt uns nun gleich das Gesetz entgegen: daß keinem Teil etwas zugelegt werden könne, ohne daß einem andern dagegen etwas abgezogen werde, und umgekehrt.

Hier sind die Schranken der tierischen Natur, in welchen sich die bildende Kraft auf die wunderbarste und beinahe auf die willkürlichste Weise zu bewegen scheint, ohne daß

---

* my italics
[29] *Ed. cit.*, p. 195 f., paragraphs 320—321.

sie im mindesten fähig wäre den Kreis zu durchbrechen oder ihn zu überspringen. Der Bildungstrieb ist hier in einem zwar beschränkten, aber doch wohleingerichteten Reiche zum Beherrscher gesetzt. Die Rubriken seines Etats, in welche sein Aufwand zu verteilen ist, sind ihm vorgeschrieben, was er auf jedes wenden will, steht ihm, bis auf einen gewissen Grad, frei. Will er der einen mehr zuwenden, so ist er nicht ganz gehindert, allein er ist genötigt an einer andern sogleich etwas fehlen zu lassen; und so kann die Natur sich niemals verschulden, oder wohl gar bankrutt werden. . . .

Wir denken uns also das abgeschlossene Tier als eine kleine Welt, die um ihrer selbst willen und durch sich selbst da ist. So ist auch jedes Geschöpf Zweck seiner selbst . . . Jenen allgemeinen Typus, den wir nun freilich erst konstruieren und in seinen Teilen erst erforschen wollen, werden wir im ganzen unveränderlich finden . . .

Nun aber müssen wir, indem wir bei und mit dem Beharrlichen beharren, auch zugleich mit und neben dem Veränderlichen unsere Ansichten zu verändern und mannigfaltige Beweglichkeit lernen, damit wir den Typus in aller seiner Versatilität zu verfolgen gewandt seien und uns dieser Proteus nirgendhin entschlüpfe.

Fragt man aber nach den Anlässen, wodurch eine mannigfaltige Bestimmbarkeit zum Vorschein komme, so antworten wir vorerst: das Tier wird durch Umstände zu Umständen gebildet . . . der Adler durch die Luft zur Luft, durch die Berghöhe zur Berghöhe.'[30]

The snake compensates for its pronounced and differentiated head by an undifferentiated body; the lizard's legs are developed at the expense of a contracted rump; whilst the long-legged frog and toad pay for their extremities by the stumpiness of their trunk.

This idea 'eines haushälterischen Gebens und Nehmens' in the budget of nature has found its poetic precipitate in the poem *Metamorphose der Tiere*, part — it is to be assumed — of that encompassing poem on the laws of organisation throughout the realms of animate and inanimate nature which Goethe meant to write during the decade preceding the composition of *Pandora*. Here again the idea of the inner purposiveness of organised forms, governed as that is by the interplay between 'Bildungstrieb' and environment, and that of the law of compensation as the principle regulating the workings of metamorphosis and *Steigerung* which Goethe shares with Plato's Epimetheus, are unequivocally expressed.

The passage I have quoted from the *Allgemeine Einleitung in die vergleichende Anatomie* was written in 1795. The dating of *Metamorphose der Tiere* is less certain. Staiger, in the wake of others, quotes 1806 as the year of its composition, whilst Gräf, Boucke and Trunz opt for an earlier date, between 1798 and 1799[31]. As we have seen, the idea of a nature poem on a large scale of which the extant poem would seem to have been intended as a part, was still in Goethe's mind as late as 1810, and connected with his *Festspiel*.

---

[30] *Erster Entwurf einer allgemeinen Einleitung in die Vergleichende Anatomie, ausgehend von der Osteologie. IV. Anwendung der allgemeinen Darstellung des Typus auf das Besondere. HA XIII,* pp. 175 ff. We might add the famous passage from *Entwurf einer Farbenlehre*, in which Goethe's general morphological principles are applied to the organ of perception, the eye, resulting in an identically structured statement: '. . . so bildet sich das Auge am Lichte fürs Licht . . .'. (*Einleitung, HA XIII, p. 323.*)

[31] Cf. *HA* I, note to p. 201, on p. 585.

In view of this evidence it seems inconceivable that Plato's presentation, in *Protagoras*, of Epimetheus as the executor of nature's supreme organising principle — the principle of metamorphosis regulated by the law of compensation — should not have arrested the poet's attention when he pondered the dialogue in connection with his own *Pandora*, or should have failed vitally to influence his own conception of that enigmatic figure[32].

Without denying that personal experiences, such as the encounter with Minna Herzlieb or Sylvie von Ziegesar, may have had their part in shaping the figure of the Titan, or indeed that he embodies features of the ageing and renouncing poet, I would then plead that the deepest resonances emanating from his blinding linguistic transports spring from another strain. In this suffering figure Goethe once again invoked, and relived, ranges of experience that had driven this poet-scientist to Italy in the first instance, dominated him there to the exclusion of almost all else and continued to reverberate in him from his return to the *Kimmerischen Norden* until he died. And the experience that is embodied in this tragic figure is the artist's impassioned quest to understand, palpably to perceive, and to produce according to, the formative laws of organising nature herself; that heroic *Abenteuer der Vernunft* he himself claims to have ventured upon, in *Anschauende Urteilskraft*. Plato's Epimetheus is the incarnation, in a mythological figure, of the law of metamorphosis; Goethe's Pandora is the embodiment of metamorphosing nature —

> In tausend Formen magst du dich verstecken —

whilst Goethe's Epimetheus is the eternal seeker after that fountainhead of all form, 'die innere Form, die alle Formen in sich begreift', that radiant and elusive power which,

> Immer wechselnd, fest sich haltend;
> Nah und fern und fern und nah;
> So gestaltend, umgestaltend —[33]

he yearns to draw into life, *sehnsüchtigster Gewalt*.

4.

I would suggest, then, that the Epimetheus of Goethe's *Festspiel* is yet another mutation of that 'belebte Fixidee', Prometheus. His is, as it were, Prometheus' third face, an older face than that of his brother as he has become, reflecting back some of the immediacy of the Titan as the young Goethe had envisaged him, and at the same time a younger face, mirroring problems and possibilities

---

[32] I cannot trace any specific reference by Goethe to *Protagoras*, either in the *Weimarer Ausgabe* or in specialist studies such as that by E. Grumach. This, however, does not detract from the likelihood of his having been acquainted with it. For, despite numerous informed and highly appreciative comments on Plato, allusions to individual dialogues are remarkably scant. Besides, in addition to his first hand reading, Goethe repeatedly used, from 1799 onwards, the summaries of the dialogues contained in Buhle's *Geschichte der Philosophie*.   [33] *Parabase*.

as yet unknown to the Father of men[34]: Epimetheus is his brother's first and last countenance.

The Prometheus of the *Festspiel* is no longer associated with the primal act of creation, as he was in the early ode and fragment. He appears, and is celebrated as, the helpmate of created man, through his theft of the divine fire. The erstwhile progenitor of Pandora, he has become her implacable enemy. 'In starrender Gesetzlichkeit', he has ensconced himself in an intermediate and derivative sphere of productivity, alienated from the gods and fashioning inert matter to consolidate the position of what is created, a living embodiment of an ever active *Spezifikationstrieb*.

His older incarnation, Epimetheus, has now taken over the role of Prometheus' youth. This 'Ur-Prometheus', as we may call him, has seen, understood and embraced Pandora; he has 'received' the vision of *Natura Naturans* and made it his own; even engendering with her two daughters, the seal of a union between what is in time and what is out of time, the finite and the infinite: Elpore and Epimeleia, those eminently human phenomena of hope for the future and care for what is past. And, at her hand, he has penetrated to the womb of being that lies beyond *Natura Naturata*,

Zum trüben Reich gestaltenmischender Möglichkeit —

an august encounter with primal chaos, too perplexing for a man to bear.

The classical Epimetheus, Plato's, had not had the power to sustain the formative task of nature entrusted to him by the gods. He had run out of resources with which to equip nature's most complex and vulnerable creation — man. A similar fate befalls Goethe's hero. He has not the strength to hold *Natura Naturans* in her most consummate and evanescent form: 'in Jugend-, in Frauengestalt'. He fails to hold that vision for three related reasons: because it eludes possession, because it is too bright and because it is too fugitive.

Pandora had held out to Epimetheus the disinterested contemplation of her 'geheimnisreicher Mitgift', the divine spectacle of nature's own 'formumformend Weben', in the airy shapes arising from her urn. 'Formung des Formlosen', mysterious yet 'gesetzlicher Gestaltenwechsel des Unbegrenzten': this is what she had revealed to him and, through it, herself. The common crowd had thronged towards the 'Luftgeburten', had tried to catch 'lieblich Götterbilder' in their hands[35]; and Epimetheus, nobler than they, yet possessive too, had said to her: 'Bleibe mein!'

---

[34] Cf. Wilamowitz-Möllendorf, *loc. cit.*, p. 6*, note 1. He writes: 'Epimetheus war er [Goethe] unmittelbar nach der Heimkehr aus Italien.'

[35] Petsch emphasises the symbolic nature of Pandora's gifts which the crowd would 'sich leibhaft aneignen'. (*Loc. cit.*, p. 24.) Altogether he surmises that the theme of the drama, had it been completed, would have been the discovery of the symbolic mode enabling the characters 'Vergangenes in ein Bild zu verwandeln' (p. 27). He speaks of 'die wundervolle Gabe, das Wirkliche symbolisch zu sehen ... ' (p. 28).

> Und eignete das gottgesandte Wonnebild
> Mit starken Armen meiner lieberfüllten Brust.

But how can any man bodily embrace a 'Bild', a principle of creative nature, let alone metamorphosing nature herself?

These words do not only signify the regression into possessiveness of one unable to sustain a symbolic mode of experiencing[36]. They pinpoint the overpowering brilliance of the vision that has laid hold of Epimetheus' mind; and its fleetingness. The vision to which Pandora's lover has exposed his naked eye is fleeting because no human eye can sustain such brightness for any length of time:

> Endlich nun doch tritt sie hervor,
> Steht mir so scharf gegen den Blick!
> Herrlich! So schafft Pinsel und Stahl! —
> Blinzen des Augs scheuchet sie fort! —

These words express but a fraction of the *unsäglichen Augenschmerz* the sight of beauty no less than of ugliness engenders in Goethe's figures; an optical and spiritual susceptibility of the most radical kind which they share with their creator. The very sharpness with which vision is etched on the retina hurts and blinds; incessantly and tormentingly, it waxes and wanes. We shall pursue this central motif in some later chapters[37].

But such unsteadiness of vision is not merely due to the almost pathological irritableness of the seeing eye. It is inherent in the nature of the objects the eye perceives. In the section *Die Absicht eingeleitet* of Goethe's morphology we read:

'Betrachten wir aber alle Gestalten, besonders die organischen, so finden wir, daß nirgend ein Bestehendes, nirgend ein Ruhendes, ein Abgeschlossenes vorkommt, sondern daß vielmehr alles in einer steten Bewegung schwanke ... Das Gebildete wird sogleich wieder umgebildet, und wir haben uns, wenn wir einigermaßen zum lebendigen Anschaun der Natur gelangen wollen, selbst so beweglich und bildsam zu erhalten, nach dem Beispiele mit dem sie uns vorgeht.'[38]

In relating these vital reflections to the figure of Epimetheus, we are on the point of delineating his third countenance. For the Prometheus of Goethe's youth and the brother of Epimetheus in the *Festspiel*, *Gestalten* do not *schwanken in einer steten Bewegung*. The young Prometheus had seized vigorously and confidently what presented itself to his eye and shaped it with untrembling hands.

> Hier sitz' ich, forme Menschen
> Nach meinem Bilde ...

---

[36] In this connection, cf. Kommerell, *Gedanken über Gedichte*, Frankfurt a. Main, 1943, p. 422 f. Also Staiger, *Goethe* II, p. 457.

[37] Cf. Chapters VIII and XIII.

[38] *HA* XIII, p. 55 f.

and:

> Hier alle meine Wünsche
> In plastischen Gestalten —:

these are entirely characteristic utterances of the Titan's youth. He perceives kinaesthetically and with monumental plasticity, and this is how he creates. And the Prometheus of the *Festspiel* has no time for Pandora and no patience for a race lusting after 'bewegtem Rauchgebilde'. He is busy beating out rigid shapes in the fire the smoky shapes of which are no more than waste-products. The knowledge that 'Die Gestalt ist ein Bewegliches, ein Werdendes, ein Vergehendes' has not been allowed to cross the threshold of Prometheus' consciousness.

But this post-Italian awareness of Goethe's is ingrained in the very fabric of Epimetheus' mind. The spiritual progeny of the morphologist Goethe and the morphologist Plato is tormented by the perpetual coming and going of the *Gestalt* he loves:

> Mühend versenkt ängstlich der Sinn
> Sich in die Nacht, suchet umsonst
> Nach der *Gestalt**. Ach! wie so klar
> Stand sie am Tag sonst vor dem Blick.
>
> *Schwankend** erscheint kaum noch das Bild;
> *Etwa nur so** schritt sie heran!
> Naht sie mir denn? Faßt sie mich wohl? —
> *Nebelgestalt schwebt sie vorbei,**
>
> Kehret zurück, herzlich ersehnt;
> Aber noch *schwankt's** immer und *wogt's,**
> Ähnlich zugleich andern und sich;
> Schärferem Blick *schwindet's** zuletzt.
>
> Endlich nun doch tritt sie hervor,
> Steht mir so scharf gegen dem Blick!
> Herrlich! So schafft Pinsel und Stahl! —
> Blinzen des Augs *scheuchet sie fort!**
>
> Ist ein Bemühn eitler? Gewiß
> Schmerzlicher keins, ängstlicher keins!
> Wie es auch streng Minos verfügt,
> *Schatten** ist nun ewiger Wert.
>
> Wieder versucht sei's, dich heran,
> Gattin, zu ziehn! Hasch' ich sie? Bleibt's
> Wieder, mein Glück? — *Bild nur und Schein!**
> *Flüchtig entschwebt's, fließt und zerinnt.**[39]

---

* my italics.

[39] The enjambment between line four of stanza two and line one of the stanza following is a powerful poetic tool to express the incessant coming and going of the *Gestalt* and the

The initiate into the mysteries of metamorphosing nature cannot grasp her image, because he himself is as labile as the *Gestalt* he would capture and has no means of mastering such inner flux. We recall the observation Riemer recorded in his diary: 'Über Pandora: über Systole und Diastole des Weltgeistes. Jene gibt die Spezifikation, diese das Unendliche.'[40] The Prometheus of Goethe's youth is systole and diastole of the cosmic spirit in one. He knows both, the artistic joy of specification and the religious ecstasy of merging with the infinite. The aged Prometheus of the *Festspiel* is all systole, all specification in the sphere of finitude. Prometheus-Epimetheus, the one with the third face, who has inherited his own creator's morphological legacy and Plato's, is pure diastole of the cosmic spirit, the infinity of metamorphosis incarnate. Like his creator in his youth, like Werther even, he calls for brush and chisel; and this Goethe was to do, desperately, on Italian soil. But this most musical of Goethe's major figures cannot fix his fleeting and floating vision and carve its iridescence in the permanence of marble[41]. He lacks the *Spezifikationstrieb* that will arrest the process of *Gestalten Umgestalten* and body forth the lasting form. The mutations evade him as he eludes himself, in uncontrollable flow and flux.

---

tension this sets up in the percipient's mind; a device which is enhanced in stanza six: first the enjambment linking and separating, at one and the same time, the crucial word *heran-ziehn* (a device mirroring the remarkable splitting up of the word *unerreich-bar* (l. 124f.) in one of Epimetheus' trimeters), finally the fraught questioning — again 'enacted' by means of an enjambment — of 'Bleibts' // Wieder, mein Glück?'

Such detailed observations help one choose between the positions adopted by Hankamer and Burckhardt on the one hand and by Petsch on the other. The first two stress the homogeneity of a poetic idiom which, for all its diversification, deliberately obtrudes its artificiality at all times. Hankamer speaks of 'das schwere, ganz unschmiegsame, brokatene Sprachkleid' (*op. cit.*, p. 162), an evocative formulation but clearly not apt in the instances I have cited; and Burckhardt, expressly under Hankamer's influence, extrapolating from the observation of the latter and arguing the 'Verselbständigung des Sprachkörpers' which intervenes between characters and readers 'als ein Trennendes' (*loc. cit.*, p. 164f.), arrives at the basic thesis that language, in *Pandora*, is a means of parodying, and renouncing, a classical ideal 'dessen Verwirklichung ihm [Goethe] zur Zeit der *Iphigenie* noch möglich schien.' (*Loc. cit.*, p. 169.) Whilst my own conclusion partially points in this direction, as will be seen, Burckhardt is in my opinion too rigid in his repudiation of Petsch's endeavour — and, to a lesser extent, of Wilamowitz-Möllendorf's — to show the differentiated use the poet makes of language and metre to characterise different figures and their mode of response. (Burckhardt, *loc. cit.*, notes 8 and 10.)

[40] Cf. note 17.

[41] Staiger, *Goethe II*, p. 461f. and *Die Zeit als Einbildungskraft des Dichters*, p. 114f.; also Petsch, *loc. cit.*, p. 24, and Kunz, ed. *HA* V, p. 526, all emphasise that the *gestaltenmischende* Epimetheus falls short of being an artist in that he lacks a definitive form drive. As against this, Hankamer regards him as an embodiment of his ageing poet-creator: 'So geht auch das Los des Dichtertums . . . auf Epimetheus über, wie sie der Betrachtende vor dem Täter, der Entsagende vor dem Erfüllten empfunden haben mochte . . .' (*op. cit.*, p. 198).

Jener Kranz, Pandorens Locken
Eingedrückt von Götterhänden,
Wie er ihre Stirn umschattet,
Ihrer Augen Glut gedämpfet,
Schwebt mir noch vor Seel' und Sinnen,
Schwebt, da sie sich längst entzogen,
Wie ein Sternbild über mir.

Doch er hält nicht mehr zusammen;
Er zerfließt, zerfällt und streuet
Über alle frischen Fluren
Reichlich seine Gaben aus.

(Schlummernd).

O wie gerne bänd' ich wieder
Diesen Kranz! wie gern verknüpft' ich,
Wär's zum Kranze, wär's zum Strauße,
Flora-Cypris, deine Gaben!

Doch mir bleiben Kranz und Sträuße
Nicht beisammen. Alles löst sich.
Einzeln schafft sich Blum' und Blume
Durch das Grüne Raum und Platz.
Pflückend geh' ich und verliere
Das Gepflückte. Schnell entschwindet's.
Rose, brech' ich deine Schöne,
Lilie, du bist schon dahin.

The fragmentation and dissolution of experience expressed in these lines is terrible and total. Goethe himself would seem to tell us so, in the distant retrospect of a late poem from the *Chinesisch-Deutsche Jahres- und Tageszeiten* where the motif of *Rose und Lilie* is once again taken up, in a significant modulation:

"Mich ängstigt das Verfängliche
Im widrigen Geschwätz,
Wo nichts verharret, alles flieht,
Wo schon verschwunden, was man sieht;
Und mich umfängt das bängliche,
Das graugestrickte Netz." —
Getrost! Das Unvergängliche,
Es ist das ewige Gesetz,
Wonach die Ros' und Lilie blüht.

In Epimetheus' vision things 'have already vanished as they are being glimpsed'. His thoughts and his lines hold together no more than the flowers that once formed a wreath. The lament at the transience of the rose is swallowed up, and terminates, in the disintegration of the lily. Thought overtakes thought and both outpace event[42]. The ultimate of *Wechsel* is accomplished here.

---

[42] Cf. Chapter XIII, sections 4 and 5.

Reflecting on the 'Um- und Umgestaltung' that is characteristic of the species of the rodents, an *unstetes Schwanken* which has given rise to a variability of forms that threaten to lose themselves in the monstrous, Goethe observes:

> 'Wer aber, der sich mit solchen Untersuchungen ernstlich abgab, hat nicht erfahren, daß eben dieses Schwanken von Form zu Unform, von Unform zu Form den redlichen Beschauer in eine Art von Wahnsinn versetzt? denn für uns beschränkte Geschöpfe möchte es fast besser sein, den Irrtum zu fixieren, als im Wahren zu schwanken.'[43]

It is this *Wahnsinn* that Epimetheus, initiate into the secret of metamorphosis, has to endure.

5.

The polarisation between Prometheus and Epimetheus, that *Doppelherme* of himself[44] as Goethe once called them, is complete. What does the poem express through this dichotomy? Ultimately, as I see it, it signifies the awareness that its creator had reached an artistic impasse. To explain this, we must once again go back to Goethe's Italian sojourn and its reverberations.

In Italy, Goethe had encountered nature as she was meant to be. Here, amidst the lush and healthy vegetation of the south, the idea of the *Urpflanze* had dawned on him. The hunch that a primal pattern metamorphosed through the various stages of one growing-process and through the variety of different organic species had come to fruition there. This insight entailed a revolution in his thinking on matters of art. To be true, art has to capture the fluid movement of a nature which is at all times in transition. To be able to do so, the artist, like the morphological student of nature, has to be in movement so as to catch her in movement. For: 'Das Gebildete wird sogleich wieder umgebildet, und wir haben uns, wenn wir einigermaßen zum lebendigen Anschaun der Natur gelangen wollen, selbst so beweglich und bildsam zu erhalten, nach dem Beispiele mit dem sie uns vorgeht.' On the other hand, the artist must master the flux which he perceives, to which — so the poem *Dauer im Wechsel* tells us — he must ruthlessly expose himself. He must select *the* pregnant moment in a continual passage of moments all of which are pregnant with dissolution and re-formation: and *the* pregnant moment is the one which carries within itself, and projects, a maximum of past and future.

> '... vollendete Kunst ... [macht] auf ihrem höchsten Gipfel keine Ansprüche auf lebendige, produktive und reproduktive Realität ..., sondern [ergreift] die Natur auf dem wichtigsten Punkte ihrer Erscheinung ..., [lernt] ihr selbst die Schönheit ihrer Proportionen ab ..., um sie ihr selbst wieder vorzuschreiben ... Die Kunst übernimmt nicht mit der Natur, in ihrer Breite und Tiefe, zu wetteifern ...; aber sie hat ihre eigne Tiefe,

---

[43] In: *Die Skelette der Nagetiere, abgebildet und verglichen von D'Alton, HA* XIII, p. 214.
[44] Letter to Zelter, June 26, 1811.

ihre eigne Gewalt; sie fixiert die höchsten Momente . . ., und so gibt der Künstler, dankbar gegen die Natur, die auch ihn hervorbrachte, ihr eine zweite Natur, aber eine gefühlte, eine gedachte, eine menschlich vollendete zurück.'[45]

To choose the pregnant moment is an act of the highest selectivity. It will inevitably gravitate towards the highest, the 'letzte Produkt der sich immer steigernden Natur', towards the 'schöne Mensch'[46]. Even this phenomenon nature succeeds in producing but rarely,

'weil ihren Ideen gar viele Bedingungen widerstreben, und selbst ihrer Allmacht ist es unmöglich, lange im Vollkommnen zu verweilen und dem hervorgebrachten Schönen eine Dauer zu geben. Denn genau genommen kann man sagen, es sei nur ein Augenblick, in welchem der schöne Mensch schön sei.'[47]

Precisely speaking, this is

'der Augenblick der Pubertät . . . Die Begattung und Fortpflanzung kostet dem Schmetterlinge das Leben, dem Menschen die Schönheit . . .'[48]

Art, then, is not nature. It cannot be nature because, where the latter organises living yet indifferent beings, the artist organises dead yet significant matter; where nature produces real structures, the artist creates the pure semblance of symbolic ones. Nature's eternal and monotonous fertility is the counterpoint of the pregnant moment singled out by art. So far the anti-naturalistic art-credo of Goethe's classicism is an organic development towards artistic maturity; and although this was helped along by the morphological insights which gained momentum in Italy, this development was bound to happen sooner or later in all conditions and under any sky[49].

But the unemotive and universal distinction between the realms of nature and art hardens into something of a dichotomy after the poet's return to the *Kimmerische Norden*. He was now faced, and faced for good, with a different nature in which any illusion of 'seeing' the *Urpflanze* or, for that matter, the *Urmensch*, was mercilessly and finally shattered. The *Einleitung in die Propyläen* speaks of the Italian venture in nostalgic tones and draws a harsh contrast between the southern dream and the northern reality. 'Werden nicht Denker, Gelehrte, Künstler angelockt, sich in ihren besten Stunden in jene Gegenden zu versetzen', Goethe asks:

[45] In: *Diderots Versuch über die Malerei, AGA* 13, p. 210.
[46] In: *Winckelmann. Schönheit. HA* XII, p. 102.
[47] *Ibid.*, p. 102f.
[48] In: *Diderots Versuch über die Malerei, AGA* 13, p. 216.
[49] For a very concise and informative statement of the classical Goethe's view of nature as *einer andren*, or *zweiten Natur* — a concept which both encompasses the basic continuity of the two spheres recognised early on, yet delimits them from one another — cf. K. R. Mandelkow, *ed. HA* Briefe 2 (1786—1805), note to letter 431, p. 486f. Mandelkow does not, however, take note of the fact that it is Goethe's specifically morphological insights which are responsible, in the first instance, for the anti-naturalistic stance of his classicistic high noon and the further developments beyond that position to the *Westöstliche Divan*.

'unter einem Volke, wenigstens in der Einbildungskraft zu wohnen, dem eine Vollkommenheit, die wir wünschen und nie erreichen, natürlich war, bey dem in einer Folge von
Zeit und Leben sich eine Bildung in schöner und steigender Reihe entwickelt, die bei
uns nur als Stückwerk vorübergehend erscheint?'[50]

And then, passing from nostalgia to sheer despair:

'Dem deutschen Künstler, so wie überhaupt jedem neuen und nordischen, ist es schwer,
ja beinahe unmöglich, von dem Formlosen zur Gestalt überzugehen und, wenn er auch
bis dahin durchgedrungen wäre, sich dabei zu erhalten.'[51]

And now come those harsh and uncompromising statements that usher
in the phase of Goethe's late classicism, such as the *cri de coeur*, in a letter to
Meyer: 'Die ewige Lüge von Verbindung der Natur und Kunst macht alle
Menschen irre . . .'[52] This position appears in a modifying context, but by no
means watered down, in the seminal statement we find in the *Einleitung in
die Propyläen*. There Goethe reaffirms his life-long conviction: 'Die vor-
nehmste Forderung, die an den Künstler gemacht wird, bleibt immer die:
daß er sich an die Natur halten, sie studieren, sie nachbilden, etwas, das ihren
Erscheinungen ähnlich ist, hervorbringen solle.' We note the *ähnlich* and
read on:

'Wie groß, ja wie ungeheuer diese Anforderung sei, wird nicht immer bedacht, und der
wahre Künstler selbst erfährt es nur bei fortschreitender Bildung. Die Natur ist von der
Kunst durch eine ungeheure Kluft getrennt, welche das Genie selbst, ohne äußere Hilfs-
mittel, zu überschreiten nicht vermag.
    Alles, was wir um uns her gewahr werden, ist nur roher Stoff; und wenn sich das schon
selten genug ereignet, daß ein Künstler durch Instinkt und Geschmack, durch Übung
und Versuche dahin gelangt, daß den Dingen ihre äußere schöne Seite abzugewinnen,
aus dem vorhandenen Guten das Beste auszuwählen und wenigstens einen gefälligen
Schein hervorzubringen lernt, so ist es, besonders in der neuern Zeit, noch viel seltner,
daß ein Künstler sowohl in die Tiefe der Gegenstände als in die Tiefe seines eignen
Gemüts zu dringen vermag, um in seinen Werken nicht bloß etwas leicht und oberfläch-
lich Wirkendes, sondern, wetteifernd mit der Natur, etwas Geistig-Organisches hervorzubringen und seinem Kunstwerk einen solchen Gehalt, eine solche Form zu geben,
wodurch es natürlich zugleich und übernatürlich erscheint.'[53]

The gulf between nature and art had indeed deepened. The old Italian
dream of the artist producing works of art that were in instinctive consonance
with nature and of necessity governed by her own formative laws had turned
to shambles. And not only because nature was now recognised to be in
constant movement, *gestaltend umgestaltend*. Nor merely because nature as
Goethe saw it on his return to the north was ugly and deformed[54]: but
because the artist in him found himself confronted by a fourfold and well-nigh

[50] *HA* XII, p. 38.
[51] *Ibid.*, p. 48.
[52] May 20[—22], 1796.
[53] *HA* XII, p. 42.
[54] Cf. *Einleitung in die Propyläen, HA* XII, p. 46, l. 14f.

impossible task: he had to discount the ugliness of the forms around him and, battling against a deterioration of his own inner vision, keep alive and perpetually reconstitute within himself the model of nature according to which he was going to work, and indeed regenerate his own model of himself as a creative force. With it, he had to be as fluid, as *beweglich*, as is nature herself, in order to catch her gliding forms, her *schwankende Gestalten*. And yet, that inner lability had to be controlled. In it, he had to discover the still pivot, the plasticity enabling him to grasp and form the pregnant moment from outer and inner flux. Fourthly and finally, he had to have the inner resilience to endure the creative troughs which were bound to beset him in the face of such a daunting task. How deep a creative exhaustion did in fact befall Goethe after his return from the Italian south, is readily apparent from a late utterance. *In Morphologie. Schicksal der Handschrift*, written in 1817, we read:

> Aus Italien dem Formreichen war ich in das gestaltlose Deutschland zurückgewiesen, heiteren Himmel mit einem düstern zu vertauschen; die Freunde, statt mich zu trösten und wieder an sich zu ziehen, brachten mich zur Verzweiflung. Mein Entzücken über entfernteste, kaum bekannte Gegenstände, mein Leiden, meine Klagen über das Verlorne schien sie zu beleidigen; ich vermißte jede Teilnahme, niemand verstand meine Sprache. In diesen peinlichen Zustand wußt' ich mich nicht zu finden, die Entbehrung war zu groß, an welche sich der äußere Sinn gewöhnen sollte, der Geist erwachte sonach, und suchte sich schadlos zu halten.'[55]

What a cleavage between ideal and reality, art and nature, what a tragic alienation from his environment and from his own artistic self do these words express!

Neither of the Titans of Goethe's *Festspiel* was able to rise to the manifold and daunting challenge with which the poet of 1807 saw himself confronted. Certainly not 'the doer', Prometheus. The massive monumentality of his speech is eloquent testimony of the fact that the robust assault on language born of a will to plasticity of form had gone stale on the poet. To be a nature in its own right, art must depart from the outward shapes of nature. It must be 'etwas Geistig-Organisches', 'eine gefühlte, gedachte, eine menschlich vollendete Natur', 'natürlich zugleich und übernatürlich'. That is to say, it must sensitively register, and master, the law of *Gestaltung Umgestaltung*

---

[55] *HA* XIII, p. 102. Cf. also the tormented words in *Schicksal der Druckschrift:* 'Zu meiner Art mich auszudrücken wollte sich niemand bequemen. Es ist die größte Qual, nicht verstanden zu werden, wenn man nach großer Bemühung und Anstrengung sich endlich selbst und die Sache zu verstehn glaubt; es treibt zum Wahnsinn, den Irrtum immer wiederholen zu hören, aus dem man sich mit Not gerettet hat, und peinlicher kann uns nichts begegnen, als wenn das, was uns mit unterrichteten, einsichtigen Männern verbinden sollte, Anlaß gibt einer nicht zu vermittelnden Trennung.' (*HA* XIII, p. 109f.) It is surprising, and sadly instructive, how frequently, and where, the mature Goethe uses the words *Wahnsinn* and *wahnsinnig;* nowhere more than in his morphological writings: an intensity that is reflected in the figure of Epimetheus.

that governs organic nature within and without, and capture the evanescent in even its most perdurable phenomena. Prometheus' poetic idiom lacks this fine fluidum of *das Übergängliche*. With literal faithfulness, it cleaves to a style once, in the long distant past, felt to be natural, and by that very literalness produces a parody of that style, marking it, and himself, as obsolete[56]. This stylistic parody in turn is but a symbol of the larger parody of nature grasped, and imitated, literally. The result is 'un-Nature', not 'übernatürlich' but 'außernatürlich': the 'starrende Gesetzlichkeit' of a classicism that is dead.

The Protean mutability of Epimetheus, that initiate into the mysteries of metamorphosis, came much closer to the sensibilities of the post-Italian poet-scientist; and even the self-same trimeter in his hands becomes a different thing altogether, not to speak of his utterances in the lyrical mode[57]. Who but the 'sehnsuchtsvolle Hungerleider' after the unattainable, the infinite, could loosen up this unyielding metre to the point of introducing an enjambment in the middle of a word, and *what* a word:

> Und irdisch ausgestreckten Händen unerreich-
> bar jene, steigend jetzt empor und jetzt gesenkt,
> Die Menge täuschten stets sie ...

This is the *Übergängliche* to a fault. But like his brother, albeit for different reasons, he too lacks the power to transmute nature into art, 'Vergangenes in ein Bild zu verwandeln'.

Even as the creative impetus of Plato's Epimetheus ran out of resources before the executor of organising nature could equip her highest product, man, even as Goethe's own Epimetheus has lost the formative principle incarnated in Pandora, so that 'gestaltenmischende' figure lacks the shaping impulse, and the medium, to translate the fugitive vision he has glimpsed into the symbolic truth of the perennial form. He has produced *real* children with Pandora; yet he has remained unable to seize the *aesthetically* pregnant moment and fashion it, unmindful of the fact that 'vollendete Kunst ... keine Ansprüche auf lebendige, produktive und reproduktive Realität macht, sondern die Natur auf dem würdigsten Punkte ihrer Erscheinung ergreift'[58]. Impassively, he endures a tragic sense of creative exhaustion and impotence, realising nothing because he cannot realise Pandora's *Hochgestalt*. His is the neoplatonic countervoice to Prometheus who hails a world of created forms regardless of the loss of vision such materialisation entails. 'Tote Werke' is

---

[56] This point is made by Burckhardt, but of the play in its entirety; a sweeping generalisation I am unable to accept. (*Loc. cit.*, p. 169.) Staiger, more convincingly, speaks of 'das Nebeneinander der Stile'. (In: *Goethe*, II, *op. cit.*, p. 474.) Wilamowitz-Möllendorf (*loc. cit.*, p. 3*), K. May, ed. *AGA* 6 (p. 1202) and Hankamer (*op. cit.*, p. 195) see the diction of *Pandora* as a phenomenon of transition caused by the fact that the poet 'mit dieser Phase seiner Entwicklung innerlich fertig war.' (Wilamowitz-Möllendorf.)

[57] Cf. note 39 and my observations on Burckhardt's findings.

[58] In: *Diderots Versuch über die Malerei*, *AGA* 13, p. 210.

what he creates; and what Proteus, in the *Klassische Walpurgisnacht*, says of those strange figures, the Telchinen, holds equally good of him and his crew:

> Das bildet, schmelzend, unverdrossen;
> Und haben sie's in Erz gegossen,
> Dann denken sie, es wäre was.[59]

Epimetheus spurns the solace of vigorously shaping the real, because every conceivable created thing, in whatever medium, represents a defection from the glory of the *Gestalt aller Gestalten*, the formative principle he has glimpsed and lost and disconsolately mourns. With Plotinus he might say:

> '... nicht die Gestalt, die in der Kunst ruhet, gelangt in den Stein, sondern dorten bleibt sie und es gehet indessen eine andere, geringere hervor, die nicht rein in sich selbst verharret, noch auch wie sie der Künstler wünschte, sondern insofern der Stoff der Kunst gehorchte.
>
> Wenn aber die Kunst dasjenige, was sie ist und besitzt, auch hervorbringt ..., so ist sie fürwahr diejenige, die mehr und wahrer eine größere und trefflichere Schönheit der Kunst besitzt, vollkommener als alles, was nach außen hervortritt.'[60]

In *Problem und Erwiderung* we read:

> 'Die Idee der Metamorphose ist eine höchst ehrwürdige, aber zugleich höchst gefährliche Gabe von oben. Sie führt ins Formlose ... Sie ist gleich der vis centrifuga und würde sich ins Unendliche verlieren, wäre ihr nicht ein Gegengewicht zugegeben: ich meine den Spezifikationstrieb, das zähe Beharrlichkeitsvermögen dessen, was einmal zur Wirklichkeit gekommen.'[61]

It is the tragedy of Goethe's intended *Festspiel* that those two great principles are dichotomously polarised in the two Titans. The systole of the *Weltgeist*, in Prometheus, has led to the contraction of an unleavened *Spezifikationstrieb* productive of arid forms; its diastole, in Epimetheus, recipient of that 'höchst ehrwürdige, aber zugleich höchst gefährliche Gabe von oben', has issued in a diffuse infinity devoid of form: a polarisation which has found its poetic precipitate in the exotic luxuriance of a language which is nonetheless artificial — 'außernatürlich' — in the extreme, to the point, at times, of being antiquarian and contrived; and intentionally so. Monumentality without animation, flux without form: these are the warring forces embodied in the two Titans; and neither principle, in its isolation, is empowered to produce that paradox of poetry, *Gestalt*, which, though *schwankend* and tremulous as nature's *Gestalten* must be, nevertheless rests pacified in the miracle of form.

We may call upon the poet to help us express this polarisation in yet another way. 'Grundeigenschaft der lebendigen Einheit', Goethe writes in *Maximen und Reflexionen*:

---

[59] *Faust II*, Act II, ll. 3806ff.
[60] In: *Wilhelm Meisters Wanderjahre, Aus Makariens Archiv, HA* VIII, p. 462f.
[61] In: *Probleme, HA* XIII, p. 35. Cf. also *AGA* 17, p. 176ff.

'sich zu trennen, sich zu vereinen, sich ins Allgemeine zu ergehen, im Besonderen zu verharren, sich zu verwandeln, sich zu spezifizieren und, wie das Lebendige unter tausend Bedingungen sich dartun mag, hervorzutreten und zu verschwinden, zu solideszieren und zu schmelzen, zu erstarren und zu fließen, sich auszudehnen und sich zusammenzuziehen.'[62]

The aptness of these epithets for the modes of being represented by the two Titans standing there, arid and opposed, requires no comment.

That 'lebendige Einheit' of which the poet speaks will be ushered in at the *gottgewählte Stunde* Eos proclaims when, seized by the might of Eros, Prometheus' son 'Phil-Eros'[63] takes the regenerative plunge into fertile flux, Epimetheus' daughter walks through chastening flames and the *Hochgestalt* of Pandora will once more materialise from the drifting mists. But in the reality of Goethe's poetic development this miracle had to await the *gottgewählte Stunde* of the *Westöstliche Divan*. It was there that the poet was to achieve a seamless and altogether ravishing blend of fluidity and form, empowering him to transcend the impasse of the aged Titans, and to let those reborn in fire and water sing:

> Mag der Grieche seinen Ton
> Zu Gestalten drücken,
> An der eignen Hände Sohn
> Steigern sein Entzücken.
>
> Aber uns ist wonnereich
> In den Euphrat greifen,
> Und im flüss'gen Element
> Hin und wider schweifen.
>
> Löscht' ich so der Seele Brand,
> Lied, es wird erschallen;
> Schöpft des Dichters reine Hand,
> Wasser wird sich ballen.[64]

---

[62] *HA* XII, p. 367, No. 21.

[63] Wilamowitz-Möllendorf draws attention to the significance of the name, which means 'der den Eros liebt'. (*Loc. cit.*, p. 8*.)

[64] *Lied und Gebilde, Buch des Sängers.*

IV Gegenständlichkeit

"Immer nach Hause."
Novalis

Transmigrations:
'Warum gabst du uns die tiefen Blicke ...'

Es schufen sich einst die Einsamen liebend,
Nur von Göttern gekannt, ihre geheimere Welt.
Hölderlin

I.

In a review of contemporary philosophical trends which had contributed to his own intellectual development, Goethe recalls how the appearance of Kant's *Critique of Pure Reason* revived the age-old controversy as to the part played by self and world in the complex encounter we call experience: 'wieviel' — so he himself has it — 'unser Selbst und wieviel die Außenwelt zu unserm geistigen Dasein beitrage.'[1] This question, he confesses with a simple 'naive realism' which is as breathtaking as it is delightful, had never seriously exercised him. 'Ich hatte beide niemals gesondert', he admits, 'und wenn ich nach meiner Weise über Gegenstände philosophierte, so tat ich es mit unbewußter Naivetät und glaubte wirklich, ich sähe meine Meinungen vor Augen.'[2]

These lines were written in 1820: that is, some half century after the unfinished spire of Straßburg Cathedral had revealed to him of its own free will the 'offenbare Geheimnis' of its intended design[3]; thirty years after he had wandered about the public gardens of Palermo, fully expecting to see the veritable 'Urpflanze' with his eyes[4]. And what he wrote in 1820 was in turn the precursor of a similar and even more momentous selfassessment, contained in the short essay written in 1823 and entitled *Bedeutende Fördernis durch ein einziges geistreiches Wort*[5].

Sparked off by the anthropologist Heinroth's observation that the poet's 'Denkvermögen *gegenständlich* sei'[6], a radiant Goethe, in the highest excitement, reviews the whole spectrum of his mental functioning in the light of this *aperçu*. Clearly it seemed to him that Heinroth had put his finger on the 'prägnanten Punkt'[7] from which could be seen to flow the specific character

---

[1] In: *Einwirkung der neueren Philosophie*, *HA* XIII, p. 26.
[2] *Ibid.*, p. 26f. Cf. Chapter VIII, section 9.
[3] *Dichtung und Wahrheit*, III, 11, p. 499. Cf. Chapter XIII.
[4] *Italienische Reise*, Palermo, Dienstag den 17. April 1787. *HA* XI, p. 266f.
[5] *HA* XIII, pp. 37ff.
[6] *HA* XIII, p. 37.
[7] *Ibid.*, p. 40.

of his sensibility in all its facets, his mode of responding as a poet no less than as a scientist or thinker. Goethe expatiates on Heinroth's remark in a manner closely reminiscent of the earlier 'ich hatte beide niemals gesondert', saying: 'daß mein Denken sich von den Gegenständen nicht sondere, daß die Elemente der Gegenstände, die Anschauungen in dasselbe eingehen und von ihm auf das innigste durchdrungen werden, daß mein Anschauen selbst ein Denken, mein Denken ein Anschauen sei'[8].

This assessment of his mode of experiencing quite consistently leads him on to the statement, a little later in the same essay: 'Der Mensch kennt nur sich selbst, insofern er die Welt kennt, die er nur in sich und sich nur in ihr gewahr wird. Jeder neue Gegenstand, wohl beschaut, schließt ein neues Organ in uns auf.'[9] The chiastic construction of the 'die er nur in sich und sich nur in ihr gewahr wird' and, within it, the bold telescoping of a binary statement demanding a connecting 'sowie' into a single one: all this, by its very style, proclaims the parity and, indeed, the extraordinarily intimate permeation of self and world[10] in a mode of experiencing in which both poles are still comprised in a primordial unity, as it were 'in einem lebendigen Ur-Ei'[11].

If this is true of his thinking, so, Goethe tells us, it is of his poetry-making. It is equally object-impregnated. 'Mir drückten sich' — so we read — 'gewisse große Motive, Legenden, uraltgeschichtlich Überliefertes so tief in den Sinn, daß ich sie vierzig bis funfzig Jahre lebendig und wirksam im Innern erhielt; mir schien der schönste Besitz, solche werte Bilder oft in der Einbildungskraft erneut zu sehen, da sie sich denn zwar immer umgestalteten, doch ohne sich zu verändern einer reineren Form, einer entschiednern Darstellung ent-gegenreiften.'[12] Here again the style tells its own story. 'Mir drückten sich . . .': he, the poet, is at the receiving end of the creative process, just as he is the grammatical object of the sentence. It is the objects themselves which are the active agents in this encounter, imprinting themselves on his mind of their own accord, there to form and re-form and finally to ripen to maturity[13].

---

[8] *Ibid.*, p. 37.

[9] *Ibid.*, p. 38.

[10] It is interesting to note that the outer 'limb' of the chiasmus, i. e. the 'die' and 'ihr', refers to the world; eloquent testimony of the fact that Goethe experiences the self as being safely cradled in its embracing presence. For a similar awareness similarly expressed through the order of words, cf. the last line of *Ein Gleiches* (*Wandrers Nachtlied II*) and *HA* I, p. 533 f., note to p. 142 *Ein Gleiches*.

[11] *Ballade, Betrachtung und Auslegung, HA* I, p. 400.

[12] *HA* XIII, p. 38. Cf. Chapters VIII and XIII.

[13] This autonomy is variously stressed: firstly by the use of verbs in their reflexive form, e. g. 'drückten sich', 'sich umgestalteten', etc.; secondly by the prevalence of organic imagery, e. g. 'lebendig und wirksam', 'entgegenreiften', 'Kern', 'Frucht', 'hervorbringt' etc. For a systematic analysis of Goethe's model of experiencing cf. Chapter XIII.

His leaning towards occasional poetry, too, seems to spring naturally from the same object-impregnated mode of experiencing. 'Aus Obigem', Goethe writes, 'erklärt sich auch meine Neigung zu Gelegenheitsgedichten, wozu jedes Besondere irgendeines Zustandes mich unwiderstehlich aufregte. Und so bemerkt man denn auch an meinen Liedern, daß jedem etwas Eigenes zum Grunde liegt, daß ein gewisser Kern einer mehr oder weniger bedeutenden Frucht einwohne . . .'[14]

With the word 'Gelegenheitsgedicht' we have arrived at the subject of this chapter, the letter-poem 'Warum gabst du uns die tiefen Blicke . . .' which the twenty-six year old Goethe sent to Charlotte von Stein on April 14, 1776. It need hardly be stressed that the majority of critics have not regarded this long and weighty poem as a 'Gelegenheitsgedicht' in the loose and depreciative sense in which the word serves as a label for many of Goethe's products, with all the implications it carries of improvisation occasioned by an extraneous and perhaps trifling event. On the contrary, the sustained magnificence and delicate discipline of a communication intended to be no more than a letter[15], even in an age when letter-writing was still regarded as an art[16], have remained a source of unceasing wonder. Yet a 'Gelegenheitsgedicht' it is, in the quite precise sense which the poet himself was to give to the word so many years later; and it is this aspect of it that I wish to single out for comment.

A 'Gelegenheitsgedicht': that is to say, a poem into which the 'Besondere irgendeines Zustandes', its 'Eigenes', its 'Kern' has entered. Here it is the unique quality of the poet's relation with Frau von Stein which has 'wandered over' into his poem and imprinted itself upon it. And indeed, how receptive the poet appears in it! receptive *vis-à-vis* a fate which has 'given' them their knowledge of one another and holds 'prepared' for them things scarcely guessed at; and receptive, above all, towards the woman he loves. The younger of the two, he appears as a learner, a pupil going through his discipleship in a school of feeling which, significantly, is envisaged as a schooling of perception; we shall have more to say about that in subsequent chapters[17]. 'Kanntest', 'spähtest', 'konntest', 'tropftest', 'richtetest', 'hieltest', vergaukeltest': every time it is she, the loved one, who is the active agent in the process of education, as, indeed, it is she who is the grammatical subject of each sentence. Goethe speaks of

jenen Wonnestunden,
Da er dankbar dir zu Füßen lag.

---

[14] *HA* XIII, p. 39.

[15] Goethe kept no copy of the poem for his own use against possible publication.

[16] Cf. Max Kommerell, *Gedanken über Gedichte, op. cit.*, p. 143 f.

[17] Cf. Chapters VIII, IX, X, XIII. For the relation between the poet-lover and the woman he loves cf. Chapter II, section 2.

In more ways than one he — the creative one with his infinite potential for giving — is at her feet, imbibing, learning and receiving himself back from Charlotte's hands.

He receives himself back from her, it is true. But it has become a different self, transformed and enhanced through the experience of loving and being loved: a self that has learnt to say 'we'. The convincing ease with which Goethe, in this poem, speaks of 'us' instead of 'me' and 'you' has often been remarked upon[18]. It eloquently testifies to the depth of the communion between the lovers, to the total and unselfconscious intimacy that exists between them. This is moving. Equally moving is the appellation '... uns armen liebevollen beiden' which introduces some of the most crucial lines of the poem, the lament at what seems to be the crowning glory of their union: their total knowledge of one another. Equally moving or perhaps even more so, not only because these words signify the completest mutual identification, but because of their quality of compassion. Compassion — 'Mit-Leid' — is suffering at one remove. It implies consciousness and distance[19]. And here it implies distance — the most tender distance, it is true, but distance none the less — of the speaker from himself, perceiving himself anew as part of a relationship which has transformed him. The poet here stands in a most complex relation to himself, one we tend to associate with the structure of consciousness evinced by the artist and, perhaps, by the actor in particular: he is creator, part of the thing created — a relationship which he has entered and which has entered him and utterly transformed him — and he is onlooker, all in one[20]. There is compassion for himself as well as her, and for the third thing — the relation — which has emerged from under their hands by virtue of their unremitting discipline and effort and the bliss and burden of their consciousness. He perceives his self, which is deeply implicated in this relationship, as though it were separate from him. His very subjectivity, permeated through and through by the object of his love and transformed by such an imprint, has itself become an object of his conscious contemplation.

---

[18] By J. Boyd in *Notes to Goethe's Poems*, Oxford 1944, Vol. I, 1749—1786, p. 114 and S. Prawer in *German Lyric Poetry*, London 1952, p. 69. In fact there is hardly an instance in the poem, outside the central stanza, of pronouns referring to the two lovers in the nominative case. 'Du' and 'wir' are all but absent, 'ich' is completely so. As in Goethe's account of his creativity in *Bedeutende Fördernis durch ein einziges geistreiches Wort*, so here, in the delineation of the lovers *vis a vis* the world: their receptivity is conveyed through the use of the dative and accusative cases.

[19] For a discussion of compassion as a characteristically aesthetic emotion, cf. my *Schiller's Drama. Talent and Integrity*, London and New York, 1974, Chapter 9, section III, p. 214f., Chapter 12, section VIII, pp. 321ff. For a contrary view, cf. E. Staiger, *Friedrich Schiller*, Zurich 1967, p. 288f.

[20] Cf. E. Bullough, 'The Modern Conception of Aesthetics', in: *Bullough, Aesthetics*, ed. E. M. Wilkinson, London 1957, p. 66f.. Cf. also Chapter IV, section 6 of this book.

This strange process finds its consummation in the central stanzas of the poem in which the poet recalls a long-past existence shared with his beloved. These stanzas, the inner heart of the poem, towards the end of which the speaker altogether ceases to refer to himself in the first person and re-emerges as a 'him', call for our close attention, both for the recollection they embody and for the mode in which this recollection is apprehended.

It is in the last few lines of Stanza III that the change-over from the 'us' of the preceding stanzas to 'you' and 'mine' begins to take place. It may be significant to note that the speaker does not in fact refer to himself in the nominative case of the first person, as an 'I'. Perhaps he is not yet quite a person? At the present he, who is so difficult of access, is being penetrated by the steady and observant gaze of his beloved in her concentrated effort to understand him:

> *Kanntest* jeden Zug in meinem Wesen,
> *Spähtest*, wie die reinste Nerve klingt,
> Konntest mich mit *einem* Blicke lesen,
> Den so schwer ein sterblich *Aug' durchdringt*.*

With rapt attention she scans him and culls her image of him from what she thus discerns. This image she gives back to him, infiltrating it into his very blood, ordering his chaos and resuscitating him. 'He' meanwhile has gone quite underground[21]. He has certainly ceased to be a 'we', ceased even to be an 'I', and momentarily seems no more than a collection of unrelated, unintegrated and warring parts: 'Zug', 'Nerve', 'heißes Blut', 'wilder irrer Lauf', 'zerstörte Brust'.

Yet a process of growing has been going on all the time. It has started at the line 'Den so schwer ein sterblich Aug' durchdringt'. Admittedly, these words express, precisely, a deep unrelatedness. At the same time, they mark a turning-point. As the accusative form of the relative pronoun tells us, the speaker is now beginning to see himself from the outside, as an object that is opaque to his own vision. He has in fact begun to receive her image of him and to see himself through her eyes. The moment this process is completed, he re-emerges, objectified and healed, as it were, in the third person[22].

> Hieltest zauberleicht ihn angebunden
> Und vergaukeltest ihm manchen Tag.
> Welche Seligkeit glich jenen Wonnestunden,
> Da er dankbar dir zu Füßen lag,

---

[21] This assimilation of the lover-speaker's personality by and in that of the beloved has its precise counterpoint in the letter-poems of the cycle of sonnets composed 1807/1808, where the person of the beloved acts as a reflecting surface, itself blank, to the person she is addressing. Cf. Chapter II, section 3.

[22] For a differing point of view, cf. S. Prawer (*op. cit.*, p. 70), who sees in this change-over to the third person a sign of disintegration.

* my italics.

Fühlt' sein Herz an deinem Herzen schwellen,
Fühlte sich in deinem Auge gut,
Alle seine Sinnen sich erhellen
Und beruhigen sein brausend Blut.

These lines tells us clearly enough that only by receiving his self from her has he become a true person with an abiding identity, an apperceiving self and at the same time a worthy one. It is here as it was in *Ganymed* and as it will be in *Bedeutende Fördernis durch ein einziges geistreiches Wort*: knowledge or experience of self involves, perhaps even presupposes, knowledge or experience of what is not self. Individuality presupposes relatedness. Only as we learn to say 'we' do we learn to say 'I'. The marvellous 'Fühlte sich in deinem Auge gut' already foreshadows Hatem's extravagant gratitude to Suleika:

Wie sie sich an mich verschwendet,
Bin ich mir ein wertes Ich . . .[23]

We must still note a strange correspondence between the matter of this central stanza and its manner. For as it describes the clarification of the speaker's senses, it is also the most purely sensuous portion of the whole poem. All reflection has ceased. The speaker sees himself, and the relationship of which he is part, as though he were watching others acting out their lives. He perceives a pure scene or picture, illuminated throughout and casting no shadow. As Kommerell has it: 'Der Dichter liest im Liebesleben der Gewesenen wie in den aufgeschlagenen Büchern eines Romans, liest Ähnliches wie das, was hier geschieht.'[24] This presupposes a state of distance. But it is one in which his subjectivity is not, indeed, denied, but illuminated and objectified[25].

Indeed, we may go further and say that, if the recollection of a past transmigration is the inner heart of the poem, it is also the secret of its mode of perception. As in a transmigration, the relationship — Charlotte's creation and his — has 'wandered over' to him, entered him and imprinted its character, its 'Besonderes', upon him in all its purity. 'Rein genau' describes the nature of the pedagogic relationship which is at the centre of the poet's recollection. But 'rein genau' no less accurately describes the quality of the speaker's apprehension of this pedagogic relationship. He perceives 'rein genau'; that is to say, he perceives the whole emotional complex of which he himself forms part, as an objective event outside him. Seized by his 'exakte sinnliche Phantasie', which Goethe knew to be at the base of all his psychic functions[26], the relationship in its entirety stands clear of him and moves

---

[23] *Westöstlicher Divan, Buch Suleika.*
[24] In: *Gedanken über Gedichte, op. cit.,* p. 147.
[25] For a diametrically opposed reading, cf. Hugo Kuhn, 'Warum gabst du uns die tiefen Blicke . . .' (in: *Dichtung und Volkstum,* 41. Band, 1941, pp. 406ff.).
[26] Cf. Goethe's *Ernst Stiedenroth, Psychologie zur Erklärung der Seelenerscheinungen, HA* XIII, p. 42. Cf. also Schiller's letter to Goethe dated August 31, 1794.

before his eyes and our own, as it were of its own accord. So autonomous does this imagined life seem to be that one cannot but recall in this context a description of his imaginative powers that the poet was to write much later in his life: 'Ich hatte die Gabe', Goethe tells us in *Das Sehen in subjektiver Hinsicht*,

> 'wenn ich die Augen schloß und mit niedergesenktem Haupte mir in der Mitte des Seh-organs eine Blume dachte, so verharrte sie nicht einen Augenblick in ihrer ersten Gestalt, sondern sie legte sich auseinander und aus ihrem Innern entfalteten sich wieder neue Blumen ... regelmäßig wie die Rosetten der Bildhauer. Es war unmöglich, die hervor-quellende Schöpfung zu fixieren, hingegen dauerte sie so lange, als mir beliebte, ermattete nicht und verstärkte sich nicht ... '

A little later he adds:

> 'Hier darf nun unmittelbar die höhere Betrachtung aller bildenden Kunst eintreten; man sieht deutlicher ein, was es heißen wolle, daß Dichter und alle eigentliche Künstler geboren sein müssen. Es muß nämlich ihre innere produktive Kraft jene Nachbilder, die im Organ, in der Erinnerung, in der Einbildungskraft zurückgebliebenen Idole freiwillig ohne Vorsatz und Wollen lebendig hervortun, sie müssen sich entfalten, wachsen, sich ausdehnen und zusammenziehn, um aus flüchtigen Schemen wahrhaft gegenständliche Wesen zu werden.'[27]

The recollection, in the poem, of a past life shared with his beloved has much of this trance-like clarity and independence from himself which time and again Goethe stresses as being the crux of his poetic imagination[28].

A past life? Some critics have read these central stanzas as confirmation of Goethe's belief in some actual pre-existence shared with Charlotte[29]. Others argue that he is expressing therein the effect the relationship is having on him in a present 'transferred to an imagined past'[30]. Others yet take the myth of metempsychosis to be a symbol of the abiding validity Goethe felt the relation with Frau von Stein to possess, outward appearances notwithstanding[31]. To take the first line of argument is, despite Goethe's letter to Wieland[32], to adopt a rather hazardous position. Besides, Goethe is deliberately ambiguous in placing this second time-dimension now into the past and now into the future. The second view is too simple in that it fails to account for the clear distinction the poem itself draws between the everyday present and the re-collected event embedded in it. Closer to the truth comes the third view which regards the central section of the poem as evoking the quintessential present within the empirical now, the 'real' as it is perceived through the

---

[27] *AGA* 16, p. 902f.

[28] Cf. p. 172. of this chapter; also Goethe to Eckermann, May 6, 1827 and March 14, 1830. Cf. Chapter XIII, section 1.

[29] This would seem to be indicated by Barker Fairley who charges Goethe with creating an illusory and escapist dreamworld. There is no hint, in Fairley's observations, that the poet himself has any distance from the illusion he is creating. (*Op. cit.*, p. 34f.)

[30] S. Prawer, *op. cit.*, p. 70f.

[31] M. Kommerell, *op. cit.*, p. 147 and E. Staiger, *Goethe* I, p. 314.

[32] April 10, 1776.

veil of the actual. As Staiger has it: 'Was war und was sein wird, ist Frau von Stein, älteste, jüngste und künftige Wahrheit.'[33]

I would go even further and suggest that the quintessential present which is perceived embedded in the ordinary time-stream is the present apprehended aesthetically. Goethe here intuitively operates with a knowledge which Schiller and, after him, Wordsworth, were to articulate discursively: that the mode of 'Erinnerung' is itself 'fernend'[34] and that in turn we perceive as 'recollected' what we perceive in tranquillity. Through the permeation of his self with an object the speaker has achieved psychical distance. This distance *demands* its appropriate expression in terms of temporal and spatial distance, and achieves this expression in the myth of pre-existence. The distance of recollection is no more than a function of the initial quality of an extraordinarily pure aesthetic experience.

The same Goethe is speaking here who, nearly twelve years later, on Italian soil, will thus speak of his encounter with the art of classical antiquity: 'Mir ward bei diesem Umgang das Gefühl, der Begriff, die Anschauung dessen, was man im höchsten Sinne die Gegenwart des klassischen Bodens nennen dürfte. Ich nenne dies die sinnlich geistige Überzeugung, daß hier das Große war, ist und sein wird.'[35] And indeed, it is the same man who, much later in his life, was to declare apodictically: 'Das meiste Neuere ist nicht romantisch, weil es neu, sondern weil es schwach, kränklich und krank ist, und das Alte ist nicht klassisch, weil es alt, sondern weil es stark, frisch, froh und gesund ist'[36]. The distant time-dimension in which the poem, too, culminates and which in these two passages is termed 'classical', does not determine the quality of experiencing of which the poet speaks: it is its result.

2.

Indeed, it might be wise to take our cue from these passages and return, not to the Orient, but to the classical age of Plato's Greece in order to explain the mythological overtones in a poem so closely concerned with the nature of perception and the role in it of self and world. For does not Plato, too, in the *Phaedrus,* resort to the myth of the transmigration of souls to symbolise their progressive perception of the truth[37]? And does not the central situation of

[33] *Op. cit.,* p. 314.
[34] In: *Bürgers Gedichte a) Rezension.* Schiller writes: 'Aus der sanftern und fernenden Erinnerung mag er dichten, und dann desto besser für ihn, je mehr er an sich erfahren hat, was er besingt ...'. Schiller is here prefiguring the aesthetic paradox E. Bullough was to term 'the antimony of distance'. (*Ed. cit.,* pp. 98 ff.)
[35] *Italienische Reise* III, 1787, *Bericht* for December.
[36] To Eckermann, April 2, 1829.
[37] *Ed. cit.,* pp. 42 ff. That Goethe had read Plato is patently clear from his letters of 1771 to 1772, especially to Herder. No doubt he drew upon this knowledge or indeed renewed it

Goethe's poem recall both, the culminating section of the *Symposium* and the crucial epistemological myth at the beginning of the Seventh Book of the *Republic*? In the *Symposium* as here it is an older woman — Diotima — who initiates her disciple — Socrates — into the mysteries of love and, with it, into the perception of the true nature of things[38]. Charlotte von Stein, in this poem, is the Diotima to Goethe's Socrates. And the perception her pupil gains is of the essence of relatedness, the Platonic Idea of Love which, in Plato's universe of discourse as well as in that of the pre-Italian Weimar Goethe, inevitably means the Idea of Platonic Love.

But such a clear perception of a relationship which was cluttered with external complications and in which, moreover, his own subjectivity was deeply and painfully involved, could not indefinitely be sustained. The absolute transport of the illuminated moment — so movingly evoked by the 'leicht angebunden', the 'vergaukeltest' and the 'Seligkeit' of the 'Wonne-stunden' spent gratefully at his Diotima's feet — by its very brilliance tempo-rarily conceals the strain of such illumination, and its ineluctible eclipse[39]. This strain, and this eclipse, the poet has articulated in the framing stanzas: in the persistent questionings of the first, through the vivid evocation, in the second, of that condition of inner blindness which is the lot of most mortals at most times, and then again in the last stanza which takes up this same theme on a different plane, now explicitly relating it to the lovers themselves who find themselves banished into a painful twilight existence.

To understand this apparently regressive movement of the poem, a glance at the cave-myth which is expounded at the outset of Book VII of Plato's *Republic*, may be helpful. Here Socrates likens the condition of ordinary men to that of prisoners chained fast in a cave, their faces fixedly turned to the wall and a source of light well behind them. The only realities such men perceive are the shadows cast onto the wall they are facing by the figures or objects passing behind them. Every movement they see and every sound they hear is inevitably referred to the shadows in front of them. When once in a while such a prisoner escapes and turns about, directly facing the light, 'would not his eyes, think you, be distressed, and would he not shrink and turn away to the things which he could see distinctly, and consider them really clearer than the things pointed out to him'[40]? In this question, Socrates expresses precisely that quality of perplexed ambivalence which informs stanzas I and II. The lovers perceive more than others, but they envy those

---

when he came to write his *Tasso* in which Platonic ideas have a central place. In this connection, cf. J. Kunz, *ed. HA* V, p. 447 f. and p. 453, note to p. 222. Cf. also my *Goethe and Lessing, op. cit.*, Chapter V, section 2 and Chapter VIII, section 1. It may be assumed that during the years between 1771 and 1780 Plato was a living possession for Goethe.

[38] *The Symposium*, Penguin Classics, Harmondsworth 1951, pp. 79 ff.
[39] For a detailed discussion of perceptual patterns, cf. Chapters VIII and XIII.
[40] *The Republic* (Golden Treasury Series) London 1935, p. 236.

others their shadow world, their 'Traumglück' and even their 'Traumgefahr', coveting their very blindness. In the central stanzas of the poem Goethe arrives at a clear and unclouded perception of the essence of relatedness, recollected 'rein genau', 'aus der ... fernenden Erinnerung'; the last stanza tells us — as do *Pandora* and *Wilhelm Meister* — the price that must be paid for such a dazzling illumination. To elucidate these lines, I suggest turning to Plato once again. 'And now consider', Socrates asks, 'what would happen if such a man were to descend again and seat himself on his old seat? Coming so suddenly out of the sun, would he not find his eyes blinded with the gloom of the place?'[41] And, again: 'Do you think it a marvellous thing, that a person, who has just quitted the contemplation of divine objects for the study of human infirmities, should betray awkwardness ... when, with his eyes still dazed, and before he has become sufficiently habituated to the darkness that reigns around, he finds himself compelled to contend ... about the shadows of justice, or images which throw the shadows, and to enter the lists in questions involving the arbitrary suppositions entertained by those who have never yet had a glimpse of the essential features of justice?'[42] This state of pained unease is the very condition of the lovers as the perception of their relation in all its luminousness becomes clouded by inner and outer impediments to their understanding:

> Und von allem dem schwebt ein Erinnern
> Nur noch um das ungewisse Herz,
> Fühlt die alte Wahrheit ewig gleich im Innern,
> Und der neue Zustand wird ihm Schmerz.
> Und wir scheinen uns nur halb beseelet,
> Dämmernd i um uns der hells e Tag.

The crucial difference between the final and the initial stages of the lovers' quest for perception could not be more accurately summed up than in the words of Socrates: '... for a sensible man will recollect that the eyes may be confused in two distinct ways and from two distinct causes, — that is to say, by sudden transitions either from light to darkness or from darkness to light.'[43]

The prevalence, in this poem, of images relating to perception, and especially to visual perception, has rightly been noted[44]. How could it be otherwise in a poem that is so centrally concerned with perception, with the illumination of the senses? And indeed, how could it be otherwise with a poet so eminently an *Augenmensch*, to whom — I shall demonstrate this point in the chapters on *Wilhelm Meister* and *Faust* — the eye was to be the symbol *par excellence* of the potential totality of human experience and freedom? 'Tiefe Blicke', 'schaun',

---

[41] *Ed. cit.*, p. 238.
[42] *Ed. cit.*, p. 239.
[43] *Ibid.*
[44] By Kuhn, *loc. cit.*, p. 421. Cf. Chapters VIII, IX, X and XIII of this book.

'wähnend', 'sehn', 'ausspähn'; 'kennen', 'dumpf', 'unversehn', 'Morgenröte', 'verstehen', 'sehn'; 'Blick', 'rein genau'; 'kanntest', 'spähtest', 'lesen', 'Aug', 'durchdringen'; 'Auge', 'Sinnen', 'erhellen'; 'ungewiß', 'scheinen', 'dämmernd', 'hellster Tag': the mere recital of these key-images enables us to trace the inner movement of the poem, from the perplexed perception of a clear relationship, via the brilliant illumination of its essence in an aesthetic dimension out of time, to a final clarification and acceptance of the basic incongruence between the actual and the true.

'Jeder neue Gegenstand, wohl beschaut, schließt ein neues Organ in uns auf.' This statement has explained itself. The clarity of Charlotte's perception imprints itself on the poet there to engender the answering, yet enhanced clarity of his total perception[45], a perception which encompasses equally the shadow-world and the world of essences, the twilight of a reality which is only half true and the blinding illumination of the true relationship. In the end, it is he, the recipient, who speaks both for himself and his beloved in that tone of consummate and compassionate consciousness which informs the poem as a whole[46].

In this poem, in which relatedness to what is outside the self helps establish the self in the first instance, we find that incessant transmigration of world to self and of self back to world which the opening paragraph of Goethe's late essay so graphically renders; an interpenetration and mutual enhancement which for Goethe at all times constituted the warp and woof of experience[47].

In a brilliant comparison of Schiller's mode of creativity with that of his great friend, Wilhelm von Humboldt describes Goethe as follows: 'Auch wo er selbst schafft, scheint er noch zu empfangen, er erscheint fast immer nur um sich schauend, und bloß aussprechend, was er sah als in sich arbeitend und forteilend . . .'[48]. In 'Warum gabst du uns die tiefen Blicke . . .' Goethe perceived and articulated what had imprinted itself upon his mind and in turn had received its imprint, in an ever ascending spiral of awareness: the Platonic Idea of his and Charlotte's love, seen now *sub specie realitatis* and now *sub specie aeternitatis*. If we in turn allow this product of the poet's active receptivity to impress itself upon us in a like manner, our perception, too, may be enhanced and we may be enabled to read a new page in the lore of love: a page filled with that very modern quality of a meditative and compassionate tenderness, culled from that very modern predicament — consciousness, with all its burdens and with all its blessings.

---

[45] Cf. M. Kommerell who writes: 'Die Freundin durchdringt ihn; er durchdringt ihr Leben miteinander.' (*Op. cit.*, p. 146.)

[46] Interestingly, Plato concludes the cave myth with a plea to 'compassionate' the soul which 'has just quitted a brighter life, and has been blinded by the novelty of darkness.' (*Ed. cit.*, p. 239.)

[47] Cf. also *Zur Morphologie. HA* XIII, p. 53.

[48] September 1800.

An Eye for the World:
Stages of Realisation in 'Wilhelm Meister'

'Mache ein Organ aus dir'

Goethe

I.

'Das Gesicht ist der edelste Sinn', we read in *Makarien's Archiv;* 'die andern vier belehren uns nur durch die Organe des Takts, wir hören, wir fühlen, riechen und betasten alles durch Berührung; das Gesicht aber steht unendlich höher, verfeint sich über die Materie und nähert sich den Fähigkeiten des Geistes.'[1] At first sight, this statement does not sound significantly different from Schiller's famous apotheosis of the eye in the 26th Aesthetic Letter. Yet how exposed is the *Augenmensch* Goethe to its force!

> Doch uns Sterbliche nötigt, ach,
> Leider trauriges Mißgeschick
> Zu dem unsäglichen Augenschmerz,
> Den das Verwerfliche, Ewig-Unselige
> Schönheitliebenden rege macht.

Thus the chorus, in the third act of *Faust II*, as Phorkyas-Mephistopheles becomes visible on the threshold of Helena's paternal home. But it is not only 'das Verwerfliche, Ewig-Unselige', ugliness, which causes 'unsäglichen Augenschmerz': quite as much it is the sight of beauty, indeed the experience of seeing as such. Goethe's optical susceptibility, the intensity and the precision of his perceiving are quite out of the ordinary and at times seem to border on the pathological. It is a gift with which he has endowed those of his characters through whom he is revealing intimate aspects of his poetic nature: Tasso, the duke in *Die Natürliche Tochter*, Epimetheus, Faust, Ottilie and Wilhelm Meister. And the power this sense exercised over the poet is no less marked in his lyrical poetry. Whether we think of an early poem such as *An Lili* (In ein Exemplar der 'Stella'), the elegy *Euphrosyne* from his middle years or indeed the *Marienbader Elegie* written in his old age, the blinding impact and the visionary, almost persecutory quality of his optical perceptions becomes, if anything, enhanced. This is how he sees Lili in his mind's eye:

> Im holden Tal, auf schneebedeckten Höhen
> War stets dein Bild mir nah;
> Ich sah's um mich in lichten Wolken wehen,
> Im Herzen war mir's da.[2]

[1] *HA* VIII, p. 480.
[2] *HA* I, p. 105.

And this is how he will see, and lose, the image of the beloved in *Marienbader Elegie*:

> Wie leicht und zierlich, klar und zart gewoben
> Schwebt, seraphgleich, aus ernster Wolken Chor,
> Als glich' es ihr, am blauen Äther droben,
> Ein schlank Gebild aus lichtem Duft empor;
> So sahst du sie in frohem Tanze walten,
> Die lieblichste der lieblichsten Gestalten.[3]

And then, later:

> Fehlt's am Begriff: wie sollt' er sie vermissen?
> Er wiederholt ihr Bild zu tausendmalen.
> Das zaudert bald, bald wird es weggerissen,
> Undeutlich jetzt und jetzt im reinsten Strahlen;
> Wie könnte dies geringstem Troste frommen,
> Die Ebb' und Flut, das Gehen wie das Kommen?[4]

The intensity of such visual impingements is by no means to be ascribed to the magnitude of the occasion alone. One look at Goethe's *Farbenlehre* teaches us that perception *per se*, and the perception of colour in particular, for him was an experience heavily charged with emotional overtones. In the section on *Sinnlich-Sittliche Wirkung der Farbe* — the title is in itself significant — we read:

'Die Menschen empfinden im allgemeinen eine große Freude an der Farbe. Das Auge bedarf ihrer, wie es des Lichtes bedarf. Man erinnre sich der Erquickung, wenn an einem trüben Tage die Sonne auf einen einzelnen Teil der Gegend scheint und die Farben daselbst sichtbar macht. Daß man den farbigen Edelsteinen Heilkräfte zuschrieb, mag aus *dem tiefen Gefühl dieses unaussprechlichen Behagens** entstanden sein.' (Para. 759).[5]

In this passage, do we not recognise the figure of Ottilie, described by the narrator as 'ein wahrer Augentrost', more beneficial to those who look upon her than is the emerald 'durch seine herrliche Farbe'? 'Wer sie erblickt, den kann nichts Übles anwehen; er fühlt sich mit sich selbst und mit der Welt in Übereinstimmung.'[6] Of the colour yellow we read: 'Das Auge wird erfreut, das Herz ausgedehnt, das Gemüt erheitert; eine unmittelbare Wärme scheint uns anzuwehen.' (Para. 769).[7] Of Gelbrot:

---

[3] *HA* I, p. 382.

[4] *HA* I, p. 385.

[5] *HA* XIII, p. 434. For a lucid exposition of Goethe's optical studies and some of the problems it presents, cf. G. A. Wells, 'Goethe's scientific Method and Aims in the Light of his Studies in Physical Optics', *PEGS* (New Series) XXXVIII, 1967—68, pp. 69 ff.

[6] I, 6, *HA* VI, p. 283.

[7] *HA* XIII, p. 496.

* my italics.

'Das angenehme, heitere Gefühl, das uns das Rotgelbe noch gewährt, steigert sich bis zum *unerträglich Gewaltsamen** im hohen Gelbroten.' (Para. 774).[8] 'Man darf eine vollkommen gelbrote Fläche starr ansehen, so scheint sich die Farbe wirklich *ins Organ zu bohren.** Sie bringt eine *unglaubliche Erschütterung** hervor und behält diese Wirkung bei einem ziemlichen Grade von Dunkelheit.' (Para. 776).[9] *Blau:* 'Diese Farbe macht für das Auge eine sonderbare und *fast unaussprechliche** Wirkung.' (Para. 779).[10] *Blaurot:* ' . . . man kann wohl behaupten, daß eine Tapete von einem ganz reinen gesättigten Blaurot eine Art von *unerträglicher Gegenwart** sein müsse.' (Para. 790).[11]

These are but a few examples for many. One might suspect the very intensity of the impact which colours make upon Goethe to preclude precision of observation. The section devoted to, say, *Physiologische Farben* teaches us otherwise. Phenomena such as after-images, reversal of colours or haloes which were thought to be hallucinatory 'weil man ihre Flüchtigkeit nicht haschen konnte'[12], are registered with patient care and explained with the utmost circumspection. Goethe himself is alive to the fact that he is here exploring subjective phenomena closely bordering on the delusory, and that it took a susceptibility as differentiated as his own to do so without blurring the distinction between the healthily and the pathologically subjective. But also as disciplined: 'Es gehört eine eigene Geisteswendung dazu', we read in *Betrachtungen im Sinne der Wanderer*, 'um das gestaltlose Wirkliche in seiner eigensten Art zu fassen und es von Hirngespinsten zu unterscheiden, die sich denn doch auch mit einer gewissen Wirklichkeit lebhaft aufdringen.' (Para. 153)[13]. Often, in phenomena such as these, the difference is one of degree only, as is the case with the duration of after-images. A healthy retina will retain these for a matter of seconds, or at most a couple of minutes, whilst a sick one will hold them for fourteen to seventeen minutes, not to speak of a case reported by Boyle in which it lasted for ten whole years. (Paras. 28 and 122). Such an extreme longevity is by no means beyond the range of Goethe's imagining. One recalls the unchanging intensity with which the marble statues of her infancy are imprinted on Mignon's imagination; also, perhaps, the tenacity of Agamemnon's image in Iphigenie's mind and the etched clarity of Chlytemnestra's dying gesture in that of Orestes[14]. But in the intermediate regions it is less easy to say where normality ends and abnormality begins. Weakness and strength are here as elsewhere often curiously interlaced, as

[8] *HA* XIII, p. 497.
[9] *Ibid.*
[10] *HA* XIII, p. 498.
[11] *HA* XIII, p. 499.
[12] *HA* XIII, p. 329.
[13] *HA* VIII, p. 306.
[14] Cf. Chapter III, section 5. The underlying reason for dwelling so extensively on the mode of perception and memory evinced by Iphigenie and Orestes in that chapter will become increasingly clearer in the present chapter and find its full explanation in the concluding one.

* my italics.

Goethe observes in the *Farbenlehre* and as, indeed, the reaction pattern of his characters goes to demonstrate. Ottilie's capacity to sustain precise and moving images of Eduard represents such an interlacing; and it is matched by Goethe's own as he relates it in *Das Sehen in subjektiver Hinsicht*, or as it becomes apparent in the poems I have cited. Goethe himself indicates some such ambiguity when he identifies the long duration of an after-image as a symptom of a weak or diseased retina, adding, however, 'so wie das Vorschweben leidenschaftlich geliebter oder verhaßter Gegenstände aus dem Sinnlichen ins Geistige deutet.' (Para. 28)[15].

It is precisely because he was so uncommonly susceptible and because visual phenomena — real and pathological — assailed him with such merciless force that Goethe's need to order them and to discipline this his native sensibility was so urgent. More than once we hear something resembling a *cri de cœur* of one bewildered by the multifariousness of the impressions he so acutely registered. Reporting on his experiments with colour-blind subjects, he writes: 'Wenn man die Unterhaltung mit ihnen dem Zufall überläßt . . . so gerät man in die größte Verwirrung und fürchtet, wahnsinnig zu werden.' (Para. 109)[16]. Strong words, these; but they are repeated, more than once, in his osteological writings. The rodents especially, with the tantalising variability of their subspecies, reduce him to despair. 'Wer aber, der sich mit solchen Untersuchungen ernstlich abgab', he asks, 'hat nicht erfahren, daß eben dieses Schwanken von Form zu Unform, von Unform zu Form den redlichen Beschauer in eine Art von Wahnsinn versetzt?'[17]. Again, a little later, he speaks of the 'sinneverwirrende Zustände'[18] induced by comparing the skeletons of those species.

It is only a morphologically trained eye and mind that help him through the jungle of mutations encountered in his botanical, zoological and optical studies. 'Das Gebildete wird sogleich wieder umgebildet', we read in *Die Absicht eingeleitet*, 'und wir haben uns, wenn wir einigermaßen zum lebendigen Anschaun der Natur gelangen wollen, selbst so beweglich und bildsam zu erhalten, nach dem Beispiele mit dem sie uns vorgeht.'[19] Similarly, in the *Allgemeine Einleitung in die vergleichende Anatomie*:

'Nun aber müssen wir, indem wir bei und mit dem Beharrlichen beharren, auch zugleich mit und neben dem Veränderlichen unsere Ansichten zu verändern und mannigfaltige Beweglichkeit lernen, damit wir den Typus in aller seiner Versatilität zu verfolgen gewandt seien und uns dieser Proteus nirgendhin entschlüpfe.'[20]

[15] *HA* XIII, p. 334.
[16] *HA* XIII, p. 355.
[17] *Die Skelette der Nagetiere, abgebildet und verglichen von D'Alton*, *HA* XIII, p. 214.
[18] *Ibid.*, p. 217.
[19] *HA* XIII, p. 56.
[20] *HA* XIII, p. 177.

His 'frischer Blick' is as 'sicher' and 'geschmeidig' as are the mutations of
the single organs within the complex of the plant or the metamorphosis of
the individual species within its general type. In *Anschauende Urteilskraft* he
claims to have risen, 'durch das Anschauen einer immer schaffenden Natur,
zur geistigen Teilnahme an ihren Produktionen . . .'[21]

The most seminal statement on his mode of perceiving is indubitably the
late essay *Bedeutende Fördernis durch ein einziges geistreiches Wort*. Enthusiastically,
he takes up Heinroth's description of his mental and perceptual *Gegenständ-*
lichkeit which he expatiates as meaning 'daß mein Denken sich von den Gegenständen nicht sondere', 'daß die Elemente der Gegenstände, die Anschauungen,
in dasselbe eingehen und von ihm auf das innigste durchdrungen werden,
daß mein Anschauen selbst ein Denken, mein Denken ein Anschauen sei.'[22]
Such an intimate reciprocal permeation of eye and object in the act of experiencing, such a mutual illumination of self and world it is which leads him to
put forth the key statement of the whole treatise, a key statement, as we shall
see, for the understanding of *Wilhelm Meister*, too: 'Jeder neue Gegenstand,
wohl beschaut, schließt ein neues Organ in uns auf.'[23] It is in this essay, too,
that Goethe reveals the longevity in himself of poetic images, that same longevity and power to metamorphose which he studies at length in the physio-
logical section of his *Farbenlehre*, as we have already seen[24]. We shall see precisely this slow maturational process of early visual imprints as being the structural law of the novel with which we are concerned in this chapter[25]. And we

---

[21] *HA* XIII, p. 30.

[22] *HA* XIII, p. 37.

[23] *HA* XIII, p. 38.

[24] *HA* XIII, p. 38. Cf. Chapter VII, p. 172. In this connection, cf. Chapter IX, section 4,
and Chapter XIII.

[25] In this basically morphological concern this chapter, and indeed this book, touch most
closely on Günther Müller's approach in his two books *Die Gestaltfrage in der Literaturwissenschaft und Goethes Morphologie* (I), Halle/Saale 1944, and *Gestaltung-Umgestaltung in
Wilhelm Meisters Lehrjahren* (II), Halle/Saale 1948. But while (II) largely concerns itself with
questions of narrated and narrative time — a detailed analysis which links on somewhat uneasily to the author's general premisses — (I) differs from my own approach in the
following two fundamental ways: a) it is not specific to *Wilhelm Meister* nor indeed to
Goethe; b) it operates with a large number of concepts derived from Goethe's morphology
and applies these — often stimulatingly and fruitfully — to literary works of art, to define
their *Gestalt* in a manner that shall bear as closely as possible on Goethe's own morphological *Gestalt*-concept. As against this, I am largely concerned with the morphology of
percepts (on which Müller does not touch). Perception and its objects, light and colour,
for Goethe represented the natural phenomenon *par excellence*, indeed the sole natural
phenomenon capable of aesthetic use, i. e. of directly symbolising moral and spiritual
events. Cf. the basic statement: 'Das Auge als ein Geschöpf des Lichtes leistet alles, was
das Licht selbst leisten kann. Das Licht überliefert das Sichtbare dem Auge; das Auge
überliefert's dem ganzen Menschen. . . . In ihm spiegelt sich von außen die Welt, von innen
der Mensch. *Die Totalität des Innern und Äußern wird durchs Auge vollendet*.'* (*WA*, II, 5,
2. Abteilung, p. 12) (* My italics). Thus the symbolism of perception served Goethe as no

shall do well to remark the poet's extraordinary receptivity *vis à vis* these nuclei of his visual imagination — a near-passivity expressed through the grammatical form of his statement — and the all but autonomous life these images lead in him.

It is indeed the autonomous life of the eye, its disposition spontaneously to produce colours that will complement the one to which it is exposed, and thus to restore a totality and harmony all its own, which makes perception the most apt symbol for specifically human and moral phenomena in the whole realm of nature. It is the aesthetic symbol *par excellence*. '. . . das Bedürfnis nach Totalität, welches unserm Organ eingeboren ist' . . . is a 'Wink, daß uns die Natur durch Totalität zur Freiheit heraufzuheben angelegt ist und daß wir diesmal eine Naturerscheinung zum ästhetischen Gebrauch unmittelbar überliefert erhalten.' (Para. 812)[26]. Thus Goethe in the section on the *Sinnlich-Sittliche Wirkung der Farbe*, which is entitled *Totalität und Harmonie*. Are we rash in suggesting that the supremely visual author of a novel whose hero's avowed concern is with 'jener harmonischen Ausbildung meiner Natur, die mir meine Geburt versagt', should make his central statement in terms of that uniquely gifted natural organ, the human eye, and that he should speak of the manifold metamorphoses which are part and parcel of human maturation — 'alles . . ., [was] sich nach und nach gebildet, aufgelöst und wieder gestaltet hatte'[27] — through the symbolism of that most versatile, delicate and differentiated of organic phenomena, human perception?

2.

'Welche sind die ersten lebhaften Eindrücke, deren du dich erinnerst?' Wilhelm asks Mariane as, bored by her lover's lengthy account of his youthful theatrical exploits, she valiantly tries to swallow her yawns. It is a question the narrator asks, and answers, in relation to the majority of his characters, and for good reason: 'denn niemand glaube die ersten Eindrücke der Jugend überwinden zu können', as the Abbé will have it later on in the novel. (II. 9)

A whole calvacade of primal impressions passes before the reader's eye, some dating back to the first years of the figure harbouring them, others received later in life, some kinaesthetic in character, others visual: but all alike formative imprints of the fiercest intensity, rapid in their onset, slow and far-reaching in their consequences and decisive for the characters' future

---

other could have done, to articulate the development of Wilhelm and other figures *within* the novel; moreover, it also became what I have elsewhere termed the dominant operational symbolism determining the — morphological — structure *of* the novel in its entirety. (Cf. my *Goethe and Lessing, Introduction*.)

[26] *HA* XIII, p. 502.
[27] *Wanderjahre* III, 14.

development. A quick glance at some of this vast amount of expositional material will readily demonstrate my point.

Starting with the *Schöne Seele*, we do indeed begin at the beginning. For her effective memory coincides with the conception, in herself, of what she calls 'die eigentliche Gestalt meines Herzens' or, later on, 'die wahrhafte Gestalt meiner Seele.' It is her spiritual birth she remembers, a gestation period ushered in by the spitting of blood, and lasting nine months. She expressly stresses the indelible impact the event made upon her: '. . . in dem Augenblick war meine Seele ganz Empfindung und Gedächtnis. Die kleinsten Umstände dieses Zufalls stehn mir noch vor Augen, als hätte er sich gestern ereignet.' Despite the visual character of this initial recollection, however, the imprint left by this trauma is in increasing measure seen to be a kinaesthetic one. She feels like a snail, the intimations of the divine are by way of soft tactile im-presses — impresses, we may add, she herself actively seeks rather than suffers — and at the climactic point of her confessions she avows: '. . . meine Seele hat nur Fühlhörner und keine Augen; sie tastet nur und sieht nicht; ach! daß sie Augen bekäme und schauen dürfte!'[28] Similarly, the Harfner, natively disposed 'zu einer Art von schwärmerischer Ruhe', becomes marked for life by the 'Genuß einer heiligen Schwärmerei' to which as a young monk he abandons himself, 'jenen halb geistigen halb physischen Empfindungen, die, wie sie ihn eine Zeitlang in den dritten Himmel erhuben, bald darauf in einen Abgrund von Ohnmacht und leeres Elend versinken ließen.' (VIII, 9). Sensuality coupled with the intensest introversion all but of necessity lead him into an incestuous union with his sister, and, thence, into the abyss of 'leeres Elend' in which we meet him. Here, too, we note the absence of formative visual imprints: 'Sein Herz war weich; die früheren Eindrücke der Religion wurden lebhaft' (*ibid.*) are the words in which the narrator describes his con-dition after the discovery of his crime; and this 'weich', echoing the words of the *Schöne Seele*, points to tactile rather than to visual sensations.

The case of the beautiful countess is perhaps most striking. Attracted to Wilhelm and teased by Philine as to whether the picture of her husband she wears in a medallion on her breast has not by chance been replaced by another's image, she presently finds herself in Wilhelm's embrace, '. . . als die Gräfin sich auf einmal mit einem Schrei von ihm loßriß und mit der Hand nach ihrem Her-zen fuhr.' (III. 12). Later we hear that the countess is deluded into thinking this momentary 'Druck' to be the beginning and cause of a cancerous condi-tion; a belief which in turn precipitates her religious conversion and with-drawal from any active part in the world. Let us add the figure of Aurelie, whose dominant impressions are the moral depravity of the aunt who brought her up — a sexual motif unequivocally sounded in the confessions of the *Schöne Seele* — and the faithlessness of Lothario, her lover, who imprinted on her,

---

[28] Cf. Chapter XIII, section I, p. 355.

by an *unglücklichen Eindruck*, an insuperable distaste of French, the language he began to use as his feelings towards Aurelie cooled; imprints, both, devoid of visual contour.

Thus we have a cluster of four figures, alike in that the primal impress upon their lives is non-visual in character, that it becomes, in every case, a fixation (the preoccupation of the *Schöne Seele* with blood has been critically noted)[29] and that, lastly, these lives, under the dominance of this imprint, are lived out in a more or less complete withdrawal into a spiritual or religiously tinted inwardness. We may say, even now, that they are lives whose fuller development is arrested; and remark on the narrator's interlacing of these diverse yet similar fates.

Book VI, containing the *Bekenntnisse einer schönen Seele*, which most fully and circumstantially trace the genesis of inwardness through tactile 'Ein-Drücke', is placed at the centre of this complex. The manuscript is introduced towards the end of the preceding book, at the terminal stage of Aurelie's illness (to whom it is read), and shortly after the doctor has given a blood-curdling account of the Harfner's mental sickness and related the unfortunate sequel of Wilhelm's embrace of the beautiful countess. 'Für den Menschen', the doctor observes between the two portions of his account, 'sei nur das eine ein Unglück, wenn sich irgendeine Idee bei ihm festsetze, die keinen Einfluß ins tätige Leben habe oder ihn wohl gar vom tätigen Leben abziehe' (V. 16). By this general reflection the narrator subtly links the three lives that have claimed our attention in Book V — Aurelie's, the Harfner's and the beautiful countess' — with that of the *Schöne Seele* in whom the whole series culminates; her spiritual development representing the optimal possibility attainable to one moulded by this type of formative experience.

By way of complete contrast, the following book opens with a poignantly powerful visual scene, the spectacle of a rainbow, symbol, for Goethe, of harmonious totality[30], and harbinger of the hope felt by the percipient, Wilhelm, 'daß die angeborne Neigung unsers Herzens nicht ohne Gegenstand bleiben werde' (VII. 1). No doubt but that this 'angeborne Neigung' is the 'unwiderstehliche Neigung' he had earlier avowed 'zu jener harmonischen Ausbildung meiner Natur', the goal he is approaching now as, under the augury of the rainbow, he is entering the orbit of Lothario, Therese and Natalie.

Another group of figures is associated with a primal imprint that is visual in character. These are figures who play a more central role in the two parts of the novel. The extremest case is that of Mignon who harbours the *Marmorbilder* of her Italian childhood in unabated intensity. Next to her, Lenardo,

[29] By E. Staiger, in: *Goethe*, II, p. 141.
[30] But cf. *Zur Farbenlehre, Sinnlich-Sittliche Wirkung der Farbe, Totalität und Harmonie, HA* XIII, p. 503, para. 814 and 815.

who, having broken his pledge to a young girl, daughter of one of his uncle's tenants, to intervene on her father's behalf, is haunted by the memory of the scene: 'Sooft ich einsam, sooft ich unbeschäftigt war', he confesses to Wilhelm, 'trat mir jenes Bild des flehenden Mädchens, mit der ganzen Umgebung, mit jedem Baum und Strauch, dem Platz, wo sie knieete, dem Weg, den ich einschlug, mich von ihr zu entfernen, das Ganze zusammen wie ein frisches Bild vor die Seele. Es war ein unauslöschlicher Eindruck, der wohl von andern Bildern und Teilnahmen beschattet, verdeckt, aber niemals vertilgt werden konnte' (*WJ*, I. 11). Gradually, on his travels, the image wanes. But on returning home, to the location of the incident, it is once again inflamed.

> 'Die Gestalt des Mädchens frischt sich auf mit den Gestalten der Meinigen ... Dabei ist das Bild, die Vorstellung, die mich quält, so angenehm, so liebenswürdig, daß ich gern dabei verweile. Und denke ich daran, so scheint der Kuß, den sie auf meine Hand gedrückt, mich noch zu brennen.' (*WJ*, I. 11).

Natalie herself expressly answers the question Wilhelm had asked of Mariane: 'Ich erinnere mich von Jugend an kaum eines lebhaftern Eindrucks, als daß ich überall die Bedürfnisse der Menschen sah und ein unüberwindliches Verlangen empfand, sie auszugleichen', she tells Wilhelm (VIII. 3). 'Unnachahmlich war von Jugend auf ihr Betragen gegen Notleidende und Hülfsbedürftige', her aunt corroborates, adding that she would always change money into whatever object was most needed in the particular case. 'Niemals erschien sie mir liebenswürdiger, als wenn sie meine Kleider- und Wäscheschränke plünderte'; and, summarising: 'Alles schien ihr gleich, wenn sie nur das verrichten konnte, was in der Zeit und am Platz war.' We may assume that the narrator attaches some considerable importance to Natalie's encounter with her future husband. And, indeed, it is presented to the reader as an intensely visual experience. But it is an experience of a totally different complexion from any other we have so far met. Natalie sees and acts. She turns 'ihre Augen nach der wunderbaren Gruppe', makes the requisite enquiries 'mit menschenfreundlicher Teilnehmung', consults with the doctors and takes in the central figure: '"*Sehen Sie nur**", sagte sie, nachdem sie einigemal hin und her gegangen war und den alten Herrn wieder herbeiführte, "*sehen Sie**, wie man ihn zugerichtet hat..." Sie ging unruhig hin und wider; es schien, *als könnte sie sich nicht von dem Anblick des Verwundeten losreißen ...*'.* Then she takes off her cloak and, having steadied him by the '*heilsame Blick ihrer Augen*'* while the surgeon treats Wilhelm's injured arm, spreads it over him (IV. 6).

There is no indication on the part of the narrator that this intense visualisation leaves any after-image in Natalie's mind; and no reason for supposing so on ours. The energy of her perception is geared to the object before her and spends itself in immediate and appropriate action. We shall presently

---

* my italics.

have more to say about her mode of perception, here and on other occasions.

There remains the central figure of the novel, Wilhelm. How would he himself have answered the question he asks of his sleepy beloved? The answer of the Wilhelm of the *Lehrjahre* would certainly be very different from that the hero of the *Theatralische Sendung* would have given. For by telescoping past and present and presenting his hero's early theatrical exploits as a series of flashbacks embedded in the framework of his first love, the poet has achieved a clustering of images overlaying one another and, therewith, a mental fabric of great denseness and poignancy. The past is, as it were, dipped into the fluidum of the present. Early visual, tactile, gustatory and even olfactory impressions all blend in the overpowering sensation of his first passion and enhance it. There is the smell of the larder in which he first discovered his puppets amongst edible booty, the puppets themselves and the secret aesthetic and erotic initiations connected with the first ill-begotten show; there is his grandfather's picture collection including the one showing 'wie der kranke Königssohn sich über die Braut seines Vaters in Liebe verzehrt' (I. 17); there is — we hear of this much later, at a most significant point — the first adolescent impression of the fisherboy's naked figure bodying forth all the glory of the human *Gestalt*, and the image of his dead body; and tinging it all, there are the enchanting images of his actress-lover, on stage, in the sweet chaos of her dressing room, and in his embrace. Insensibly, the image he had made himself of the muse and that of his beloved, aesthetic and erotic impulses, merge. 'In der kleinsten Abwesenheit ergriff ihn ihr Andenken' (I. 9). 'Alles, was in den innersten Winkeln seiner Seele bisher geschlummert hatte, wurde rege. Er bildete aus den vielerlei Ideen mit Farben der Liebe ein Gemälde auf Nebelgrund, dessen Gestalten freilich sehr ineinander flossen; dafür aber auch das Ganze eine desto reizendere Wirkung tat' (I. 9). His transports assume an almost visionary force: 'Es sind keine Träume, meine Liebste!' he writes to Mariane:

'Wie ich an Deinem Herzen habe fühlen können, daß Du in Liebe bist, so ergreife ich auch den glänzenden Gedanken und sage — ich will's nicht aussagen, aber hoffen will ich, daß wir einst als ein Paar gute Geister den Menschen erscheinen werden, ihre Herzen aufzuschließen, ihre Gemüter zu berühren und ihnen himmlische Genüsse zu bereiten, so gewiß mir an Deinem Busen Freuden gewährt waren, die immer himmlisch genennt werden müssen, weil wir uns in jenen Augenblicken aus uns selbst gerückt, über uns selbst erhaben fühlen.' (I. 16).

In the opening section of *Die Metamorphose der Pflanzen*, Goethe describes the first rudimentary organs, the cotyledons, which emerge immediately above the seed and break the soil. Forerunners of the leaves proper, these always appear in couples or clusters, even when the subsequent leaves grow around the stem in alternating positions:

'es zeigt sich also hier eine Annäherung und Verbindung der Teile, welche die Natur in der Folge trennt und voneinander entfernt. Noch merkwürdiger ist es, wenn die Kotyledonen als viele Blättchen um Eine Achse versammlet erscheinen, und der aus ihrer Mitte sich nach und nach entwickelnde Stengel die folgenden Blätter einzeln um sich herum hervorbringt . . . '³¹

Through telescoping and interlacing, in the final version of the novel, present and past impacts and developmental trends, the poet achieved that rich clustering and first proliferation or expansion which he had observed in the growth of plants³². The morphological device the poet employed in the final version of his novel enabled him to create an immensely rich if undifferentiated primal imprint on the mind of his young hero, an imprint far exceeding that of any other figure of the novel, by reason of its massed complexity. We may recall in passing that Goethe may well have been conscious of the morphological procedure he adopted, either at the time of revising the *Urmeister* or in retrospect. For in the *Tag- und Jahreshefte* up to 1780, we find the remark: 'Die Anfänge des "Wilhelm Meister" wird man in dieser Epoche auch schon gewahr, obgleich nur kotyledonenartig: die fernere Entwickelung und Bildung zieht sich durch viele Jahre.'³³

3.

'Niemand glaube die ersten Eindrücke der Jugend überwinden zu können', says the Abbé who joins Wilhelm and the theatrical company on their river trip (II. 9). And this maxim is fully confirmed by the after-life the formative impressions we have observed lead in the mind of their recipients. Their power and longevity, their fixed tenacity or, alternatively, their capacity to merge with other impressions and metamorphose without yet losing their distinctive quality, are enormous. It is some of these patterns and their effects on the development of those affected that we must now seek to trace.

In some instances the force of these imprints is annihilating. This is patently so in the instances of Mignon, the Harfner, the beautiful countess and her husband, and Aurelie. These figures are persecuted by the percepts to which they have been exposed and which they can do nothing to mitigate or dispel, by salutary contact with reality. As a result, they withdraw into the barren inwardness of hallucinatory fantasies, and all further development is cut off. The Harfner's deluded belief that he will harm, and be harmed by, a young child proves more powerful than the healing routine of ordered activities devised by the doctor. Nothing can shake the count's premonition that he is fated to die, nor the countess' belief that the physical impress of her husband's medallion has caused her to contract cancer. Aurelie acts out the trauma of her betrayal in her feverish portraits of Ophelia and Orsina and wastes away.

³¹ *Zur Morphologie. Der Inhalt bevorwortet*, *HA* XIII, p. 68.
³² For a repetition of this phenomenon, at a later stage of the plants' growth, cf. also *ibid.*, p. 73.
³³ *HA* X, p. 431.

And so does Mignon — *sich verzehren* is the word Goethe uses — once her helpless longing for Italy has been reanimated by her equally helpless adolescent
longing for Wilhelm. She literally consumes herself; her heart, 'dieses erste
Organ des Lebens' as Natalie has it, and the only organ for the world that
passionate child possesses, contracts without an answering object and stands
still. As Goethe has it in *Maximen und Reflexionen*: 'Die Botaniker haben eine
Pflanzenabteilung, die sie incompletae nennen; man kann eben auch sagen,
daß es inkomplette unvollständige Menschen gibt. Es sind diejenigen, deren
Sehnsucht und Streben mit ihrem Tun und Leisten nicht proportioniert sind.'[34]
     In the more visually disposed figures the tenacity and precision of the
actual after-images left by the primal imprint is astonishing. In the *Farbenlehre*
we read:

'Daß Bilder sich bei Augenkrankheiten vierzehn bis siebzehn Minuten, ja länger auf der
Retina erhielten, deutet auf äußerste Schwäche des Organs, auf dessen Unfähigkeit, sich
wieder herzustellen, so wie das Vorschweben leidenschaftlich geliebter oder verhaßter
Gegenstände aus dem Sinnlichen ins Geistige deutet.' (Para. 28).[35]

Such retention and wilful reanimation of powerful after-images — the *Farbenlehre* explores this possibility, too — is characteristic of Mignon and Lenardo, to
a less pathological degree of Hersilie, but above all of Wilhelm himself. It
is Lenardo who most poignantly formulates this haunting after-life: 'Ein leb-
hafter Eindruck ist wie eine andere Wunde', he says to Wilhelm; 'man fühlt
sie nicht, indem man sie empfängt. Erst später fängt sie an zu schmerzen
und zu eitern' (*WJ*, I. 11). Both, the fixity of Lenardo's injurious impression
and Mignon's immutable *Marmorbilder* —

                    Und Marmorbilder stehn und sehn mich an —

testify to a dangerous weakness in their constitution — a *grillenhafte Schwäche*
Lenardo's inborn conscientiousness is called — to a passivity unable to throw
off one-sided affects and to restore the harmonious totality of the person.
Only the presence of the disturbing object and the activity directed towards
it can heal the imagination by freeing it from its slavery: and such presence,
in its fuller sense, is denied to Mignon, and is the secret goal of Lenardo's
pilgrimage. Both the doctor and Wilhelm know about the all-healingness of
Gegenwart; the former when he says 'wie sehr die Gegenwart eines geliebten
Gegenstandes der Einbildungskraft ihre zerstörende Gewalt nimmt und die
Sehnsucht in ein ruhiges Schauen verwandelt' (VIII. 3), the latter when
he insists on seeing the dead Mignon, exclaiming: 'Das Unglück, das wir mit
Augen sehen, ist geringer, als wenn unsere Einbildungskraft das Übel gewaltsam in unser Gemüt einsenkt' (VIII. 5).
     Just how forcibly the image can embed itself in the imagination, a *cri de coeur*
of Hersilie's — half-serious, half-humourous as is her wont — goes readily to

[34] *HA* XII, p. 532.
[35] *HA* XIII, p. 334.

demonstrate. After a good deal of to-ing and fro-ing between father and son she receives an irresistibly charming message from the young Felix and laments: 'und der kleine Schalk ist mir gegenwärtiger als je, ja es ist mir, als ob sein Bild sich mir in die Augen hineinbohrte' (*WJ.* II. 10).

But it is to Wilhelm that we must turn if we would gain a full impression of the after-life the primal percept continues to lead in the recipient and the vicissitudes to which it — and he — are exposed.

Wilhelm, too, knows something of the annihilating power of sudden impressions on the mind. When he sees Norbert's shadow hurrying away in the dark from Mariane's door, we read: 'Wie einer, dem der Blitz die Gegend in einem Winkel erhellte, gleich darauf mit geblendeten Augen die vorigen Gestalten, den Zusammenhang der Pfade in der Finsternis vergebens sucht, so war's vor seinen Augen, so war's in seinem Herzen' (I. 17). But, as the narrator tells us in the following chapter, such a total eclipse is 'eine Wohltat'. The extreme brightness that had assailed Wilhelm's eye, had produced a state 'der äußersten Überspannung und Unempfindlichkeit.' (*Farbenlehre* Para. 8)[36]. The darkness into which it is plunged restores the organ, as well as its owner, to a condition 'der höchsten Abspannung und Empfänglichkeit'[37]. Wilhelm's nature is given a respite to recuperate. Besides, the darkness in which he finds himself enveloped, is a sign of resilience, of potential freedom and autonomy, testifying not only to the 'große Regsamkeit der Netzhaut', but symbolically exemplifying

> 'den stillen Widerspruch, den jedes Lebendige zu äußern gedrungen ist, wenn ihm irgendein bestimmter Zustand dargeboten wird ... Wie dem Auge das Dunkle geboten wird, so fordert es das Helle; es fordert Dunkel, wenn man ihm Hell entgegenbringt, und zeigt eben dadurch seine Lebendigkeit, sein Recht, das Objekt zu fassen, indem es etwas, das dem Objekt entgegengesetzt ist, aus sich selbst hervorbringt.' (Para. 38).[38]

And indeed, this eclipse is only a temporary one. As Wilhelm recovers, he comes to experience the truth, both of the Abbé's remark quoted at the outset of this section, and of Lenardo's sad observation that a strong impression is 'wie eine andere Wunde' which hurts and festers after the event. In his instance the pain of the wound is all the greater, since the imprint of Mariane, indelible itself, is 'kotyledonenartig' intertwined with all his other formative impressions, notably with his early aesthetic and artistic experiences. As the narrator has it: 'Der Streich hatte sein ganzes Dasein an der Wurzel getroffen' (II. 1). Thus the pain is reanimated by a variety of objects and memories and the wound is opened up, if anything, more deeply with the passing of time. His artistic aspirations and, especially, the picture of the sick prince are part-elements of this rudimentary conglomeration; and these will always appear

---

[36] *HA* XIII, p. 330.
[37] *Ibid.*
[38] *HA* XIII, p. 337.

coupled with his lost love and themselves reawaken the memory of it. For Goethe was in no doubt but that artistic creativity is biological creativity transferred to another medium, and that Protean Eros moves uncertainly between the artistic and the human domains[39]. As for the picture of the lovesick prince, this emblem of incestuous loving is seen, surely, not only as the biological phenomenon it will be in the case of the Harfner and Sperata and in the many instances, mainly in the *Wanderjahre*, where father and son are erotically bound up with the same woman and stand in a relation of potential rivalry: more importantly, it signifies any form of loving that is too close and basically inward turned, in that the beloved does not in truth represent an objective pole other than the self and separate from it. The danger of such loving — e. g. Wilhelm's and Mignon's — is ever present throughout this novel, and it is because it is so pressing that its figures have to become 'die Entsagenden'. Wilhelm, too, will be exposed to its force once again, at the peak of his development. Thus, the excessive closeness of his relation to Mariane is paradigmatic in itself and by its association with the picture of the prince, the imprint of which will indeed accompany him into full maturity.

It is not possible to trace in isolation the after-life of Mariane's image in Wilhelm's mind. For, contrary to the behaviour of primal imprints as we have observed it in other figures of the novel, the percept of Mariane and the whole cluster of impressions associated with it, is swept up, *kotyledonenartig*, in a movement of progressive metamorphoses, as it merges with such fresh impressions as Wilhelm encounters on his journey through life. This unrecognised tenacity has its dangers, but also its corresponding advantages. The dangers are hinted at in the *Farbenlehre*, where we read: 'Wir blicken von einem Gegenstand auf den andern, die Sukzession der Bilder scheint uns rein, wir werden nicht gewahr, daß sich von dem vorhergehenden etwas ins nachfolgende hinüberschleicht' (Para. 19)[40]. In the novel itself, the Abbé is mercilessly lucid about the handicaps of trailing along past impressions and, above all, warping or injurious ones. Tongue in cheek, he illustrates his contention by the example of a gifted young actor whose unfortunate early predilection for puppet shows had destined him 'die jugendlichen Eindrücke, welche nie verlöschen, denen wir eine gewisse Anhänglichkeit nie entziehen können, von einer falschen Seite zu empfangen' (II. 9). In a more forward-looking vein he asserts: 'Mit je lebhafterm Sinn er das Unreine in seiner Jugend angefaßt und nach seiner Art veredelt hat, desto gewaltsamer wird es sich in der Folge seines Lebens an ihm rächen, indem es sich, inzwischen daß er es zu überwinden suchte, mit ihm aufs innigste verbunden hat' (II. 9). And then, yet more directly alluding to Wilhelm's recent past: 'Wer früh in schlechter, unbedeutender Gesellschaft gelebt hat, wird sich, wenn er auch später eine

---

[39] *Cf.* my *Goethe and Lessing*, Chapter V, section 2.
[40] *HA* XIII, p. 333.

bessere haben kann, immer nach jener zurücksehnen, deren Eindruck ihm
zugleich mit der Erinnerung jugendlicher, nur selten zu wiederholender
Freuden geblieben ist'. (*Ibid.*). This is quite true. Long after his association
with Serlo and his meticulous efforts to interpret the figure and meaning of
Hamlet, Wilhelm comes to the first rehearsal of the play and examines the
décor, only to relapse into memories of a similar scenery in Mariane's epoch
and to indulge himself in hopes that he might see her again. When, a little
later, Philine is seen, and finally departs, with a young person wearing an offi-
cer's uniform such as Mariane had worn, Wilhelm is beside himself: 'Lassen
Sie mich das Mädchen sehen', he beseeches Philine, 'sie ist mein, es ist meine
Mariane! Sie, nach der ich mich alle Tage meines Lebens gesehnt habe, sie,
die mir noch immer statt aller andern Weiber in der Welt ist! . . . sagen Sie
ihr, daß ich hier bin, daß der Mensch hier ist, der seine erste Liebe und das
ganze Glück seiner Jugend an sie knüpfte' (V. 15). And *this* after the protracted,
if ambivalent, dilly-dallying with Philine, after the impact made by Mignon
and Aurelie, after falling deeply in love with the beautiful countess and with
her sister, the 'Amazon'! 'Was einem angehört, wird man nicht los, und wenn
man es wegwürfe.'

And yet this survival of the primary imprint in later mutations is as healthy
and organic as is the metamorphosis of the early cotyledons into the leaves,
the calyx and the bloom of one and the same plant. There is continuity about
such a development, and the original energy is not lost, but preserved and
progressively refined. Impression is superposed upon impression in a steady
upward and outward growth.

Of Mignon's effect on Wilhelm we read: 'Diese Gestalt prägte sich Wil-
helmen sehr tief ein' (II. 4). All Wilhelm's innate need to help is stirred into
urgent life at the sight of this lonely figure, and he longs 'dieses verlassene
Wesen an Kindesstatt seinem Herzen einzuverleiben, es in seine Arme zu
nehmen und mit der Liebe eines Vaters Freude des Lebens in ihm zu erwecken.'
(II. 8). Yet, when he finally calls her 'Mein Kind!' and pledges himself never
to leave her, his mind is brimful with the image of Philine. Identifying with
young Friedrich's rage against the successful *Stallmeister* who has won her
favour, he watches their fight 'nachdenklich und beschämt':

'Er sah sein eignes Innerstes, mit starken und übertriebenen Zügen dargestellt; auch er
war von einer unüberwindlichen Eifersucht entzündet; auch *er*, wenn ihn der Wohlstand
nicht zurückgehalten hätte, würde gern seine wilde Laune befriedigt, gern mit tückischer
Schadenfreude den geliebten Gegenstand verletzt und seinen Nebenbuhler ausgefordert
haben; er hätte die Menschen, die nur zu seinem Verdrusse da zu sein schienen, vertilgen
mögen.' (II. 14).

Wilhelm's perceptual household evidently stands in some need of clearing up.

The first glimpse of the countess initiates a new growing-phase. She makes
a deep impression on him: 'Ihre Schönheit, Jugend, Anmut, Zierlichkeit und
feines Betragen machten den angenehmsten Eindruck auf ihn', we read

(III. I), and soon two pairs of eyes are caught up in an enchanted traffic. 'Sich wechselseitig anzusehen, war ihnen ein unaussprechliches Vergnügen, dem sich ihre harmlosen Seelen ganz überließen . . .' (III. 8). It is at this point of a dawning visual passion that Wilhelm spontaneously understands why Racine should have grieved to death, for no other reason than the Sun-King averted his eye from him.

The prank thought up by the baroness, that Wilhelm surprise the countess in the guise of her husband, fans his love and, with it, reanimates past images, stronger or weaker as the case may be, but in any case welling up unbidden: 'Jeder weibliche Reiz, der jemals auf ihn gewirkt hatte', we read,

'zeigte sich wieder vor seiner Einbildungskraft. Mariane erschien ihm im weißen Morgen-kleide und flehte um sein Andenken. Philinens Liebenswürdigkeit, ihre schönen Haare und ihr einschmeichelndes Betragen waren durch ihre neueste Gegenwart wieder wirksam geworden; doch alles trat wie hinter den Flor der Entfernung zurück, wenn er sich die edle, blühende Gräfin dachte, deren Arm er in wenig Minuten an seinem Halse fühlen sollte, deren unschuldige Liebkosungen er zu erwidern aufgefordert war.' (III. 10).

The premature entry of the returning count foils Wilhelm's hopes. But not his excited imagination. He idolises the countess and etches her image ever more sharply upon his mind. 'Er sah sie oft im Lesen an, als wenn er diesen Eindruck sich auf ewig einprägen wollte', the narrator reports (III. 12). At the fatal goodbye he discovers his own initials engraved on the bracelet the countess is wearing and, fired by this token of a mysterious affinity, declares: 'Ihr Bild steht unauslöschlich in meinem Herzen' (*ibid.*); and this avowal of the impression she has made upon him is sealed by the fatal embrace in which he presses her to his breast.

This renewed vivification of his being leads to yet another expansion, a further growing spurt. And again the composite imprint on his mind under-goes a further metamorphosis. Exhilarated by the countess' evident warmth of feeling, gratified by the gift of money the baron has bestowed upon him at the parting, and excited by his theatrical success, the whole mass of his mind is stirred up:

'In dieser glücklichen Exaltation fuhr er fort . . . ein langes Selbstgespräch zu unter-halten, in welchem er . . . sich eine tätige und würdige Zukunft ausmalte. Das Beispiel so vieler edlen Krieger hatte ihn angefeuert, die Shakespearische Dichtung hatte ihm eine neue Welt eröffnet, und von den Lippen der schönen Gräfin hatte er ein unaussprech-liches Feuer in sich gesogen. Das alles konnte, das sollte nicht ohne Wirkung bleiben.' (IV. 1).

This effect, at first, takes the form of a thoroughgoing regression. Poetically masqueraded, Wilhelm takes over the principalship of the chequered company and heroically undertakes to conduct them to their chosen destination through a horde of marauders. It is in the unexpected encounter with these characters, and transported back to the frame of his first youth, that Wilhelm, setting eyes on Natalie, enters on the new, and crowning, phase of his career.

4.

The impression left on him by this fugitive apparition — *Erscheinung* is the word with which the narrator introduces her — exceeds all previous ones by reason of its visionary force. 'Er hatte seine Augen auf die sanften, hohen, stillen, teilnehmenden Gesichtszüge der Ankommenden geheftet; er glaubte nie etwas Edleres noch Liebenswürdigeres gesehen zu haben.' Insensible of all but her, and the 'heilsame Blick ihrer Augen', he lets the surgeon extract the bullet from his arm. As she steps closer so as to cover him with her uncle's cloak,

'wirkte der lebhafte Eindruck ihrer Gegenwart so sonderbar auf seine schon angegriffenen Sinne, daß es ihm auf einmal vorkam, als sei ihr Haupt mit Strahlen umgeben, und über ihr ganzes Bild verbreite sich nach und nach ein glänzendes Licht . . . Die Heilige verschwand vor den Augen des Hinsinkenden; er verlor alles Bewußtsein, und als er wieder zu sich kam, waren Reiter und Wagen, die Schöne samt ihren Begleitern verschwunden.' (IV. 6)

This visionary experience is deemed so important that it is recounted, in full detail, twice more, not to mention later allusions. When the apparition has vanished, Wilhelm lies quite still, wrapped in Natalie's cloak from which electric sparks seem to exude, and giving himself over to the powerful impress she had made on him. 'Er sah noch den Rock von ihren Schultern fallen, die edelste Gestalt, von Strahlen umgeben, vor sich stehen, und seine Seele eilte der Verschwundenen durch Felsen und Wälder auf dem Fuße nach' (IV. 7). And again, during his recovery:

'Unaufhörlich rief er sich jene Begebenheit zurück, welche einen unauslöschlichen Eindruck auf sein Gemüt gemacht hatte. Er sah die schöne Amazone reitend aus den Büschen hervorkommen, sie näherte sich ihm, stieg ab, ging hin und wider und bemühte sich um seinetwillen. Er sah das umhüllende Kleid von ihren Schultern fallen; ihr Gesicht, ihre Gestalt glänzend verschwinden.'

And this time the narrator adds: 'Alle seine Jugendträume knüpften sich an dieses Bild. Er glaubte nunmehr die edle, heldenmütige Chlorinde mit eignen Augen gesehen zu haben: ihm fiel der kranke Königssohn wieder ein, an dessen Lager die schöne, teilnehmende Prinzessin mit stiller Bescheidenheit herantritt' (IV. 9).

A number of recurrent features in these accounts command our interest. To begin with, the enhanced quality of the image, as compared to former ones, both as regards its power and its content. As for the latter: Mariane had appeared to him in her negligé, an image devoid of all but sensual associations. These had been carried over into the image of Philine's lush hair and insinuating ways, but her *Liebenswürdigkeit* had entered into the picture. The pitch of the image he has of the *Gräfin* is altogether raised: she is *edel* and *blühend*, and her caresses are *unschuldig*. The more refined of these earlier associations are taken over and blended into the image of the 'Amazone':

'Er glaubte nie etwas Edleres noch Liebenswürdigeres gesehen zu haben.' Yet for all that the nobler features of the earlier imprints are preserved, the imprint, in its new metamorphosis, is immeasurably enhanced and attains to the force of a veritable revelation. The halo and the falling garments account for this *Steigerung:* for what the falling cloak reveals[41] is at first 'ihre schöne Gestalt', then 'die edelste Gestalt' and, finally, a face and form which are all incorporeal radiance. On a later occasion Wilhelm will refer to her as to 'diese Gestalt aller Gestalten' (VII. 5), a superlative epithet preserving the memory of and including all the earlier forms that have filled his imagination at the more rudimentary stages of his development, and reserved only for Helena beside Natalie who, in the initial vision, is finally called 'die Heilige'.

Here again, as with Mariane and the beautiful countess, the fresh impress animates 'alle seine Jugendträume'. The whole mass of his mind is stirred. But it is significant that what is thus reanimated is no longer the memory of his earlier loves, but the aesthetically distilled essence of his youth: artistic images and, especially, the visual one of the sick prince, crowd in; and these will remain firmly associated with the figure of Natalie (VIII. 2 and 3).

The 'Steigerung' which is perceptible, both from the features attributed to Natalie's image and the associations it evokes, is epitomised, as it were, in the halo in which she appears to him. Goethe devotes detailed attention to the phenomenon of the nimbus in his optical treatise. He gives various examples of its occurence and arrives at the conclusion that the phenomenon is the result of the independent activity of the eye which, perceiving a dark image that is moving against a lighter background, of itself produces the bright halo surrounding it as a complementary phenomenon (Para. 30). As she bends

---

[41] William Larret associates Natalie's cloak with 'the mantle of poetry', at least in *Wilhelm Meisters Theatralische Sendung*, where her appearance and the gift she bestows upon Wilhelm virtually form the conclusion of the novel. With the shift of emphasis from Wilhelm's preparation for a poetic and theatrical vocation to his development towards human wholeness, the significance of Natalie and her cloak changes, too. In: 'Wilhelm Meister and the Amazons. The Quest for Wholeness', in: *PEGS* XXXIV, (New Series) 1968—69, pp. 37 ff. Larret traces Wilhelm's development to aesthetic wholeness through his association with various women, amazons all, although in different senses, Natalie being the closest approximation to Schiller's, Humboldt's and Goethe's own aesthetic ideal whose wholeness, transcending the division between the sexes, has certain hermaphroditic features about it. 'Natalie in her form, function and character is the Juno of the Lehrjahre' Larret writes. (p. 55.) He certainly shows a relevant and interesting aspect of Wilhelm's quest for wholeness, as reflected in the ascending order of the female figures with whom he associates. But in the Juno-like characterisation of 'die schöne Amazone' I miss something of Natalie's specific delicacy, a quality she not only projects directly — as in her famous 'Nie oder immer' which is ineffably sweet rather than just devoid of sex — but which is indirectly reflected throughout the *Wanderjahre*, in figures resembling her, such as Maria or die Schöne-Gute or Hilarie, and in situations such as the idyll on the Lago Maggiore which receives its tenderness from her absence.

down to cover Wilhelm with her uncle's cloak, Natalie moves, and Wilhelm's eye spontaneously produces 'das geforderte helle Bild um das dunkle' (Para. 30): at the moment of her shedding her husk to help him, an optical phenomenon assumes the force of a revelation. This revelation is a double one. It is about the object Wilhelm perceives — Natalie in her incomparable perfection. At the same time it is about the mode of his perception and the percipient himself: for 'das Auge ... zeigt eben dadurch seine Lebendigkeit, sein Recht, das Objekt zu fassen, indem es etwas, das dem Objekt entgegengesetzt ist, aus sich selbst hervorbringt' (Para. 38). Wilhelm has a right to Natalie in that his mind and eye evince that same harmony and totality which is the hallmark of her existence[42].

This eye, this mind has a predestined affinity with the object it perceives, and perceives creatively. Natalie's *after-image*, metamorphosing as the bond is strengthened, incessantly hovers before him, guiding him, and slowly becomes a *Vorbild* he seeks to approximate, spiritually no less than physically. Shortly before their final union, he mentally compares the image of the Amazon as she had appeared to him at the first with that 'seiner neuen gegenwärtigen Freundin ...; jenes hatte er sich gleichsam geschaffen, und dieses schien fast *ihn* umschaffen zu wollen' (VIII. 2).

And yet, what fluctuations, what evanescence and what precariousness attend even this most cherished of *Gestalten*! Dreamlike, she comes and goes,

---

[42] Larret comes to much the same conclusions, but I consider the way by which I reach these — i. e. through the analysis of the phenomenon of perception — as being more central to Goethe. H. Reiss has devoted some attention to the development of perceptual material in *Wilhelm Meisters Lehrjahre*, in an attempt to demonstrate the poetic organisation of the novel on the verbal level. He traces Wilhelm's development from 'Fleeting images which merely hover' to those of 'representative art' which 'express more durable values'. (In: 'On some Images in *Wilhelm Meisters Lehrjahre*', *PEGS* (New Series) XX, 1949, p. 125 f.) Reiss' analysis of this image-complex and others is designed to show 'the development of his [i. e. Wilhelm's] rational faculties and of his capacity to approach artistic form.' (p. 137.) Many good detailed observations notwithstanding, Reiss does not show any awareness of the wealth of significance, and ambiguity, the symbolism of perception held for Goethe: the fact escapes him that 'hovering' forms are not a sign of a primitive state of confusion, but the tragic hallmark of *Erscheinungen, Gestalten per se*, so that it becomes impossible to trace a linear development from immaturity to maturity in simple terms of the solidity of our percepts. Neither does Reiss seem acquainted with Goethe's optics; a fact which leads him to put a radically untenable interpretation on, say, the longevity of Mignon's early visual imprint. He maintains that the validity of the percept, i. e. 'its relation to reality', 'is measured by the precision and duration of the image.' (p. 123.) As I am concerned to show in this and other chapters, the last criterion he adduces — i. e. the duration of the image — is a very dubious one indeed, necessitating distinctions Reiss fails to make. Thus he concludes that 'Mignon's yearning expresses a desire for a firmer grasp of reality. In her song 'Kennst du das Land' she longs for the *Marmorbilder* (21, 233) where the image is no longer hovering, but has been given firm shape.' (p. 123.) Such a reading is equally at odds with the intention of the text and with Goethe's scientific views as expressed in *Die Farbenlehre*.

scarcely more material than an apparition. 'Oft kam ihm die Geschichte wie ein Traum vor, und er würde sie für ein Märchen gehalten haben, wenn nicht das Kleid zurückgeblieben wäre, das ihm die Gewißheit der Erscheinung versicherte.' And after a long period, in which her image is all that Wilhelm has to hold on to, she materialises once again, slowly and uncertainly, only to disappear from our sight, and Wilhelm's, throughout the length and breadth of the *Wanderjahre*. We shall encounter such transience of cherished forms again — Tasso experiences it, and the father of Eugenie, the speaker of the poems *Euphrosyne* and *Marienbader Elegie*, the Faust of the Helena acts and Epimetheus; and we shall see that even Hermann experiences Dorothea in all the fugitiveness of the human form: *schwankende Gestalten*, all of these, by more than one law. *Schwankende Gestalten* because all forms of nature, and her organic forms above all, *schwanken* 'in einer steten Bewegung', and *schwankend* because the artist is pledged 'wetteifernd mit der Natur etwas Geistig-Organisches hervorzubringen', 'etwas das ihren Erscheinungen ähnlich sei'; which he is only able to do 'wenn wir die Art, wie sie bey Bildung ihrer Werke verfährt, ihr wenigstens einigermaßen abgelernt haben.' The human eye, itself part of nature and ever changing in the forms it presents to the mind and the imagination, is eminently fitted to catch nature's fleeting phenomena; and what eye more so than Goethe's, supremely suceptible and disciplined to capture the lawful flux of sensations — *Bildung und Umbildung* — not only of the *objects* of perception but of the perceptual *process* itself?

Natalie's *Gestalt* is *schwankend*, then, because this novel is a novel about the perception of the world — 'an eye for the world' — and because not only the world of external objects but also the perceiving eye, itself governed by the morphological law of *Gestalten-Umgestalten*, is an object of discourse. The Amazon is offered to the eye and withdrawn again; and in the end nothing but her quintessential *Gestalt* is capable of being held in the creative vision of the *Entsagende*.

But long before such ultimate internalisation is achieved in the living present, what fugitiveness and fluctuations of the beloved's image need to be endured! Perhaps because it is so blinding, Wilhelm cannot sustain it in the etched clarity with which he had perceived it at first. Insensibly, it merges with that of the beautiful countess, her sister, whose handwriting he will later confuse with Natalie's: '... eine Erscheinung verwandelte sich in die andere, ohne daß er imstande gewesen wäre, diese oder jene festzuhalten' (IV. 11). The release of all inhibitions in sleep ushers in an even greater confusion. Bewildered by Aurelie's death and by the unexpectedly favourable impression Lothario has made on him, he dozes off in the early hours of the morning; and in his dream all the images stored up in his unconscious well up, merging and separating and merging again: Aurelie and Mariane and Philine, Frau Melina, the Harfner and the children, Friedrich, Laertes, his

father and *die schöne Amazone* who magically saves his Felix from water and
fire and walks hand in hand with the dreamer.

Wilhelm is entering what Goethe, in *Die Metamorphose der Pflanzen*, calls
the *Blüten- und Fruchtstand* of his development. Imprints that had been
received separately, one after the other, overlap and anastomose, as do the
leaves of the plant in the formation of the calyx. 'Diese Kraft der Natur',
we read in that treatise,

'welche mehrere Blätter um eine Achse versammlet, sehen wir eine noch innigere Verbindung bewirken und sogar diese zusammengebrachten modifizierten Blätter noch
unkenntlicher machen, indem sie solche untereinander manchmal ganz, oft aber nur zum
Teil verbindet, und an ihren Seiten zusammengewachsen hervorbringt. Die so nahe
aneinandergerückten und -gedrängten Blätter berühren sich auf das genauste in ihrem
zarten Zustande, anastomosieren sich ... und stellen uns die glockenförmigen oder
sogenannten *einblätterigen Kelche* dar, welche ... uns ihren zusammengesetzten Ursprung
deutlich zeigen ...'[43]

This simultaneity and renewed undifferentiatedness of growth, which precedes the final flowering of the plant, is a repetition of the phenomenon
characteristic of its 'erste Kindheit': the formation of cotyledons immediately
above the seed. Is it accidental that Wilhelm's entry into the penultimate
phase of his development, a phase characterised by the consistent overlaying
and partial merging of the imprints he has been receiving one by one, should
be inaugurated by a dream, which signifies a return to the undifferentiated
psychic life of childhood, and a dream, moreover, closely packed with figures
he has earlier on encountered?

Deeply preoccupied with Natalie, 'diese Gestalt aller Gestalten', Wilhelm
meets and half falls in love with Therese. He lets himself be persuaded to give
Mignon and Felix into her keeping. They depart, and, alone, he daydreams:

'Der schöne Knabe schwebte wie eine reizende ungewisse Erscheinung vor seiner Einbildungskraft, er sah ihn an Theresens Hand durch Felder und Wälder laufen, in der
freien Luft und neben einer freien und heitern Begleiterin sich bilden ...

Presently he offers her his hand in marriage. Her letter of acceptance, however,
sees him blanch. 'Mit Entsetzen fand er lebhafte Spuren einer Neigung gegen
Natalie in seinem Herzen.' Yet, when, in the presence of the woman he
loves, the news is received that Therese is free to marry Lothario, the strength
of the impression she has made on him becomes apparent: '... das schöne
Bild verläßt mich auf ewig. So lebe denn wohl, du schönes Bild! und ihr
Bilder der reichsten Glückseligkeit, die ihr euch darum versammelt!' (VIII. 4).
What a powerful imprint, and how close to overlaying that of Natalie! And
strangely enough, the ultrasensible Therese reacts, on the eve of *her* happiness,
with a passionate vision which curiously corresponds to Wilhelm's own: on
hearing that she is free to marry Lothario, she fiercely exclaims:

[43] *HA* XIII, p. 74.

'Mein erster Traum, wie ich mit Lothario leben würde, ist weit von meiner Seele weg-
gerückt; der Traum, wie ich mit meinem neuen Freund zu leben gedachte, steht noch
ganz gegenwärtig vor mir. Achtet man mich so wenig, daß man glaubt, es sei so was
Leichtes, diesen mit jenem aus dem Stegreife wieder umzutauschen?' (VIII. 4).

This all but fatal mistake is accompanied by other blurrings of Natalie's
image, more temporary, but significant nonetheless. There is the momentary
flare-up of his passion for Mariane when Barbara tells him of her wretched
fate. Keenly interested in Therese and magically drawn to the 'herrliche
Amazone', his 'edler Schutzgeist', as he apostrophizes her at the beginning of
the chapter, these feelings are all but swept away as he listens to Barbara's
account of her mistress' fidelity. The past is all-powerful. 'Wo hast du sie?
Wo verbirgst du sie?' he impetuously asks the old woman. 'Ich glaube dir
alles, ich verspreche dir alles zu glauben, wenn du mir sie zeigst, wenn du
sie meinen Armen wiedergibst. Ihren Schatten habe ich schon im Fluge gesehen, laß mich sie wieder in meine Arme fassen! ... Komm, daß ich sie mit
diesem Licht beleuchte! daß ich wieder ihr holdes Angesicht sehe!' What else
should have induced the narrator to interpolate this account, and Wilhelm's
passionate aberration, in the midst of an epoch belonging to Therese and,
ultimately, Natalie, if not the desire to show the simultaneous clustering of
imprints received turn by turn before the final flowering of vision? Error is
built into error with every morphological deliberation.

Then there is the confusion between the handwritings of the beautiful
countess and Natalie, and the brief confusion of Natalie with the portrait of her
aunt, *die schöne Seele*, whom she so uncannily resembles: a last stage of that
Steigerung of the image developing in Wilhelm which we have been observing
all along. For as it will soon be said, it is Natalie who is in truth a '*schöne
Seele*'. The last husk is shed. Wilhelm recognises the *Gestalt* his active eye is
fitted to perceive; and, with it, recovers the image of the lovesick prince
which has been imprinted upon his mind's eye from his earliest youth onwards, symbol of a loving that is too inward turned and close. As he enters
the hall of Natalie's home, he sees '... eine Muse, die seinem Großvater gehört
hatte ... Darauf trat er in den Vorsaal, und zu seinem noch größern Er-
staunen erblickte er das wohlbekannte Bild vom kranken Königssohn an der
Wand' (VIII. 2). Later, he says:

'... ich werde mich des Eindrucks von gestern abend zeitlebens erinnern, als ich herein-
trat und die alten Kunstbilder der frühesten Jugend wieder vor mir standen. Ich erinnerte
mich der mitleidigen Marmorbilder in Mignons Lied; aber diese Bilder hatten über mich
nicht zu trauern, sie sahen mich mit hohem Ernst an und schlossen meine früheste Zeit
unmittelbar an diesen Augenblick.'

The primal imprint has expanded and reached maturity. All others are
absorbed in it and enhance the energy and purity of the emerging *Gestalt*[44].

---

[44] It may well be argued that this phase of Wilhelm's development in which the maturing
image of Natalie is superposed, and at times threatened, by a proliferation of other im-

The alternation of sad and happy events assailing Wilhelm 'hatten sein Innerstes ganz aus aller Fassung gebracht, einer Leidenschaft zu widerstehn, die sich des Herzens so gewaltsam bemächtigt hatte' (VIII. 10). The seed of his loving has come to full bloom; and at the moment of fulfilment a final, tremendous expansion takes place, as it does — so we learn from *Die Metamorphose der Pflanzen* — in the development from calyx to flower: 'du kommst mir vor wie Saul, der Sohn Kis, der ausging, seines Vaters Eselinnen zu suchen, und ein Königreich fand', Friedrich comments. What an enlargement[45]! And it is from his hands that Wilhelm receives the 'flower' of his life: 'Wie meint Ihr, Freund, . . . als wir Bekanntschaft machten, als ich Euch den schönen Strauß abforderte, wer konnte denken, daß Ihr jemals eine solche Blume aus meiner Hand empfangen würdet?' (VIII. 10). Might it have been at this climactic stage of his hero's development that, nearing Sicily and pursuing the spectre of the *Urpflanze*, Goethe uttered the prayerful wish that in that paradisical land the last books of his *Meister* might flourish? One of the last entries in the *Italienische Reise*, before he finally set sail, reads: 'Möge meine Existenz sich dazu genugsam entwickeln, der Stengel mehr in die Länge rücken und die Blumen reicher und schöner hervorbrechen.'

pressions, bears some resemblance to the interaction of the *vertikale Tendenz* with the *Spiraltendenz* which Goethe describes in *Spiraltendenz der Vegetation* (*HA* XIII, pp. 130ff.). Of the *vertikale Tendenz* we read: 'Diese ist anzusehen wie ein geistiger Stab, welcher das Dasein begründet und solches auf lange Zeit zu erhalten fähig ist. . . . es ist dasjenige, was bei den Bäumen das Holz macht . . .' (p. 132). 'Das vertikal aufsteigende System bewirkt bei vegetabilischer Bildung das Bestehende, seinerzeit Soleszidierende, Verharrende . . .' (p. 133). As against this we read of the *Spiralsystem*: 'Das Spiralsystem ist das Fortbildende, Vermehrende, Ernährende, als solches vorübergehend, sich von jenem gleichsam isolierend. Im Übermaß fortwirkend, ist es sehr bald hinfällig, dem Verderben ausgesetzt; an jenes angeschlossen, verwachsen beide zu einer dauernden Einheit als Holz oder sonstiges Solide.' (p. 133.) The energy of Natalie's image represents the *vertikale Tendenz*, the *geistige Stab* or, as Goethe has it a little later on in the same essay, the *Stütze*, 'as it were the skeleton' of Wilhelm's growth. The proliferation of this image into Therese, Mariane, the beautiful countess, even the *schöne Seele*, represents the *Spiraltendenz, fortbildend, vermehrend, ernährend* as we have seen, because these excrescences feed and refine the dominant energy rather than luxuriating in isolation from it. Were they to do so, they would soon sap it, as Goethe observes in the essay (p. 135 f.). As it is, these 'spiral' accretions nourish the principal image, and in a unified growth eventually form a *dauernde Einheit*, i. e. an indelible eidetic image of Natalie. In this connection, cf. Chapter XIII, section 3, and S. Alexander, *Beauty and other Forms of Value* (p. 68 f.).

45 Günther Müller deplores 'die so nachdrückliche Fassung des Endresultats, . . . so mager wirkt sie vor der Weite und Tiefe des ganzen Werks.' (*Op. cit.* (I), p. 30.) He does so in a most commendable context, namely in pursuit of his thesis 'daß Dichtung nicht in der Aussage von Denkresultaten gipfelt, sondern in der Gestaltbildung ihre eigentliche Wirklichkeit erreicht.' (p. 30.) To reply to his stricture here that Wilhelm's image of enlargement articulates the morphological law of his total development and voices the final phase of expansion would seem like carrying coals to Newcastle!

5.

'Daß die Geschlechtsteile der Pflanzen durch die Spiralgefäße wie die übrigen Teile hervorgebracht werden, ist durch mikroskopische Beobachtungen außer allen Zweifel gesetzt', we read in *Die Metamorphose der Pflanzen* (Para. 60). It is evident, Goethe argues,

'daß der weibliche Teil so wenig als der männliche ein besonderes Organ sei, und wenn die genaue Verwandtschaft desselben mit dem männlichen uns durch diese Betrachtung recht anschaulich wird, so finden wir jenen Gedanken, die Begattung eine Anastomose zu nennen, passender und einleuchtender.' (Para. 69).

It is strange that the Harfner — a brother of the marchese as it turns out — should rest the defence of his incestuous union with his sister Sperata on precisely this analogy from the world of plants. 'Seht die Lilien an', he passionately exclaims:

'entspringt nicht Gatte und Gattin auf *einem* Stengel? Verbindet beide nicht die Blume, die beide gebar, und ist die Lilie nicht das Bild der Unschuld, und ihre geschwisterliche Vereinigung nicht fruchtbar? Wenn die Natur verabscheut, so spricht sie es laut aus; das Geschöpf, das nicht sein soll, *kann nicht werden**, das Geschöpf, das falsch lebt, wird früh zerstört. Unfruchtbarkeit, kümmerliches Dasein, frühzeitiges Zerfallen, das sind ihre Früchte.' (VIII. 9).

Nature's verdict disproves the Harfner, more even than his own remorse. Mignon, 'das Knaben-Mädchen' as she will be called, does not reach the fullness of womanhood and dies early; and

So laßt mich scheinen, *bis ich werde**,

she begs in her parting song[46]. And of the Harfner's 'kummervollen Nächte' we learn not only through his lyrics —

Ihm färbt der Morgensonne Licht
Den reinen Horizont mit Flammen,
Und über seinem schuld'gen Haupte bricht
Das schöne Bild der ganzen Welt zusammen —:

we have the doctor's description of his hollow and horrified emptiness (VII. 4). The result of his too close relatedness is a self incapable of entering into any relation whatever with what is outside it:

'Seit vielen Jahren hat er an nichts, was außer ihm war, den mindesten Anteil genommen, ja fast auf nichts gemerkt; bloß in sich gekehrt, betrachtete er sein hohles, leeres Ich, das ihm als ein unermeßlicher Abgrund erschien ... ich weine meine Tränen alle mir selbst und um mich selbst. Nichts ist mir grausamer als Freundschaft und Liebe ...'

---

[46] For an interpretation of Mignon's plea which complements the one given here, cf. Larret (*loc. cit.*, p. 48 f.).

* my italics.

These are the fruits of unmediated closeness. What is natural on the lower rungs of nature, becomes a monstrous travesty of nature in the human domain. Naturalness, amongst humans, requires the altogether unnatural taboo of distance. Wilhelm, in his relation to Mignon, is in constant danger of overstepping this taboo. When her love for him becomes manifest — 'die lange und streng verschlossene Knospe war reif', we read — and he, confused by a surge of primitive passions, locks her in his embrace, 'floß ein Strom von Tränen aus ihren geschlossenen Augen in seinen Busen' (II. 14). This is not a communion between related yet distinct beings: it is a communion of one being with itself, that *Anastomose* of which Goethe speaks in his treatise on the metamorphosis of plants[47].

The picture of the sick prince who consumes himself for the love of his mother is Goethe's shorthand for those abysses of nature. And this picture, part of Wilhelm's primal imprint, is firmly associated with his relationship to Natalie. As he finds her, he finds this mental possession of his earliest youth, and the ring of his life-cycle, broken before, closes upon itself.

There is no doubt that, through the cypher of this picture, the poet is indicating the dangers of too close a feeling-bond between Wilhelm and Natalie. They are as alike as blood relations. Natalie's nature is to help — *hilfreich* is the epithet constantly associated with her — even as Wilhelm's first youthful impulse had been to help his drowned friend, the fisherman's son. It is this moment of impotence which implanted the seed of his calling in him.

The deep affinity between the lovers is stressed by Therese in a curious attempt to persuade herself that *this* of all facts makes Wilhelm suited to *her*, Natalie's friend. 'Wenn ich hoffe, daß wir zusammen passen werden', Therese writes to Natalie,

> 'so gründe ich meinen Anspruch vorzüglich darauf, daß er Dir, liebe Natalie, die ich so unendlich schätze und verehre, daß er Dir ähnlich ist.... Wenn ich an ihn denke, vermischt sich sein Bild immer mit dem Deinigen, und ich weiß nicht, wie ich es wert bin, zwei solchen Menschen anzugehören.' (VIII. 4).

In this piece of rationalisation we may discern something of the irony that pervades the *Wahlverwandtschaften*. Therese thinks she chooses, but the lovers are in fact chosen by the deep affinity that governs their natures.

When Wilhelm exclaims that, in entering Natalie's home, he has entered a temple 'und Sie sind die würdige Priesterin', he knows by anticipation, as it were, that to be worthy of her humanity, and his own, he must renounce the immediacy prescribed by untutored nature. The very pictures he sees around him — that of the *kranke Königssohn* who is tended by the beautiful, sympathetic princess, amongst them — tell him that he is on the right way: for 'diese Bilder hatten über mich nicht zu trauern, sie sahen mich mit hohem Ernst an'.

---

[47] *HA* XIII, p. 83 f.

Basically, we know from the moment he sets eyes on his 'Amazone', that theirs will be the way of mediacy and renunciation for the sake of a common concern: for 'Das Kind lag zwischen ihnen beiden auf dem Teppich und schlief sanft' (VIII. 2). This constellation will be repeated once again, at the climactic moment of the final chapter. Mignon is dead, Felix seems to have drunk Augustin's poison, the latter has slashed his wrists. The three lives closest to Wilhelm's roots are in eclipse. In this passionate turmoil he sits on a stool in front of Natalie;

> 'er hatte die Füße des Knaben auf seinem Schoße, Kopf und Brust lagen auf dem ihrigen, so teilten sie die angenehme Last und die schmerzlichen Sorgen und verharrten, bis der Tag anbrach, in der unbequemen und traurigen Lage; Natalie hatte Wilhelmen ihre Hand gegeben, sie sprachen kein Wort, sahen auf das Kind und sahen einander an.'[48]

It is during this night spent in distance and nearness, a night that seals their union, that Augustin puts an end to his incest-stained life.

6.

Distance and nearness, nearness through distance and across it, this is the shape of Wilhelm's and Natalie's loving, and this will be the theme of *Die Wanderjahre* which reflect this exemplary relation in endless metamorphoses and *wiederholten Spiegelungen*.

The second part of the novel begins with the story of St. Joseph the Second. It is indeed a *Wiederholte Spiegelung*[49] of Wilhelm's relation to the 'schöne Amazone', in the precise sense in which Goethe uses the term in the essay bearing its name. For in the holy wilderness in which Wilhelm finds himself, he encounters a man, like himself married to a woman who has loved 'nie oder immer', as the 'schöne Amazone' has it of herself, and whose healing bond with that woman is sealed over a young child belonging to another. St. Joseph, too, has an essentially visionary experience of the strange woman, the moment he sets eyes on her: 'Es war mir, als wenn ich träumte', he recalls to Wilhelm,

> 'und dann gleich wieder, als ob ich aus einem Traume erwachte. Diese himmlische Gestalt, wie ich sie gleichsam in der Luft schweben und vor den grünen Bäumen sich herbewegen sah, kam mir jetzt wie ein Traum vor, der durch jene Bilder in der Kapelle sich in meiner Seele erzeugte. Bald schienen mir jene Bilder nur Träume gewesen zu sein, die sich hier in eine schöne Wirklichkeit auflösten.' (I. 2).

---

[48] E. Bahr has noted this point and the close resemblance of the emotional situation here to that depicted in 'St. Joseph der Zweite'. (In: *Die Ironie im Spätwerk Goethes etc.*, *op. cit.*, p. 92 f.)
[49] Cf. Bahr, *op. cit.*, p. 92.

Throughout the night of Maria's confinement, he relates, 'hatte ich die schöne Gestalt vor Augen, wie sie auf dem Tiere schwankte und so schmerzhaft freundlich zu mir heruntersah'[50].

This is essentially the constellation Goethe describes in *Wiederholte Spiegelungen*. One man who cherishes a long-standing and deeply imprinted vision meets another 'in welchem das Bild sich gleichfalls eingedrückt hat' (Para. 7). 'Hier entsteht nun in der gewissermaßen verödeten Lokalität die Möglichkeit, ein Wahrhaftes wiederherzustellen, aus Trümmern von Dasein und Überlieferung sich eine zweite Gegenwart zu verschaffen und Friederiken von ehmals in ihrer ganzen Liebenswürdigkeit zu lieben' (Para. 8). In precisely this manner Wilhelm recovers Natalie, as in *'einer zweiten Gegenwart'*, in the reflection he encounters in the dilapidated monastery that is the home of the 'holy family'. More than that: just as Näke's 'passion' for Friederike was inspired by Goethe's lyrics, so the carpenter's life and love are mirrorings of the picture-stories which have surrounded him from his youth onwards, and on which he models his ways. The congruence of this opening episode of the *Wanderjahre* with Goethe's essay is as striking as it is significant: for it is the optical law of repeated mirrorings and the enhancement of the images thus reflected that determines the structure of the second part of the novel, as we shall presently see.

'Und hat nicht selbst das Zusammentreffen dieser beiden Liebenden etwas Ähnliches mit dem unsrigen?' Wilhelm writes. Wilhelm and Natalie, at their first encounter, hold the sleeping Felix between them. Joseph, at long last permitted to see Maria, enters the room of her confinement. 'Frau Elisabeth . . . hub etwas vom Bette auf und brachte mir's entgegen: in das weißeste Zeug gewickelt den schönsten Knaben. Frau Elisabeth hielt ihn gerade zwischen mich und die Mutter, und' — we hardly trust our eyes as we read on —

> 'auf der Stelle fiel mir der Lilienstengel ein, der sich auf dem Bilde zwischen Maria und Joseph als Zeuge eines reinen Verhältnisses aus der Erde hebt. Von dem Augenblicke an war mir aller Druck vom Herzen genommen . . . (I. 2).

The lily, symbol of the too intimate union of incest in the first part of the novel, returns here once again, at the opening of the second: but now, in this delicate intertwining of nature and nurture, it appears as the symbol of that chaste relatedness grounded in suprapersonal concerns which emerges as the common goal of the *Entsagenden*. As Makarie has it: 'Von Natur besitzen wir keinen Fehler, der nicht zur Tugend, keine Tugend, die nicht zum Fehler werden könnte' (*WJ.*, I. 10)[51].

---

[50] Note the 'schweben' and 'schwanken' in the depiction of an archetypal situation as expressive of permanence and universality as is ever possible, and in this connection cf. note 42.

[51] In another context, W. Benjamin draws attention to the ambiguity of the lily as a symbol of innocence: 'Die strengen Linien des Gewächses, das Weiß des Blütenkelches verbinden

7.

In this second part of the novel, Natalie is removed from our sight, and Wilhelm's fortunes become interlaced with, and at times overshadowed by, a host of other figures which claim our attention, some familiar, some new to the reader, some appearing in the main plot, others in the stories with which it is interspersed, and many gliding from the one fictional frame into the other. Yet the human constellations and the themes that have made up the fabric of the *Lehrjahre* recur, in multiple metamorphoses and mirrorings, removed and at the same time enhanced, throughout its continuation. And indeed, the symbol of the *kranke Königssohn* has lost none of its power. How many triangular entanglements there are, as often as not involving father and son in an unconscious incestuous rivalry over the same woman! We need only think of *Die pilgernde Törin*, of *Der Mann von funfzig Jahren* with its double plot woven around Hilarie and the beautiful widow, both of whom attract father and son, of Lucidor who is promised by his father to the wrong bride, and, last but not least, of the curiously vacillating relation of Hersilie to Felix and his father, to convince ourselves of the continuing importance of this motif. If to this list we add the triple betrayal in *Nicht zu weit* and the ambiguous position of Lenardo *vis à vis* the courting *Gehilfe* and the dead fiancé, or *Gatte*, of 'die Schöne-Gute' (the relation to her dead lover is never fully spelt out and this enigmatic purity places her in the immediate vicinity of the 'schöne Amazone' and Joseph's wife Maria), we have a picture of confused relationships to match any presented in the *Lehrjahre*. And so, too, the blurred identities we encounter in the *Wanderjahre* — 'das nußbraune Mädchen' = Valerine = Nachodine = Frau Susanne = 'die Schöne-Gute' is but one example for many — carry on a pattern that is familiar to us from the first part of the novel. And as for the mental turmoil, the loss of 'innere Gestalt', be it that of one individual or of a human configuration, there is no instance in the *Lehrjahre* to match the chaos that overtakes the major in *Der Mann von funfzig Jahren* when, returning at night from an inspection of his estates, he espies his son and Hilarie skating hand in hand over the inundated fields; nor indeed a passage to match the eerie intensity of his approach:

'Da blickten sie auf und sahen im Geflimmer des Widerscheins die Gestalt eines Mannes hin und her schweben, der seinen Schatten zu verfolgen schien und selbst dunkel, vom Lichtglanz umgeben, auf sie zuschritt ... Sie vermieden die immerfort sich herbewegende Gestalt, die Gestalt schien sie nicht bemerkt zu haben und verfolgte ihren geraden Weg nach dem Schlosse. Doch verließ sie auf einmal diese Richtung und umkreiste mehrmals das fast beängstigte Paar.' (*WJ*, II. 5).

sich mit den betäubend süßen, kaum mehr vegetabilen Düften', he remarks, in: *Illuminationen*, Frankfurt/Main 1961, p. 121.

The inner counterpart to this evocation of menacing anonymity is evoked as follows: 'Auszumalen ist nicht *die innere Gestalt** der drei nunmehr nächtlich auf der glatten Fläche im Mondschein Verirrten, Verwirrten', the narrator reports; and a little later continues to describe the *innere Gestalt* of the father thus:

'Bedauern wir den guten Mann, dem diese Sorgen, diese Qualen wie ein beweglicher Nebel unablässig vorschwebten, bald als Hintergrund, auf welchem sich die Wirklichkeiten und Beschäftigungen des dringenden Tages hervorhoben, bald herantretend und alles Gegenwärtige bedekkend. Ein solches Wanken und Schweben bewegte sich vor den Augen seines Geistes; und wenn ihn der fordernde Tag zu rascher, wirksamer Tätigkeit aufbot, so war es bei nächtlichem Erwachen, wo alles Widerwärtige, gestaltet und immer umgestaltet, im unerfreulichsten Kreis sich in seinem Innern umwälzte. Dies ewig wiederkehrende Unabweisbare brachte ihn in einen Zustand, den wir fast Verzweiflung nennen dürften, weil Handeln und Schaffen, die sich sonst als Heilmittel für solche Lagen am sichersten bewährten, hier kaum lindernd, geschweige denn befriedigend wirken wollten.' (II. 5).

What visual precision in the evocation of the nocturnal scene, and what controlled knowledge of a pathological instability in which every mental contour is obliterated by a chaos of metamorphosing images!

The world of persons and relationships, in the *Lehrjahre* still capable of being ordered and stored up in the neat files of the *Turmgesellschaft*, seems to have proliferated into an impenetrable jungle of passions run amok. Where is Therese's ideal of a 'moral diet'? Where Wilhelm's notion of a 'reinen und sichern Tätigkeit'? Where is the soil in which the lily, 'Zeuge eines reinen Verhältnisses', may grow?

'Die Sehnsucht verschwindet im Tun und Wirken', Lenardo writes; and: 'mache ein Organ aus dir', Jarno-Montan impresses on Wilhelm. It is in the direction pointed by these words that we must seek the answer to our question.

The character in the *Wanderjahre* who is most relentlessly driven by *Sehnsucht* is Lenardo himself; and we may do well to turn our attention to this figure and follow him on his pilgrimage, to gain some clue as to how and where it is appeased.

There seems to be some natural affinity between given human beings and some objects. They talk to him and he understands them, their behaviour, their needs and their uses. Such an affinity was soon to become manifest between Lenardo and technical tools. 'Von Jugend auf entwickelte sich in ihm eine gewisse muntere, technische Fertigkeit, der er sich ganz hingab und darin glücklich zu mancher Kenntnis und Meisterschaft fortschritt', Makarie relates of her travelling nephew (I. 10); and Lenardo himself confirms the truth of this account: 'Unter den frühsten meiner Fähigkeiten, die sich nach und nach durch Umstände entwickelten', he tells Wilhelm,

'tat sich ein gewisser Trieb zum Technischen hervor, welcher jeden Tag durch die Ungeduld genährt wird, die man auf dem Lande fühlt, wenn man bei größeren Bauten,

---

* my italics

besonders aber bei kleinen Veränderungen, Anlagen und Grillen ein Handwerk ums andere entbehren muß und lieber ungeschickt und pfuscherhaft eingreift, als daß man sich meistermäßig verspäten ließe.' (III. 4).

Lenardo duly acquires a lathe and other carpenters' tools. He scarcely remembers ever having played, 'denn alle freien Stunden wurden verwendet, etwas zu wirken und zu schaffen.' (*Ibid.*) He found that he had to invent tools to serve specific purposes, 'und wir litten nicht wenig an der Krankheit jener Techniker, welche Mittel und Zweck verwechseln, lieber Zeit auf Vorbereitungen und Anlagen verwenden, als daß sie sich recht ernstlich an die Ausführung hielten.' (*Ibid.*) He had, in fact, contracted the craftman's addiction to his medium, toying with it, exploring its possibilities, together with the conditions of its application. Thus, discovering ever new fields of employment for his skills and studying what was needful, he had become an expert in all aspects of the homecraft of weaving which, being conducted in secluded valleys, was especially dependent on the versatility of a mobile technician. 'Diese Neigung, diese ausgebildete Gabe' was to fit him for the task of travelling to those secluded parts on behalf of the society, to select craftsmen suited to emigrate to the new world. Thus, even as he searches for the girl he had let down, the longing to find her is tempered by the gratification of exercising his masterly skills.

The first lap of his pilgrimage to find the 'nußbraune Mädchen' turns out to be a mistaken one. Misled by the name Valerine, and supposing it to be that of the girl for whom he searches, he and Wilhelm arrive at the estate of a flourishing farmer. The mistress of the house is not at home, and the landowner invites his guests to come into the fields with him; the friends duly consent and we read:

'... der Landmann hatte seinen Grund und Boden, den er unumschränkt besaß und beherrschte, vollkommen gut inne; was er vornahm, war der Absicht gemäß; was er säete und pflanzte, durchaus am rechten Ort;' (I. 11).

We remember Goethe's enthusiastic description of George Batty's agricultural expertise, in the diary entry which begins with the words: 'Gedancken über den Instinckt zu irgend einer Sache'[52], and we recognise the same instinct of the man for his land here. They belong to one another by a deep affinity. The soil, 'den er vollkommen gut "inne hatte"', is part of him, the 'Land-Mann', as it were. It informs him of its needs and he responds to its demands with perfect appropriateness. Or, rather, his hands do the responding: for, as Odoard tells the crafsmen who have opted to remain in Europe: 'die Bekenner sollten mit der Hand wirken, und die Hand, soll sie das, so muß ein eigenes Leben sie beseelen, sie muß eine Natur für sich sein, ihre eignen Gedanken, ihren eignen Willen haben' (III. 12). This intimate understanding of his hands the *Landmann* explains to his guests in a charming way:

---

[52] Cf. Chapter IV, sections 3 and 4.

'Er führte sie auf seinen Hof, zeigte ihnen seine Werkzeuge, den Vorrat derselben sowie den Vorrat von allem erdenklichen Geräte und dessen Zubehör: "Man tadelte mich oft", sagte er dabei, "daß ich hierin zu weit gehe; allein ich kann mich deshalb nicht schelten. Glücklich ist der, dem sein Geschäft auch zur Puppe wird, der mit demselbigen zuletzt noch spielt und sich an dem ergötzt, was ihm sein Zustand zur Pflicht macht."' (I. 11).

On their way they meet the *Geschirrmacher*, an important figure in the secluded rural district in which they find themselves, in that he knows and is able to repair all the utensils used in the various crafts, especially the spinning wheels and looms required by the spinners and weavers. Lenardo finds 'einen sehr verständigen, in gewissem Sinne gebildeten, seiner Sache völlig gewachsenen Mann' (III. 5), as joyful in the exercise of his craft as the *Landmann* had been before him. Again we observe the affinity of man and object: the figure of speech chosen by the narrator here is loaded with more than its conventional meaning: man and *Sache* have grown up together, indeed, they *have* grown together, as the centaur is one with his horse.

This deep, bodily affinity of worker and work is even more striking in the case of the spinners, masters of a craft to which Lenardo feels magically drawn and amongst whom he will discover, by the law of that inner logic which governs this novel, the woman he loves. 'Die Spinnerin sitzt vor dem Rade, nicht zu hoch; ... Mit der rechten Hand dreht sie die Scheibe und langt aus, so weit und hoch sie nur reichen kann, wodurch schöne Bewegungen entstehen und eine schlanke Gestalt sich durch zierliche Wendung des Körpers und runde Fülle der Arme sich vorteilhaft auszeichnet' (III. 5). This description of harmonious movement would seem to be of aesthetic rather than functional significance. That this is not so, however, becomes apparent from the following passages in which the processing of the finer cotton is described, which, carefully skeined and combed, is wrapped into a paper bag and thence spun from the hand:

'Dieses Geschäft, welches nur von ruhigen, bedächtigen Personen getrieben wird, gibt der Spinnerin ein sanfteres Ansehen als das am Rade; kleidet dies letzte eine große, schlanke Figur zum besten, so wird durch jenes eine ruhige, zarte Gestalt gar sehr begünstigt. Dergleichen verschiedene Charaktere, verschiedenen Arbeiten zugetan, erblickte ich mehrere in *einer* Stube und wußte zuletzt nicht recht, ob ich meine Aufmerksamkeit der Arbeit oder den Arbeiterinnen zu widmen hätte.' (III. 5).

A pre-established harmony, in which mental and bodily make-up determines the mode of activity, whilst that activity in turn moulds character and frame; a mutual choice governed by affinity and beautifully expressed in the *double entendre* of the word 'zugetan'[53].

---

[53] Such a demonstration of thematic continuity should dispel the criticism, so often voiced, that what is felt to be a mass of technical detail has remained unassimilated into the poetic organism of the work as a whole. For a complementary argument to my own, cf. Lange who argues that Goethe's concern, in the *Wanderjahre*, was the portrayal 'of a society in transition' (*loc. cit.*, p. 59), of 'a synthetic panorama of contemporary experience.' 'To

Lenardo has all along been guided in his search of the 'Schöne-Gute' by a description of her sent to him by Wilhelm. We read:

'Häuslicher Zustand, auf Frömmigkeit gegründet, durch Fleiß und Ordnung belebt und erhalten, nicht zu eng, nicht zu weit, im glücklichsten Verhältnis der Pflichten zu den Fähigkeiten und Kräften. Um sie her bewegt sich ein Kreislauf von Handarbeitenden im reinsten, anfänglichsten Sinne; hier ist Beschränktheit und Wirkung in die Ferne, Umsicht und Mäßigung, Unschuld und Tätigkeit.' (II. 6 and III. 5).

Already in the *Lehrjahre* the Abbé had maintained: 'man könne nichts tun, ohne die Anlage dazu zu haben, ohne den Instinkt, der uns dazu treibe ... es gibt keine unbestimmte Tätigkeit' (*LJ*, VIII. 3); and Jarno-Montan says to Wilhelm: 'Der Mensch versteht nichts, als was ihm gemäß ist' (*WJ*, I. 3). We have seen the truth of those maxims in the instance of Lenardo, the husbandman, the utensil-maker and, in enhanced measure, of the spinners. They are born and made for their job, as it is made for them. It fits them like their skin; it is entirely integral to them and their inborn aptitudes, and that is why they understand it. The depth and closeness of such an interlocking, in turn, makes for a certain limitation of scope, the limitation of the professional, the specialist. It is the old story of the 'Ehstand des Künstlers mit seinem Instrument', as Goethe has it in his diaries, an intimacy of attunement which results in an air of domesticity.

So far the description Wilhelm has sent to Lenardo of the sphere of activity in which he will find his 'Schöne-Gute' corresponds to what we have seen for ourselves, here and in related instances. But what about that 'Wirkung in die Ferne'? Lenardo himself queries the aptness of this description. 'Nur eine Wirkung in die Ferne will mir nicht gleichermaßen deutlich scheinen', he demurs. Yet Wilhelm is correct, and correct in more ways than one: 'der beste, wenn er *eins* tut, tut er alles, oder, um weniger paradox zu sein, in dem *einen*, was er recht tut, sieht er das Gleichnis von allem, was recht getan wird', Jarno-Montan had explained to Wilhelm (*WJ*, I. 4), and clearly this eager but diffuse young man had marked his words. But he is more correct than he could have known at the time of writing to Lenardo; for how could he have guessed that 'die Schöne-Gute', herself the active centre of an ordered circle, is sufficiently alive to the symbolic character of her humble pursuits to be worthy of becoming the companion of Makarie, that loftiest of all figures of *Die Wanderjahre*, whose own life is a mysterious circling around the sun?

convey this experience in its compelling actuality he represented certain aspects of it, not in a symbolic key, not transposed, but through the sober description of technical and scientific processes.' (p. 60.) This to me seems a most subtle and completely satisfying answer to those who — like Grillparzer — deny the inner unity of the novel and bolster up their charge by reference to the chunks of unassimilated discursive material it is supposed to contain. Cf. also Bahr's emphasis on 'obscuritas' as the stylistic principle of the novel. (*Op. cit.*, p. 102.)

Indeed, Montan's paradoxical maxim opens vaster perspectives before our eyes as well. Those affinities between man and object, worker and work which we have observed on a small scale, operate on higher levels and in more elevated spheres, in exactly the same fashion and with the same precision. Montan himself — counterpoint to Makarie — offers us an example. He is attuned to the stony world of the mountains. He can read them and in the letters of 'Felsen und Zacken' decipher the writing of nature. 'Die Natur hat nur *eine* Schrift', he laconically explains to the literary Wilhelm, 'und ich brauche mich nicht mit so vielen Kritzeleien herumzuschleppen' (I. 3). Allied with him is the *Bodenfinderin*,

> 'eine Person . . ., welche ganz wundersame Eigenschaften und einen ganz eigenen Bezug auf alles habe, was man Gestein, Mineral, ja was man überhaupt Element nennen könne. (III. 14).

Later, when she joins the servants on Makarie's estate, we are told 'man habe sie oft das Werkzeug niederlegen und querfeldein über Stock und Steine springen sehen, auf eine versteckte Quelle zu, wo sie ihren Durst gelöscht'; which feat she repeated day in day out, in varied locations and never missing her objective (III. 15).

This enigmatic affinity of the soil-diviner to the element is really no more mysterious than those other ones we have seen to operate on more mundane levels. In every instance, we are confronted with a native attunement between a person and an object, a self and a given aspect of the world, and from that interaction an organ has developed which constitutes an unfailing link between the two spheres. Hersilie, magically attracted to Wilhelm and his impetuous son, and finding the key to Felix's mysterious chest which is in her keeping, excitedly writes: 'Da sehen Sie nun, in was für einen Zustand mich die Freundschaft versetzt: ein famoses Organ entwickelt sich plötzlich, Ihnen zuliebe; welch ein wunderlich Ereignis!' (III. 2). 'Das unnützeste Geschöpf von der Welt', as Friedrich calls his wife Philine, has made a similar discovery — her 'gefräßige Schere':

> 'Legt ihr ein Stück Tuch hin, stellt Männer, stellt Frauen ihr vors Gesicht: ohne Maß zu nehmen, schneidet sie aus dem Ganzen . . . und das alles ohne Papiermaß. Ein glücklicher geistiger Blick lehrt sie das alles, sie sieht den Menschen an und schneidet, dann mag er hingehen, wohin er will, sie schneidet fort und schafft ihm einen Rock auf den Leib wie angegossen.' (III. 4).

In one instance, and an important one, we watch such an 'organ' being disclosed before our very eyes. Hilarie, on Lago Maggiore, shows a sensitive understanding of the young painter's pictures of Mignon and is eventually persuaded to produce her own efforts. However, her work shows signs of timidity. Presently, excited by the painter's developed talent and freedom,

> 'fühlt sie sich . . . erweckt, was von Sinn und Geschmack in ihr treulich schlummerte; . . . und so schließt sich die schönste Fähigkeit unvermutet zur Fertigkeit auf: wie eine Rosenknospe, an der wir noch abends unbeachtet vorübergingen, morgens mit Sonnen-

aufgang vor unseren Augen hervorbricht, so daß wir das lebende Zittern, das die herrliche Erscheinung dem Lichte entgegenregt, mit Augen zu schauen glauben.' (II. 7).

By and by, we have moved into the sphere of visual perception from which we started, and we realise that, in discussing the development of an active organ for the mastery of some aspect of the objective world, we have been speaking all along of that *gegenständliche Anschauen* which Goethe recognised to be the key to his own connection with the world. What is true of him could be affirmed by his fictional characters as well: 'daß die Elemente der Gegenstände, die Anschauungen in dasselbe [i.e., das Denken] eingehen und von ihm auf das innigste durchdrungen werden, daß mein Anschauen selbst ein Denken, mein Denken ein Anschauen sei.'[54]

And thus we come to Wilhelm, Natalie and Makarie, the crowning triad of the novel. As we have seen, the seed of his future calling was implanted in Wilhelm when the splendid form of the fisherman's boy lay dead before him and he was sensible of his utter helplessness. Relating this early erotic experience and its sad outcome in a letter to Natalie, he perceptibly dillydallies and evades the point of his story. Again he comes back to the accident, the discussion that followed it and his own childish resolution to miss no opportunity 'alles zu lernen, was in solchem Falle nötig wäre, besonders das Aderlassen'. But, he adds, he was distracted by his passion for the theatre. Apologising for his dilatoriness, he pleads:

'sollte es dem Verständigen, dem Vernünftigen nicht zustehen, auf eine seltsam scheinende Weise ringsumher nach vielen Punkten hinzuwirken, damit man sie in *einem* Brennpunkt zuletzt abgespielt und zusammengefaßt erkenne, einsehen lerne, wie die verschiedensten Einwirkungen den Menschen umringend zu einem Entschluß treiben, den er auf keine andere Weise, weder aus innerm Trieb noch äußerm Anlaß, hätte ergreifen können?' (II. 11).

Then, at last, after an allusion to the talk with Montan, in which the latter had impressed on him: 'Mache ein Organ aus dir', he comes to the point. It is the medical instrument bag he had seen on the occasion when he first met Natalie which has brought about a silent revolution in his life:

'Du erinnerst dich gewiß jenes Bestecks, das euer tüchtiger Wundarzt hervorzog, als du dich mir, wie ich verwundet im Walde hingestreckt lag, hülfreich nähertest? Es leuchtete mir damals dergestalt in die Augen und machte einen so tiefen Eindruck, daß ich ganz entzückt war, als ich nach Jahren es in den Händen eines Jüngeren wiederfand.' (II. 11).

Jarno had recognised the significance this 'fetish' had for his friend and had taken him to task over his indolence 'auch ihren Gebrauch zu verstehen und dasjenige zu leisten, was sie stumm von dir fordern' (II. 11). Wilhelm had confessed 'daß mir dies hundertmal eingefallen ist; es regte sich in mir eine innere Stimme, die mich meinen eigentlichen Beruf hieran erkennen ließ ... doch jede Stunde löschte den Vorsatz aus.' 'So ergreif ihn jetzt',

[54] *HA* XIII, p. 37.

Jarno had replied, scoffing at Wilhelm's high endeavours to be a spiritual Jack of all trades. 'Narrenpossen ... sind eure allgemeine Bildung und alle Anstalten dazu[55]. Daß ein Mensch etwas ganz entschieden verstehe, vorzüglich leiste, wie nicht leicht ein anderer in der nächsten Umgebung, darauf kommt es an, und besonders in unserm Verbande spricht es sich von selbst aus.'

It is through the illuminated perception of the tool of his calling, under the *heilsame Blick* of the woman he loves, that Wilhelm's 'organ' for that calling which will connect him with the world in 'einer reinen und sichern Tätigkeit' has been disclosed to him. And we may add that, through Wilhelm's — and his own — dilatoriness in revealing the full significance of this all-important object, the narrator enacts as it were the slow and devious development of his hero towards his eventual goal.

This perception of need is immeasurably more differentiated in Natalie, and she arrives at her vocation without any error or diversion. In fact, she is born to it. We have dwelt on her response to Wilhelm's mishap and remarked on her concentrated perception of his condition and his needs. We have already cited the first memory she has of herself: 'Ich erinnere mich von Jugend an kaum eines lebhaftern Eindrucks', she confesses, 'als daß ich überall die Bedürfnisse der Menschen sah und ein unüberwindliches Verlangen empfand, sie auszugleichen'. This is how she continues her self-assessment; and we must take careful note of her recurrent references to the act of perceiving which lend their characteristic mark to her account:

'Das Kind, das noch nicht auf seinen Füßen stehen konnte, der Alte, der sich nicht mehr auf den seinigen erhielt, das Verlangen einer reichen Familie nach Kindern, die Unfähigkeit einer armen, die ihrigen zu erhalten, jedes stille Verlangen nach einem Gewerbe, den Trieb zu einem Talente, die Anlagen zu hundert kleinen notwendigen Fähigkeiten, diese überall zu entdecken, schien mein Auge von der Natur bestimmt. Ich sah, worauf mich niemand aufmerksam gemacht hatte; ich schien aber auch nur geboren, um das zu sehen. ... meine angenehmste Empfindung war und ist es noch, wenn sich mir ein Mangel, ein Bedürfnis in der Welt darstellte, sogleich im Geiste einen Ersatz, ein Mittel, eine Hülfe aufzufinden.'

'Sah ich einen Armen in Lumpen, so fielen mir die überflüssigen Kleider ein, die ich in den Schränken der Meinigen hatte hängen sehen; sah ich Kinder, die sich ohne Sorgfalt und ohne Pflege verzehrten, so erinnerte ich mich dieser oder jener Frau, der ich bei Reichtum und Bequemlichkeit Langeweile abgemerkt hatte; sah ich viele Menschen in einem engen Raum eingesperrt, so dachte ich, sie müßten in die großen Zimmer mancher Häuser und Paläste einquartiert werden. Diese Art, zu sehen, war bei mir ganz natürlich, ohne die mindeste Reflexion ...' (VIII. 3).

---

[55] This transition from the emphasis on 'allgemeine Bildung', which is the goal of the *Lehrjahre*, to the specialisation demanded in the *Wanderjahre* is a development anticipated in the diaries of the young Goethe. There, too, the strenuous cult of universality in the end is seen not to do justice to the one gift Goethe possessed 'ganz entschieden' — his poetic genius. This discovery leads, not indeed to the abandonment of his multifarious activities, but to the gradual formulation of a more complex model of wholeness. (Chapter IV. sections 5 and 6.)

It is because Natalie *sees* need rather than feeling or vaguely sensing it, as Wilhelm tends to do, with an incomparable urgency and precision, in fact with what Goethe, in relation to himself, terms 'exakte sinnliche Phantasie', that she emphatically dissociates herself from the Abbé's precept to let people learn through their errors: 'Wer nicht im Augenblick hilft, scheint mir nie zu helfen, wer nicht im Augenblicke Rat gibt, nie zu raten', she declares with some passion.

Natalie has an inborn aptitude for and affinity with goodness, and the organ through which she is unfailingly connected with her calling is that all but immaterial organ, her loving eye. She sees what it takes to be good, as Goethe 'saw' the *Urpflanze*, 'mit unbewußter Naivität', in a flawless *gegenständlichen Anschauung*. The elements of her perception enter into her imagination and thinking and permeate it, and in turn her thinking and her imagination seize upon the iniquitous situation with which her eye has presented her, until she comes up with a solution and acts on it: plundering wardrobes, supplying shelter or clothing — e. g. the cloak with which she covers Wilhelm — or doing whatever else the' Augen-Blick' requires to be done.

Early on in the novel, Wilhelm's friend Werner had painted a glowing picture of the virtues of commerce — the counterpart to Wilhelm's *Muse* — praising it as the great mediator between demand and supply in the world; Lothario and Therese had conversed about similar topics — 'aber gewissermaßen ward unser Gespräch zuletzt immer ökonomisch, wenn auch nur im uneigentlichen Sinne' (VII. 6). In the *Wanderjahre*, a great deal of thought will be expended on how to balance supply and demand in the remote mountain regions in which the spinners practise their homecraft. It is Natalie who, of all figures in the novel, has the liveliest *sinnliche Phantasie*, the most unerringly *gegenständliche Anschauung* of supply and demand in the specifically human domain, the moral sphere. Because she cannot but fulfil a need as soon as she has perceived it, she answers Wilhelm's question: 'Sie haben nicht geliebt?', by replying: 'Nie oder immer.' It is for this reason that her brother may tease her and poor Wilhelm, saying: 'Ich glaube, du heiratest nicht eher, als bis irgendwo eine Braut fehlt, und du gibst dich alsdann nach deiner gewohnten Gutherzigkeit auch als Supplement irgendeiner Existenz hin' (VIII. 7). Friedrich is not altogether off the mark. But in a world governed by mysterious affinities, and between two hearts endowed with an unerring organ for the good, the outlook is favourable.

8.

'Das Auge hat sein Dasein dem Licht zu danken. Aus gleichgültigen tierischen Hülfsorganen ruft sich das Licht ein Organ hervor, das seinesgleichen werde, und so bildet sich das Auge am Lichte fürs Licht, damit das innere Licht dem äußeren entgegentrete.' These introductory sentences of the *Farbenlehre* describe the stage of realisation that all-transcending figure Makarie has reached. She has 'an eye for the world'. Her eye is her integral organ for the cosmos. Its totality comprehends the totality without, and she lives in a perpetual *Gegenständliche Anschauen* of what it mirrors. Her *inneres Licht*, that sun which is not darkened by even the brightest light of the outward sun, goes out towards the heavenly orb, circling around it in an ever ascending spiral. In citing from the various passages in which Markarie's mode of being, which is a mode of seeing, is described, we must again take note of the recurrent emphasis placed on the act of perceiving:

'Wie man von dem Dichter sagt, die Elemente der sichtlichen Welt seien in seiner Natur innerlichst verborgen und hätten sich nur aus ihm nach und nach zu entwickeln, daß ihm nichts in der Welt zum Anschauen komme, was er nicht vorher in der Ahnung gelebt: ebenso sind, wie es scheinen will, Makarien die Verhältnisse unsres Sonnensystems von Anfang an, erst ruhend, sodann sich nach und nach entwickelnd, fernerhin sich immer deutlicher belebend, gründlich eingeboren.' (I. 10).

Thus Angela to Wilhelm. Towards the end of the novel this account is supplemented by a statement found amongst Makarie's archives. There we read of her movement around the sun, in circles which increasingly outsoar our solar system, and of the inner cause of such affinity: 'Sie erinnert sich von klein auf ihr inneres Selbst als von leuchtendem Wesen durchdrungen, von einem Licht erhellt, welchem sogar das hellste Sonnenlicht nichts anhaben konnte. Oft sah sie zwei Sonnen, eine innere nämlich und eine außen am Himmel . . .' (III. 15).

With such creative totality of perception as hers, we would expect all Makarie's faculties to be developed into aptitudes, all her aptitudes to be enhanced to the highest sublimity and precipitated in the noblest and aptest activity. Such implications of her mode of perceiving are in fact confirmed:

'alle Fähigkeiten wurden an ihr lebendig, alle Tätigkeiten wirksam, dergestalt daß sie allen äußeren Verhältnissen zu genügen wußte und, indem ihr Herz, ihr Geist ganz von überirdischen Gesichten erfüllt war, doch ihr Tun und Handeln immerfort dem edelsten Sittlichen gemäß blieb. Wie sie heranwuchs, überall hülfreich, unaufhaltsam in großen und kleinen Diensten, wandelte sie wie ein Engel Gottes auf Erden . . .' (III. 15).

Natalie helps in the moment — Goethe's 'Augenblick'! — for the moment. The elements of her perception are material, even though they are incandesced with her loving: children and the infirm, nakedness and hovels are what she sees; and such seeing gives rise to remedial actions aimed at bettering the physical world. Makarie's perception sees only the spiritual elements of the world, and it is with the clarification of these that her actions are concerned. It is she that transforms a jungle of confused and tangled passions into a gossamer web of affinities:

'es war, als wenn sie die innere Natur eines jeden durch die ihn umgebende individuelle Maske durchschaute. Die Personen, welche Wilhelm kannte, standen wie verklärt vor seiner Seele, das einsichtige Wohlwollen der unschätzbaren Frau hatte die Schale losgelöst und den gesunden Kern veredelt und belebt.' (I. 10).

She resolves the inner conflicts that darken mind and soul of the characters in the novella *Der Mann von funfzig Jahren*. Both the mature and more vulnerable partners of that foursome find peace and inner clarification through the penetrating power of her moral perception. They seek her help, knowing 'daß jene Treffliche, im Vorhalten eines sittlich-magischen Spiegels, durch die äußere verworrene Gestalt irgend einem Unglücklichen sein rein schönes Innere gewiesen und ihn auf einmal erst mit sich selbst befriedigt und zu einem neuen Leben aufgefordert hat' (II. 5). Her mirror is 'magic' in that it does not merely clarify: it creates. It is in her proximity that the tiresome Lydie first gains a human face and, with it, our sympathy, much to our suprise.

If Makarie is vouchsafed a *Gegenständliches Anschauen* of an almost mystical intensity and scope, her human goodness lies in transmitting some of this power of perception to those around her. This is the significance of her *sittlich-magischer Spiegel*. Those that perceive themselves in it, perceive themselves *gegenständlich*, as though they were another: they accept what they see with a dispassion that is sympathetic, and are pacified by such purity of vision. And such pacification in turn is a mighty transforming agent. One might sum up her influence in the words the narrator interpolates in a *Zwischenrede*: it is to be hoped, 'es werde allen und jeden, wenn sie sich ins Leben zu finden wissen, ganz erwünscht geraten' (II. 7).

But it is not only Makarie who transmits the power to perceive the world *gegenständlich*. Others possess this capacity in a lesser measure and pass it on. It is Lothario above all — whose own mode of perceiving is *gegenständlich* in a high degree as is attested by his strange encounter with the *Pachterstochter* he once loved — who presents a clear mirror to those around him, in which they perceive themselves and the world. 'Er führt, wo er auch sei, eine Welt mit sich' it is said of him (VIII. 5). To transmit a *gegenständliche Anschauung* of the intricacies of an individual life and its interrelations is, of course, the purpose of the scrolls stored up in the archives of the *Turmgesellschaft* whose founding members, on Jarno's admission, had no higher ambition 'als die Welt zu kennen wie sie war'; 'Wir wollten mit eignen Augen sehen', Jarno characteristically adds (VIII. 5).

Wilhelm's perception is educated by the greatest variety of agents: through Shakespeare, through Aurelie, Lothario, Therese, Jarno, the Abbé and the scroll containing his own life's story — 'er sah zum erstenmal sein Bild außer sich, zwar nicht, wie im Spiegel, ein zweites Selbst, sondern wie im Porträt ein anderes Selbst', we read (VIII. 1) — through the young painter who 'opened his eyes' to the beauties of nature whose 'offenbares Geheimnis' he for the first time beheld through his companion's sensibilities (*WJ.*, II. 7); through the anatomical sculptor who teaches him 'sich den Zusammenhang dieses lebendigen Wunders' — i. e., of the human form — 'immer vor Geist und Auge zu erneuern' (*WJ*. III. 3); and, last but not least, through

his own son, Felix, whose inquisitiveness about everything his eye sees
rouses his shamefaced father to emerge from his own fog of vagueness:
'Wilhelm sah die Natur durch ein neues Organ', we read (VIII. 1); and
there can be no doubt that it is the youth's reckless experimentations with
life as much as the manifold starts and stops of his own career which bring
home to him the justice of Jarno-Montan's all-important words:

> 'Denken und Tun, Tun und Denken, das ist die Summe aller Weisheit, von jeher
> anerkannt, von jeher geübt, nicht eingesehen von einem jeden. Beides muß wie Aus- und
> Einatmen sich im Leben ewig fort hin und wider bewegen; wie Frage und Antwort sollte
> eins ohne das andere nicht stattfinden. Wer sich zum Gesetz macht, was einem jeden
> Neugebornen der Genius des Menschenverstandes heimlich ins Ohr flüstert, das Tun
> am Denken, das Denken am Tun zu prüfen, der kann nicht irren, und irrt er, so wird
> er sich bald auf den rechten Weg zurückfinden.' (II. 9).

But Wilhelm has yet another organ of perception, an antenna he shares
with Makarie alone, of all the figures that crowd the pages of this novel.
This is his power of anticipation.

The intimations of the 'jungen, zärtlichen, unbefiederten Kaufmannssohn'
who soars above reality 'auf den Flügeln der Einbildungskraft' (I. 1 and I. 3),
at first seem vague enough. For all the intensity with which his imagination
'schwebte', or even 'brütete', 'über der kleinen Welt' of his puppet-show and,
later, of his first live play, it did not forewarn him of the fact that parts have
to be known to be successfully acted. The portrait he paints of the poet as
'Lehrer, Wahrsager, Freund der Götter und der Menschen' seems true
enough in itself, but barely applicable to Wilhelm whose knowledge of people
and their motives is lamentable; indeed, we become suspicious when the
'unbefiederte Kaufmannssohn' paints the poet's being in his own colours, in
the likeness of a bird, 'gebaut..., um die Welt zu überschweben, auf hohen
Gipfeln zu nisten und seine Nahrung von Knospen und Früchten, einen
Zweig mit dem andern leicht verwechselnd, zu nehmen' (II. 2): it all sounds
too etherial, and it brings to mind the occasion, much later, when Wilhelm
is already maturing, on which he will come to feel the lash of Aurelie's
tongue: 'mein feiner Paradiesvogel' she calls him and, on being asked the
meaning of this appellation, explains: 'Man sagt, sie hätten keine Füße, sie
schwebten in der Luft und nährten sich vom Äther' (V. 10). Yet it is this
self-same Aurelie who marvels at his inborn knowledge of things: 'Ohne die
Gegenstände jemals in der Natur erblickt zu haben, erkennen Sie die Wahrheit im Bilde; es scheint eine Vorempfindung der ganzen Welt in Ihnen
zu liegen...' (IV. 16). And does not *der Sänger* of the Harfner's ballad
compare himself to a bird? Perhaps we must after all take Wilhelm's belief in
his anticipatory knowledge of things seriously.

After his first encounter with Natalie, which becomes interlaced with the
images of his youth, he asks himself:

> 'Sollten nicht ... uns in der Jugend wie im Schlafe die Bilder zukünftiger Schicksale
> umschweben und unserm unbefangenen Auge sichtbar werden? (IV. 9).

Shortly after his arrival at Makarie's home, and before he has learnt anything concerning that woman's strange relation to the solar system, Wilhelm is deeply impressed by the starry sky, more glorious to the *Schauenden* than he had ever perceived it to be. Overwhelmed, he lapses into musing; and these are his thoughts:

> '"Darfst du dich in der Mitte dieser ewig lebendigen Ordnung auch nur denken, sobald sich nicht gleichfalls in dir ein beharrlich Bewegtes, um einen reinen Mittelpunkt kreisend, hervortut?"' (I. 10).

Is not his perception here anticipating Makarien's own awareness of two suns, one inner and one outer one, and the movement of her self around 'die Weltsonne'? These facts are not revealed until the end of the novel, and the narrator gives no clear indication as to whether the relevant records from her archives are at any point made available to Wilhelm.

Later that same night Wilhelm is awakened by Makarie's astronomer to admire the planet Venus which is just then heralding the rise of the sun in unusual brightness. Wilhelm looks, marvels and calls what he has seen a miracle. Told by the astronomer that he could see nothing miraculous about an otherwise lovely sight, he explains that the star he had just seen in reality was the continuation as it were of the same star he had dreamt a few seconds earlier. He had perceived Makarie on her chair moving heavenward, and her face had turned into a luminous star which, ascending through the ceiling, had merged with the starry heavens, seeming to engulf it. 'In dem Augenblick wecken Sie mich auf' — another of those pregnant uses of the word *Augen-Blick* —

> 'schlaftrunken taumle ich nach dem Fenster, den Stern noch lebhaft vor meinem Auge, und wie ich nun hinblicke — ... Dieser wirkliche, da droben schwebende Stern setzt sich an die Stelle des geträumten, er zehrt auf, was an dem erscheinenden Herrliches war, aber ich schaue doch fort und fort, und Sie schauen ja mit mir, was eigentlich vor meinen Augen zugleich mit dem Nebel des Schlafes hätte verschwinden sollen.' (I. 10).

Miracle indeed, the astronomer exclaims: Wilhelm had in his dream anticipated the destiny sooner or later in store for Makarie.

It is two days after this nocturnal vision that Makarie's young companion, Angela, reveals the mysterious relation of her mistress to the solar system; and she introduces her account as follows:

> 'Wie man von dem Dichter sagt, die Elemente der sichtlichen Welt seien in seiner Natur innerlichst verborgen und hätten sich nur aus ihm nach und nach zu entwickeln, daß ihm nichts in der Welt zum Anschauen komme, was er nicht vorher in der Ahnung gelebt: ebenso sind, wie es scheinen will, Makarien die Verhältnisse unsres Sonnensystems von Anfang an, erst ruhend, sodann sich nach und nach entwickelnd, fernerhin sich immer deutlicher belebend, gründlich eingeboren.' (I, 10).

Wilhelm's anticipations have confirmed the truth of what 'man von dem Dichter sagt'[56]. They have, moreover, confirmed that, although he may not be a poet in the specific sense of the word, his creator has richly endowed him with his own poetic sensibility, with his sensitive receptivity, his own slow and organic mode of harbouring imprints received early on, until they reach eventual maturity, in short with his own *Gegenständlichkeit* of perception and, last but not least, with his own power of anticipation. For of himself Goethe affirmed, curiously enough in connexion with the genesis of *Wilhelm Meister*, that 'der Dichter durch Antizipation die Welt vorwegnimmt'[57], and, in a more general vein: 'Hätte ich nicht die Welt durch Antizipation bereits in mir getragen, ich wäre mit sehenden Augen blind geblieben.'[58] Finally, Wilhelm's anticipation of Makarie's being and destiny argues not only the existence of some deep bond between these two figures; it suggests that they move in a universe itself governed by mysterious affinities.

9.

The world in the second part of *Wilhelm Meister* has, as we have seen, enormously expanded. New figures, new groups of figures even, have sprung into existence, individual destinies have receded in comparison with the collective problems that have to be faced in an industrial age demanding an increase in specialisation, and eyes are turned to the new world, beyond the narrow confines of the old. Such proliferation of material necessitated a new, and more complex, narrative technique. The movement of the principal plot became slacker and more devious; individual portraits and personal configurations tended to be pursued in separate novellas inserted like islands in the main stream of the action, or like tributaries joining it. Figures conceived in such a separate fictional frame step out of it and are absorbed in the ampler framework of the main plot. Such are Hilarie, Flavio and 'die schöne Witwe' from *Der Mann von funfzig Jahren*, 'das nußbraune Mädchen' who emerges as Makarie's companion, Odoard, tragic hero of *Nicht zu weit* who becomes the leader of one section of the society, to mention only some. Other figures belonging to the main plot slip into the inserted narrations and out of them again: Wilhelm and Lenardo in their search for 'das nußbraune Mädchen', the barber who becomes the hero of *Die neue Melusine*, St. Christoph who narrates, and plays a leading part in, *Die gefährliche Wette*, and so on.

---

[56] H. Reiss traces the motif of the bird but contradistinguishes the mode of Wilhelm's association with it from that of the Harfner and concludes that, in the case of the hero, it articulates a development from free-roaming fancy to self-restraint coupled with imaginativeness. (*Loc. cit.*, pp. 127 ff.)

[57] *HA* X, p. 430f.

[58] Goethe to Eckermann, February 26, 1824.

In addition to this criss-cross between different strata of reality, there are constant mirrorings of one part of the main plot in another, or as between portions of the main plot and the inserted narratives[59]. Lenardo in many ways resembles Wilhelm, and both alike search for a woman who is as much a sister as a wife and can be theirs only at the price of radical renunciation. Wilhelm may not live with Natalie, whom he had called 'die würdige Prieste-rin' on first seeing her again. Nachodine's dying father pledges his daughter and Lenardo to one another, saying: 'Das soll kein irdisches, es soll ein himm-lisches Band sein; wie Bruder und Schwester liebt, vertraut, nützt und helft einander, so uneigennützig und rein, wie euch Gott helfe.' (III. 13). And these words, as well as Wilhelm's sentiments, are echoed in the words 'die Schöne-Gute' speaks as a sort of epilogue: '"In die Nähe soll man nicht hoffen", rief sie aus, "aber in die Ferne"'. The parallel is obvious; and the lov-ing of both friends is once again mirrored in the story of *St. Joseph der Zwei-te* — a powerful reflector of most themes occurring in *Die Wanderjahre* — in which the lily joins, and separates, husband and virgin wife, 'als Zeuge eines reinen Verhältnisses'. On the other hand, what a counterpoint Lenardo's romantic and protracted search for the *Pachterstochter* of his youth makes to Lothario's visit to his early love, also a *Pachterstochter*, where he experien-ces a sense of perfect fulfilment 'in der sonderbarsten Gegenwart zwischen der Vergangenheit und Zukunft, wie in einem Orangenwald, wo in einem kleinen Bezirk Blüten und Früchte stufenweis nebeneinander leben' (VII. 7). Here is 'Im Gegenwärtigen Vergangnes', with all longing pacified in the purest of *Gegenständliches Anschauen*.

Again, Lucidor, hero of *Wer ist der Verräter?*, reflects features of Wilhelm. He, too 'war von tiefem Gemüt und hatte meist etwas anders im Sinn, als was die Gegenwart erheischte'; he too all but marries the wrong girl; and it is impossible not to recognise in the mischievous *Junker* who cuts the Gordian knot a reflection of Friedrich, the *enfant terrible* who with unceremonious cheek saves the situation at the end of the *Lehrjahre*. Stories such as *Die neue Melusine* and *Die gefährliche Wette* echo themes that run through both parts of the novel: the disparity between capacity and achievement — 'Jeder . . . grei-fe mit allen seinen Fertigkeiten so weit umher, als er zu reichen fähig ist' (I. 6) — and the fatal disparity between powerful imprints and the ability to absorb them in action, Mignon's fate and the Harfner's. The manifold trian-gular situations of the *Lehrjahre*, involving more often than not two men and one woman, are reflected in similar ones encountered in the second part of the novel, both in and out of the main plot: and everywhere we come upon the father-son motif which is so insistently sounded in the picture of the 'kranke Königssohn'.

---

[59] Cf. Lange (*loc. cit.*, pp. 59 ff.) and Bahr (*op. cit.*, pp. 98 ff.).

Strangest of all perhaps is the resurrection of Mignon in the *Wanderjahre*. A real if enigmatic presence in the fictional frame of the first part, her after-image is caught in the mirror of the young artist's imagination who (like the young Näke in search of Goethe's Friederike) follows her in the tracks of her childhood and, 'leidenschaftlich eingenommen . . . von Mignons Schicksalen, Gestalt und Wesen', paints a series of pictures of the *anmutige Scheinknabe*, as she is called. The enhanced art-image of the dead child powerfully radiates back into the company of the living, Wilhelm amongst them, and affects an almost magic *Steigerung* of sentiments that had hitherto remained unspoken. 'Das Vorgefühl des Scheidens' which had animated this strange group floating there on Lago Maggiore, tied by close bonds of emotion, yet doomed to remain footloose and distant from one another, discharges itself as the dead child's

> Kennst Du das Land, wo die Zitronen blühn,
> Im dunklen Laub . . .

is sounded. And 'unter dem hehren Himmel, in der ernst-lieblichen Nacht-stunde, eingeweiht in alle Schmerzen des ersten Grades der Entsagenden', all alike experience the distilled essence of longing pacified by presence and purified by art.

It is as though the participants in this nocturnal episode — the most con-summate piece of lyricism in the whole of the *Wanderjahre* — saw their in-dividual conditions, their memories and the strange relationships of the present moment reflected back and transfigured in Makarie's 'sittlich-magischen Spie-gel', a transforming agent which recollects 'Vergangnes, Abwesendes traum-artig' and distances 'das Gegenwärtige, als wäre es nur Erscheinung, geister-mäßig'. And this indeed is the effect of all those 'Spiegelungen' which inter-connect the two parts of the novel, the several portions of the main plot of *Die Wanderjahre* as well as the main narrative, with the stories that are inserted in it. As the fictional figures of the novellas step out of their framework, and mingle with the figures belonging to the principal action, the ontological status of the latter becomes steadily more uncertain: what had seemed real enough, through its merging with what is real at one remove, becomes 'gei-stermäßig entfernt'. Conversely, those figures who, like Mignon, are re-animated in the minds of the living or join their company, attain to a 'dream-like' presence. And both, the characters and configurations of the main plot and those that have their being in the interpolated narratives, through their repeated mirroring become ever more transparent and enhanced in what is gradually revealed as being a symbolic reality. In the end, structure and thema-tic development coincide: a thicket of confused longings and tangled relation-ships becomes clarified into a network of affinities between 'Entsagende': reflected back as they appear in a maze of mirrors, these figures and con-figurations become, as it were, abstract to themselves; and we, too, perceive them, and the relations between them, symbolically, as an intimation of some ultimate and encompassing pattern of correspondences. What else is the irony of symbolic indirection but the renunciation of immediacy objectified in a supremely 'reflective' form?

But our account of Makarie and, indeed, the quotation from the *Farbenlehre* we cited in the context of that figure at the outset of the previous section is not, so far, complete. We have not yet mentioned the fact that Makarie is more than a percipient of the solar system, however *gegenständlich* that perception may be. Expressly and repeatedly we are told 'daß sie nicht sowohl das ganze Sonnensystem in sich trage, sondern daß sie sich vielmehr geistig als ein integrierender Teil darin bewege.' Thus Angela to Wilhelm; and this vital piece of information is repeated at the end of the novel where we read: 'Im Geiste, der Seele, der Einbildungskraft hegt sie, schaut sie es nicht nur, sondern sie macht gleichsam einen Teil desselben' (III. 15). In exact correspondence, the passage from the *Farbenlehre* I have partially cited, reads on as follows: 'Jene unmittelbare Verwandtschaft des Lichtes und des Auges wird niemand leugnen; aber sich beide zugleich als eins und dasselbe zu denken, hat mehr Schwierigkeit.'[60]

If, then, it is true that 'nur von Gleichem werde Gleiches erkannt'[61], we must concede that, in the marginal instance of Makarie at least, our reading of the affinity between subject and object, between self and world, as it is symbolically disclosed through the phenomenon of perception, is not sufficiently radical; and, so too, our understanding of what Goethe means by an 'organ of perception' falls short of the truth. In the case of Makarie at least, the notion of an affinity between her and the cosmos must give way to that of an ultimate identity; and to say that she has, or is, an organ for the perception of that cosmos must be corrected as meaning that she is connected or integrated with it by some kind of anastomosis. On the same lines, we would have to argue that the 'Land-Mann' is an integral and integrating part of the land he cultivates, the inborn 'organ' he has developed for it linking the two in an affinity which is as rooted in bodily reality as it is mystical. Finally, Wilhelm is magically connected with threatened lives: it is no accident that his son comes to grief and all but drowns within sight of his father; and the instrument bag, Wilhelm's 'organ', becomes as it were the life-line ensuring the survival of both.

I think that we are correct in accepting this more radical interpretation Goethe puts on the affinity between self and world as symbolised by the phenomenon of perception, and in adjudging it to be valid for the novel we have considered. In the end, the notion of *Gegenständliches Anschauen* which is central to it, transcends any dichotomous distinction between subject and object, self and world, and indeed any possibility of separating them at all.

---

[60] *HA* XIII, p. 324.
[61] *Ibid.*

In the essay *Einwirkung der neueren Philosophie* Goethe recounts the excitement
aroused by the Kantian question 'wieviel unser Selbst und wieviel die Außenwelt zu unserm geistigen Dasein beitrage.' 'Ich hatte beide niemals gesondert',
is his simple comment[62]; and the failure, or unwillingness, to do so, which is
strongly corroborated by the position maintained in *Bedeutende Fördernis
durch ein einziges geistreiches Wort*, in my opinion is not accounted for by pointing
to the 'naive realism' of a philosophically indifferent mind, but springs from
a mystical belief in an ultimate identity of 'Selbst' and 'Außenwelt', a belief
approximated throughout *Wilhelm Meister* and incarnated through an act of
dichterische Antizipation in the figure of Makarie.

In *Betrachtungen im Sinne der Wanderer* we read:

> 'Alles, was wir Erfinden, Entdecken im höheren Sinne nennen, ist die bedeutende Aus-
> übung, Betätigung eines originalen Wahrheitsgefühles, das, im stillen längst ausgebildet,
> unversehens mit Blitzesschnelle zu einer fruchtbaren Erkenntnis führt. Es ist eine aus dem
> Innern am Äußern sich entwickelnde Offenbarung, die den Menschen seine Gottähnlich-
> keit vorahnen läßt. Es ist eine Synthese von Welt und Geist, welche von der ewigen
> Harmonie des Daseins die seligste Versicherung gibt.'[63]

This 'ewige Harmonie des Daseins', this ultimate oneness of the stuff of
which mind and matter, self and world, eye and light are spun was, I suggest,
the sacred credo of a poet who was, to an all but unique degree, an *Augenmensch* and, in the last resort, something of a mystic.

> Wär nicht das Auge sonnenhaft,
> Die Sonne könnt' es nie erblicken;
> Läg' nicht in uns des Gottes eigne Kraft,
> Wie könnt' uns Göttliches entzücken?

---

[62] *HA* XIII, p. 26.
[63] *Betrachtungen im Sinne der Wanderer*, *HA* VIII, p. 302.

V The Symbolic Mode

> This is the use of memory:
> For liberation — not less of love but expanding
> Of love beyond desire, and so liberation
> From the future as well as the past.
>
> T. S. Eliot

'Verwandte Engelsbilder':
Apotheosis of an Artist ('Die Wahlverwandtschaften')

Unmöglich scheint immer die Rose,
Unbegreiflich die Nachtigall.

Goethe

I.

Die Wahlverwandtschaften has been intriguingly described as the 'roman édu-catif de la jeune fille'[1]; and although something in our mind refuses to cast this most complex and profoundly ambiguous of Goethe's works into so straight and linear a mould, there is undoubtedly some truth in this appellation in relation to the figure of the young heroine. Development there is to be discerned, and the poet has marked this fact — and his special sympathy for Ottilie — by the progression in the epithets accompanying her career. *Das liebe* and *schöne Kind*, as she is called in early portions of the novel, gives way to *das herrliche* and, eventually, das *himmlische Kind*. Yet, as these epithets tell us clearly enough, a child she remains to the end; and there seems no question but that we are not confronted, in her case, with a linear development from youth to human maturity as we are, say, in the figure of Meister, or Wolf-ram's Parzival, or Thomas Mann's Hans Castorp.

And what a child she is! With her bad school reports, her stiff and un-developed hand, her profound inarticulacy which, if anything, grows more pronounced as she lapses, towards the end, into unbroken silence, and, most of all, the breathtaking unconsciousness with which, blithely and without so much as a tremor of conflict, she intrudes upon the marriage of the woman she reveres as a second mother![2] And how touchingly naive are her gestures, going down on her knees before Charlotte, which embarrasses the latter no less than its explanation, and that gesture of supplication the *Gehülfe* describes,

---

[1] By J. F. Angelloz, *Goethe*, Paris 1949, p. 258. E. L. Stahl, too, implies *Die Wahlverwandt-schaften* to be a *Bildungsroman*, or, at least, to contain strong elements of a *Bildungsroman*. In 'Die Wahlverwandtschaften' (*PEGS* XV, 1945) we read: 'if in *Werther* Goethe represents a "Bildungsroman" in reverse . . ., in *Die Wahlverwandtschaften* he offers the spectacle of steadily mounting human achievement.' (p. 89, cf. also p. 91.)

[2] This unconsciousness has often been noted and has received various and opposing inter-pretations. W. Benjamin uses it as evidence for her 'Scheinhaftigkeit' and her lack of moral fibre. (In: *Illuminationen*, Frankfurt/Main 1961, pp. 121 ff.). As against this, Hankamer perceives, correctly in my opinion, the parallel between Ottilie's 'schuldlose Schuld' and that of the Paria woman and accounts for both by Goethe's tragic conception of fate. (*Op. cit.*, pp. 293 ff.) Staiger does not ask this specific question but notes that organic slowness of her development as a whole which comes closest to the interpretation essayed

which is enacted before our eyes when Eduard crosses her resolution to renounce him, appearing at the inn, on her way to the *Pension*. 'Sie drückt die
flachen Hände, die sie in die Höhe hebt, zusammen und führt sie gegen die
Brust, indem sie sich nur wenig vorwärts neigt und den dringend Fordernden
mit einem solchen Blick ansieht, daß er gern von allem absteht, was er verlangen oder wünschen möchte'. This, and the gesture with which she tries
to re-unite husband and wife, after the episode at the inn: 'Mit Eifer und Gewalt
faßt sie die Hände beider Ehegatten, drückt sie zusammen und eilt auf ihr
Zimmer.' How can she hope to undo all that has been done and to do all
that has been left undone — by herself as much as by the others — by such
an ineffably naive command?[3]

No, Ottilie is and remains a child, a stranger in the sophisticated and
articulate emotional climate into which she has been transplanted. And this
impression is not gainsaid by the heroically simple manner in which she resolves the moral knot.

The objection will at once be raised that Ottilie's diaries reveal, not at all
a child's mentality, but a highly reflective and knowing mind[4]. This is, of

---

here and resolves the critical problem that has exercised others, in an encompassing
fashion. 'Bei beiden [i. e. Ottilie and Hermann] vollzieht sich die Bildung des Geistes
organisch wie die des Körpers. So wenig der Körper befähigt ist, Entwicklungsphasen
zu überspringen, vermag der Geist in seinem echten, natürlichen Wachstum etwas zu
fassen, was vorzeitig an ihn herantritt'. (*Op. cit.*, II, p. 488.)

[3] Again, Benjamin rejects this gesture and the sensibility from which it springs, outright
and on moral grounds. 'Pflanzenhaftes Stummsein, wie es so groß aus dem Daphne-Motif
der flehend gehobenen Hände spricht, liegt über ihrem Dasein und verdunkelt es noch in
den äußersten Nöten . . .' (*op. cit.*, p. 122.). The operative word is *pflanzenhaft*. For Benjamin,
morality is insolubly rooted in language; it is of its essence a linguistic act. 'Daher wird,
in dem vollkommenen Schweigen der Ottilie, die Moralität des Todeswillens, der sie
beseelt, fragwürdig.' (*Ibid.*) From this rationalistic approach to morality, and to mental
phenomena altogether, springs the vitriolic attack Benjamin levels against Gundolf who
maintains the thesis that '. . . nach Analogie des Verhältnisses von Keim, Blüte und Frucht
ist auch Goethes Gesetzesbegriff, sein Schicksals- und Charakterbegriff in den Wahlverwandtschaften zu denken.' (*Op. cit.*, p. 554.) Granting his philosophical and more
specifically epistemological premisses, Benjamin's condemnation of Ottilie follows with
necessity. Clearly he has not pondered Goethe's own criticism of Schiller's *Jungfrau von
Orleans*, which finds fault, precisely, with her premature consciousness of her moral
transgression (diary-entry of May 27, 1807, *AGA Tagebücher*, p. 276f.); nor indeed is
Benjamin consistent in the position he maintains: for in the same essay he adopts the very
morphological language he criticises Gundolf for using, criticising Ottilie's diaries —
which are a central concern of this chapter — for their tendency "allzufrüh die Keime der
Erinnerung aufzudecken und das Reifen ihrer Früchte zu vereiteln . . .' (p. 124). Benjamin
is trying to have his cake and eat it, too.

[4] A point first stressed in the contemporary reactions of Abeken (*HA* VI, p. 630f., para. 7)
and Rochlitz, in a letter to Goethe, November 5, 1809. Cf. also G. Schaeder in: *Gott und
Welt. Drei Kapitel Goethescher Weltanschauung*, Hameln 1947, p. 316. Schaeder asks the
question whether such mature reflections could come from someone so young, but answers
it in the affirmative. Similarly Hankamer, *op. cit.*, p. 253; H. Reiss in: *Goethes Romane*,

course, true; and the question arises whether the author has been consistent in the presentation of this, his favourite character. To be sure, he has safeguarded himself doubly: by pointing to the red thread that is woven into the plait of her musings — her attachment to Eduard — which serves to connect her utterances and to make them her own, as it were; and by having the narrator tell us, twice, that some, or even most, of these reflections are excerpts copied from unnamed sources, a device on his part which cleverly exonerates him from any charge that her thoughts fly higher than her intellect permits. Besides, has he not, by this part explanation, brought Ottilie into line with one of the most striking features of the milieu in which she moves — its imitativeness? There is, in this novel, an all-pervading air of decadence or, at least, of derivativeness. Everybody tries his hand at imitating something — Charlotte and the *Hauptmann* imitate nature in their landscape gardening, the whole company imitates great scenes of art in their living *tableaux*, Luciane imitates apes, Eduard imitates the saintliness of his beloved, and so on[5]. It seems quite in keeping with all this artificiality that Ottilie should copy the wisdom of others and support her labile existence on such a prop.

And indeed, the theme of art does seem a thread connecting these diaries with plot and inner action of the novel, a thread quite as tough and recognisable as is Ottilie's attachment to Eduard. Art plays an enormous part in the leisured and genteel existence of this priviliged group, and increasingly becomes an overt theme of their discourse. Landscape gardening[6], at the time in which

---

Bern 1963, p. 185; F. Stopp in 'Ottilie und "Das Innere Licht"', in: *German Studies presented to Walter Horace Bruford*, London 1962, p. 121; and, with explicit stress on the organic mode of maturation reflected in the diaries, E. Staiger, *op. cit.*, II, p. 492. By way of contrast, Stöcklein, ed. *AGA* 9, p. 688, deplores the 'scharf geprägten Aphorismen Ottiliens.' Hankamer refers to Ottilie's diaries as testifying to 'einer so klaren und bewußt lebenden Natur', but nonetheless, and in my opinion correctly, stresses an underlying profound moral unconsciousness. (*Op. cit.*, p. 296.)

H. B. Nisbet and H. Reiss, in their edition of *Die Wahlverwandtschaften* (Oxford 1971) actually pinpoint the problem, saying: '[its] philosophical content is surprisingly profound for a young girl.' (p. XVIII.) The scope and maturity of Ottilie's reflections are stressed by the authors (p. XVIII). Similarly also Stahl (*loc. cit.*, p. 93). The depth of Ottilie's preoccupation with art has been noted by H. G. Barnes, in: *Die Wahlverwandtschaften. A Literary Interpretation*, Oxford 1967 (p. 55) and by Nisbet and Reiss, *ed. cit.*, p. XLIV; the authors write:'... certainly the phrasing of Ottilie's diary leaves no doubt that a heightened consciousness is at work in the telling of the story.' (p. XXIV.) Whose heightened consciousness, one might ask? The narrator's? The author's who stands behind the narrator? We almost have here an implicit admission that Ottilie's voice is that of her creator.

[5] This aspect is especially emphasised by Paul Stöcklein in: *Wege zum späten Goethe*, Hamburg 1960 and ed. *AGA* 9, pp. 708 ff.

[6] For a highly individual reading of these semi-artistic landscaping activities as profoundly narcissistic in character and reflecting Eduard's dominant character trait, cf. F. Stopp '"Ein Wahrer Narziss". Reflections on the Eduard-Ottilie Relationship in Goethe's "Wahlverwandtschaften"', in: *PEGS* (New Series) XXIX, 1959—60, pp. 58 ff.

the novel is set, was considered to be an art, and it is as such that we must consider Charlotte's attempts to groom nature, with the help of Eduard and the *Hauptmann*. Her *Mooshütte* with its carefully framed view and its artificial flowers; the maze of paths leading up to it; the bolder plans for a *Lustgebäude* which reveals, all of a sudden, a new and different world, wilder than the familiar scene in which the main building is set; the united ponds which are to restore an illusion of untampered nature in the midst of an overcultivated scenery; the English park Eduard and the *Hauptmann* are busy creating in lieu of the French symmetries reminiscent of a bygone era: all these are so many attempts to graft art onto a willing nature. And indeed, the whole style of life, the mastery of conversation, the refinement of manners, the tact which prevail in this company, testify to aesthetic sensibilities which treat the whole of life, in all its varied manifestations, as a rightful medium of the higher art of living. Even Eduard's grafting of his beloved trees — a bit of rejuvenating magic significantly placed at the opening of the novel — and the romantic wilderness in which Ottilie and he lose themselves during the outing of the two couples, seem to form part of the picture: nature, even where it grows according to its own laws, is either being actively refined or voluntarily answers to the fastidious demands of this group of people by presenting a pleasantly romantic yet civilized front which nowhere offends eyes and sensibilities reared in the expectation of beauty.

The second part of the novel does not merely confirm this impression: it enhances it. The young architect moves to the fore of the scene and, with him, art: the re-modelling of the graveyard; the restoration of the church and the decoration of the little chapel which is to be Ottilie's and Eduard's last resting-place — variations in a minor key on the construction of the *Lustgebäude* which analogously presides over the first part of the novel — the collection of finds from ancient burial sites he carries with him in his pretty little chest, so much like the one Eduard has given to Ottilie; the portfolio of mediaeval drawings and, of course, the caleidoscope of *tableaux*: all these multifarious artistic or semi-artistic activities crowd the pages of the second part of the novel, and form the incongruous backcloth against which the tragic events are played out, and a foil for the final *tableau*, Ottilie's lying in state and the architect's vigil at her coffin.

'Semi-artistic': it has often been remarked, and rightly so, that most of these goings-on, however tasteful and fastidiously executed, have an air of *déja vu* about them. Copies of originals are passed around and these, in turn, are copied. Nowhere does there seem to be a breath of originality or bold invention; and Luciane's passion for apes, Nature's born imitators, seems an apt if acid comment on all the aping of life in the raw that is going on, a comment from which not even Eduard's mode of death, by his own resigned admission, is being exempted.

2.

It is with this background in mind that we must turn to Ottilie's diaries. To come to them is to come, perhaps, from Goethe's anacreontic lyrics to his 'Künstlergedichte', or, for that matter, from the erudite niceties of Belriguardo to the lonely figure of Tasso. Wherever Ottilie got these excerpts from, this much we may confidently assert: these jottings are not copied from anyone in her milieu; they seem to be lifted straight from the diary of a practising artist, or maybe so many echoes of a mental dialogue such an artist might hold with himself in the quiet of his workshop[7]. Let us look at a few instances of the kind of observation we find amongst her entries.

Take her remarks on the art of portraiture, for example. Here is a young girl in love. One would expect her to clamour for a picture of her beloved as she sees him. She does nothing of the sort. Quite on the contrary, she is well aware that personal idiosyncrasies have no place in this art, and that the portrait painter, intent on culling the objective essence of his model, yet beset by contradictory subjective expectations, faces an impossible task he is entitled to hold in contempt.

Looked at more closely, her sympathy for the portrait painter's plight springs from two related sources. To her, a picture is the visible projection of an inner image — the artist's image which, through the finished product, is transmitted to the onlooker. And she is much concerned with the value of the images an artist transmits, and with the effect and function of images thus brought to bear on the imagination. 'Die Kunst beschäftigt sich mit dem Schweren und Guten', she apodictically states. And it has an educative function. Thus she repudiates, with a vehemence that is striking from one so gentle, Luciane's monkey picture-book, the whole genre of caricature which looks for the animal behind the human mask, and indeed all presentations of natural phenomena pictured out of their natural environment, solely for their exotic thrill; frowning on the presentation of anything other than man, for the reason 'daß das Menschenbild am vorzüglichsten und einzigsten das Gleichnis der Gottheit an sich trägt . . . Dem einzelnen bleibe die Freiheit, sich mit dem zu beschäftigen, was ihn anzieht, was ihm Freude macht, was ihm nützlich deucht; aber das eigentliche Studium der Menschheit ist der Mensch.' These are hardly the words of a romantic young girl fresh from finishing school. Rather do they betray the conviction of Goethe who, towards the end of his Roman stay, extolled the human figure as the *non plus ultra* of all human knowledge and activity[8]. The images with which we surround ourselves determine the quality of our being. Let our eyes be nourished only by the

---

[7] For the relation of women to art, cf. *Faust II*, Act I (*Weitläufiger Saal mit Nebengemächern*): 'Denn das Naturell der Frauen // Ist so nah mit Kunst verwandt.' (l. 5106f.)

[8] Cf. Chapter V, sections 6 and 7.

noblest symbols — the human being, not degraded to the likeness of what is beneath us on the ladder of organic being, but bodied forth in the image of the divine. This is Ottilie speaking, and this is serious thinking on the effect and function of art, in the mainstream of the tradition of Socrates and Plato and worthy of Goethe's and Schiller's didactic thinking at the peak of their classical noon.

But it is Ottilie's more intimate observations on the interaction between artist and world, and on the artist's relation to his own art-making and its products, that come as the real shock of surprise as we leaf about in her diary entries. Take for instance the two correlated remarks: 'Es gibt keinen größern Trost für die Mittelmäßigkeit, als daß das Genie nicht unsterblich ist', and: 'Selbst im Augenblicke des höchsten Glücks und der höchsten Not bedürfen wir des Künstlers.' How does she know about that ultimate human sorrow that there is no permanence except in form, the knowledge Goethe expressed in, say, the poem *Dauer im Wechsel* and Schiller, when he wrote: 'Der Mensch kann nichts als was Form ist, sein eigen nennen'[9], or in *Nänie*? And how does she come by the cynical insight that mediocrity, like the eternal Judas that it is, rejoices at the downfall of those that have, and dispense, the life that alone can save man from the unsung anonymity of the beast? We think we hear Faust say

> Die Wenigen, die was davon erkannt,
> . . . .
> Hat man von je gekreuzigt und verbrannt,

or the more muted tones of the aged Goethe:

> Sagt es niemand, nur den Weisen,
> Weil die Menge gleich verhöhnet . . .

Or take this amazing statement: 'Man weicht der Welt nicht sicherer aus als durch die Kunst, und man verknüpft sich nicht sicherer mit ihr als durch die Kunst.' Who was likely to instruct her about that race of seers who are the professional misfits of this world? Who would have explained to her the wisdom of a tradition that insists on a blind Homer? Or the inexorable fate of a Beethoven who wrote *an die ferne Geliebte* and who composed the Pastoral Symphony as a stone-deaf man? How could she know of the 'Disproportion des Talentes mit dem Leben' of a Pushkin or Tolstoi, a Grillparzer or a Kleist, a Mörike or a Nietzsche, a Michelangelo or a van Gogh, a Schubert or a Tschaikowsky, a Wilde or a Gide, a Rilke, a Kafka, a Tonio Kröger or a Dr. Faustus, who heartrendingly wrote about, or composed in stone or sound what they failed to live? How could she know of the disponibility of the creative Eros which disengages itself from the rigours of binding relationships and shuns their consummation to articulate them all the more authentically?[10]

---

[9] In *Anmut und Würde*.
[10] Cf. Chapters I and II of this book and my *Goethe and Lessing*, Chapters V, VI and VII.

Finally and most importantly, what could she know about Goethe's most sacred credo, the belief that the formative laws of Nature and art are identical, so that the artist, however withdrawn from this or that level or range of human experience, will give exemplary utterance to it, because Nature and the world themselves speak through him?[11] It is an *aperçu* of fathomless depth to which Ottilie gives expression here, and such are the sureness of her insight and the succinctness of her formulation that one begins to wonder whether the source of such knowledge must not be herself.

As a final example take Ottilie's musings about the relation of the artist to his work of art and the mutations this relation undergoes in diverse social structures. Ottilie notes at the beginning that the opening remark stems from 'the young artist', referring, presumably, to the architect. This is what we read — and the passage is worth quoting *in toto*: 'Wie am Handwerker so am bildenden Künstler kann man auf das deutlichste gewahr werden, daß der Mensch sich das am wenigsten zuzueignen vermag, was ihm ganz eigens angehört. Seine Werke verlassen ihn so wie die Vögel das Nest, worin sie ausgebrütet worden.' So far, supposedly, the architect, that temperate young man whose whole demeanour, notably his quiet renunciation of the girl he so dearly loves, gives us no reason to think of him as of one ruled by the laws of elemental nature. And yet it is precisely from one in whom this mode of experiencing in organic rhythms is dominant that these words would seem to stem. From one who knows, as the Goethe of the early poems *Der Wandrer* or the slightly later *Nektartropfen* knew, no less than the aged author of *Novelle* that, for all that art is a second nature — the poet's works are here compared to young birds — 'Menschenkraft mit der ewig lebenden und fortwirkenden Natur sich in dem ernstesten Streite erblicken lassen.'[12] 'Hoch baut die Schwalb' am Architrav, // Unfühlend, welchen Zierat // Sie verklebt', the wanderer had sadly mused as he walked past the ruins of the old temple, now the habitation of natural beings — the swallows and the humble folk who live in the shadow of its ruined columns. Such grief at the transience of all, at the precarious confirmation of his creativity the artist receives from the forms he has created, at the perishableness of those forms themselves which are as shortlived as birds, informs the remark Ottilie ponders, together with the sense of consolation that the cruel law governing the artist's existence is the law of creative Nature; 'gestaltend, umgestaltend'. Is this the wisdom of the architect, or not rather her own, or that of her creator? And how she drives on from this starting insight! We read — and these observations are now given as being her own:

'Der Baukünstler vor allem hat hierin das wunderlichste Schicksal. Wie oft wendet er seinen ganzen Geist, seine ganze Neigung auf, um Räume hervorzubringen, von denen er

---

[11] Cf. Goethe's letter to Zelter, October 30, 1808 and *Italienische Reise*, III. Teil, Rome, September 6, 1787.

[12] *Novelle, HA* VI, p. 493 f.

sich selbst ausschließen muß! Die königlichen Säle sind ihm ihre Pracht schuldig, deren größte Wirkung er nicht mitgenießt. In den Tempeln zieht er eine Grenze zwischen sich und dem Allerheiligsten; er darf die Stufen nicht mehr betreten, die er zur herzerhebenden Feierlichkeit gründete, so wie der Goldschmied die Monstranz nur von fern anbetet, deren Schmelz und Edelsteine er zusammengeordnet hat. Dem Reichen übergibt der Baumeister mit dem Schlüssel des Palastes alle Bequemlichkeit und Behäbigkeit, ohne irgend etwas davon mitzugenießen. Muß sich nicht allgemach auf diese Weise die Kunst von dem Künstler entfernen, wenn das Werk wie ein ausgestattetes Kind nicht mehr auf den Vater zurückwirkt? Und wie sehr mußte die Kunst sich selbst befördern, als sie fast allein mit dem Öffentlichen, mit dem, was allen und also auch dem Künstler gehörte, sich zu beschäftigen bestimmt war![13]

Ottilie's observations amount to nothing less than a biting sociological critique of the psychology of the artist and the history of art. She shows herself fully aware of the sort of problem which exercised Goethe in Italy and in its precipitate, *Die Propyläen*, and Schiller in his preface to *Die Braut von Messina*. How much more acute is the artist's predicament in a civilisation in which, through climatic and social conditions, the rift between his creation and himself becomes absolute in that the created product becomes a private possession inaccessible to him? This was what Goethe could, and did, observe in Italy: the feedback from the works of art themselves to the artists that had created them, was fatally lessened in a civilisation in which — unlike that of classical antiquity (slaves do not count in the reasoning of that period) — art became the private property of the rich and privileged who could afford to lock themselves up in and with their treasures. This development was bound to blight that constant *Steigerung* of artistic achievement through a process of *wiederholte Spiegelungen* in the mind of any given artist. The artist of old would see his art and that of others before him, permeate himself with it and produce incessantly enhanced creations, approximating ever more closely to the ideal before him: and as that ideal was the summit of the whole of organic nature, so he was, in turn, a second nature destined to bring forth a summit out of himself, to create forms that were the fitting manifestations of *Natura Naturans: beseelte Gestalt*. This is the *Steigerung* articulated in the passage from the *Winckelmann* essay I have quoted elsewhere[14]. Like her creator, Ottilie is imbued with this noble and esoteric conception of nature and art[15] producing, from a common and secret spring, ever higher forms of nature and art[16]: and with the conviction that modern civilisation inhibits such a creative feedback and such progression as ensues from it.

---

[13] For an interesting reading of this diary entry cf. F. Stopp, 'Ein Wahrer Narziss', *loc. cit.*, pp. 81 ff.. Stopp argues that 'Eduard is the artist who has created the temple of their mutual love, though in the outcome he may not approach nearer to the altar than the lowest step.' A persuasive enough reading as long as this passage is treated in isolation, but lacking ultimate conviction in the wider context in which I seek to view it.

[14] In Chapter V, section 8.

[15] December 1787, *Bericht. HA* XI, p. 456.

[16] *Ibid.*

Such a credo is primarily gained through the actual experience of making art, and only secondarily propounded in discursive terms. What Ottilie knows, then, are insights sprung from the deepest strata of the creative intelligence; and we must seriously envisage the possibility that Goethe intended to body forth in this figure, incongruously placed in a sterile environment in which the springs of creation have dried up, a creative artist in her own right. But what is the medium in which this strange young artist works? And exactly what is it that she creates?

3.

A preliminary answer readily springs to mind. Of course, she helps the architect as he decorates the ceiling of the chapel: she paints the robes of the angels that will look down upon her and Eduard in their last sleep, 'heitere, verwandte Engelsbilder'; leaving the faces themselves, the last one of which looks exactly as she does, to the practised hands of the young architect. The inception of this work is so important that I propose to quote the passage in full. 'Die Frauen waren zu ihm aufs Gerüste gestiegen', we read; 'und Ottilie bemerkte kaum, wie abgemessen leicht und bequem das alles zuging, als sich in ihr das durch frühern Unterricht Empfangene mit einmal zu entwickeln schien, sie nach Farbe und Pinsel griff und auf erhaltene Anweisung ein faltenreiches Gewand mit soviel Reinlichkeit als Geschicklichkeit anlegte.'

The operative word in this passage is 'das Empfangene'. Ottilie may or may not be something of an artist. What is certain is that she shares the supremely receptive disposition of her creator. Like his, her mode of perceiving is *gegenständlich* and *anschauend*. Forms have imprinted themselves on her mind, and there continue quietly to gestate. But at a given moment, in this instance through the answering forms her eye perceives, such dormant creativity is galvanised into activity. The forms she had received begin to develop, spontaneously and autonomously as the use of the reflexive verb testifies, and the fact that it is not the volitional she, but the *Empfangene* that is the grammatical and logical subject governing the statement[17]. And what is thus animated, operates in and through her, permeated by the model that she had perceived, and undistorted by her subjectivity.

But it is to the paragraph which follows upon a short digression regarding Charlotte's state of mind that we must turn for an elucidation of the question in what sense, and in what medium, Ottilie is a creative artist. It is after a short interpolation that we read, in a paragraph placed on its own:

---

[17] For an analysis of this type of statement and what it tells us regarding Goethe's creative mode, cf. Chapter VII, and especially Chapter XIII, section 1.

'Wenn gewöhnliche Menschen, durch gemeine Verlegenheiten des Tags zu einem leidenschaftlichen ängstlichen Betragen aufgeregt, uns ein mitleidiges Lächeln abnötigen, so betrachten wir dagegen mit Ehrfurcht ein Gemüt, in welchem die Saat eines großen Schicksals ausgesäet worden, das die Entwicklung dieser Empfängnis abwarten muß und weder das Gute noch das Böse, . . . was daraus entspringen soll, beschleunigen darf und kann.'

This passage has been variously interpreted by commentators as referring to Charlotte or Ottilie respectively[18]. I consider that the immediate context in which it is placed as well as the verbal fabric in which it is imbedded unequivocally argue that the author is here speaking of the more tragic of the two figures — Ottilie. To be sure, Charlotte has conceived and is expecting her child. In that sense, she carries the seed of a life which cannot be hurried in its development and which may bring good or evil. But in truth it is Ottilie who has conceived the seed of a great destiny which cannot, and *may not* — the poet expressly adds this 'may not' — precipitately see the light of day; she of whom the word 'conception' is now used for the second time, and in a significant *Steigerung*: for as she had begun actively to body forth the holy forms she had received in her youth — *das Empfangene* — so now the seeds of the spiritual conception she has experienced — *Empfängnis* — begin to swell and ripen in her, under their own impetus. Art is the analogue, and has become the metaphor, of spiritual creativity. And we are not surprised that Goethe articulates this higher creativity in the self-same terms in which he is wont to describe biological or artistic process: in morphological terms.

4.

It has been noted that, whilst the first book of *Die Wahlverwandtschaften* has polarity for its theme and structural principle, the organising middle of theme and form in the second book is the principle of *Steigerung*[19]. More precisely speaking, it is concerned with the *Steigerung* of Ottilie's patent receptivity to an active creativity of its own kind.

Ottilie has long since received Eduard's imprint; not bodily, for he fears even that the medaillon with her father's picture which she wears around her neck should injure her at a touch, and begs her to remove it[20]. But her changing handwriting, which has become his own, and her piano playing, so

---

18 B. v. Wiese unequivocally refers it to Ottilie in *ed. HA* VI, p. 667. For an opposed, if implied, view cf. H. G. Barnes, 'Bildhafte Darstellung in den *Wahlverwandtschaften*', *Dt. Vierteljahrsschr.*, JG 30, 1956. XXX. Band, p. 45, also in his book (*op. cit.*, p. 174).

19 Cf. Schaeder, *op. cit.*, pp. 313 ff. Most more recent critics concur with Schaeder in regarding *Steigerung* as the structural principle, no less than as the law of Ottilie's personal development, throughout Book II.

20 The ambivalence of Eduard's request has been variously noted. Cf. Stöcklein, ed. *AGA* 9, p. 694, and F. Stopp, 'Ein Wahrer Narziss', *loc. cit.*, p. 67 f.

totally adapted to his wayward fluting, show how indelible an impress he has left on her soul. What she has thus conceived — 'die Saat eines großen Schicksals' — she carries within her, hopefully and in a truly astonishing unconsciousness of the human and moral implications of her passion. Hers is the unconscious abandon to her condition of one pregnant, which even Eduard's departure and the news of Charlotte's pregnancy are not able effectively to undermine. On this note of enhanced life the first part of the novel closes.

As against this, the second part, opening as it does with the dispute about the graveyard and the discussions this prompts, sounds the note of death[21]; and this is faithfully reflected in Ottilie's first diary entries. Eduard has gone; and she begins — we have touched on this already — to reflect on the role of the picture as a second presence, as it were. The picture he has imprinted on her soul is living there, with an independent life of its own. It is growing and so is her relation to it, and him. She herself tells us so in the second paragraph of her diary extracts — a passage which forcibly reminds one of the many statements of her creator about the autonomous life poetic images led in his conscious, or unconscious, mind, in a process of gestation he in no way helped or hurried[22]. But actual presence has become picture, image. And with these Ottilie now lives, in full cognisance of the difference. A long process of sublimation and rarification of what is no longer palpable presence has begun; and Ottilie willingly submits to this process — which will end in her voluntary death — as willingly as she submits to the autonomous life of those images in her. The concluding entry of the first series of excerpts from her diaries clearly indicates the direction in which she is moving:

> 'Wenn man die vielen versunkenen, die durch Kirchgänger abgetretenen Grabsteine, die über ihren Grabmälern selbst zusammengestürzten Kirchen erblickt, so kann einem das Leben nach dem Tode doch immer wie ein zweites Leben vorkommen, in das man nun im Bilde, in der Überschrift eintritt und länger darin verweilt als in dem eigentlichen lebendigen Leben. Aber auch dieses Bild, dieses zweite Dasein verlischt früher oder später.'

Ottilie is slowly moving into a spiritual dimension in which solid, material being assumes the translucency of the symbol — a metaphorical existence which is nevertheless inscribed with her name, and Eduard's. Her receptivity, strong as ever, is refined and begins to be permeated by the semblances of things.

It is immediately after that moving entry — moving because it testifies to the rapidity of Ottilie's inner, if silent, development — that the narrator shows her picking up brush and paint and executing those angels, the last one of which so strikingly resembles her; and it is here that, in a highly significant

---

[21] A motif particularly emphasised by Benjamin, *op. cit.*, pp. 81 ff.
[22] Cf. section 8 of this chapter, Chapters VII, VIII and XIII (section 1); also *HA* VI, p. 695, note to 350, 38.

modulation, he progresses from the burgeoning of what she has *received* — *das Empfangene* — to the secret life of the seed she has *conceived* — *Empfängnis.* Here indeed is *Steigerung:* the breakthrough from receptivity to creativity has begun. But it is noteworthy that this does not issue in a change of her mental mould: the grammatical construction in the first of these paragraphs, which we have noted, tells us as surely as does the second paragraph *expliciter* that, even when she is creative, Ottilie evinces a supreme receptivity. She is not the maker. Something makes itself in her. Is this not an astonishing resemblance to Goethe, the Goethe of *Bedeutende Fördernis durch ein einziges geistreiches Wort?*

It is in the same morphological terms Goethe has used in the vital passage — 'die Saat eines großen Schicksals' — that Ottilie continues to speak of the creative development that has been engendered in her. A number of entries speak of sowing and growing and harvesting in the cycle of the seasons. At first, these jottings appear somewhat random. It is only as we realise that they are placed, without fail, in the immediate vicinity of utterances which have to do with her personal development and of reflections about art, that the narrator's purpose becomes clear: he treats of Ottilie's spiritual creativity in terms of her artistic creativity, and of both in the strain of organic natural creativity.

This technique becomes all the more striking in the degree in which her spiritual development outstrips the natural domain; surest sign that her growing sublimation represents a refinement rather than a denial of her nature, and that the poet wishes us to remain mindful of the biological genesis even of the highest manifestations of her specific creativity in the spiritual domain, and of mental creativity *per se*[23].

A few examples will establish my point. The third chapter of the second book concludes on the words:

'Das Jahr klingt ab. Der Wind geht über die Stoppeln und findet nichts mehr zu bewegen; nur die roten Beeren jener schlanken Bäume scheinen uns noch an etwas Munteres erinnern zu wollen, so wie uns der Taktschlag des Dreschers den Gedanken erweckt, daß in der abgesichelten Ähre soviel Nährendes und Lebendiges verborgen liege.'[24]

---

[23] Benjamin stresses the 'naturalness' of Ottilie's development, and of the mode of her dying — she has not cared for food in her happier moments either — but uses this trait as evidence of her moral inadequacy. (*Op. cit.*, p. 122.) As against this, Staiger and Stöcklein assign a wholly positive significance to this trait which sharply distinguishes her from her human environment, as already Gundolf had done.

[24] Hankamer quotes this passage and comments: 'In dieser Tagebuchnotiz Ottiliens ist die Stimmung gefaßt, in welcher der erste Teil endet und der zweite beginnt: das Gefühl des Zu-Ende und die erwachende Sehnsucht, über die schmerzhafte Wirrnis des vergänglichen Lebens hinauszugelangen und in einem anderen Leben Frieden zu finden.' In this somewhat quietistic reading the specifically creative overtones of Ottilie's musings — and the imagery in which they are couched — are overlooked.

This is the old paradox of life in death: 'Except a corn of wheat fall into the ground and die . . .'. The fifth chapter ends with the laconic statement: 'Säen ist nicht so beschwerlich als ernten.' At the end of the ninth chapter we read:

'Man läßt sich den Winter auch gefallen. Man glaubt sich freier auszubreiten, wenn die Bäume so geisterhaft, so durchsichtig vor uns stehen. Sie sind nichts, aber sie decken auch nichts zu. Wie aber einmal Knospen und Blüten kommen, dann wird man ungeduldig, bis das volle Laub hervortritt, bis die Landschaft sich verkörpert und der Baum sich als eine Gestalt uns entgegendrängt.'

These examples show, not only that Ottilie experiences in terms of natural process, but also that creative process is in fact at work in her. In them, we perceive a clear acceleration. Firstly, the last quoted example is patently more intimate and expressive of her inner life than the previous ones. This 'Landschaft' is a *Landschaft der Seele*. Secondly, this last reflection transcends the cycle of the seasons within which her imagination had moved on the earlier occasions. It is a new burgeoning of life, in a fresh cycle, inaugurated after the caesura of winter and death, that she envisages. It is with this awareness in mind that we must interpret her description of the full bodiliness the *Gestalt* of the *Baum* assumes — (Ottilie is associated with trees: Eduard planted his beloved plane trees the day she was born) — the bodiliness with which it impresses itself on her perception. This spring is the timeless spring after her death, this *Gestalt* the apotheosis of her living form.

A similar progression is perceptible in the reflections on her own development and on art, which appear so closely linked with the above ones. The first entry here quoted — about the secret life winter harbours — is preceded by the following statement:

'Man mag sich stellen, wie man will, und man denkt sich immer sehend. Ich glaube, der Mensch träumt nur, damit er nicht aufhöre zu sehen. Es könnte wohl sein, daß das innere Licht einmal aus uns herausträte, sodaß wir keines andern mehr bedürften.'

As always, Ottilie — whose eyes are called 'ein wahrer Augentrost' — is envisaged as an extraordinarily perceptive, and receptive, creature. What she sees in the daytime imprints itself on her inner eye and continues to lead an autonomous life there, even into her dreams. We know how spontaneously patterned these dream-images are: the narrator tells us so, in relation to the visions of Eduard that animate her imagination in the moments between waking and sleeping. She perceives him in strange war-like attire: 'Die Gestalt, bis aufs kleinste ausgemalt, bewegte sich willig vor ihr, ohne daß sie das mindeste dazu tat, ohne daß sie wollte oder die Einbildungskraft anstrengte.' And we are forcibly reminded of the many statements we have from Goethe's hand about his *gegenständliches Anschauen*, in *Bedeutende Fördernis durch ein einziges geistreiches Wort*, in *Ballade*, in *Das Sehen in subjektiver Hinsicht* as well as in conversations recorded by Eckermann, dated January 18 and May 6, 1827. I have quoted the relevant passage in the last named essay in an earlier chapter. Ottilie seeing Eduard moving in her imagination, Ottilie stressing that we dream only to continue seeing, presents us with the same phenomenon the poet describes with regard to himself; and here, in the diary entry we are considering, this 'exakte sinnliche Phantasie', as Goethe calls it, the inner perception of what she has faithfully received, is on the point of being bodied forth, creatively, in independent shape. Perception of what? we may ask. Of her illuminated self[25]?

The second entry we have quoted — 'säen ist nicht so beschwerlich als ernten' — is preceded, in an exactly analogous fashion, by reflections of a more patently personal nature. There are four of them, starting with the statement we have already considered at length, that art is the surest way both of evading and of appropriating the world. The *aperçus* that follow progressively link the sphere of art with her personal predicament and, in addition, evince a definite progression within themselves. This is how they run: 'Selbst im Augenblick des höchsten Glücks und der höchsten Not bedürfen wir des Künstlers.' — 'Die Kunst beschäftigt sich mit dem Schweren und Guten.' — 'Das Schwierige leicht behandelt zu sehen, gibt uns das Anschauen des Unmöglichen.' Statements, all of them, testifying to the spiritual process silently at work in her. Again she *sees* 'das Schwere und Gute', she *perceives* the task to execute the difficult lightly: and again this inner perception stops short, just, of being bodied forth, as it comes upon the boundaries of the 'Unmögliche'.

The entry at the end of the ninth chapter, in which her imagination transcends the bounds of natural cyclic progress and envisages a spring after death, is followed up by a statement which curiously hovers between personal confession and natural observation. We read:

> 'Alles Vollkommene in seiner Art muß über seine Art hinausgehen, es muß etwas anderes, Unvergleichbares werden. In manchen Tönen ist die Nachtigall noch Vogel; dann steigt sie über ihre Klasse hinüber und scheint jedem Gefiederten andeuten zu wollen, was eigentlich singen heiße.'

As in the preceding reflection about a new spring inaugurating a new organic cycle, this observation, too, marks a radical caesura, and a radical metamorphosis unexpectedly springing from such an incision. The nightingale transcends its native species without leaving it. It becomes a model of it, or a symbol. And the emergence of a new, creative, faculty — song — in its total immateriality is underscored by the choice of the patently physical attribute of the class it represents and transcends: 'jedem Gefiederten'. In both of these coupled statements, then, transcendence is the keynote. The impossible, the difficult executed lightly, before which Ottilie's imagination had boggled in the preceding series of entries, in the natural art of the nightingale has become simple fact. And in this statement which moves on all three levels at once —

---

[25] Chapter 7, Section 1, p. 176f.

natural, artistic and spiritual — we may see an adumbration of Ottilie's decisive breakthrough to her specific creativity, the creativity, as we might now call it, of transcendence.[26]

Both these coupled reflections foreshadow her farewell to the world and her separation from herself. We must not forget that they occur in the same series of entries in which she speaks of the artist's works relinquishing the artist as birds will leave their nest — the image of the nightingale by itself confirms this connection. What Ottilie is hatching in her inward self — 'die Saat eines großen Schicksals' — is growing to maturity, about to leave its progenitor and to transcend him.

5.

As soon as the ceiling of the chapel is painted, the architect requests Charlotte and Ottilie not to enter the building for a little while. During this time he arranges for a beautiful flooring and a stained glass window to be put in place.

Ottilie enters unaccompanied. 'Durch das einzige hohe Fenster fiel ein ernstes, buntes Licht herein', we read; and the narrator describes the ensuing scene as follows:

'Ottilie freute sich der bekannten, ihr als ein unbekanntes Ganze entgegentretenden Teile. Sie stand, ging hin und wider, sah und besah; endlich setzte sie sich auf einen der Stühle, und es schien ihr, indem sie auf- und umherblickte, als wenn sie wäre und nicht wäre, als wenn sie sich empfände und nicht empfände, als wenn dies alles vor ihr, sie vor sich selbst verschwinden sollte; und nur als die Sonne das bisher sehr lebhaft beschienene Fenster verließ, erwachte Ottilie vor sich selbst und eilte nach dem Schlosse.'

This episode enacts precisely that inner state in which we left Ottilie at the end of the preceding section. She perceives repeatedly and attentively, and what she so perceives is both known and unknown to her, within her and before her eyes, herself and not herself. The fledgling birds are about to

---

[26] In this connection, cf. F. Stopp, 'Ottilie and "Das Innere Licht"', *loc. cit.*, p. 121 f.. Discussing some of the diary entries with which we are here concerned, Stopp writes: '... the achievement of perception, of fully realized harmonious autonomy, whether in art, life, or nature, requires a process of self-transcendence, in which the creative impulse passes into another mode of being.' I could not agree more. Stopp points out that the term 'das innere Licht' is used both by Goethe and by G. H. von Schubert, in his *Ansichten von der Nachtseite der Naturwissenschaften*. Without being able to say for sure whether Goethe read that book, he stresses the parallelism between Ottilie's development as analysed by him and Schubert's Lecture 12 describing 'how, when Nature is about to make a signal leap forward, prototypes of future organs appear at the lower level in forms which are apparently retrogressive, useless, and even a hindrance to the organisms concerned ...' (p. 122). Surveying Ottilie's development in terms of perceptual imagery — i. e. the progression from the beauty of her eyes to the eventual truth of her 'insight', as Stopp and I do — the parallel with Schubert would seem compelling.

leave their nest. The inner light is about to step forth, to be the sole source of illumination. And what she perceives, as yet refracted by the coloured glass, is the Holy she herself has been instrumental in creating. It is a solemn sight[27].

After Luciane's departure, the architect devises one last *tableau* in which Ottilie is to take the main part. Luciane herself had shone on three such occasions in which well known paintings had been imitated. The spectators had felt themselves transported into another world, 'nur daß die Gegenwart des Wirklichen statt des Scheins eine Art von ängstlicher Empfindung hervorbrachte', as the narrator significantly has it.

Ottilie's *tableau* is of a different kind. It is not modelled on any work of art, but a free presentation of the adoration of the holy child in the manger. Ottilie is a 'scheinbare Mutter' — a fact which is underscored by the presence of Charlotte, herself pregnant — and the lighting effects are elaborate and patently of the most artificial: yet the semblance that is created is pure and unalloyed by any thought of a deviant reality. This impression is due to the fact that Ottilie *is* what she *acts*. She does not imitate another's art, she herself *is* art which transcends all known art as the nightingale, by its song, transcends 'jedes Gefiederte'. 'Ottiliens Gestalt, Gebärde, Miene, Blick übertraf aber alles, was je ein Maler dargestellt hat', the narrator comments. 'Und wer beschreibt auch die Miene der neugeschaffenen Himmelskönigin?', he goes on to ask: 'Die reinste Demut, das liebenswürdigste Gefühl von Bescheidenheit bei einer großen, unverdient erhaltenen Ehre, einem unbegreiflich unermeßlichen Glück bildete sich in ihren Zügen, sowohl indem sich ihre eigene Empfindung, als indem sich die Vorstellung ausdrückte, die sie sich von dem machen konnte, was sie spielte.' Ottilie recreates the Queen of Heaven, *die neugeschaffene Himmelskönigin*, as the narrator significantly has it. Or perhaps it would be truer to say that the inner image of the holy Mother bodies itself forth visibly, of its own, without her making. It is Ottilie's humility, her happiness at this undeserved honour, which answer to the requirements of her part; and once again we recognise the autonomous nature of this creation in the reflexive form the poet uses: 'bildete sich'; formed itself.

The holy Mother holding the holy child: what more fitting symbol could the poet have found to express the nature of Ottilie's creativity? For Ottilie creates the Holy in herself, and that inner light is now being shown stepping forth and being the sole source of the outer illumination[28].

---

[27] For a different but compatible interpretation cf. W. Emrich, *Die Symbolik von Faust II*, Frankfurt/Main, Bonn 1957, pp. 319 ff.

[28] Both Stöcklein (*ed. AGA* 9, p. 709) and Staiger (*op. cit.*, II, p. 504) stress the questionableness of the *lebenden Bilder;* Staiger, in particular, the moral and aesthetic *Fragwürdigkeit* of the last, which 'will escape no thoughtful reader'. But whilst Ottilie's own reaction makes its moral inappositeness perfectly clear, the narrator most carefully distinguishes

But Ottilie is both, mother and child, creator and creation, nest and bird. She bodies forth the Holy and she is herself on the way to holiness[29]. And thus the initial 'Nacht- und Niedrigkeitsbild' is transmuted into a 'Tag- und Glorienbild'. We read: '... eine ganz unendliche Hellung umgab sie.' 'Das ganze Bild war alles Licht, und statt des völlig aufgehobenen Schattens blieben nur die Farben übrig'. 'Das ganze Bild': these words remind us that the image evoked before the reader's eyes is a symbol prefiguring what has in reality not yet been achieved. Small wonder that, on becoming conscious of herself through the entry of the *Gehülfe*, Ottilie, with characteristic truthfulness and humility, should perceive the discrepancy of ideal and reality and experience an annihilating self-illumination!

'Wie im zackigen Blitz fuhr die Reihe ihrer Freuden und Leiden schnell vor ihrer Seele vorbei und regte die Frage auf: ... "wie wenig wert bist du, unter dieser heiligen Gestalt vor ihm zu erscheinen, und wie seltsam muß es ihm vorkommen, dich, die er nur natürlich gesehen, als Maske zu erblicken?" ... Ihr Herz war befangen, ihre Augen füllten sich mit Tränen, indem sie sich zwang, immerfort als ein starres Bild zu erscheinen ...'

She has seen truly. The vessel is not yet consecrated, semblance and lived reality as yet cleave apart, for herself if not for the others. The time is not yet ripe for the 'herrliche Kind' to perceive and revere her likeness in a 'Tag- und Glorienbild'.

6.

But all the time the creative process continues to work in a soul in which 'die Saat eines großen Schicksals ausgesäet worden.'

'Der Frühling war gekommen',

we read at the beginning of the ninth chapter,

'später, aber auch rascher und freudiger als gewöhnlich. Ottilie fand nun im Garten die Frucht ihres Vorsehens; alles keimte, grünte und blühte zur rechten Zeit; manches, was hinter wohlangelegten Glashäusern und Beeten vorbereitet worden, trat nun sogleich der endlich von außen wirkenden Natur entgegen ...'.

---

between the aesthetic inadmissibleness of Luciane's *tableau* where 'die Gegenwart des Wirklichen statt des Scheins eine Art von ängstlicher Empfindung hervorbrachte' and the pure semblance — the word 'scheinen', or cognate forms, occurs five times in the description — of Ottilie's *tableau* which admittedly transcends art and *prefigures* the — imminent — reality of her holiness.

[29] Both Benjamin and Stöcklein stress Ottilie's virginity, the one labelling it as dubious (*op. cit.*, p. 121), the other in a positive vein (*ed. cit.*, p. 704 and 706). Gundolf argues that Charlotte's child is 'auf mystische Weise ihr Kind' (*op. cit.*, p. 573), but that she is debarred from the motherhood she wished for, 'dumpf und blind', up to the moment of the catastrophe. I would go further and contend that the Christ child held by the 'scheinbare Mutter' is the symbol of her enhanced spiritual motherhood, more true than the natural motherhood of Charlotte.

Ottilie works hand in hand with nature, and with the gardener who tends his plants with that same 'stille Konsequenz' with which the seed implanted in her develops; endeavouring, like her, 'in jeder Jahreszeit, in jeder Stunde das ganz Gehörige zu tun'.

This phase of Ottilie's development is set in an entirely vegetative frame; her growth, like that of the artist, is deeply in tune with the laws that govern organic nature. Charlotte's ill-begotten son has been born, and paradoxically it is Ottilie, *die scheinbare Mutter*, yet the more truly creative of the two, who nurses the young life. '. . . und so trug sie es am liebsten selbst heraus, trug das schlafende, unbewußte zwischen Blumen und Blüten her, . . . zwischen jungen Sträuchen und Pflanzen, die mit ihm in die Höhe zu wachsen durch ihre Jugend bestimmt schienen.'

It is in this proximity to Nature and to the quiet working out of her laws that gentle illumination comes to Ottilie about her self and her situation in the world:

> 'Ottilie fühlte dies alles so rein, daß sie sichs als entschieden wirklich dachte und sich selbst dabei gar nicht empfand. Unter diesem klaren Himmel, bei diesem hellen Sonnenschein ward es ihr auf einmal klar, daß ihre Liebe, um sich zu vollenden, ganz uneigennützig werden müsse; ja in manchen Augenblicken glaubte sie diese Höhe schon erreicht zu haben.'

It is not so much the heroism of her renunciation as the purity of her perception which lends this passage its characteristic stamp. *Rein, klar, hell* —: these are the operative words of the narrator's account. Unlike the occasion when she first encountered her likeness in the dimly lit chapel, she now perceives her self uncoloured by hope or fear, in the clear light of day, as it is in truth. Again we note the *Gegenständlichkeit* of her perceiving; and conclude that the selflessness of her loving springs as much or more from the impartial objectivity of her perceiving as from any specifically moral root[30].

Her development appears to have come full cycle. The narrator seems to indicate that much; for at this point of his chronicle he reverts to an image first introduced when he had related Ottilie's breakthrough to creativity, artistic and spiritual. Then he had used the metaphor of sowing — the sowing of a great destiny — intermittently taken up, as we have seen, in her diary entries. Now the image recurs, in a key which curiously hovers between the major and minor:

---

[30] To stress this naturalness of Ottilie's morality is to be at one with those critics who themselves emphasise the harmonious continuity of her metamorphosis; i. e. Schaeder, Stöcklein, Staiger, Hankamer and Stopp. Such a reading, however, could be claimed as confirmatory evidence by Benjamin who denies Ottilie any title to morality, let alone sanctity, on the grounds that her development is a vegetative one and lacks the clear element of moral self-abnegation which is commonly (if erroneously) associated with Schiller's concept of sublimity.

'Daß der Herbst ebenso herrlich würde wie der Frühling, dafür war gesorgt. Alle sogenannten Sommergewächse, alles, was im Herbst mit Blühen nicht enden kann und sich der Kälte noch keck entgegenentwickelt, Astern besonders, waren in der größten Mannigfaltigkeit gesäet und sollten nun, überallhin verpflanzt, einen Sternhimmel über die Erde bilden.'

This is the last sentence of the narrative of that chapter — Chapter IX — and it dismisses us with a host of resonances. It is autumn. The cycle of the seasons is drawing towards its end. Ottilie, too, had envisaged it as the season of her harvesting and had looked to spring as to a time beyond time of unearthly transcendence. Autumn, moreover, is the time for asters, *Astern*. A star itself, the name of the flower is cognate with the word *Stern*. Asters, however, are strange flowers. They proliferate but bear no fruit[31]. And it is asters more than any other flowers which Ottilie will save up this autumn for the celebration of Eduard's birthday, the day which will see her lying dead, her head adorned with 'einen Kranz von Asterblumen..., die wie traurige Gestirne ahnungsvoll glänzten.' And she will lie, at the very end, under the 'azurne Himmel' of the chapel vault, with its 'Blumen- und Fruchtgehänge, ... welche Erde und Himmel gleichsam zusammenknüpfen sollten', 'heitere, verwandte Engelsbilder' looking down on her and Eduard.

No, the imagery of 'Stern' and 'Astern', the way the poet has deployed it, tells us that her development is not yet at an end. The rich blooming of the vegetation suggests a peaceful completion of the cycle which is not to be for her. Organic nature, here as always in this novel, holds out an oracle which turns out to be erroneous. Its peaceful paths are to be crossed, twice, by an eruption of elemental forces which inhibit Ottilie's slow and vegetative growth, among the growing plants, and inaugurate a more drastic process of maturation[32].

True, when the lovers unexpectedly meet again by the lakeside, and lie in one another's embrace, we read: 'Die Hoffnung fuhr wie ein Stern, der vom Himmel fällt, über ihre Häupter weg. Sie wähnten, sie glaubten einander anzugehören'. But the shooting star is as treacherous and as evanescent as the starry vault of asters that carpet the earth. Charlotte's child will die, and Ottilie, barren like the flowers of her choice, will not give Eduard a son that has her eyes by rights. The treachery of demonic forces by which this misbegotten fruit of an adulterous union dies, which will lead the lovers together once more when, by all the laws of nature, Ottilie may expect never to set eyes on him again, will exact a dearer toll from her. She will have gently to part with the nature which has so far cradled her unconscious growing and protected it. She will have to transcend nature in herself, in

---

[31] Cf. Stöcklein, *ed. AGA* 9, p. 704 and 706.
[32] This 'heroic' phase of Ottilie's development is convincingly presented by Hankamer, *op. cit.*, pp. 286 ff.

order to become the *bekannte* yet *unbekannte* Holy she has bodied forth, outside herself, in symbols: first on the ceiling of the chapel and then in the living *tableau* which found her not yet ready to shine in a 'Tag- und Glorienbild'. To become what she represented then, to body forth in truth that inner light in its radiance and be illuminated by it, she will have to be as immaterial as the nightingale's song, as spectral and translucent as the trees in winter time[33].

7.

The lovers have met and Charlotte's child has drowned. She and the Major spend this night holding a sad vigil, seated opposite one another in silence. Towards morning, they turn over in their minds the malignity of demonic powers which will not be pacified; and Charlotte, her will broken in the face of such unreasoning resistance, resolves to agree to the dissolution of a marriage the fruit of which lies dead. All this time Ottilie, in a death-like trance, has lain on the floor, her head in the lap of her maternal friend.

The words she eventually speaks are too well known to be repeated here. All we are here concerned with is the rapid transition from the deepest unconsciousness to the most cruel consciousness about herself and her condition, and the manner in which that change is effected. It is a turning-point, we now learn, Ottilie has experienced already once in her life, as a child, soon after her mother died. Then, too, she had lain on Charlotte's lap in a half-dead trance, and had taken in the words in which Charlotte had adumbrated her future, as she does now again. What interests us here is the extraordinary receptivity Ottilie evinces on both these occasions.

'Ich schlief nicht, ich wachte nicht; ich schlummerte',

she tells Charlotte.

> 'Ich vernahm alles, was um mich vorging, besonders alle Reden sehr deutlich; und doch konnte ich mich nicht regen, mich nicht äußern, . . . nicht andeuten, daß ich meiner selbst mich bewußt fühlte. Damals sprachst du mit einer Freundin über mich . . . Ich faßte alles wohl auf und genau . . . Ich machte mir nach meinen beschränkten Einsichten hierüber Gesetze . . . Aber ich bin aus meiner Bahn geschritten . . .'.

In her somnambulist state, Ottilie evinces, as she had done on that earlier occasion, the highest degree of perceptiveness. She perceives all, seeing and hearing what is said about her, in impartial yet sympathetic judgment. And what she thus perceives falls into her soul and imprints itself there as though the wheels of a powerful vehicle had run across it. Without the ability to do anything about it, she receives the indelible imprint of her law, the law of her being. Like a pair of tracks it is laid down in her, and she must walk in

---

[33] Cf. F. Stopp, 'Ottilie and "Das Innere Licht"' (*loc. cit.*) for a very similar reading; also G. Schaeder (*op. cit.*) who, like myself, sees Ottilie's 'genius' as an essentially religeous one (p. 321).

their groove; she is being enlightened: 'nach einem schrecklichen Ereignis klärst du mich wieder über meinen Zustand auf . . .' and, more definitely: 'Auf eine schreckliche Weise hat Gott mir die Augen geöffnet . . .'.

This is the girl who is so relentlessly exposed to the influx of the forces about her, to the elemental forces she registers with painful precision, the girl who is utterly defenceless in her loving of Eduard, stamped through and through with his being, the girl who will find no protection against 'die ungeheuer zudringenden Mächte' which assail her, other than the liquidation of an organisation so susceptible. This pathological susceptibility is at the same time the stuff of her creativeness. The impress of the law she perceives with the force of such *Gegenständlichkeit* moulds her very being, and moulds it, slowly, into the uncorrupted purity with which she has perceived it.

Ottilie's vow never to set eyes on Eduard again is broken, through no fault of her own. This last demonic assault on her sensibilities issues in a final *Steigerung* of her creative resources. She transcends the nature that she is. She *is* nature in the highest degree, elemental nature, as open to the impress of her surroundings as water, the most labile of elements. But through the very sharpness and truthfulness with which she receives impressions, and the inborn willingness to be led to the perception of ever more rarified forms, she has created a powerful mechanism against her own lability. Her own developing nature has imprinted on her an indelible image of her own self — a being at the summit of nature, producing in and of itself a *gesteigerte Natur*, an essence that is wholly creative and imperishable: and this creative core of her being is now set free, through the encounter with the demonic forces of elemental nature. Calling upon the Holy in herself which surrounds us, 'unsichtbar', she outstrips the lower registers of nature, as the song of the nightingale outstrips the feathered bird. She liberates the Holy in herself by no act of denial, let alone of repression: simply by living that sublimation which is her innate gift and — as always — the mainspring of her creativeness, and thus, gradually, shedding her material husk. The food she will henceforth take is sublimated in the highest degree. She nourishes what is pure song in her — the transcendent Holy — which becomes 'sichtbar' in the measure in which her physical frame becomes translucent and disembodied. The diminution of her physical self is the outward manifestation of the 'Heilige, das, uns *unsichtbar** umgebend', alone affords protection from the immensity of the demonic forces that assail her sensitivity.

Not that she negates nature, the nature she has become in an incessant organic process of *Steigerung*. Her susceptibility remains unchanged and, with it, the insoluble attachment to the man who has inscribed her being as with an indelible stamp. For her, unlike Eduard, there is no breath of denial about those parting days. They are all mellowness. As Charlotte accompanies

* my italics.

the Major's competent violin playing, so Ottilie adapts herself to Eduard's
wayward fluting as uncannily as she had done at the first burgeoning of
their love. To Ottilie, this fulfilment of the spiritual nature she has become
and this transcendence of the nature she once was, this being ineffably close
and at the same time ineffably removed, appears as a 'selige Notwendigkeit'.
She is true to her law: 'geprägte Form, die lebend sich entwickelt'. Of her
as of Eduard the narrator writes:

> 'Nach wie vor übten sie eine unbeschreibliche, fast magische Anziehungskraft gegenein-
> ander aus. Sie wohnten unter Einem Dache; aber selbst ohne gerade aneinander zu denken,
> . . . näherten sie sich einander. Fanden sie sich in Einem Saale, so dauerte es nicht lange,
> und sie standen, sie saßen nebeneinander. Nur die nächste Nähe konnte sie beruhigen,
> und diese Nähe war genug; nicht eines Blickes, nicht eines Wortes, keiner Gebärde,
> keiner Berührung bedurfte es, nur des reinen Zusammenseins. Dann waren es nicht zwei
> Menschen, es war nur Ein Mensch im bewußtlosen, vollkommnen Behagen, mit sich
> selbst zufrieden und mit der Welt. Ja, hätte man eins von beiden am letzten Ende der
> Wohnung festgehalten, das andere hätte sich nach und nach von selbst, ohne Vorsatz, zu
> ihm hinbewegt.'

The capitalised numeral 'Ein', the recurrence of 'an'- or 'nebeneinander' (spelt
as *one* word), and the final merging of the two sexes in the neuter form of 'eins'
und 'das andere' bespeak complete fulfilment. The two are one. Nature holds
sway; but it is nature pacified, a symbolic nature that has transcended itself
and of itself become sacred[34].

Here is a foretaste of that spring, past the wintry end, which Ottilie had
foreseen, looking at the wintry bareness of the trees. Translucent, yes, but
adumbrating a new unearthly bodiliness and the fullness of their resurrected
Gestalt — that *Gestalt* of the Holy which, imperishable as only a work of art
can be[35], Ottilie will embody as she lies dead, *ein verwandtes Engelsbild*
herself, still generating life in those that come to see and touch her.

8.

Goethe, I would suggest, loved this figure so deeply, because in her creativeness
he had created a likeness of his own artistic self[36]. With her, he shared that
extraordinary susceptibility and receptivity to impressions from the world, to
elemental forms within and without; a disposition which led to a life-long lability and to that 'exakte sinnliche Phantasie', that *Gegenständlichkeit* of perceiving and producing which puts its unique stamp on him, as poet and man.
Like his Ottilie, he could only master this, his innate lability because he was
an *Augenmensch* supremely gifted to perceive truly and objectively. And like
her, his enormous receptivity enabled him to assimilate influences from the

---

[34] Cf. v. Wiese, ed. *HA* VI, p. 666 and 668.
[35] Cf. Emrich, *op. cit.*, p. 320.
[36] Cf. Chapters VII, VIII and especially XIII for the following observations.

outside and creatively to transmute them into inmost and enriching possessions: witness his appropriation of classical culture in the *Roman Elegies*,
and of Eastern modes in the *Westöstliche Divan;* and witness Ottilie's
appropriation of the insights of others in those diary entries which, paradoxically, become the most powerful organs of her creativity. To her, he gave
his own formative *nisus*, that shaping-impulse which made him model and
chisel his human form as we see him doing in his diaries and in the
Italian Journey, until his life was a work of art transcending, perhaps, his other
creations; and so, too, it is in the medium of life that Ottilie works, until she
transcends herself and is bodied forth like a work of art in imperishable form.
Like her creator, Ottilie is nature, deepest nature, exposed to the demonic
although not demonic herself. Like him, she creates according to the law of
her nature which is indelibly imprinted on her and truly perceived. And like
those uncorrupted models of nature's workings, the plants to which Goethe
devoted so much care and thought, her, and his, development proceeds slowly
and spontaneously, according to nature's law. Whatever vicissitudes they
encountered from without or within, they completed their course, guided
by an inborn law which led them to body themselves forth in ever purer,
ever more translucently symbolical *Gestalten*. Like the plant whose stalk
becomes leaf and whose leaves become petals and organs of procreation, they
metamorphosed from organic stage to organic stage, preserving their basic
structure, yet reproducing it in ever more refined forms. From the deepest
unconsciousness to the most penetrating consciousness they went, and beyond,
to a creative frame encompassing unconsciousness and consciousness in one
state transcending both: Goethe from that somnambulist frame in which he
wrote to Herder 'Jetzt versteh ich's tue die Augen zu und tappe'[37], to that
high-water mark of clarity, at the end of his Italian journey, when he records:
'Genug, ich habe schon jetzt meinen Wunsch erreicht: in einer Sache, zu der
ich mich leidenschaftlich getragen fühle, nicht mehr blind zu tappen'[38]; and
beyond that again to his penultimate letter to his friend W. von Humboldt, in
which we read:

'... durch eine geheime psychologische Wendung, welche vielleicht näher studiert zu
werden verdiente, glaube ich mich zu einer Art von Produktion erhoben zu haben, welche,
bei völligem Bewußtsein, dasjenige hervorbrachte was ich selbst noch billige, ohne
vielleicht jemals in diesem Flusse wieder schwimmen zu können; ja was Aristoteles und
andere Prosaisten einer Art von Wahnsinn zuschreiben würden.'[39]

Ottilie, from the somnambulist state in which she first hears the law of her
life pronounced, from her sleepwalking love for Eduard, to that second a-
wakening of which she says: 'Auf eine schreckliche Weise hat Gott mir die Au-

---

[37] Letter to Herder, July 1772.
[38] *Italienische Reise*, Zweiter Römischer Aufenthalt, Rome, February 22, 1788.
[39] December 1, 1831.

gen geöffnet, in welchem Verbrechen ich befangen bin'; and, beyond such cruel clarity, to that unconscious-conscious state in which the narrator describes, for the last time, the concord of division transcended: 'Dann waren es nicht zwei Menschen, es war nur Ein Mensch im bewußtlosen, vollkommnen Behagen.'

As so often, it was Schiller who, long before the figure of Ottilie was conceived, prophetically articulated the law of Goethe's creativity — the self-same law Goethe was to implant in his beloved creation: 'Sie sind wirklich, solang Sie arbeiten, im Dunkeln und das Licht ist bloß *in* Ihnen, und wenn Sie anfangen zu reflektieren, so tritt das innere Licht von Ihnen heraus und bestrahlt die Gegenstände Ihnen und andern.'[40]

[40] Letter to Goethe, Jena, January 2, 1798.

'Das flücht'ge Ziel':
'Die natürliche Tochter'

'Etiam disiecti membra poetae'

Horace

I.

I am not aware that the fact has received attention that of all Goethe's major dramatic figures Eugenie, heroine of *Die Natürliche Tochter*, alone is assigned a poem which is expressly of her own composition[1]. We would expect such a device on the poet's part in Goethe's *Tasso*, a drama centred in creative genius, the tragedy of which is inseparable from such a gift pursued absolutely, to the exclusion of all other values. But although it has been ingeniously shown that in some portions of Tasso's speeches his own voice and his own poetic idiom do indeed take over and can be clearly distinguished from the voice and idiom the author has lent to the other figures of the play, these portions have been acclaimed as representing no more than early conceptions of what might, on closer application, become full-blown poetic utterances[2]. Besides, as I have tried to show elsewhere, there may be some legitimate doubt as to the poetic viability of these rudimentary conceptions[3]. Again, it might conceivably be possible to regard Epimetheus' wonderful lines

> Wer von der Schönen zu scheiden verdammt ist,
> Fliehe mit abgewendetem Blick . . .

as his poem rather than yet another piece of his creator's superb lyricism. Epimetheus no doubt is a character of predominantly artistic endowment; and to hear a poem from his own lips would, perhaps, not be an untoward expectation. Yet this *Festspiel* is so overflowing with lyricism of the purest water that by the same token we would have to address the blacksmiths as the authors of their song, or regard Epimeleia as the creator of the stanza beginning with the words:

> Ach! warum, ihr Götter, ist unendlich
> Alles, alles, endlich unser Glück nur!

---

[1] The sonnet 'Natur und Kunst . . .', given over to *Nymphe* in *Was wir bringen*, is expressly described by her as being 'eines Dichters alter Spruch'. Iphigenie's 'Parzenlied' is similarly introduced.

[2] By E. M. Wilkinson in: *'Torquato Tasso'. The Tragedy of the Poet.* In: E. M. Wilkinson and L. A. Willoughby, *Goethe Poet and Thinker*, London 1962, pp. 75 ff.

[3] In: *Goethe und Lessing*, Chapter VII, section 4.

It is Goethe's genius which, blurring all boundary lines between his characters, overflows into their utterances, shedding its rainbow radiance over them. But, most importantly, nowhere is the claim put forward that these lyrics are in fact the characters' own poetry.

Now this is precisely the claim put forward on behalf of and by Eugenie as she conceives, and with slow deliberation writes, the poem she will presently lock away in the hidden wall-cabinet in her room, this being the safest place that she can think of.

We are not quite unprepared for this event: for almost the first thing the duke, her father, tells the king about his daughter is that she is blessed, if not with the imagination of a poet, then at least with a poetic fancy.

> Mit welcher Leichtigkeit, mit welchem Sinn
> Erfreut sie sich des Gegenwärtigen,
> Indes ihr Phantasie das künft'ge Glück
> Mit schmeichelhaften Dichterfarben malt.

A lively awareness of the present and an imagination that masters the shades of the poet's palette, these could well be the endowment of a creative mind in the making.

This impression is strengthened by the manner of Eugenie's poetic venture, to say nothing of the quality of its outcome. We learn that she has in the past written poems to give pleasure to her father, and that these come to her unbidden,

> wie mir's der Muse Gunst
> Bei manchem Anlaß willig schenken mag.

And this account of inspiration has the ring of authenticity. Something, some shapes, are hovering before her inner eye. This event is as independent of her as is the influx of shapes the poet records in the first line of the first *Faust* Prologue:

> Ihr naht euch wieder, schwankende Gestalten...

we read there; and here, quite analogously,

> Verlaß mich! Eben schwebt mir's heiter vor,
> Ich muß es haschen, sonst entschwindet's mir.

The shape that has announced itself in this imperious manner crystallises instantly. No sooner has she rid herself of the *Hofmeisterin* than it is there —

> Ich hab' es ganz, und eilig fass' ich's auf —

and she commits it to paper, reciting the words to herself aloud as she pens them.

We might expect Eugenie's elation to take the form of a lyrical effusion, most likely boldly improvised in a free metrical form. This would be entirely appropriate to the mental frame and the artistic temper of a young girl in all likelihood no older than her creator when he wrote the great hymns of his own *Sturm und Drang*. What in fact she produces is a perfectly turned, and beautiful, sonnet. This is how this 'birth' poem runs:

> Welch Wonneleben wird hier ausgespendet!
> Willst du, o Herr der obern Regionen,
> Des Neulings Unvermögen nicht verschonen?
> Ich sinke hin, von Majestät geblendet.
>
> Doch bald getrost zu dir hinauf gewendet
> Erfreut's mich, an dem Fuß der festen Thronen,
> Ein Sprößling deines Stamms, beglückt zu wohnen,
> Und all mein frühes Hoffen ist vollendet.
>
> So fließe denn der holde Born der Gnaden!
> Hier will die treue Brust so gern verweilen
> Und an der Liebe Majestät sich fassen.
>
> Mein Ganzes hängt an einem zarten Faden,
> Mir ist, als müßt' ich unaufhaltsam eilen,
> Das Leben, das du gabst, für dich zu lassen.

For a young girl writing some time in the 'eighties of Goethe's own century — Goethe's drama is set just before the outbreak of the French Revolution — this is an astonishing poem; and Goethe assuredly meant it to be registered as such by his readers or spectators. For the sonnet is perhaps the most highly wrought and taxing of all Western lyrical genres: set as to length and intricate rhyme scheme, its form demands a maximum of emotional and intellectual discipline, and mercilessly shows up the dilletante's technical shortcomings. There is no fumbling here; it is all there, the antithesis, in the first two quartets, between the blinding fall and the trusty upward look, between the *geblendet* and the *vollendet* which are the rhyme words of their respective last lines; there is the momentary resting, in the first tercet, in this condition — 'Hier will die treue Brust so gern verweilen' — and then, in the last, the unexpected turn, the turn towards a loss of self decreed by some mysterious fate: 'Mir ist, als müßt' ich unaufhaltsam eilen . . .'. This last turn is prefigured in the first line of the poem, indeed in the whole first quartet, which speaks of the outgoing of life from the *Herr der obern Regionen* without mention of a return, and significantly couples this statement with the surrendered humility of her kneeling. In the first tercet this outpouring of life seems to be contained: the speaker would 'sich fassen', 'an der Liebe Majestät'. But the possibility of the young life, the *Sprößling*, being thus sustained at and by its source is envisaged only to be put into question by the last tercet, in which the 'ausgespendet' with its sense, almost, of squandering, is echoed, enhanced and finally accepted in the impulse of the 'I' to pour itself out and lose itself.

The strength of this sonnet lies in the dialectic between its strict tectonic form and the irresistible impetus towards fluidity that is contained by it, only just. The form of the sonnet is, as Erich Trunz has evocatively called it,

'randfest'. In this instance it stays, and cups — but only just — its subject:
the overwhelming need of the self to spend itself and merge with what lies
beyond it. A brief comparison with *Mächtiges Überraschen*, the introductory
poem of the sonnet cycle written some seven years later, will illuminate this
point. There, too, the fluid elemental force — *Ein Strom* — flows out from its
source, this time towards an obstacle which arrests its course and finally contains it. But whereas in this later sonnet the restless impulse to stream away
towards its destination is articulated in the first tercet, and comes to rest in
what Kommerell calls 'die reine gesättigte Spiegelung' of the last triplet, here,
in Eugenie's poem, the order is reversed. The first tercet gives voice to the
momentary containment, whilst in the second one, by a sudden turn, the centrifugal movement towards self-loss takes over and carries all before it. In
some sense this turn runs against the grain of the sonnet form itself, which
tends to come to rest at the end and to curl in upon itself, as it were, pacified,
contained within its own bounds, such collectedness being the appropriate
expression of the intellectual mastery which is the hallmark of the genre.
Eugenie's sonnet, too, is rounded and, in that sense, contained. The 'ausgespendet' of the first line is enhanced, and echoed, in the rush of the I to spend
itself at the end. But such containment is a purely formal one. As we have seen,
the centrifugal impulse which governs the end runs counter to the exigencies
of the form. And indeed, this impulse carries the speaker beyond the closed
form of the poem she has just rounded off. For almost straightaway she
questions:

> Doch ist es wohl genug? Hier quillt es fort,
> Hier quillt es auf! —

The impulse to spend herself has not been stayed and transmuted by her fashioning of a form. Perfect as it is, the vessel of her sonnet does not contain the
force that has generated it. It overflows its rim and her imagination, still
moving in images of fluid, strains forward to the '*ungemeßne** Wonne' of the
day that will see her birth into the world[4].

Goethe, I think, wanted us to register the formal perfection of Eugenie's
poem on the one hand, and on the other the incommensurability of the
creative thrust behind it — enunciated in imagery of fluid — with the closed
form she has created. The 'dämonisch' which characterises the obstacle in
Mächtiges Überraschen, in this poem belongs to a formative drive which does
not come to rest within the confines of the form it has wrought.

---

[4] Cf. J. Müller, *Goethes Sonette — Lyrische Epoche und motivische Kontinuität* (p. 14); cf. also
H. J. Schlütter (*op. cit.*, pp. 75 ff.). H. Wolff considers Eugenie's sonnet as reflecting the
poetic endeavours of Sylvie von Ziegesar who, according to the author, is the inspiring
genius of *Die Natürliche Tochter*. (*Op. cit.*, p. 80.)

* my italic.

If we now look back to the sonnet-scene and the crucial scene it precedes, as a whole, we may discern a striking parallelism between their rhythm and the movement which informs that poem itself, as well as with the fashioning process from which it has sprung. Eugenie has suffered her fall — she recapitulates this event to the *Hofmeisterin* — and has found herself both elevated and elated by the king's promise to effect her entry into public life. She is rapturous at the prospect which fills the *Hofmeisterin* with the gloomiest forebodings, and feels at peace in the promised proximity to her king, the lord 'der obern Regionen'. She wants to come to terms with this new condition; and this, to her, means that she must compose it in words, must collect herself alone, in the deepest secrecy. The *Hofmeisterin* urges Eugenie to talk to her and share her happiness. And, interestingly, she compares the confidences to be exchanged to the delighted inspection by two youngsters of a secret *Schmuck*, concealed in the *Herzens geheimste Fächer*. This 'opening' Eugenie rejects, the same girl who, a few moments afterwards, will override the *Hofmeisterin's* anxious cautions and rummage through the treasure chest sent to her, on completion of her poem. On the contrary, she abruptly withdraws at this very point to write her sonnet — the sonnet which brims over beyond its bounds — and with solemn secrecy commits this treasure, 'meines Lebens Glück', to a concealed wall-cabinet the secret of which her own 'rastlose Tätigkeit' has ferreted out, a cabinet, moreover, she herself knows not to be safe. It is as coming in the wake of these events that we must interpret the untimely prising open of the secret treasure which has been entrusted to her keeping[5]. It is as though the fashioning impulse itself had released energies which, well incapsulated before, can now no longer be contained, which she had shown every sign of containing before its onset. Looking forward to the

---

[5] For the dramatic function and the symbolic import of the treasure chest, cf. K. May, *ed. AGA* 6 who argues that in her transgression of her father's request Eugenie has failed symbolically in a symbolic test and shows 'den Keim ... zu unabsehbar entartender menschlicher Hybris' (p. 1195). Staiger argues that Eugenie's fate could not have been averted, even had she not opened the chest (*op. cit.*, II, p. 392), but in another context, in the wake of Emrich, concedes it a symbolic import which he himself does not integrate into his reading of the drama but which is central to my own. 'Das Innere' — i. e. *der Schrein* — 'ist jeweils der Sinn, der "Geist", Eugenies strahlender, aber bisher unsichtbarer Adel, *der dichterische Genius**, der sich im stillen bildet, um einst die Welt zu verklären' (p. 469). (My italics.) Whether he means the italicised words to refer to Eugenie or to the child in the *Zauberflöte* he is discussing, is not clear from the context. Closest to my reading comes Emrich who argues that 'Kästchen ... sind Ausdrucksformen des Geheimnisses selbst, sozusagen das Geheimnis des Geheimnisses.' (*Op. cit.*, p. 109f.) As regards *Die Natürliche Tochter*, he considers the dangerousness of the chest to have a doubled significance: firstly the dangerous and labyrinthine nature of the world is symbolically concentrated in the box (p. 198), and secondly 'ruht dies Gefährliche im eigenen "Mut", im *Überschwang des Daimon**, der den Helden ahnungslos ins Verderben zieht und unterirdisch wieder mit dem spezifisch *Innerpoetischen**, dem Höheren in der Brust des Helden, zusammenhängt' (p. 198). (My italics.)

king's birthday feast which is to mark her own 'birth' — 'neugeboren durch sein Wort' — her formative drive is activated, shapes for itself a mould that will not hold it, seeks for itself a hiding place that will not safely conceal it and finally thrusts beyond its goal, like a stream or a bird, to reveal itself[6]. Eugenie impatiently putting on adornment upon adornment, saying:

> Der Schein, was ist er, dem das Wesen fehlt?
> Das Wesen, wär' es, wenn es nicht erschiene?

and imperiously affirming:

> O meine Liebe! Was bedeutend schmückt,
> Es ist durchaus gefährlich . . .
> Unwiderruflich, Freundin, bleibt mein Glück . . . :

this is not, as one critic has made her out to be, 'a glamour girl, intent above all on being admitted to the inner circle of courtlife', or 'a young society girl'[7]: the imagery of adornment and the invitation to share her secret, which the poet has placed on the lips of her companion, fall on deaf ears. She is rather, I would suggest, the embodiment of a formative drive fated, by some mysterious decree, to overshoot the mark and to step forth into the light of the public day before the time is ripe for such a self-revelation.

2.

A number of critics, notably J. Kunz and K. May[8], have stressed the prevalence in Goethe's drama of images derived from the biological sphere of organic life, and allied imagery denoting artifacts, such as a ship or a town. This observation is correct in itself, as is also their assumption that in such images of compound structures the crumbling social and political hierarchy of Eugenie's country and, perhaps, the whole of Western Europe at the time immediately preceding the outbreak of the French Revolution is mirrored. To deny such macrocosmic resonances would be as foolish as to fight against windmills. We have Goethe's own word for it that, in *Die Natürliche Tochter*, he created for himself a receptacle in which to deposit, 'mit geziemendem Ernst', his protracted reflections about the Revolution and its consequences; and the extant text as well as the schemes for its continuation bear out the propriety of such a reading. *Die Natürliche Tochter*, let it be categorically stated, *is* about 'Entfernten Weltgetöses Widerhall', that is to say, about the birthpangs heralding this mighty socio-political cataclysm, and the fate of Eugenie *does*, as a number of critics have persuasively argued, reflect the im-

---

[6] Cf. the parallel symbolism in *Der Zauberflöte Zweiter Teil*, where Tamino's and Pamina's enshrined child arises from its chest as 'ein Genius'.
[7] Cf. H. Böschenstein, 'Goethes *Die Natürliche Tochter*', in: *PEGS* (New Series) XXV, 1955—56, p. 34 and p. 40.
[8] J. Kunz, *ed. HA* V, pp. 481 ff. and K. May, *ed. AGA* 6, p. 1191.

possibility of the individual to maintain itself against the encroachment of the anonymous masses[9]. Yet it has also been recognised time and again that *Die Natürliche Tochter* is an exceedingly complex composition moving on a number of levels and articulating a number of coexistent or conflicting insights. These levels and these insights have been identified differently by different critics; but the vast majority of scholars have found it indispensable to operate with a pluralistic conception in their handling of this play[10].

If then there can be little doubt that the organic imagery pervading this drama and associated verbal patterns bear on the hierarchical order of the social whole we see giving before our eyes, we are not out of step with prevailing views in suggesting that this same body of imagery may simultaneously be articulating another meaning-stratum concealed in the dense verbal weave of this play. I would suggest that this whole body of imagery may, in addition to its overt meaning and on its deepest level, have a microcosmic signification. It may illuminate an inter-personal configuration between the central figures of the tragedy, and this inter-personal configuration may, in its turn, itself be the outward reflection, and magnification, of some ultimate internal configuration which, but for such a process of externalisation in a number of related figures, would altogether resist poetic formulation in virtue of its complexity.

To start with the intermediate level of meaning on which images of organic and associated structures bear on the relationships between the various characters that figure in the play: in our consideration of Eugenie's sonnet a good deal has already emerged regarding the nature of her relationship with the king. The latter, it has universally been recognised, is a weak figure; and something of that has already transpired at the beginning and at the end of Eugenie's encomium. To her he is the fount of life. To him she would give all. Yet the poem speaks of no feedback of energy from the sustaining *Herr der obern Regionen*. All we hear is:

> Welch Wonneleben wird hier ausgespendet...

and, in a more ominous strain:

> Mein Ganzes hängt an einem zarten Faden,
> Mir ist, als müßt' ich unaufhaltsam eilen,
> Das Leben, das du gabst, für dich zu lassen.

---

[9] Cf. especially E. Staiger in: *Goethe*, II, pp. 375 ff., also R. A. Schröder, 'Goethes Natürliche Tochter', in: *Gesammelte Werke in fünf Bänden*, Berlin and Frankfurt/Main 1952, II, p. 484.

[10] Cf. for example R. Peacock in: 'Goethes "Natürliche Tochter" als Erlebnisdichtung', in: *Dt. Vierteljahrsschr.*, JG 36 (1962) Heft, 1, who openly operates with the concept of two tragedies, a political one and 'ein subjektives Gefühlsdrama' (p. 1 f.), and S. P. Jenkins, 'Goethes *Natürliche Tochter*', in: *PEGS* (New Series), XXVIII, 1958—59 who emphatically argues that the play is integrated but moves, at one and the same time, on different levels of experience, necessitating a continual adjustment of critical focus (p. 41).

This sense that the life that is fed into her overlord drains away never to return to the donor, to the reader does not come as a complete surprise. After her fall, overwhelmed at the king's gracious recognition of her, Eugenie had faltered in uttering her gratitude. For, she asks,

> Was fehlte dir? was wäre dir zu bringen?

and goes on to answer her own question, sadly saying:

> Die Fülle selber, die zu dir sich drängt,
> Fließt, nur für andre strömend, wieder fort . . .

But the images Eugenie uses in this scene and, later, in her poem, cut deeper. They suggest a secret leaking out of power in the representative of the realm to whom she is attached by inextricable, and fatal, bonds. And the poet is much concerned to give substance to this suspicion by a number of small verbal hints. When the duke introduces the impetuous amazon to her overlord, he answers the king's question as to who she is, saying:

> Da du gebietest, darf ich sie vor dich
> Als meine Tochter stellen.

An awkwardness dictated by metrical considerations, we ask, meaning no more than 'darf ich sie dir als meine Tochter vorstellen'? The unusual concreteness of the turn of phrase is certainly kept before our mind in the stichomythic exchange between father and daughter that follows upon the king's departure.

> Eugenie: Von altem Heldenstamme grünt er auf.
> Herzog: Die Kraft *entgeht** vielleicht dem späten Zweige.
> Eugenie: Die Schwäche zu *vertreten** sind wir da.

Imperceptibly, the poet is building up, by the use of such verbs as *vor-stellen*, *ent-gehen*, *ver-treten* in their original, concrete signification, a cumulative picture of life-sap escaping from a living whole. The duke, Eugenie and the king himself all contribute to this emerging characterisation, the king above all when, in an extended metaphor, he likens the state to a leaking ship and prays for such 'volle Kraft' as may be felt to be an animating force throughout the crumbling realm and hold it together; Eugenie as, in response to his appeal for loyalty, she falls at her monarch's knees with 'Bedeutender Gebärde *dringend Streben**', and enthusiastically envisages a time when the nobles of the realm will rally to him,

> Um ihn sich *drängen**, seine Brust zu schützen,

and again later, after she has written her poem, when she exclaims:

> Beflügelt *drängt** sich Phantasie *voraus**,
> Sie trägt mich vor den Thron und *stellt mich vor**,
> Sie gibt im Kreise mir —.

* my italics.

Such ardently protective gestures bespeak one most sensitively aware of strength ineluctably draining away from the fount and guardian of life, the King's life on which her own absolutely depends, and prepared to stop the leak with her own body and, if need be, with the blood that courses in her veins.

I have chosen this last formulation advisedly. For, underlying those strangely concrete formulations of stopping a gap, or leak, is the submerged image of vital sap, or fluid, escaping from the central life-force, that force which should be sustaining the vitality of the common weal and Eugenie's own. And that image links the king's predicament with Eugenie's fate, prophetically enunciated in her sonnet and borne out, later, in bitter reality, by her banishment overseas. The king's lament at the oncoming revolution is overwhelmingly couched in images of waters unleashed to mingle and dissolve what is only viable as long as it is discreet.

We read:

> O diese Zeit hat fürchterliche Zeichen:
> Das Niedre schwillt, das Hohe senkt sich nieder,
> Als könnte jeder nur am Platz des andern
> Befriedigung verworrner Wünsche finden,
> Nur dann sich glücklich fühlen, wenn nichts mehr
> Zu unterscheiden wäre, wenn wir alle,
> Von *einem* Strom vermischt dahingerissen,
> Im Ozean uns unbemerkt verlören.
> . . .
> Laßt endlich uns den alten Zwist vergessen,
> Der Große gegen Große reizt, von innen
> Das Schiff durchbohrt, das gegen äußre Wellen
> Geschlossen kämpfend nur sich halten kann.

That same closing of the ranks the king urges when he pledges the *Herzog* and Eugenie to secrecy. Only the strictest solidarity can empower a will which, exposed to intrigue, is buffeted about as helplessly as a ship on a storm-tossed sea.

Such imagery is taken up in Eugenie's sonnet in a twofold fashion. She is a shoot of the royal stem,

> ein Sprößling deines Stamms;

and this image is charged with the association of sapped vitality which the *Herzog* had introduced when he had warned Eugenie, earlier on, that

> Die Kraft entgeht vielleicht dem späten Zweige . . .,

an association which had in its turn been prefigured by the king's ominous words about the perforated ship; whilst the penultimate line of her poem —

> Mir ist, als müßt' ich unaufhaltsam eilen,

— takes up the king's ominous vision of separate lives being swept into an ocean of anonymity and dissolved therein.

Even more crucial is the appellation of the king in the first tercet of Eugenie's sonnet:

So fließe denn der holde Born der Gnaden!

she says, adding the hope that at his breast, in the sustaining embrace of his life-force, she may contain her life and suckle in sustenance in return for the strength she has given: a vain hope as beginning and end of the sonnet indicate, and an ominous misreading in the light of the shared awareness, already in the first act, that the vitality of the king and the realm he represents is steadily draining away into impotence and amorphousness, in much the same manner in which Eugenie's own creative energy seeps through the containing form she has herself composed and loses itself 'unaufhaltsam', in an impulse towards elemental boundlessness.

We must beware of the temptation to label with too great definiteness the configuration that is expressed in the relationship between Eugenie and her monarch. This relation works on more than one level and expresses more than one inner configuration. To reduce it to any one exclusive signification would be to reduce the bafflingly rich symbolism that pervades this play, and personal constellations which patently point beyond themselves, to the dry dust of allegory.[11]

Nevertheless we must attempt to indicate something of the significance, on one level of the tragedy, which we may have sensed the configuration between Eugenie and her monarch to possess. The weak and fickle king — whether the decree sealed by him which the *Hofmeisterin* produces later on is genuine is left open — would seem to be the presiding force of an hierarchic organisation of which Eugenie is a part. The head of the state of which she is a citizen, of course; but over and above that, the controlling agency of an internal economy of which Eugenie is the productive 'nisus'[12], to use one of Goethe's favourite words to describe the fashioning impulse in himself. It is because this creative economy is no longer discreet but about to dissolve, because 'der Herr der obern Regionen' has become unsure of himself and uncertain of his willingness or ability to sanction the life-force he represents, that Eugenie's creative thrust remains errant and spends itself in an elemental void. The king and Eugenie between them suggest a creative organisation imperilled by some fatal leak, such that the formative energies embodied in her being — taking the word in its aesthetic sense over and above its socio-political meaning — are set free, capable neither of sustaining the organising power of their entelechy nor of being sustained by it.

[11] Cf. S. P. Jenkins, 'Goethe's *Die Natürliche Tochter*', p. 63.

[12] J. Kunz, *ed. cit.*, comes closest to this reading, defining Eugenie as 'jenes Wesen, in dem sich gleichsam die Kräfte des Organismus sammeln; ihr ist es aufgegeben, die Gestaltenenergien zu bewahren, damit aus ihnen in einer günstigen Stunde die Erfüllung aufzublühen vermag. Eugenie ist es, die die Erinnerung an das Telos des Ganzen durch die Zeit des Vergessens hindurchträgt' (p. 483).

Even more caution is needed to articulate the configuration obtaining between the *Herzog* and his child. Here we must take note of the fact that Goethe has renamed his heroine, the name of the author of the memoirs from which he drew much of his tragic fable being Stéphanie-Louise de Bourbon-Conti. Such renaming, as well as the anonymity of the other characters in the play, has been explained by R. A. Schröder[13] and M. Gerhard[14] as springing from the poet's desire to veil a reality too close to the contemporary scene to be experienced, as he intended it to be, in its representative, typical character; and this is no doubt true. On the other hand, Goethe chose a name which is highly suggestive in its own right, a fact alluded to by J. Kunz and K. May. Eugenie, feminine derivative of Eugene (this itself is significant) means 'well- or nobly born'. But beyond that the further etymological origin of this name would seem worthy of our attention. 'Eugenie' is cognate with 'genius', the original meaning of which is 'generative power'. The hypothetical Indo-European root of the word is *gen which means 'to beget, to produce'. By the same token, 'Eugenie' is also cognate with the latin word 'genus' which means not only 'kind' or 'clan', but 'sex' and 'gender'. This latin word, in its turn, derives from, and is cognate with, the Greek 'γονή' which, interestingly enough, means both, 'that which is begotten, offspring', and 'that which generates, seed, semen; genitals', as well as 'the act of generation'.

The name Goethe gave to his heroine, then, means begetter, begetting organ, act of begetting and thing begotten, all in one. This comprehensive spectrum of meaning hints at a very close relation indeed between Eugenie and her father. How close a relation it is, may be seen from the fact that Goethe consigned Eugenie's mother, who plays a considerable role in the memoirs of Stéphanie-Louise de Bourbon-Conti, to limbo. The importance of Eugenie being the illegitimate offspring of the duke has been noted by most critics, though the significance of this fact has been variously assessed. We can scarcely put our mind at rest with the observation that Goethe's own son, August, was an illegitimate child as well, and that, therefore, the story of Stéphanie-Louise de Bourbon-Conti captured his sympathy[15]. The parallelism is obvious but does not assist our understanding of the play in its own frame of reference. I would suggest that, by virtually dropping the role of the mother, the poet hinted at the existence of an unusually close bond between father and child, and moreover suggested that the true nature of this bond is not to be found on a straightforward biological level. If the meanings contained in Eugenie's name have not provided a sufficient clue as to the nature of this relationship, we may turn to Max Kommerell to help us further along. In his analysis of *Die Ballade vom vertriebenen und zurückkehrenden Grafen* Kommerell establishes the

---

[13] *Op. cit.*, p. 480.
[14] Melitta Gerhard, 'Goethes Erleben der französischen Revolution im Spiegel der "Natürlichen Tochter"', *DV* 1, 1923, p. 305.
[15] By R. Peacock, *loc. cit.*, p. 4f.

closest parallel between Goethe's poem and the tragedy with which we are
here concerned. Both, he argues, are Goethe's ways of coming to terms with
the French Revolution, and both, in their different ways, deal with the theme
of 'das edle Blut im Exil'. 'Zweifach ist es vorgestellt', he writes of Goethe's
ballad: 'denn es ist nicht Person; als Vater und Kind, zeugend und gezeugt,
zeitkundig und naiv-blühend. Eine Tüchtigkeit des Wesens, die sich steigert
im abgöttisch geliebten Kind: das ist auch der Vater Eugeniens im politischen,
das ist der Vater Galatheens im kosmischen Drama.'[16] Of the Graf in Goethe's
ballad we read that the 'Dichter und der vertriebene Edle zu einer Person
werden'; hence Kommerell concludes, still à propos of the ballad, with the
question: 'Ist da nicht der Dichter, wenn er unter den andern erscheint, das
Hohe in verkannter Gestalt? Ist da nicht der vertriebene Edle die Maske des
Dichters?'[17]

I should like to take up the thread of Kommerell's argument where he leaves
off and suggest that the creative configuration he identifies in Goethe's ballad
in fact holds good for his classical drama as well. I would urge that what
Goethe presented in that central constellation between father and daughter
is 'nicht Person', but one and the same inner, indivisible and creative configuration of the creator in relation to his emergent product, seen now from one
aspect and now from the other. The aspect of that total configuration which
is embodied in the *Herzog* is that of the begetter, whilst in the figure of Eugenie
the poet has articulated the complementary aspect, that of the act of begetting
and of the creation that is begotten.

                                            3.

In the opening section of this chapter we saw Eugenie in the act of fashioning
a poem, and we considered this product of her imagination as the reflection
of a creative impetus which cannot be contained but flows past its goal,
beyond the vessel it has wrought for itself. In the following section we connected this 'leaking out' of Eugenie's creative energy with the precarious
configuration into which she is placed in the hierarchical structure of which
she is the most vital part.

We may now begin to see that heart-scene of the finished drama — Eugenie
violating the discreetness and secrecy of the creational act (the two are closely
linked) and bursting out of its confines into unbounded openness — as the governing symbol of her being and her fate. Her sonnet, contained and yet overflowing its rim, her wall-cabinet, concealed yet discovered by her curiosity
and others' and anything but safe, her treasure chest, decreed to remain sealed
and yet unlocked and displayed — are not all these so many concentric circles

---

[16] In: *Gedanken über Gedichte, op. cit.*, p. 400.
[17] *Op. cit.*, p. 414 f.

in which, layer upon layer, the quintessential *Gestalt* of her being is revealed?[18] In these progressive characterisations, Eugenie gradually emerges as the personification of a creative force which, once activated, cannot, by some untoward concatenation of inner and outer circumstances, be restrained from relinquishing its harbouring context to manifest itself fully, and comes to grief in such self-manifestation. And that harbouring context, that native shelter is, precisely, the duke, her begetter.

In a reading of *Die Natürliche Tochter* which principally concerns itself with problems of character and motivation, S. P. Jenkins describes the *Weltgeistliche* as 'one of the most evil characters in any literature, and one we do not expect to find in the work of a poet who created such an amusing and at times almost amiable Mephistopheles.'[19] The reason for this condemnation is, of course, the bewildering course the *Weltgeistliche* adopts to convince the duke that his daughter has died: '. . . this he does by the most vivid, crude and cruel details one could imagine, using the most hideous methods of mental and emotional torture, intensifying the lie just because it is a lie.'[20]

Miss Jenkins is correct in discerning a startling discrepancy between the exigencies of the objective situation and the means adopted by the *Weltgeistliche* to bridge the gap. All that was needed for the plot as Goethe envisaged it was that Eugenie should be radically removed, and the best way of ensuring this was to pronounce her dead, in such a manner as to exclude any possibility of even her dead body being viewed. This aim could certainly have been accomplished by some much simpler and less hurtful cover-story, such as that Eugenie fell into a ravine or a river and that her body could not be recovered.

The question arises why Goethe, who by nature shunned the theatrical exploitation of evil and suffering, should have chosen to expose the duke to such an annihilating onslaught of a malignity serving no compelling dramatic purpose. The question becomes more urgent as we call to mind the fact that here, too, Goethe, true to his bent, avoided the dramatic presentation of the duke's first reception of the news of Eugenie's death. As with most dramatic turning-points in this play — the fact has been critically noted[21] — this peak-moment, like that of her abduction or of her vain pleading with the people to rise to her aid, has been relegated offstage: the duke has heard the news,

---

[18] The centrality of these motifs is stressed by Goethe himself in conversation with J. D. Falk. Falk reports Goethe as saying: 'Was jener geheimnisvolle Schrank verberge, was ich mit dem ganzen Gedichte, was ich mit dem Zurücktreten der Fürstentochter in den Privatstand bezweckte — darüber wollen wir uns in keine nähere Erklärung einlassen.' (January 25, 1813.) I would submit that the *Gedicht* referred to in the closest proximity to the mysterious wall-cabinet means, not primarily the dramatic poem as a whole, but Eugenie's own sonnet, which was, after all, to be re-discovered by the king.

[19] *Loc. cit.*, p. 49.

[20] *Loc. cit.*, p. 50.

[21] Amongst others by K. May in: 'Goethes "Natürliche Tochter"', in: *Goethe* 4, p. 156f., and Staiger, *Goethe*, II, p. 382.

and has been granted the balm of sleep. And it is one of the two chief
intriguers, the *Sekretär*, who gives a deeply humane and understanding account
of this healing retreat into the unconscious, which we recognise as being
characteristically Goethean.

> Er schläft! Ich segnet' ihn, als ich ihn sah
> Bewußtlos auf dem Pfühle ruhig atmen.
> Das Übermaß der Schmerzen löste sich
> In der Natur balsam'scher Wohltat auf.

With such compassionate lines at the beginning of those two gruelling scenes,
and the master villain's magic words of comfort to the stricken duke at their
end — his 'der Geist' which, like the 'Ist gerettet' at the end of *Faust I*, opens
up entirely new perspectives and restores the suffering duke at one stroke —
we must abandon Miss Jenkins in her quest for psychological consistency
and concur with E. Staiger's assessment of the poet's intentions: 'Oft ist es
nicht wichtig, *wer* etwas sagt', Staiger argues: '*was* gesagt wird ist bedeutsam'.[22]
'Niemand kommt hier durch, der auf folgerichtiger Charakterisierung be-
harrt.'[23] And, summing up: 'Der dritte Aufzug ist abstrakt in seiner Gleich-
gültigkeit gegenüber der handlungsmäßigen Realität, abstrakt aber eben deshalb, weil das Letzte, der innerliche Bereich, mit einer ungeheueren Anstrengung verteidigt werden muß.'[24]

Staiger's assessment of this crucial scene is in my view correct as far as it
goes. But why is the *Weltgeistliche* made in the first place to torture the duke
in a manner and degree which so radically exceeds the requirements of the
plot, and what precisely is the 'innere Bereich' he helps the duke discover
by such seemingly incongruent means?

He himself charts the course he will follow, in the introductory conversation
with the *Sekretär* which precedes the appearance of the duke. Expatiating on
the resolution that Eugenie must be accounted by her father 'als ewig tot',
he outlines his programme as follows:

> Der Irrtum soll im ersten Augenblick
> Auf alle künft'ge Zeit, gewaltig wirken.
> An ihrer Gruft, an ihrer Leiche soll
> Die Phantasie erstarren. Tausendfach
> Zerreiß' ich das geliebte Bild und grabe
> Dem Sinne des entsetzten Hörenden
> Mit Feuerzügen dieses Unglück ein.
> Sie ist dahin für alle, sie verschwindet
> Ins Nichts der Asche. Jeder . . .
> . . . .   vergißt, . . .
> . . . .   daß auch sie
> Im Reihen der Lebendigen geschwebt.

[22] *Goethe*, II, p. 381.
[23] *Goethe*, II, p. 383.
[24] *Goethe*, II, p. 384.

These are crucial words. They show that the lies the *Weltgeistliche* will presently produce are not primarily aimed at the duke's common sense and power of understanding. To convince him that Eugenie is dead and beyond recall would, as I have shown, be an easy undertaking. It would also be an incomplete and ill-conceived undertaking. For Eugenie is not so much her father's physical possession. Her existence is rooted in his 'Phantasie' — the self-same power her father first stresses in relation to Eugenie herself, in his description of her to the king — and any assault to eradicate her must first and foremost be aimed at this domain. What the *Weltgeistliche*, on the basis of his assessment of the duke, deems necessary is nothing less than a murder of the second power: a murder of her image — her *Bild* — in his mind.

The *Weltgeistliche* has divined the arena of the ensuing battle correctly; and it is through his taking aim with such merciless precision that the true nature of the duke's relation to his daughter is gradually borne in on us. To reveal this inner configuration is the overriding poetic purpose of his exquisite malignity.

Goethe may or may not have been careless in his psychological motivation of the villainous *Weltgeistliche* who offers the duke battle on the piece of ground which is his most vital domain and, in doing so, causes him to entrench himself in a position made invincible by the very force of his own attack. Certainly he was most careful in preparing us for the insight this savage duel will bring, the insight into the recesses of his being in which Eugenie is most firmly rooted. In scene 6 of the opening act he gives us an important clue. Eugenie has fallen down the cliff and is miraculously restored to her father, unhurt. The shock of the near-catastrophe seems to have ebbed away, and reality and the concerns it brings are once again exacting their *ungeheure Recht*. In such a frame of mind father and daughter bid each other farewell; and at this point, unexpectedly and with overwhelming force, the duke's imagination takes over. '. . . lebe wohl', he says, and continues thus:

> Doch ach! indem ich scheide,
> Befällt mich grausend jäher Furcht Gewalt.
> Hier lagst du tot in meinen Armen! Hier
> Bezwang mich der Verzweiflung Tigerklaue.
> Wer nimmt das Bild vor meinen Augen weg!
> Dich hab' ich tot gesehn! So wirst du mir
> An manchem Tag, in mancher Nacht erscheinen.
> War ich, entfernt von dir, nicht stets besorgt?
> Nun ist's nicht mehr ein kranker Grillentraum,
> Es ist ein wahres, unauslöschlichs Bild:
> Eugenie, das Leben meines Lebens,
> Bleich, hingesunken, atemlos, entseelt.

Already here, in the face of his unhurt daughter, the duke's imagination triumphs over plain reality. Before ever the *Weltgeistliche* has appeared and poisoned the father's mind with his fabrications, the very *Bild* he plans to

implant in him is engraven in him *unauslöschlich*, '*mit Feuerzügen*'. We must
take note of the tenuousness of physical reality for this man — the tenuousness, at least, of the reality of his daughter's physical existence — and of the
extreme violence with which her image, in this case the image of the dead
Eugenie, lays hold on an imagination of the most irritable susceptibility. It
is indelible in its vehemence, and in this, for him, lies its claim to being true,
truer and more tenacious than the palpable reality before him.

It seems then that Eugenie, in her physical reality, leads a fragile existence
in her father's imagination; and this impression is borne out in the second
scene of Act III, in his encounter with the *Sekretär* which again precedes
that with the *Weltgeistliche*. The *Sekretär's* comforting words:

> O möchte doch das viele, das dir bleibt
> Nach dem Verlust, als etwas dir erscheinen ...

are desperately brushed aside by the bereft father as 'ein geistverlassner,
körperlicher Traum'. The real sting is contained in the word 'erscheinen'.
To the *Sekretär* it means 'appear'. To the duke, 'erscheinen' has the force
of a vision; and, dismissing such comfort as the *Sekretär* offers to him as
'mindless' and 'physical', his thoughts once again painfully gravitate towards
the 'Bild' of his daughter as he sees her, even now, in his mind's eye:

> Wie schwebte beim Erwachen sonst das Bild
> Des holden Kindes dringend mir entgegen!

he laments; and significantly continues:

> Hier fand ich oft ein Blatt von ihrer Hand,
> Ein geistreich, herzlich Blatt, zum Morgengruß.

These words, and the secretary's reply, recall Eugenie's writing her sonnet,
her eager 'Eben schwebt mir's heiter vor'; and we realise that father and daughter are made of the same stuff. The urgent and fugitive vision that besets their
imagination, *das flücht'ge Ziel*, this alone to them is supremely real and true.
So real and so true, indeed, that before the force of its onset the duke loses
sight of reality and momentarily abandons himself to the 'heil'ge Anschaun'
of paternal joys which are, or so he has been led to believe, for ever forfeited.
He awakens to the *Sekretär's* reminder that all this is now lost, with surprise
almost, asking:

> Verlor ich's? War es doch im Augenblick
> Vor meiner Seele noch im vollen Glanz.
> Ja, ich verlor's!

And now that, what to him had possessed the authenticity of vision, is exposed
as a delusion, he calls down upon himself and upon 'was mir in seiner Dauer
Stolz erscheint', the same destruction which has overtaken the radiant and
fragile image by which he has lived. All is 'schwankende Gestalt'; yet what
of it, if even her *Gestalt* has but precariously and momentarily 'im Reihen der

Lebendigen geschwebt', if the only thing that is exempt from transience is her dead form,

> Ein Schreckliches, nun ewig Bleibendes . . .?[25]

Routed from the stronghold of life, the duke now encamps himself in the last entrenchment that is left, death itself, and passionately fights to preserve Eugenie's lifeless form[26]. This is where the *Weltgeistliche* comes onto the scene to begin his subtler attack. The duke pleads for her dead body to be embalmed:

> Laß uns . . .
> Das unschätzbare Bild zusammenhalten!
> Ja! die Atomen alle, die sich einst
> Zur köstlichen Gestalt versammelten,
> Sie sollen nicht ins Element zurück.

But he is routed even from his position in the camp of death. 'Ach! das zerstörte Bild!' the *Weltgeistliche* sighs and continues to paint a picture of destruction which is Kleistean in its demoniacal ferocity:

> Laß mich verhehlen, wie sie, durchs Gebüsch,
> Durch Felsen hergeschleift, entstellt und blutig,
> Zerrissen und zerschmettert und zerbrochen,
> Unkenntlich, mir im Arm zur Erde hing.

But as the *Weltgeistliche* attacks the duke ever more relentlessly, he forces out of him an ever more refined and creative response. Begging him to stay, the duke asks him:

> Ein schön entworfnes Bild,
> Das wunderbar dich selbst zum zweitenmal
> Vor deinen Augen zu erschaffen strebt,
> Hast du entzückt es jemals angestaunt?
> O hättest du's! du hättest diese Form,
> Die sich zu meinem Glück, zur Lust der Welt
> In tausendfält'gen Zügen auferbaut,
> Mir grausam nicht verstümmelt, mir die Wonne
> Der traurigen Erinnrung nicht verkümmert!

The begotten that, mysteriously and autonomously ripening towards perfection, surpasses the highest dreams of its begetter and transforms him: this, surely, is Goethe the artist speaking, the *Augenmensch* who, himself overwhelmed and seared by the sight of beauty, lent his voice to Faust as he invokes Helena from the shades —

> Hab ich noch Augen? Zeigt sich tief im Sinn
> Der Schönheit Quelle reichlichstens ergossen? —

---

[25] In this connection, cf. Chapters VIII, XI, sections 4, 5 and 6, and XIII, section 3.

[26] Cf. Goethe's own words: 'Wenn ich an meinen Tod denke, darf ich, kann ich nicht denken, welche Organisation zerstört wird.' (*Maximen und Reflexionen*, *HA* XII, No. 1057.)

the creator of Epimetheus, of Wilhelm Meister who is transformed by the form he himself had harboured and nurtured in his mind — this is the author of the supreme artist's credo: 'Eine geistige Form wird aber keineswegs verkürzt, wenn sie in der Erscheinung hervortritt, vorausgesetzt daß ihr Hervortreten eine wahre Zeugung, eine wahre Fortpflanzung sei. Das Gezeugte ist nicht geringer als das Zeugende, ja es ist der Vorteil lebendiger Zeugung, daß das Gezeugte vortrefflicher sein kann als das Zeugende.'[27] And when the duke laments the silent dissolution of the 'Götterbild', comparing the bliss of the time

> Wenn über werdend Wachsendem vorher
> Der Vatersinn mit Wonne brütend schwebte . . .

with the evil eye of despair now which turns to 'Moder nach und nach . . . die Lust des Lebens' —: what is he invoking in these words if not the ecstasy of the artist in the act of creation, and the artist's inconsolable bereavement as his creation is given over to decay, and the creative power in him turns to dust and ashes?

Like the figure of King Lear[28] on the heath, the duke, in an imperious gesture, wants to turn the world into a wilderness and to transform the 'Tempel der Genesung' he has been building to commemorate Eugenie's restoration to life, into a monument to chaos and transience. To both, chaos as well as transience. The archaic disorder around him is to commemorate and reflect the dissolution of her precious form, and the collapse of that high, creative configuration in himself which was his while he harboured her evolving form. This, which now has come to nothingness, is what he wants to immortalise. In a scene compounded of timeless arrest and death, the duke is building a monument of despair to Eugenie's sleeping beauty and to the sleep in which, for a timeless moment, he had found succour from the gruesome spectacle of time and transience.

This evocation of the stillness which was his while he harboured her and she was there, in the inviolateness of perfection, ushers in a transition to a new key. One more lament, the most grievous of all, at having lost her and, in her, himself:

> Daß ein Besitz so fest sich hier erhält,
> Wenn das Verlorne fern und ferner flieht,
> Das ist die Qual, die das geschiedene,
> Für ewig losgerißne Glied aufs neue
> Dem schmerzergriffnen Körper fügen will.
> Getrenntes Leben, wer vereinigt's wieder?
> Vernichtetes, wer stellt es her?

But even these lines mourn not only her loss, and the pain of it. They affirm the indivisible oneness of him and her, in one *Hochgestalt* of creativity. The

---

[27] *Wilhelm Meisters Wanderjahre, Aus Makariens Archiv, HA* VIII, p. 464, No. 27.
[28] Goethe read *King Lear* at the time of the conception of *Die Natürliche Tochter*.

begotten has been wrenched from the begetter and, like one maimed, he perpetually hallucinates the presence of the severed limb. And in that supremacy of felt truth over the actual reality lies the seed of his salvation. From the beginning, the mental image, now of the dead Eugenie, now of the living child, had proved more powerful than the bare bone of reality. Always that frail and urgent image had interpolated itself between him and her physical existence, between him and her physical loss. Always, for him, the real Eugenie had precariously 'im Reihen der Lebendigen geschwebt'; and always her 'Bild' had hovered about him, with the invincible power of a vision. The 'spectre' of the real had ever been magically and effortlessly exorcised by 'meiner Tochter liebliche Gewalt'. And now, too, the very pain of bereavement restores her, as the pain of severance will restore the sensation of the severed limb. She is his, as she said she would be, a vivid and radiant thread that is woven into the very fabric of his imagination, and the *Weltgeistliche*, by denuding him of every false support, has helped to crystallise his consciousness of such an imperishable possession. He has experienced in himself the truth of the words the *Weltgeistliche* will eventually speak:

> Nicht in das Grab, nicht übers Grab verschwendet
> Ein edler Mann der Sehnsucht hohen Wert.
> Er kehrt in sich zurück und findet staunend
> In seinem Busen das Verlorne wieder.

It is the experience of separation which ushers in that final, inalienable nearness, that sense of imperishable possession. Goethe was to articulate it at the end of Act II and then again at the end of the Helena act of *Faust II*, in late poems such as *Hochbild* and *Äolsharfen*; and he articulated it already here, in *Die Natürliche Tochter*. When Eugenie stands before him safe and sound, her father laments:

> Eugenie, das Leben meines Lebens,
> Bleich, hingesunken, atemlos, entseelt.

But, whispered by a ghostly voice, we seem to hear the word which will restore her to him. The missing word is the one the *Weltgeistliche* will pronounce when she is gone: 'der Geist'. For

> ... das Leben ist die Liebe,
> Und des Lebens Leben Geist.

It is only when the duke has lost Eugenie's physical presence that she is truly his. 'Mein Geist im Bilde', as the poem *Äolsharfen* has it —: this is Eugenie's legacy to her father[29].

---

[29] For a very similar interpretation, cf. Schröder, who speaks of 'Stufen der Entsagung, des Verzichtes. Man könnte auch mit gelehrtem Terminus sagen, es seien Stufen erhöhter Abstraktion; und so wäre der Begriff des Verzichtes unmittelbar gegenwärtig. Auf der letzten Stufe entblüht der höchsten Entsagung die höchste Bejahung, dem ... absoluten Verzicht der unverlierbare Besitz.' (*Op. cit.*, p. 474.)

Everywhere in Goethe's poetry it is the same: it is renunciation, and renunciation alone, that ushers in the pacified present of the symbolically fulfilled moment. Here, in *Die Natürliche Tochter*, the *Weltgeistliche* will answer the duke's agonised question as to what or who will reunite what is severed, saying:

> Der Geist!
> Des Menschen Geist, dem nichts verlorengeht,
> Was er von Wert mit Sicherheit besessen.
> So lebt Eugenie vor dir, sie lebt
> In deinem Sinne, den sie sonst erhub,
> Dem sie das Anschaun herrlicher Natur
> Lebendig aufgeregt; so wirkt sie noch
> Als hohes Vorbild, schützet vor Gemeinem ...
> So fühle dich durch ihre Kraft beseelt!

'Was er ... mit Sicherheit besessen': But what is *sicher* in the world of *Die Natürliche Tochter*, indeed in Goethe's world? Eugenie's physical existence is radically insecure — her fall had presaged that from the beginning. She, like all else in the calvacade of living forms, is subject to constant change and a prey, finally, to transience. Like all else, she is a *schwankende Gestalt*. Even before her fall and her eventual eclipse, every breath she draws means a constant process of *gestalten, umgestalten*, a perpetual breaking down and re-forming of such elements as make up her *Gestalt*. Her form, her living form already, is in that constant flux the poet mourns in the poem *Dauer im Wechsel*. It is a mere fluke of time and chance 'daß auch sie im Reihen der Lebendigen geschwebt'. Nothing is easier than to banish her from that hovering calvacade; and sooner or later she is fated to leave the procession altogether. What is 'secure', lasting and utterly resistant to destruction is, paradoxically, her image, that frail and radiant after-image of her *Gestalt* which has indelibly imprinted itself on her father's susceptible mind, on his very retina, and there leads an autonomous life, the constancy and power of which far exceed that of the physical existence in which it is rooted. That physical base may be eroded, destroyed or otherwise removed from sight. Its *Gestalt*, hovering yet constant, frail yet tenacious, luminous in the extreme, remains. The after-image becoming a *Vorbild* —: what a daring transmutation, and how profoundly Goethean![30]

> Schwebe vor,
> Wohin ich wandle, zeige mir den Weg
> Durch dieser Erde Dornenlabyrinth!
> Du bist kein Traumbild, wie ich dich erblicke;
> Du warst, du bist.

Eugenie's *Geist im Bilde*, and only that, is her father's possession, as intangible as it is timeless, grounded in renunciation — abstraction, as R. A. Schröder

---

[30] Cf. Chapter XIII, section 3.

has finely remarked, is a mode of renunciation[31] — leading him back to his own creativeness and, thus, exempt from loss.

> Die Gottheit hatte dich
> Vollendet einst gedacht und dargestellt.
> So bist du teilhaft des Unendlichen,
> Des Ewigen, und bist auf ewig mein.

It is the *Weltgeistliche* who has nursed to ripeness this inner security of the duke, the security, surely, of the artist who, shorn of all false supports, in the end finds it deep in himself, in the carrying element of his creativeness. Such consolidation in a position of fathomless exposure is needful. For the words of Ottilie, in *Die Wahlverwandtschaften*, are ever true, 'daß der Mensch sich das am wenigsten zuzueignen vermag, was ihm ganz eigens angehört. Seine Werke verlassen ihn so wie die Vögel das Nest, worin sie ausgebrütet worden.'[32]

4.

Even early on in his development, the duke has repudiated the secretary's imputation that he loves his child with the self-centred impetuosity of a lover[33]; and he compares this mental frame with the contemplative bliss of a father

> der entzückt,
> In heil'gem Anschaun stille hingegeben,
> Sich an Entwicklung wunderbarer Kräfte,
> Sich an der Bildung Riesenschritten freut.

It is the word 'Bildung' which is of interest in the present context. In Goethe's morphology we may read the following passage which is as crucial to my purpose in this chapter and to the argument advanced in this book as a whole as any:

'Der Deutsche hat für den Komplex des Daseins eines wirklichen Wesens das Wort Gestalt. Er abstrahiert bei diesem Ausdruck von dem Beweglichen, er nimmt an, daß ein Zusammengehöriges festgestellt, abgeschlossen und in seinem Charakter fixiert sei.

---

[31] *Op. cit.*, p. 474 and p. 487. Cf. note 29.

[32] *Die Wahlverwandtschaften*, II, 3, *HA* VI, p. 374.

[33] H. Wolff disputes the duke's assertion, maintaining that the person here lamenting is 'nicht mehr ein Vater, sondern ein Liebhaber, dessen Klagen nur notdürftig dem Schmerz eines Vaters angepaßt sind.' Needless to say, '. . . die schmerzlichen Klagen des Herzogs um die verlorene Tochter in Akt III sind im Grunde Goethes eigene Klagen', for Sylvie von Ziegesar. (In: *Goethe in der Periode der Wahlverwandtschaften*, p. 80.) This reductionist biographical approach, which Wolff pursues *vis à vis* the sonnets, *Pandora*, *Wilhelm Meisters Wanderjahre* as well as *Die Wahlverwandtschaften* and *Die Natürliche Tochter*, has been appropriately dealt with by H. J. Schrimpf, in 'Silvie von Ziegesar und die Goetheschen Altersdichtungen aus der Zeit von 1802 bis 1809. Auseinandersetzung mit H. M. Wolffs Buch "Goethe in der Periode der Wahlverwandtschaften"'. In: *Dt. Vierteljahrsschr.*, JG 29, 1955.

> Betrachten wir aber alle Gestalten, besonders die organischen, so finden wir, daß
> nirgend ein Bestehendes, nirgend ein Ruhendes, ein Abgeschlossenes vorkommt,
> sondern daß vielmehr alles in einer steten Bewegung schwanke.'

Everything that we have so far said about the precariousness of Eugenie's own being, as well as of the configuration in which she is encompassed together with her father, reads like a glossary on these words. She is *schwankende Gestalt*, and so is the creative configuration of which she forms a part. But Goethe's own statement does not end here. He adds an important rider. We read: 'Daher unsere Sprache das Wort Bildung sowohl von dem Hervorgebrachten, als von dem Hervorgebrachtwerdenden gehörig genug zu brauchen pflegt.'

It is in this double sense that Goethe employs the word *Bildung* in the duke's description of his paternal joys. Eugenie is his *Bildung* in the sense that she is the creation he has brought forth. But she is also his *Bildung* in the sense that in her person she embodies the act of bringing forth. She is the incarnation of her begetter's generative power, and this, we may remember, is the original meaning of the word 'genius', itself cognate with the name Eugenie, which the poet has given to her. Thus a curious ambivalence attaches to the heroine, that *Bildung* so idolised by her begetter. She is both a figure, a *Gestalt*, though of necessity, as we now see, a *schwankende Gestalt;* and she is also a generative force — a dynamic aspect here indicated by the word 'Riesenschritten' — a formative process productive of form, yet not itself form. This ambiguous status is reflected in Eugenie's sonnet, formed, yet straining beyond its bounds; it goes a long way towards accounting for the deep precariousness her father feels attaching to her possession; and it explains her character and her fate.

Eugenie's extraordinary vitality has been commonly noted. R. Peacock especially has emphasised her sheer *joie de vivre* as the necessary foil to the obsession with death Goethe evinces in this drama. 'Sie ist eine Gestalt von stürmischer Vitalität', we read, and 'sie ist zunächst vital-heroisch, nicht sentimental-idyllisch.'[34] This reading is, if anything, a low-key statement of the picture the poet is evoking for us. The Goethe of the turn of the century did not use words like 'Frevels Glück', 'Taumel', 'ungemessne Wonne', 'Raserei', 'tollkühner Übermut', 'unbedingte Freiheit' or — time and again — 'Verwegne' lightly. Descriptions such as that of her

> Überkühner Mut, mit dem du dich,
> Als wie ans Pferd gewachsen, voll Gefühl
> Der doppelten, centaurischen Gewalt,
> Durch Tal und Berg, durch Fluß und Graben schleuderst,
> Wie sich ein Vogel durch die Lüfte wirft ...

[34] *Loc. cit.*, p. 13.

or the duke's 'posthumous' characterisation —

> Ins Wasser tauchend, schwimmend, schien sie mir
> Den Elementen göttlich zu gebieten . . .

— seem to say more. They bespeak an elemental, demonic, a mythological force even, deeply at one with nature, rather than denoting any person at all. Especially the last quoted description is worthy of our attention: water-imagery, for Goethe, is always closely associated with creativity — this I have shown elsewhere[35]; and in this description the heroine emerges as the genius of this element, gifted with that ultimate virtuosity in exposure to elemental flux which is the hallmark of the artist. How like her father is she in finding security in the groundless insecurity of life itself! Again, her credo of carelessness is reminiscent of Egmont, himself a figure driven by demonic powers:

> Dem Ungemeßnen beugt sich die Gefahr . . .

she raps, and:

>   Das Glück
> Und nicht die Sorge bändigt die Gefahr;

and, perhaps most impressively:

>   Was bedeutend schmückt,
> Es ist durchaus gefährlich.

And finally, her fall: At the risk of momentarily shocking my readers, I would contend that there is much of Penthesilea's *Raserei* prefigured in this, her insane and somnambulist plunge into the depths.

>   Sie allein besinnt
> Sich keinen Augenblick und nötiget
> Ihr Pferd von Klipp' zu Klippe, grad herein . . .

the Graf recounts. And she herself confirms his story, echoing:

>   Ja, nun weiß ich alles.
> Dort oben hielt ich, dort vermaß ich mich
> Herab zu reiten, grad herab. Verzeih!
> Nicht wahr, ich bin gestürzt?

These are the words of a sleepwalking demon — Egmont compares himself to a sleepwalker and Goethe thought of him as such, and Penthesilea, sister to Käthchen, sleepwalks throughout the whole of her tragic career — and moreover they are the deeds and words of a being that is curiously sexually indeterminate. H. Böschenstein has critically noted that 'Eugenie on occasion comes perilously and uncomfortably close to being a woman of masculine resoluteness'[36]. And this comes closer to the mark than his observation, on

[35] Cf. Chapter I and my *Goethe and Lessing*, Chapter XI.
[36] *Loc. cit.*, p. 39.

the preceding page, that 'Iphigenie and Eugenie stand for pious feeling and gentle persuasion'[37]. More consistently, Peacock argues: 'das Bild, das schließlich vor unsern Augen triumphiert, ist das der Amazonentochter', in which he sees the master-key to Eugenie's character and actions[38]. True, but not enough. The blend, in her, of masculine and feminine traits is as bewildering and bewitching as in Mignon who, embracing Wilhelm with all the marks of womanly passion, insists on wearing the clothes of a boy and then dons a trailing angel-robe and longs for the time when

> Sie fragen nicht nach Weib und Mann.

Eugenie's form, too, is to hover between life and death, embalmed in her fathers imagination,[39] as her excited heart had hovered between masculine and feminine drives; now asking for adornments as any young girl would do, now donning them with martial pomp, like Penthesilea when she is about to gird herself for battle with Achilles.

> Nun sprich vom Tode nur! Sprich von Gefahr!
> Was zieret mehr den Mann, als wenn er sich
> Im Heldenschmuck zu seinem Könige,
> Sich unter seinesgleichen stellen kann?
> Was reizt das Auge mehr als jenes Kleid,
> Das kriegerische lange Reihen zeichnet?
> Und dieses Kleid und seine Farben, sind
> Sie nicht ein Sinnbild ewiger Gefahr?
> Die Schärpe deutet Krieg, womit sich, stolz
> Auf seine Kraft, ein edler Mann umgürtet.
> O meine Liebe! Was bedeutend schmückt,
> Es ist durchaus gefährlich. Laß auch mir
> Das Mutgefühl, was mir begegnen kann,
> So prächtig ausgerüstet, zu erwarten.
> Unwiderruflich, Freundin, bleibt mein Glück.

The tenor of these words is characterised by the *Hofmeisterin's* retort, murmured in an aside:

> Das Schicksal, das dich trifft, unwiderruflich.

The most Schillerian ending to any scene he ever wrote, this exchange has been called[40]; certainly, I would say, the most Greek in feeling. It is the voice of a sexless and disembodied spirit we hear, the voice of one possessed by the imperious need to make itself fully manifest, to *erscheinen* in and to the world, in the heightened consciousness, which belongs to the tragic personage, that to do so is to accept the supreme challenge of its destiny.

---

[37] *Loc. cit.*, p. 38.
[38] *Loc. cit.*, p. 7. Cf. also K. May, *ed. AGA* 6, p. 1194.
[39] For the motif of beauty embalmed cf. Emrich, *op. cit.*, p. 320.
[40] By Schröder, *op. cit.*, p. 478.

We hear, in fact, the voice of Euphorion, hermaphroditic himself, irresistibly drawn to danger and death, arming himself for it and courting it as by some prior and intimate understanding with his destiny —

> Und der Tod
> Ist Gebot,
> Das versteht sich nun einmal —

and accomplishing it:

> Doch! — und ein Flügelpaar
> Faltet sich los!
> Dorthin! Ich muß! ich muß!
> Gönnt mir den Flug!

Euphorion-Byron, late genius of poetry who steps forth into life to fulfil his unconditional calling with martial ecstasy —: that is Eugenie. And if this Icarus seeks to fly, as a fitting expression of his demonic upward thrust — Mignon dons a pair of wings, too — so does the heroine of Goethe's classical tragedy, herself the embodiment of an unbounded creative drive.

Eugenie is pervasively, and fatally, associated with the imagery of birds and flying. After her fall her anguished father scolds her

> ... überkühner Mut, mit dem du dich ...
> Durch Tal und Berg, durch Fluß und Graben schleuderst,
> Wie sich ein Vogel durch die Lüfte wirft ...

This description does not evoke the image of effortless soaring — 'dem Geier gleich' — but the violent assault on gravity in which a body mindlessly flings itself through space and through looming obstacles, *as though* it had wings. This same impression, if anything, enhanced, emerges from the father's lament. Blaming himself that he had done nothing to curb her insane raging while there was yet time, he says:

> Da sollt' ich strafen die Verwegenheit,
> Dem Übermut mich scheltend widersetzen,
> Verbieten jene Raserei, die sich
> Unsterblich, unverwundbar wähnend, blind,
> Wetteifernd mit dem Vogel, sich durch Wald
> Und Fluß und Sträuche von dem Felsen stürzt.

And who could mistake the image that is implicit in the *Weltgeistliche's* description of her dangling dead body, the image of a bird with its broken wing limply hanging over his cupped arm?

> Laß mich verhehlen, wie sie, durchs Gebüsch,
> Durch Felsen hergeschleift, entstellt und blutig,
> Zerrissen und zerschmettert und zerbrochen,
> Unkenntlich, mir im Arm zur Erde hing ...

When, after her crazy downward plunge, Eugenie stands unharmed before her father, he promises to consecrate the ground onto which she fell, 'zum ew'gen Denkmal', building a 'Tempel ... der Genesung'.

> Hier soll kein Schuß,
> Solang' ich lebe, fallen, hier kein Vogel
> Von seinem Zweig, kein Wild in seinem Busch
> Geschreckt, verwundet, hingeschmettert werden.

Impotent desire to stay an elemental force that cannot be stayed, a fugitive form that cannot be arrested, any more than the 'flücht'ge Ziel' by which king and duke and Eugenie were carried past their goal, into the wilderness which will presently engulf her life-force and his dream! Embodiment of a demonic formative drive which strains past the shelter of the containing form towards boundlessness and de-composition, Eugenie herself, we now realise, is this 'flücht'ge Ziel'.

Quite unequivocally, her birdlike flight is linked with the aesthetic sphere which we have by now identified as being her native domain.

> Beflügelt drängt sich Phantasie voraus . . .

she enthusiastically exclaims as she has completed her sonnet and, with that thrust which cannot be contained, flies ahead in imagination to the 'great day', the birth anniversary of the king when she is to step forth into manifest life. And the same image recurs once again when she beseeches the *Gerichtsrat* to give her a ray of hope:

> Und wenn du täuschen solltest! — Wäre nur
> Für Augenblicke meiner Phantasie
> Ein zweifelhafter, leichter Flug vergönnt . . .

she pathetically begs; and we note not only the bat-like, moth-like uncertainty of a flight which is the dubious flight into an illusion, but also the epithet *leicht* which patently contrasts with the violence with which, earlier on, she had tossed herself vertically downwards, in her boundless zeal to *erscheinen*, to step forth into manifest being. Now, close to the moment when she will step back into harbouring concealment, in the '*Hafen*-Stadt', and renounce her quest to be 'ein offenbar Geheimnis', as the Graf has it, her formative *nisus* has attained a new ethereal quality — *leicht* — and her flight is adapting itself to the hovering motion of the winged creatures of the night into which she will herself dis-appear.

Yes, Eugenie is birdlike, and in the blindness of her desire to fly into the light, disregarding all obstacles and coming to grief against them, even more like a moth. Such associations bring her into the closest proximity to *Knabe Lenker*,

> . . . die Verschwendung, die Poesie;
> . . . der Poet, der sich vollendet,
> Wenn er sein eigenst Gut verschwendet,

whose treasures, recklessly tossed into midair, turn into 'frevle Schmetterlinge'; and even more to the creator of *Selige Sehnsucht* and of *Tasso*. As Tasso emerges from the cocoon of his creative engrossment and seeks the light of the 'neue Tag', dazed, with faltering steps, so Eugenie steps forth from the pupa stage of her creativeness into the day of manifest life uncertainly, *geblendet*. There we read:

Here:

> Unsicher folgen meine Schritte dir,
> O Fürstin, und Gedanken ohne Maß
> Und Ordnung regen sich in meiner Seele.

> O verzeihe mir
> Die Majestät! wenn aus geheimnisvollem,
> Verborgnem Zustand ich, ans Licht auf einmal
> Hervorgerissen und geblendet, mich,
> Unsicher, schwankend, nicht zu fassen weiß.

Tasso, rejected by a world which repudiates his elemental productive drive, retraces his steps, first into imaginary banishment — into the duke's most outlying estate of which he will take care against the day when life will once again return to it — and then into the bitterer banishment of his inwardness, the shelter he had prematurely relinquished[41]. Eugenie, banished from the

> Regionen, wo mir eben
> Die neue, heitre Sonne sich erhebt...,

seeks refuge in a remote house belonging to the *Gerichtsrat*, 'alt und halb verfallen'. This she passionately chooses, rather than the *wohlgelegne Gut* the *Gerichtsrat* offers to her, exclaiming:

> Nein! In das altverfallne laß mich ziehn,
> Zu meiner Lage stimmt es, meinem Sinn.
> Und wenn er sich erheitert, find' ich gleich
> Der Tätigkeit bereiten Stoff und Raum.
> Sobald ich mich die Deine nenne, laß,
> Von irgendeinem alten zuverläss'gen Knecht
> Begleitet, mich, in Hoffnung einer künft'gen
> Beglückten Auferstehung, mich begraben.

How much like Tasso's imagined refuge, and how much like him in the loving depiction of the vivid detail and the telling touch! More crucially, do we not discern in these last two lines the echo of Tasso's prayer, as he once more affirms the need of his nature to bury himself in the cocoon of his creativeness, and looks forward to some distant and uncertain resurrection? Symbolic burial, banishment, and hope of some future resurrection here and there[42]. And banishment not merely from a world that repudiates them, but a more tragic banishment, in both cases, from creative fulfilment of the

---

[41] Cf. my *Goethe and Lessing*, Chapter VII.

[42] The motif of Eugenie's 'fall' and resurrection is explored by Kunz, *ed. HA* V, p. 484, and p. 500, note to line 2913; also by S. P. Jenkins, with more specifically biblical connotations. Miss Jenkins traces the parallelism between the dramatic plot and the Joseph story which is itself a prefiguration of 'the life, death and resurrection of Christ'. (*Loc. cit.,* p. 59.)

self. Tasso has completed his poem and delivered it to his patrons. The creation he harboured has become autonomous, as independent of him as the fledgling birds that leave their one-time nest. The creative drive which, not long before, was contained by the vessel he was fashioning, now has become object-less. It is still there, but it flows out into a void.

And Eugenie? She, too, is creative drive, generative force. In a mighty and irresistible thrust, she had striven to step forth into the manifest being of a lasting and definite *Gestalt*. She had asked:

> Der Schein, was ist er, dem das Wesen fehlt?
> Das Wesen, wär' es, wenn es nicht erschiene?

These words are not as esoteric as they are usually made out to be. As

> Natur hat weder Kern noch Schale,

so Eugenie, a supremely creative *Wesen*, has sought to step forth into the appearance of a visible and lasting *Erscheinung*[43]. This legitimate wish is not granted to her; it cannot be granted to her in the world of a drama in which creativity is neither trusted nor sanctioned, in which the creative economy is impaired, in that head and generative drive cleave apart; it cannot be fulfilled in a universe of discourse in which every *Gestalt*, and especially the supremely creative *Gestalt aller Gestalten*, is conceived as *schwankend* and radically insecure, destined, as Goethe has it in *Pandora*,

> Erst verborgen, offenbar zu werden,
> Offenbar, um wieder sich zu bergen.

Thus Eugenie tragically withdraws from her native claim to appearance and dis-appears into the seclusion of latency whence she came, hoping for the day when she may be fully manifest and play her destined role as the acknowledged genius of the creative economy which has failed her, to which she is pledged. That this is the burden of her hibernation, and of her longed-for resurrection, becomes apparent from the role the *Gerichtsrat* assumes.

It is in this figure, in the *Hafenstadt*, that she finds the shelter that her father had been to her. He had looked for his destiny in vain:

> Doch du *erscheinest**: ich empfinde nun,
> Was ich bedurfte. Dies ist mein Geschick.

She will dis-appear again from his sight as soon, almost, as she appeared to him and to the world. Yet, with that same insuperable reliance on her *Geist*

---

[43] At one point, E. Staiger comes close to this interpretation, when he writes: 'Eugenie verschwindet wieder aus der Welt, noch ehe sie völlig erschienen ist.' (In: *Goethe, op. cit.*, II, p. 400.) But this formulation does not do justice to his emphasis, throughout his reading, on the impossibility for Eugenie to survive the onslaught of the political and social forces of anonymity.

* my italic.

im Bilde, on the permanence and power of her shining essence which her father had evinced, he will live by the after-image of that brief *Erscheinung* and let it be a guiding power to him, an inextinguishable *Musterbild*. And in this act of renunciation he will possess her in perpetuity and truth, as her father had done before him.

The development within the *Gerichtsrat* echoes to a nicety that within Eugenie's father, and both together tell us the same about the nature and destiny of the mysterious figure at the centre of the tragedy, Eugenie. Stepping forth from the concealment of its beginning, the genius of creativity, unable to find embodiment in a *Gestalt* that is immune from destruction in an enfeebled economy ruled by a fickle power, withdraws from its disastrous incarnation into phenomenality, awaiting a second coming when the world will sustain the visible glory of its revelation. This precious offspring of creative nature must, by a tragic decree, abstain from being 'ein offenbar Geheimnis'. In an uncreative world it must shroud itself — Eugenie appears shrouded in the final acts of the play — into the mystery from whence it came, unrevealed.

5.

It do not claim this reading to be an easy one. An easy reading cannot be expected of a play whose central figure *is* 'ein Geheimnis', as we hear time and again, who not only is given a treasure which must not be prematurely opened, but herself *is* this treasure[44]. Mystery is of the essence of Eugenie's being, and we cannot expect altogether to lift a veil of secrecy in which the poet has himself shrouded ranges of experience so deep and so intimate as to deliberately conceal them from the prying eye.

Fortunately, Goethe himself, at a less fraught moment of his life, has given utterance to those very same ranges of experience in a poem which is considerably less intractable to the critical understanding. I mean the elegy *Euphrosyne*, written in 1797/98 and published in 1799, that is to say, the year in which the poet conceived *Die Natürliche Tochter*. The remarkable similarity between the main personage of that elegy, the idealised figure of the young actress Christiane Becker, and the heroine of Goethe's tragedy has, to my knowledge, not been noted; yet her destiny, and the poetic dimension in which it is placed, experienced and interpreted, may afford us a valuable key for our understanding of what Goethe could and would not fully reveal in the *Geheimnis* which is at the centre of his tragedy.

In this elegy, written when the news of the early death of his favourite young actress-pupil hit him on his third Swiss journey, her spirit, newly dead, appears to him and eloquently reminds him of the culminating moments

---

[44] Cf. note 5 of this chapter.

of their relationship. It is a curiously complex relationship, in which the speaker — Goethe himself — appears as father, teacher and lover in one. Euphrosyne appears and at once identifies herself as the child genius who had acted the part of the doomed young Prince Arthur in Shakespeare's *King John*, in a rehearsal preceding the public performance of the play, during which Goethe himself had taken over the part of King John's chamberlain, Hubert. Pledged to gouge out the young prince's eyes, Hubert is moved by his innocence and beauty to let him be; but the young prince, in a desperate plunge from the walls of the prison in which his pretender-uncle has incarcerated him, leaps to his death. It is the rehearsal of these scenes that Euphrosyne recalls, and the timeless moment in which her paternal friend and mentor had clasped the play-acting young actress, seemingly dead and shattered, in his arms. She now reminds him of how profoundly shocked he was at her pretended death; and how he had mused, not only on the uncertainty of human life in general, but on that most cruel reversal of Nature's benign law, the young dying before the old.

> Alles entsteht und vergeht nach Gesetz; doch über des Menschen
> Leben, dem köstlichen Schatz, herrschet ein schwankendes Los.

And holding 'den Zerschmetterten' (the word occurs twice) — the boy Arthur played by the young Christiane — he had given himself over to an unrestrained lament at the grievousness of transience:

> Als du, zur Leiche verstellt, über die Arme mir hingst . . . :

these are the words in which the dead Euphrosyne evokes this strange scene, a prefiguration, as it was to turn out, of her actual death not many years after. And now her spirit has returned, beseeching the poet to bestow on her a name which, amongst the nameless and *gestaltlosen* shades that crowd Hades, will vouchsafe some permanence to her *Gestalt*, even in death.

It is impossible to miss the threads that ply between Goethe's elegy and his classical tragedy: the supremely talented young artist, a boy-girl at the moment the poet chooses to highlight in the poem, 'rehearsing' her incumbent death; the lament of the father-lover who had harboured her early genius, at the fickleness of the human form epitomised, as it were, in one whose creativeness entitled her above all others to permanence of *Gestalt*, and the plea to be granted that after-life which only the poet can bestow by the act of naming, which will defeat the anonymity of the forces of death, thus preserving her *Geist im Bilde*: all this is a prefiguration, *en miniature*, of *Die Natürliche Tochter*. Everything is there: the young creative talent associated with sexual indeterminacy, the violent reaction of the father to the seeming death that will usher in the actual death, the image of the shattered form hanging over the *Weltgeistliche's* arm, and, most of all, the recovery of what is lost from the onset of anonymity through the power of creative remembrance, of poetic naming — Eugenie is the only figure in the drama to have a name, and what a name!: here, surely, in this elegy, we have the lyrical nucleus of what the tragedy, this long-extended elegy, was to articulate, and conceal, in the mode of tragic utterance.

The appearance of Euphrosyne is heralded by clouds, and it is engulfed in clouds that she disappears; she steps forth from the *bewegte Gebild* of those most fugitive of forms and is led back into moving clouds by the God Hermes. Into this setting of transience — for clouds in their constant transformation are this poet's archetypal symbol of the ineluctable transience of all that has shape[45] — Goethe has placed his most powerful lyrical lament over the passing of a young life which, by reason of its creative genius, had the supreme title to permanence of *Gestalt;* and he has transcended this lament by the affirmation of its perdurability, paradoxically, in the faithful eye and mind of its creator. And this, the ineluctable transience of a supremely creative entelechy, its radical insecurity in the real world and its continuing existence *im Bilde*, we must take to be the meaning and the fate Goethe embodied in the figure of his 'Liebling', Eugenie. Another Eurydice, led into the realm of the shades by Hermes, the *köstlicher Schatz* of such human lives is both lost to Orpheus — the speaker of the poem, and the duke — and restored to them through the power of the creative spirit, in — as Staiger has it — 'einer ungeheueren Anstrengung'[46].

6.

'Hat man sich nicht ringsum vom Meere umgeben gesehen, so hat man keinen Begriff von Welt und von seinem Verhältnis zur Welt.' This statement, made on arrival in Sicily, reflects the general tenor of Goethe's poetic utterances about water and his relationship to the element. Labile in the extreme and attuned to the fact that permanence, for a poet of all mortals, is to be sought, and found, in the midst of flux, he extolled the life-giving force of water throughout his long career, and set up its self-renewing circulation to its source as the fitting symbol of the human, and especially the creative, condition[47]. Water, to him, overwhelmingly was the cradle of formed growth; and 'jenes Meer'

> Das flutend strömt gesteigerte Gestalten . . .

was to receive its final poetic apotheosis in the rapturous acclaim given to it at the end of *Klassische Walpurgisnacht*.

It is in this spirit of reverence for water as an essentially creative force that the duke, in *Die Natürliche Tochter*, had looked forward to the day when

[45] Cf. Chapter XIII, section 4.
[46] In: Goethe, II, p. 384.
[47] Cf. note 35 of this chapter.

he would initiate Eugenie into the mysteries of *terra firma* and the boundless sea:

> So hofft' ich, ihr des Reichs bebaute Flächen,
> Der Wälder Tiefen, der Gewässer Flut
> Bis an das offne Meer zu zeigen, dort
> Mich ihres trunknen Blicks ins Unbegrenzte
> Mit unbegrenzter Liebe zu erfreun.

And so, too, Eugenie had recalled their common wish:

> Ans Meer versprach er mich zu führen, hoffte
> Sich meines ersten Blicks ins Unbegrenzte
> Mit liebevollem Anteil zu erfreun —.

Father's and daughter's hopes, we know, tragically founder. The *unbegrenzte* sea, when she does reach its shores, rings her from every side, an implacable enemy to all her hopes of self-realisation[48]. To Eugenie, this tragic turn comes as a bolt from the blue. To us, it is less of a surprise. For from the beginning of the play the allusions to the fluid element, now covert, now open, had spelt danger and even treacherousness. When Eugenie had vainly looked for a gift she might bring to her sovereign, sadly observing:

> Was fehlte dir? Was wäre dir zu bringen?
> Die Fülle selber, die zu dir sich drängt,
> Fließt, nur für andre strömend, wieder fort ...

we had registered the ominous implications of her words: the draining away from the centre of the vital economy of which he is the head and she the heart, of the energies fed into it. Such implications had been confirmed by her sonnet — framed, we remember, in images of water — in which she had envisaged her life-force as irresistibly streaming away to a *holde Born der Gnaden* which, we had reason to suspect, had itself sprung a leak. Neither in such images nor indeed in that which the duke uses of the king — of the degenerate bough the sap of which escapes — had there been a suggestion of that wholesome circulation of energies issuing from their vital centre and replenishing themselves: *this* is the mark of a healthy organism, to express which Goethe time and again resorted to the symbolism of coursing water. If, thus, the vitality and resilience of the economy of which Eugenie forms part was called into question early on, its viability was soon to be challenged openly, in the self-same imagery of water. Accepting Eugenie's pledge of loyalty, the king himself had evoked the spectre of a political and social hierarchy in danger of impotence and dissolution. What was firm and per-

---

[48] An ineluctable fact which makes Staiger's statement 'Wohl weht die Gnade fühlbar wie ein leiser Hauch vom Gestade des Meeres über Eugenie und den Mönch ...' (*op. cit.*, p. 397) strangely incongruent and inept. For all his critical acumen and stylistic mastery, such lapses at times make one wonder what depth-dimensions in the works he discusses have altogether escaped him.

manently structured, he had prophetically seen as being about to be engulfed by chaos: and chaos had been invoked in images of a swelling tide, merging what is structured and viable, and carrying it towards loss of identity and final obliteration in an ocean of anonymity; to which metaphor he had added that of the leaking ship.

It will be seen that water, in its amorphousness, has emerged as the symbol of dissolution of what is permanent and structured, as the symbol of chaos *per se*[49]. There is no reference to the life-renewingness of just such fluidity, to the aspect of the element which, throughout Goethe's poetry, predominantly colours his references to that force. And a symbol of chaos, of regression into sheer unstructuredness, it will henceforth remain throughout this tragedy, in the Faustean curse the bereaved duke will call down upon everything

> Was mir in seiner Dauer Stolz erscheint

as in the vision of the monk, towards the end of the play, of the ocean engulfing the edifices of the *Hafenstadt*.

Much has been said about the prevalence of organic imagery in this play; and it is certainly to be found there, as we have seen for ourselves. But the fact has gone largely unobserved that, from fairly early on in the tragedy, organic images — except on Eugenie's lips — tend to be replaced by images of artifacts. It is the leaking ship, the tide-invaded town which are battered into shapelessness. This is important; for, from the beginning onwards, we have had our qualms about the viability of an organisation in which there is no feedback of energies; the organisation, precisely, in which Eugenie's life-force is allowed to stream away uncupped and unreplenished, so that she can say:

> Mir ist, als müßt' ich unaufhaltsam eilen,
> Das Leben, das du gabst, für dich zu lassen,

so that, in the end, she finds her life unsupported by the whole:

> Die zum großen Leben
> Gefugten Elemente wollen sich
> Nicht wechselseitig mehr mit Liebeskraft
> Zu stets erneuter Einigkeit umfangen.
> Sie fliehen sich, und einzeln tritt nun jedes
> Kalt in sich selbst zurück.

---

[49] It is interesting that in a personal context, too, Goethe resorted to the imagery of water in its chaotic aspect when discussing the French Revolution. A propos of Soulavie's *Mémoires historiques et politiques du règne de Louis XVI*, he writes to Schiller: 'Im ganzen ist es der ungeheure Anblick von Bächen und Strömen, die sich, nach Naturnotwendigkeit, von vielen Höhen und aus vielen Tälern gegen einander stürzen und endlich das Übersteigen eines großen Flusses und eine Überschwemmung veranlassen, in der zugrunde geht wer sie vorgesehen hat so gut, als der sie nicht ahndete.' (March 9, 1802.)

Is the poet, by such a transposition of the imagery of organisms onto the inferior plane of artifacts — even Eugenie's *gefugt*[50] does not ring quite true in an organic context — indicating that the structure with which he is in this play concerned, in which Eugenie's generative force is of no avail, is already on the point of deteriorating into a concatenation of lifeless atoms loosely bound together and unable to resist the onrush of the elements? Such a reading would certainly lend compelling force to her fate: the eclipse or at least the unredeemed taboo that is placed on the manifestation of a supremely creative form.

Be this as it may, it is Goethe's favourite element, water, which in this unfinished trilogy emerges as the arch-enemy of formed life and man's striving for permanence. Now that *die Hochgestalt* of his life, Eugenie, has gone, the duke calls upon all the powers of that same unleashed element to lay low and utterly destroy what there may be left of form — worthless all, since she is given over to dissolution: like Lear he cries:

> So strömt, ihr Klagen, denn!
> Zerstöre, Jammer, diesen festen Bau,
> Den ein zu günstig Alter noch verschont.
> Verhaßt sei mir das Bleibende, verhaßt,
> Was mir in seiner Dauer Stolz erscheint,
> Erwünscht, was fließt und schwankt. Ihr Fluten, schwellt,
> Zerreißt die Dämme, wandelt Land in See!
> Eröffne deine Schlünde, wildes Meer,
> Verschlinge Schiff und Mann und Schätze!

Eugenie herself, in her hemmed-in despair, wants to end her life in the waves:

> Empfangt mich dann, ihr Wellen, faßt mich auf
> Und fest umschlingend senket mich hinab
> In eures tiefen Friedens Grabesschoß.

And so, too, the monk, in a vision of sombre power, foresees the victory of the chaotic element over all the artifices of man's making. He sees 'der Gebäude Pracht', 'die felsengleich getürmten Massen', 'der Plätze Kreis, der Kirchen edlen Bau', and in the light of day he sees

> alles für die Ewigkeit
> Gegründet und geordnet.

But come the night,

> Da stürmt ein Brausen durch die düstre Luft,
> Der feste Boden wankt, die Türme schwanken,
> Gefugte Steine lösen sich herab,
> Und so zerfällt in ungeformten Schutt
> Die Prachterscheinung. Wenig Lebendes

---

[50] This is a point that has been overlooked in Kunz's otherwise admirable analysis of organic and allied imagery. (*Ed. cit.* V, pp. 481 ff.)

> Durchklimmt bekümmert neuentstandne Hügel,
> Und jede Trümmer deutet auf ein Grab.
> Das Element zu bändigen, vermag
> Ein tiefgebeugt, vermindert Volk nicht mehr,
> Und rastlos wiederkehrend füllt die Flut
> Mit Sand und Schlamm des Hafens Becken aus.

In this tragedy the creative element — 'die Lebensfeuchte', or 'diese holde Feuchte', as Goethe caressingly has it in the second *Faust* — is the enemy of all that is formed, not merely by virtue of its amorphousness. It is evil throughout, poisoned itself and engendering slow death by poisoning. This is the horror of the isles to which Eugenie, embodiment of the creative force *per se*, is to be banished. The words in which the *Gerichtsrat* depicts her place of exile are unparalleled in the poetic *opus* of Goethe for the venomous force which is seen pervading these seagirded strips of land — with one exception. For ever, he laments, her tragic fate has vitiated the joy that used to fill him at the sight of the ocean. For

> Fern am Rande
> Des nachtumgebnen Ozeans erblick' ich
> Mit Not und Jammer deinen Pfad umstrickt!
> . . .
> Der Sonne glühendes Geschoß durchdringt
> Ein feuchtes, kaum der Flut entrißnes Land.
> Um Niederungen schwebet, gift'gen Brodens,
> Blaudunst'ger Streifen angeschwollne Pest.
> Im Vortod seh' ich, matt und hingebleicht,
> Von Tag zu Tag ein Kummerleben schwanken.
> O die so blühend, heiter vor mir steht,
> Sie soll so früh, langsamen Tods, verschwinden!

Schweben, schwanken, verschwinden: Eugenie, genius of creativity, is not only to vanish from the eyes of a world not ready to regenerate itself through her: she is to dis-appear in water-locked lands where her very *Gestalt*, token of her creative force, is to be given over to slow and hideous erosion. And that the treacherous element, breeding poison in the low-lying no-man's-land of life, will attack not only her bodily form but the *innere Gestalt* of her creativity as well, becomes plain from Eugenie's ensuing words:

> Entsetzen rufst du mir hervor! Dorthin?
> Dorthin verstößt man mich! In jenes Land,
> Als Höllenwinkel mir, von Kindheit auf,
> In grauenvollen Zügen dargestellt.
> Dorthin, wo sich in Sümpfen Schlang' und Tiger
> Durch Rohr und Dorngeflechte tückisch drängen,
> Wo, peinlich quälend, als belebte Wolken
> Um Wandrer sich Insektenscharen ziehn,
> Wo jeder Hauch des Windes, unbequem
> Und schädlich, Stunden raubt und Leben kürzt.

Clouds, for Goethe, are the archetypal symbol of fertile flux. But these 'living clouds' formed by swarming insects are devoid of any mental association bar that of the deepest, and most agonising, disorientation. They are the venom of inner chaos personified.

Never — except in the passage from *Der Mann von funfzig Jahren* quoted in an earlier chapter[51] — has this poet used imagery of clouds and mists to evoke such violence of revulsion before the annihilating force of a confusion that erodes the very fibre of a mind: never, except here, in Eugenie's speech, where the 'Widerwärtige, gestaltet und immer umgestaltet', is envisaged even more revoltingly, in the form of sickening swarms of insects.

We must face the fact that, in this tragedy, the benign connotation of water, mist and clouds which accrues to these images virtually throughout Goethe's work — I have demonstrated this for the *Faust* drama in its entirety[52] — is radically rescinded. And it is not rescinded by one character and in one place as is the case in the fourth and fifth acts of *Faust II*. Here, a large body of water-associated imagery is built up on all levels of discourse and deployed by a variety of figures otherwise carefully distinguished: the king, the duke, the *Weltgeistliche* — who foresees that Eugenie will be engulfed in an ocean of anonymous destruction — the *Hofmeisterin*, the *Gerichtsrat*, the monk and Eugenie herself: and at all hands this huge body of imagery assumes a radically negative connotation. We cannot gainsay the fact that this imagery here emerges as the poet's imagery, that the connotation which cumulatively accrues to it is that intended by the poet, and that it directly contributes to the total statement this play is making: the tragic eclipse of a creative force in a world which cannot sustain it, in a natural environment, even, which is set on eroding it at its very core. How can we square such an import with the picture we have of Goethe? And can we adduce it to explain the fact that the tragedy remained unfinished in the form it was originally envisaged, that is to say, a trilogy?

7.

It is time now, at the end of this enquiry, to make allusion to Goethe's mental and physical frame at the time he worked on *Die Natürliche Tochter*, the discussion of which customarily prefaces any analysis proper of the play in its own right. Such biographical data — and rich use has been made of them in the studies of Hankamer, Staiger, Gerhard, Peacock, to mention only some — have an unfortunate way of obtruding themselves between the critic and his proper material, the extant work of art, prejudicing its reading from the start. We tend to be left with a host of biographical details on the one hand, and with a condemnation of, or apologia for, the

---

[51] Chapter VIII, section 7.
[52] In my *Goethe and Lessing*, Chapter XI. Cf. especially p. 293 f.

'marmorkalte'[53] reticence Goethe is supposed to have evinced *vis-à-vis* his dramatic materials, or with the demonstration that we are really dealing with two plays, the one abstractive and remote, the other pulsing with Goethe's life-blood and eloquent of his personal trauma. By postponing the consideration of the poet's personal predicament to the end, I hope to have avoided any such form of circular reasoning.

But of course it is necessary to consider the frame from which this most radically tragic of Goethe's tragedies sprang in the first instance. The *Tag- und Jahreshefte* for the year 1801 tell us of the 'grimmige Krankheit'[54] which befell the poet on January 2 of that year, of its outward course, its apparent ebbing away and 'die krankhafte Reizbarkeit'[55] it left behind. We know that the year following still found Goethe in a precarious frame, and as late as February 17, 1803 Schiller writes to Humboldt that Goethe lived in monastic seclusion and, without being exactly ill, had not stirred from the house for months on end. And we hear that he fainted on the one occasion when he set foot in his garden.

It is during these years of living through what is evidently a profound psychosomatic crisis that Goethe worked on *Die Natürliche Tochter*, a play first conceived in 1799, that is to say, a year after *Euphrosyne*. What inroads the first onset of the illness made on his total constitution, psychic as well as physical, becomes apparent from a curious formulation in the description of the event in the *Tag- und Jahreshefte* for 1801. After an unconsciousness lasting some nine days in which his friends feared for his life and lost all semblance of composure, he came to and recovered sufficiently to take in hand, a little more than a fortnight after first falling ill, the translation of Theophrastus' book *Von den Farben*. 'Innerlich hatte ich mich indessen schon wieder so gestaltet ...' we read; and in these strange words we readily recognise traumatic ranges of experience which found their direct precipitate in the tragedy which is concerned with the radical precariousness of the human *Gestalt* and which he was going to set about writing as the year wore on. There follows, in the *Annalen*, a reference to the resumption of his work on *Faust*. In all probability this meant the *Helena-Fragment*, another evocation, from waves and flux, of a highly uncertain *Gestalt*, a *Gestalt*, moreover, doomed to recede back into the shades from whence she, for a short while, appears. Then Goethe reports recalling the chill reception the Jena circle had given to his rendering of *Tancred* at the end of the year preceding. They had scolded him 'daß ich mich mit französischen Stücken, welche bei der jetzigen Gesinnung von Deutschland nicht wohl Gunst erlangen könnten, so emsig be-

---

[53] A charge levelled at Goethe as early as February 29, 1804, by Huber, in *Die Neue Leipziger Literaturzeitung* and echoed by Fr. Th. Vischer in: *Goethes Faust, Neue Beiträge zur Kritik des Gedichtes*, Stuttgart 1875, p. 87f.

[54] *HA* X, p. 450.

[55] *HA* X, p. 456.

schäftige und nichts Eigenes vornähme . . .'. 'Ich rief mir daher die "Natürliche Tochter" vor die Seele, deren ganz ausgeführtes Schema schon seit
einigen Jahren unter meinen Papieren lag[56].'

Every one of these recollections adds an unobtrusive splinter to fit the fine
mosaic of the play as we have come to know it. The beginnings of the re-
organisation of a mind that had all but disintegrated and was frail and shaken
in the extreme; the preoccupation with the supremely *schwankende Gestalt*
of the *Helena-Fragment;* and finally the turn to *Die Natürliche Tochter* in a
frame which caused others at any rate to doubt his creativeness, as though
to prove its undiminished potency to them and to himself. In this connection
a letter to the composer J. F. Reichardt, written on February 5 of that year,
comes to mind. Written during the time of his convalescence, Goethe relates the
course of his illness and recounts the anecdote of Haller who, having fallen
down a flight of stairs, promptly tested his mental capacities by repeating from
memory the names of Chinese emperors in chronological order. 'Mir ist nicht
zu verdenken', he continues, 'wenn ich ähnliche Proben anstellte. Auch hatte
ich Zeit und Gelegenheit in den vergangenen vierzehn Tagen mir manche
von den Fäden zu vergegenwärtigen, die mich ans Leben, an Geschäfte, an
Wissenschaft und Kunst banden.' We recall Eugenie's words, in her sonnet,
'Mein Leben hängt an einem zarten Faden'. Is the occupation with *Die
Natürliche Tochter* one of those tests undertaken to prove to himself and
others that his creative powers were functioning unimpaired? We shall never
know. Certainly the formulation 'Ich rief mir daher (sic!) die "Natürliche
Tochter" vor die Seele' rings slightly different from his usual descriptions of
the beginnings of poetic ventures. Whether we think of the opening line
of the first prologue of *Faust,* or of the accounts Goethe gives of his creative
stirrings in essays such as *Bedeutende Fördernis durch ein einziges geistreiches Wort*
or *Das Sehen in subjektiver Hinsicht:* it is always he who obeys or endures a
visitation. Here he does the inviting himself, with a purpose, and in a tone
that is a trifle more peremptory than one would expect from one so
receptive[57]. However, we can establish no more than that this poetic venture
got off the ground at a time when the poet's own creative *Gestalt* was only
just mending and he was far from fully trusting his creative powers.

As we know from the *Annalen,* Goethe, 'durch einen auf Erfahrung
gestützten Aberglauben, daß ich ein Unternehmen nicht aussprechen dürfe,
wenn es gelingen solle'[58], kept this work secret even from Schiller 'und
erschien ihm daher als unteilnehmend, glauben- und tatlos'[59]. As we also
know from the *Tag- und Jahreshefte* for 1803, Goethe attributed the fact that

[56] *HA* X, p. 451 f.
[57] Cf. Chapter XIII, section 1.
[58] *HA* X, p. 452.
[59] *Ibid.*

the trilogy was not completed to the premature publication and performance of its first part. This explanation has been pooh-poohed by most critics, who consider it to be a rationalisation and even a mystification of whatever real reasons lay behind the failure. Staiger does not consider 'daß sich der Aberglaube schon früher bestätigt habe' and quotes *Faust*, *Wilhelm Meister* and *Hermann und Dorothea* in support of his thesis[60]. However, one could equally well cite Goethe's total seclusion at the time of writing *Werther*, of *Egmont*, and, on the Sicilian voyage, *Tasso*, in support of Goethe's own contention, not to mention the self-characterisation of his mode of productivity in *Dichtung und Wahrheit*[61].

This brings us to the reason he advances for having had to abandon his trilogy, in the *Tag- und Jahreshefte* for 1803. The first part of *Eugenie*, as he often calls it, was written, performed and printed. The second was going to be set in Eugenie's refuge, the third in the capital, 'wo mitten in der größten Verwirrung das wiedergefundene Sonett freilich kein Heil, aber doch einen schönen Augenblick würde hervorgebracht haben'[62]. This is all Goethe reveals of his plans, and although we do not know what role the recovered sonnet would have played — critics customarily regard it as providing proof positive of the heroine's loyalty to the king — the stress the poet lays on it and it alone[63] would seem to vindicate the importance I have attached to it in the reading advanced here.

After commenting on the good reception the public gave to the first, completed, part, Goethe continues:

> ... 'allein ich hatte den großen unverzeihlichen Fehler begangen, mit dem ersten Teil hervorzutreten, eh' das Ganze vollendet war. Ich nenne den Fehler unverzeihlich, weil er gegen meinen alten geprüften Aberglauben begangen wurde, einen Aberglauben, der sich indes wohl ganz vernünftig erklären läßt.
> Einen sehr tiefen Sinn hat jener Wahn, daß man, um einen Schatz wirklich zu heben und zu ergreifen, stillschweigend verfahren müsse, kein Wort sprechen dürfe, wie viel Schreckliches oder Ergötzendes auch von allen Seiten erscheinen möge. Ebenso bedeutsam ist das Märchen, man müsse bei wunderhafter Wagefahrt nach einem kostbaren Talisman, in entlegensten Bergwildnissen, unaufhaltsam vorschreiten, sich ja nicht umsehen, wenn auf schroffem Pfade fürchterlich drohende oder lieblich lockende Stimmen ganz nahe hinter uns vernommen werden.
> Indessen war's geschehen, und die geliebten Szenen der Folge besuchten mich nur manchmal wie unstete Geister, die wiederkehrend flehentlich nach Erlösung seufzen.'[64]

Schatz? Talisman? Eugenie herself is that *Schatz*, that *Talisman*. She has been sent a *Schatzkasten* that must not be opened before its time. And that

---

[60] *Goethe*, II, p. 391.
[61] III, 15, *HA* X, p. 48. Cf. Chapter VI, section 1.
[62] *HA* X, p. 458.
[63] Cf. note 18 of this chapter.
[64] *HA* X, p. 459.

treasure box symbolises herself, her father's secret treasure, the knowledge of which he allows to seep out and to become 'ein offenbar Geheimnis', in the same manner in which Eugenie entrusts her treasure, her poem —

das Geheimnis,
Das größte, das ich je gehegt,

her 'Lebens Glück' — to a secret cabinet she knows not to be proof, in the same manner in which that 'Geheimnis', her sonnet itself, overflowed its bounds. And so, too, she is a talisman. Resolving to take the hand the *Gerichtsrat* has offered her in marriage, she says:

An ihn will ich mich schließen! Im Verborgnen
Verwahr' er mich, als reinen Talisman.

Eugenie's being, creativity 'stepping forth' into a world that cannot sustain or sanction it, and carried upon an element that has turned treacherous at its source, appearing and dis-appearing, harboured yet mysteriously unrealised and abandoned — what is this import of the tragedy if not the story of its premature *Hervortreten*, its genesis? The theme of the tragedy is recorded on the grooves of the poetic matrix from which it sprang. 'In dem Plane bereitete ich mir ein Gefäß, worin ich alles, was ich so manches Jahr über die französische Revolution und deren Folgen geschrieben und gedacht, mit geziemendem Ernste niederzulegen hoffte[65].' Thus Goethe. Eugenie and her father are this vessel: he the harbouring begetter and she the generative force as well as the progeny: a creative configuration which proved not sufficiently sturdy and discreet to keep its integrity inviolate in a wasteful and brittle economy of forces encroaching upon its form and undermining it.

In a crisis such as Goethe lived through at the time when he wrote *Die Natürliche Tochter*, returning 'von der nahfernen Grenze des Totenreichs', as he writes to Reichardt in the letter from which I have already quoted, every stirring, even into life, brings back memories of the silent crumbling that beset the journey into near-dissolution. At such a time of pathologically heightened susceptibility to, say, noise[66], every moment, every productive moment even, is experienced as a precarious ridge between formation and dissolution, between becoming and dying. To such a sensibility every moment appears as a moment pregnant with the almost bodily awareness that de-composition is lurking in every growing-point, at the very heart of the productive process. In this sense, *Die Natürliche Tochter* is a tragedy enacting 'the pregnant moment' — a crucial aesthetic term shared by Schiller and Goethe in these years — as none other, excepting only Schiller's *Wallenstein* trilogy[67]. Informed by profound dread stemming from the immediate proximity of a

---

[65] *Tag- und Jahreshefte*. Ende Juni 1823. Quoted *HA* V, p. 477.
[66] *HA* X, p. 455 f.
[67] Cf. my *Schiller's Drama. Talent and Integrity*, London and New York 1974, Chapter XI.

violent biological trauma, it is a tragedy about a becoming that is at every point a dying. Eugenie needs no secret warrant from the king decreeing exile and slow death. She carries it within her, at every eager step she takes into life. Her every step forward into appearing is a step backward into dis-appearing; and words of foreboding, such as her own

> Die Tage schreiten vor, und ahnungsvoller
> Bewegen sich nun Freud' und Schmerz heran ...

like a Greek chorus accompany her Janus-faced creativity at its every move.

Thus Goethe conceived her, and thus he fashioned her, uncertainly, the spectre of transience looming behind him, and her. And what of the 'Märchen, man müsse bei wunderhafter Wagefahrt nach einem kostbaren Talisman ... unaufhaltsam vorschreiten, sich ja nicht umsehen ... '? At first sight this reads incongruously in connection with this tragedy, despite the identification, in it, of the talisman with the figure of Eugenie. The association, however, becomes crystal-clear when we think of Eugenie's sister, Euphrosyne, and once again scrutinise Goethe's words about his tragedy with her in mind. In that poem the God Hermes takes Eurydice back to the shades. Orpheus is nowhere mentioned; but the reader is invited to recognise him — who could not retrieve Eurydice because he looked back to assure himself that she was there — in the disconsolate figure of the speaker. And the creator of *Die Natürliche Tochter*? How could he but 'look back' when, having just returned from his 'kurze Reise', he was so little sure yet of his creative powers, when every step forward into creation still echoed the terrors of the path 'rückwärts ... in Chaos und Nacht' he had trod but a little while before, steps he was barely beginning to retrace? Through Goethe's words, do we not glimpse the figure of that mythological seer and singer, winding his way up from the netherworld, uncertainly looking back on the 'flücht'ge Ziel' of his desiring — Eurydice or Euphrosyne or Eugenie — *schwankende Gestalten* all of them between being and non-being whom no fearful love may reprieve from transience, except through the pious act of naming them in poetic utterance?

> Denn aus dem Purpurgewölk, dem schwebenden, immer bewegten,
> Trat der herrliche Gott Hermes gelassen hervor.
> Mild erhob er den Stab und deutete; wallend verschlangen
> Wachsende Wolken, im Zug, beide Gestalten vor mir.

VI Dauer im Wechsel

'We step and do not step into the same river:
We are, and we are not.'

Heraclites

A delicate Balance:
'Hermann und Dorothea'

I.

Erstaunte euch nicht auf attischen Stelen die Vorsicht
menschlicher Geste? War nicht Liebe und Abschied
so leicht auf die Schultern gelegt, als wär' es aus anderm
Stoffe gemacht als bei uns? Gedenkt euch der Hände,
Wie sie drucklos beruhen, obwohl in den Torsen die Kraft steht.
Diese Beherrschten wußten damit: so weit sind wirs,
Dieses ist unser, uns so zu berühren. Stärker
stemmen die Götter uns an. Doch dies ist Sache der Götter.
Rilke, Duineser Elegien, 2. Elegie.

Happily there are signs that the modish deriding of Goethe's Homeric idyll
may have had its day. Emil Staiger's sensitive reading[1] and, more recently,
Oskar Seidlin's[2], have sharpened our eyes to the daringness of Goethe's venture. It is a threatened idyll the poet has created for us, these critics urge;
and both stress the delicate balance between stability and insecurity, a balance,
precisely, such as will ensure its continuing life. Staiger locates insecurity in
the spirit of the times, in the 'Geist der vorwärtsschreitenden Zeit', ... the
'Ungeist, der wiedererstandenen alten Nacht'[3]; that is to say, in the revolu-
tionary unrest which reverberates through the poem, and ultimately in the
precariousness of a poet's position who seeks to permeate such incongruous
materials with the spirit of antiquity. Seidlin goes further. He perceives
'radikale Ungesichertheit' at the heart of the poem. The 'radikale Ungesichert-

---

[1] Staiger, *Goethe*, II.

[2] 'Über Hermann und Dorothea'. In: *Klassische und moderne Klassiker. Goethe/Brentano/Eichen-
dorff/Gerhart Hauptmann/Thomas Mann*, Göttingen 1972.

[3] *Op. cit.*, p. 254. In stressing the dialectical juxtaposition of the forces of unrest as represented by the French Revolution and those of order and eternal natural law, Staiger moves
in the tradition of F. Gundolf, *Goethe*, p. 501, R. A. Schröder, *ed. cit.*, pp. 566ff., M. Gerhard, 'Chaos und Kosmos in Goethes "Hermann und Dorothea"', *Monatshefte für deutschen Unterricht* (Madison, U.S.A.) 34, 1942 and E. Trunz, *ed. HA* II, p. 699. H. Freiherr
v. Maltzahn rejects a narrowly political interpretation geared to the contemporaneous
events: 'Was er sagt, gilt aber weniger dem einmaligen historischen Ereignis als jedem
Versuch, Ordnung und natürlich gewachsene Lebensformen zu stören.' (*Ed. AGA* 3,
p. 788.) 'Das Epos ist kein historisches Gemälde, es ist das Stilleben eines "glücklichen
Winkels", dessen problemlose patriarchalische Ruhe der Künstler mit sympathisierender
Beschaulichkeit verklärt' (p. 789). Similarly, Richard Samuel characterises the work as
'breit und behäbig', expressive of 'das Ideal des mäßigen Lebens.' (In: 'Goethes *Hermann
und Dorothea*', *PEGS* (New Series) XXXI, p. 103.

heit' of those who shape fortuitous events in a spirit of unerring truthfulness
and risk what they would have and hold rather than take it away sullied. Both
Hermann and Dorothea, according to Seidlin, experience a crisis of truthfulness: he when he blurs the true motive for wanting to leave his home, and
she when she is similarly tempted in order to gain a home. Thus Seidlin
places the epos in the immediate vicinity of *Iphigenie*, an illuminating parallel
which, however, tends to stress the tragic possibilities 'des nach innen geführ-
ten Menschen', rather than more specifically epic motifs[4].

I should like to take Staiger's and Seidlin's thinking a little further and in
a somewhat different direction. This much is certain: Goethe himself stressed
the bipolar character of his epic, when he wrote to his friend Heinrich
Meyer: 'Ich habe das reine Menschliche der Existenz einer kleinen deutschen
Stadt in dem epischen Tiegel von seinen Schlacken abzuscheiden gesucht und
zugleich die großen Bewegungen und Veränderungen des Welttheaters aus
einem kleinen Spiegel zurück zu werfen getrachtet.'[5] On the one hand, the
German small-town idyll, a stable and ordered microcosm; on the other,
those mighty movements and mutations perceptible on the cosmic plane. But
across such bipolarity relating to the thematic structure there plays another
one, connected with the fashioning process: and this would seem to reverse
the direction of the overt statement. Through distilling the pure human
essence of the small-town reality, this reality — an idyll — comes to mirror
those non-idyllic events which are perceptible on the cosmic stage. That is
to say, comes to be a symbol expressive of these events. For a symbol, to
Goethe, is 'ein im geistigen Spiegel zusammengezogenes Bild'[6]. It is important to emphasise this dialectic. For no interpretation which assumes — as
does Staiger's[7] — that stasis and movement are separate poles relating to the
diverse portions of the subject, is able to do justice to the complexity indicated by Goethe's own statement. According to that, stasis *itself* reflects
movement, and thus we must seek the latter at the very heart of the small-
town idyll considered to be the epitome of a now suspect conservatism.

But Goethe's statement is of additional interest because of the imagery it
deploys. Both images — one metallurgic and the other optical — are far from
random choices. We shall encounter both in positions of patent significance
in the work itself; and, seeing that they make their appearance here, in an
aesthetic statement about his poem, the possibility suggests itself that, inside
the poetic organisation, they may function as 'operational symbols', that is

---

[4] *Loc. cit.*, pp. 30—37.

[5] December 5, 1796. In this connection, cf. Goethe's letter to Staatsrat Schultz, dated
July 8, 1823, in which Goethe comments, in the same image of the mirror, on his reaction
to a translation of the epos into Latin, this time with obvious reference to his essay *Wiederholte Spiegelungen*, composed a few months earlier, in January of that year.

[6] In: *Kunstgegenstände, AGA* 13, p. 868.

[7] And as do the critics grouped together with Staiger in note 3.

to say, as symbols marking the point where the fashioning energies enter the overt import and modify it[8]. If so, they would signify, roughly, that it takes a process of melting down to reveal the true configuration of a phenomenon, and that furthermore the symbolic truth thus gained, like the image reflected back from a small mirror, is both like and unlike the reality it reflects: like it, yet distorted, not only in that what is left will appear as right, but also because the medium of the reflecting surface, being more or less even, will show a rippling reflection. Moreover, the reflection of a large area in a *small* mirror requires a convex surface: and this will cause the central portions of the image to appear disproportionately magnified, like the embossed face of a curving shield.

2.

Much has been written about the saturated plasticity of language and imagery in *Hermann und Dorothea*. In true Homeric fashion, inner events have become scenic and address themselves to the eye — indeed, almost, to the hand of the fashioning artist. This is the monumental moulding of one who, till his fortieth year, was torn between the immaterial medium of words and the material one of pencil, wash or clay; whose eye had been trained to extraordinary precision during his Italian sojourn; a language such as only another poet-painter, Gottfried Keller, was to achieve in German letters.

Many instances of this felt-through plasticity spring to mind: the opening scene of the 'Wirt zum Goldenen Löwen' sitting in the porch of his house, together with his wife, musing with placidity on the train of misery which is moving past this little town, and on their own reactions; joined, later on, by the apothecary with whom they share a good vintage wine inside the house, away from the commotion. There are the vivid scenes of flight and confusion just witnessed and reported by the latter; the remembered scene of the parents' betrothal; the encounter between son and mother under the pear tree; the meeting of the lovers by the well and, later on, their first embrace, on the way home; the twice repeated description of Dorothea — a Hodler or a Thoma portrait in words; and, of course, the entry of the splendid young couple into the parents' home, through a door that seems almost too small to let them through.

Two features about these scenic pictures — and there are many I have not singled out for mention — are particularly striking. They are monumental, to be sure, especially those connected with the young couple; but not in the static fashion which we associate with the figures of, say, Hebbel's Judith or Mariamne. Like Cellini's statues, they stand in space, limpid, with the air flowing about them, inviting the reader, almost, to walk around them to feel them in their volume and displacement. And, as in a Cellini sculpture, there is

[8] In *Goethe and Lessing*, p. XII.

a subliminal ripple of movement vibrating through the pacified form. They are still, but not static. Always the poet introduces his most moulded and felt-through visions as moments in movement[9], and even where there is complete repose, a vestigial tremor remains. For action in verbal depiction, the mother's walk as she goes in search of her son springs to mind. It has been said that Goethe was here minding Lessing's caution to the painter in words, in *Laokoon*. Words which are successive sounds in time — so Lessing had argued — cannot imitate painting which has to do with contemporaneous signs in space, except by indication, in so far as the poet resolves the simultaneous picture and lets it emerge before our eyes sequentially, in the form of an action[10]. The load of the fruit on the apple and pear trees is made palpable as the mother, in passing, props them up on their supports. The grapes, half hidden beneath the vineleaves, are glimpsed as she ascends the steps from below. But is Goethe just being the obedient pupil of Lessing? He that had transcended the sequential character of language by fashioning in it the consummate tranquillity of *Wandrers Nachtlied II* where stillness and silence are evoked by means of movement and sound[11]? The physical properties of a medium do not define the bounds of its aesthetic possibilities, as Goethe proved time and again, and as a modern critic has convincingly urged[12]. No — Goethe's images and scenes, however tranquil, are astir with secret movement, and for a different reason from that urged by the older writer. Either the scenes themselves are animated by some vestigial tremor, or their stasis is used as a counterpoint to enhance the dynamics of their immediate vicinity. To what end the poet follows this poetic law, we shall presently see. First some illustrations.

The example that immediately springs to mind is the meeting of the young couple by the well. In one of the most exquisite passages of the poem, the two lovers together look into the mirror of its waters and there see their image reflected, slightly rippling in the rippling sky.

> Also sprach sie und war die breiten Stufen hinunter
> Mit dem Begleiter gelangt; und auf das Mäuerchen setzten
> Beide sich nieder des Quells. Sie beugte sich über, zu schöpfen;
> Und er faßte den anderen Krug und beugte sich über.
> Und sie sahen gespiegelt ihr Bild in der Bläue des Himmels
> Schwanken und nickten sich zu und grüßten sich freundlich im Spiegel. (VII)

[9] A point stressed by W. v. Humboldt in his *Ästhetische Versuche. Th. 1. Über Göthes Hermann und Dorothea*, Braunschweig 1799. Cf. *HA Briefe* 2, p. 588, note to 631.

[10] How little this corresponds to what the poet is in fact doing, may be seen from Goethe's letter to Schiller of April 8, 1797. There we read: 'Diejenigen Vorteile, deren ich mich in meinem letzten Gedicht bediente, habe ich alle von der bildenden Kunst gelernt ... Auf dem Theater würde man große Vorteile davon verspüren ... So erschienen mir diese Tage einige Szenen im Aristophanes völlig wie antike Basreliefe und sind auch gewiß in diesem Sinne vorgestellt worden.'

[11] A point made by F. Nolte in *Lessings 'Laokoon'*, Lancaster, PA 1940, p. 93 f.

[12] *Ibid.*

Staiger has commented this passage beautifully: stressing, on the one hand, the Greek chastity with which the inner event — the slightly giddied awakening of the young people to their love — is articulated in the outer, the swaying reflection in the well; on the other urging that there is a translucency about this and many other images in Goethe's epos which marks it as post-Homeric and essentially modern: 'Erst wenn ein Allgemeines, Geistig-Seelisches und die Anschauung schon als verschieden erfahren und nachträglich wieder vereinigt werden, entsteht Symbolik dieser Art.'[13]

Both these mutually complementary observations are true. But I would urge that the rippling movement which animates this all but sculpted scene is not exclusively geared to the portrayal of the specific inner event it illuminates. It is entirely typical of Goethe's idiom here as a whole. We note the word 'schwanken', placed at the head of a line, the second limb of an enjambment which enhances the hovering quality of the image, as does also the rhythmically equivalent 'nicken' which once again takes it up.

Hermann, 'der wohlgebildete Sohn', is first brought before our eyes as he enters through the door of his home, and so, too, the parents will first set eyes on the 'herrliche Paar' as they pass through the door of the homestead, almost dwarfing it.

> Aber die Tür ging auf. Es zeigte das herrliche Paar sich,
> Und es erstaunten die Freunde, die liebenden Eltern erstaunten
> Über die Bildung der Braut, des Bräutigams Bildung vergleichbar;
> Ja, es schien die Türe zu klein, die hohen Gestalten
> Einzulassen, die nun zusammen betraten die Schwelle.

The typifying sculpturesque epithets — 'wohlgebildet', 'herrlich', 'Bildung' — are counterbalanced by the movement of the figures they characterise. And the low door emphasises, by contrast, both the movement and the monumental stature of the 'hohen Gestalten', as indeed the 'Mäuerchen' of the well had done and the swaying corn through which they had passed on their way homeward. It is at such points that we observe the action of the small mirror through which the large events of the world are reflected: magnifying the human figures at the centre of the idyll and casting back their image arrested, as it were, in a ripple of movement: fitting symbols, somehow, of those cosmic movements in which they have part. And how Hermann's first entry is heralded by thunderous commotion! The very first we hear of him is how he masters his horses —

> Was der Junge doch fährt, und wie er bändigt die Hengste!

the father proudly exclaims. The first line of the second canto records his entry; but we have been prepared for this event by the tumultuous approach of his horsedrawn carriage, 'der mit gewaltiger Eile nun donnert unter den

[13] In *Goethe*, II, p. 255.

Torweg.' It has been suggested that Hermann's 'steeds', picturesquely described here and elsewhere, in all probability are no more than farm horses
and that the poet idealises them heroically in an attempt ironically to underpin
the incongruence between the Homeric mould and the German small-town
reality[14]. A kind of alienation device, then. I do not think that this comment
is entirely apt. Whatever they are 'in reality', Hermann's steeds are true
steeds, partaking of the magnification and movement in which the youth
himself is consistently portrayed and supporting this stylisation towards
monumental stature in movement[15]. We meet the same delicate balance
between stasis and dynamism when Hermann — by now, like Egmont, firmly
associated with his horses — awaits the return of the parson and the apothecary from the refugee camp, idly standing by the well which will presently see this reunion with Dorothea. We read:

> Und sie eilten und kamen und fanden den Jüngling gelehnet
> An den Wagen unter den Linden. Die Pferde zerstampften
> Wild den Rasen; er hielt sie im Zaum und stand in Gedanken,
> Blickte still vor sich hin und sah die Freunde nicht eher,
> Bis sie kommend ihm riefen und fröhliche Zeichen ihm gaben.

Hermann's immobile stance is not merely pinpointed by the rapid approach
of his friends; in a subtler manner it is gainsaid by the restiveness of his
horses who reflect the goings on in his unconscious.

Soon after, the image is taken up again, this time in a significant intensi-
fication. The parson has taken over the carriage and is escorting his nervous
companion home. Hermann has resolved to speak to Dorothea there and then.
Of the youth we read:

> Lange noch stand der Jüngling und sah den Staub sich erheben,
> Sah den Staub sich zerstreun; so stand er ohne Gedanken.

Again, that same stillness with an undercurrent of unrest — his own horses'
unrest — and more: the phantom-like flux before the dreamer's unseeing
eyes belies the stasis of the image. In his mind's vision, in the rising and
falling cloud of dust, forms come and go[16]. We shall leave the sturdy dreamer
to his airy nothings and for a moment or two observe how the poet instils
life into a truly stationary object by means of juxtaposition and parallel.

Take, for instance, that imposing table round which the 'Wirt zum Goldenen
Löwen' sits with his men friends, in the shade, drinking wine and imbibing
renewed faith in the constancy of their clouded fortunes. Here, surely, in the

---

[14] By Seidlin, *op. cit.*, p. 26. Similarly, R. Samuel stresses the incongruence of Homeric topoi
and sees their justification in the irony which obviates 'jeden Verdacht von Sentimentali-
tät . . . .' (*Loc. cit.*, p. 97.).
[15] And expressive of the life-force animating Hermann, as L. A. Willoughby has shown in
'The Image of the Horse and Charioteer', *PEGS* (New Series) XV, p. 64f.
[16] Cf. Chapter XIII, section 4.

glänzend gebohnten,
Runden, braunen Tisch, er stand auf mächtigen Füßen . . .

Goethe has carved a symbol of indestructible stability: into that table he has compacted all the solidity of ordered lives embedded in a structured social whole itself sustained by a benign nature. And yet, how problematic does this symbol become by its juxtaposition to a world that is upside down! The massive table stands, defiant of time and decay, securely planted on its sturdy legs, the right way up. But in the two adjacent pictures nothing is the right way up: all is topsy turvy. Homes have spilt their content. What was once shelter and inside, has been turned inside out and is mercilessly and chaotically displayed: the sieve and the woollen blanket incongruously crown the wardrobe, the sheet covers the mirror; homely utensils are strewn about in disorderly disarray. The naked newly-born sways high on top of the swaying cart. Homes have been piled onto the jolting vehicles and, in a huge arc, crash down from them into the wayside ditch. The picture the mother will sketch of the past conflagration is the exact mirror image of this[17]. On the one hand, the charred remains of the 'hohlen Mauern und Essen'; on the other, the sorry rows of chests and beds stacked alongside the village-green.

It is in such a setting of devastation that the poet asks us to experience the table indestructibly implanted on its 'mächtigen Füßen'; and in yet another context, of which more presently. Into such a framework the poet has placed the first description of Dorothea in the midst of chaos, a powerful figure exuding tranquillity and order as, 'mit starken Schritten', she leads the oxen-drawn cart with the new life on it, 'klüglich', in a scene of seething chaos.

Back to the Homeric dreamer. What forms had passed before his eyes while his friends had spotted the splendid figure of his beloved? The poet who had left him musing in the void at the end of the sixth canto, tells us, in the introductory lines of the canto that culminates in the meeting of the lovers by the well. Like one dazzled by the rays of the sinking sun, Hermann's inner eye had been filled with luminous after-images of Dorothea:

> Wie der wandernde Mann, der vor dem Sinken der Sonne
> Sie noch einmal ins Auge, die schnell verschwindende, faßte,
> Dann im dunkeln Gebüsch und an der Seite des Felsens
> Schweben siehet ihr Bild; wohin er die Blicke nur wendet,
> Eilet es vor und glänzt und schwankt in herrlichen Farben:
> So bewegte vor Hermann die liebliche Bildung des Mädchens
> Sanft sich vorbei und schien dem Pfad ins Getreide zu folgen.

---

[17] This aspect of the fable — chaos in the midst of the seemingly indestructible law and order of Hermann's community — is forgotten or suppressed by critics who, like v. Malt-zahn, put the exclusive emphasis on the *glücklichen Winkel*, or who polarise chaos and cosmos and treat them as belonging to different strata within the epos. Cf. note 3.

And, lo and behold, from this most fugitive of phenomena — the uncertainly hovering after-image on the retina — the real *Gestalt* of his beloved materialises:

> Aber er fuhr aus dem staunenden Traum auf, wendete langsam
> Nach dem Dorfe sich zu und staunte wieder; denn wieder
> Kam ihm die hohe Gestalt des herrlichen Mädchens entgegen.
> Fest betrachtet' er sie; es war kein Scheinbild, sie war es
> Selber.

3.

At first sight it seems as though 'das Bild der schön erwachsenen Jungfrau', once it has materialised from mental flux, is exempt from the poetic law the poet has so consistently obeyed. Here, if anywhere, is a perfectly reposeful figure exuding the stillness of a sculpted form. Twice her portrait is evoked for us; and what could be less in transit than this archetypal young woman, a refugee, it would seem, only in name?

> Und ihr werdet sie bald vor allen andern erkennen;
> Denn wohl schwerlich ist an Bildung ihr *eine* vergleichbar.
> Aber ich geb' euch noch die Zeichen der reinlichen Kleider:
> Denn der rote Latz erhebt den gewölbeten Busen,
> Schön geschnürt, und es liegt das schwarze Mieder ihr knapp an;
> Sauber hat sie den Saum des Hemdes zur Krause gefaltet,
> Die ihr das Kinn umgibt, das runde, mit reinlicher Anmut;
> Frei und heiter zeigt sich des Kopfes zierliches Eirund;
> Stark sind vielmal die Zöpfe um silberne Nadeln gewickelt;
> Vielgefaltet und blau fängt unter dem Latze der Rock an
> Und umschlägt ihr im Gehn die wohlgebildeten Knöchel.

What classical composure and timeless calm! A Phidias or a Mantegna or a Hodler would have seen the tranquil essence of young womanhood thus. Everything about this graceful and monumental figure — she does seem more than life-size, being at the centre of the reflecting epic mirror — is at rest, planted there, or so it seems, for ever. Except for one thing: Dorothea's ankles — 'die wohlgebildeten Knöchel' — which (and this comes, almost, as a shock, for up to this point the unruffled neatness of her contour has evoked the image of one in repose) are envisaged in actual movement:

> Und umschlägt ihr im *Gehn** die wohlgebildeten Knöchel.[18]

Is this a coincidence, a whim of the poet's fancy? Hardly. For it is one of these shapely ankles this deft and sturdy young woman sprains as she descends the steps of the vineyard on the way, with her timid lover, to her future home[19].

---

* my italics

[18] This sense of movement is retained in the apothecary's description of Dorothea's skirt which 'Reichlich *herunterwallt* zum wohlgebildeten Knöchel'. (My italics.)

[19] R. Samuel regards this incident as one of those ironic interpolations carefully calculated to dispel the merest suspicion of sentimentality. 'Wie eine kleine humorvolle Phrase eine

The poignancy of this nocturnal trip and this accident would be hard to miss. The homeless one, burdened by present need and past sorrow, courted under false pretences by an inexperienced youth, is here taken to fit her footloose existence into the conservatism of respectable small-town lives. The harsh tensions of this moment are eloquently rendered by her slip and by Hermann's rigid reaction[20]:

> Aber sie, unkundig des Steigs und der roheren Stufen,
> Fehlte tretend, es knackte der Fuß, sie drohte zu fallen.
> Eilig streckte gewandt der sinnige Jüngling den Arm aus,
> Hielt empor die Geliebte; sie sank ihm leis' auf die Schulter,
> Brust war gesenkt an Brust und Wang' an Wange. So stand er,
> Starr wie ein Marmorbild, vom ernsten Willen gebändigt,
> Drückte nicht fester sie an, er stemmte sich gegen die Schwere.

'Starr wie ein Marmorbild': we marvel at the counterpoint of stasis and dynamism at this climactic moment, and ask ourselves how such untried strength will be able to encompass the imperilled life entrusted to its care. And indeed, the polarisation of the fugitive and the firm, the transient and the secure, is subtly yet powerfully underscored by atmospheric means. The weather has been fine and dry, just right for harvesting, as the father has told us; as fine and constant as it had been that memorable night twenty years before[21] when a conflagration had seized the town and Hermann's parents had found one another over the smouldering ruins of their homesteads. And now again, as Hermann leads home his bride from across the Rhine, elemental forces announce their presence. As they are hurriedly descending we are told that

"romantische Szene" entsentimentalisiert, zeigen die so lyrisch gestimmte Rückkehr der beiden Liebenden und der Zwischenfall mit Dorotheas verstauchtem Fuß. Goethe verwendet eben nicht den Begriff verstaucht, sondern gebraucht die Wendung: "es knackte der Fuß" (VIII, 90), wie denn gelegentlich alltägliche Phrasen einen Gegensatz zu den gespreizten Homerischen Formen darstellen . . . .' (*Loc. cit., p.* 97.)

[20] Cf. A. W. Schlegel's lovely — and Goethean — description of Hermann: 'Wie schön gedacht ist es, beim Hermann die kraftvolle Gediegenheit seines ganzen Wesens mit einem gewissen äußeren Ungeschick zu paaren, damit ihn die Liebe desto sichtbarer umschaffen könne!' In: *Allgemeine Literatur-Zeitung,* Jena und Leipzig, 1797, 11., 12. und 13. Dezember. Schlegel seems to have in mind the words of Wilhelm Meister when he reflects on his image of Natalie as she first appeared to him and as he now knows her: 'jenes hatte er sich gleichsam erschaffen, und dieses schien fast ihn umschaffen zu wollen' (VIII, 2). His words anticipate from afar those of Doctor Marianus, at the end of *Faust II* (ll. 11096—11099). Nevertheless, he does not quite appreciate the degree of Hermann's rigidity here and the extent to which he will have to become *umgeartet* before he is able to shelter Dorothea's wounded existence.

[21] Gerhard notes the doubled reference to the fact that the weather is just right for harvesting and regards it as underpinning the pervading sense of a lawful benign nature. This is so, but the ominous overtones accompanying both references must not escape us: they are the counterpoint that is woven into the fable and its verbal texture at every point. (*Loc. cit., p.* 421.)

> mit schwankenden Lichtern durchs Laub überblickte der Mond sie,
> Eh' er, von Wetterwolken umhüllt, im Dunkeln das Paar ließ.

'Schwankend' is how Dorothea had described herself when she had accepted Hermann's proposition to hire her as a maid;

> Denn ein wanderndes Mädchen ist immer von schwankendem Rufe.

'Schwankend' had been the refugees' carts with their top-heavy, topsy-turvy loads; 'Wankend' the cornfields they had walked through on their way to the house; 'wild' and 'schwankend' Hermann knows life to be; wherefore salvation lies not with him 'der zur schwankenden Zeit auch schwankend gesinnt ist'[22]. 'Schwankend' had been the image of Dorothea that had presaged her actual *Gestalt;* 'schwankend' the lovers had seen their reflected image in the well; and in words curiously reminiscent of those Tasso addresses to Antonio after the cataclysm, Dorothea, shaken still by her fall and the pain of it, says at the last:

> O verzeih, mein trefflicher Freund, daß ich, selbst an dem Arm dich
> Haltend, bebe! So scheint dem endlich gelandeten Schiffer
> Auch der sicherste Grund des festesten Bodens zu schwanken.

4.

No, the figure of Dorothea is not exempt from the poetic law the poet observes throughout the presentation of his epos, for all its saturated plasticity and for all its seeming repose. On the contrary, the rippling movement that informs even its most statuesque scenes, in her — the most monumentally heroic and sculpted figure of all — has been precipitated into a climactic episode, to wit, her threatened fall. Nor is her figure exempt from the knowledge which prompted this poet, time and again, to invoke *schwankende Gestalten*[23]. For how could Dorothea be different from 'was in schwankender Erscheinung schwebt' — *Gestalt?* How precarious Goethe knew every *Gestalt* to be, how close to the flux of becoming and dissolving, how subject to the law of life which, like the Goddess Campura, is for ever 'gestaltend, umgestaltend'! The poet of *Hermann und Dorothea* created what the scientist knew: 'Betrachten wir aber alle Gestalten, besonders die organischen, so finden wir, daß nirgend ein Bestehendes, nirgend ein Ruhendes, ein Abgeschlossenes vorkommt, sondern daß vielmehr alles in einer steten Bewegung schwanke.' And again, definitively: 'Die Gestalt ist ein Bewegliches, ein Werdendes, ein Vergehendes.'

---

[22] These words have been cited time and again as containing the central message of the poem — idyllic and patriotic. They do — but we must not be deaf to the precarious context into which they are placed by the doubled recurrence of the word 'schwankend'.
[23] Cf. Chapters VI, VIII, X, XII and XIII.

In another, aesthetic context to which Emil Staiger first drew attention in the present connection[24], Goethe delineates the *Gestalt* even more radically. In his *Winckelmann* essay we read: '... das letzte Produkt der sich immer steigernden Natur ist der schöne Mensch.'[25] This, he argues, is a rare achievement and, worse, necessarily a transitory one: 'Denn genau genommen kann man sagen, es sei nur ein Augenblick, in welchem der schöne Mensch schön sei.'[26] In *Diderots Versuch über die Malerei* this moment is further defined as that of reaching sexual maturity: 'Die Begattung und Fortpflanzung kostet dem Schmetterlinge das Leben, dem Menschen die Schönheit.'[27] This moment of maximal beauty was the configuration Goethe had to capture in a poem concerned with the process of maturation — a passing configuration articulating, with the greatest degree of definition, what lay before it and what would issue from it. This peak-configuration he termed the pregnant moment: fraught with highest significance, and thus seeming to arrest the passing form, yet ineluctably transient[28].

We may now appreciate the poetic law which prompted the poet to present even the most plastically visualised scenes of his epos with a subliminal tremor rippling through the contours, as though in subterranean flux. Flux in permanence, movement in stasis, had to be the stylistic principle and, indeed, the thematic core of his epos, for flux in permanence and movement in stasis is nothing less than nature's own law. And although, to the post-Italian classical Goethe, there seemed to be fixed, between nature and art, an unbridgeable gulf, — 'eine ungeheure Kluft'[29] — yet he deemed it the noblest business of the artist to penetrate beneath the scarred skin of a sickly northern nature to the perennial laws operative in it and to bring forth, 'wetteifernd mit der Natur, etwas Geistig-Organisches'[30].

Thus we see that even the peak of the narrative, the glorious couple — *die herrlichen Gestalten* — entering through the porch of Hermann's home into maturity, had to be shown in transit. For 'genau genommen' it is only one moment beauty can claim for itself: the moment before Hermann will lead his bride to his little room in the attic of his parents' home — the room Dorothea spies from afar —

> Daß dir werde die Nacht zur schöneren Hälfte des Lebens
> Und die Arbeit des Tags dir freier und eigener werde ...,

as the mother so beautifully has it.

---

[24] In *Goethe*, II, p. 226 and in *Die Zeit als Einbildungskraft des Dichters*, Zürich 1963, p. 134.
[25] *Schönheit*, *HA* XII, p. 102.
[26] *Ibid.*, p. 103.
[27] *AGA* 13, p. 216.
[28] Cf. my *Schiller's Drama. Talent and Integrity*, Chapter XI, sections 1, 2 and 3, in which I have dealt at some length with Goethe's conception of the pregnant moment.
[29] *Einleitung in die Propyläen*, *HA* XII, p. 42.
[30] *Ibid.*

We see it clearly: the rippling reflection of the lovers in the depths of the well, the threatening break of the weather, the 'schwankenden Lichter' of the perfect circle of the moon, about to be drowned in engulfing clouds, the darkness, Dorothea's slip —: all these touches spring from the deepest strata of this poet-scientist's creative imagination. They articulate his knowledge of flux at the heart of seeming permanence, of movement at the pregnant moment which would seem to arrest perfection in perfect stasis.

What else is the metre Goethe chose for his Homeric idyll but modelled flow, rhythmicized repose? What else does the encounter between the *Bürger-sohn* and the transient *Erscheinung* of the fleeing girl betoken but the marriage between permanence and flux[31]? And what of the French Revolution beating on the gates of the little town? Has not the poet arrested in the vessel of this subject what he still hoped to capture in *Die Natürliche Tochter* — the clash between the perdurable and the passing? Here, in this threatened idyll, he succeeded in containing his deepest dread and in encompassing the fugitive in the firm.

This dread the poet has articulated in the parting words of Dorothea's dead fiancé[32]. And is it coincidence that his reflections on transience and those of the apothecary flank the entry of the 'herrliche Paar' into the climactic moment of their lives? Any more than that the description of Dorothea's tranquillity in flight is flanked by pictures of utter devastation?

> Nur ein Fremdling, sagt man mit Recht, ist der Mensch hier auf Erden;

these are the hollow sounds from the lips of a young man that lies dead; and:

> 'Lebe glücklich', sagt' er. 'Ich gehe; denn alles bewegt sich
> Jetzt auf Erden einmal, es scheint sich alles zu trennen.'

These words do not only presage the finality of his own parting. They presage, just as much, the fugitiveness of the *Hochgestalt* of Hermann and Dorothea as it is now, at the brief moment of their consummation. That peak-constellation is bound to pass away. In the knowledge that we are strangers in transit it is needful not to cling to what we love but to hold it lightly.

> Liebe die Liebenden rein und halte dem Guten dich dankbar!
> Aber dann auch setze nur leicht den beweglichen Fuß auf . . .,

the dead man had said to Dorothea; careful words of resignation which, from across the gulf of a century and a half, hail those of a radically threatened poet of our own century which I quoted at the head of this chapter. Perhaps it was from the Greeks, those masters of the pacified present, that Goethe had learnt the consummately light gesture of resignation which informs his Homeric idyll. It is a paradoxical possibility we may gainsay only at our peril.

---

[31] Cf. W. v. Humboldt's beautiful characterisation of the Hexameter in: *Gesammelte Schriften, Akademie-Ausgabe*, Berlin 1968, Vol. III, p. 147; also Trunz, *ed. HA* II, p. 671.
[32] Cf. Gerhard, *loc. cit.*, p. 419.

5.

It is hardly necessary to say that the dead man's words echo back to Dorothea's nocturnal slip — the *knackende Knöchel*[33]; an accident mirroring the as yet unresolved tensions of the situation and the as yet unclarified desires in Dorothea's soul. What is far less obvious is another echo, back across the gulf of some ten years which separated Goethe from a strange episode of his first Italian sojourn[34].

We have spoken of his frantic attempts, in the last three months of his Italian stay, from Christmas 1786 to Easter 1787, to model — a human foot[35]. After what he himself called a veritable passiontide, he gave up, packed his bags and resigned himself to two related things: to becoming an exile from Rome and returning 'home', to the *Kimmerischen Norden;* and to the knowledge that, however perfectly he could see, he was not a creative visual artist, but a poet. And in renouncing the supreme grace of permanence bodied forth in an imperishable form external to the *schwankende Gestalt* of his own inwardness and independent of it, he died the death which was the harbinger of his true rebirth: the birth of the poet destined to body forth airy nothings in an immaterial medium and to endure such inwardness, unaided by any external props[36]. Perhaps only an artist so exposed to the rhythm of transience was fitted to fulfil the artist's true task, 'wetteifernd mit der Natur, etwas Geistig-Organisches hervorzubringen' — to exhibit permanence in flux, *Dauer im Wechsel.*

What else is the foot he modelled — that shapely base of the most articulated of natural forms, the human *Gestalt* — if not that longed-for prop, a palpable charm against transience? And what the sacrifice of that obsessive dream, if not the acceptance of transience as the condition of true creativity?

Such acceptance of permanence in flux *and* flux in permanence is reflected in that inner movement which pulsates through the pages of Goethe's Homeric epos. It is poignantly reflected in the ugly cracking of Dorothea's ankle. To be sure, no one dies in that idyll. The new-born child looks at his mother *mit gesunden Augen*, the lovers are united and will add a ring to the chain of the generations. But Dorothea herself wears a ring betokening an earlier bond, a bond death has broken. And who but someone that has gone through inner death could meaningfully repeat those strange words her fiancé had spoken?

> Du bewahrst mir dein Herz; und finden dereinst wir uns wieder,
> Über den Trümmern der Welt, so sind wir erneute Geschöpfe,
> Umgebildet und frei und unabhängig vom Schicksal . . .

[33] Cf. note 19.
[34] Cf. Chapter V, sections 7 and 8.
[35] Chapter V, section 7, p. 224 ff.
[36] Chapter V, section 8, p. 234.

Erneut, umgebildet —: esoteric words, these, which we might expect in a poem such as *Selige Sehnsucht* or in the last choruses of *Faust II*. Here they seem extravagant. Yet this is the beating heart of this poem, its delicate intertwining of *Stirb und Werde*.

6.

Goethe almost tells us so in the symbol of the ring, the sight of which had struck Hermann's love silent. The dead man who had given it to Dorothea, had thus taken his leave:

> 'Lebe glücklich', sagt' er. 'Ich gehe; denn alles bewegt sich
> Jetzt auf Erden einmal, es scheint sich alles zu trennen.
> Grundgesetze lösen sich auf der festesten Staaten,
> Und es löst der Besitz sich los vom alten Besitzer.
> . . .
> Uns gehört der Boden nicht mehr; es wandern die Schätze;
> Gold und Silber schmilzt aus den alten, heiligen Formen;
> Alles regt sich, als wollte die Welt, die gestaltete, rückwärts
> Lösen in Chaos und Nacht sich auf und neu sich gestalten . . .'

We know this imagery. It recalls the metallurgic metaphor the poet had used in the letter to Heinrich Meyer quoted at the beginning of this chapter. He had hoped to burn the small-town reality which was to be the subject of his poem clean of all its dross 'im epischen Tiegel', until only the pure human truth of it remained: and therewith — *zugleich* — reflect the great movements and mutations of the cosmic scene, as through a small mirror. We have seen the reflection of these great movements and mutations — and not merely those caused by the French Revolution but those inexorable ones ordained by the law of Nature herself — in the language, imagery and thematic structure of the epos: everywhere there is movement in stasis, flux at the heart of seeming permanence. The most radical formulation of the precariousness of formed life the poet has saved up to the end. Possessions change owners; yes. The dead youth's ring may have been taken off his finger, and Dorothea, once his, will be another's wife. But this is the least of it. The very form of things, their time-hallowed *Gestalt*, is a prey to change. It is smelted down and, maybe, resurrected, *erneut, umgebildet*, in a new and unrecognisable shape.

Throughout the cantos of this epos the poet has prepared us for the emergence of this ultimate metaphor of transience. The little town burnt down and the parents joined hands over the ruins; and, mindful of this rebirth, the mother welcomes her son's decision 'zu frein im Krieg und über den Trümmern'. There was continuity in the parents' courtship. The same lives were burnt into a new form by that disaster. But sometimes the element wreaks irreparable damage. The old judge reminds Hermann's friends of this possibility when they ask him what good war and flight have revealed. He replies:

> Ihr erinnert mich klug, wie oft nach dem Brande des Hauses
> Man den betrübten Besitzer an Gold und Silber erinnert
> Das geschmolzen im Schutt nun überblieben zerstreut liegt.

These words are given their human displacement in the parting speech of
Dorothea's fiancé, a noble youth, we are told, striving for noble liberty 'im
ersten Feuer des hohen Gedankens'. This vessel is melted down, this form is
wasted. What continuity there is, is tenuous in the extreme. It is true, the
pastor places the parents' rings on the fingers of the new couple. And he
places the ring Dorothea receives above the one from her old fiancé. Yet
the bond that old ring signified has been terminated; the bond that is initiated
now is a new one, with new partners, and in it the old ones die and are
reborn: 'Ein Band ... das völlig *gleiche* dem alten.' In every deeper sense
the old metal has been melted down, a unique *Gestalt* — that of the fiancé,
and the emotional configuration between those lovers[37] — has been broken
up, and new, and different, life has sprung from the melting pot. The words
from *Die Natürliche Tochter* come to mind:

> Getrenntes Leben, wer vereinigt's wieder?
> Vernichtetes, wer stellt es her?

For all Hermann's resolution to stand fast 'in schwankenden Zeiten', the
lesson these few fateful hours teach him is the need for radical exposure to
transience. He had stood 'starr wie ein Marmorbild' at the climactic moment
and had all but lost the girl he loves. He had been rigid because of the ring on
her finger. He could not yet assimilate the truth that every becoming is a
surrendering, a dying, of his own old form or that of another. It is a lesson
the corn knows and the earth he tills. And he knows it, too, when finally he
says:

> Und nun ist das Meine meiner als jemals ...;

for he couples his resolution to hold and defend what is his with the readiness
to obey the call of the hour and to surrender it all again. He has learnt to
hold life lightly.

7.

'Das Allerstarrste freudig aufzuschmelzen' Goethe acclaimed as his greatest
delight some ten years after writing *Hermann und Dorothea*, in the cycle of
sonnets connected with Minna Herzlieb; a credo he was to reiterate, years
later yet, in Faust's magnificent words 'Doch im Erstarren such ich nicht
mein Heil'. The rigidity of the sonnet form was the recalcitrant medium

---

[37] Goethe himself uses the term *innere Gestalt* to denote the configuration of a relationship
involving two or more individuals. Cf. *Wilhelm Meisters Wanderjahre, Der Mann von funfzig
Jahren, HA* VIII, p. 214, l. 20.

which vouchsafed a deeper renewal, in love and poetry: 'Sonettenwut und Raserei der Liebe'. The small-town idyll burnt clean of the dross of its rigidities served as the small mirror in which the poet, with infinite loving care and not a little self-irony at his own delight in moulding what he knew to be in transit, was able to reflect the cosmic spectacle of transience in permanence, held in a delicate balance. As a *schwebendes Bild* Dorothea's first love desires to be remembered. If we see Goethe's poem thus, a *schwebendes Bild* itself, we, a generation in transit, may acclaim this our heritage as 'das Meine meiner als jemals', knowing, as few have known before us, that we may hold fast to nothing if we would stay close to the life-process; for

> Alles regt sich, als wollte die Welt, die gestaltete, rückwärts
> Lösen in Chaos und Nacht sich auf und neu sich gestalten.

The grateful Moment:
The Element of Time in 'Faust'

> We, till shadowed days are done,
> We must weep and sing
> Duty's conscious wrong,
> The Devil in the clock . . .
>
> W. H. Auden, Twelve Songs

I.

Despite a wise warning that the popular image of Faust as he depicts himself in answer to the question

> Hast du die Sorge nie gekannt?

may not be Goethe's own but a projection of the 'incessant doing and striving and achieving' of the Bismarck-era[1], that ghost seems hard to lay. The image of a Faust rushing through a world he finds eternally wanting, dissatisfied and restless, is still abroad; and Goethe's glory is still seen in having bequeathed to the Western world the legacy of man created in its likeness, that of an idealistic activist[2].

Had he done so, he would scarcely have earned the gratitude of a generation which has tasted the fruits of idealist activism in two world wars and their sequels and is turning to the East in a search for other models of being. Besides, he would have shattered his own image, the image some of us cherish of him. For how can we square our mental picture of a poet as still and exquisitely receptive as the author of, say, 'Dämmrung senkte sich von oben', as alive to the 'Übergängliche' as the creator of the final choruses of *Faust II*, with the arrogant and imperatorial strutting of one who says of himself:

> Ein jed' Gelüst ergriff ich bei den Haaren,
> Was nicht genügte, ließ ich fahren,
> Was mir entwischte, ließ ich ziehn.
> Ich habe nur begehrt und nur vollbracht
> Und abermals gewünscht und so mit Macht
> Mein Leben durchgestürmt . . .?

[1] Staiger, *Goethe*, II, p. 351.
[2] A notion to which even that most liberal critic, Ernst Cassirer, subscribes. Cf. *Freiheit und Form. Studien zur deutschen Geistesgeschichte*, Berlin 1918, p. 413.

How immature is this roaring through the empty stretches of time, this noisy attempt to deafen himself to its silent flow, to beat it in a senseless race leading to a senseless goal. If this were all there is to *Faust*, or to Goethe, we would be wasting our time troubling ourselves about either.

Yet it must be admitted that the rush through time, and the fear of its emptiness, seems to be of the very essence of the drama, and, with it, a good deal of noisy posturing. Take, for instance, Faust's summary of his expectations *after* the wager has been concluded:

> Laß in den Tiefen der Sinnlichkeit
> Uns glühende Leidenschaften stillen,
>
> . . .
>
> Stürzen wir uns in das Rauschen der Zeit,
> Ins Rollen der Begebenheit!
> Da mag denn Schmerz und Genuß,
> Gelingen und Verdruß
> Mit einander wechseln, wie es kann;
> Nur rastlos betätigt sich der Mann.

Such words bear very closely on his reply to *Sorge*, at the end of the play. As the devil well knows, they, and the attitude they reveal, seem expressly designed to outshout *Sorge* and that most haunting of human experiences, the silent passage of the moments. 'The Devil in the clock' it is — to quote Auden's words — whom Faust would seem to want to silence by making a pact with Mephistopheles; him whom he wants to drown when he utters the solemn pledge:

> Dem Taumel weih' ich mich, dem schmerzlichsten Genuß,
> Verliebtem Haß, erquickendem Verdruß.

Much has been written about these oxymora. 'So spricht kein Wollüstling', writes Thomas Mann. 'So spricht ein Aktivist, der nicht den Genuß sucht, sondern das *Leben*, und der sich nur insofern dem Teufel verschreibt, wie eben ein Mensch des Geistes das tut, der sich dem Leben verschreibt.'[3] And Petsch, in his commentary on *Faust*, flatly asserts:

'Dieser Faust ist gar nicht imstande, im "flachen Leben" zugrunde zu gehen; dazu hat seine Hinwendung zur Sinnlichkeit . . . viel zu viel "Methode", ist noch viel zu sehr von Ideen getragen. . . . er . . . [hat] trotz alles Aufwallens lang zurückgehaltener Triebe und Leidenschaften immer ein gewisses theoretisches Verhältnis zu seiner eigenen Lebenslinie behalten . . .'[4]

Both critics are correct in urging that his is a passion of a highly reflective order, a thirst *for* passion felt in the mind rather than the thirst *of* passion unselfconsciously goading a man on to his goal. Faust's passion, it must be

---

[3] In: *Adel des Geistes. Sechzehn Versuche zum Problem der Humanität*, Stockholm 1955, p. 606.

[4] In: *Goethes Werke*, Festausgabe vol. V, *Dramen I: Faust*, bearbeitet von Robert Petsch, Leipzig 1925, p. 30f.

remembered, has no object at the time at which he is speaking. Nonetheless his frantic words bespeak a shallowness of the second power, the shallowness of one who is afraid of the intimacy and stillness of pure being in the mysterious dimension of time.

Be this as it may, this much has become clear from these introductory remarks: Faust's understanding of and relation to time is at the heart of Goethe's drama; and we shall do well to pursue this theme — the central theme of the play as I see it — within the play and outside it. To help us into our subject, I can think of no more fitting 'text' than the so-called 'Cosmogenic Myth' at the end of Part II, Book 8 of *Dichtung und Wahrheit*[5]; that is to say, the poet's retrospective account of the homespun credo of his youth. It is a credo to which the aged poet clearly still subscribes; his reflections at the end of his account patently tie it in with his mature thinking[6]; and, seeing that it spans his life from its beginnings to the years of discretion, we cannot hope to find a more reliable guide to the drama which was his companion through sixty odd years of his life, or indeed to his poetic *opus* in so far as it bears upon the phenomenon of time[7].

2.

The 'Cosmogenic Myth' is a statement on man in the predicament of temporality. Let us look at it from this point of view.

In it, Goethe posits the infinite productivity of the godhead which leads it to proliferate itself in the form of a trinity. Such a proliferating of the productive force is inherent in its infinity, 'da sich ... Produktion nicht ohne Mannigfaltigkeit denken läßt'[8]. However, having become a triune god, the divinity had exhausted its capacity for adequate self-manifestation, in a circle of beings every one of which was 'ebenso bestehend lebendig und ewig als das Ganze ... '[9]. What was not exhausted and worked on unabated was the divine productive drive. Thus, between them, the trinity engendered a fourth being. This of necessity contained a contradiction 'indem es, wie sie, unbedingt und doch zugleich in ihnen enthalten und durch sie begrenzt sein

[5] *HA IX*, pp. 351 ff.
[6] *Ibid.*, p. 353, ll. 4—24.
[7] Eduard Spranger assigns the 'Cosmogenic Myth' a central position in Goethe's world view. 'Der Jugendmythos enthält wie im Keim Goethes ganze zukünftige Weltanschauung', he writes. 'Das heißt: er deutet das Gerüst an, das immer irgendwie im Hintergrunde des Bewußtseins liegt und die Ausdrucksweise, die Wahl der Bilder und Symbole bestimmt.' In: *Goethes Weltanschauung*, Leipzig (no date), p. 25. For detailed information about Goethe's sources, cf. *HA* IX, pp. 725 ff. The editor — E. Trunz — states that Goethe's early interest in Pansophism never waned and that he returned to this intellectual domain at about 1800 in connection with his studies for *Faust*.
[8] *Dichtung und Wahrheit*, II, 8, *HA* IX, p. 351.
[9] *Ibid.*

sollte'[10]. This fourth being was Lucifer, incongruous in that he shares the infinite productivity of the divine which had perpetuated itself in him, yet contingent on and delimited by the absolute being that has engendered it. This basic incongruence was to be repeated twice more, in the angels and, later on, in man. First, the angels. The divine productivity has now been delegated to Lucifer, and it is he that creates the angels in his likeness. Like himself in relation to the triune god, they are 'unbedingt, aber in ihm enthalten und durch ihn begrenzt'[11]. For the second time we stand *vis à vis* the predicament of infinity ensconced within the walls of finitude, though of the shape this finite condition takes in the case of beings of this order it is difficult to say anything with certainty.

This much, however, Goethe himself tells us: glorying in his own infinite productivity and the fruits thereof — the heavenly hosts surrounding their creator — Lucifer, and along with him part of the angels, forget about their actual contingency. This act of forgetfulness constitutes the primordial ingratitude towards the infinite from which they issue, which delimits them, and from which their estate is sharply divided by reason of their being finite: a denial and an ingratitude to which, clearly, Goethe attaches the utmost importance[12] in that it is a charge he will bring once more against man, the last in the row of cosmic paradoxes.

This ungrateful denial of his contingency ushers in Lucifer's concentration in and upon his own self, a concentration into which part of the angels followed him, engendering that heaviness, density and darkness we designate by the name of matter. The other half of the angels escaped this process of self-condensation by remaining mindful of their own contingency and turning towards their infinite origin. The more Lucifer, and with him the rebellious angels, turned in upon themselves in a pretended infinity, 'je unwohler', Goethe deliciously surmises, 'mußte es ihm werden, sowie allen den Geistern, denen er die süße Erhebung zu ihrem Ursprung verkümmerte.'[13]

For a while the Elohim look upon this undelectable spectacle of an infinite productive force fruitlessly concentrating its ill-directed powers on and against itself — *sich aufreiben* is the term Goethe uses — and ponder whether to let ungrateful creation grind itself to atoms. Eventually they step in, lending all being the capacity to expand and, therewith, to reverse its direction and to return to its origin. This was to be the epoch in which light made its appearance and to which we date back what we call creation proper.

However, some mediating link was still required to bridge the gap between the infinite and the contingent, the original triune creators and their creations: 'und so wurde der Mensch hervorgebracht, der ... sich aber

[10] *Ibid.*
[11] *Ibid.*
[12] *Ibid.*, l. 23 and p. 352, l. 39.
[13] *Ibid.*, p. 351.

freilich dadurch abermals in dem Falle Luzifers befand, zugleich unbedingt und beschränkt zu sein'[14]; and, this being his condition throughout all manifestations of his being, a condition, moreover, accompanied by perfect self-awareness and a vigorous will, man foreseeably became 'zugleich das Vollkommenste und Unvollkommenste, das glücklichste und unglücklichste Geschöpf'[15] in the whole of living creation. Before long, he played Lucifer's game and, forgetting his own finite status, forgot his dependence on and the gratitude due to his infinite creator. This emancipation in a specious autonomy on the part of a finite being, Goethe reiterates in conclusion of his account proper, is 'der eigentliche Undank'[16], a defection from the primordial rhythm of creation which is a perpetual flowing out from and returning of what is created to its infinite source and origin; wherefore it is our bounden duty, 'indem wir von einer Seite uns zu verselbsten genötiget sind, von der andern in regelmäßigen Pulsen uns zu entselbstigen nicht zu versäumen'[17].

In the foregoing report I have purposely refrained from putting any interpretation upon the 'infinite yet contingent condition' in which Lucifer and the angels are described as being. The reason for such abstinence lies in the fact that Goethe himself rests content with the bare bones of his basic declaration, and that I possess little or no direct access to those higher orders of being on which to rely for its further elucidation! Thus it remains to be seen whether the *Faust* drama itself may eventually contribute to its fuller understanding; an uncertain hypothesis, admittedly, in view of the ambiguous status Mephistopheles enjoys in it[18]. When the same definition recurs, however, for the third time, in relation to our own kind, the critic finds himself in an altogether more favoured position. Not only can he resort to Goethe's own full statement on the *condition humaine* in the paradigmatic figure at the heart of his *Faust* drama; he also has his own immediate experience of that condition to draw on, in order to elucidate Goethe's professed credo; and this is no doubt the angle from which the poet expected us to approach his three-tiered mental edifice.

The condition of created beings in general and of man in particular, then, which Goethe articulates in the 'Cosmogenic Myth', is, I would suggest, that of beings placed in time and space. As the alternation of day and night and the cycle of the seasons tell us, we are beings in the flow of time. And the events of ageing, degeneration and death unequivocally inform us of the fact that we are in a time-stream that is irreversible and unidirectional. Analogously

---

[14] *Ibid.*, p. 352.
[15] *Ibid.*
[16] *Ibid.*
[17] *Ibid.*, p. 353.
[18] The ambiguity of Mephistopheles' status is discussed by Th. Mann in *Adel des Geistes, op. cit.*, p. 599 — Mann argues that this is a deliberate strategy on the part of the poet — and by Staiger, *Goethe*, II, p. 332, in a similar vein.

we are located in space. We are bound to one more or less constant object in space — our bodies. We cannot be in two places at the same time or enter a different shape altogether.

Of the two, our being in time would seem to be the more basic condition. True, we are tied to our bodies and, through them, to space. And we inevitably experience objects in space. But our conception of space has turned out to be more elastic than we thought, as recent findings about our expanding and contracting universe have taught us. What seems a less flexible mode of our experiencing is our being in an irreversible stream of time, a condition only temporarily transcended by mystic and allied experiences, and never finally invalidated. However, we readily transpose temporal events or experiences into spatial terms, and *vice versa*, as we shall see.

This temporality is, I think, the *condition humaine* Goethe pinpoints in his 'Cosmogenic Myth'. In it, he has articulated the basic paradox of human experience. We are infinitely productive beings — Goethe himself, in reflecting on what precisely drew him to the Prometheus myth, stressed his productivity in an otherwise contingent position as the one indubitable basis of his being and the effective link with that mythological figure[19] — we have perfect consciousness and a vigorous will to translate this productivity into infinite action in the dimension of reality, and yet we are in the finite husk of our mortal bodies. We are gods in pygmies' skins.

This basic paradox of human experience has made us question the meaningfulness of our existence time and again, and in one way or another — Goethe himself stresses this at the end of the reflections with which we are here concerned — all religions are attempts of coming to terms with it. It is not a paradox confronting animals or, indeed, children. It is adult men and women that experience this incongruity as a monstrous paradox, and this paradox becomes more monstrous in the measure in which productivity is felt to be potentially infinite in the first place. Goethe himself derived a defiant conviction in his indestructibleness from the sheer mockery of this contradiction: 'Die Überzeugung unserer Fortdauer entspringt mir aus dem Begriff der Tätigkeit', he proclaimed to Eckermann; 'denn wenn ich bis an mein Ende rastlos wirke, so ist die Natur verpflichtet, mir eine andere Form des Daseins anzuweisen, wenn die jetzige meinem Geist nicht ferner auszuhalten vermag'[20]. Time is always wrong; it is an outrage that should not have happened in the first place.

3.

These reflections have levered us almost imperceptibly into the heart of the problem with which Goethe grapples in his *Faust*. Infinite man straitjacketed

[19] Cf. *Dichtung und Wahrheit*, III, 15, *HA* X, p. 48 f. and Chapter VI, section 1.
[20] On February 4, 1829. Cf. also Goethe's letter zo Zelter dated 19 March, 1827.

in a finite garb, faced with the annihilating fact of temporality; this is the beating heart of the tragedy.

A great deal of this temporal predicament the poet has transposed into spatial terms. This is especially true of the young author of the *Urfaust*, with his unerring flair for the immediate, the scenic possibility; and a quick run through its short sequences will demonstrate my point.

The titanic figure of the *Nacht* scenes has incarcerated himself in a prison cell of his own making. He carries infinity in his breast. Yet, as he looks at his surroundings, his eye glances off walls stacked to the ceiling with papers and with books, a dim and claustrophobic shell crammed to bursting with implements and junk, refusing entry even to the light of the moon.

> Weh! steck ich in dem Kerker noch?
> Verfluchtes dumpfes Mauerloch . . .

he exclaims. One roomful of shambles is what his inner infinity has yielded; and this *Kerker* ironically reflects back to him his boundless craving for the total meaning of life, for that life itself. And, desperate and incredulous alike at this monstrous incongruency, he sums up what he sees, saying:

> Das ist deine Welt! das heißt eine Welt!

About to flee from his *Kerker* 'hinaus ins weite Land', his eyes are arrested by Nostradamus' book and the sign of the macrocosm. Here is the whole universe, infinite vistas to mirror the infinite vision of his mind. But what he can thus take in at a glance is an abstract, one more diagram in one more book, infinity scaled down to the proportions of a peep-show. He turns away from this shrunken image of his infinite vision and invokes the spirit of the Earth itself, living emanation of the very fullness of the life he craves. But inevitably, this huge presence in its immediacy to him appears condensed and, in this condensation, overpowering. The 'breasts' of life elude him; they are both too potent and too small; and, *Übermensch* that he is, he is rudely rejected, 'ein furchtsam weggekrümmter Wurm'.

No sooner has the anticlimactic sense of let-down ebbed away — a *descrescendo* brilliantly envisaged in the steadily declining stature of the figures that succeed the towering Faust on the stage — than Faust's travelling companion stands by his side, ready to take him into the wide world. After a sobering first stop at Auerbach's tavern Faust at last enters real life, as he enters the sphere of Gretchen. We know hers to be a very small world. More precisely speaking, it is encompassed in 'ein kleines, reinliches Zimmer', as the stage direction has it. The towering giant, standing there on the threshold of life, does not notice the tragic irony of the words with which he hails the infinity he feels beckoning to him:

> In dieser Armut welche Fülle!
> In diesem Kerker welche Seligkeit!

he rapturously sighs as he is entering the sphere of her domesticity; and for all the charm her tiny world exercises over him, for all his fervent belief that *der große Hans* can be *der kleine Hans* and yet hold the universe in her embrace, infinity eludes him in the finite. His vast dreams contract into a nightmare as soon as the narrow gates of reality fall to behind him. Gretchen expects his child, and the idyll abruptly contracts into a *bürgerliches Trauerspiel*. All the crippling constrictions of Gretchen's existence — constrictions brilliantly anticipated and projected in spatial terms, as the courting couples alternate in the garden and Faust's boundlessness becomes ever more apparent against the backcloth of Gretchen's *milieu*[21] — converge in Gretchen's *Kerker*, the confinement into which Faust's craving for infinity has led them both. With the all-important difference that Gretchen chooses to remain in it, whilst he walks out, a broken man on a world tour just begun, sponsored by a shady travel agency.

From books to life, from *Kerker* to *Kerker*: this, in spatial terms, is the tragic movement of the *Urfaust*. A giant had sought for a universe fit for one like him to roam in and had found a burrow made for mice. This giant bears the Cain's mark of Lucifer, of the fallen angels. He is the archetypal man accursed with their predicament. Teeming with infinite productivity, he has forgotten his finitude and the finitude of the world in which created beings are placed. He has forgotten the condition of all beings bar divinity itself: 'zugleich unbedingt und beschränkt zu sein'.

It would be easy to show in considerable detail how the poet has projected his theme — the temporality of man — in its own dimension, the dimension of time. We need only point to Faust's awareness, in his opening speech, of the relentless march of the years; to the timeless simultaneity of the sign of the macrocosm which *fails* to give him satisfaction; to his wooing of the spirit of life who presides over cradle and grave, who weaves

> . . . am sausenden Webstuhl der Zeit;

for it is *in* time that this 'Ebenbild der Gottheit' would, by a frontal assault on time's elusiveness, capture infinity[22]. We would register the indecent haste

---

[21] For the more ambiguous aspects of Faust's courting under the management of Mephistopheles, cf. Barker Fairley, *Goethe's Faust. Six Essays*, Oxford 1952, p. 48 f. W. v. Humboldt criticised Goethe's conception on the grounds that Goethe spoilt the first meeting of the lovers by interpolating the 'rohe' and 'undelikate' episodes between Frau Marthe and Mephistopheles. 'Goethe hätte sie nicht sollen einander begegnend spazieren gehen lassen. Denn so oft ich nun lese, was Grete sagt, seh ich schon im Geiste immer wieder die unausstehliche Marthe auf sie zukommen.' (Letter to Caroline von Dacheröden, May 24, 1790). Humboldt misses both the economy and the ambiguity the poet achieved by this alternation which is as shrewd as it is beautiful.

[22] In this connection, cf. Wilkinson and Willoughby in: *Goethe Poet and Thinker (op. cit.)*, p. 113 f.

with which this impetuous lover demands to make love, no sooner than he has set eyes on Gretchen; his despairing plea for the infinity of the productive moment —

> Ihr Ende würde Verzweiflung sein.
> Nein, kein Ende! kein Ende! —

which, paradoxically, issues in the most time-bound process of human lives, the inexorable procession of counted hours from conception through birth to the unending confinement of parenthood; the uncanny racing of time as the courting couples alternate in the garden and the urgent movement of one relationship towards its appointed climax is ever more vividly borne in on us by the contrast it makes to the stationariness of the other; the anguish of the 'Unmensch ohne Zweck und Ruh', trying to shrink 'die Zeit der Angst' and to accelerate the cataclysm; and, finally, the frantic battle against contracting time, the race to outwit the moments that separate Gretchen from death and damnation.

But at this point we shall do well to change focus and shift our attention to the drama in its completed form. For it is in this later version that the poet has conceptually explored his theme of temporality to the full. The Prologue in Heaven enunciates this theme; indeed, it anticipates the final formulation it will find at the end of the drama: permanence in transience, *Dauer im Wechsel*, is the leitmotif that is sounded here by the angels, and reiterated, and refined, by the Lord's

> Und was in schwankender Erscheinung schwebt,
> Befestiget mit dauernden Gedanken.

But the Faust of Part I is far from envisaging any such possibility of reconciling the infinite with the finite. He is infinite productivity cruelly incarnated in time; and according to which aspect of his self he contemplates, he feels as great as a god or as wretched as a worm. This incongruence, this duplicity indeed, he expresses in the intimation:

> Zwei Seelen wohnen, ach! in meiner Brust,
> Die eine will sich von der andern trennen . . .

The one, his body's soul, cleaving worm-like to the earth, craving to lose itself in temporality, to plunge, 'mit derber Liebeslust', 'in das Rauschen der Zeit'; the other, his divine soul, straining away from life and time into the loftiness of its own timeless past.

These are the alternatives that present themselves to the god-man: infinite, yet doomed to finitude, he must either forfeit his divine potential by coming to terms with the contemptible moment and become contemptible himself; or he must shun 'the Devil in the clock' and have no truck with finitude. In the one case he will sell his identity; in the other, life in time.

So radical is the incongruence of man's condition — the divine incarnate in mortal shape, infinity in the shackles of temporality — that there seem no means to bridge the domains in which his dual being has part: he must altogether repudiate life in time, or become corrupt in it. For infinity and finitude are radically incompatible and contradictory conditions, each bound to cancel out the other; and any being uniting these two conditions in one frame is not one, but two, doomed either to self-loss or to unreality.

These two possibilities Faust envisages with every clarity. The first, that of loss of the self in time, significantly while he is still a child of seclusion, before ever he has set foot out of his monastic cell into the world of life and time. Shattered by his encounter with the *Erdgeist* and uncertain whether to obey its mighty pull towards a confrontation with life, he reflects:

> Dem Herrlichsten, was auch der Geist empfangen,
> Drängt immer fremd und fremder Stoff sich an;
> Wenn wir zum Guten dieser Welt gelangen,
> Dann heißt das Beßre Trug und Wahn.
> Die uns das Leben gaben, herrliche Gefühle,
> Erstarren in dem irdischen Gewühle.

This is what we might call the tragedy of realisation in the dimension of time. Every statement here speaks of a time sequence: 'immer fremd und fremder'; 'wenn ... dann', 'das Gute, das Beßre'; and finally the process of slow congealing expressed in the last couplet. Faust here describes the process of realisation in terms of a process of accretion and gradual suffocation. In time *das Herrliche* — the word occurs twice — that is to say, the infinite we received for our heritage, is cluttered up by a matter radically foreign and inimical to it. And as vision shrinks in the process of realisation —

> Wenn wir zum Guten dieser Welt gelangen,
> Dann heißt das Beßre Trug und Wahn —

so, eventually, *das Herrliche* itself atrophies, that infinite productivity which is our eternal part and the fount of our life.

And now comes the long and dreary procession of temporal possessions — 'Haus und Hof', or 'Weib und Kind', or 'Feuer, Wasser, Dolch und Gift': eating their way into the very fabric of the heart, cluttering up its pores, they usher in *Sorge*, the grey demon which erodes the quality of the moment, the very quality of life in time which remains unlived:

> Du bebst vor allem, was nicht trifft,
> Und was du nie verlierst, das mußt du stets beweinen.

Realisation of the infinite 'im Zeitenstrudel' means loss of the infinite, loss of life-quality. Paradoxically and ironically, it even means the erosion of time.

Sorge, here as in *Egmont*, means that the present moment is continually swallowed up by the spectre of the next one looming over it[23].

The alternative to the tragedy of realisation is the tragedy of non-realisation. Faust is equally lucid in the manner in which he envisages this choice. He confronts it as Mephistopheles, elegantly dressed in tight-fitting clothes this time, advises him to do likewise and start on his trip into the world. We know Faust's answer:

> In jedem Kleide werd' ich wohl die Pein
> Des engen Erdelebens fühlen . . .

he says. And these words usher in the lament of the incarnated spirit at the disaster of incarnation — which is the disaster of temporality — *per se*. This is not the lament of his 'body's soul', the one that would cleave to the earth 'mit klammernden Organen', in the desperate hope of losing itself in the 'Rauschen der Zeit'. It is the lament of the pure spirit, isolated and austere, ascetic and proud, alienated from all that is mortal, shuddering at the barest breath of life in time which rasps out its incessant 'No'. Lament of a spirit which cruelly aborts every intimation of earthly joy 'mit eigensinnigem Krittel', who feels his every creative vision to be mocked by 'tausend Lebensfratzen'.

> Der Gott, der mir im Busen wohnt,
> Kann tief mein Innerstes erregen;
> Der über allen meinen Kräften thront,
> Er kann nach außen nichts bewegen;
> Und so ist mir das Dasein eine Last,
> Der Tod erwünscht, das Leben mir verhaßt.

What is he lamenting if not the impotence of the god incarnated in the temporal medium 'des engen Erdelebens', a condition such as he feels to be ever and ineradicably alien?

---

[23] For differing interpretations of *Sorge*, cf. P. Stöcklein, *Wege zum späten Goethe*, Hamburg 1949, pp. 93 ff., M. Kommerell, *Geist und Buchstabe der Dichtung*, Frankfurt/Main 1962, and E. Staiger, *Goethe*, III, p. 434 f.. Stöcklein's interpretation of Faust's first encounter with *Sorge*, and the transcending of *Sorge* by the rejuvenating force of tears is sensitive and, in my view, correct (cf. esp. p. 110); but it is disjointed from his reading of *Sorge*, at her last appearance, as constituting an attack against the *vis unitiva* of Faust's soul (p. 122) which 'trifft nur die Physis von Faust, . . . während der Seelenkern, zwar erschüttert, dennoch jeder Verminderung und jeden Todes spottet.' (p. 151.) Besides, Stöcklein introduces the related experience of *Reue* as relevant for the aged Faust (pp. 117 ff.). This reading Kommerell and Staiger reject, in my view correctly. Guilt and remorse in their view are foreign to the *Sorge* Faust encounters. (Cf. Kommerell, pp. 95 ff.) Staiger roundly and rightly declares: 'Die Sorge spricht, nichts als die Sorge, der Dämon, den Goethe von lange her kennt, der Egmonts Tod zu verdüstern droht . . .' (*Goethe*, III, p. 435).

There seems to be no third possibility that might bridge these two unaccept-
able alternatives or altogether transcend them. Infinite productivity cannot
accomodate itself to finitude and befriend it. One or the other is sacrificed
in the confrontation: the infinite spirit, or life in time. And neither the tragedy
of realisation nor the tragedy of non-realisation is a viable option for one
who is neither worm, nor god, but embodied spirit, that two-legged paradox
we call man.

4.

The same two alternatives would seem to be in Faust's mind as he settles for
the devil. The agreement into which Faust enters with Mephistopheles is as
every student knows a wager, that is to say, a provisional arrangement. It
is provisional, precisely, in that it depends on the interpretation Faust will
ultimately place upon the phenomenon of time. It would not be true to say
that the outcome will depend on his evaluation of time 'when his hour has
come'. His evaluation of time, rather, will usher in 'his hour': it will end
life in time for him, one way or another. And it will end life in time for him
in one of two radically different ways, expressed in the two radically divergent
formulations he puts forward to Mephistopheles, a fact to which not sufficient
attention has been paid.

At the first, preceding his formal terms, Faust bitterly scoffs at the devil's
arts:

> Was willst du armer Teufel geben?
> Ward eines Menschen Geist, in seinem hohen Streben,
> Von deinesgleichen je gefaßt?

he asks, very much in the desperate tenor in which, in the preceding
conversation, he had shrugged off the very possibility of coming to any
sort of terms with finitude. All the devil is likely to give him, he suggests, is
what he already has in plenty — a restless spirit and a radical distrust of life
in time. Time is worthless and fickle, and so are all things that are beholden
to time.

It is in this frame — an idealistic frame *par excellence* — that Faust proffers
his first formulation to the devil:

> Werd' ich beruhigt je mich auf ein Faulbett legen,
> So sei es gleich um mich getan!
> Kannst du mich schmeichelnd je belügen,
> Daß ich mir selbst gefallen mag,
> Kannst du mich mit Genuß betrügen,
> Das sei für mich der letzte Tag!
> Die Wette biet' ich!

If the devil can lull him into forgetfulness of his degrading servitude to the
moment, any moment, for all are equally worthless; if he can trick him into

coming to terms with the element and the shady business of 'becoming real'; if he can drown his spirit in the puddle that is time, well and good. Let time come to an end for him. What matter? For in any case time is the conqueror:

> Das sei für mich der letzte Tag!

This is the final challenge Faust's infinite and imperatorial spirit flings into the face of finitude. He flings it, contemptuous of finitude and confident that it will never mute his *heilige Unzufriedenheit*. 'The Devil in the clock' will never be silenced by Mephistopheles and his time-killing amusements.

But these are not Faust's final words; and his second challenge reads very differently from his first. All of a sudden, and almost despite himself, as it were, a new possibility suggests itself to him. This is neither the tragic possibility of non-realisation — he has opted for that, in his first formulation of the wager. Nor yet is it the alternative and equally tragic possibility of realisation. At least, not quite. But what — and this is entirely new — if time were not always and under all possible conditions worthless? If finitude could throw up a moment that is in itself 'schön', worthwhile? What if the infinite spirit were to be mirrored in a surpassing moment, one moment of grace which is *in* time yet not *of* it? If this were conceivable, then the fetters with which the devil would shackle him would no longer be fetters; for the finite would be redeemed and the infinite spirit would be free and at home in what up to now had seemed its prison house. 'The Devil in the clock' would be silenced by pure being; the end of Faust would signify, not the victory of worthless time, but its redemption; it would signify the infinite marrying with the finite in that ultimate paradox which transcends the paradox even of the human condition 'zugleich unbedingt und beschränkt zu sein' —: the paradox of the timeless moment.

This, I take it, is the meaning towards which Faust gropes his way as he formulates the terms of the wager for a second time, significantly — and this point has escaped attention — at a moment which is itself out of the time-dimension shared by the two speakers: for the wager has already been agreed, and 'time is up'.

> Werd' ich zum Augenblicke sagen:
> Verweile doch! du bist so schön!
> Dann magst du mich in Fesseln schlagen,
> Dann will ich gern zugrunde gehn!
> Dann mag die Totenglocke schallen,
> Dann bist du deines Dienstes frei,
> Die Uhr mag stehn, der Zeiger fallen,
> Es sei die Zeit für mich vorbei!

At this point in the drama, Faust himself is scarcely conscious of what he is saying in a pictorial language by which he may well intend to express no more than 'then my hour will have struck'. What in fact the poet foreshadows in

these words is the total re-interpretation and re-evaluation the phenomenon of
time will have undergone by the end of the drama, at the hero's death and
after it, a re-evaluation no longer in quantitative but in qualitative terms. If
the measurable futility of mere succession can be transcended by the inherent
value of the significant moment, the ticking of the clock and the movement
of its hands across its face will cease to be of consequence. 'Der Augenblick
ist Ewigkeit': time and finitude will be redeemed and, in losing his wager
and his life, Faust will have won both[24].

By the deep ambiguity of the second, and final, formulation of the wager
Goethe has prepared us for the irony of an ending which is significantly
couched in the self-same symbolism:

Die Uhr steht still — ...

Mephistopheles announces;

Der Zeiger fällt.

the Chorus responds;

Er fällt, es ist vollbracht.

the devil comments. What do these biblical words betoken on the chorus'
lips? Assuredly not that Faust has been vanquished by the 'letzten, schlechten,
leeren Augenblick' and that a neater alternative to the futility of life in time,
as it has just been enacted, would be 'das Ewig-Leere'. What is accomplished
is that Faust has affirmed the infinite *in* the finite *and* is saved; that, in
losing the wager according to his sights, he has won it in terms of the deeper
meaning the poet has put upon his lips. Time and finitude are redeemed;
and so, at last, is man: 'geeinte Zwienatur'.

5.

But the Faust who is here negotiating with the devil, even the Faust who,
with the aid of the devil, will lead the emperor to victory and found a coastal
empire of his own, is very far from any such solution. His very alliance
with the devil means that he assaults and rapes the finite in an attempt to make
it bear infinite dividends —: infinite love, infinite money, infinite beauty and
infinite power. Wilfully oblivious of his contingent condition and spuriously
claiming the infinity that belongs to the triune god, he is, for all his striving,
indeed because of it, a brother of Lucifer and, like him, a creature of paradox,
unhappy in a skin that pinches him, divided.

Indeed, the Faust we encounter immediately after the wager is concluded,
seems to have regressed beyond the mature solution he had groped for in

---

[24] In my interpretation of the wager and the implications of this for the import of the drama
as a whole, I find myself in total agreement with Staiger. (II, p. 350 and III, p. 448).

his second formulation, beyond the more modest terms even he had envisaged at the first go. Intensely frightened by the rushing past of time, he had asked:

> Rast nicht die Welt in allen Strömen fort...

He has no desire but to drown its din in the greater noise of violent and tormenting fairground distractions. This is the force of his

> Stürzen wir uns in das Rauschen der Zeit,
> Ins Rollen der Begebenheit!

Noise and movement to drown noise and movement, to drown the unendurable anguish of having to be 'in time'.

And what of the speech with which the *Fragment* sets in, the one that starts with the lines:

> Und was der ganzen Menschheit zugeteilt ist,
> Will ich in meinem innern Selbst genießen ...?

Commentators have regarded these words as articulating the representative, *stellvertretende,* character Faust will assume in the matured conception of the play as Goethe saw it now. I regard them as the culminating expression of Faust's luciferic denial of finitude, an inflation of the scope and intensity of his experiencing beyond their natural bounds which cannot but end in the disaster Faust's words themselves anticipate; and the devil is right when he persiflages this frantic borrowing of infinite and artificial powers in a quest for infinite and artificial experience and mockingly calls his charge 'Herrn Mikrokosmus'. And, for all that the critics say, Mephistopheles is right when he predicts, at the end of the wager scene, that Faust as he is now, idealistic, activist, driven by his strained visions of infinity, will drown in 'flache Unbedeutenheit': not because he is shallow or lacking in displacement, but because his frenzied anguish of time and finitude will drive him into the arms of time and finitude, in the distracted endeavour to escape the torment of 'the Devil in the clock'. It will drive him to Gretchen, and to the undermining of her true little world by the frenetic intensity of his passion, and to that first flash of self-knowledge, after a few moments of quiet being, in the seclusion of *Wald und Höhle*.

> So tauml' ich von Begierde zu Genuß,
> Und im Genuß verschmacht' ich nach Begierde ...,

he says, blaming his devilish companion for the inferno in his breast. But it is he himself, not Mephistopheles, who fans this conflagration, fearful of the streaming of the moments and intent on foisting infinity upon their frailty. Thus it is precisely as Mephistopheles had said it would be, at the end of the wager scene:

> Ihm hat das Schicksal einen Geist gegeben,
> Der ungebändigt immer vorwärts dringt,
> Und dessen übereiltes Streben
> Der Erde Freuden überspringt.

The greed for *Begierde im Genuß*, what is this if not greed for greed, greed infinitely multiplied which detests the finite and nonetheless busies itself blowing it up to infinite dimensions? Mephistopheles is not the cause of such inflation. He is its agent, rather, the embodiment of Faust's own luciferic striving to infuse infinity into his finite condition by whipping it up into an infinite intensity. And Faust's striving is and remains luciferic, whether it is directed to infinity of feeling or to infinity of possessions.

> Es irrt der Mensch, solang' er strebt:

Man — so the 'Cosmogenic Myth' has told us and so the *Faust* drama seems to tell us once again — does not err *despite* the fact that he strives. It is *because* he strives unconditionally, infinitely, denying the finitude of the temporal life into which he is placed and his own contingent condition, that he goes astray. We badly need to reverse the customary emphases in our evaluation of Faust's *hohes Streben*[25].

The catastrophic nature of such boundlessness, forcing infinity onto finite material in the frantic effort to deny finitude and time, becomes patent to Faust himself in the closing portion of *Wald und Höhle*:

> Bin ich der Flüchtling nicht? der Unbehauste?
> Der Unmensch ohne Zweck und Ruh',
> Der wie ein Wassersturz von Fels zu Felsen brauste
> Begierig wütend nach dem Abgrund zu?

Faust is the *Flüchtling* from finitude, the *Unbehauste*, in that he refuses to make his home in it. Revulsed by the consciousness of being finite and yet doomed to extinction, terrified by the stream of time, he whips himself up to a noise and movement sufficient to drown 'das Rauschen der Zeit'; and, rushing faster than the receding flight of moments, forestalls the end in a cataclysm more fearful than any natural end might be.

It is the same Faust — still or again — whom we encounter in the fourth and fifth acts of the second part of the tragedy. He is an old man, and the sands of time are running out fast when he conceives of his heroically puerile plan to conquer the sea. The results of such an undertaking may be heroic, though the devil assures us of its futility; but the motives driving him to it are puerile[26].

---

[25] Staiger writes: 'Seine Größe ist es, daß er sich nie dem unablässigen Weiterschreiten des Geistes entzieht; sein Verhängnis, daß er als Weiterschreitender nie sich selbst genügt und die Ruhe der Stufe nicht kennt.' (*Op. cit.*, II, p. 350).

[26] Of Faust's coastal empire E. Trunz writes: 'Die Faust-Dichtung zeigt aber auch zugleich, daß der Tatendrang seine Problematik hat; denn die Tätigkeit an sich kann auch der sittlichen Weltordnung entgegengesetzt sein, sie kann dämonisch sein. Fausts Ziel, das tätig-freie Volk auf dem neuen Lande, ist gut. Aber sein Weg, dieser Weg mit Hilfe Mephistos und seiner dämonischen Helfer, ist schlecht. Auch der Gewaltherrscher Timur im „Westöstlichen Divan" ist ein Tätiger, aber im böse-dämonischen Sinne. Da sind die

What exactly is it that makes him decide to give battle to the element? His motives are complex and some of them I have sought to elucidate elsewhere[27]. But one motive, surely, a very powerful one which assumes especial importance in the present enquiry, is the revulsion he feels at the sight, and sound, of the ocean's rhythmic beat. With a noisy tirelessness that is inane, the surf assaults the beach with a gigantic show of strength, only to disperse again, withdrawing from the

>stolz erreichten Ziel;
>Die Stunde kommt, sie wiederholt das Spiel.

In the spectacle of the tides coming and going with the futility of sheer empty succession, Faust sees the very epitome of time as he experiences it. So radical is his revulsion from time, which makes a mockery of infinity, in which, by definition almost, 'es ist nichts geleistet' because it comes to an end, that he sees it exactly as he sees the sea before him: as a sheer succession of empty, worthless moments, temporal prophet of the devil's 'Ewig-Leere'. *Because* they are finite and run out, the content of the successive moments, whatever it might be, is *a priori* experienced and repudiated as worthless, exactly as worthless as the busy surging of the sea which has neither *Zweck* nor *Ziel*. There is no gainsaying the fact that this is a nihilistic conception of time, much as that of Mephistopheles who contends that for a thing to be over is tantamount to its not having been at all:

>Vorbei und reines Nicht, vollkommnes Einerlei!
>. . .
>'Da ist's vorbei!' Was ist daran zu lesen?
>Es ist so gut, als wär' es nicht gewesen . . .

This is the devil speaking. Yet it expresses Faust's experience of life as soon as he thinks of it in terms of time — and when does he cease to think of it in these terms? — and it is in a desperate if unconscious attempt to stop the senseless surging of time itself that he turns his rage against the sea.

In the fifth act the poet has once more presented Faust's craving for a spurious infinity in grandiose spatial visions: Faust's coastal empire is brought before our eyes, a colossal aggregate of atoms to delude him into thinking that he is mirroring himself in an infinity of his own making. Yet atoms, piled up for the sake of piling up atoms, like the succession of empty moments, are mere quantities of atoms. And no quantity, however closely approximating to infinity, but that could not be more infinite or is able adequately to reflect back the quality of infinite productivity. Faust's huge edifice rests on an

---

Grenzen.' In: 'Das Vergängliche als Gleichnis in Goethes Dichtung', in: *Goethe* 16, 1954, p. 49. For a similar assessment, cf. also Staiger, *Goethe*, III, pp. 430ff.. Staiger, too, draws the parallel between Faust and Timur (p. 433).

[27] In: *Goethe and Lessing*, Chapter XI, sections 5 and 6.

illusion, even as the shifting sands on which it is built will fall back to the element from which he has uncertainly snatched it[28].

We may see in this coastal empire the spatial evocation of two speeches of his we know. In and through this artificial world, he has made good the claim he has enunciated after the conclusion of the wager, the ambition that he would

> ... mein eigen Selbst zu ihrem Selbst erweitern ...;

in and through this world he has 'realised' his striving for infinity and, in doing so, has lost — as he knew one does —

> Die uns das Leben gaben, herrliche Gefühle ...

His possessions, huge accretions to his self clustering around him, have suffocated, almost, the living heart and, having attained the good things of this life, he is denying 'das Beßre'. Ensconced in finitude massed to all but infinite proportions, Faust has become all too real; and, in worshipping a graven image of his own divinity, has all but forfeited the access to his origins.

But he himself is dissatisfied with what he has, for the first time for good cause; and in the reason he gives for his dissatisfaction we once again glimpse the shadow of his temporal predicament. Mephistopheles is extolling Faust's colossal achievement. Tongue in cheek, he points out

> daß hier, hier vom Palast
> Dein Arm die ganze Welt umfaßt.

It is this reiterated 'hier' which makes Faust explode with a sudden burst of irritation:

> Das verfluchte *Hier*!
> Das eben, leidig lastet's mir ...

he exclaims. It is the eternal here and now that is for ever incomplete and nagging him: there is yet one little particle still missing in all this infinity of massed atoms that shakes the potentate. And now he comes out with the grotesque reason for his disgruntlement, a reason of which he is himself ashamed. He craves the lime trees that stand in the grounds of the ancient couple Philemon and Baucis:

> Die wenig Bäume, nicht mein eigen,
> Verderben mir den Weltbesitz.

---

[28] M. Kommerell writes: 'Alles Angeraffte ist Stoff des Todes. Der Lebendigste, der am meisten an sich rafft, ist auch der Verfallenste, weil seine Selbstgestaltung den Haushalt der Natur am meisten gekostet hat.' In: *Geist und Buchstabe der Dichtung*, p. 96. And: '... Was ist Magie? Steigerung, Beschleunigung dieses Weltverbrauchs, welcher der Ernährungsprozess der Selbstheit ist. Das Wesen dieses Selbst ist Gefräßigkeit' (p. 23).

These trees he would transform into a look-out from which to view the infinity of his achievement, so as

> Zu sehn, was alles ich getan,
> Zu überschaun mit einem Blick
> Des Menschengeistes Meisterstück ...

We see it: mathematical infinity is a concept of continuous movement. However much it is approximated, so it recedes. It is, in fact, the *ad nauseam* infinity of greed:

> So sind am härtsten wir gequält,
> Im Reichtum fühlend, was uns fehlt.

So far Faust's dissatisfaction has been expressed in spatial images. But behind his greed for space, there lurks his dread of time. He has silenced 'the Devil in the waves'. He has stopped the surging of the tide. But there is still something else that reminds him of the soft movement of time, the consciousness of which erodes life:

> Des Glöckchens Klang, der Linden Duft
> Umfängt mich wie in Kirch' und Gruft.
> Des allgewaltigen Willens Kür
> Bricht sich an diesem Sande hier.
> Wie schaff' ich es mir vom Gemüte?
> Das Glöcklein läutet, und ich wüte.

Mephistopheles knows very well that it is not the fragrance of the lime trees but 'the Devil in the clock' that drives his companion frantic. Sardonically, he replies:

> Natürlich! daß ein Hauptverdruß
> Das Leben dir vergällen muß.
> Wer leugnet's! Jedem edlen Ohr
> Kommt das Geklingel widrig vor.
> Und das verfluchte Bim-Baum-Bimmel,
> Umnebelnd heitern Abendhimmel,
> Mischt sich in jegliches Begebnis,
> Vom ersten Bad bis zum Begräbnis,
> Als wäre zwischen Bim und Baum
> Das Leben ein verschollner Traum.

What exquisitely hilarious verses, and how perfectly they hit the nail on the head! By their very triteness — Mephistopheles is a master of the banal — they evoke the futility of anything surveyed from too great a distance; and this is precisely what Faust does, permitting the awareness of time to intrude into his unconscious and letting it erode all innocent immediacy of participation. Seen like that, in the bird's-eye perspective of Faust's look-out, all shrinks into equal insignificance, and the mystery of a human life in its slow and rich progression from infancy to death — one thinks of Faust's own intimations as he stands musing by the four-poster bed in which Gretchen

was born — becomes as emptied of meaning as the mere succession of
moments measured by the clock, or the slick platitude of Mephistopheles'
'Vom ersten Bad bis zum Begräbnis'.

To the last, time remains Faust's enemy, even as, blinded, he goads on his
workmen to dig more ditches in less seconds, even as, in his parting vision,
he claims:

> Es kann die Spur von meinen Erdentagen
> Nicht in Äonen untergehn . . .,

deluding himself into thinking that he has aggrandised finite entities — finite
atoms or finite moments — into a genuine infinity. To the last, this half-
brother of Lucifer dreads and despises finitude. In thrall to the 'Devil in the
clock', afraid of pure being, 'und wär's ein Augenblick', and masterfully
decreeing that the temporal become infinite, he remains its contemptuous
slave: a god incarnated into a temporality he spurns yet serves, unable to
redeem it.

6.

And yet, there have been the gracious moments of *Anmutige Gegend*, Faust's
castle and Arcadia. These scenes are suffused with the illumination that had
briefly visited Faust as he had once more spelt out the terms of the wager
in a kind of afterthought. Then he had conceived of time, not as a quantity
of successive moments, but as a potentially qualitative event. Through the
imagery he had used, he had groped his way towards that ultimate paradox
transcending the paradox even of the human condition — the paradox of
the timeless moment. In such an experience the god incongruously incarnated
in temporality might come to rest, for in it time itself, that constant rush of
successive moments, stands still, redeemed of transience. Perhaps, or so it
had seemed, the infinite and the finite could after all be reconciled in a fashion
that did not involve magic, the magic of aggrandising the finite to be what
it could never be, by a direct onslaught of powers fanned into an unnatural
intensity[29]. Perhaps letting go was the answer, rather than whipping along
the moments and straining the atoms towards a specious infinity beyond their
enduring and bound, sooner or later, to crumble.

Letting go — this is what Faust experiences as he awakens from the crash
of Gretchen's world and his own.

It is a soft and silvery night which cradles the sleeping Faust in timeless
'Kindesruh'. Silently, the hours flow by, and

> Duty's conscious wrong,
> The Devil in the clock

---

[29] For a similar reading of Faust's magic, cf. Staiger, *Goethe*, III, p. 437 f.

are utterly appeased. The raindrops shimmer, the 'Zitterperle' on the dewy leaves glistens, 'große Lichter, kleine Funken' are mirrored in the sparkling lake. All is limpid, light bathed in light.

As Faust opens his eyes, the rising sun, climbing over the mountain tops, by and by illuminates the slopes, the valley, the chasms. As it appears over the ridge of the hills, suddenly the whole scene is enveloped in radiance:

> — und, leider schon geblendet,
> Kehr' ich mich weg, vom Augenschmerz durchdrungen.

For one moment he stands face to face with the infinite, as he had done when he had invoked the *Erdgeist*. He is overwhelmed now as he was then. But whilst, in that earlier confrontation, he had stood his ground until he was forced to turn away cringing, he now voluntarily averts his eye from the 'Flammenübermaß' and turns to the transfigured earth,

> Zu bergen uns in jugendlichstem Schleier.

Reverting to the earth is not anticlimactic. For the earth itself is bathed in infinite radiance. Every dewy shrub, even down to the bottom of the valley, reflects it back to him[30]. The *jugendlichste Schleier* between him and the infinite does not blanket that sight. Like the *Schleier* handed to the speaker in the poem *Zueignung*,

> Aus Morgenduft gewebt und Sonnenklarheit . . .,

it mediates the absolute to him, veiling *and* revealing what cannot be endured naked[31]. The Faust who is allowing his pulses to be quickened by contact with the earth which lies, 'neu erquickt', at his feet, at long last experiences the regenerative rhythm of which Goethe speaks in his 'Cosmogenic Myth', that *Entselbstigung* in which, alive to our finitude, we gratefully and humbly return to our origins.

Thus his resolution:

> So bleibe denn die Sonne mir im Rücken!

is as far as is ever possible from signifying an act of abdication of his infinite heritage. He affirms it, in truth, by letting go of his 'krampferstarrten' effort to persist, isolated, in his own infinity, allowing himself instead to flow out

---

[30] A very similar reading is given by Trunz, 'Das Vergängliche als Gleichnis in Goethes Dichtung', *loc. cit.*, p. 36 and p. 53. Cf. also *HA* III, ed. Trunz, p. 537f., and Staiger, *Goethe*, III, pp. 278ff., whose interpretation follows Emrich, *Die Symbolik von Faust II*, pp. 88ff.

[31] For the symbol of the *Schleier*, cf. Emrich's basic formulations (*op. cit.*, pp. 51ff.). Emrich writes: 'Entscheidend und überraschend an diesem Urbild des Schleiers ist, daß seine ursprüngliche Funktion, das Verschleiern und Verhüllen, nicht mehr in erster Linie gemeint ist. Der Schleier ist aus "Morgenduft gewebt und Himmelsklarheit." Er klärt auf, erhellt, macht das Verworren-Nebulose transparent' (p. 53).

and be rejuvenated at his source. It is perhaps his first grateful moment, experienced, not as a god, nor as a worm, but as a man.

And now he sees before him what he has just experienced within himself. Quietly and joyfully, he perceives the *Wassersturz* to which he had likened himself in those anguished moments in *Wald und Höhle*, vying with time itself in a frenzied rush to a catastrophic end. But now he sees differently, and what he perceives becomes transformed in the act of perceiving. He perceives his being outside himself there, in the soaring mountain stream, and he apprehends it as a symbol, not only of himself, but of humankind: 'das menschliche Bestreben'. The 'I' of the earlier Faust has given way to the 'you' or the 'we' of one who looks upon himself symbolically, in a symbol[32].

And what is the adequate symbol of 'das menschliche Bestreben'? There is finitude, too, in the *Wassersturz* he now perceives. In fact, no more transient phenomenon could readily be conceived. But there is infinity in it, too, not the loathsome infinity of eternal futile repetition, the fruitless assault of fruitless waves upon the beach, which is all the nihilist sees, but the infinity of a force perpetually issuing from and returning to its source, in perpetual renewal. Like the youthful stream in *Mahomets-Gesang* which

> Jauchzet wieder
> Nach dem Himmel

even as it courses seaward from its source, this *Wassersturz*, too, perpetually returns heavenward, to its origin,

> Hoch in die Lüfte Schaum an Schäume sausend.

Here is being in time; but a force that does not exhaust itself in its downward rush, in that it is ever renewed; and a force which, for all its dynamic movement, seems to hover in mid-air, in its own cloud of spray. The infinite in the finite, stillness in movement, being in time, yet not devoured by time: this is how Faust now perceives himself.

But high above the hovering element there flowers another phenomenon, more ethereal yet and more gracious, as befits this '*Anmutige*' *Gegend*: the miracle of the rainbow. Exempt from gravity, the arc of the rainbow forms a floating bridge, spanning the infinite and the finite. A bridge, not only in that it rests upon the earth and soars heavenward, but in that every one of the myriads of refreshing[33] droplets of which it consists, elemental and transient in the extreme, reflects the infinite light in all but the totality of its spectrum. It is but a brief moment that this miraculous marriage between the immaterial and the material, the infinite and the finite lasts — but what a

---

[32] For the *Verfremdung* of the hero as he sees himself in, and as, a symbol, cf. Emrich, *op. cit.*, p. 90.

[33] That *Kühle*, i. e. that refreshment vouchsafed by the symbolic mode, be it in art or in the symbolic perception of the world, is equally stressed in the poem *Zueignung*, ll. 99—100.

transcending 'Augen-Blick' it is! For in that rich spectacle, the spectrum of the light, eye and mind perceive the vision that answers, more than any other, to their own need and capacity for wholeness of experience; experience not of the blinkered here and now, but of phenomena in the totality of their condition. It is the full spectrum of the human condition Faust now perceives in the phenomenon of the rainbow as he 'reflects':

> Der spiegelt ab das menschliche Bestreben . . .

and:

> Am farbigen Abglanz haben wir das Leben.

'Das menschliche Bestreben' no longer signifies the repudiation of finitude as worthless, be it in ascetic denial or by whipping it along with disgust. It means 'geeinte Zwienatur', as the angels will have it later, man in the totality of his condition, which is both 'unbedingt und beschränkt'. In the rainbow, that hymn of water to the sun, Faust recognises the symbol of the union between the infinite and the finite and of man's possibility to grasp the one in the other.

But what are we to make of the concluding line of Faust's speech:

> Am farbigen Abglanz haben wir das Leben . . .?

Faust, we had said, grasps the infinite in the finite which reflects it in its splendour and totality. What does this 'grasp' signify? In what manner do we 'have' life in its colourful reflection? We cannot grasp, or have, or possess a reflection, any more than we can a sigh or a smile. And yet he 'has' the infinite in the finite, he 'has' life in its reflected image.

To help us answer this question, we may profitably ask how this reflection itself comes about and in what manner we perceive it. The rainbow is a phenomenon which arises when sun and rain first meet. It is an evanescent phenomenon, and one that will only come about while the air is saturated with moisture. Were the sun to move too close or its heat to be too consuming, this passing phenomenon would not take place in the first instance. Distance is the inexorable condition of its short flowering; and, indeed, distance is the condition of our perceiving the iridescence of the illuminated drops: as soon as we move too close, iridescence turns into a blurred glare.

The Faust that perceives the human condition in its totality, sees it, and in it himself, in a representative way. To see thus implies distance, the very distance that is involved in the act of perceiving as such, the very distance on which the phenomenon of the rainbow depends in the first instance. What he thus perceives at a distance, cannot be possessed after the fashion in which he sought to possess Gretchen and will seek to possess Helena when he first lays hands on her apparition. Like the perception of the phenomenon of the rainbow in its evanescent *Gestalt*, true 'having' presupposes distance, and the renunciation of all possessiveness from the start. When Faust says:

> Ihn schau' ich an mit wachsendem Entzücken . . .

his words are expressive of that disinterested perception of pure being, in all the frailty that attaches to this as to any other *Gestalt* in Goethe's world. He perceives creatively, symbolically, without laying hands on the form revealed to him in an 'Augen-Blick' in which he has as though he had not, which, though *in* time, is not *of* it.

Goethe has most consummately enunciated this esoteric mode of 'having', in which distance and nearness ineffably blend, at the end of the first prologue to *Faust*:

> Was ich besitze, seh' ich wie im Weiten,
> Und was verschwand, wird mir zu Wirklichkeiten.

7.

Wirklichkeiten: no single word could characterise more aptly the plurality of dimensions into which we are led in the second act of *Faust II*, and the flowering of a new dimension altogether in the timeless moment of Faust's union with Helena, in the act following.

Much has been written about the blurring of space and, particularly, of time in the *Klassische Walpurgisnacht*, by Kommerell, Emrich, Staiger and Trunz, to mention only some notable contributors to this theme[34]. It is out of such blurred temporal perspectives that, at the beginning of the third act, 'die Gestalt aller Gestalten', Helena, emerges, fresh from Troy and actually a little sea-sick —:

> Noch immer trunken von des Gewoges regsamem
> Geschaukel . . .

and yet, in her own consciousness, already a poetic myth belonging to posterity.

Much has been said about the brief and blinding apparition of the Grecian queen, and especially about the precariousness of her existential status, as it is gradually borne in on the reader and on herself[35]. From the beginning, her anchorage in human time had been in question. The crowded sequences of her love life had threatened to burst time at its seams, and placed a heavy strain on the credulity of all except the philologists, as Chiron had already pointed out[36]. The myth of her 'posthumous' affair with Achilles had been adduced, finally to erode any conception of her as a real being existing in a single and

---

[34] Staiger offers some exemplary formulations characterising the iridescence of the *Walpurgisnacht* itself and the function of such blurrings *vis à vis* the Helena-act. (*Goethe*, III, p. 327 and p. 357.) Cf. also Emrich, *op. cit.*, pp. 257 ff.

[35] Cf. Kommerell, *op. cit.*, p. 58: 'Man sollte nicht glauben, daß in der Nähe der Schönheit das Lebensgefühl so unsicher werde. Aber es ist so. Hier wird das Drama Künstlerdrama.' Also Staiger, *Goethe, op. cit.*, III, pp. 357 ff., and especially p. 366. For a very interesting discussion of the genesis of the Helena drama, cf. Emrich, *op. cit.*, pp. 308 ff.

[36] ll. 7427 ff.

irreversible stream of time: a fact welcomed by Faust who bases his hopes on precisely this reversal of the law of temporality, demonstrated in already one precedent:

> So sei auch sie durch keine Zeit gebunden!
> Hat doch Achill auf Pherä sie gefunden,
> Selbst außer aller Zeit.

To such a doubling of the time-dimension in which she has her mythological being there corresponds a doubling of her existence in space. At the time of her re-appearance, after 'her time', she is said to have lived in two places at one and the same time, with Paris in Ilion and with Achilles in Aegypt. Phorkyas levels this multiple charge against her:

> Doch sagt man, du erschienst ein doppelhaft Gebild,
> In Ilios gesehen und in Ägypten auch.

and:

> Dann sagen sie: aus hohlem Schattenreich herauf
> Gesellte sich inbrünstig noch Achill zu dir!

And this doubled attack on her being unequivocally in the time and space in which she, somewhat uncertainly, feels herself to be — alive, fresh from Troy, Menelaus' wife, now ominously ordered to prepare a sacrifice on returning to her father's house and childhood home — shatters her belief in the singleness of a reality which, from the beginning, had been shadowed by the suspicion that she might after all be a poetic myth as well as a person here and now.

> Selbst jetzo: welche denn ich sei, ich weiß es nicht ...

she confesses; and, fainting, exclaims:

> Ich schwinde hin und werde selbst mir ein Idol.

As I have indicated and as critics have observed, this ontological insecurity is carefully prepared from the start. Helena's opening words:

> Bewundert viel und viel gescholten, Helena,

place her being into a perspective which exceeds the bounds of its own reality; her vivid evocation of her childhood and the homely familiarity of the surroundings to which she has returned seem expressly designed — and this, too, has been shown[37] — to combat her incipient sense of disorientation without, however, succeeding in doing so. For in the concluding words of that same speech she once again lapses into confusion, envisaging herself as a mythological being in the after-life of posterity

> Von dem die Sage wachsend sich zum Märchen spann.

---

[37] By Oskar Seidlin, in: *Von Goethe zu Thomas Mann. Zwölf Versuche*, Göttingen 1963, p. 71 f.

The unbridled invectives between her and the Choreatides in which each had
charged the other with being embodiments of primal night and pre-human
chaos, to Helena had invoked

> Unsel'ger Bilder Schreckgestalten . . .
> Die mich umdrängen, daß ich selbst zum Orkus mich
> Gerissen fühle, vaterländ'scher Flur zum Trutz.

And her question:

> Ist's wohl Gedächtnis? war es Wahn, der mich ergreift?
> War ich das alles? Bin ich's? Werd' ich's künftig sein . . .?

finds its annihilating answer in the relentless, ever accelerated duologue
between Phorkyas and herself in which her chequered career is re-enacted and
her uncertain claim to an existence in a single time-space continuum is
decisively invalidated.

The meaning of Helena's swoon and of her famous words

> Ich schwinde hin und werde selbst mir ein Idol . . .

has been variously interpreted. At the one extreme of the critical spectrum
stands Emrich who writes: 'Die Idolszene hat keinen anderen Sinn, als den
Prozess schrittweiser Ablösung eines überirdisch zeitlosen Bildes von seinem
zeitlichen Sein zu beschreiben . . .'[38], and again, more poignantly yet: 'die
Abspaltung des "Bildes" vom "Leben" ist . . . das Thema . . .'[39]. At the
other extreme, Seidlin persuasively argues that this moment represents the
nadir in Helena's breakthrough from 'mythischer Umstrickung'[40] to a 'Selbst-
findung' in a 'neuem personalistischem Lebensgefühl'[41] anchored in time and
space.

In appraising this vital breakthrough into a new time-dimension — for as
such it has been universally recognised — I must ask my readers to bear in
mind some of our findings in previous chapters of this book. We have
gained some insight into the radical precariousness of the human form in
Goethe's world. *Gestalten* materialise and disappear again, almost as soon as
they have been glimpsed. Eugenie, Natalie, Pandora, Euphrosyne, Ottilie,
Mignon and Euphorion, even Dorothea —: all these are *Gestalten* in transit,
waxing and waning in an ineluctable process of *Gestaltung-Umgestaltung*.

It is into such a pervasive context of objective as well as subjective precariousness of all that is phenomenal that I would place the brief and blinding
apparition of the Grecian queen. 'Die Gestalt aller Gestalten', her actual
span is bound to be as brief as that of all beauty. And, being the embodiment

---

[38] *Op. cit.*, p. 316.
[39] *Op. cit.*, p. 319.
[40] *Von Goethe zu Thomas Mann*, p. 80.
[41] *Ibid.*, p. 87.

of a beauty that is singular, and surpassing, she experiences herself symbolically, as being in that condition of waxing and waning which accompanies
the awareness of mental form. In a fierce existential crisis, exactly analogous
to that in which the duke works his way to the true, mental, reality of
Eugenie, she abstracts and emancipates her quintessential *Gestalt* from her
empirical, historical form, and, blinded by a searing flash of recognition,
perceives her life 'im Bilde, in der Überschrift'[42]:

> Ich schwinde hin und werde selbst mir ein Idol.

As with Eugenie, and indeed Ottilie, Mignon and Makarie, the steady
diminution of her phenomenality which accompanies her *Hervortreten*, liberates
her imperishable — one feels inclined, almost, to say her 'spectral' — form.
Her real existence in time and space is *aufgehoben* — using the word in its
threefold Hegelian sense — in her pure semblance. The time-dimension of
her hybrid being, which the poet took the greatest care to complicate and
undermine from the start, is shed like a husk as, after a total eclipse of her
shaky empirical self, she awakens to her timeless condition of being, as it were,
the distilled essence of form *per se*, 'die Gestalt aller Gestalten'.

Faust on his part undergoes a parallel metamorphosis. In a development
that has already begun in *Anmutige Gegend* he has effectively ceased to be an
individual dramatic character confined in the bounds of his own time and
space and destiny. The sixteenth century scholar has metamorphosed into a
mediaeval knight at the time of the fourth crusade. A mature man already
in *Anmutige Gegend*, we now encounter him at the peak of his life, *herrscher-
lich* and imposing in his manliness, it is true, but in no way suggesting the
passage of twenty years, the time that is supposed to have elapsed since the
conquerors 'aus cimmerischer Nacht' started building the Gothic castle in
which he now receives the Grecian queen. On the contrary, the 'jungholdeste
Schar . . . von Jünglingsknaben' that surrounds him suggests that he has not
only been transported into an earlier period of human history, but that, in
addition, he has stepped out of the dimension of his own biological life-
stream. For a while he stands in the motionlessness of consummate manhood,
at the zenith of his being; then, at the death of his son, Euphorion-Byron,
he overtakes his own life-span by several centuries. It is as impossible to fit
this simultaneity of successive phases — extending over some seven hundred
years, from the thirteenth to the nineteenth century — into any system of
temporal coordinates as it was in the case of Helena.

As he has entered into a new season of life and history, so he is transported into a new spatial dimension, from the north to the classical south,
from the 'hochgewölbten, engen, gotischen Zimmer' of the first part to a

---

[42] *Die Wahlverwandtschaften*, II, 2.

castle near Sparta which, although Gothic, seems more classical in its symmetries than Helena's archaic home,

> plumpes Mauerwerk,
> Das eure Väter, mir nichts dir nichts, aufgewälzt,
> Zyklopisch wie Zyklopen . . .

But the distant place to which he is removed is not only the historical Sparta
to which Helena returns after the fall of Troy; it is the scene of the great
migrations, of the Nordic conquerors and the fourth crusade, the scene, finally,
which will become associated, through Euphorion's death, with the Greek war
of liberation —: the Hellas of the mind[43].

This point of intersection in time and space, the south invaded by the
north, the soil of classical antiquity fructified by the sediment of three thousand years of history, Goethe has chosen for his setting. In it, he claims to
have unrolled scenes conforming 'aufs genauste' to the three unities of the
classical drama. And rightly so. For 'in der Fülle der Zeiten', between the
fall of Troy and the battle of Missolonghi, he captured the symbolic moment,
the marriage of north and south, antiquity and modernity, Faust and Helena,
even as the place in which that marriage is set, transcends any specific
historical locality already before the landscape expands into the eternal pleni-
tude of Arcadia.

The incredible 'Wechselrede'[44], the dialogue in which that marriage is symbolically enacted, falls into two more or less even parts, divided by the inter-
locution of the chorus. In the first portion Faust remains Faust as Helena
remains Helena: he leading, questioning, seeking, she flexibly responding,
tuned in with the moment. His operative words are entirely characteristic
of his Faustean, striving self: *Herz, Brust, Sehnsucht, überfließen, fragen, Geist*.
Her responses are equally characteristic in the purity of their containment;
the rhyme words she supplies being *mitgenießt, Glück* and *Hand*. And this

---

[43] Kommerell writes: 'Er [Faust] bedeutet den geschichtlichen Moment mit allen Gnaden
und Lasten, zugleich . . . den goethischen Moment der Italienreise.' (*Op. cit.*, p. 59.) Cf.
also Schröder: 'Goethes "Flucht nach Italien" ist in aller Munde . . . seiner und Schillers
"Flucht nach Griechenland" . . . ist man nicht immer mit gleicher Liebe und gleichem
Verständnis nachgegangen.' In: 'Zu Hermann und Dorothea', *Werke, ed. cit.*, II, p. 571.

[44] For interpretations of this dialogue, cf. Kommerell, *op. cit.*, p. 62; Staiger, *Goethe*, III,
p. 377 f.; Seidlin, *op. cit.*, p. 82 and p. 88 (cf. also note 24), Trunz, *ed. HA* III, p. 594 f.,
E. M. Wilkinson, in: 'Goethe's *Faust*: Tragedy in the diachronic Mode' (in: *PEGS*
(New Series) XLII, 1971—72, pp. 127 ff) and my *Goethe and Lessing*, p. 286. All critics
named are aware of the fact that Goethe is here articulating an erotic event, and the two
last named expatiate on the fact that this scene is an example of the overlay of different
imports which may be operating simultaneously in a given piece of writing, semantic,
erotic and aesthetic, or semantic, erotic and cultural, as the case may be. But — as Helena
and Professor Wilkinson would be the first to agree — 'c'est le ton qui fait la musique.'

slight distance which as yet remains to be bridged is mirrored in the marginal suspense between his uncompleted utterance and her chiming response.

In the second portion of the duet this last fraction of time and suspense has vanished. In perfect mutual concord, each voice sings its part, utterly responsive to the other, yet resting within itself, bounded within its own rhyming couplets. And here, in that second portion, an exchange of roles is completed which, side by side with the individually coloured utterance, has already begun in the first part. Already there Faust had hailed the present which looks neither to the future nor yet to the past. He that had so shunned the unfathomed depth and silence of pure being, had entrusted himself to the unsupported moment, without looking for any grounds or sureties, saying:

> Schatz ist sie, Hochgewinn, Besitz und Pfand;

words which remind us from afar of those spoken by the duke after the first storm of anguish at Eugenie's near-disaster has passed:

> Das Leben ist des Lebens Pfand; es ruht
> Nur auf sich selbst und muß sich selbst verbürgen.

Now, as the lovers' voices are heard again, both speak from the depths of pure duration, he more surely than she. They speak in muted tones, with bated breath, as though out of a trance they know to be a trance, lest they break in upon their own and the other's somnambulist knowledge of their strange condition, destroying the ineffably fragile present they hold in trembling hands. Helena feels herself as being both near and far, as Faust knew already in *Anmutige Gegend* one must be, truly to possess. Only if they remain at a distance, can the love of rain and sun be consummated in 'des bunten Bogens Wechseldauer'. The words Helena speaks only 'zu gern', are not 'Hier bin ich! hier' but 'Da bin ich! da', suggesting a presence that stands free from itself, as it were, in an awareness encompassing both immediacy and distance, present and past[45].

In this somnambulist state, Helena, 'die Gestalt aller Gestalten', knows about the 'otherness' of beauty, that precarious configuration of

> . . . was in schwankender Erscheinung schwebt,

in a realm between life and death, and knows

> . . . daß auch sie
> Im Reihen der Lebendigen geschwebt.

Like Euphrosyne, she knows the miracle of being revived and held, in a timeless moment, in the creative vision of one loving; and to the life-giving

---

[45] For a similar use of the demonstrative pronoun 'da', cf. the poem *Im Gegenwärtigen Vergangnes*.

presence of that unknown saviour who sustains her 'Geist im Bilde' all her being is gratefully pledged:

> In dich verwebt, dem Unbekannten treu.

Like Faust *vis à vis* the rainbow in *Anmutige Gegend*, she feels what permanence she has mysteriously flowering from the abyss of transience —

> Ich scheine mir verlebt und doch so neu —

and bows to the law of such frail and mysterious flowering.

It is Faust who, from the depths of pure duration, speaks the words which will round her tremulous utterance with a final firmness:

> Durchgrüble nicht das einzigste Geschick!
> Dasein ist Pflicht, und wär's ein Augenblick[46].

The revival of beauty, that most precarious of phenomena, from ephemeral flux through the force of the creative vision is a singular event:

> Errungen Liebe gegen das Geschick!

It must be cherished with a surpassing care which puts all care behind it[47]. It must be experienced in the depth of pure being from which Faust now speaks. To endure such pure being — *Da-Sein* — unflinchingly and quietly, as Faust now does, is the transcendent achievement of a man who had shunned and devalued its stillness throughout his life by summoning 'the Devil in the clock'. Throughout his long and stormy career, from the *durch-grübelnde* hours in his study to the obsessed last minutes on the shores of his illusory empire, these are the only moments in which this figure dares expose himself fully to the silent force of the *Augenblick* and 'be there', even as Helena says 'Da bin ich! da'; dares to 'be there' without eroding the present by reflection or by whipping it along. And indeed, *Da-Sein* in this sense is a feat achieved only in the rarest configuration of external and internal circumstances. Who can achieve this feat? Who can — as Goethe once put it — 'im Augenblick zum Lächeln kommen'[48]? The incomparable Egmont above all; the poet of the *Roman Elegies* — gloriously in league with the goddess *Gelegenheit* — of the *Italian Journey* and of *Hermann und Dorothea*, of some pacified lyrics such as *Wandrers Nachtlied* II or *Dämmrung senkte sich von oben*. But for the rest? Werther and Tasso never, Iphigenie only during a

---

[46] Cf. Staiger, *Goethe*, III, p. 378 and Kommerell who writes: 'Augenblick ist für Goethe kein Zeitpunkt, sondern ein Akt und das Gelingen dieses Aktes.' (*Op. cit.*, p. 105.)

[47] Kommerell writes: 'Das Leben im Augenblick ist eine bedeutende sittliche Anweisung Goethes. Mit ihr erscheint er . . . in vertraulicher Nachbarschaft zu Stifter, der gesagt hat: "Sehet die Lilien auf dem Felde an."' (*Op. cit.*, p. 105.) Cf. also Stöcklein, *Wege zum späten Goethe*, p. 117.

[48] In a letter to Zelter, June 26, 1811.

few unclouded moments, Wilhelm Meister during the brief moment at the end of the *Lehrjahre* when the ring of his life closes as Natalie joins her being to his, Epimetheus only in a past with Pandora which is irretrievably gone, Eugenie never and the lovers in *Die Wahlverwandtschaften* perhaps in those strange and still days preceding Ottilie's death.

No, *Da-Sein* is the most difficult of human achievements[49], not *gegeben* — to use Kantian language — but *aufgegeben*. It is, indeed, *Pflicht*, and none more sacred in an existence worthy of being called human. But not a *Pflicht* such as implies striving towards an ideal as yet unattained and receding into an ever more unbridgeable distance. The *Pflicht* which Faust means here, in this dreamlike knowing, signifies, not the awareness of 'duty's conscious wrong', not the challenge to strive. All striving terminates in the state of aesthetic totality — and this is what Faust now experiences in his creative union with Helena. One can only be open to it and live it: for it is a transcendent state of grace. *Pflicht*, as Faust uses the word here, in his somnambulist awareness, paradoxically means the abnegation of all activist striving, its *Aufgehobensein* — again in Hegel's sense — in the utterly pacified moment[50].

And what an *Augenblick* it is, to live which Faust sees as his highest duty! It is the *Augen-Blick* of Helena, 'Gestalt aller Gestalten', whom even Phorkyas had acknowledged as the

> . . . hohe Sonne dieses Tags,
> Die verschleiert schon entzückte, blendend nun im Glanze herrscht . . .;

the sun Lynkeus saw 'marvellously rising in the south' —

> Diese Schönheit, wie sie blendet,
> Blendete mich Armen ganz . . . —

the sun which, on rising even,

> Der hohen Mutter, dem Geschwister
> Das Licht der Augen überstach.

Lynkeus had not been able manfully to sustain the *Augen-Blick* of such a blinding light. He had been overpowered as Faust had once been, by the spectacle of the *Erdgeist*. And it is as a lyrically youthful foil to the maturity of the latter that he plays his part in this scene[51]. For in the radiant figure before him, Faust now 'has' the infinite light, in all the glory of its spectrum reflecting his own totality, and barely veiled. He possesses this figure the way

---

[49] In this connection, cf. the conversation with Eckermann, January 27, 1824, and the poem *An Werther*.

[50] Cf. Bahr, *op. cit.*, p. 160. For a differing interpretation, cf. Seidlin who writes: 'Man lese: Dasein ist Verpflichtung — und Fausts Wesenswandlung ist bezeichnet von der ästhetischen Lebenshaltung des *Am farbigen Abglanz haben wir das Leben* hin zu dem leidenschaftlichen Aktionsprogramm des *Nur der verdient sich Freiheit wie das Leben, der täglich sie erobern muß.*' (*Op. cit.*, p. 88.)

[51] Cf. Staiger, *Goethe*, III, p. 376.

we may possess the infinite: 'am farbigen Abglanz', in a mode of possessing shot through with renunciation, which matches the translucency of the phenomenon in which the infinite is veiled and revealed: 'fern und nah', 'immer neu und immer gleich', quietly revering its 'Wechseldauer' in a moment which, though embedded in the flow of time, is itself lifted out of time and not of it.

That flow of time had been pressing before Helena had found refuge with Faust, in the excited scenes in which death at the hand of Menelaus had seemed imminent. It will become audible again with Phorkyas' vehement entry and the signals, explosions, trumpet blasts and martial music accompanying her appearance, reminding the lovers of the all-engulfing reality of transience. Once again its flow will be arrested, in the internal landscape of Arcadia in which, during untold timeless moments, the mysterious union between Helena and Faust is consummated whilst the Chorus is lost in the timelessness of sleep; and once again, this fermata of life, in which the genius of poetry is engendered, will end, this time for ever, as Euphorion, impatient of his embodiment and striving, like his father, for infinity, leaps to his death.

But for all that these few timeless seconds are embedded in transience, Faust has, in a grateful moment, embraced the infinite in the finite and not found it wanting. He has flown out to his origins and returned to himself, refreshed. For:

> In der Erde liegt die Schnellkraft,
> Die dich aufwärts treibt; berühre mit der Zehe nur den Boden,
> Wie der Erdensohn Antäus bist du alsobald gestärkt.

As a grateful son of the earth, 'unendlich' yet 'beschränkt', willingly given over to the *leise Umstrickung* of 'dieser Lüfte liebliches Geweb', he has entered into his divine heritage[52].

8.

As we know, Faust will not experience the stillness and the gratitude of pure being again, at least not during his earthly span. His vision of a fulfilled future and the words that break from his lips:

> Zum Augenblicke dürft' ich sagen:
> Verweile doch, du bist so schön!

are a pale copy of the translucent saturation of the lived presence with Helena. He has lost, and won, the wager with the devil, yes. But he has done so, not *because* of the conditional mood of the 'dürfte' — a philological nicety reminis-

---

[52] Trunz writes: 'Im höchsten Glück vereinigen sich die unmittelbare Nähe des Du und der religiöse Schauer ... Ein Hinausgelangen über die Grenzen der Ichheit ist nur möglich in der Liebe und in dem großen kosmischen Eingehen in eine höhere Welt.' (In: 'Das Vergängliche als Gleichnis in Goethes Dichtung', *loc. cit.*, p. 52.)

cent of the tidying up of Helena's love-life at which Chiron mocks — but because the future *Augenblick*, even though it hangs hypothetically in mid-air, is a moment of inherent quality heralded, even now, by one greatly worth having. But never again does he achieve the quality of pure and appeased *Da-Sein* he has shared with Helena.

Faust's striving after that encounter will be as insatiable as it had been before; and never will his symbolic vision fail him as radically as when he seeks to achieve the mathematical infinity of his coastal empire. The infinity of such symbolic seeing, it has been well argued, is preserved in an artistic organisation in which everything mirrors everything else[53], and in the openness of a dramatic form which, transcending even the hero's mortal span, has every appearance of stretching on *ad infinitum*, an eventuality only ruled out by the poet's death[54]. To Faust himself the totality of symbolic vision is lost. Instead of gratefully receiving the infinite in the finite, he aggrandises the finite to the proportions of a spurious infinity, and the executors of his will groan beneath his imperious yoke.

> Wer immer strebend sich bemüht,
> Den können wir erlösen ...

the angels proclaim in double-spaced print; and this is true in as much as such *Streben* is the primordial manifestation of man's infinitely productive nature[55]. And yet such *Streben*, unconditionally pursued, is man's — and Faust's — luciferic heritage and stands in need of redemption. Without the upward glance of the grateful moment in which man, alive to his finitude, hails and reveres the eternal in the 'Abglanz' of the temporal, the double rhythm of which the 'Cosmogenic Myth' tells us remains incomplete.

Faust's life has been singularly poor in such grateful, and appeased, upward glances through the mediating veil of the finite. It takes the communion of saints and the mobilisation of all the heavenly hosts, complete with Mater Gloriosa and Gretchen, to redeem the luciferic *Streber* by coaxing such a loving upward glance out of him, sufficient

> [Ihn] zu seligem Geschick
> Dankend umzuarten.
>
> Komm! hebe dich zu höhern Sphären!
> Wenn er dich ahnet, folgt er nach ...

Mater Gloriosa advises Gretchen; and in the final words of the drama the Chorus Mysticus pronounces that this delicate marriage between the infinite and the finite has been achieved, and, with it, the goal of redemptive love:

> Das Ewig-Weibliche
> Zieht uns hinan.

---

[53] By Emrich, *op. cit.*, p. 79.
[54] By Fairley, *op. cit.*, p. 43.
[55] E. Spranger writes: 'Daß der Mensch sich an seiner Welt nicht genügen läßt, unterscheidet ihn von allen Wesen, die wir kennen.' (*Op. cit.*, p. 19.)

Ewig, but, for all that, still *weiblich*.

But what, in the context of our enquiry, is the force of those much debated words:

> Alles Vergängliche
> Ist nur ein Gleichnis . . .?

What in particular is the force we should accord to the 'nur'? Critics over-whelmingly concur in the judgment that it signifies a pejorative meaning. 'Do not worry', they might paraphrase this meaning: 'What is ephemeral is nothing but an image of the infinite, the absolute. It is of no consequence in itself.' Such a reading strains against the structure of that final stanza, con-sisting as it does of four exactly parallel statements in each of which what is predicated is an affirmation. 'Ist nur ein Gleichnis'; 'Hier wird's Ereignis'; 'Hier ist's getan'; 'Zieht uns hinan': every one of these predicates forms part of one progressive, and encompassing, affirmative statement. Should only the first one reverse the movement and signify a negation?

Worse still, such a reading would make complete nonsense of the argument I have put before my readers in this chapter. In my view, it would make complete nonsense of Goethe's *Faust* and, in the end, of Goethe. What these precious lines in truth say is something like this: 'Take comfort. What seems but transient has the ultimate dignity of being translucent to the eternal, translucent with eternity. The infinite is worthily represented, and preserved, in the finite, even as the light in the full glory of its spectrum is preserved, and mirrored, in every single one of the myriad of pellucid droplets which together make up the earthly miracle of the rainbow.' 'Time is the mercy of eternity', as Blake so beautifully has it.

The 'nur' as Goethe uses it here, at the end of his *Faust*, is as daring an affirmation of a deeply humanistic credo as is Schiller's use of it in the heart-sentence of the *Ästhetische Briefe*: 'Denn, um es endlich auf einmal heraus-zusagen, der Mensch spielt nur, wo er in voller Bedeutung des Worts Mensch ist, und *er ist nur da ganz Mensch, wo er spielt*.'[56]

But Goethe's 'nur' signifies even more. Let us once more turn to Goethe's 'Cosmogenic Myth'. Towards the end of it, the aged poet reflects on the implications of his youthful credo as he has developed it. Man, acutely con-scious of his infinite heritage, yet destined, like Lucifer and the fallen angels, to be 'zugleich unbedingt und beschränkt', and impotent to realise in time the infinity he feels to be his legacy, is bound to be the most wretched of creatures, for ever imprisoned in his mortal husk. Finitude and temporality are bound to be experienced as a preposterous and degrading condition. Reflecting on this state of things, Goethe concludes that we are compelled to acknowledge the existence of some redemptive agency, not merely as a logi-cally necessary concept, but as a *fait accompli*: 'Nichts ist in diesem Sinne

---

[56] Fifteenth Letter.

natürlicher', we read, 'als daß die Gottheit selbst die Gestalt des Menschen annimmt, die sie sich zu einer Hülle schon vorbereitet hatte, und daß sie die Schicksale derselben auf kurze Zeit teilt, um durch diese Verähnlichung das Erfreuliche zu erhöhen und das Schmerzliche zu mildern.'[57] '. . . diese große, den Menschen unentbehrliche Wahrheit', Goethe adds, has been cast into various moulds by the different imaginations at work in the manifold religions and philosophical systems which of necessity adopted it. No one name is mentioned; but the existence of a mediator who redeems the finitude he descends to share with us is affirmed as springing from the very direness of the human predicament.

The mediator who speaks in the parables Goethe knew and loved, who is himself the incarnate symbol of our redemption in finitude; the phenomenal which speaks in parables Goethe never tired of listening to, which is the incarnate symbol of the eternal in temporality; poetic language, which speaks in parables, which is the incarnate symbol of the un-speakable —: are not these sets of symbolisms connected by some hidden link? Is not the poet telling us here as everywhere else that the *Vergängliche*, 'wohl beschaut', discloses a redemptive organ in us for the apprehension of the noumenal, the supremely redemptive organ[58]? Of course the transient, which mediates the eternal, veils the eternal even as it reveals it. Of course it remains 'farbiger Abglanz', 'heilig öffentlich Geheimnis', and we 'have' it only at a distance, in the mode of serene and reverent renunciation. All this is implied in the 'nur' of

> Alles Vergängliche
> Ist nur ein Gleichnis,

as part and parcel of the humanistic affirmation of the here and now.

Could it be that the double force of this 'nur', mediating as well as redemptive, humbling as well as uplifting, ironically pointing beyond the sphere it gratefully acclaims, hints, in a one-word parable, as it were, both, the incarnate paradox at the heart of poetic language as well as the incarnate paradox at the heart of the religion which served Goethe for a framework in these closing scenes? We cannot tell[59]. What is certain is that both symbolisms have

---

[57] *Dichtung und Wahrheit*, II, 8, *HA* IX, p. 535. For an analogous use of *erhöhen* and *mildern*, used in connection with the function of poetry, cf. *AGA* 11, p. 986f.

[58] 'Wer die Natur als göttliches Organ leugnen will, der leugne nur gleich alle Offenbarung.' (*Maximen und Reflexionen*, *HA* XII, p. 365, No. 2.)

[59] Staiger notes the fact that neither God nor Christ is explicitly mentioned in the last scene, but rejects any inference from that as foolish. (*Goethe*, III, p. 466.) Emrich treats of the role of the mediator in Goethe's works and thought and establishes a close link between that conception and the dialectic of infinity and finitude which is the central concern of this chapter; a dialectic he sees enacted in the redemptive formulation 'Es ist vollbracht' on the one hand and the nihilistic one 'Es ist vorbei' on the other. (*Op. cit.*, pp. 403 ff.) 'Fausts Tod begreift beides in sich,' Emrich writes, 'das Erfüllen und Vollenden der Zeit

created obstinate stumbling-blocks to our comprehension. But then, symbols always will, and none more so than the symbol of the symbol.

und das sinnlose Abbrechen und Verenden im Zeitlauf . . . ' ' . . . die Zeit wird Herr, der Greis liegt hier im Sand' (V. 11589ff.). 'In diesen mephistophelischen Hohn "die Zeit wird Herr" mischt sich der Goethesche realistische Zweifel an der empirischen Wirklichkeit der Vision von der Unverlöschlichkeit der "Spur von meinen Erdentagen".' I could not agree more.

VII   Schwankende Gestalten

'Do you see yonder cloud that's almost in the shape of a camel?'
'By the mass, and 'tis a camel, indeed.'
'Methinks it is a weasel.'
'It is backed like a weasel.'
'Or like a whale?'
'Very like a whale.'

Shakespeare

'Ihr naht euch wieder, schwankende Gestalten'

I.

'Wir hören von einer besondern Einrichtung bei der englischen Marine', writes the narrator of *Die Wahlverwandtschaften*, towards the beginning of Part Two of the novel: 'Sämtliche Tauwerke der königlichen Flotte, vom stärksten bis zum schwächsten, sind dergestalt gesponnen, daß ein roter Faden durch das Ganze durchgeht, den man nicht herauswinden kann, ohne alles aufzulösen, und woran auch die kleinsten Stücke kenntlich sind, daß sie der Krone gehören.'[1]

There is such a red thread that is woven into all the chapters and pages of this book. At the conclusion of it my task must be to isolate it and submit it to my readers' inspection. To do so means touching on, and disturbing, every part of the fabric I have woven, and this will inevitably entail repetition. Such a prospect does not unduly alarm me. For it is only by showing the presence of the red thread through all the ramifications of my argument that I shall be able to demonstrate the closeness of its weave. Moreover, such a procedure promises a further gain. Having unravelled the fabric of my argument and found its every strand to terminate in the interconnecting thread, we may marvel at the rich density of its fibre. And that is gain indeed. For the thread that runs through my argument, with which it is all bound up, is not my own. It belongs to Goethe. And to display the substance and resonance of a single line of Goethe's by a summarising exegesis covering largely familiar ground, carries its own reward.

'Ihr naht euch wieder, schwankende Gestalten': it is this line, the opening line of the *Faust* drama, which, I sometimes think, contains the whole of Goethe *in nuce;* certainly it contains the distilled essence of this study. Let us look at this line slowly and deliberately, word by weighty word, and gather up the threads that radiate out from it and terminate in it again.

'Ihr naht euch': a two-term intransitive verb, governing a dative object, is here used transitively, in its reflexive form. We do not know the identity of the approaching agents until later in the line, nor their direction and aim. This is divulged in the following line as being the *trübe Blick* of an 'I' which is not introduced until the third line. The first three words, then, are expressive of pure, and intensified, activity on the part of agents whose identity is taken for granted, and whose connection with their object is left open. An approach

[1] II, 2.

is made; we are not told by whom, still less to whom. The mere fact is emphatically registered.

I suggest that these three words contain, in extreme condensation, all we have had occasion to say about the *Gegenständlichkeit* of Goethe's mode of perceiving. This has been called, by myself and others, an object-permeated mode. He does not approach the object; the objects approach him; a mode of relatedness expressed linguistically by the fact that the *objects* of cognition, being the active agents, appear as the grammatical *subjects* of a given cognitive statement. The paradigm of this kind of statement is to be found in the essay *Bedeutende Fördernis durch ein einziges geistreiches Wort* where Goethe's distinctive mode of perception, and cognition, is the express subject of discourse. There we read 'daß die Elemente der Gegenstände, die Anschauungen in dasselbe [i. e. das Denken] eingehen ...'[2]. The objects 'wander over' and enter into him. Throughout the essay the emphasis on the direction of the perceptual or cognitive process, as well as the grammatical form in which this is expressed, remain the same. 'Jeder neue Gegenstand, wohl beschaut, schließt ein neues Organ in uns auf'[3]; 'Mir drückten sich gewisse große Motive ... so tief in den Sinn ...'; 'da sie sich denn zwar immer umgestalteten, doch ohne sich zu verändern ... einer entschiednern Darstellung entgegenreiften'[4]; '... wozu jedes Besondere irgendeines Zustandes mich unwiderstehlich aufregte'[5]; 'bis die Idee der Pflanzenmetamorphose in mir aufging'[6]; '... indem ich deutlich vor Augen sah, daß alle Gegenstände, die ich seit funfzig Jahren betrachtet ... hatte, gerade die Vorstellung ... in mir erregen mußten ...'[7]; 'ich raste nicht, bis ich einen prägnanten Punkt finde, ... der vieles freiwillig aus sich hervorbringt und mir entgegenträgt ...'[8].

In every one of these instances the object of perception figures as the grammatical and logical subject, and in the majority of them the verb, denoting activity, is used reflexively.

The same basic position is maintained in other autobiographical statements cast, more often than not, in the same telling mould. Especial importance attaches to the passage from *Das Sehen in subjektiver Hinsicht* which I have already quoted[9], to the conversations with Eckermann of January 18 and May 6, 1827 and March 14, 1830[10], as to the related statement about the

[2] *HA* XIII, p. 37.
[3] *Ibid.*, p. 38.
[4] *Ibid.*
[5] *Ibid.*, p. 39.
[6] *Ibid.*
[7] *Ibid.*, p. 40.
[8] *Ibid.*
[9] In Chapter IX, section 3.
[10] Conversation of January 18, 1827: 'Ich habe ... niemals die Natur poetischer Zwecke wegen betrachtet. Aber weil mein früheres Landschaftszeichnen und dann mein späteres Naturforschen mich zu einem beständigen genauen Ansehen der natürlichen Gegenstände

peculiar character of the ballad in *Ballade, Betrachtung und Auslegung*[11]. We may once more recall an illuminating passage occurring in *Zur Morphologie*. There we read:

'Wenn der zur lebhaften Betrachtung aufgeforderte Mensch mit der Natur einen Kampf zu bestehen anfängt, so fühlt er zunächst einen ungeheuern Trieb, die Gegenstände sich zu unterwerfen. Es dauert aber nicht lange, so dringen sie dergestalt gewaltig auf ihn ein, daß er wohl fühlt, wie sehr er Ursache hat, auch ihre Macht anzuerkennen und ihre Einwirkung zu verehren.'[12]

The *Selbstschilderung* of the year 1797 presents a closely similar picture:

'Eine Besonderheit, die ihn sowohl als Künstler als auch als Menschen immer bestimmt, ist die Reizbarkeit und Beweglichkeit, welche sogleich die Stimmung von dem gegenwärtigen Gegenstand empfängt . . . er darf nicht lesen, ohne durch das Buch bestimmt zu werden, er ist nicht gestimmt, ohne daß er . . . tätig . . . etwas Ähnliches hervorzubringen strebt.'[13]

Again, the *Italienische Reise* offers a very striking instance of the way objects enter and permeate Goethe's own way of seeing:

'Meine alte Gabe, die Welt mit Augen desjenigen Malers zu sehen, dessen Bilder ich mir eben eingedrückt, brachte mich auf einen eignen Gedanken. Es ist offenbar, daß sich das Auge nach den Gegenständen bildet, die es von Jugend auf erblickt, und so muß der venezianische Maler alles klarer und heiterer sehen als andere Menschen.'[14]

Goethe then relates going for a canal trip in that self-same light; and, 'so sah ich das beste, frischeste Bild der venezianischen Schule'[15]. This case of *Wiederholte Spiegelungen* — from art into life and thence, almost, back into art — clearly depends on that gift of letting objects enter and transform him, to the point of a merger, which Goethe describes in the opening sentence.

---

trieb, so habe ich die Natur bis in ihre kleinsten Details nach und nach auswendig gelernt, dergestalt, daß, wenn ich als Poet etwas brauche, es mir zu Gebote steht und ich nicht leicht gegen die Wahrheit fehle.' (*AGA* 24, p. 215.)

Conversation of May 6, 1827: 'Es war im Ganzen . . . nicht meine Art, als Poet nach Verkörperung von etwas Abstraktem zu streben. Ich empfing in meinem Innern Eindrücke, und zwar Eindrücke sinnlicher, lebensvoller, lieblicher, bunter, hundertfältiger Art, wie eine rege Einbildungskraft es mir darbot; und ich hatte als Poet nichts weiter zu tun, als solche Anschauungen und Eindrücke in mir künstlerisch zu ründen und auszubilden . . .' (*AGA* 24, p. 636).

Conversation of March 14, 1830: 'Ich hatte sie [his ballads] alle schon seit vielen Jahren im Kopf, sie beschäftigten meinen Geist als anmutige Bilder, als schöne Träume, die kamen und gingen und womit die Phantasie mich spielend beglückte. Ich entschloß mich ungern dazu, diesen mir seit so lange befreundeten glänzenden Erscheinungen ein Lebewohl zu sagen . . .' (*AGA* 24, p. 725 f.).

[11] *HA* I, p. 400 f.
[12] *Das Unternehmen wird entschuldigt. HA* XIII, p. 53.
[13] *HA* X, p. 530.
[14] *HA* XI, p. 86 f.

In conclusion, we might allude to the delightful episode related in *Dich-tung und Wahrheit*. After a long study of the Straßburg minster, Goethe comes up with the theory that the completed spire was not executed as originally planned. Asked by the custodian who had told him so, he replies: 'Der Turm selbst ... Ich habe ihn so lange und aufmerksam betrachtet, und ihm so viel Neigung erwiesen, daß er sich zuletzt entschloß, mir dieses offenbare Geheimnis zu gestehn.'[16] Goethe's 'zarte Empirie, die sich mit dem Gegenstand innigst identisch macht und dadurch zur eigentlichen Theorie wird'[17], had not misled him; and in this account we once again note the entirely characteristic way of linguistically enacting the primacy of the object in the cognitive act: the *Turm* is the logical agent as well as the grammatical subject, and the active disclosure of its open secret to the recipient is rendered through the reflexive form of the verb.

This active approach on the part of the object — 'Ihr naht euch' — is thoroughly familiar to us from Goethe's poetic works. We need only think of the sonnet that 'comes' to Eugenie or of the way in which Wilhelm — in a situation exactly parallel to that Goethe describes in the *Italienische Reise* — learns to see the beauties of nature on Lago Maggiore through the young painter's eyes[18]. More importantly, figures of consequence almost invariably enter the lives of characters by way of a spontaneous approach. Euphrosyne, or the Muse in the poem *Zueignung*, appear unbidden, and so do Dorothea and Pandora and the beautiful Amazon, to mention only a few from the multitude of examples we could recall. It would be tedious to make an exact count of the number of times the narrator, in *Wilhelm Meister*, uses statements answering to the formula 'Diese Gestalt drückte sich ihm tief ein', with its strong suggestion of leaving a kinaesthetically perceptible imprint: the total might well run into three figures.

Such consistent use of one and the same model of verbalising a cognitive encounter sharpens our attention to the possibility that the introduction of another perceptual model may carry some significance. As we saw in the chapter on Goethe's Italian sojourn, he was suddenly and unaccountably harrowed about his competence as a practising visual artist in the midst of the keenest application. It is in this context of creative self-doubt, soon to become certainty of impotence, that the poet adopts a different model of speech. 'Lebhaft vordringende Geister' he writes, obviously making his own accounts, press on from mere aesthetic enjoyment to insight and from there to active art-making: and this is where, he dolefully concedes, serious confusions set in[19]. Again, there is the description, in the *Tag- und Jahreshefte* for

[15] *HA* XI, p. 87.
[16] III, 11, *HA* IX, p. 499.
[17] *Wilhelm Meisters Wanderjahre, Betrachtungen im Sinne der Wanderer*, *HA* VIII, p. 302.
[18] *Wilhelm Meisters Wanderjahre*, II, 7, *HA* VIII, p. 229.
[19] *Italienische Reise, Zweiter Römischer Aufenthalt*, September 1787, Bericht. *HA* XI, p. 409f.

the year 1801, of the beginnings of *Die Natürliche Tochter*. He had been desperately ill at the beginning of that year, we recall, and was eager to disprove his friends who had begun to suspect a waning of his creative powers. 'Ich rief mir daher die "Natürliche Tochter" vor die Seele . . .', we read[20]. It is interesting that, in the instance of two creative ventures which were to prove abortive, Goethe relinquishes his customary model of being approached — the model exhibited in 'Ihr naht euch wieder' — and adopts a radically opposed one in which the mind approaches the object, making the overtures to it on its own account.

A third instance concerns the perceptual mode associated with Natalie's aunt, *die schöne Seele*. Her '"Hang" zu dem Unsichtbaren'[21] prompts her to approach God time and again; and 'er stieß mich nicht weg, auf die geringste Bewegung zu ihm hinterließ er einen sanften Eindruck in meiner Seele, und dieser Eindruck bewegte mich, ihn immer wieder aufzusuchen.'[22] This pattern — a reversal of the one that is customary to Goethe — persists throughout the chapter. At the crucial point in her spiritual development, when she discovers her sinfulness and her need for redemption, we read: 'Ein Zug brachte meine Seele nach dem Kreuze hin, . . . ein Zug war es, ich kann es nicht anders nennen . . . ein Zunahen . . .'[23]; and there are many other examples testifying to the direction in which her religious experiencing proceeds. Seeing that, in autobiographical contexts, Goethe tends to envisage unproductive or abortive encounters with the object-world as being initiated by the experiencing subject, we may well extrapolate from this fact and ask whether the narrator here, in *Bekenntnisse einer schönen Seele*, is calling the validity of her object — the divine experienced as a person — in question. This possibility cannot be gainsaid. It is worthy of note that, at the end of her confessions, the *schöne Seele* herself raises the issue of the reality of her *unsichtbaren Freund* in the form of a question. Aggrieved that her nephew and nieces are on educational grounds removed from her sphere of influence, she reaffirms her faith, asking: 'Warum sollte er nicht einen göttlichen Ursprung, nicht einen wirklichen Gegenstand haben, da er sich im Praktischen so wirksam erweist?'[24]

I have pointed out that the grammatical form of the statement with which we are concerned, and in particular the use of a verb denoting activity in its reflexive form, suggests an unusual degree of autonomy on the part of the impinging agents or forces. The percipient is largely passive — we shall come back to this: it is the objects which announce their presence to him

---

[20] *HA* X, p. 451.
[21] *HA* VII, p. 359f.
[22] *Wilhelm Meisters Lehrjahre*, Book VI, *HA* VII, p. 373.
[23] *Ibid.*, p. 394.
[24] *Ibid.*, p. 420. In this connection, cf. Chapter VIII, section 2.

and spontaneously act. The famous description, in *Das Sehen in subjektiver Hinsicht*, of plant-like eidetic images evolving in him may be taken as an exemplar[25]. Those eidola — *Idole* Goethe calls them — 'unfold, grow, expand and contract' entirely of their own accord; so, too, the ballads that visit him, come and go at will, as he tells Eckermann *à propos* of *Die Braut von Korinth*[26]. Much the same picture emerges from *Bedeutende Fördernis durch ein einziges geistreiches Wort*, both as regards the quasi-independent life archetypal poetic motifs lead in him and as regards the gradual evolution, in whatever sphere, of a *prägnante Punkt* 'der vieles freiwillig aus sich hervorbringt und mir entgegenträgt . . .'. In the great majority of these instances the verbs employed denote an activity that is organic: *gestalten, umgestalten, entfalten, wachsen, ausdehnen, zusammenziehen, entgegenreifen, hervorbringen*: these are the key words we encounter time and again, and they point to the morphological sphere.

The autonomy of the encroaching object is, as we have had occasion to see, no less well marked in the poetic domain. Lili's image, that of Lida in *Jägers Abendlied* or the image of the beloved in *Marienbader Elegie* are there, moving, hovering. Euphrosyne steps out of clouds into a full and sharply delineated life. Pandora and Eugenie lead their independent existence in the minds uf Epimetheus and the duke. Of Natalie's image Wilhelm can say: ' . . . dieses schien fast ihn umschaffen zu wollen'; (note the 'wollen'). Mariane 'flehte um sein [Wilhelm's] Andenken', as does the *nußbraune Mädchen* for Lenardo's (as indeed does the *natürliche Tochter* for Goethe's own). The instrument-bag which will determine Wilhelm's life pierces his eyes, incandescent with a magic life of its own. The key which is to unlock the realm of the mothers glows and grows in Faust's hand.

Most striking perhaps is the autonomous life things lead in the mind of Ottilie, 'ein Gemüt, in welchem die Saat eines großen Schicksals ausgesäet worden, das die Entwicklung dieser Empfängnis abwarten muß und weder das Gute noch das Böse, weder das Glückliche noch das Unglückliche, was daraus entspringen soll, beschleunigen darf und kann.'[27] If this statement comes closest of all to the description of Goethe's own creational processes, it is Ottilie, too, who most resembles her creator in the precision of her eidetic memory. Her images of Eduard, not indeed as she has seen him in reality, yet evolving with perfect naturalness and order, call to mind those of plants and rose-windows which spontaneously produced and maintained themselves in the author of *Das Sehen in subjektiver Hinsicht*[28].

---

[25] *AGA* 16, p. 902.
[26] On March 14, 1830. Cf. note 10.
[27] *Die Wahlverwandtschaften*, II, 3, *HA* VI, p. 371.
[28] Cf. Chapter IX, section 3.

2.

'Ihr naht euch wieder'. Still the identity of the visitors is not disclosed, and still we do not know who it is that the unknown agents seek out. Clearly, the speaker takes the knowledge of both for granted. In the context of *Zueignung* the force of the *wieder* is, of course, readily explained. Those shapes which first approached the speaker in 1769, appear again now, on June 24, 1797, and with them the memories of the figures who were associated with their first appearance. Most of these are now dead, the others have dispersed. The scene has changed out of all recognition.

This repetition of an encounter with meaningful objects, and the passage of time as between one encounter and the next, is highly characteristic of Goethe. Again we must refer to the relevant passage in *Bedeutende Fördernis durch ein einziges geistreiches Wort*, and the corroborating conversation with Eckermann, in which the poet speaks of a creative gestation period of forty to fifty years, during which imprints made early on in life 'ripened towards' a more definite presence, 'einer entschiednern Darstellung'. Clearly, the figures of Faust and Prometheus were such repeated visitors — *belebte Fixidee*, as Goethe has it in relation to the latter; and the motifs, not only of some ballads but also of an epic work like *Die Jagd*, conceived in 1797 and executed as *Novelle* some thirty years later, testify to the longevity of creative nuclei once conceived. And Goethe's allusion to the morphological law that governs the relation of the lyrical end of *Novelle* to the rest of the work testifies to the organic nature of its incubation process as a whole[29]. Another visitor who kept knocking at the door of Goethe's mind was the *Urpflanze* and the idea of the metamorphosis of ascending organic forms. It positively haunted him.

The force of that *wieder* reverberates through Goethe's poetic works, in widely different significations as we shall see and, indeed, have seen. Goethe's own repeated sensibility, first to Lotte in Wetzlar, then to Maxe Brentano at Schloß Ehrenbreitstein, is reflected in the repeated cycle of the seasons and the enhanced agony they bring to his Werther. The figure of the beloved in the cycle of sonnets draws on diverse personal encounters. Iphigenie and Orestes are time and again visited by the spectres of their begetters, and that mental deposit will be stirred up and re-structured by the influx of impressions and memories newly formed. Elpore's touching and futile 'ja doch' is little more than a promise of 'wieder' to a lover racked by the waxing and waning of the beloved's shape. Again and again the picture of the *kranke Königssohn* presents itself, in memory or reality, to greet Wilhelm; and the medical instrument-bag periodically turns up, to remind him of his true vocation. Two springs and two autumns, rich with asters, pass by, and their repetition

---

[29] January 18, 1827.

enables us to gauge the maturation of the seed 'eines großen Schicksals' which Ottilie nurses to ripeness. Faust, promised that he will soon see 'Helena in jedem Weibe', turn by turn encounters Gretchen and the Grecian queen and Gretchen again. The betrothal of Hermann's parents is re-enacted in that of the young lovers, and their rings, added to that of Dorothea's dead fiancé, inaugurate another cycle of life, another 'wieder'. And finally there is the simultaneous 'wieder' in the technique of *Wiederholte Spiegelungen* Goethe was to employ in such late works as the *Westöstliche Divan*, *Wilhelm Meisters Wanderjahre* and *Faust II*: figure is cyclically mirrored in figure, motif in motif, event in event.

But such organic evolution of experience as is consistently reflected throughout Goethe's writings, is purchased at a high price. At times, such slow ripening will result in verses which are almost magically saturated with natural process; say, the poem from the *Westöstliche Divan*

> An vollen Büschelzweigen,
> Geliebte, sieh nur hin!

But then what so approaches also wanes. What has come so unbidden may go again beyond recall; and who will guarantee that it will come back, and in what form?

> Wer kann der Raupe, die am Zweige kriecht,
> Von ihrem künft'gen Futter sprechen?
> Und wer der Puppe, die am Boden liegt,
> Die zarte Schale helfen durchzubrechen?

It is for the poet as it is for his characters. Given such deep receptivity, almost passivity, as they evince *vis à vis* their own rhythms of experiencing and the objects of such experiencing, nobody can guarantee continuity, least of all they themselves. The Goethe that impotently wrestled with the visual arts in Italy and came close to the brink of insanity did not know by what miraculous resurrection this creative death would be transcended, of all unlikely things, in his *Tasso;* the Goethe who bade farewell to his 'künstlerische Blick' on his third visit to the Bodetal, resigned himself to cultivating his scientific 'organ' and wrote that he hoped 'auch diese Epoche' — the very epoch he was then living — 'historisch, als schon vorübergegangen zu betrachten'[30], could not foretell that he was spoiling for a creative bout which was going to yield the cycle of sonnets, *Die Wahlverwandtschaften* and *Pandora;* and the poet of these esoteric works of transition could not dream that the poetic rebirth of the *Westöstliche Divan* lay around another corner.

---

[30] Letter to Reinhard, October 7, 1810. For similar utterances, cf. letter to Schiller, May 22, 1803, letter to Jacobi, May 10, 1812, *Dichtung und Wahrheit* III, 14 (*HA* X, p. 32), *Aus Makariens Archiv* (*HA* VIII, p. 465, No. 35), conversation with Jenny v. Pappenheim, February 14, 1830 (*AGA* 23, p. 664) and letter to W. v. Humboldt, December 1, 1831.

As it is with the poet himself, so with his characters. Tasso himself picks up the image his creator had used in the poem *Ilmenau*, the image of the caterpillar who knows he is spinning himself to his death, and only remotely dreams of 'das neue Sonnental' in which he will spread his wings, 'rasch und freudig'. Epimetheus patiently lives through a deep creative self-alienation, unrelieved by any certainty of Pandora's *Wiederkunft*. The centenarian Faust lives out a loveless life, insensible of the renewed metamorphosis about to release him from his 'Puppenstand'. Wilhelm wretchedly and passively awaits the return of the *schöne Amazone* after a visitation as brief as it was dazzling. The duke, and Ottilie, fight a heroic battle knowing that for them there is no 'wieder' in the ordinary sense of the term and that they must recover the reality they have lost 'im Bilde' or 'in der Überschrift', by a long and painful process of sublimating perceptual reality into eidetic memory[31].

This sense of bereavement suffered by a faceless presence — we still do not know the identity of the speaker of 'Ihr naht euch wieder' — assailed by forces that come and go at their own will, can be terrible and absolute. We recall the distraught speaker of *Euphrosyne*, enveloped in 'unbezwingliche Trauer', filled with 'entkräftender Jammer', when the beloved visitation has gone; the sustained elegiac strains of the duke in *Die Natürliche Tochter;* Epimetheus' lyrics, now incantatory in their power, now near-incoherent; Faust's agony when Helena dissolves; and most of all, perhaps, Tasso's desolation when he stands bereft, both of his poem and of the princess who was the inspiring force of his genius[32].

3.

There can be no doubt but that the extreme receptivity expressed in the 'Ihr naht euch wieder', with the pre-eminence of the object in the experiential encounter, its autonomous coming and going, signifies an unusual lability on the part of the experiencing subject. Unnamed, anonymous as it were, it seems the playball of such forces as assail it. And these forms are now identified — as indeed they must be — as 'schwankende Gestalten'. Flux enters flux, uncertain shapes impinge upon a supremely susceptible and malleable consciousness.

We have spoken of 'schwankende Gestalten' in every conceivable context, at great length, and we have used the words in a number of widely different connotations. The time has come now to break down that tantalisingly elusive concept, to isolate its different meanings and to reassemble them in such an order as will exhibit the different phases of the experiential encounter

---

[31] In connection with eidetic imagery and memory, cf. S. Alexander, *Beauty and other Forms of Value, op. cit.*, pp. 65 ff. and E. H. Gombrich, *Art and Illusion*, London 1962, p. 262.
[32] Cf. my *Goethe and Lessing*, Chapter 7, pp. 156 ff.

we consider to be characteristically Goethean, as well as its pathological
variants. At the back of our minds will be the question by what right
Gestalten, for Goethe, are overwhelmingly experienced as *schwankend*. Is it *de
facto*, because of the ineradicable lability of an experiencing mind so overpowered by the shapes assailing it that it has not yet declared its identity and,
maybe, lacks a firm identity of its own? Or is it *de jure*, in virtue of the
inherent character of the objects perceived, in virtue perhaps of the inherent
character of the perceiving subject as it is revealed to dispassionate enquiry?

There is no doubt but that in Goethe's poetic world *Gestalten* appear to
the percipient as overwhelmingly *schwankend*. As often as not they materialise
from drifting clouds or mists, for a brief span attain a maximum of dazzling
clarity, and vanish like apparitions, grievously mourned. Of them all one
might say what Eos says of Pandora, at the end of the *Festspiel*:

> Erst verborgen, offenbar zu werden,
> Offenbar, um wieder sich zu bergen.

The application of these lines to Eugenie, heroine of *Die Natürliche Tochter*,
is self-evident; they are no less true of Helena, Euphrosyne, Natalie or indeed
Dorothea, to mention only some of the fluctuating forms that have occupied
our attention. In the instance of Helena the poet has employed intricate
alienation-devices to undermine our belief, and indeed her own, in her own
empirical reality; and the double role of Eugenie throughout the heart-scenes
of the drama as one lamented dead yet in fact alive, but in eclipse, would
seem to be dictated by a similar technique, aimed at making us question the
true status of her existence. In this connection I had no qualms to instance
Euphrosyne, arguing that her brief appearance from the realm of the dead
does not constitute an exceptional case, but is merely the most radical formulation of the precariousness associated for Goethe with all organic forms
per se. We may add an observation we have already alluded to: although we
know that Natalie lives on and joins the emigrants to the New World, it is
her actual disappearance, after a brief period of being reliably 'there' and
merging her existence with that of Wilhelm, throughout the length and
breadth of the *Wanderjahre* which determines our *aesthetic* response to this key
figure. She comes and vanishes again, like Goethe's other *Gestalten* and, indeed,
as she had done after her first apparition: and no doubt it was the poet's
intention, by thus radically withdrawing her presence, to make her appear
as ephemeral and precariously moored in the present as are his other *Gestalten*.

In so consistently pursuing this poetic technique — for it is no less than
that — Goethe was motivated by a variety of objectives which we shall
consider turn by turn. Of these one of the most important was the desire to
be faithful to the laws of human perception. In considering the various ways
in which *Gestalten* appear as *schwankend* we shall be retracing these laws step
by step and build up, as it were, a morphology of perception.

At the base of Goethe's perceptual household, and indeed that of his characters, we have discerned a quite unusual susceptibility to visual impressions. 'Der Eindruck bestimmt ihn', we read in Wilhelm's *Lehrbrief*, and the application of this statement is more universal than the immediate context suggests. To render something of the all-decisive force of visual impressions, especially first or early ones, I have used the term 'imprint' familiarised by the work of Konrad Lorenz and other ethologists.

These impressions engender percepts which are as tenacious as they are volatile — 'flüchtig' is the word Goethe himself likes to use. They are tenacious in that they temporarily give rise to after-images on the retina, and/ or because they may cause eidetic images which can be renewed, and retained, in the imagination or memory at will. *Das Sehen in subjektiver Hinsicht* draws a sharp distinction between these two kinds of images — Goethe refers to them as *Blendungsbild* and *Nachbild* respectively and attributes the longevity of the *Blendungsbild* (which we would nowadays call 'after-image') to a neurotically heightened sensibility, and the vividness and tenacity of the *Nachbild* (by which he means our eidetic images) to a healthy state of enhanced psychic activity[33]. In his poetic practice, however, the two kinds of image run fluid into one another, a powerful after-image (in the modern sense of the word) leading to eidetic imagery which is in turn refreshed and fructified by subsequent visual impressions and thus ever more deeply engraven upon memory and imagination. As an example of such a compound mental phenomenon we may cite Wilhelm's first impression of the *schöne Amazone* which, leaving a powerful after-image, becomes an eidetic memory; and this, re-fertilised by his renewed encounter with Natalie, develops a doubled energy capable, now, of altogether transforming him[34]. A *Nachbild* actually becoming a *Vorbild*: it is largely with this evolution of perceptual material that we shall be concerned in the following pages.

But these primal imprints are also of the most ephemeral. As we have seen on various occasions, the very violence of the initial visual impact is the reason for its mutations and eventual disappearance. In virtue of its tendency towards totality, the eye will of its own provide phenomena complementary to those affecting it or otherwise assert its inborn autonomy and restore its equilibrium[35]. In a healthy organism, the after-image left by a strong light will mutate, reverse and disappear in a matter of seconds, or at most minutes[36]. Both in the section on pathological colours in *Zur Farbenlehre* and in *Das Sehen in subjektiver Hinsicht* a greater longevity of the primal image on the

---

[33] *AGA* 16, p. 901.

[34] In this connection, cf. Chapter VIII, section 4 and Note 44.

[35] Cf. *Zur Farbenlehre. Sinnlich-Sittliche Wirkung der Farbe*. 'Totalität und Harmonie', *HA* XIII, pp. 501 ff.

[36] *Ibid. Physiologische Farben*, para. 23, *HA* XIII, p. 333.

retina is ascribed to a weakness of the organ or an abnormal condition of the subject[37]. It is clear that we are confronted with such a pathological suscept-ibility in the case of the injured Wilhelm who is haunted, throughout his convalescence, by the radiant after-image of the *schöne Amazone*. It is equally clear that this condition is only a temporary one giving way, eventually, to a phantasmagoria of other impressions crowned by the renewal, at greater depth, of the best-loved image.

More pathological is the fixation of the primal imprint in the instances of, say, Werther, Mignon, the Harfner, Orestes and Iphigenie and Lenardo. These figures are exemplars of initial imprints that have become fixed, and such a fixation on the perceptual level in its turn signifies a stagnation or stunting of development extending over the whole psychic organism. Mignon 'sees' the marble busts of her first youth stand and gaze at her. Lotte's black eyes have bored themselves into the fabric of Werther's mind and monopolise it 'hier, . . . wo die innere Sehkraft sich vereinigt.' Orestes lives with the image of his mother's beseeching eyes and his own desperate response:

Doch sein geschwungner Arm traf ihre Brust.

It is as though life had been arrested and his mind been frozen at that agonised split second before his dagger came down. Iphigenie, similarly, lives with two conflicting images: that of the 'göttergleiche Agamemnon' and that of being dragged to the altar, by whom she dare not think or say. Lenardo has the image of the 'nußbraune Mädchen' etched on his retina, in the very act of supplication. All these characters are as in a beauty sleep. While the after-image stands thus fixed in their minds and imaginations — Goethe himself, in the section on pathological colours, speaks of 'eine Art von Paralyse' — their psychic development towards maturation is arrested; and in the case of Mignon the poet has given expression to this arrest by associat-ing her with hermaphroditic features.

It is only when these 'Fixideen' are permitted to come into renewed contact with reality and are fructified by fresh impressions, that their paralysing hold resolves and, with it, inner stagnation terminates. Werther, Mignon and the Harfner, all past-orientated in the highest degree, are denied such vivifying contact and perish. Orestes' obsession with his retributive murder is re-animated, and resolved, through the hallucinated image of retribution in reversal. 'Komm, schwinge deinen Stahl' he incites his sister: and this is the precise parallel of the earlier 'Doch sein geschwungner Arm traf ihre Brust'. Analogously, Iphigenie's fixation on herself being sacrificed is re-animated, and resolved, through the obverse phantasy of herself sacrific-ing her brother. The reversal, in both cases, complements and completes the

---

[37] *Ibid. Pathologische Farben*, paras. 121—126; *HA* XIII, p. 357. Cf. also *Physiologische Farben*, para. 28, *HA* XIII, p. 334. *Das Sehen in subjektiver Hinsicht*, Seite 168, *AGA* 16, p. 901.

spectrum of experience and liberates the mind; a restoration of totality in which the perceptual enlargement symbolically enacts a psychic event[38]. Similarly, Iphigenie's fixation on her actual, remembered father is absorbed into an ampler father-image in which Thoas, 'der mir ein zweiter Vater ward', may be included together with all that bears the imprint of the divine. Lenardo's crippling attachement to the past image of the suppliant girl, finally, is 'aufgehoben' in the liberating presence of the *Schöne-Gute*.

As we leave the domain of the 'Fixidee' and enter that of the 'belebte Fixidee', we enter the sphere of morphologically healthful evolution; and it is here, in this sphere, that we encounter a whole phantasmagoria of *schwankende Gestalten*. But here, too, in the sphere of animated images, we must make reference, first of all, to a deviation which is the polar opposite of the fixed imprint. This is the condition in which, literally, flux enters flux and perceptual chaos ensues. Never has Goethe depicted this state more poignantly than in his decription of the major, in *Der Mann von funfzig Jahren*, whose inner eye is plagued by torments '[die] wie ein beweglicher Nebel unablässig vorschweben', 'gestaltet und immer umgestaltet, im unerfreulichsten Kreis'; such a welter of aimlessly mutating images being, of course, the perceptual symbol of his own 'innere Gestalt' which is disorientated and *schwankend* in the highest degree.

---

[38] A great deal could be said about the psychological processes that are re-activated, and completed, by this reversal. Orestes' expectation of being murdered represents the masochistic reversal of those sadistic impulses which have underlain — for all the external compulsion under which he acted — the murder of his mother, a classically Oedipal act of aggression. Analogously, Iphigenie, herself the victim of her father's aggression, reverses the Electra pattern in her phantasy of murdering her brother. This phantasy is not only fed by deeply unconscious motives of revenge, but more specifically by the woman's revenge at having been — almost — penetrated. In this anguished phantasy Iphigenie acts out, and comes to terms with, that deep-seated resentment of being a woman and envy of the other sex which critics have noted in general terms.

Such depth-psychological implications are there, in the plot and in the verbal texture. To deny them would be obscurantist, to discern them is to recognise one of the hallmarks of great poetry, its anticipatory knowledge of configurations which have only been discursively formulated in more recent times. Sophocles' *Oedipus* trilogy and Shakespeare's *Hamlet* are outstanding examples of art prefiguring later insights which, in the first case, even derive their nomenclature from their literary source, and we have stopped being squeamish about this being so. Lastly, it is this fine symmetry even on the deepest psychological strata which endows this play with its exquisite balance. If nevertheless I have chosen not to include these observations in the text of Chapter 3, it is because, although what the *poem does* in fact say is inexhaustible, the reading of the text should to some extent be guided by what the *poet intended* to say within its poetic economy. Although a poetic text may embody a case-history, it is not one and taste forbids it to be treated as such. To inform us about the absence of menstrual cycles in *Iphigenie* — as does R. Eissler in his monumental psychoanalytical study of Goethe — does not, in my view, enhance our aesthetic appreciation of the play as Goethe intended it. (In: *Goethe. A Psychoanalytic Study*, 1775—1786, Detroit 1963, Vol. I, p. 318.)

As against this, Wilhelm, Faust and the duke, Eugenie's father, and, for
that matter, the speaker of the letter-poem to Frau von Stein experience an
evolution of the perceptual material they assimilate; and this evolution reflects
to a nicety their steady trend towards personal maturity. The violence of the
primal visual imprint these figures have received borders on a visionary
transport. We have seen the vitality and energy with which the images of
Natalie and Eugenie dominate the real. The strength of Helena's impact on
Faust —

> Hab ich noch Augen? Zeigt sich tief im Sinne
> Der Schönheit Quelle reichlichstens ergossen? —

may be left to speak for itself.

In all three instances the visual experience is accompanied by a desire to
possess the object of the experience. Faust lays hands on Helena — and here
his name, 'Fauste', itself becomes symbolic; the duke, over-anxious for his
daughter's life, fights a desperate rearguard-action for the possession, and
preservation, of Eugenie's dead body; and Wilhelm confesses that 'diese
Gestalt aller Gestalten' has fanned in him 'das unüberwindliche Verlangen
des Besitzes'.

Such mingling of image and desire, such possessive cleaving of the percipient to the physical substratum of the mind's vision is a transitional state
which eventually gives way to the disinterested perception of the pure
Gestalt. This enhancement of the quality of perception is, as we have seen,
accomplished in a series of mental steps. Through the various combinations
it enters and mutations it undergoes, the initial image is progressively filtered
of its grosser ingredients: we have observed this process in some detail in the
chapter on *Wilhelm Meister*, and the same is true both of Faust's mental image
of Helena as it emerges from the cavalcade of impressions assailing him in the
Klassische Walpurgisnacht, and of the duke's image of Eugenie as it survives
the gruelling transformations it undergoes at the hands of the *Weltgeistliche*.
Similarly, the image of the love relationship at the centre of 'Warum gabst
du uns die tiefen Blicke' is progressively clarified. The image is, furthermore,
stripped of its material supports — we have watched this process in the case
of *Faust* and *Die Natürliche Tochter* — a refinement brought about by the progressive alienation of the *Gestalt* from its own empirical reality. This weaning
is achieved, in *Die Natürliche Tochter*, by the fiction of Eugenie's death; in
Faust, by that self-alienation of Helena who assumes mythological status in
her own eyes, in *Wilhelm Meister*, through Natalie's Nazarene 'Nie oder
immer' and, in Goethe's letter-poem, through the transplantation of the
present love relationship into the dimension of the recollected past. In all
these instances, this separation of image from reality and the internalisation
of the pure eidetic image — Emrich speaks of the 'Prozess schrittweiser
Ablösung eines überirdisch zeitlosen Bildes von seinem zeitlichen Sein'[39],

---

[39] *Die Symbolik von Faust II*, p. 317.

and, more pithily, of the 'Abspaltung des "Bildes" vom "Leben"'[40] — involves the experience of bereavement. Faust loses Helena when he seeks to grasp her, and will lose her again after a timeless moment of disinterested possession; the lovers of Goethe's letter-poem mourn a fulfilment which has become uncertain recollection; the duke suffers all the torments of bereavement before he can say, virtually:

> Denn das Leben ist die Liebe,
> Und des Lebens Leben Geist.

And Wilhelm? At the point when he is able to say: . . . 'nun sind ihre Eigenschaften so tief in dein Gemüt geprägt, als ihr Bild jemals in deine Sinne', which is the point of maximal internalisation of Natalie's eidetic image, he is ready to continue: 'Ängstlich ist es, immer zu suchen, aber viel ängstlicher, gefunden zu haben und verlassen zu müssen[41].' He is enunciating the fate of Faust and the duke as well as anticipating his own: to find, in Goethe's world, is to renounce. It is to retrieve what has been gainsaid on the empirical level, in the disinterested perception of the pure eidolon: the symbolic 'Vorbild' of the real, stripped of all material supports.

4.

The speaker has not yet presented himself or put his cards on the table. When he will do so, in the second line, it will be synecdochically, by way of identifying himself with the 'trüben Blick' of his youthful self. We note that this second line retains the grammatical form of the first. The approaching agents, now identified as 'schwankende Gestalten', continue to be in pre-eminence. It is they that present themselves to his turbid gaze, as it will be they that, later, will press in upon a self willing to submit to their forceful clamouring and to their violent impingement.

That this self is as labile and nebulous as the forms which assail it there seems little doubt. And we are forced to ask the outright question: are the *schwankenden Gestalten*, with which we have been so largely concerned in this book, a function of the artistic sensibility, of that almost boundless receptivity and even passivity we have found to be associated with it, a psychic structure that is not gainsaid by the passage we are discussing? And, furthermore: if the percipient himself is *schwankend*, what exactly does this signify? Is the uncertainty of his vision due to the pathology of a character which, passively bombarded by overwhelmingly strong impressions, is a perpetual prey to the kind of disorientation which is produced by acute stress? Or is the

[40] *Ibid.*, p. 319.
[41] *Wilhelm Meisters Lehrjahre*, VIII, 7.

tremulousness of his vision a controlled phenomenon, governed by the
self-same law that causes the forms in the object-world to be *schwankend*?

In answer to the first of these questions we must turn to Goethe's morphology which he himself claims to encompass 'die Lehre von der Gestalt, der
Bildung und Umbildung der organischen Körper'[42]. We note that the words
'Gestalt' and 'Bildung und Umbildung der organischen Körper' are used
synonymously, interchangeably. And we must once more allude to a seminal
passage we have already cited, because it contains the unequivocal answer to
our first question, the question as to whether *Gestalten* are *schwankend* in
themselves or merely appear to be so to the heightened susceptibility of the
artistic mind: 'Betrachten wir aber alle Gestalten', we read in *Die Absicht
eingeleitet*,

> besonders die organischen, so finden wir, daß nirgend ein Bestehendes, nirgend ein
> Ruhendes, ein Abgeschlossenes vorkommt, sondern daß vielmehr alles in einer steten
> Bewegung schwanke ... Wollen wir also eine Morphologie einleiten, so dürfen wir nicht
> von Gestalt sprechen; sondern, wenn wir das Wort brauchen, uns allenfalls dabei nur die
> Idee, den Begriff oder ein in der Erfahrung nur für den Augenblick Festgehaltenes
> denken.'[43]

Gestalten, and organic forms in particular, are in the highest degree
schwankend — a phenomenon which paradoxically evinces every constancy:
stet is the word Goethe uses — and the percipient, himself part of organic nature,
is not excluded from this law. The very word *Gestalt* is an abstraction denoting
what in actual experience is a fugitive concatenation which is but momentarily
arrested in and by the experiencing consciousness.

We may see, then, that it is the morphological insight of the scientist which
prompts the poet to present *Gestalten*, to his characters' perception as well as
to our own, as being in a state of flux. The ontological precariousness of a
Helena or an Eugenie, the evanescence of Epimetheus' vision even, are no
more than extreme statements of a law holding equally true in the stable world
of a Hermann. They appear *schwankend* because they are, in fact, *schwankend;*
because, by the inexorable law of organic beings, 'Das Gebildete wird sogleich
wieder umgebildet'[44].

It is for this reason that the coming and going of the human form in
Goethe's world is so often associated with those most mutable of phenomena
— clouds and drifting mists. Helena materialises out of clouds in both her
appearances and dissolves into clouds at the end; and in the opening scene
of Act IV of the second part, Faust glimpses the shape of the *Gestalten* he has
most loved in the fugitive shapes of clouds; Euphrosyne comes out of a
cloud and is swallowed up again in a cloud; Eugenie's place of exile is envisaged as infested by insects tormenting the traveller like 'belebte Wolken';

---

[42] *Betrachtung über Morphologie überhaupt, HA* XIII, p. 124.
[43] *Zur Morphologie. Die Absicht eingeleitet, HA* XIII, p. 55 f.
[44] *Ibid.,* p. 56.

Epimetheus sees Pandora as a 'Nebelgestalt', her gifts are 'Luftgeburten', 'Rauchgestalten'; Epimenides' vision is blurred by 'Nebelrauch'; and even the comely and robust figure of Dorothea materialises from the cloud of dust into which Hermann is abstractedly gazing. It is not different with the most cherished figures of Goethe's lyrical poetry: Lili, the muse, Lida and Ulrike — they all wax and wane in the 'formumformend Weben'[45] of clouds and drifting mists, now dazzlingly clear, now blurred, constantly metamorphosing as does the element in which they manifest their changing contour to the percipient; to which we must add the 'Dunst und Nebel' from which the 'schwankende Gestalten' of the *Faust*drama beckon to the speaker.

So, too, the archetypal association of man and the human condition with the most transient of the elements, water, is readily explained once we are mindful of the position adopted by the morphologist Goethe. The symbolism of such poems as *Mahomets-Gesang*, *An den Mond*, *Gesang der Geister über den Wassern* or *Mächtiges Überraschen* becomes transparent as soon as, together with Goethe, we envisage man as being in a perpetual process of *Gestaltung, Umgestaltung*. Thus, when the speaker or dramatic character cannot endure the tragic precariousness of the human form, the sense of outrage turns against the fruitless surging of the element — witness the duke and the *Gerichtsrat* in Acts III and V of *Die Natürliche Tochter*, the aged Faust *vis à vis* the inane assault of the waves on the beach, or the speaker of the *Marienbader Elegie* who asks:

> Wie könnte dies geringstem Nutzen frommen,
> Die Ebb' und Flut, das Gehen wie das Kommen?

And surely Tasso is voicing his creator's own boundless susceptibility to that waxing and waning of forms, when he compares himself to the 'sturmbewegte Welle' which 'schwankt' in response to the flux he perceives all around him.

Perhaps the most radical statement of the precariousness of all forms is to be found in the poem *Dauer im Wechsel*, originally published under the rubric *Gott und Welt*, that is to say, in a group of poems concerned with the dialectic of transience and permanence as envisaged by the mature poet-scientist[46]. In these lines, which are as elegiac as they are inexorable, Goethe answers in one the two questions we asked a little earlier on in this chapter: both are *schwankend*, the forms of organic nature and the percipient: the latter because he — his lips, his feet, his hands, his whole body, his very eyes in the act of perceiving — is part of organic nature, and because, in order to grasp the flight of phenomena, he must be nimble enough to keep pace with the movement which surrounds him on all sides.

---

[45] *Sprüche*, *HA* I, p. 325.
[46] For a sensitive reading of *Dauer im Wechsel*, cf. E. Staiger, *Die Zeit als Einbildungskraft des Dichters*, pp. 109 ff.

This *Schwanken* 'in einer steten Bewegung', which the morphologist Goethe identifies as the condition of all forms, is poetically enacted by one recurrent device which adumbrates Epimetheus' lament,

> Rose, brech ich deine Schöne,
> Lilie, du bist schon dəhin.

The evocation of a given form or configuration, the very enunciation of its existence, is overtaken, and preceded, by the statement of its dissolution. As things are named they are already obsolete. The 'Blütenregen' races ahead of the wind that will cause it, the foliage is already questionable as it begins to provide shade, and the gales that will disperse it are a mental fact as the now fallow autumn leaves dangle from the branches. The *Regenguss* which transforms the *holde Tal* precedes its mention; and the identity of the river is already denied in the 'ach' that precedes its evocation. The loving lips and the nimble foot are 'weggeschwunden' even as they are named; and the giddy rush towards the element of what used to be the 'I' of the speaker is prefigured in the hollowness of the words in which that spectral configuration is evoked:

> Und was sich an jener Stelle
> Nun mit deinem Namen nennt,
> Kam herbei wie eine Welle,
> Und so eilt's zum Element.

Schwankende Gestalten indeed, this procession of waning shapes overtaking one another in a swift and silent race towards extinction! The percipient, himself part of this cavalcade, must move along more swiftly — so the concluding stanza of this poem is telling us — than do the phenomena themselves, the external ones and the flight of images before his eyes. He must do so — and here poet and morphologist speak with one voice — to capture *Form* and *Gehalt* of what is so fugitive: he must be able 'Einzelheiten ... wie im Fluge [wegzufangen]'[47], um das gestaltlose Wirkliche in seiner eigensten Art zu fassen'[48], or, as he has it elsewhere, 'mannigfaltige Beweglichkeit lernen, damit wir den Typus in aller seiner Versatilität zu verfolgen gewandt seien und uns dieser Proteus nirgendhin entschlüpfe'[49]. This flexibility of perceiving and experiencing it is which alone will lead 'zum lebendigen Anschaun der Natur ...'[50]

But such 'Beweglichkeit' of the morphologically trained eye and imagination must now be sharply distinguished from mere passive lability.

---

[47] *Die Lepaden, HA* XIII, p. 203.
[48] *Wilhelm Meisters Wanderjahre. Betrachtungen im Sinne der Wanderer*, No. 153, *HA* VIII, p. 306.
[49] *Allgemeine Einleitung in die vergleichende Anatomie, HA* XIII, p. 177.
[50] *Zur Morphologie. Die Absicht eingeleitet. HA* XIII, p. 56.

It presupposes a relentless discipline, 'eine eigene Geisteswendung'[51], or, as Goethe formulates it more uncompromisingly in *Das Sehen in subjektiver Hinsicht*, 'strenge sinnliche Abstraktion . . ., eine eigene und methodische Folge von Abhärtungen, Übungen und Fertigkeiten'[52]. And indeed, the morphologically trained awareness — be it that of the poet or the scientist — must forge for itself linguistic tools fitted to capture objects 'die man mehr Tätigkeiten als Gegenstände nennen kann',[53] in that they are in constant movement. In our short analysis of the poem *Dauer im Wechsel* we have identified one of the many semantic devices employed to enact flux in language without arresting it in the process of articulation.

In the chapter on *Pandora* we have sought to enter the workshop from which that problematic poem came, and tried to visualise some of the difficulties besetting the poet in the period of his late classicism, after the return from the Italian south. His aesthetic and scientific convictions between them had rendered obsolete that will towards a plastically saturated language which had been characteristic of his earlier art. The morphologist had recognised all forms, especially organic ones, to be *schwankend*, and the aesthetician had diagnosed the defectiveness of the model of form with which modern and especially northern artists are forced to operate. Both these insights had given rise to an increasingly anti-naturalistic view of art. Its aim cannot be to represent the 'Naturwirklichkeit' of objects. Art must re-create, from the inside and from the bottom upward, as it were, nature's formative processes as they become manifest in her fugitive phenomena: must learn 'wie sie bei Bildung ihrer Werke verfährt'[54] and, 'wetteifernd mit der Natur, etwas Geistig-Organisches hervorzubringen'[55], etwas, das 'ihren Erscheinungen ähnlich ist'[56].

This view of art entailed 'eine strenge sinnliche Abstraktion' from the static appearance of objects, and a versatility of eye and mind fitted 'ihre Flüchtigkeit [zu] . . . haschen . . .'[57]. Thus it placed the greatest premium on that innate receptivity and suceptibility of the percipient we so persistently stressed in the first sections of this chapter. But, also, it entailed the morphologist's firm check on the pathological lability of the percipient as well as on the model of natural form and creative process with which he operates, a model which, in modern Western culture, has ceased to be normative and lapsed into degeneracy.

[51] *Wilhelm Meisters Wanderjahre. Betrachtungen im Sinne der Wanderer*, No. 153, *HA* VIII, p. 306.
[52] *AGA* 16, p. 894.
[53] *Zur Farbenlehre. Nachbarliche Verhältnisse, HA* XIII, p. 492.
[54] *Einleitung in die Propyläen, HA* XII, p. 44.
[55] *Ibid.*, p. 42.
[56] *Ibid.*
[57] *Zur Farbenlehre. Physiologische Farben, HA* XIII, p. 329.

The late classicistic Goethe thus saw himself confronted by the doubled, and daunting, challenge of achieving a controlled exposure to flux, a problem towards which much of his late work gravitates. We need only think of the poems *Vermächtnis* and *Eins und Alles*, or, for that matter, *Dauer im Wechsel;* not to speak of the *Westöstliche Divan* and of *Faust* or *Pandora* in the dramatic domain. Basically, it is a return, at a higher level of specialisation, to the problem that had already exercised the writer of the diaries we discussed, anxious to submit to his unconscious creative cycles and yet to exercise a measure of effective control over such inner fluidity[58].

Artistically, the answer morphologist and poet alike found to this problem — a problem sharpened by the insubstantiality of language set against the objectivity and supportiveness of material media — was the discovery of that Archimedian aesthetic pivot, the pregnant moment. In arresting the pregnant moment, for all that it is fugitive in itself, the artist captures the typical in the evanescent, the *Urphänomen* in the transient phenomenon. We may recognise such pregnant moments *par excellence* in Lothario's visit to his former love, the *Pachterstochter*, and Wilhelm's condensed experience of 'Vergangenheit und Gegenwart in Eins'[59], as he goes to see Mignon's embalmed body. '"Welch ein Leben", rief er aus, "in diesem Saale der Vergangenheit!"' To which, looking at the presentations of all the archetypal if transient moments of human lives, he adds:

> 'man könnte ihn ebensogut den Saal der Gegenwart und der Zukunft nennen. So war alles und so wird alles sein! ... Hier dieses Bild der Mutter, die ihr Kind ans Herz drückt, wird viele Generationen glücklicher Mütter überleben. Nach Jahrhunderten vielleicht erfreut sich ein Vater dieses bärtigen Mannes, der seinen Ernst ablegt und sich mit seinem Sohne neckt. So verschämt wird durch alle Zeiten die Braut sitzen und bei ihren stillen Wünschen noch bedürfen, daß man sie tröste, daß man ihr zurede; so ungeduldig wird der Bräutigam auf der Schwelle horchen, ob er hereintreten darf.'[60]

5.

In the preceding quotation I have omitted the most arresting statement of all. Standing there in the hall where 'Vergangenheit' is 'beständig', 'das Künftige voraus lebendig', where 'der Augenblick ist Ewigkeit', Wilhelm, overwhelmed, exclaims: 'Nichts ist vergänglich, als der eine, der genießt und zuschaut[61].' These are some of the most precious words ever to have flowed from Goethe's pen: they are precious in virtue of their selflessness.

Such selfless participation in perception was no easy thing to come by, least of all for one so alive to the *ungeheure Recht der Gegenwart*, so relentlessly exposed to the violent impingement of things upon his senses and his

---

[58] Cf. Chapter IV, sections 5 and 6.
[59] *Dichtung und Wahrheit*, III, 14, *HA* X, p. 32. Cf. Note 30 of this chapter.
[60] *Wilhelm Meisters Lehrjahre*, VIII, 5.
[61] *Ibid.*

sensibility. It is a long way from the boundless receptivity we have stressed in the opening sections of this chapter, and the lability which is inseparable from it, to the marvellously mature words Wilhelm finds in the *Saal der Vergangenheit;* indeed to the sense of permanence in flux, *Dauer im Wechsel,* which informs Goethe's later works in their entirety. The secret of this development lies in the selflessness of a perception which became ever more filtered of its grossly personal ingredients and ever more disinterested. And the secret of such selfless perception, in turn, lay in the ability, and willingness, to perceive coherent orders of phenomena. Whether Iphigenie sees 'Am Ende dieser schönen Reihe sich geschlossen . . .'; whether Faust, in *Wald und Höhle,* perceives 'die Reihe der Lebendigen . . .'; whether the duke, in *Die Natürliche Tochter,* speaks of parents relishing 'ihr Stufenglück in wohlgeratnen Kindern'; or indeed whether the speaker of *Grenzen der Menschheit* envisages the gods as they *reihen* 'viele Geschlechter . . . an ihres Daseins unendliche Kette': the experience that is articulated of the clamorous and evanescent now as embedded in a series of nows, in past and future, remains constant; and the artist's disinterested perception is a match to that of the thinker, the scientist and the aesthetician. The essay *Der Versuch als Vermittler von Objekt und Subjekt,* with its emphasis on the patient ordering of the single phenomenon as it is manifested in the single experiment, in a coherent sequence of connected phenomena, is paradigmatic for Goethe's procedure in his optical and morphological studies. Analogously, Goethe asks the artist to envisage cyclic motifs and develop them, 'die ganze Reihe durch'[62], from their beginning to their organic end. He himself followed his own precept in *Hermann und Dorothea,* with its cycle of the seasons and generations, and, in a different manner, in such late works as the *Westöstliche Divan, Faust II* and *Wilhelm Meisters Wanderjahre,* with their cyclic structure and the patterned proliferation of the individual motif in a fabric of *Wiederholte Spiegelungen.* Such ironic recurrence in a highly 'reflective' order is the stylistic precipitate of that serenity of perception become absolutely selfless which informs the *Divan* poetry and has become incarnate in the figures of Natalie and Makarie. 'Nie oder immer' is the answer all Goethe's later poetry gives to the besetting problem of *Dauer im Wechsel;* and nowhere has the poet given more consummate expression to that light-footed renunciation than in the poem *Im Gegenwärtigen Vergangnes:*

> Nun die Wälder ewig sprossen,
> So ermutigt euch mit diesen,
> Was ihr sonst für euch genossen,
> Läßt in andern sich genießen.
> Niemand wird uns dann beschreien,
> Daß wir's uns alleine gönnen;
> Nun in allen Lebensreihen
> Müsset ihr genießen können.

[62] *Vorschlag, AGA* 13, p. 1064.

This is Goethe's selflessness and renunciation, as it is his Ottilie's: a selflessness and renunciation that are inseparably tied up with the innate object-orientatedness of his perceiving. But what a long and arduous way from the phantom-like fluidity of the shapes encroaching on his eyes — 'Ihr naht euch wieder, schwankende Gestalten' — to the serene participation of one who finds it in him to say 'Nichts ist vergänglich, als der eine, der genießt und zuschaut'! It is the way from the delusory *Nachbild* to the eidetic *Vorbild*, from the fluctuating violence of primal perceptual imprints to the sublimation and internalisation of the eidolon distilled in tranquil recollection: the long and disciplined road from the first assault by 'flüchtigen Schemen' to their pacified apprehension as 'wahrhaft gegenständliche Wesen'[63].

Goethe's selflessness conquered the transience that is writ large across the *Faust* drama, indeed across the first line of its opening prologue; he never denied it. At the end of the *Prolog im Himmel* the Lord will say:

> Und was in schwankender Erscheinung schwebt,
> Befestiget mit dauernden Gedanken.

And this is no more than we have seen Goethe himself doing. Yet even there he acknowledges the radical precariousness of phenomenal being for one as exposed with his every fibre to time and life as he was himself. And even there, in the Lord's words, the poet's language remains sufficiently 'beweglich und bildsam'[64] to enact what will ever remain true for one mortal and as susceptible to the risks of sentience as was this artist. *Gedanken* internally rhymes with *Schwanken*. The stabilising force of *dauernde Gedanken* reaches that far and no further. Thus far flux is contained. The last part of that first line, however, with its helplessly trailing dactylic inflection

> . . . [schwanken]der Erscheinung schwebt . . .

is banished beyond the domain made safe by human stability. In the last resort, 'was in schwankender Erscheinung schwebt', remains hovering in outer space, tremulous as *schwankende Gestalten* will be, unmoored, utterly without support. In such uncharted zones only the artist's trust in all-nature's 'Stirb und Werde' will avail.

---

[63] *Das Sehen in subjektiver Hinsicht, AGA* 16, p. 903.
[64] *Zur Morphologie. Die Absicht eingeleitet, HA* XIII, p. 56.

Index

I Goethe's Works

Small numerals against the page number refer to footnote numerals in text.

II Names

Names of characters from Goethes' works are indexed under the title of the work in which they appear.

Raphael (Raffaelo Santi) 14, 116, 120, 130
Reichardt, Johann Fr. 290, 292
Reinhard, Karl Friedrich Graf von 358[30]
Riemer, Friedrich Wilhelm 7, 9, 146
Roche, Marie Sophie de La 33[47]

Salzmann, Johann Daniel 12[19]
Sartorius, Caroline 11[16], 43 ff.
Sartorius, Georg 153 and [28]
Schiller, Friedrich von 8, 23, 176, 178, 181,
    199, 230[3], 246[30], 276, 285, 289, 290, 292,
    300[10], 340[43], 346, 358[30]
Schlegel, August Wilhelm 305[20]
Schönemann, Anne Elisabeth (Lili) 42[23], 45,
    78[21], 89, 99, 367
Schubert, G. H. von 243[26]
Schultz, Christoph Ludw. Fr., Staatsrat 298
Shakespeare, William 270, 363[38]
Socrates 179 f.

Sophocles 363
Stein, Charlotte A. E. von 29[43], 38, 45, 63 f.,
    78[21], 90 ff., 109, 173—181 passim, 367
Stolberg, Auguste Luise, Gräfin zu 9[7], 10[14],
    94

Tischbein, Johann Heinrich Wilhelm 118 f.

Valéry, Paul 22[35]

Werner, Zacharias 59
Wieland, Christoph Martin 177
Willemer, Marianne von 42[23], 43, 50
Winckelmann, Johann Joachim 63, 123, 137
Wordsworth, William 178

Zelter, Karl Friedrich 8[2], 11[15], 18, 162,
    235[11], 318[20]
Ziegesar, Sylvie von 35, 42, 59[45], 151 f.[25],
    153, 156

III   Themes, Concepts, Images and Key Words